Table of Contents

Beginning
XSLT

Introduction

Welcome

Welcome to Beginning XSLT, a comprehensive introduction to the Extensible Stylesheet Language Transformations.

Who is this Book For?

This book introduces those with a little knowledge of markup languages (HTML, XML, etc.) to the exciting world of XSLT. No prior programming knowledge is assumed or needed. This is a Wrox *Beginning* ... series book, so we will aim to teach you everything you need to know from scratch. This book will be equally beneficial to designers and programmers alike.

What's Covered in this Book

This book is divided into two parts. The first part introduces XML and XSLT bit by bit, gradually demonstrating the techniques that you need to generate HTML (and other formats) from XML. The second part pulls the theory together by looking at some of the other things that you can do with XSLT, including generating formats other than HTML, pulling information out of a variety of XML formats, and validating XML.

Part 1: Theory

The aim of the first part of this book is to teach you the skills that you need to use XSLT. The first part is made up of 13 chapters. The chapters in this section follow on from each other – each one assumes that you've read the earlier chapters – so really you should go through them in order.

Because each of these chapters introduces new material, they contain a lot of exercises (Try It Outs) that you can follow to try out the new techniques that you read about. In addition, each chapter has a set of review questions at the end to reinforce the information that you've taken in.

1. **Beyond HTML** – introduces this book, outlines the problem that XML and XSLT address, and describes the example TV Guide web site that will be used in the rest of the book.

2. **Introducing XML** – introduces XML and XHTML, discusses the design of markup languages, and describes how you can apply stylesheets to XML. If you already know about XML then you may want to skip this chapter, although you may find it useful to go through the review questions to refresh your memory. Here you'll move the HTML for the TV Guide that we've looked at in this chapter into XHTML and into an XML format.

3. **Creating HTML from XML** – introduces simplified XSLT stylesheets and describes how to create HTML pages using them. In this chapter, you'll create a stylesheet that transforms the TV Guide XML that you generated in the previous chapter into a basic HTML page for a daily listing.

4. **Templates** – introduces templates as a way of breaking up larger XSLT stylesheets into separate components, each handling the generation of a different portion of the HTML page. Here you'll create your first full XSLT stylesheet for the TV Guide, and make your stylesheet more maintainable.

5. **Conditions** – discusses ways of creating conditional portions of an HTML page, depending on the information that's available to the script. In this chapter, you'll tackle the creation of some more complex HTML, whose structure depends on the information that's available about a program, for example, adding an image to the page if a program has been flagged.

6. **Variables, Expressions, and Parameters** – examines how to store pieces of information in variables so that you can reuse them, and how to pass parameters between templates and into XSLT in order to change the HTML that's created. Learning about variables and parameters will allow you to simplify your stylesheet, and to create a stylesheet that can be used to generate guides for different series when passed the name of a series.

7. **Paths** – looks at how to extract information from source XML. While this chapter has a lot of theoretical content, it will equip you with the skills to move around XML information with ease.

8. **The Result Tree** – explores the various methods of creating parts of an HTML document. In this chapter, you'll learn how to create conditional attributes, how to add comments within an HTML page, and several techniques that give you more control over the precise look of the HTML that you generate.

9. **Sorting and Numbering** – introduces methods for sorting the components that you generate in the HTML page, and describes how to number items within the page. For example, you'll see how to list programs alphabetically or by the time that they're shown, and you'll learn how to assign each program a unique number.

10. **IDs, Keys, and Groups** – shows you how to follow links between separate pieces of information, how to pull them together within an HTML page, and how to group data together. While trying these techniques out on the TV Guide, you'll see how to manage when data about series is kept separate from the data about individual programs, and you'll learn how to group together programs by the time at which they show, for example, rather than the channel that they are shown on.

11. **Named Templates and Recursion** – introduces you to how to use recursion (when a template calls itself) within XSLT. Here you'll learn how to develop a number of utility templates that allow you to perform calculations (such as the total duration of a number of programs) or repeat a piece of content a certain number of times.

12. **Building XSLT Applications** – discusses how to manage XSLT stylesheets that are divided between several files, and how to generate HTML based on information from multiple separate XML documents. Here you'll learn how to create stylesheets that hold utility code that you can use in all the stylesheets for the TV Guide web site. You'll also learn what to do when the TV Guide information is divided between several physical files.

13. **Extensions** – introduces several extensions to XSLT that are provided by different implementations, and examines how to write your own. In this chapter, you'll learn how to use extensions to create a single stylesheet that can generate a page for each program and for each series, from a single command.

Part 2: Practice

The aim of the second part of this book is twofold. Firstly, it provides you with more examples, and in particular examples that don't necessarily involve the same XML format as used in the first part of the book, or involve transformations to things other than HTML. Secondly, it pulls together the techniques that you've learned in isolation in the first part of the book, so that you get a feel for how a stylesheet is developed from scratch.

These chapters generally walk through the generation of a stylesheet, and round off with a set of ideas for future development of the stylesheet that give you an opportunity to try out your XSLT skills. The chapters are:

14. **Dynamic XSLT** – discusses how to use XSLT in two environments which have built-in support for running transformations: Internet Explorer, and Cocoon (a Java servlet). In this chapter, you'll learn the principles of client side and server side transformations, and see how to put them into practice to create dynamic XSLT applications. For example, you'll learn how to create forms that let users request summaries of particular TV series, so that the series guides are created on demand rather than in a single batch.

15. **Creating SVG** – introduces you to SVG, Scalable Vector Graphics, which is a markup language that represents graphics. You'll learn the basics of SVG, and experiment with it to create a pretty, printable image displaying the programs showing during a particular evening.

16. **Validating XML with Schematron** – discusses how XSLT and XPath can be used to test aspects of an XML document to make sure that it follows a particular markup language. This chapter is an opportunity to test your understanding of how to access and test information in a source document.

17. **Interpreting RSS with XSLT** – examines RSS (RDF Site Summaries) as a way of receiving syndicated information from other sites. In this chapter, we'll examine how to use TV listings and news received from other online sources in our own TV Guide.

What You Need to Use this Book

As XML is text-based, all you need to create an XML or XSLT file is a simple text editor, such as Notepad that comes with Windows. However, to see the XML, XSLT, or HTML that we will create in the book, you really need Internet Explorer 6 (or version 5 or 5.5 with MSXML 3.0 installed in replace mode). More importantly, in order to run the XSLT transformations in this book, you will need at least one XSLT processor. The three major XSLT processors are:

- **MSXML** from Microsoft – available at http://msdn.microsoft.com/
- **Saxon** from Michael Kay – available at http://saxon.sourceforge.net/
- **Xalan** from the Apache Project – available at http://xml.apache.org/

Conventions

You will encounter various styles of text and layout as you browse through the book. These have been used deliberately in order to make important information stand out. These styles are:

Try It Out – An Example

'Try It Out' is our way of presenting a practical example. Whenever something important is being discussed, you will find this section. This will help you understand the problem better.

> **Important information, key points, and additional information are displayed like this to make them stand out. Don't ignore them!**

If you see something like `TVGuide.xml`, you will know that it's a file name or an object name. A function will be shown as `function()` and HTML, XML, and XSLT elements will be shown as `<element>`.

When first introduced, new topics and names will appear as **Important New Topic**.

Words that appear on the user interface or menu names are written in a different font, such as Control Panel.

Code in this book has several fonts. If it is a word that we are talking about in the text, it's a distinctive font (for example, when discussing the command line tools like MSXSL). If it is a command or a block of code that you can type in as a program and run, then it's in a gray box like this:

```
<H1>TV Guide</H1>
```

If you are executing a command from the command line then it's in the following style:

>msxsl HelloWorld2.xml HelloWorld.xsl -o HelloWorld.msxsl.html

Sometimes you will see the code in a mixture of styles, like this:

```
<castlist>
  <member>
    <character gender="female">Zoe Slater</character>
    <actor>Michelle Ryan</actor>
  </member>
  <member>
    <character gender="male">Jamie Mitchell</character>
    <actor>Jack Ryder</actor>
  </member>
</castlist>
```

This is meant to draw your attention to code that is new, or relevant to the surrounding discussion (in the gray box), whilst showing it in the context of the code you have seen before (on the white background).

Downloading the Source Code

As you work through the examples in this book, you might decide that you prefer to type all the code in by hand. Many readers do prefer this, because it's a good way of getting familiar with the coding techniques that are used.

If you are one of those readers who like to type in the code, you can use our files to check the results you should be getting. They should be your first stop if you think you have typed in an error. If you don't like typing, then downloading the source code from our web site is a must! Either way it will help you with updates and debugging.

Whether you want to type in the code or not, we have made all the source code for this book available at our web site:

http://www.wrox.com.

Tell Us What You Think

Our commitment to readers doesn't stop when you walk out of the bookstore. We understand that errors can destroy the enjoyment of a book and can cause many wasted and frustrated hours, so we seek to minimize the distress they can cause.

Let us know how much you liked or loathed the book, and what you think we can do better next time. You can send your comments, either by returning the reply card in the back of this book, or by email to feedback@wrox.com. Please be sure to mention the book title in your message.

Errata and Updates

We have made sincere efforts to minimize the errors in the text and in the code. However, no one is perfect and mistakes do occur. If you find an error in one of our books, like a spelling mistake or a faulty piece of code, we would be very grateful for feedback. By sending the errata, you may save other readers from hours of frustration, and of course, you will be helping us provide even higher quality information. Simply email the information to Support@wrox.com. Your information will be checked and, if correct, posted to the errata page for that title, or used in subsequent editions of the book.

To find errata on the web site, go to http://www.wrox.com/, and simply locate the title through our Advanced Search or title list. Click on the Book Errata link, which is below the cover graphic on the book's detail page.

Technical Support

We have said in the above section that you can send your queries to the support staff, who are the first people to read them, by using the email address mentioned above, but please remember to write the specific book title and the last four numbers of the ISBN in the subject line. They have files on the most frequently asked questions and will answer anything general immediately. They also answer general queries about the book and the web site.

Deeper queries are forwarded to the technical editors responsible for each book. They have experience with the general programming language or particular product and are able to answer detailed technical questions on the subject. Once an issue has been resolved, the editor can post details on the errata sheet on the web site.

Finally, in the unlikely event that the editors can't answer your problem, they will forward the request to an author. We try to protect our authors from any distraction from their main job. However, we are quite happy to forward specific book-related queries to them. All Wrox authors help with the support on their books. They will either mail the reader directly with their answer, or send their response to the editor or the support department who will then pass it on to the reader.

p2p.wrox.com

p2p (**Programmer to Programmer™**) is a community of programmers sharing their problems and expertise. A variety of mailing lists cover all modern programming and Internet technologies. Links, resources, and an archive provide a comprehensive knowledge base. Whether you are an experienced professional or a web novice you'll find something of interest here. You could have author as well as peer support on these mailing lists. The mailing lists are moderated to ensure that messages are relevant and reasonable, which means that postings do not appear on the list until they have been read and approved.

Be confident that your query to p2p is not just being examined by a support professional, but also by the many Wrox authors and other industry experts present on our mailing list.

Beginning
XSLT

1

Beyond HTML

Welcome to *Beginning XSLT*, a book that will lead you through the basics of markup and transformations, on the way equipping you with the skills you need to create XML-based web sites and other XML applications.

This chapter is an introduction to the book as a whole. We're going to look at the starting point of the journey to using the Extensible Markup Language (XML) and the Extensible Stylesheet Language for Transformation (XSLT), and examine some of the reasons that you might want to make the journey in the first place. We'll also take a look at the example that we'll be using throughout this book – a web-based TV Guide.

HTML and Markup

As we start this book, it is assumed that you already know about the Hypertext Markup Language (HTML) and have some experience in using it to create web pages. HTML is probably the most popular markup language in existence, but markup languages as a whole have been around for a long time. In its purest form, authors and proofreaders have been using markup to pass on instructions to the typesetters who would lay out a document since the invention of printing. In computer terms, markup began to be used in the early 1970s, first GML (the Generalized Markup Language), then SGML (the Standard GML) since the 1980s, and currently XML (which will be discussed in the next chapter).

The basic concept of **markup** is that instructions about how a document should be processed are embedded within that document. If you look at the HTML source code, you'll know that a web page appears as it does because of **elements** in the HTML page. Elements consist of a start tag, some content, and usually an end tag. The elements that you use around a piece of text determine the way that it appears within the page. Often the name of the element is all that's important. For example:

```
<H1>TV Guide</H1>
```

An `<H1>` element like the one above will be displayed set on its own, on a line (rather than inline with the text that follows it), in a larger font than normal, and perhaps in bold, depending on the client. Elements with different names are treated differently. For example, the following:

```
<EM>important</EM>
```

An <EM> element such as the one above will be displayed inline with the text that surrounds it, and usually in italic. The element markup tells the application (the browser) how the text that it contains should be treated.

Elements are the building blocks of an HTML page, the most important type of markup that it contains. Sometimes the elements have **attributes** that alter the way the text is displayed as well. For example:

```
<TABLE BORDER=1>...</TABLE>
```

Here, the table is given a border one pixel wide because of the BORDER attribute on the <TABLE> element.

Presentational Elements

We've described the elements that we looked at above in terms of how they are presented, but the name is also meaningful in other ways. An <H1> element is a heading, in fact a level 1 heading in a page. An <EM> element is emphasized text, information that is particularly important in the context where it's used. A <TABLE> element denotes tabular information – not simply a layout, but also associations between cells in the same row and in the same column. In other words, the name of an element indicates the **semantic meaning** of a piece of text.

These examples of elements come from a fairly early age of HTML. As web browsers developed, HTML authors demanded more control over the presentation of HTML and this led to the introduction of a number of elements (and attributes) that did not have anything to do with the semantic meaning of a piece of text, but everything to do with how the text should be displayed. For example:

```
<FONT SIZE=7><B>TV Guide</B></FONT>
```

Here, the text "TV Guide" appears large and bold (exactly as it did with the <H1> element) because of the <FONT> and <B> elements. However, this time there is no indication as to what role the text "TV Guide" plays within the document. It could be that all the text on the page is large, and the text "TV Guide" simply fits in with the rest of that. It could be that the text "TV Guide" is the most important piece of information on the page. There is no way of knowing. All we can tell is how a browser should present the information.

Why is this a problem? Well, there are two reasons:

- Other applications, for example web-crawlers that index web pages, might want to make use of the information on the page. When a web-crawler sees an <H1> element, it knows that whatever is inside that <H1> element is an important phrase because it has been placed in a heading. On the other hand, the <FONT> element has no particular meaning, so without some very sophisticated heuristics, it's impossible for the web-crawler to tell whether the phrase is important or just needs to look pretty.

- The pages are harder to maintain. If the designers decide that the web site needs a new look, all the HTML pages have to be altered to bring their format into line. If the web site needs new content, the person authoring the HTML needs to be very careful to make sure that the same design is used on the new content.

These problems don't just arise when you use the `<FONT>` element – they arise whenever you use an element to change the appearance of some content rather than reflect its meaning. Common examples are tables being used to arrange components on a page, or `<BLOCKQUOTE>` elements being used to indent information. But what are the alternatives?

Separating Content and Presentation

We need a way of making information held on web pages readable and maintainable, while making them look pretty at the same time. A good solution to this problem is to keep the content of the page separate from the instructions that govern how it should be presented. This separation means that the content and the presentation instructions can be changed independently:

- The same document can be presented in lots of different ways, just by changing the presentation instructions
- Different information can be displayed consistently, by reusing the same presentation instructions with different documents

The separation of content from presentational information can occur at several stages in the process of generating an HTML page. Indeed, especially if the page is generated dynamically, you can combine several methods of adding presentation to content at different stages in the process of generating the page.

Using Stylesheets to Add Presentation

At the web browser end, you can make a distinction between the element that indicates the meaning of a particular component of a page (heading or paragraph, emphasis or variable) and the way in which that element should be displayed using Cascading Style Sheets (CSS). The web browser uses the instructions contained within the CSS stylesheet to render the HTML page to the viewer, as demonstrated in the following diagram:

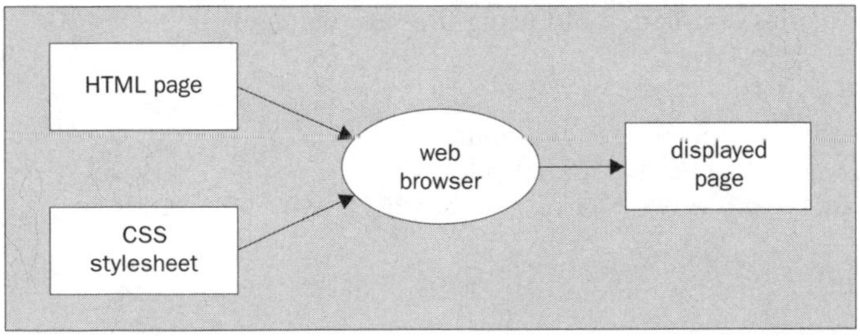

Cascading Style Sheets are made up of a number of rules that associate a particular style with particular types of elements. For example, you can state that `<H1>` elements should be displayed in an extra-large font and bold using:

```
H1 { font-size: x-large; font-weight: bold; }
```

Similarly, you can state that <EM> elements should be in italics using:

```
EM { font-style: italic; }
```

If you wanted to change the look of these elements, for example by making the <H1> elements appear in blue and italic and the <EM> elements in bold, then you could change the styles that they're associated with within the CSS stylesheet, without touching the HTML pages themselves:

```
H1 { font-size: x-large; font-style: italic; }
EM { font-style: italic; }
```

This makes updating web pages to give them a new design much easier than it is when purely presentational elements are used to indicate the style of individual pieces of text. It also helps to achieve consistency of styles across a page, and across documents, enabling you to reuse the same style instructions in multiple locations.

On top of this, you can use the `class` attribute on most HTML elements to add styles of different sorts across elements. The `class` attribute is particularly useful when combined with the elements <DIV> and <SPAN>, which enable you to add styles to blocks and phrases. The <DIV> element gives a generic block-level division in the page, while the <SPAN> element can be used around any phrase without implying a particular semantic meaning in the way that <EM> or other phrase-level elements would.

For example, imagine a list that describes the cast members for a particular TV program. We could use separate bullet points giving the character followed by the actor who plays them. The list should appear (for now) as follows:

- **Zoe Slater** Michelle Ryan
- **Jamie Mitchell** Jack Ryder
- **Sonia Jackson** Natalie Cassidy
- ...

To get this view with pure HTML, you could have something like the following HTML snippet, in which the character names are made bold using the <B> element:

```
<UL>
  <LI><B>Zoe Slater</B> Michelle Ryan
  <LI><B>Jamie Mitchell</B> Jack Ryder
  <LI><B>Sonia Jackson</B> Natalie Cassidy
  ...
</UL>
```

But what happens if you now want the actor names to be bold, while the character names are in italics? You have to go through the document, and all the similar documents, changing the HTML source. Instead, you can use CSS to indicate the meaning of the names within the list items, with <SPAN> elements and `class` attributes:

```
<UL class="castlist">
  <LI>
    <SPAN class="character">Zoe Slater</SPAN>
    <SPAN class="actor">Michelle Ryan</SPAN>
  <LI>
    <SPAN class="character">Jamie Mitchell</SPAN>
    <SPAN class="actor">Jack Ryder</SPAN>
  <LI>
    <SPAN class="character">Sonia Jackson</SPAN>
    <SPAN class="actor">Natalie Cassidy</SPAN>
  ...
</UL>
```

Now to make the character names italic and the actor names bold, you could use the following:

```
.castlist .character { font-style: italic; }
.castlist .actor { font-weight: bold; }
```

Assigning a class to the `<UL>` element for the cast list ensures that you can style actor and character names in different ways in different places within the HTML page, and allows you to style the cast list `<UL>` in a different way from other `<UL>` elements in the page.

Generating HTML Pages Using Scripts

Another method that you can use to separate content from presentation is to use a database, or many separate files, to hold the information for the HTML pages and write a script to construct the HTML from that set of information. The web server, or sometimes web browser, constructs the HTML page from the components stored within the database or file store:

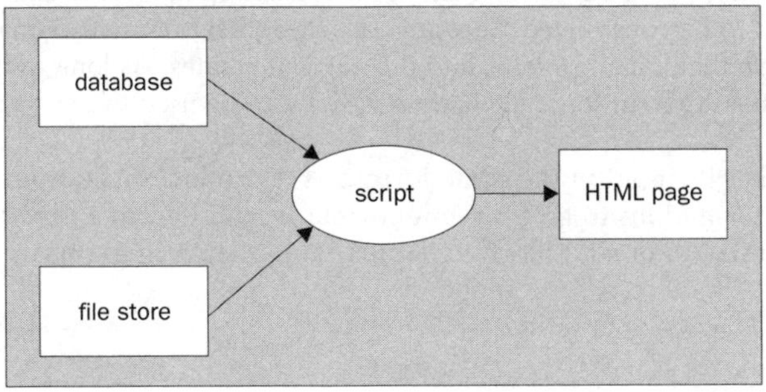

This approach is most effective when the information that is presented in the HTML page is reused in many places, such that you can reuse the same information, stored once within the database, at many locations. It is also best when the HTML page that is generated from the database or file store is supplemented with a CSS stylesheet that defines the way in which the HTML elements should be displayed:

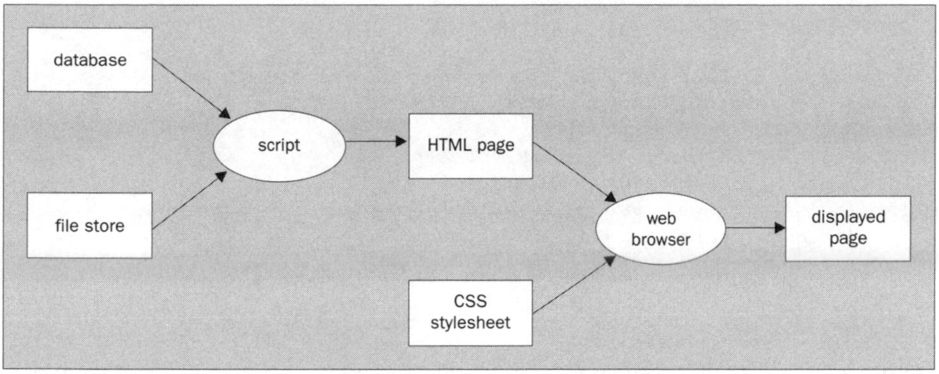

This is a powerful combination because the scripts that generate HTML pages are likely to be more complex than the stylesheets that add the look-and-feel to the HTML page. When the site design changes, the CSS stylesheet can be changed more easily than the script that generates the HTML page can.

Another powerful feature of this approach is that the same database or file store can be used to generate many different kinds of pages – not just HTML, but also other formats, such as Wireless Markup Language (WML) for WAP phones or Scalable Vector Graphics (SVG) for graphics.

There are several technologies around that enable you to write scripts for generating HTML pages, such as Java Server Pages (JSP) or Active Server Pages (ASP). In this book, we'll be looking at one particular technology that also fits into this niche – XSLT.

Unlike Java or Visual Basic, XSLT is a language that is specifically designed to fit in the "script" slot in the above diagram. This design has two facets. Firstly, it's designed to create markup languages, such as HTML, WML, or SVG, very easily, by seeing the content of these markup languages as elements and attributes rather than as strings that need to be constructed. Secondly, it's designed to use other markup languages as the source of the information that it incorporates into the pages it creates. As long as the database or file store in the above diagram creates XML in some form, then XSLT can be used to create HTML.

The fact that XSLT takes its input in the same format as it produces its output means that you can set up a series of XSLT transformations to go from one format to another, in a **pipeline**. The following diagram shows the kind of organization that a (fairly complex) application might have:

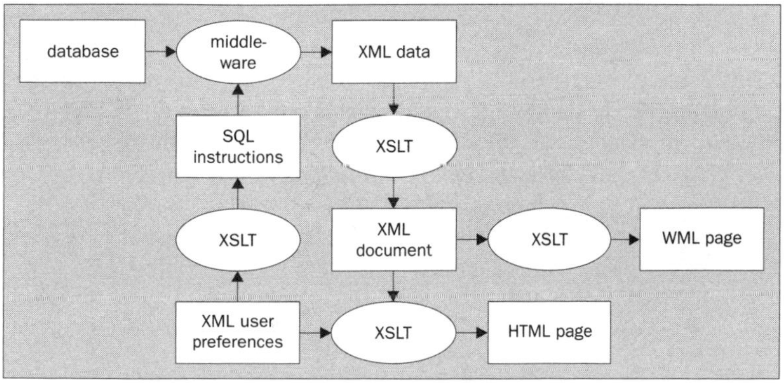

If we start from the XML user preferences in the above diagram, we can see how XSLT might be used on a web server. The user preferences, held in XML, might define what information users have access to or are interested in, as well as preferences about how they like information to be displayed. Since they are in XML, you can use XSLT to transform these user preferences into a set of SQL instructions that are fed into some middleware in order to extract the relevant information from the database into another XML file.

XML files extracted from databases tend to be quite hard-to-manage affairs, so rather than going straight from that into a final display format, another XSLT stylesheet could be used to format it into an intermediate format which holds information that's common to several final formats – for example, it might format dates and numbers into something that's more human readable than the internal database formats. This XML document is then transformed by XSLT into two separate formats: WML for WAP phones and HTML for web browsers. The same XML user preferences from which the SQL instructions were derived might feed in to this process as well, to guide the format of the page.

The TV Guide Site

During the course of this book, we'll be working on a case study involving the construction of a web site for a TV Guide. The TV Guide web site shows what's on, for a number of channels, over a week. It will give an overview of each program, listing its cast, directors, writers, and producers, just as you would get from a hardcopy of the TV Guide. To give you an idea of the organization of the site, have a look at the following site map:

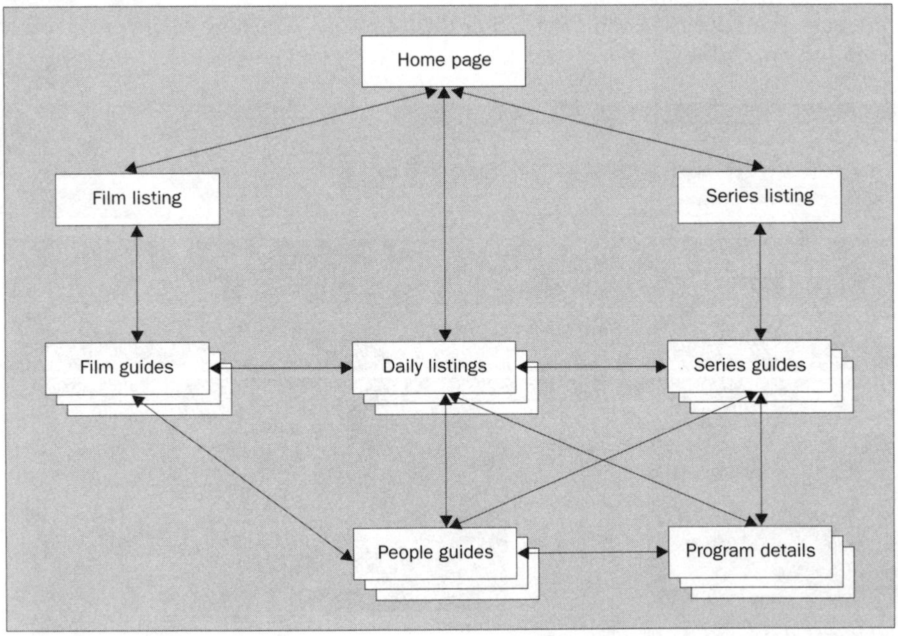

The home page links to:

- A listing of the films showing during the next week
- An alphabetical listing of the series whose episodes are being shown
- One page for each day of the week, showing the programs on each channel

Then there are several sets of pages that are interlinked. The film listing and the daily listings provide links to details on each of the films that are shown during the week. The series guides and daily listings provide links to details on the programs that are being shown. All these sets of pages link to individual pages for each of the people involved in the TV shows – actors, characters, writers, directors, and producers.

The web site provides some supplementary information as well as the official descriptions of the programs, including a rating for most of the programs. The web site can also be tailored for each user. For example:

- Users can flag programs and series that are particularly interesting to them
- Users can provide sets of keywords that might occur in titles or descriptions of programs that they might be interested in
- Users can change the structure and design of the pages, such as the colors and fonts used

Sample Page

An example page from the TV Guide web site is the following, which gives the programs showing on Thursday 5th July in a table:

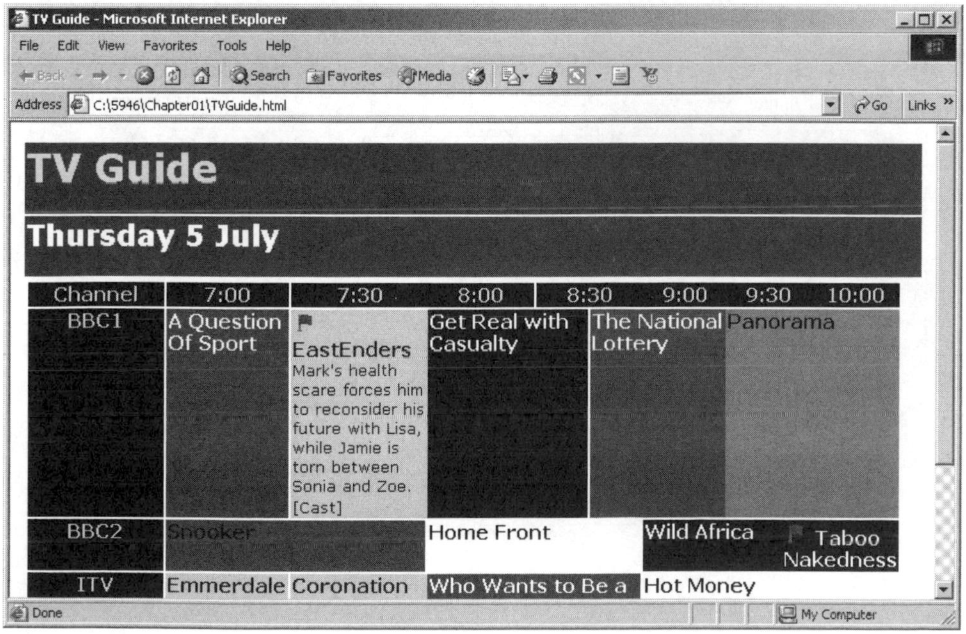

As we start on the TV Guide web site, the HTML pages mix content with presentation very freely. The HTML source for the above page (`TVGuide.html`) is as follows:

```
<HTML>
<HEAD>
  <TITLE>TV Guide</TITLE>
  <SCRIPT type="text/javascript">
    function toggle(element) {
      if (element.style.display == 'none') {
        element.style.display = 'block';
      } else {
        element.style.display = 'none';
      }
    }
  </SCRIPT>
</HEAD>

<BODY>
  <BASEFONT face="Verdana, sans-serif">
  <TABLE>
    <TR>
      <TD bgcolor=#CC0000><FONT color=yellow><H1>TV Guide</FONT></H1>
    <TR>
      <TD bgcolor=#CC0000><FONT color=white><H2>Thursday 5 July</FONT></H2>
    <TR>
      <TD>
        <TABLE width="100%">
          <TR bgcolor=black>
            <TH width="16%"><FONT color=yellow>Channel
            <TH colspan=6 width="12%"><FONT color=yellow>7:00
            <TH colspan=6 width="12%"><FONT color=yellow>7:30
            ...
          <TR>
            <TH bgcolor=black valign=top><FONT color=yellow>BBC1</FONT>
            <TD colspan=6 bgcolor=green valign=top>
              <FONT color=white><B>A Question Of Sport</B></FONT><BR>
            <TD colspan=6 bgcolor=pink valign=top>
              <IMG src="flag.gif" alt="[Flagged]" width=20 height=20>
              <B>EastEnders</B><BR>
              <FONT size=2>Mark's health scare forces him to reconsider his
              future with Lisa, while Jamie is torn between Sonia and Zoe.
              <SPAN onclick="toggle(EastEndersCast);">[Cast]</SPAN></FONT>
              <BLOCKQUOTE id="EastEndersCast" style="display: none;">
                Zoe Slater <B>Michelle Ryan</B><BR>
                Jamie Mitchell <B>Jack Ryder</B><BR>
                Sonia Jackson <B>Natalie Cassidy</B><BR>
              </BLOCKQUOTE>
              ...
        </TABLE>
  </TABLE>
</BODY>
</HTML>
```

This HTML demonstrates presentation information embedded in the content of the page and HTML elements being used purely to provide presentational cues. For example:

- Almost the entire page is wrapped within a <TABLE> element, so that the headings at the top of the page can have a red background
- The background of the cells is determined by a `bgcolor` attribute on the <TD> or <TH> element, while the color of the text is determined by separate <FONT> elements within the cells themselves
- A <BLOCKQUOTE> element is used to indent the list of cast members, each of which is placed on a new line using a <BR> element
- Individual words or phrases are highlighted using <B> or <I> elements, which provide styling information but say nothing about the meaning of the phrase or word

Adding CSS

The first step in separating the presentational information from the content of the TV Guide page is to add a CSS stylesheet to style the components of the page rather than using embedded presentational attributes and elements. To make this change, purely presentational elements are removed, and may be replaced by <DIV> and <SPAN> elements with appropriate classes. Taking the examples listed above:

- The wrapping <TABLE> element, which was purely added for presentational purposes, can be removed, because background colors can be added to blocks of text without using table cells.
- The `bgcolor` attributes and <FONT> elements can be removed, and the style of a cell determined by whether it is a heading cell (<TH>) or a normal cell (<TD>).
- The cast members are conceptually items in a list, not lines in a quotation. With CSS, they can be represented as items in a list (using a <UL> and <LI> elements) – the bullet points can be omitted by controlling the style of the <UL> element.
- The meaning of the words and phrases can be indicated with generic <SPAN> elements with appropriate `class` attributes rather than presentational elements.

Making these changes gives a very different set of HTML, `TVGuide.css.html`:

```
<HTML>
<HEAD>
  <TITLE>TV Guide</TITLE>
  <LINK rel="stylesheet" href="TVGuide.css">
  <SCRIPT type="text/javascript">
    function toggle(element) {
      if (element.style.display == 'none') {
        element.style.display = 'block';
      } else {
        element.style.display = 'none';
      }
    }
  </SCRIPT>
</HEAD>

<BODY>
```

```
    <H1>TV Guide</H1>
    <H2><SPAN class="day">Thursday</SPAN> 5 July</H2>
    <TABLE width="100%">

      <TR>
        <TH width="16%">Channel
        <TH colspan="6" width="12%">7:00
        <TH colspan="6" width="12%">7:30
        ...

      <TR>
        <TH class="channel">BBC1
        <TD colspan="6" class="quiz">
          <SPAN class="title">A Question Of Sport</SPAN><BR>
        <TD colspan="6" class="soap">
          <IMG src="flag.gif" alt="[Flagged]" width="20" height="20">
          <SPAN class="title">EastEnders</SPAN><BR>
          Mark's health scare forces him to reconsider his future with Lisa,
          while Jamie is torn between Sonia and Zoe.
          <SPAN onclick="toggle(EastEndersCast);">[Cast]</SPAN>
          <DIV id="EastEndersCast" style="display: none;">
            <UL class="castlist">
              <LI>
                <SPAN class="character">Zoe Slater</SPAN>
                <SPAN class="actor">Michelle Ryan</SPAN>
              <LI>
                <SPAN class="character">Jamie Mitchell</SPAN>
                <SPAN class="actor">Jack Ryder</SPAN>
              <LI>
                <SPAN class="character">Sonia Jackson</SPAN>
                <SPAN class="actor">Natalie Cassidy</SPAN>
            </UL>
          </DIV>
        ...
    </TABLE>
  </BODY>
  </HTML>
```

The style is added to this HTML page using a CSS stylesheet, which is referenced using the `<LINK>` element in the `<HEAD>` element of the HTML page. In fact, using CSS gives a lot more control over the exact styling of the components of the page – more control over the size of the fonts used, greater flexibility in the spacing of blocks of text, and so on. An example CSS file for this page (`TVGuide.css`) is as follows:

```
BODY, TABLE {
     font-family: Verdana, sans-serif;
     font-size: 8pt;
}

TABLE {
```

```
    width: 100%;
}

TD, TH {
    vertical-align: top;
    margin: 0;
}

H1 {
    background: #C00;
    color: yellow;
    padding: 0 0.2em;
    margin: 0;
}

H2 {
    background: #C00;
    color: white;
    padding: 0 0.2em;
    margin: 0;
}

TH {
    background: black;
    color: yellow;
    font-size: 1.2em;
}

.soap {
    background: pink;
}

.news {
    background: gray;
}

.entertainment, .quiz {
    background: green;
    color: white;
}

.sport {
    background: red;
}

.documentary {
    background: navy;
    color: white;
}

.film {
    background: black;
```

```
        color: white;
    }

    .title {
        font-size: 1.2em;
        font-weight: bold;
    }

    .castlist {
        margin: 0em;
        padding: 0.5em 1em;
    }
    .castlist li {
        display: list-item;
        list-style-type: none;
    }
    .character, .actor {
        display: inline;
        background: transparent;
        color: black;
        margin-bottom: 0em;
        padding: 0em;
        font-weight: normal;
        font-size: 1em;
    }
    .actor {
        font-weight: bold;
    }
```

This CSS file creates the following rendered page from `TVGuide.css.html`:

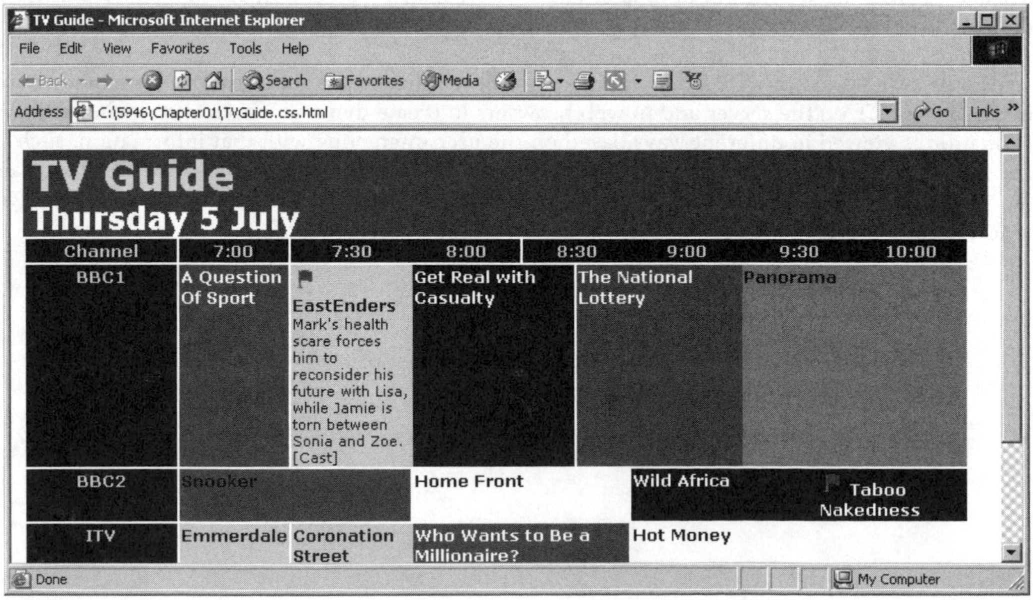

Not only can this CSS file be easily updated to change the style of the page, it also has the benefit that it can be shared across many files, ensuring that there's a consistent design to each of the pages on the site. When the style of the site needs to be changed, the only file that needs to be changed is the CSS file that controls the appearance of the pages.

Adding XSLT

We've also looked at the first method of separating content and presentation; taking the sample page from the TV Guide as the base, we've moved from an HTML style that mixes content and presentation to one where the presentational information is contained in a CSS stylesheet. The rest of this book will focus on the second method of separating content and presentation, by generating the HTML page from raw XML data using XSLT.

To use XSLT at all, we need to have the data that makes up the page in a format that can be used by XSLT, and that means XML. In the next chapter, we'll introduce XML and XHTML. We'll move the HTML for the TV Guide that we've looked at in this chapter into XHTML and into an XML format that we'll use as the source data for the rest of the book.

Once we've got an XML source file, we can create HTML from it. We'll start off simply, just building a simple listing of programs from some XML, but gradually make that stylesheet more and more sophisticated, eventually recreating a table like the one that we've seen in this chapter. We'll see how XSLT can be used to format, reorder, and filter information, to create the various different pages for the web site from the same core set of information, and create conditional content based on user preferences or access to information, such as adding flags to programs and highlighting keywords.

XSLT can be used in several ways and in several places within an application, as we've seen from the example showing XSLT used to create SQL instructions, intermediate XML formats, and final presentational formats. We're going to start by concentrating on creating presentation formats (in particular HTML) using XSLT, but in later chapters we'll also look at how XSLT is incorporated into larger applications.

In particular, we'll see how XSLT can be used to pull in information from user preferences, and how you can use XSLT on the server and in web browsers to create dynamic applications where the same information is viewed in different ways based on the user interacting with that information, such as resorting tables or showing or hiding parts of the page. We'll also look at how to use XSLT to transform to and from other XML formats, so that you can create a series of transformations that take you from one format to another.

Summary

In this chapter, we've seen the problems encountered with many HTML pages, where the pertinent information that they convey is mixed with presentational elements. We've seen how the mix of content and presentation on a page makes the page harder to interpret by other applications, and harder to maintain, particularly when the design of a site needs to change.

You've learned about two methods of separating content from presentation: using CSS to give color and style to an HTML page, and using scripts, in particular XSLT, to generate the HTML page itself, based on information stored in a more accessible and reusable format (such as a database or a file store).

The problems, and the use of CSS, have been illustrated in this chapter using the example web site that we'll be looking at throughout this book – an online TV Guide. We've also looked, briefly, at the kinds of features that we'll be able to add to our online TV Guide using the XSLT that you'll learn through this book.

Beginning
XSLT

2

Introducing XML

In the last chapter, we started looking at how to separate content from presentation. We took an HTML page with a lot of presentational elements in it and replaced them with more generic elements (<SPAN> and <DIV>) and lots of CSS.

In this chapter we're going to go one step further and separate the **dynamic information** in the page, the content that we'll want to change over time, from the **static information** that stays the same over a longer period. We're going to store this dynamic information as a separate XML file so that it can be repurposed – used in other places in addition to this web page, such as in other web pages, or presented in a different form such as WML for WAP phones. By the end of the chapter we'll have an XML document on which we can use a variety of **XSLT** stylesheets in the rest of the book.

The material that you learn in this chapter is essential for the rest of the book because everything else we look at, including XSLT, is based on XML. In this chapter you'll learn:

- What XML is and where it comes from
- How to make HTML XML-compliant
- How to create some XML to hold the information that you have
- What things to bear in mind when you're designing a markup language
- How to write a description of your markup language
- How to use CSS to present an XML document

Markup Languages

When you think of the Web, you think of HTML, the Hypertext Markup Language. Like a natural language, there are two parts to a markup language: its **vocabulary** and its **grammar**.

The vocabulary tells you the names of the components that you can use in a document. Those things are:

- **Elements** like <P> and <A>
- **Attributes** like `class` and `href`
- **Entities** like ` ` and `é`

The grammar tells you the rules that tie the parts of the vocabulary together. These are rules like:

- An <A> element has an `href` attribute
- A <UL> element can contain one or more <LI> elements
- The <HEAD> element must contain a <TITLE> element

Now, you could imagine a different markup language that used a different vocabulary and grammar. Instead of a <P> element, it might use the name <para>; rather than having <H1> to <H6> for headings, it might use <section> elements with <title> elements inside them, and so on.

Extending HTML

Why would you need this other language? Well, have another look at the HTML that we have created for our TV guide. HTML has elements that allow us to say that a particular word or phrase is a link or should be emphasized, but it doesn't let us state that this part of the TV description is the title of the program, that bit its running length, this other section lists its cast, and so on. Identifying those parts is important for two reasons:

- It affects the way that information looks on the page. As we've seen in the last chapter, the presentation of a piece of content is often tied to its meaning. If we had elements to indicate the meaning of these words and phrases, we would be able to display them in different ways with CSS.
- It helps other people, and more importantly applications, look at the page and draw some conclusions about the information that it contains. If we used <B> to indicate the program's title and the name of a character, then all an application could tell was that those phrases should be in bold. If we had more descriptive element names, like <title> and <character>, then the application could distinguish between the two and could actually make use of that information.

The idea of applications being able to make sense of web pages by looking at the names of the elements that are used within them is at the heart of the idea of the "Semantic Web".

Try It Out – Changing CSS Classes to Elements

We're currently using the `class` attributes on HTML elements and using <SPAN> and <DIV> elements in our HTML page to indicate the meaning of the parts of the page. This is fine as far as it goes, but it doesn't give us the flexibility and control that an element and attributes would. For example, currently the `TVGuide.html` HTML page contains the following structure for cast lists:

```
<UL class="castlist">
  <LI>
    <SPAN class="character">Zoe Slater</SPAN>
    <SPAN class="actor">Michelle Ryan</SPAN>
```

```
  <LI>
    <SPAN class="character">Jamie Mitchell</SPAN>
    <SPAN class="actor">Jack Ryder</SPAN>
  <LI>
    <SPAN class="character">Sonia Jackson</SPAN>
    <SPAN class="actor">Natalie Cassidy</SPAN>
</UL>
```

In this structure the cast list contains a number of character-actor pairs, but there's nothing in the grammar of HTML that determines this – it's just a rule that we know about. We assume that this rule holds true in the CSS that we use to present the cast list. Instead, we could design a markup language that used elements to mark up the cast list using elements – `castlist1.xml`:

```
<castlist>
  <member>
    <character>Zoe Slater</character>
    <actor>Michelle Ryan</actor>
  </member>
  <member>
    <character>Jamie Mitchell</character>
    <actor>Jack Ryder</actor>
  </member>
  <member>
    <character>Sonia Jackson</character>
    <actor>Natalie Cassidy</actor>
  </member>
</castlist>
```

Using elements means that it's easy to write the grammar for the cast list:

- `<castlist>` elements contain one or more `<member>` elements
- `<member>` elements contain a `<character>` element followed by an `<actor>` element
- `<character>` and `<actor>` elements contain text

It also means that we can add attributes to these elements if we want to, perhaps indicating the gender of the different characters as we do in `castlist2.xml`:

```
<castlist>
  <member>
    <character gender="female">Zoe Slater</character>
    <actor>Michelle Ryan</actor>
  </member>
  <member>
    <character gender="male">Jamie Mitchell</character>
    <actor>Jack Ryder</actor>
  </member>
  <member>
    <character gender="female">Sonia Jackson</character>
    <actor>Natalie Cassidy</actor>
  </member>
</castlist>
```

Including structured information would be a lot harder to do using just the `class` attribute in HTML. Even if we did include it in the `class` attribute, it would be hard to use because you have to be able to list all the possible classes in order to use them. While that's easy for an attribute like gender – its value can be either 'male' or 'female' – if we were to include the character's age, or the date the actor joined the series, then it would become impossible.

> **Using your own elements and attributes to mark up your information gives you more flexibility in how to represent it and makes it more accessible and meaningful to other people and programs.**

Meta-Markup Languages

You'll notice in the example we used above that the new markup language for the cast list still uses the same general syntax as HTML – tags are indicated with angle brackets, attributes with names, and values are separated by an equals sign. A document written in this new markup language would look much the same as the same document written in HTML, except that the names of the elements and attributes might change and perhaps things would be moved around a little.

But how do you decide that this is the syntax you will use? Why not use parentheses to indicate elements and slashes to escape special characters? Well, you could, and some markup languages do, but HTML, along with a number of other markup languages, is based on the ISO standard **SGML**, the **Standard Generalized Markup Language**. SGML is what's known as a **meta-markup language** – it doesn't define a vocabulary or a grammar itself, but it does define the general syntax that the members of a family of markup languages share.

The benefit of sharing a meta-markup language is that you can create basic applications that can handle *any* markup language in that family. An SGML **parser** can read and interpret SGML because it recognizes, for example, where an element starts and ends, what attributes there are, what their values are, and so on. SGML editors can support authors who are writing in SGML-based markup languages by adding end tags where necessary. Standard tools can format and present SGML no matter which SGML-based markup language is used in a particular document. Indeed, SGML-based markup languages have been used in many large projects; HTML is just the most popular of these languages.

However, SGML has some drawbacks as a meta-markup language that mean it doesn't quite fit the bill as a meta-markup language for the Web. The most important of these drawbacks is that it is *too* flexible, *too* configurable, which means that the applications such as web browsers that read it and manipulate it have to be fairly heavy weight. You can see some of this in HTML – certain elements in HTML, like `<LI>`, don't need to have close tags whereas others, like `<EM>`, do. Other markup languages in the SGML family use close tags without names in, and so on. The variation that SGML allows means that any application that covers all the possibilities is going to be huge.

XML: The Extensible Markup Language

What the Web needed was a cut-down version of SGML, a meta-markup language that gave just enough flexibility, but retained its simplicity. This is the role of **XML**, the **Extensible Markup Language**.

XML is a meta-markup language, like SGML, but it's specifically designed to be easy to use over the Web, to be human-readable and straightforward for applications to read and understand. The XML Recommendation was released by the W3C in February 1998, and the "Second Edition", which just incorporates the errata from the first edition, was released in October 2000. You can download a copy of the XML Recommendation from http://www.w3.org/TR/REC-xml.

There are now lots of tools that can help you to author XML and to write applications that use XML. One important group of these tools is XML parsers. XML parsers know the syntactic rules that XML documents follow and use that knowledge to break down XML documents into their component parts, like elements and attributes. This process is known as **parsing** a document.

Most XML parsers make the information held in the document available through a standard set of methods and properties. Most parsers support **SAX**, the Simple API for XML. SAX parsers generate events every time they come across a component in an XML document, such as a start tag or a comment. Several parsers also support **DOM**, the Document Object Model, which is an API defined by the W3C. DOM parsers hold the structure of the XML document in memory as a tree.

> *You can find out more about the SAX and DOM APIs in* Beginning XML, 2nd Edition*, ISBN 1-861005-59-8, from Wrox Press.*

> **XML is a meta-markup language that defines the general syntax of markup languages for use on the Web and elsewhere.**

There are a large and growing number of markup languages that are based on XML, that are part of the family that follow the syntactic rules that are defined by XML. There are markup languages in all areas – documentation, e-commerce, metadata, geographical, medical, scientific, graphical, and so on – often several. Because all these languages are based on XML, you can move between them very easily – all you have to learn is the new set of elements, attributes, and entities. So what are the syntactic rules that these markup languages all have in common?

XML Rules

We've already seen that HTML is a markup language that uses SGML, and how XML is a cut-down version of SGML. As you might expect, then, the syntax that XML defines involves a lot that's familiar from HTML: it has elements and attributes, start tags and end tags, and a number of entities for escaping the characters that are used as part of the markup.

In this section, we'll go through the rules that govern XML documents in general. These rules are known as **well-formedness constraints**, and XML documents that follow them are known as **well-formed documents**. Unlike with HTML, where browsers are notoriously lazy about checking the HTML that you give them, XML has to be well-formed to be recognized and usable by XML applications. When people talk about an XML document or XML message then they are talking about well-formed XML.

Well-formedness constraints are distinct from the rules that come from the vocabulary and grammar of a particular markup language (like HTML). An XML document that adheres to the rules of a particular markup language is known as a **valid document**; we'll see how to declare the rules that a valid document must follow later in this chapter.

Try It Out – Testing Whether an XML Document is Well-Formed

Before we launch into a look at what the well-formedness rules are, we'll first look at how to check whether an XML document is well-formed or not. Knowing how to check well-formedness will enable you to try out different examples as we go through the individual rules.

Most XML editors will let you test whether a document you create is well-formed and show you the error if it isn't. If you're not using an XML editor, you can test whether a document is a well-formed XML document by opening it in Internet Explorer: by default a well-formed XML document will display as a collapsible tree.

Try looking at the `castlist2.xml` XML document that we created earlier in this chapter using Internet Explorer. You should see a tree representation of the XML file, as follows:

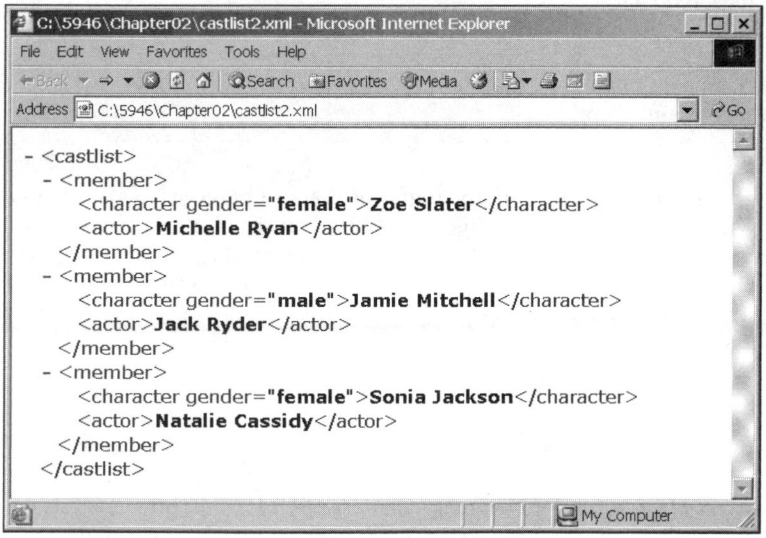

You can click on any of the minus signs next to the start tags of the elements to collapse those elements. For example, the following screenshot shows all the `<member>` elements collapsed except for the first:

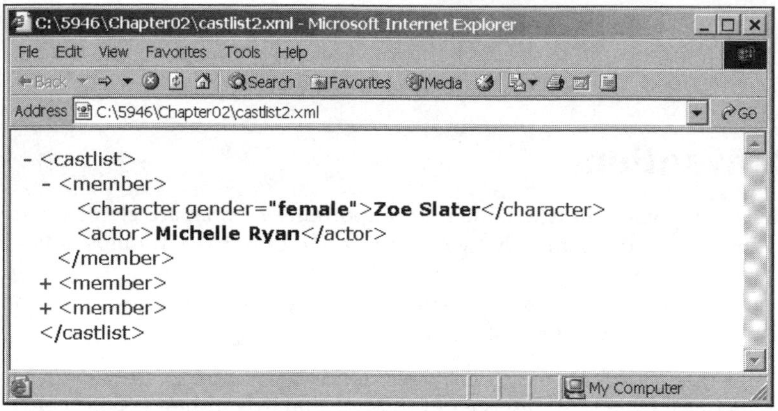

Now try adding the extension `.xml` to the `TVguide.html` file from the last chapter to create `TVGuide.html.xml`. Adding this extension will make Internet Explorer treat the HTML file as an XML file. But the HTML file doesn't adhere to XML rules, so you get an error reported, as follows:

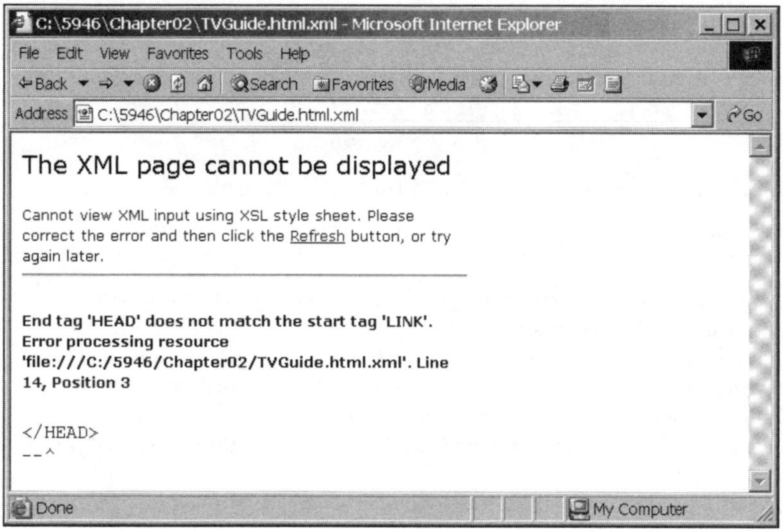

By simply opening your document in Internet Explorer, you can use any error messages that it shows you to identify the problems in your XML documents.

XHTML

As you've seen, HTML doesn't follow the XML rules. However, you can turn HTML into **XHTML**. In the XHTML 1.0 Recommendation at http://www.w3.org/TR/xhtml1, XHTML is called "The Extensible HyperText Markup Language", but really its subtitle, "A Reformulation of HTML 4 in XML 1.0", is more accurate. As we've seen, HTML is a markup language in the SGML family; XHTML is the same markup language (the same vocabulary and grammar) as HTML, but this time in the XML family.

In the rest of this section, we'll take the HTML document that we put together in the last chapter and turn it into XHTML bit by bit. By the end of this section, you'll be able to open up the XHTML document with an `.xml` extension in Internet Explorer, and it will display as a tree.

Naming Conventions

Names are used in several places in XML, the most important of which are element names, attribute names, and entity names. In general, the names that you use in XML only have to follow a few rules:

- Names can contain letters, digits, hyphens (-), periods (.), colons (:), or underscores (_), but they must start with a letter, colon, or underscore.
- Names cannot start with `xml` in any case combination (that is, they can't start with `XML` or `Xml` either) as these names are reserved for XML standards from the W3C.
- Names should only use a colon if they use **namespaces**, which are ways of indicating the markup language that a particular element or attribute comes from. We will see more about namespaces in the next chapter.

The following table compares a few valid and invalid names:

Invalid XML Names	Valid XML Names
`2nd`	`second`
`XmlDoc`	`Doc`
`tv:castlist:member`	`tv.castlist.member`

There aren't any fixed conventions for names in XML so if you're designing your own markup language you can use whatever naming convention you like. However, XML is case-sensitive, so if you use a particular case convention for the name of an element in a start tag, you must use the same convention in the end tag. Many markup languages use camel case, where new words are indicated by a capital letter, either starting with an uppercase letter (for example, `CastList`) or lowercase letter (`castList`). Several markup languages use lowercase with hyphens (`cast-list`) or capital-case with periods (`Cast.List`).

> *As we'll see later on, XSLT uses a naming convention of all lowercase with hyphens separating words, for example* `<value-of>`.

The first big difference between HTML and XHTML is that whereas you can use any case you like for the names of elements and attributes in HTML, in XHTML they are standardized to all be lowercase. If you revisit the HTML that we looked at earlier in the chapter, and change all the element and attribute names to use lowercase, creating `TVGuide2.html`, you can see the (small) difference that this makes. For example, the cast list now looks like:

```
<ul class="castlist">
  <li>
    <span class="character">Zoe Slater</span>
    <span class="actor">Michelle Ryan</span>
  <li>
```

```
    <span class="character">Jamie Mitchell</span>
    <span class="actor">Jack Ryder</span>
  <li>
    <span class="character">Sonia Jackson</span>
    <span class="actor">Natalie Cassidy</span>
</ul>
```

XHTML uses all-lowercase element and attribute names.

Elements in XML

This section looks at the main component in an XML document – the elements – and the rules that they must follow.

End Tags

In XML, all elements must have both start and end tags, each holding the name of the element, with the name in the closing tag prefixed with the / character.

Therefore, unlike in HTML, every element in XHTML has to have an end tag. The HTML that we looked at before didn't have end tags for the <LI> elements; the equivalent XHTML must look like:

```
<ul class="castlist">
  <li>
    <span class="character">Zoe Slater</span>
    <span class="actor">Michelle Ryan</span>
  </li>
  <li>
    <span class="character">Jamie Mitchell</span>
    <span class="actor">Jack Ryder</span>
  </li>
  <li>
    <span class="character">Sonia Jackson</span>
    <span class="actor">Natalie Cassidy</span>
  </li>
</ul>
```

Empty Elements

Some elements, such as <IMG> and <BR> in HTML, don't have end tags because they don't contain anything. In XML, these **empty elements** can use a special syntax: a forward-slash before the closing angle bracket of the start tag rather than having an end tag.

Here are a couple of examples from XHTML:

```
<img src="star.gif" />
<br />
```

I put a space before the forward-slash out of habit – it's not necessary in XML, but including one in XHTML means that older browsers that only understand HTML don't balk at empty XHTML elements, particularly those that don't have attributes such as `<br>` and `<hr>`.

This syntax means exactly the same thing to an XML application as having a start tag immediately followed by an end tag:

```
<img src="star.gif"></img>
<br></br>
```

Nested Elements

Elements in XHTML have to nest properly inside each other – you can't have the end tag in the content of an element unless its start tag is also within that element. In fact, this is the case in HTML as well (it's a rule from SGML) but some web browsers don't pick up on errors where elements overlap each other. For example:

```
Some <B>bold and <I>italic</B> text</I>.
```

should be:

```
Some <B>bold and <I>italic</I></B><I> text</I>.
```

The Document Element

Finally, XML only allows there to be a single element at the top level of the document, known as the **document element**. This element contains everything in the XML document. In XHTML, the document element is the `<html>` element, for example. Compare the XML documents in the following table to see the difference:

Well-formed XML Document	Non-well-formed XML Document
`<Chars>`	`<Char>Zoe Slater</Char>`
`<Char>Zoe Slater</Char>`	`<Char>Jamie Mitchell</Char>`
`<Char>Jamie Mitchell</Char>`	`<Char>Sonia Jackson</Char>`
`<Char>Sonia Jackson</Char>`	...
...	
`</Chars>`	

Elements nest inside each other to form a hierarchy, with the document element at the top of the hierarchy. Elements must have a start and end tag, although empty elements can use a special syntax.

Attributes in XML

XML attributes are always name-value pairs associated with an element, with the value given in quotes following an equals sign after the name of the attribute. You can use either single or double quotes for any particular attribute value, but they must match: if you start the attribute value with a single quote, then you must use a single quote to end it.

Like element names, attribute names must be valid XML names. However, unlike elements, there are some attributes that are built in to XML. These attributes are:

- `xml:lang` – indicates the language of the element, its attributes, and its contents
- `xml:space` – controls whether whitespace is retained (`preserve`) or dealt with by the application (`default`)
- `xml:base` – provides the base URI for the element, its attributes, and its contents

In addition to these attributes, there is a class of special attributes known as namespace declarations, as we'll see later, all of which begin with the string `xmlns`.

As well as forcing attributes to use quotes around values, XML differs from SGML in that it cannot have Boolean attributes which are indicated solely by their name, without a value – the presence of a Boolean attribute implies a true value and its absence a false one. Boolean attributes occur in several places in HTML, most especially in forms. Take an example drop-down menu in HTML:

```
<SELECT name="channels" multiple>
  <OPTION selected>BBC1
  <OPTION selected>BBC2
  <OPTION>ITV
  <OPTION selected>Channel 4
  <OPTION>Channel 5
</SELECT>
```

The `<SELECT>` element can take a `multiple` Boolean attribute and the `<OPTION>` element can take a `selected` Boolean attribute. These Boolean attributes aren't allowed in XML because every attribute must have a value. Instead, each of these attributes takes a value equal to the name of the attribute. Thus the equivalent in XHTML (remembering to use lowercase and to add end tags) would be:

```
<select name="channels" multiple="multiple">
  <option selected="selected">BBC1</option>
  <option selected="selected">BBC2</option>
  <option>ITV</option>
  <option selected="selected">Channel 4</option>
  <option>Channel 5</option>
</select>
```

All attributes must use either single or double quotes. Boolean attributes have values that are equal to their name.

Entities, Characters, and Encodings

There are several characters that are significant in XML – a less-than sign signals the start of a tag, for example. But what if you want to include one of these characters in the data that the XML document holds, such as a less-than sign in some code held by an XML element? In these cases, you have to **escape** the character so that an XML parser knows that it's not part of the markup you're using in this particular instance. As in HTML, the significant characters in XML markup are escaped with **entities**. This means that the ampersand, which indicates the start of an entity, also has to be escaped. These special characters should be familiar from HTML:

- < – less-than sign (<)
- > – greater-than sign (>)
- " – double quotes (")
- ' – single quotes or apostrophe (')
- & – ampersand (&)

You have to use < to escape the less-than sign and & to escape ampersands wherever they occur in attribute values or element content. You only have to use " in an attribute value that's delimited by double quotes and ' in an attribute value that's delimited by single quotes (these are the only places where they are significant). The only time you have to use > to escape a greater-than sign is after a double close square brackets (]]). But if in doubt, use the entity!

The big difference between HTML and XHTML in this regard lies in the fact that these are the only entities that are recognized in XML applications. In HTML, you're used to having a whole range of other entities at your disposal, giving symbols, accented characters, and things like non-breaking spaces. These aren't available as entities in XML, but they are available in different guises.

XML uses **Unicode** to represent characters. Unicode is a standard that assigns numerical values to characters in almost every language under the sun, as well as symbols and mathematical notations. Using Unicode means that XML supports internationalization fairly easily. Almost all Unicode characters can be included in your XML document if you use a **character reference**. A character reference looks a bit like an entity – it starts with an ampersand (&) and ends with a semicolon (;) – but it has a hash (#) right after the ampersand. The hash is followed by the number of a character in Unicode, either as a decimal or in hexadecimal if the number starts with an 'x'. For example, a lowercase e with an acute accent could be represented as any of:

```
&#233;
&#xE9;
&#xe9;
```

*One good place to find numbers for the characters that you're used to from HTML is Section 24 (*Character entity references in HTML 4*) in the HTML 4 Recommendation at http://www.w3.org/TR/html401. To find the numerical values for all characters, go to the Unicode site at http://www.unicode.org/.*

Try It Out – Using Character References

One of the characters in EastEnders is called Zoe, and so far we've glossed over the fact that it should be spelt with an ë as the last character. It's easy to use an ë in HTML, because HTML defines the entity `ë`. We'll use a simple HTML document (`eastenders.html`) to look at this in detail, containing just the information about EastEnders. In the `eastenders.html` HTML document, we can use this entity as follows:

```
<ul class="castlist">
  <li>
    <span class="character">Zo&euml; Slater</span>
    <span class="actor">Michelle Ryan</span>
  </li>
  ...
</ul>
```

The HTML browser shows the `ë` entity as an ë character when you view `eastenders.html` and click on the [Cast] link:

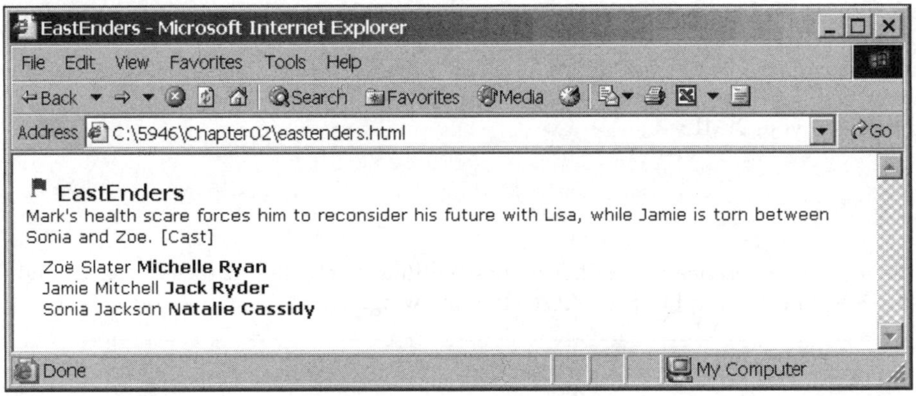

However, try using the `ë` entity in the `castlist3.xml` XML document, as follows:

```
<castlist>
  <member>
    <character gender="female">Zo&euml; Slater</character>
    <actor>Michelle Ryan</actor>
  </member>
  ...
</castlist>
```

When you open up this document in Internet Explorer, you get an error message:

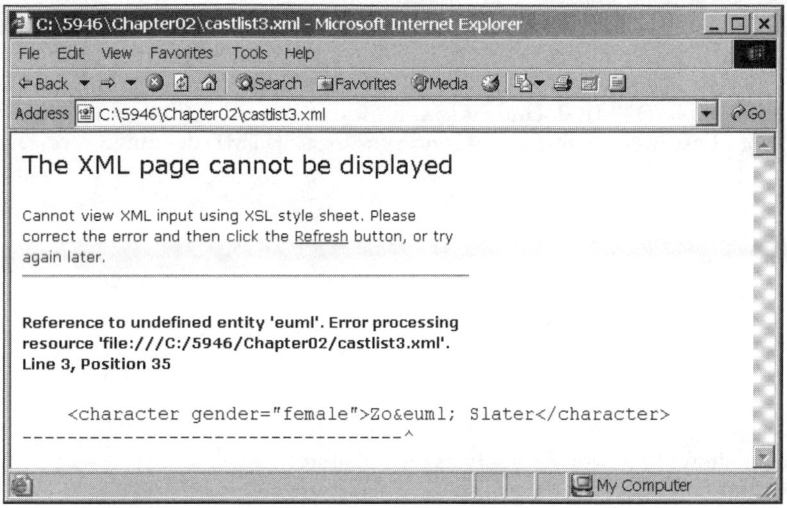

The XML parser in Internet Explorer doesn't recognize the `ë` because it's not a character reference and it's not one of the five entities that are built in to XML. Instead, you have to use a character reference for the ë character. If you look at the definitions in HTML, you'll see that the ë character is assigned the number 235, which equates to EB in hexadecimal. Therefore, you can use either of the following character references to get an ë in your XML:

```
&#235;
&#xEB;
```

If you replace the `ë` reference with either of these entities, to create `castlist4.xml`, and then load `castlist4.xml` into Internet Explorer, you'll see the following:

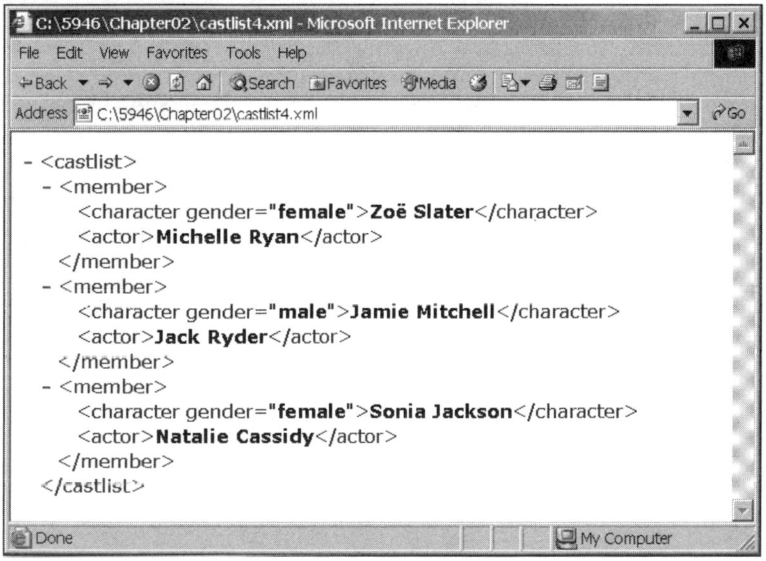

The XML parser in Internet Explorer recognizes the character reference and decodes it. Internet Explorer displays the ë character despite the fact that you used a character reference for it. You can use character references for any of the data in the file – text in element content or attribute values. Try using   in place of spaces, for example.

The XML Declaration

You can also just include any character in your document as it is, natively, but if you do so then you need to make sure that the application that uses your XML can understand the **encoding** that you use when you save your document. An encoding is a way of representing characters with bytes. Some encodings, like **UTF-8** and **UTF-16**, map very closely onto the Unicode character numbers whereas others, like **ISO-8859-1** and **Shift-JIS**, are specifically designed for representing characters in particular languages. Applications that are designed for a particular locale usually expect the encoding that's used in that locale – programs in the US will usually assume ISO-8859-1, while those in Japan will assume Shift-JIS.

All XML applications must understand UTF-8 and UTF-16, so if you have an editor that saves files in one of these encodings then you don't have to do anything special. In fact, ASCII uses the same encoding as UTF-8, so you're also OK if you only use ASCII characters. However, if you have an editor that uses a different encoding – such as Notepad in Windows 98, which uses ISO-8859-1 – then you need to indicate what encoding you've used for the document.

You can indicate the encoding of your XML document using an **XML declaration**. If you use an XML declaration, it must be the very first thing in your document, on the first line, without even a space in front of it. The basic XML declaration looks like:

```
<?xml version="1.0"?>
```

Having this at the start of a file indicates that the file is XML and that it conforms to version 1.0 of XML (which is the only version of XML that there is right now).

If you don't include an XML declaration in your XML document, then an XML application will assume that it's encoded using UTF-8 or UTF-16. If you want to indicate the encoding that you're using, you can do this in the XML declaration. For example, to indicate that your XML document has been saved using ISO-8859-1, you should use:

```
<?xml version="1.0" encoding="ISO-8859-1"?>
```

You can see here that the XML declaration contains a couple of things that look like attributes. These are known as **pseudo-attributes** because they look like attributes but, unlike real attributes, they don't live in the start tag of an element.

> **There are only five entities built in to XML, and you must always use < to escape less-than signs and & to escape ampersands. You can use character references to include non-ASCII characters, or include them directly as long as you use an XML declaration to specify the encoding that you save your document in.**

Try It Out – Changing the Encoding of an XML Document

In the previous section, you worked out various ways of including an ë character in the `castlist4.xml` XML document. Now try including the ë character as an ë character instead, to give `castlist5.xml`, which looks like the following:

```
<castlist>
  <member>
    <character gender="female">Zoë Slater</character>
    <actor>Michelle Ryan</actor>
  </member>
  ...
</castlist>
```

Open up the document in Internet Explorer. If you're using an editor that saves in something other than UTF-8 or UTF-16, then you will get an error like the one shown in the following screenshot:

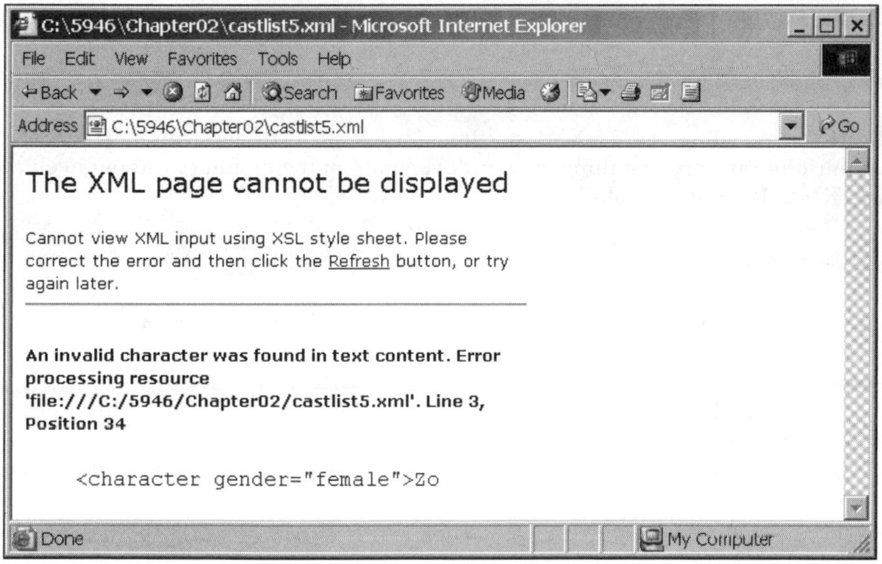

Probably your editor saves documents using ISO-8859-1, but we haven't included an XML declaration yet, so the XML parser thinks that the document is encoded using UTF-8. When the XML parser comes across the bytes that make up the character ë in ISO-8859-1, it tries to interpret them as bytes in UTF-8, and therefore can't figure out what the character is and shows the error message.

Now add the XML declaration to state that you're using ISO-8859-1 to save the file, to create `castlist6.xml` as follows:

```
<?xml version="1.0" encoding="ISO-8859-1"?>
<castlist>
  <member>
    <character gender="female">Zoë Slater</character>
    <actor>Michelle Ryan</actor>
```

```
  </member>
  ...
</castlist>
```

When you open this file up in Internet Explorer, you should see the collapsible tree as before, this time with the XML declaration that you used shown at the top, as follows:

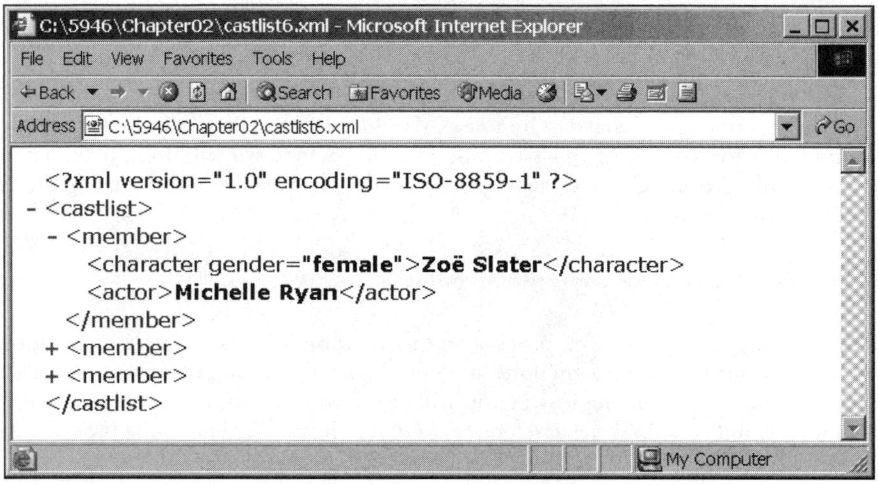

If Internet Explorer still gives you an error, your editor is using some other encoding when it saves the file. You need to read your editor's documentation to find out what encoding it's using, and then state that encoding within the `encoding` pseudo-attribute in the XML declaration.

Other Components of XML

There are three other components of XML documents that we haven't yet touched on:

- Comments
- Processing instructions
- CDATA sections

Comments

Comments in XML (and therefore in XHTML) work in exactly the same way as those in HTML. They start with the four characters `<!--` and end with the characters `-->`. You can have anything you like between the start and end of a comment; they can stretch over as many lines as you like and you don't have to escape any characters within them. The only thing you need to watch out for is that you cannot have two hyphens next to each other in the middle of a comment, because that would make the parser think that it was the end of the comment. Here is an example:

```
<!-- Document written February 18th 2002 -->
```

Comments can go just about anywhere in the document body, but not inside a start tag or an end tag, nor within an empty element tag. You can even spread a comment over several lines if you wish.

Processing Instructions

A component in XML that you probably won't have seen in HTML is the **processing instruction**. As their name suggests, processing instructions (or **PI**s) are instructions destined for the application that processes the XML document. Processing instructions start with `<?`, are immediately followed by a name and then some content, and end with `?>`.

Processing instructions aren't used very often, but there's one use for processing instructions that is particularly relevant for this book, and that's to link an XML document with a stylesheet that can be used to present it. For example, if we were writing the TV guide in XML (which we will do in detail later in this chapter), then we could link it to the CSS stylesheet (`TVGuide.css`) for formatting it using the `xml-stylesheet` processing instruction:

```
<?xml-stylesheet type="text/css" href="TVGuide.css"?>
```

You can see here that the `xml-stylesheet` processing instruction contains a couple of pseudo-attributes. The syntax of the content of processing instructions in general isn't something that's fixed in XML, but the application that understands the processing instruction will know what to do with it. The only limit on the content of a PI is that it must not contain the characters `?>`, as that indicates the end of the processing instruction.

Processing instructions can control the processing of an XML document.

CDATA Sections

There are a couple of elements in HTML where the normal parsing of HTML is suspended, namely in `<SCRIPT>` and `<STYLE>` elements. Things work differently in these elements because they contain content that isn't HTML, but that may use characters such as less-than signs, which are usually used as part of markup, in other ways. Take a simple piece of JavaScript in HTML, for example:

```
<SCRIPT type="text/javascript">
  function validHour(hour) {
    if (hour >= 0 && hour < 24) {
      return true;
    }
    else {
      return false;
    }
  }
</SCRIPT>
```

Here, the less-than sign and the ampersand character have all been included in the HTML literally rather than being escaped. As we've already seen when looking at entities, this isn't legal XML – you have to escape less-than signs and ampersands throughout the document. In XHTML, you could therefore use:

```
<script content="text/javascript">
  function validHour(hour) {
    if (hour >= 0 &amp;&amp; hour &lt; 24) {
      return true;
    }
    else {
      return false;
    }
  }
</script>
```

However, it's difficult to read code that's been escaped like this and it's tedious to write. If you have an element that contains lots of characters that you need to escape, you can use a **CDATA section.** CDATA stands for "character data", and a CDATA section indicates that a piece of text only contains characters, so the meaning of the characters is no longer significant. CDATA sections begin with the special series of characters `<![CDATA[` and end with the sequence `]]>`.

In this example, we can create a CDATA section to wrap around the JavaScript code:

```
<script content="text/javascript">
  <![CDATA[
  function validHour(hour) {
    if (hour >= 0 && hour < 24) {
      return true;
    }
    else {
      return false;
    }
  }
  ]]>
</script>
```

One problem with doing this is that browsers that don't recognize XHTML will not know how to interpret the CDATA section, and will report it as a JavaScript syntax error. To avoid this, you can use JavaScript comments to comment out the CDATA section:

```
<script content="text/javascript">
  // <![CDATA[
  function validHour(hour) {
    if (hour >= 0 && hour < 24) {
      return true;
    }
    else {
      return false;
    }
  }
  // ]]>
</script>
```

Even better, you can use an external JavaScript file to hold the script and then refer to it:

```
<script content="text/javascript" src="TVGuide.js" />
```

As you might expect, the only sequence of characters that *isn't* allowed in a CDATA section is the sequence used to close it,]]>.

> **CDATA sections are a way of saving you from having to escape characters using entities.**

Moving to XHTML

Most web browsers can understand XHTML, so converting your HTML documents into XHTML is a good way to start the journey to using XML. The easiest way to convert an HTML document into XHTML is to use HTML Tidy from Dave Raggett at W3C. You can get HTML Tidy from http://www.w3.org/People/Raggett/tidy/.

Let's review the changes that you have to make to your HTML to turn it into XHTML:

- Change the names of elements and attributes to lowercase
- Add end tags if they are missing
- Use empty element syntax for empty elements
- Make sure that the elements don't overlap each other
- Add matching quotes to all attribute values
- Turn Boolean attributes into normal attributes by giving them their name as a value
- Change any entity references in your document into character references
- Add an XML declaration that specifies the encoding that you're using to save the file
- Wrap the content of <script> and <style> elements in CDATA sections

Try It Out – Converting HTML to XHTML

If we follow these steps with the HTML document that we looked at in the last chapter, then we get the following document, TVGuide.xhtml:

```
<?xml version="1.0" encoding="ISO-8859-1"?>
<html>
<head>
  <title>TV Guide</title>
  <link rel="stylesheet" href="TVGuide.css" />
  <script type="text/javascript">
    // <![CDATA[
    function toggle(element) {
      if (element.style.display == 'none') {
        element.style.display = 'block';
      }
      else {
```

```
        element.style.display = 'none';
      }
    }
    // ]]>
  </script>
</head>

<body>
  <h1>TV Guide</h1>
  <h2><span class="day">Thursday</span> 5 July</h2>
  <table>
    <tr>
      <th>Channel</th>
      <th colspan="6">7:00</th>
      <th colspan="6">7:30</th>
      ...
    </tr>
    <tr>
      <th class="channel">BBC1</th>
      ...
      <td colspan="6" class="soap">
        <img src="flag.gif" alt="[Flagged]" width="20" height="20" />
        <span class="title">EastEnders</span><br />
        Mark's health scare forces him to reconsider his future with Lisa,
        while Jamie is torn between Sonia and Zoe.
        <span onclick="toggle(EastEndersCast);">[Cast]</span>
        <div id="EastEndersCast" style="display: none;">
          <ul class="castlist">
            <li>
              <span class="character">Zo&#235; Slater</span>
              <span class="actor">Michelle Ryan</span>
            </li>
            ...
          </ul>
        </div>
      </td>
      ...
    </tr>
    ...
  </table>
</body>
</html>
```

When you view `TVGuide.xhtml` in Internet Explorer, it has exactly the same appearance as the original HTML file, `TVguide.html`:

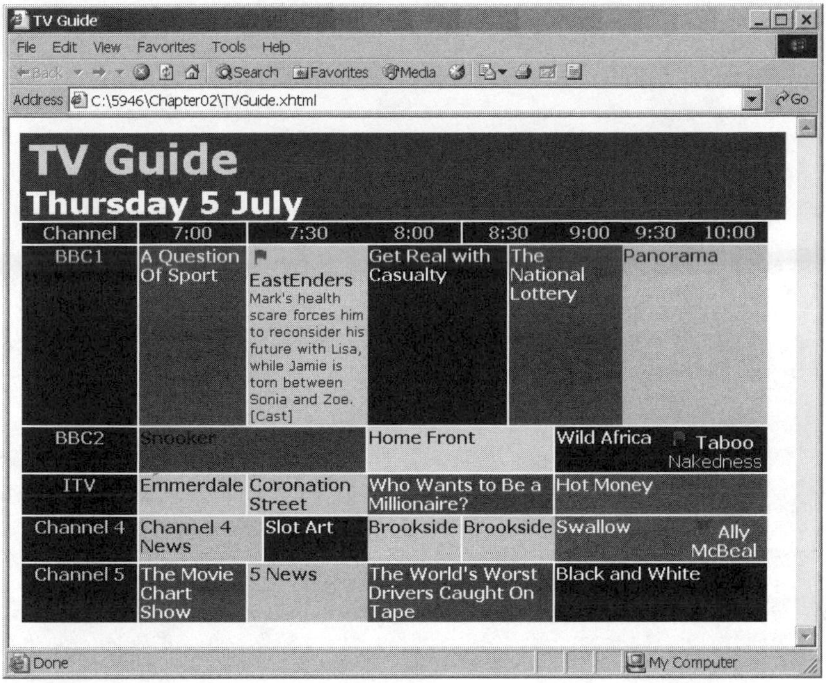

Creating Markup Languages

Despite the fact that it uses XML, XHTML, like HTML, is still oriented around the presentation of documents. Looking at the kind of elements that XHTML uses illustrates this: `<p>` for paragraphs, `<em>` for emphasis, `<ul>` for unordered lists, and so on. XHTML elements are designed to mark up documents, not for data, and they're certainly not tailored for the data that we're using.

To get the full benefit of XML, we need to design our own markup languages or reuse an existing one if we can find one that fulfils our requirements. We can design a markup language to hold the information in our TV guide; one that specifically indicates what a cast list is, what a program title is, and so on.

In this section, I'll briefly go through some of the issues involved in designing your own markup language and look at how to articulate the rules that you come up with so that an application can check whether an XML document adheres to those rules. Both these topics are big areas, so we won't have space to go into a lot of detail on them, but I'll show you enough to get by and point you in the direction of more information if you're interested.

Designing Markup Languages

Designing a markup language involves two steps:

1. Analyzing how the information fits together and how it will be used in your system

2. Deciding how to represent this in XML

The amount of time that you spend on each of the steps is up to you. XML is not an end itself, but rather a means of storing and transferring information within a larger computer system. As such, you have to think about what information is relevant and how it is going to be used within your system. Just as with designing a database or any other component of a computer system, the more effort you put into analysis, the more rigorous your solution will be, but for some smaller applications it can be going overboard to carry out a lot of analysis.

The kinds of questions that you need to ask are:

- What are the main kinds of information that are used in the system?
- How do these different bits of information fit together?
- What do you need to know about the information items?
- Which parts of the application use what information?
- Is the information transient or does it hang around and get reused?

You can often get the answers to these questions by looking at existing markup languages, databases, programs, and so on that use the kind of information you're interested in. Answering these questions should give you models of the data that you use in your system and the processes that use that data.

Try It Out – Creating a Data Model

In the case of our TV guide, the main kinds of information (which are often known as concepts or entities) are:

- TV guide
- Channels
- Programs
- Series
- Cast members
- Characters
- Actors
- Writers
- Directors
- Producers

There are bits of information about each of these concepts that it's useful to know about for our TV guide. These are known as properties. Properties in this example are things like:

- The start and end date for the TV guide
- The names of the channels
- The start date and time for a program, and its duration, title, and description

- The title and a description for each series
- The names of the characters, actors, writers, directors, and producers

We can see links between these different bits of information, known as relations:

- A TV guide contains listings for a number of channels
- Each channel shows a number of programs
- Programs may belong to a series
- Programs have a cast list which is made up of a number of cast members
- Each cast member is a pairing between a character and an actor
- Both individual programs and series as a whole can have writers, directors, and producers
- Characters, actors, writers, directors, and producers are all people

It's often useful to represent all this information in a diagram. The following diagram shows each of the concepts as a rectangle. A concept's associated properties are shown inside its rectangle. The lines between the rectangles show the relationships between the concepts. An asterisk at the end of a line indicates a one-to-many relationship. For instance, the asterisk above the program rectangle (and next to the line from the channel rectangle) indicates that each channel can contain one or many programs.

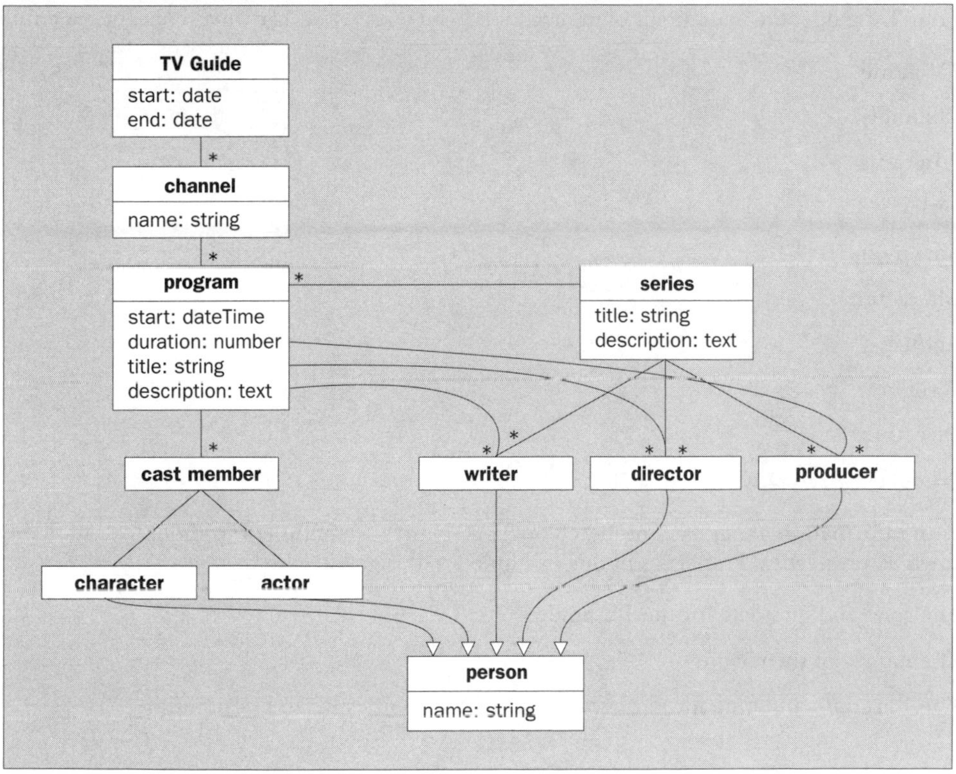

An information model is the starting point for designing a markup language.

Once you have this type of model, you need to map it onto an XML structure. In the rest of this section, we'll look at how you do this mapping and the different choices you might make while doing it, but before we start, it's worth getting our priorities in order.

Deciding Our Criteria

Whenever you design something, you need to know the requirements of the design. Knowing what your requirements are helps you to make decisions because it enables you to tell the difference between a good design (one that meets the requirements) and a bad design (one that doesn't).

There are usually four types of requirements in systems involving XML:

- **Human readability** – how easy it is for someone to understand the XML document.

  This is especially important if people have to author the XML documents by hand, but is also relevant for people programming applications that deal with the XML.

- **Processing efficiency** – how easy it is for an application to process the XML document.

  The ease with which relevant information can be accessed within your XML document affects how simple it is to program applications that use it, and the speed with which they work. Different types of applications make different demands on markup languages, so it's not the case that one design will suit every type of processing.

- **Size** – how big the XML document is.

  XML is a verbose syntax – one of the initial requirements for XML was that it not be too concerned about verbosity – and it compresses well, so size is rarely crucial. However, it can be important in storage, processing, and transmission.

- **Extensibility** – how easy it is to reuse or make changes to the markup language later on?

  Extensibility involves giving room in a markup language for people to add their own extras and designing parts of the structure so that they can be used easily elsewhere. Both increase the lifespan and utility of the markup language. Of course, you don't have to worry about this if you never make explicit any rules about how your elements and attributes should fit together (such as in a schema or DTD).

These types of requirements have to be balanced against each other for any particular project, and even for particular XML documents within an application. You might not care very much about size when storing some information, for example, but when that same information needs to be transmitted over the Internet then it starts to be an issue.

In our example, human readability and extensibility are the most important aspects because we're going to be using this as an example throughout the book, and I want you to be able to understand the examples we use, as well as to be able to extend the markup language to illustrate particular points. Processing efficiency is also important – we're going to be processing this with XSLT, and we want that XSLT to be fairly simple. Size, on the other hand, isn't really important.

> **How an XML document is going to be used has a big effect on how it is best structured.**

Deciding on a Naming Convention

The second decision to make before progressing onto the really hard work is to decide what naming convention to use. You'll remember from earlier in the chapter that there is no prescribed naming convention for XML markup languages, but that XML is case-sensitive, so you have to be consistent in whatever naming convention you use.

Naming is relevant in several places in markup languages:

- Element names
- Attribute names
- Enumerated values for elements and attributes
- Entity names

You may wish to adopt different naming conventions for the different types of names that you use in your document.

There are several case conventions that you might use. You can use camel case, where the first letter of each new word is indicated with a capital letter, or you can separate words with hyphens, underscores, or periods and use all lowercase or all uppercase. Case convention is really a matter of preference, although it can be helpful to use a case convention that makes your markup stand out from the languages that you're using to process it. In this book we'll be using XSLT, which uses all-lowercase words, separated by hyphens, to process our XML, and we'll also be using XHTML, which uses lowercase names, so using something that stands out from both of those would be useful.

A second thing to consider when deciding on names is how much abbreviation to use. Using abbreviations can make a big difference to the size of the document that you create and the amount of typing you have to do to create it! For example, look at an alternative way of representing the table we're using in our XHTML:

```
<table>
  <table-row>
    <table-cell>Channel</table-cell>
    <table-cell>7:30</table-cell>
    <table-cell>8:00</table-cell>
  </table-row>
  <table-row>
    <table-cell>BBC1</table-cell>
    <table-cell>...</table-cell>
    <table-cell>...</table-cell>
  </table-row>
  ...
</table>
```

With this naming scheme, the markup dominates the content of the table, making it harder to work out what the document is saying. On the other hand, it's a lot less ambiguous than the XHTML markup – it's a lot clearer what `<table-row>` means than what `<TR>` means.

Along the same lines as the issue of abbreviation is the question of how much context to add to element and attribute names. Some markup languages add a lot of context. For example, the cast list could be marked up as follows:

```
<Cast.List>
  <Cast.Member>
    <Cast.Member.Character>Zoe Slater</Cast.Member.Character>
    <Cast.Member.Actor>Michelle Ryan</Cast.Member.Actor>
  </Cast.Member>
  <Cast.Member>
    <Cast.Member.Character>Jamie Mitchell</Cast.Member.Character>
    <Cast.Member.Actor>Jack Ryder</Cast.Member.Actor>
  </Cast.Member>
  <Cast.Member>
    <Cast.Member.Character>Sonia Jackson</Cast.Member.Character>
    <Cast.Member.Actor>Natalie Cassidy</Cast.Member.Actor>
  </Cast.Member>
</Cast.List>
```

Much of each of the names here is irrelevant, a repetition of context from higher up the hierarchy, and again the longer names swamp the content of the document, making it harder to work out what's going on.

For the purposes of the examples in this book, then, I will use camel case names, starting with an uppercase letter for elements and a lowercase letter for attributes. I will not use abbreviations, but neither will I add context information to element names. So the cast list will look like:

```
<CastList>
  <CastMember>
    <Character>Zoe Slater</Character>
    <Actor>Michelle Ryan</Actor>
  </CastMember>
  <CastMember>
    <Character>Jamie Mitchell</Character>
    <Actor>Jack Ryder</Actor>
  </CastMember>
  <CastMember>
    <Character>Sonia Jackson</Character>
    <Actor>Natalie Cassidy</Actor>
  </CastMember>
</CastList>
```

The naming convention that you use doesn't matter, as long as it's consistent so that it's easy to guess what the name of an element or attribute will be.

Mapping to Elements and Attributes

Now that we know what our priorities are and how we're going to name everything, we can start thinking about the components that we're going to use in our markup language. We need to decide what elements and attributes we're going to have and what kind of values they can take.

Generally a data model will have two components:

- A number of objects, concepts, or classes, important things in the domain
- Properties or attributes, important information about those things

The important distinction between properties and concepts is that the values that properties take are **primitive** or **simple** values. Properties have values that cannot be broken down any further, like numbers, dates, and strings. A concept, on the other hand, is **structured** or **complex**. The value of a concept has to be broken down into separate properties.

You have to use elements to hold structured or complex information in an XML document, so each of the concepts in the TV guide model can map onto an element in our XML structure. However, you can represent properties as either elements or attributes. Whether you use an element or attribute for a particular property is largely a matter of preference, although here are a couple of guidelines:

- Use an element if you might want to add more structure later on. For example, I might later want to add markup within descriptions or break down people's names into forenames and surnames.
- Use an attribute if the property holds information about information (**meta-information**). For example, the start and end dates for the TV guide are information about the information held in the TV guide, not a feature of the TV guide itself.
- If in doubt, use an element.

Try It Out – Deciding Whether to Use Elements and Attributes

In our TV guide the concepts include:

- TV guide
- Program
- Series
- Cast member
- Actor
- Character

The properties are things like:

- A program's start date and time
- A series' title
- A character's name

Using these mapping rules and the naming conventions that we've decided, we can come up with preliminary structures for those concepts and properties in the information model for our TV Guide. These elements aren't arranged in a document yet – we're just looking at what the concepts and their properties might look like as elements and attributes individually:

```
<TVGuide start="date" end="date">...</TVGuide>
```

```
<Channel>
  <Name>string</Name>
  ...
</Channel>
```

```
<Program>
  <Start>dateTime</Start>
  <Duration>duration</Duration>
  <Title>string</Title>
  <Description>text</Description>
  ...
</Program>
```

```
<Series>
  <Title>string</Title>
  <Description>text</Description>
  ...
</Series>
```

```
<Character><Name>string</Name></Character>
<Actor><Name>string</Name></Actor>
<Writer><Name>string</Name></Writer>
<Director><Name>string</Name></Director>
<Producer><Name>string</Name></Producer>
```

While you're looking at the simple values that you need to hold in your XML document, it's worth thinking about how to represent them and what rules will govern whether a value is acceptable for that element or attribute. The closer the representation that you use is to the one used by the source or destination of the data, the easier it will be to process. Another factor that might influence the representations that you use is the availability of a standard representation, which we'll come on to soon.

> **You can hold simple data in either attributes or elements, but you have to use elements to hold structured information.**

Representing Relationships

In the last section, we created some basic XML for the important information in our TV guide. What we didn't do, though, was fit that information together to show how the parts related to each other. We need to represent things like:

- A TV guide has listings for a number of channels
- A channel shows a number of programs
- A program has a number of cast members
- A program may be part of a series
- A cast member is a pairing of a character and an actor

There are two ways of representing this kind of information in XML: by **nesting** and by **reference**.

Using nesting involves placing the element representing one piece of information within the element it's associated with. For example, we could show that a TV guide is made up of a number of channels by nesting the <Channel> elements within the <TVGuide> element, and show that a channel shows a number of programs by nesting the <Program> elements within the corresponding <Channel> elements:

```
<TVGuide start="date" end="date">
  <Channel>
    <Name>string</Name>
    <Program>...</Program>
    <Program>...</Program>
    ...
  </Channel>
  <Channel>
    <Name>string</Name>
    <Program>...</Program>
    <Program>...</Program>
    ...
  </Channel>
  ...
</TVGuide>
```

When you use nesting to indicate a one-to-many relationship, it's sometimes worth using a **wrapper element** to hold the nested elements. Using a wrapper element makes it easy to see where the list begins and ends, especially if you have several other elements nested in the same parent element. For example, we could use a wrapper element called <CastList> to hold all the <CastMember> elements in a <Program>:

```
<Program>
  <Start>dateTime</Start>
  <Duration>duration</Duration>
  <Title>string</Title>
  <Description>text</Description>
  <CastList>
    <CastMember>
      <Character><Name>string</Name></Character>
      <Actor><Name>string</Name></Actor>
    </CastMember>
    <CastMember>
      <Character><Name>string</Name></Character>
      <Actor><Name>string</Name></Actor>
    </CastMember>
    ...
```

```
    </CastList>
    ...
  </Program>
```

Using references involves referencing a set of information using a unique identifier. For historical reasons, these identifiers and references often use attributes rather than elements, but you can use either, especially if you are using XSLT to process your XML. A good example where references would be appropriate here is in representing the link between a program and a series. We don't really want to nest the <Series> element inside the <Program> element because that would mean repeating the information about the series multiple times in the TV guide, whenever a program in that series was shown. On the other hand, we don't want to nest the <Program> element within the <Series> element because that would break the association between the channel and the program.

Instead, we could use the title of the series as a unique identifier for that series, and use that title within the information about the program. In the following code, a program references the EastEnders series by its title. In the following example, we have two <Series> elements, the first of which defines the series at the top level of the document:

```
<Series>
  <Title>EastEnders</Title>
  <Description>Soap set in the East End of London.</Description>
</Series>
```

The second <Series> element, used inside the <Program> element, gives a pointer to the series description (notice that the <Title> element here is empty as it represents the title of the episode, and the EastEnders series does not use episode titles):

```
<Program>
  <Start>2001-07-05T19:30:00</Start>
  <Duration>PT30M</Duration>
  <Series>EastEnders</Series>
  <Title></Title>
  <Description>
    Mark's health scare forces him to reconsider his future with Lisa, while
    Jamie is torn between Sonia and Zoe.
  </Description>
  ...
</Program>
```

Using references allows you to reuse the same information without repeating it. The referenced material may be in the same document as the references to it (you could nest the <Series> elements within the <TVGuide> element) or it could be in a separate document (you could create a `series.xml` document that contains the <Series> elements). However, using too many references may make it hard to work out how all the information ties together.

You can use nesting or references to show the links between different sets of information in your document. References prevent duplication of information, but generally lead to documents that are harder to process.

TV Guide XML Document

It's always helpful to create a sample XML document when you design a new markup language, both to show people what you mean it to look like and to test that the decisions you've made hold up against data in the real world. So here's a sample document for our TV guide – `TVGuide.xml`:

```
<?xml version="1.0" encoding="ISO-8859-1"?>
<TVGuide start="2001-07-05" end="2001-07-12">
  <Channel>
    <Name>BBC1</Name>
    ...
    <Program>
      <Start>2001-07-05T19:30:00</Start>
      <Duration>PT30M</Duration>
      <Series>EastEnders</Series>
      <Title></Title>
      <Description>
        Mark's health scare forces him to reconsider his future with Lisa,
        while Jamie is torn between Sonia and Zoe.
      </Description>
      <CastList>
        <CastMember>
          <Character><Name>Zoe Slater</Name></Character>
          <Actor><Name>Michelle Ryan</Name></Actor>
        </CastMember>
        <CastMember>
          <Character><Name>Jamie Mitchell</Name></Character>
          <Actor><Name>Jack Ryder</Name></Actor>
        </CastMember>
        <CastMember>
          <Character><Name>Sonia Jackson</Name></Character>
          <Actor><Name>Natalie Cassidy</Name></Actor>
        </CastMember>
        ...
      </CastList>
      <Writers>
        <Writer><Name>Nick Saltrese</Name></Writer>
        <Writer><Name>Julie Wassmer</Name></Writer>
      </Writers>
      <Director><Name>Stewart Edwards</Name></Director>
      <Producer><Name>Emma Turner</Name></Producer>
    </Program>
    ...
  </Channel>
  ...
</TVGuide>
```

We also have a supplementary document – `series.xml` – that holds information about TV series:

```
<SeriesList>
  ...
  <Series>
```

```
    <Title>EastEnders</Title>
    <Description>Soap set in the East End of London.</Description>
  </Series>
  ...
</SeriesList>
```

This XML structure is the structure that we'll use throughout this book as the basis of our XSLT transformations. We've got a sample document, and we've discussed the rules that the document follows, but to share that description with other people, and to enable computers to check our documents, we need to write down those rules in a formal way. In the next section, we look at how to validate markup languages by describing them with DTDs and schemas.

Validating Markup Languages

Earlier in this chapter, we looked at the differences between well-formed XML documents, which follow the rules governing the syntax of XML, and valid XML documents, which follow the specific rules for a particular markup language. To enable an application to check whether a document you write is valid, you have to tell it the rules governing the vocabulary and grammar of the markup language that you're using. Validating helps you check the XML that you generate and the XML that you receive, to make sure that it has the structure that you're expecting.

> *Chapter 16 looks at how to validate XML documents using XSLT.*

There are two general ways of defining a markup language: using a **document type definition**, or **DTD**, and using a **schema**.

Document Type Definitions

DTDs are the basic means of defining XML structures. They use a similar syntax for describing markup languages to that which SGML uses, rather than XML, and they are fairly restricted in the rules that they allow you to put together about a markup language. However, DTDs are well-supported: most XML editors enable you to validate an XML document against a DTD and most applications that use XML will use a DTD if one is available.

Associating Documents with DTDs

You can associate a DTD with an XML document using a **DOCTYPE declaration** at the top of your XML document, just underneath the XML declaration. A DOCTYPE declaration can link to an external DTD or define an internal DTD, or do both. For example, you could link your XHTML document to an external XHTML DTD with the following:

```
<?xml version="1.0" encoding="ISO-8859-1"?>
<!DOCTYPE html PUBLIC "-//W3C//DTD XHTML 1.0 Strict//EN"
          "DTD/xhtml1-strict.dtd">
<html>
...
</html>
```

The string after the PUBLIC keyword is known as a **public identifier** and it gives a unique identity for the markup language. Some applications might be able to recognize the public identifier and use that to access their own set of internal rules to apply to the document. After the public identifier comes the **system identifier**, which is a relative file path to the DTD for the XML document.

An internal DOCTYPE declaration for our TV guide XML might look like the following:

```
<?xml version="1.0" encoding="ISO-8859-1"?>
<!DOCTYPE TVGuide [
<!ELEMENT TVGuide (Channel+)>
<!ATTLIST TVGuide
    start CDATA #REQUIRED
    end   CDATA #REQUIRED>
<!ELEMENT Channel (Name, Program+)>
...
]>
<TVGuide start="2001-07-05" end="2001-07-12">
...
</TVGuide>
```

This code snippet shows that the <TVGuide> element can contain one or more <Channel> elements and has two attributes: start and end. The <Channel> element contains a <Name> element followed by one or more <Program> elements.

Writing DTDs

There isn't enough space here to go into how to write DTDs in detail, but there's one aspect of DTDs that will be useful for you to know about: defining **entities**.

> *You can find details of DTD syntax in* Beginning XML, 2nd Edition*, ISBN 1-861005-59-8, from Wrox Press.*

If you remember back a couple of sections, we talked about how XML only uses five entities to escape the special characters in XML, and doesn't support all those useful entities that you have in HTML. Well, you can use a DTD to define whatever entities you want. These can be character entities, for example for a non-breaking space or an é character, or longer ones if you want, holding standard or repeated text or XML, such as disclaimers.

You can define an entity with an entity definition, which gives the name of that entity and the value it holds. For example, you could define a   entity for a non-breaking space (which is   as a character reference) with:

```
<!ENTITY nbsp ' '>
```

Naturally, the XHTML DTD includes all the entities that you can use in HTML. If you want to use them in your XML document, you can define **parameter entities** (which are entities that can be used within a DTD) for the files and include them in an internal DTD. To use these entities in the TV guide document, for example, we could use:

```
<!DOCTYPE TVGuide [
<!ENTITY % HTMLlat1 SYSTEM "xhtml-lat1.ent">
%HTMLlat1;
<!ENTITY % HTMLsymbol SYSTEM "xhtml-symbol.ent">
%HTMLsymbol;
<!ENTITY % HTMLspecial SYSTEM "xhtml-special.ent">
%HTMLspecial;
]>
```

These `.ent` *files are available along with the XHTML DTDs from* *http://www.w3.org/TR/xhtml1*.

You can use DTDs to define entities and make it easier to include non-ASCII characters in your document.

Try It Out – Defining Entities

Earlier in this chapter, we looked at a couple of ways of including an ë character in the cast list XML document and found that the usual HTML entity `ë` wouldn't work. Let's look now at how to define an entity for that character, so that we can use the `ë` entity in our XML document.

We'll start off with an internal DTD, in `castlist7.xml`. You need to create a `DOCTYPE` declaration in the XML document, and put the entity definition inside this `DOCTYPE` declaration, as follows:

```
<?xml version="1.0" encoding="ISO-8859-1"?>
<!DOCTYPE castlist [
<!ENTITY euml '&#235;'>
]>
<castlist>
  <member>
    <character gender="female">Zo&euml; Slater</character>
    <actor>Michelle Ryan</actor>
  </member>
  ...
</castlist>
```

Have a look at this XML document using Internet Explorer, and you should see the ë character without any problems. The `DOCTYPE` declaration is indicated at the top of the page, but Internet Explorer doesn't show you its contents, as follows:

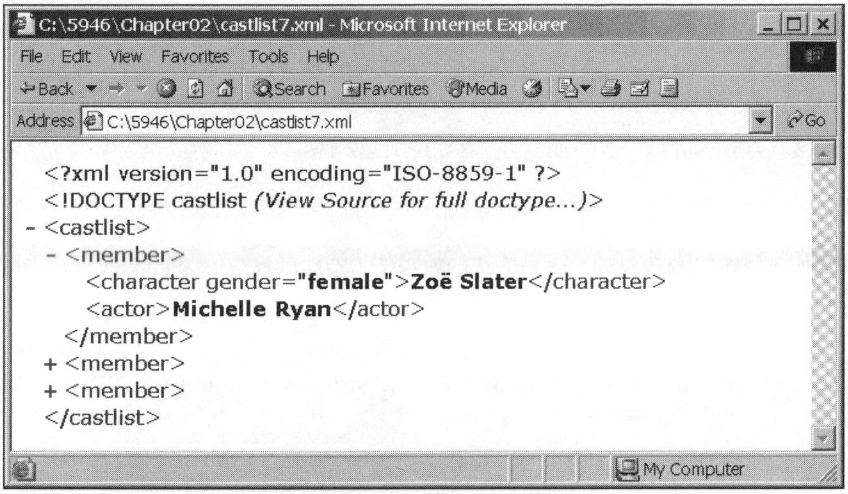

Now try moving the content of the `DOCTYPE` declaration into its own file, `castlist.dtd`. The DTD document is very small, only containing one line:

```
<!ENTITY euml '&#235;'>
```

In the `castlist8.xml` XML document, you need to point to this external DTD from the `DOCTYPE` declaration. Change the `DOCTYPE` declaration from `castlist7.xml` so that it reads:

```
<?xml version="1.0" encoding="ISO-8859-1"?>
<!DOCTYPE castlist SYSTEM 'castlist.dtd'>
<castlist>
  <member>
    <character gender="female">Zo&euml; Slater</character>
    <actor>Michelle Ryan</actor>
  </member>
  ...
</castlist>
```

Moving the entity definition to an external DTD makes absolutely no difference to how Internet Explorer displays the XML document.

Finally, try using the entity definitions available from XHTML. Download the three entities files from http://www.w3.org/TR/xhtml1 and reference them from your `castlist.dtd` DTD, as follows:

```
<!ENTITY % HTMLlat1 SYSTEM "xhtml-lat1.ent">
%HTMLlat1;
<!ENTITY % HTMLsymbol SYSTEM "xhtml-symbol.ent">
%HTMLsymbol;
<!ENTITY % HTMLspecial SYSTEM "xhtml-special.ent">
%HTMLspecial;
```

Now you can use whatever entities you like from HTML within your `castlist8.xml` document.

Schemas

Schemas are XML documents that define a particular markup language. There are several different schema markup languages around; at the time of writing three schema languages are heading the field:

- **XML Schema** from W3C – the official W3C schema language
- **RELAX NG** – a schema language currently being developed by the Oasis standards organization
- **Schematron** – a very flexible rule-based schema language

Each of these schema languages is able to articulate different kinds of rules that might apply to your markup language. Indeed, often it's worth using several of these schema languages in combination, depending on how rigorous you need the validation to be.

There obviously isn't space here to go into any of these schema languages in detail, but it is worth looking briefly at one aspect of XML Schema – the data types that it defines. The XML Schema Recommendation is split into three parts: a primer, a document on structures like element and attribute declarations, and a document on the data types that you can use in an XML Schema. The data types document is particularly relevant because it specifies standard ways of representing values of various types. These standard data types are likely to be adopted very widely, so using them will not only make writing schemas easier, but also make it easier to translate documents using your markup language into another markup language.

The formats that are particularly relevant are:

- **Dates and times** – use ISO 8601 formats, including:
    - **dateTime** – `CCYY-MM-DDThh:mm:ss` for example, `2001-07-05T19:30:00` for 7:30 pm on 5th July 2001
    - **date** – `CCYY-MM-DD` for example, `2001-07-05` for 5th July 2001
    - **time** – `hh:mm:ss` for example, `19:30:00` for 7:30 pm
- **durations** – use `PnYnMnDTnHnMnS` for example, `PT30M` for 30 minutes
- **boolean** – use `true` or `false`, or `1` or `0`
- **language** – use language specifications as defined by RFC 1766, for example, `en-US` for US English

You can find the XML Schema data types Recommendation at http://www.w3.org/TR/xmlschema-2/. *If you want to learn more about XML Schema in general, then you should have a look at* Professional XML Schemas, *ISBN 1-861005-47-4, from Wrox Press.*

XML Schema defines how to represent various data types, and you should use these representations if you can.

Presenting XML

The reason that HTML is so ubiquitous is because there are lots of applications that understand HTML. HTML editors and most importantly web browsers know how to parse HTML, and they know how to present HTML – they know that an `<H1>` element should be large and bold, that a `<TABLE>` element and its content defines a table, that an `<EM>` element should be rendered in italics, and so on. As we saw in the last chapter, these presentational rules might be overridden by CSS, but usually the default behavior of the web browser gives a baseline, with CSS tweaking the details.

On the other hand, a web browser has absolutely no idea about what to do with an XML document. It can't know how a `<CastList>` element should be displayed because it doesn't know anything about our TV guide XML. However, we can still use CSS to tell the browser how to display the XML.

Presenting XML with CSS

The CSS that you use for XML documents is similar to that for HTML documents, except that the names that you use in the CSS rules are those of the XML elements rather than the HTML elements.

One thing that's particularly important in CSS for XML documents is the `display` property. The `display` property governs the general layout of the content of the element within the page, for example, whether it should create a new block, be rendered inline, be a list item, and so on. The `display` property is also useful for *hiding* certain parts of the document if you don't want them to be displayed, which you can do by setting it to the value `none`.

As an example, here is a CSS file – `TVGuide.xml.css` – for displaying the TV guide XML:

```
TVGuide {
  font-family: Verdana, sans-serif;
  font-size: small;
}
Duration, Writer, Director, Producer {
  display: none;
}
Start {
  margin-top: 1em;
  display: block;
}
Channel Name, Series, Title {
  display: block;
  margin-bottom: 0em;
  padding: 0.3em;
}
Channel Name {
  margin-top: 1em;
  background: #C00;
  color: white;
  font-weight: bold;
  font-size: 1.44em;
}
Series {
```

```
    background: black;
    color: yellow;
    font-weight: bold;
    font-size: 1.2em;
  }
  Title {
    background: black;
    color: white;
  }
  CastList {
    display: block;
    padding: 0.5em 1em;
  }
  CastMember {
    display: list-item;
    list-style-type: none;
  }
  Character Name, Actor Name {
    display: inline;
    background: transparent;
    color: black;
    margin-bottom: 0em;
    padding: 0em;
    font-weight: normal;
    font-size: 1em;
  }
  Actor Name {
    font-weight: bold;
  }
```

You can use CSS to style XML in the same way as you use it with HTML.

Associating Stylesheets with XML

In HTML, you can either nest CSS within a `<STYLE>` element or use a `<LINK>` element to point to a separate CSS file. An XML document can't use either of these methods because a web browser doesn't know what these elements mean for a random markup language. So how does the web browser know to use this CSS with the XML document without having a `<LINK>` element to point to it? Well, you might remember the `xml-stylesheet` processing instruction from earlier in this chapter:

```
<?xml-stylesheet type="text/css" href="TVGuide.css"?>
```

If you add this processing instruction to the top of your XML document, right underneath the XML declaration, then an XML-aware and CSS-capable web browser (like Internet Explorer) will use the CSS stylesheet you point at to display the XML document. The top of `TVGuide2.xml` looks like:

```
<?xml version="1.0"?>
<?xml-stylesheet type="text/css" href="TVGuide.css"?>
<TVGuide start="2001-07-05" end="2001-07-12">
```

```
...
</TVGuide>
```

> **The `xml-stylesheet` processing instruction links a document to a stylesheet that can be used to present it.**

Try It Out – Viewing XML with CSS

Save the CSS shown in the last section as `TVGuide.xml.css` and add an `xml-stylesheet` processing instruction to the `TVGuide.xml` file that we've developed, pointing to the `TVGuide.xml.css` file, to create `TVGuide2.xml`. Now open the `TVGuide2.xml` file in Internet Explorer. Instead of the collapsible tree that you saw before, you'll see something that looks like an HTML page:

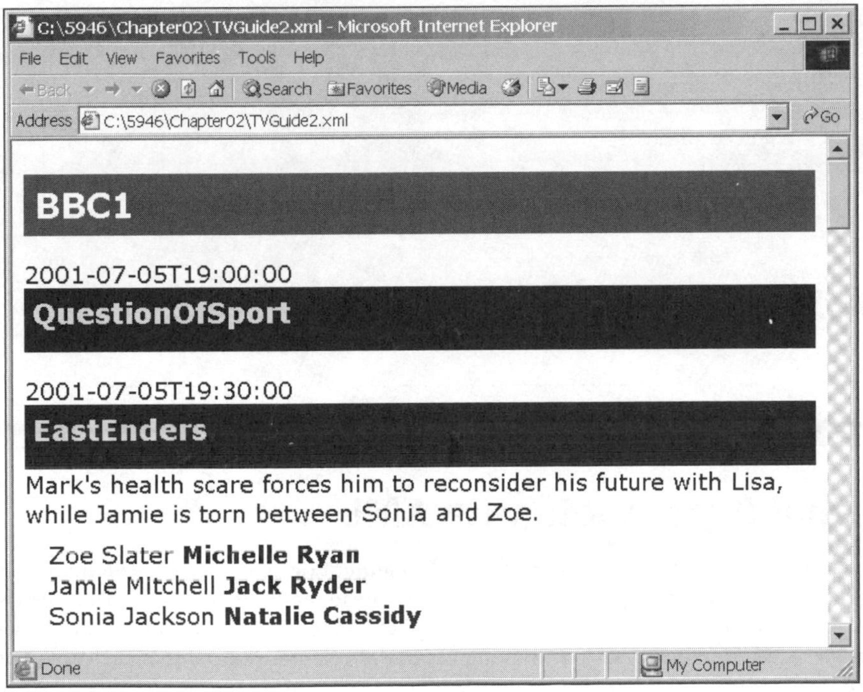

You can play around with the CSS to hide and show different parts of the XML document.

Limitations of CSS

We've managed to get a reasonably nice view of our XML document using CSS, but it isn't perfect – in fact it looks nothing like the pretty display that we had with our HTML document. CSS has several limitations that stop us from getting the display the way we want with the XML that we have:

- The XML elements are displayed in the order that they're given in the XML document. We can't make the start time of a program display after the series title, for example.
- CSS can't display attributes. We can't use CSS to display the start and end dates of the TV guide as they're held in attributes.
- Element content is shown exactly as it is. Our XML specifies the start date/time of a program using a standard date/time format that isn't particularly easy to read, but we can't use CSS to reformat it.
- You can't add much in the way of text. CSS2 allows you to add text or images before or after elements, but this is not supported in many browsers and CSS2 gives no support for adding static content like headings, descriptions, or disclaimers when displaying XML.
- Content held in other documents is hard to access. We've put the information about the series that programs can be part of in a separate document, but we can't now access that information and display it in the page.
- An element can only be of one type. If you want to use CSS to display tables, you have to have elements that follow the same kind of structure as tables in HTML. We couldn't display the TV guide as a table with each column being a different channel, for example.
- CSS doesn't support dynamic content. We can't create links from our page, much less use scripting to show and hide parts of the page.

All in all, CSS is fairly limited when it comes to displaying XML documents, especially ones that are **data oriented** like ours is, where the structure of the XML doesn't necessarily mirror the way that we want to see it.

> **You can't use CSS to restructure your XML or your data, which is a big limitation.**

Summary

This chapter has given a speedy introduction to XML. XML is a meta-markup language: it defines a syntax that a family of markup languages should follow. Documents that follow these rules are known as well-formed XML documents. An HTML document can be turned into an XHTML document by making it follow XML rules.

But the real power of XML comes from being able to make up your own markup language. You can design a markup language that is specifically designed to hold the information that you need it to hold for your application. Once you've designed it, you can describe the language using a DTD or a schema. Having a DTD or schema enables applications to check whether a document adheres to the rules of your markup language – to validate XML documents.

We've created an XML document that holds the dynamic information in our HTML page, the core set of information that makes up our TV guide. We can render this XML document using CSS, but it doesn't look anything like the HTML document that we had in the first place.

So haven't we painted ourselves into a corner? We did have a lovely HTML page that displayed the information we had in the way that we wanted to see it, gave us links and images, and had dynamic content. Now we have an XML document that we can't view in the way we want to view it. What's the point of that? Well, the content that our XML document holds can now be used by applications without them having to wade through lots of irrelevant HTML. This means our TV guide can be **repurposed** – used by lots of different applications in lots of different ways.

However, we still want to be able to use that information in the way that we were originally using it – to display it on a web page. To do that, we need a mechanism for transforming our XML into something that web browsers can understand more easily, back to the HTML that we had originally. And to do that, we need XSLT, which leads us nicely on to the next chapter.

Review Questions

1. Why is it beneficial to use your own elements and attributes rather than using HTML?
2. What are the relationships between XML, SGML, HTML, and XHTML?
3. What naming convention does XHTML use?
4. What are the differences between start tags, end tags, and empty element tags?
5. What is the term for the element in an XML document that contains all the other elements in the document?
6. What two ways could you use to give an attribute a value that contains an apostrophe?
7. How do you translate Boolean attributes from HTML to XHTML?
8. What two characters must always be escaped using entities within an XML document? Which other three characters can be represented by entities in an XML document?
9. What four ways could you use to include a non-breaking space character in an XML document?
10. In which two XHTML elements are `CDATA` sections most useful, and why?
11. What considerations do you need to take into account when you're designing an XML-based markup language?
12. What kinds of information can attributes hold?
13. What two ways can you use to indicate an association between different sets of information in an XML document?
14. How do you associate a DTD with an XML document?

15. What is the difference between a well-formed XML document and a valid XML document?

16. Name some schema markup languages.

17. How can you associate a stylesheet with an XML document?

18. What are the limitations of using CSS to style XML?

Beginning
XSLT

3

Creating HTML from XML

In the last chapter, we developed two main XML documents. The first was an XHTML document – the same HTML document that we started with in the first chapter, but represented in XHTML. The XHTML document gets displayed just like an HTML document would, but you can also edit it and display it like XML, in a tree. The XHTML document doesn't really take full advantage of XML, though. We're still stuck using a markup language that doesn't really tie in with the content of our document. So the second XML document we developed used a markup language we specifically invented to hold information for our TV Guide.

The XML document written in the specialized markup language is a lot cleaner – it doesn't say anything at all about the way in which a particular piece of information should be presented. On the other hand, that's its big weakness – even people who are used to reading XML will find it a lot harder to work out what TV program is showing when and on what channel. Somehow we need to add information to the XML document to say how it should be shown on a web page.

In this chapter, we'll start looking at XSLT as a way of telling a browser how to display an XML document. This whole book is about XSLT, so we're not going to cover everything, just enough to get an XML document displayed as an HTML page. In this chapter, you'll learn:

- What the goals of XSLT are and how it fits with other XML standards
- How to use XSLT processors to transform XML into HTML
- How to write simplified stylesheets
- What XSLT namespaces are
- How to access information from an XML document
- How to iterate over elements in an XML document
- How to get a value into an attribute

XSL: The Extensible Stylesheet Language

XML goes a long way towards making information accessible – it's a text-based format that you can use to hold data on different platforms and in different kinds of applications. But just because some information is held in XML that doesn't mean that it's immediately useful. You still need to write a program to manipulate the data. The most common thing that you'll want to do with XML is to present that information – as HTML pages on the Web, as WML pages on WAP phones, as PDF documents for printing, and so on.

The W3C started developing a standard language for presenting information held in XML in 1998, around the time XML was being finalized. This language was named the Extensible Stylesheet Language (**XSL**). The goal of XSL was to develop a stylesheet language that could overcome the limitations of CSS that we saw at the end of the last chapter – a stylesheet language that could restructure information and add things like headings to a page. To manage this, XSL borrowed heavily from **DSSSL** (Document Style Semantics and Specification Language), which is the main stylesheet language that's used in SGML applications. Another early design decision was that XSL should use **XML syntax** to represent the rules about how XML should be presented – XSL should be an XML-based markup language.

Not long into the development of XSL, it became clear that there were really three parts to the stylesheet language:

- A markup language for describing presentational details, like the margin around a block or the color of a table cell
- A markup language for defining how to map from some XML into the presentational markup language
- An expression language for pointing to information in an XML document and performing calculations

The Extensible Stylesheet Language therefore split into two markup languages and a third text-based language. The first markup language is purely presentational and describes how **formatting objects** should be laid out on a page. This language is known as XSL Formatting Objects or **XSL-FO**. The second markup language defines how to **transform** from any XML-based markup language into another markup language (or into plain text). This language is known as XSL Transformations or **XSLT**. The third, text-based language is used within XSLT to point to pieces of information in an XML document, and this is the XML Path Language or **XPath**.

XSL-FO is a fairly large markup language in its own right, so we're not going to have space to cover it in detail in this book, but you don't need to know about XSL-FO in order to use XSLT to transform into other useful markup languages, such as XHTML. XSL-FO is usually used as an intermediary format on the way to something like PDF or PostScript, for printing, although it's feasible that browsers will start supporting it in the future.

XSL is made up of two markup languages: XSL-FO for describing how information should be displayed and XSLT for describing how to transform from one markup language to another format. XSLT uses a third language, XPath, to select parts of XML to process and to perform calculations.

An XML document that is written in XSLT is commonly known as an **XSLT stylesheet** and it's usually given the extension `.xsl`. Each XSLT stylesheet describes how a set of XML documents – the **source** documents – should be converted into other documents – the **result** documents – whether they are XSL-FO, XHTML, comma-delimited text, or in any other text-based format such as HTML. Usually, an XSLT stylesheet will take source documents written in one particular markup language, such as the TV guide XML that we're using, and produce a result in another markup language that can be used by a specialist application, such as XHTML for presentation in a browser.

To perform a transformation, XSLT needs to be able to point to information in the source document, so that it can process it and include it in the result, and this is where XPath comes in. The most important role of XPath is to collect information from an XML document by navigating through the document. A secondary role of XPath is as a general expression language, to allow you to perform calculations, such as averaging the ratings given to TV programs.

The XSLT Recommendation is available at http://www.w3.org/TR/xslt and the XPath Recommendation is available at http://www.w3.org/TR/xpath.

XML documents written in XSLT are known as stylesheets. Stylesheets can transform source XML documents into result documents in a range of formats.

Using XSLT Processors

To use XSLT, you need an **XSLT processor**. XSLT processors are applications that understand what to do with XSLT stylesheets. You tell an XSLT processor to use a particular stylesheet with a particular XML document, and it runs the stylesheet to give you a result:

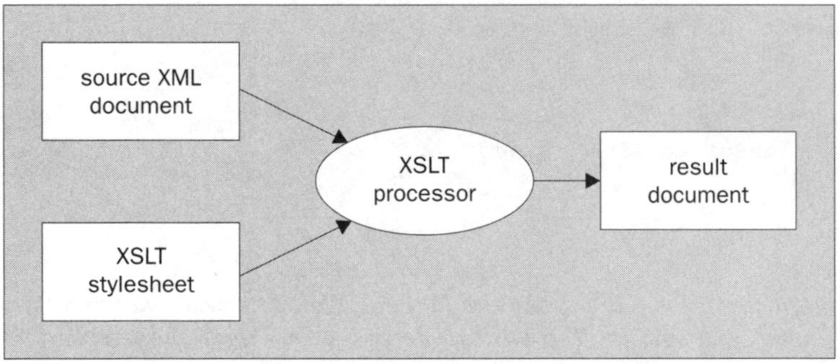

There are lots of different XSLT processors available for different platforms, many of which are free and open source. The three major XSLT processors are:

- **MSXML** from Microsoft – download from http://msdn.microsoft.com/
- **Saxon** from Michael Kay – download from http://saxon.sourceforge.net/
- **Xalan** from the Apache project – download from http://xml.apache.org/

There are lots and lots of other stand-alone XSLT processors that you can use. Go to http://www.xmlsoftware.com/xslt/ for a complete list. There are also XSLT processors embedded in frameworks and applications, for example, the `System.Xml.Xsl` class in Microsoft's .NET framework.

These three processors have all been around for some time and have gone through a lot of testing, so they're pretty much guaranteed to be conformant to the XSLT Recommendation. However, they do often differ in little ways, and in particular in the types of error message that they give when there's something wrong with your stylesheet, so sometimes it's useful to try a stylesheet with several processors to help isolate what's wrong with it.

XSLT stylesheets are interpreted by XSLT processors, which generate a result from source XML.

In the rest of this section, I'll describe how to use each of the three main XSLT processors. As is traditional, we'll use a very simple Hello World example. The XML document for this example is `HelloWorld.xml`, which looks like:

```
<?xml version="1.0" encoding="ISO-8859-1"?>
<greeting>Hello World!</greeting>
```

The `HelloWorld.xsl` stylesheet is also very straightforward. It looks a lot like a well-formed HTML document:

```
<?xml version="1.0" encoding="ISO-8859-1"?>
<html xmlns:xsl="http://www.w3.org/1999/XSL/Transform"
      xsl:version="1.0">
  <head>
    <title>Hello World Example</title>
  </head>
  <body>
    <p>
      <xsl:value-of select="/greeting" />
    </p>
  </body>
</html>
```

The more astute amongst you will have noticed that this XML document contains a special attribute, beginning with `xmlns`. This attribute declares a namespace and associates the namespace with the prefix `xsl`. As we'll see later on, prefixes are used on element and attribute names to say what markup language they come from.

Using MSXML

MSXML is Microsoft's XML parser, schema validator, and XSLT processor rolled into one package. MSXML comes with Internet Explorer, so if you have Internet Explorer installed on your machine, you will have a version of MSXML as well.

MSXML is mainly used with **client-side transformations**. In a client-side transformation, the source XML and the stylesheet for transforming it are both shipped to a client (like Internet Explorer) and then the client carries out the transformations and displays the result. Of course, you can use this facility to automatically transform and view XML documents on your machine – they don't have to come from a distant server.

You can also run MSXML from a script in Internet Explorer or server-side from ASP pages. You'll learn more about this in Chapter 14, when we look at writing dynamic applications using XSLT.

You have to be careful with MSXML because there are several different versions. MSXML only supports XSLT in version 3 and above. The version that comes with Internet Explorer 5 and 5.5 is MSXML2, which doesn't support XSLT. MSXML3 comes with Internet Explorer 6, but you can install it in replace mode to make it work in Internet Explorer 5 and above.

MSXML2 does support a transformation language, but it's based on an early version of XSL and isn't XSLT. You can tell that a stylesheet is using this transformation language by the fact that it uses the namespace `http://www.w3.org/TR/WD-xsl` *rather than* `http://www.w3.org/1999/XSL/Transform`.

To work with XSLT in Internet Explorer, you need to either download and install Internet Explorer version 6 or download and install MSXML3. To make it work automatically, you have to install MSXML3 in replace mode by running a utility called `xmlinst` to replace the existing MSXML2 with MSXML3. You cannot use MSXML4 to get automatic transformations with Internet Explorer; you must use MSXML3.

There is a very useful FAQ on MSXML available at http://www.netcrucible.com/xslt/msxml-faq.htm. *You might also find Chris Bayes's site at* http://www.bayes.co.uk/xml *useful for identifying what version of MSXML you have installed.*

There are two other tools available from Microsoft (http://msdn.microsoft.com/downloads/) that you will find helpful if you're using MSXML to transform your documents:

- IE XML tools – gives a context-menu option for viewing the result of XSLT transformations in Internet Explorer
- MSXSL command-line utility – allows you to carry out transformations using MSXML from the command line

You can use MSXML4 through the MSXSL command-line utility. You can also use it if you run the transformation from a client-side or server-side script.

Try It Out – Transforming with MSXML

The easiest way to transform XML with MSXML is to use Internet Explorer to activate the transformation. In the last chapter, you saw how you could associate a stylesheet with an XML document by adding an `xml-stylesheet` processing instruction at the top of the XML document. In that example, we used a CSS stylesheet. Now, we want to associate the `HelloWorld.xml` document with the `HelloWorld.xsl` stylesheet. Edit `HelloWorld.xml` to add an `xml-stylesheet` processing instruction and create `HelloWorld2.xml` as in the following:

```
<?xml version="1.0" encoding="ISO-8859-1"?>
<?xml-stylesheet type="text/xsl" href="HelloWorld.xsl"?>
<greeting>Hello World!</greeting>
```

Now, when you open up the XML document in Internet Explorer, Internet Explorer reads the `xml-stylesheet` processing instruction and retrieves the `HelloWorld.xsl` stylesheet. Internet Explorer uses MSXML to process the stylesheet and shows you the result in an HTML page. You should see something like the following screenshot:

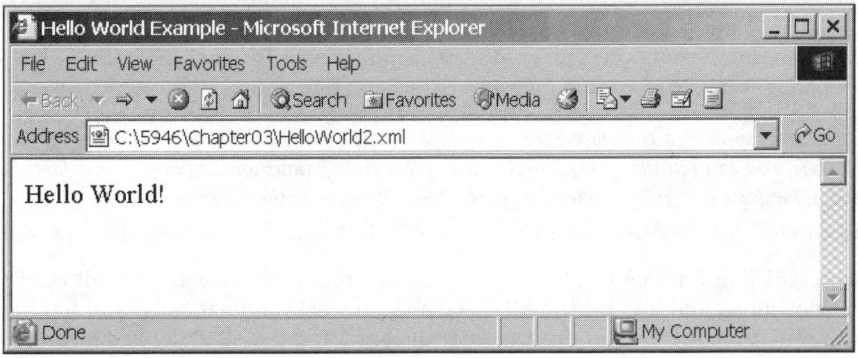

You can see that the XSLT stylesheet's been used properly because the title bar of the window shows the title that we used in the XSLT stylesheet. You can check the XML source by viewing the source of the document (either through the View Source option in the context menu or through the Source option in the View menu). The XML document will probably open up in Notepad:

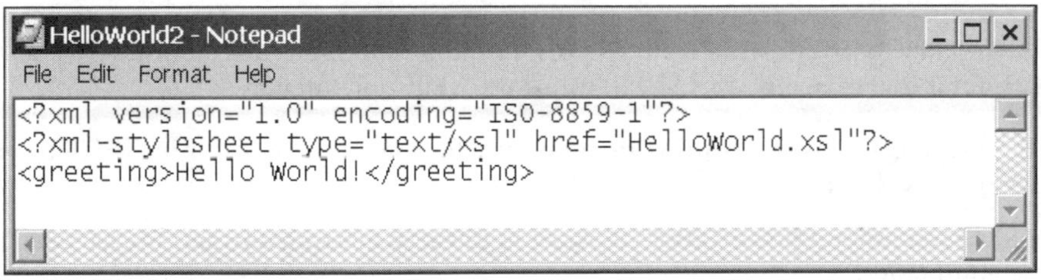

If you've installed the Internet Explorer XML tools, then you can also view the source code of the result of the transformation. Open the context menu and select the View XSL Output option. Another window will open up to show you the result of the transformation:

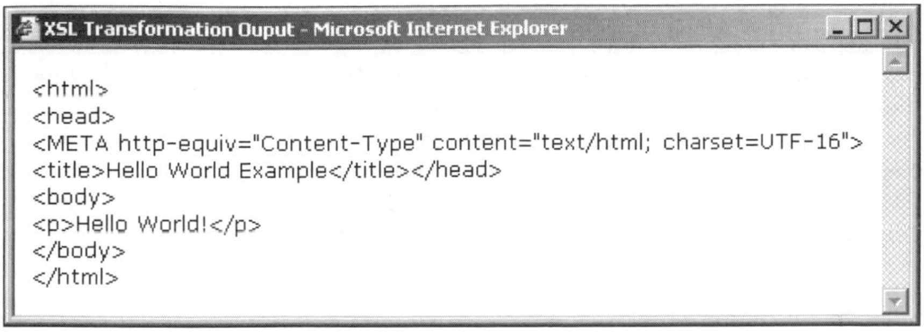

Notice that the result of the transformation is encoded in UTF-16 rather than ISO-8859-1. We'll get on to how you control the encoding of the result of a transformation in Chapter 8, but the encoding of the result really doesn't matter when you're doing a client-side transformation because in fact the result is never saved as a physical file, only manipulated by Internet Explorer in memory.

If you've installed the XSLT command-line utility, then you can also run transformations from the command line. It will make things easier if you have the MSXSL executable in your path, so either edit your `PATH` environment variable or copy/move `msxsl.exe` into the `System32` directory on your machine.

Now open a command prompt in the directory in which you've saved `HelloWorld2.xml` and type the following command line:

>msxsl HelloWorld2.xml HelloWorld.xsl -o HelloWorld.msxsl.html

MSXSL ignores the `xml-stylesheet` processing instruction, and instead uses whatever stylesheet you specify on the command line. In the above command line, we direct the output to `HelloWorld.msxsl.html`. If you now open up `HelloWorld.msxsl.html` in a text editor, you'll see the same result for the transformation:

```
<html>
<head>
<META http-equiv="Content-Type" content="text/html; charset=UTF-16">
<title>Hello World Example</title></head>
<body>
<p>Hello World!</p>
</body>
</html>
```

If your text editor doesn't understand the UTF-16 encoding, then you may find that `HelloWorld.msxsl.html` looks strange, with spaces or Å characters every other character. This is because UTF-16 stores each character as two bytes, but editors that don't understand UTF-16 interpret the first of each of these bytes as a separate character. It's a good idea to find an editor that understands UTF-16 – I use EditPlus from http://www.editplus.com/.

Using Saxon

Saxon is an open source XSLT processor written in Java by Michael Kay. There are two flavors of Saxon: the full Java version and a stand-alone version for Windows named Instant Saxon. The full Java version is useful if you want to use XSLT transformations within Java applications, but for most purposes Instant Saxon is sufficient.

As with MSXSL, it makes things easier if you have the Saxon executable in your path, so once you've installed it, either edit your `PATH` environment variable or move `saxon.exe` into the `System32` directory on your machine.

Try It Out – Transforming with Saxon

Open a command prompt in the directory in which you've saved `HelloWorld2.xml` and type the following command line:

>saxon -o HelloWorld.saxon.html HelloWorld2.xml HelloWorld.xsl

This command line directs the output of the transformation to `HelloWorld.saxon.html`. If you open this HTML file up, you'll see a document similar (though not identical) to the one produced by MSXML:

```
<html>
   <head>
      <meta http-equiv="Content-Type" content="text/html; charset=utf-8">
      <title>Hello World Example</title>
   </head>
   <body>
      <p>Hello World!</p>
   </body>
</html>
```

There are three differences between the two results. First, Saxon indents the output, MSXML doesn't. Second, MSXML uses a `<META>` element whereas Saxon uses a `<meta>` element (though this doesn't matter since HTML is not case-sensitive). Finally, MSXML uses UTF-16 as its default output encoding, whereas Saxon uses UTF-8 (this is reflected in the `content` attribute of the `<meta>` element).

You can also use the `xml-stylesheet` processing instruction in `HelloWorld2.xml` to get Saxon to use that processing instruction to identify the stylesheet that it should use to transform the XML document. If you want Saxon to use the `xml-stylesheet` processing instruction, you need to add the `-a` flag to the command line and remove the reference to the stylesheet, as follows:

>saxon -a -o HelloWorld.saxon.html HelloWorld2.xml

Using Xalan

Xalan is another open source XSLT processor written in Java, but it doesn't have an "instant" version. To use it, you need to download and install it, then add the location of the `xalan.jar` and `xerces.jar` files to your `CLASSPATH` environment variable. Xerces is the XML parser that Xalan uses by default.

Like Saxon, you can use Xalan in any Java application. The place where Xalan is used most is within the **Cocoon** servlet. Cocoon is a servlet that sits on a web server and manages the transformations of XML documents into HTML, which it then sends back to the client. These transformations are known as **server-side transformations** because they occur on the server.

Try It Out – Transforming with Xalan

Once you have it set up, you can run Xalan on the Hello World example using the following command line:

```
>java org.apache.xalan.xslt.Process -IN HelloWorld2.xml -XSL HelloWorld.xsl
    -OUT HelloWorld.xalan.html
```

The result from Xalan also differs a little from the other two processors:

```
<html>
<head>
<META http-equiv="Content-Type" content="text/html; charset=UTF-8">
<title>Hello World Example</title>
</head>
<body>
<p>Hello World!</p>
</body>
</html>
```

Like MSXML, Xalan hasn't indented the output. Like Saxon, it has saved the result in UTF-8 rather than UTF-16.

Simplified Stylesheets

Hopefully you'll have been able to get at least one of the processors to transform the `HelloWorld2.xml` document into HTML. Now let's have a closer look at the `HelloWorld.xsl` stylesheet so we can see what it's doing. Here's the stylesheet again:

```
<?xml version="1.0" encoding="ISO-8859-1"?>
<html xmlns:xsl="http://www.w3.org/1999/XSL/Transform"
      xsl:version="1.0">
  <head>
    <title>Hello World Example</title>
  </head>
  <body>
    <p>
      <xsl:value-of select="/greeting" />
    </p>
  </body>
</html>
```

The first thing you'll notice is that the document element of the XML document is an `<html>` element rather than one with a name that indicates that the XML document is a stylesheet. This is because this stylesheet is a **simplified stylesheet**. Simplified stylesheets are intended for basic transformations, and are a good first step on the road to more complicated stylesheets. We'll start seeing more complicated (and more representative) stylesheets in the next chapter.

The second thing that you should notice from the XSLT stylesheet is that it's a well-formed XML document. It has elements, attributes, and an XML declaration. XSLT stylesheets have to be well-formed XML documents.

Try It Out – Checking the Well-Formedness of Stylesheets

Even with practice, it's often difficult to write well-formed XML in a normal text editor (although XML editors can help a lot). One of the main types of errors you'll find as you write XSLT stylesheets just occur because you've made a mistake with the XML. To see what happens when you try to transform XML with a non-well-formed stylesheet, try changing `HelloWorld.xsl` so that it's not well-formed: take away the close tag for the <p> element, for example, to create `HelloWorld2.xsl`:

```
<?xml version="1.0" encoding="ISO-8859-1"?>
<html xmlns:xsl="http://www.w3.org/1999/XSL/Transform"
      xsl:version="1.0">
  <head>
    <title>Hello World Example</title>
  </head>
  <body>
    <p>
      <xsl:value-of select="/greeting" />
  </body>
</html>
```

Now try transforming `HelloWorld2.xml` with this non-well-formed stylesheet. The XSLT processor will report an error with the stylesheet. For example, using MSXML at the command prompt you should get the following error reported:

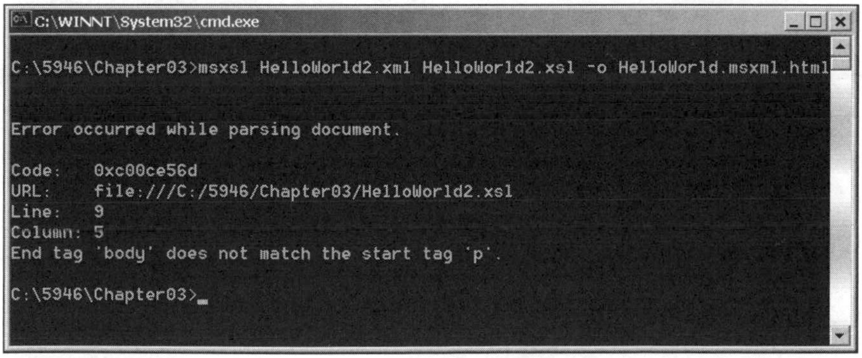

Alternatively, amend `HelloWorld2.xml` to reference the new non-well-formed stylesheet and save it as a new file called `HelloWorld2a.xml`:

```
<?xml version="1.0" encoding="ISO-8859-1"?>
<?xml-stylesheet type="text/xsl" href="HelloWorld2.xsl"?>
<greeting>Hello World!</greeting>
```

If you try to open this file in Internet Explorer you'll get the following error:

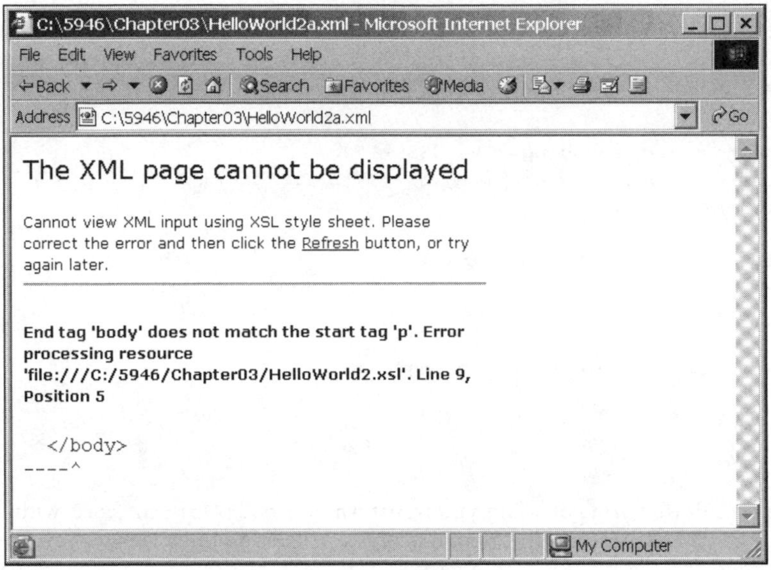

You can also open up an XSLT stylesheet directly within Internet Explorer to see whether it is well-formed. Try opening the original (well-formed) `HelloWorld.xsl` stylesheet in Internet Explorer. You should see the following:

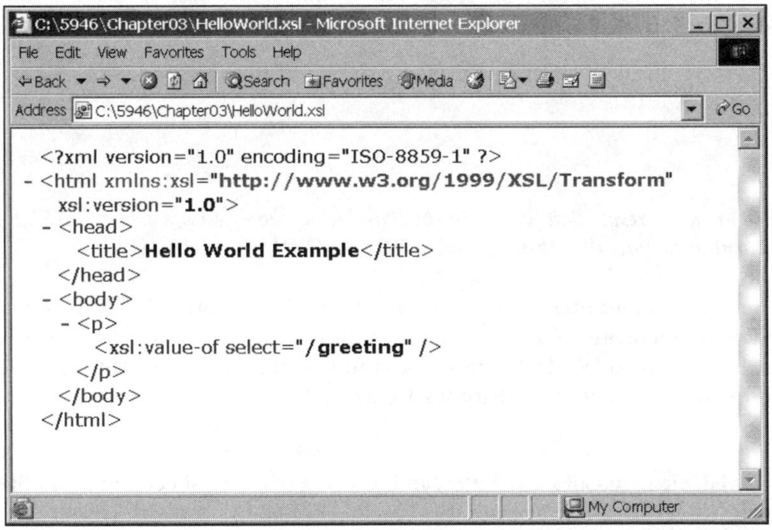

XSLT stylesheets must be well-formed XML documents; you can check the well-formedness of stylesheets in exactly the same ways as you can check normal XML documents.

Literal Result Elements

Most of the elements in the stylesheet are well-formed HTML elements. These elements are given literally in the stylesheet just as if you were creating a normal HTML document. The lines containing the start and end tags of these elements are highlighted below:

```
<?xml version="1.0" encoding="ISO-8859-1"?>
<html xmlns:xsl="http://www.w3.org/1999/XSL/Transform"
      xsl:version="1.0">
  <head>
    <title>Hello World Example</title>
  </head>
  <body>
    <p>
      <xsl:value-of select="/greeting" />
    </p>
  </body>
</html>
```

Now look at the result that you got when you transformed `HelloWorld2.xml` with `HelloWorld.xsl`. You'll see that the elements that you gave in the stylesheet are output literally in the result:

```
<html>
   <head>
      <meta http-equiv="Content-Type" content="text/html; charset=utf-8">
      <title>Hello World Example</title>
   </head>
   <body>
      <p>Hello World!</p>
   </body>
</html>
```

The one element in the result that wasn't in the stylesheet is the `<meta>` *element. XSLT processors add this element automatically whenever you create an HTML document.*

When you include an element literally in a stylesheet so that it's output in the result, these elements are known as **literal result elements**. You'll also have noticed that the text that you included in the stylesheet (namely the "Hello World Example" text in the `<title>` element) was also included literally in the result, and you'll see later that attributes are as well.

Any non-XSLT elements and attributes, and any text in a stylesheet, are given literally in the result. Elements that are generated like this are known as literal result elements.

The <xsl:value-of> Instruction

The one element in `HelloWorld.xsl` that isn't output literally to the result is the `<xsl:value-of>` element. The `<xsl:value-of>` element is a special element that the XSLT processor recognizes as an **instruction**. The `<xsl:value-of>` element takes a single attribute called `select`. When the XSLT processor encounters an `<xsl:value-of>` instruction in the stylesheet, it inserts the value specified by the `<xsl:value-of>` element's `select` attribute.

In the Hello World example, the `<xsl:value-of>` instruction tells the XSLT processor to insert the value of the `<greeting>` element from the source document (`HelloWorld2.xml`) in the result. The `select` attribute holds an XPath – `/greeting`. The XPath acts a bit like a file path. It tells the processor to go to the very top of the document and then down to the `<greeting>` element.

We'll look at a few more XPaths a bit later on in this chapter.

> **The `<xsl:value-of>` instruction gives the result of evaluating the XPath held in its `select` attribute as some text in the result document.**

The XSLT Namespace

We can see from the result of the transformation that the XSLT processor recognizes the `<xsl:value-of>` element as an XSLT instruction, but how does it know not to output `<xsl:value-of>` as a literal result element in the same way as it does with the other elements?

Stylesheets are a particular example of a problem in XML: what do you do when you have a document that contains a mixture of elements and attributes from different markup languages? It would be possible, even likely, that elements and attributes from different markup languages would have the same names, and so you need a way of distinguishing between them. XML distinguishes between elements and attributes from different markup languages with **namespaces**.

Most markup languages have their own namespace, which is identified with a unique identifier – a **namespace URI**. Namespace URIs are often (though not always) URLs. For example, the namespace URI for XSLT is:

```
http://www.w3.org/1999/XSL/Transform
```

You've seen this URL in the Hello World example. Let's look at the `HelloWorld.xsl` stylesheet again:

```
<?xml version="1.0" encoding="ISO-8859-1"?>
<html xmlns:xsl="http://www.w3.org/1999/XSL/Transform"
      xsl:version="1.0">
  <head>
    <title>Hello World Example</title>
  </head>
  <body>
```

```
      <p>
        <xsl:value-of select="/greeting" />
      </p>
    </body>
  </html>
```

The XSLT namespace is the value of the `xmlns:xsl` attribute on the `<html>` element. Attributes that start with `xmlns` have a special significance in XML; they're known as **namespace declarations**. A namespace declaration associates a short string, known as the **namespace prefix**, with a namespace URI. The prefix is the part of the attribute name after the colon. In this case, the XSLT namespace URI is being associated with the prefix `xsl`.

You can also have namespace declarations that don't specify a prefix. For example, we could add a namespace declaration without a prefix to the stylesheet, one that points to the XHTML namespace. Here's the file `HelloWorld3.xsl`:

```
  <?xml version="1.0" encoding="ISO-8859-1"?>
  <html xmlns:xsl="http://www.w3.org/1999/XSL/Transform"
        xmlns="http://www.w3.org/1999/xhtml"
        xsl:version="1.0">
    <head>
      <title>Hello World Example</title>
    </head>
    <body>
      <p>
        <xsl:value-of select="/greeting" />
      </p>
    </body>
  </html>
```

A namespace declaration that doesn't specify a prefix indicates the **default namespace**. So now the default namespace of our stylesheet is the XHTML namespace.

When an XML parser goes through a document, it looks at each element and attribute and tries to work out what namespace the element or attribute belongs to. It treats the name of each element and attribute as a **qualified name** or **QName** for short – a name that is qualified by the namespace to which the element or attribute belongs. If a qualified name contains a colon (`:`), then the part before the colon indicates a namespace prefix. The part after the colon is known as the **local part** or **local name** of the element. So in the case of `<xsl:value-of>`, the prefix is `xsl` and the local part is `value-of`.

Once it's worked out what prefix is being used in a particular qualified name, the XML parser tries to work out which namespace URI the prefix has been associated with by looking at the namespace declarations. In this case, the prefix `xsl` has been associated with the XSLT namespace, so the XML parser knows that the `<xsl:value-of>` element is part of the XSLT namespace.

By convention, the XSLT namespace is usually associated with the prefix `xsl`*. In this book, I use* `<xsl:value-of>` *to indicate the* `value-of` *element in the XSLT namespace even though you can use a different prefix for it if you want to.*

Qualified names that don't have colons are treated a little differently. If an element's name doesn't contain a colon, then the element belongs to the default namespace. On the other hand, if an attribute's name doesn't contain a colon, then the attribute doesn't belong to any namespace.

When the XML parser passes on information about the XML document, it tells the application about the namespace to which the element or attribute belongs. So the XSLT processor sees some XML where every element and attribute has a namespace.

Let's look back at the `HelloWorld3.xsl` stylesheet again, with the default namespace declaration that we included. Most of the elements don't have a prefix, so they are in the default namespace, which is the XHTML namespace. The `<xsl:value-of>` element does have a prefix, `xsl`, which is associated with the XSLT namespace, so `<xsl:value-of>` is part of XSLT. The `xsl:version` attribute has a prefix as well, so it is also part of XSLT. On the other hand, the `select` attribute on `<xsl:value-of>` has no prefix, and attributes without a prefix don't use the default namespace, so that attribute is in no namespace. Let's have a look at the XML document as a tree to make this clearer:

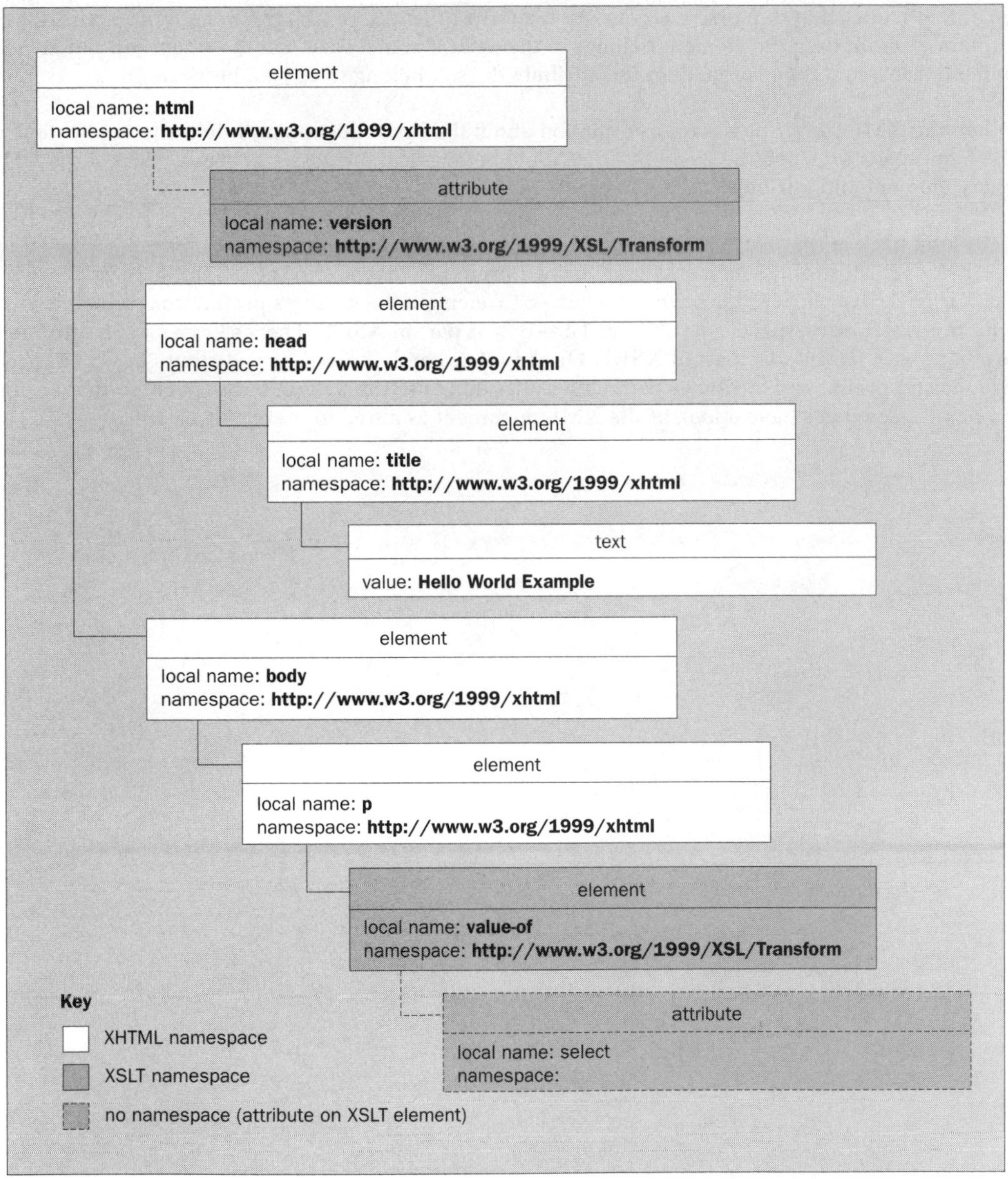

Namespaces allow you to distinguish between elements and attributes that come from different markup languages. A namespace declaration associates a prefix with a namespace URI in a particular document. Elements and attributes that use that prefix belong to that namespace. Elements that don't have a prefix belong to the default namespace, if one is declared with an `xmlns` attribute.

Try It Out – Controlling Namespaces

The prefix that you use in a particular XML document for a namespace doesn't matter, as long as the namespace URI is the same. Try editing the `HelloWorld.xsl` XSLT stylesheet so that you use a different namespace prefix, `test:`, instead, to give `HelloWorld4.xsl`:

```
<?xml version="1.0" encoding="ISO-8859-1"?>
<html xmlns:test="http://www.w3.org/1999/XSL/Transform"
      test:version="1.0">
  <head>
    <title>Hello World Example</title>
  </head>
  <body>
    <p>
      <test:value-of select="/greeting" />
    </p>
  </body>
</html>
```

Now change the `href` attribute in `HelloWorld2.xml` to `HelloWorld4.xsl` to use this stylesheet and save the new file as `HelloWorld2b.xml`; you'll see that it makes no difference to the result of the transformation. The XSLT application uses the namespace URI of the element or attribute to work out whether it's an XSLT instruction (if it has a namespace URI of `http://www.w3.org/1999/XSL/Transform`) or a literal result element (otherwise); it doesn't care about the prefix that you use.

The XML parser will give an error if you try to use a prefix but you haven't specified a namespace declaration for that prefix. Try removing the namespace declaration for the XSLT namespace, to give `HelloWorld5.xsl`:

```
<?xml version="1.0" encoding="ISO-8859-1"?>
<html xsl:version="1.0">
  <head>
    <title>Hello World Example</title>
  </head>
  <body>
    <p>
      <xsl:value-of select="/greeting" />
    </p>
  </body>
</html>
```

Now amend `HelloWorld2.xml` to reference `HelloWorld5.xsl` and call the new file `HelloWorld2c.xml`. If you try to open `HelloWorld2c.xml` in Internet Explorer, then you'll see the following error:

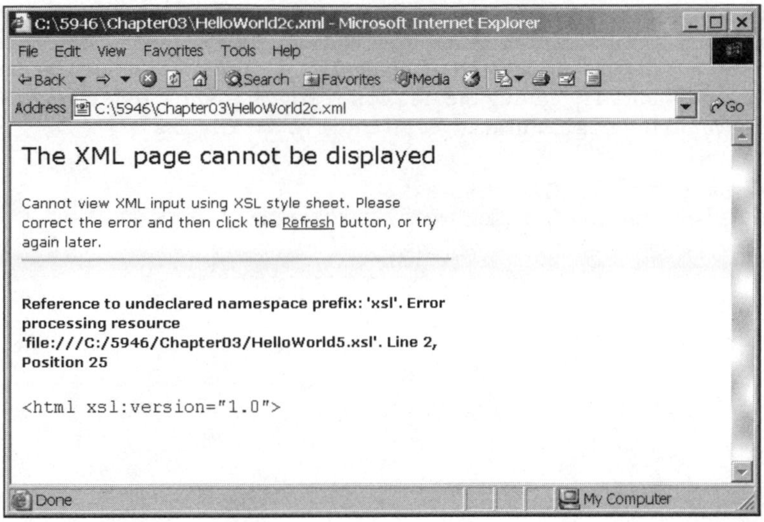

The XML parser can't work out what namespace the `xsl` prefix is supposed to indicate.

The XSLT stylesheet is still a well-formed XML document. Namespaces work at a level above basic XML syntax.

The other kind of change that you can try out is using a different namespace URI for the namespace declaration. Try the following stylesheet, `HelloWorld6.xsl`:

```
<?xml version="1.0" encoding="ISO-8859-1"?>
<html xmlns:xsl="http://www.example.com/bogus/namespace"
      xsl:version="1.0">
  <head>
    <title>Hello World Example</title>
  </head>
  <body>
    <p>
      <xsl:value-of select="/greeting" />
    </p>
  </body>
</html>
```

This is one of those times when the processor that you use makes a difference. MSXML and Xalan treat the `<xsl:value-of>` element as a literal result element – they just include it in the result in the same way that they include the other elements in the stylesheet, to give:

```
<html xmlns:xsl="http://www.example.com/bogus/namespace" xsl:version="1.0">
  <head><title>Hello World Example</title></head>
  <body>
    <p>
      <xsl:value-of select="/greeting" />
    </p>
```

```
  </body>
</html>
```

On the other hand, Saxon raises an error because it doesn't find a `version` attribute in the XSLT namespace on the document element, so it doesn't believe that `HelloWorld6.xsl` is a stylesheet:

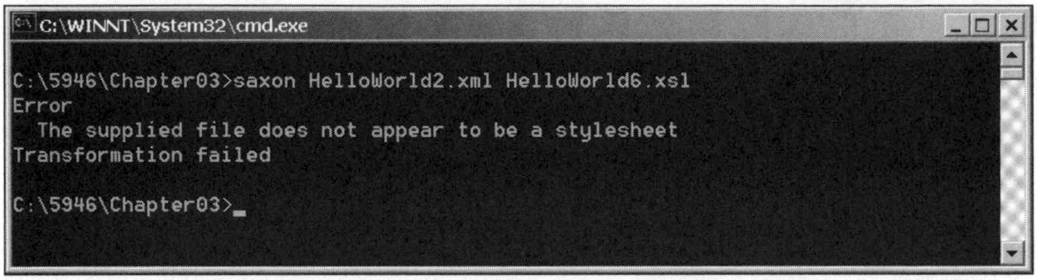
C:\WINNT\System32\cmd.exe
C:\5946\Chapter03>saxon HelloWorld2.xml HelloWorld6.xsl
Error
The supplied file does not appear to be a stylesheet
Transformation failed
C:\5946\Chapter03>_

Simplified stylesheets like the one that we're using here must have an `xsl:version` attribute on the document element, but some XSLT processors accept any XML document as a stylesheet, in which case they copy the XML document as the result of the transformation. The `xsl:version` attribute indicates the version of XSLT that is used in the stylesheet, which will always be `1.0` at the moment, since there is no other version of XSLT.

Generating HTML Pages

We've looked through a nice simple example of how to create an HTML page using a simplified stylesheet. Now it's time to try to use what you've learned about XSLT with our TV Guide.

We've got two main XML files associated with our TV Guide:

- `TVGuide.xhtml` – an XHTML version of the original HTML TV Guide
- `TVGuide.xml` – an XML file that just holds the information about the programs in the TV Guide

We want to generate some HTML that looks something like `TVGuide.xhtml`, but use the information from `TVGuide.xml` to fill in the details. You've seen from the Hello World example that a simplified XSLT stylesheet for generating HTML looks a lot like a well-formed HTML file. We can use `TVGuide.xhtml` as a template for the stylesheet to transform `TVGuide.xml` into HTML.

As a first step, we should use a simple version of `TVGuide.xhtml` so that it's a bit easier to manage – filling in the table cells properly would involve some complicated calculations that we should leave for a later chapter. So instead, we'll just list the programs that are on for each channel. We'll start with some XHTML that looks like:

```
<?xml version="1.0" encoding="ISO-8859-1"?>
<html>
<head>
  <title>TV Guide</title>
  <link rel="stylesheet" href="TVGuide.css" />
  <script type="text/javascript">
    function toggle(element) {
      if (element.style.display == 'none') {
        element.style.display = 'block';
      }
      else {
        element.style.display = 'none';
      }
    }
  </script>
</head>
<body>
  <h1>TV Guide</h1>
  <h2 class="channel">BBC1</h2>
  ...
  <div>
    <p>
      <span class="date">2001-07-05T19:30:00</span><br />
      <span class="title">EastEnders</span><br />
      Mark's health scare forces him to reconsider his future with Lisa,
      while Jamie is torn between Sonia and Zoe.
      <span onclick="toggle(EastEndersCast);">[Cast]</span>
    </p>
    <div id="EastEndersCast" style="display: none;">
      <ul class="castlist">
        <li>
          <span class="character">Zoe Slater</span>
          <span class="actor">Michelle Ryan</span>
        </li>
        <li>
          <span class="character">Jamie Mitchell</span>
          <span class="actor">Jack Ryder</span>
        </li>
        <li>
          <span class="character">Sonia Jackson</span>
          <span class="actor">Natalie Cassidy</span>
        </li>
        ...
      </ul>
    </div>
  </div>
  ...
</body>
</html>
```

In Internet Explorer, TVGuide.xhtml looks like the following:

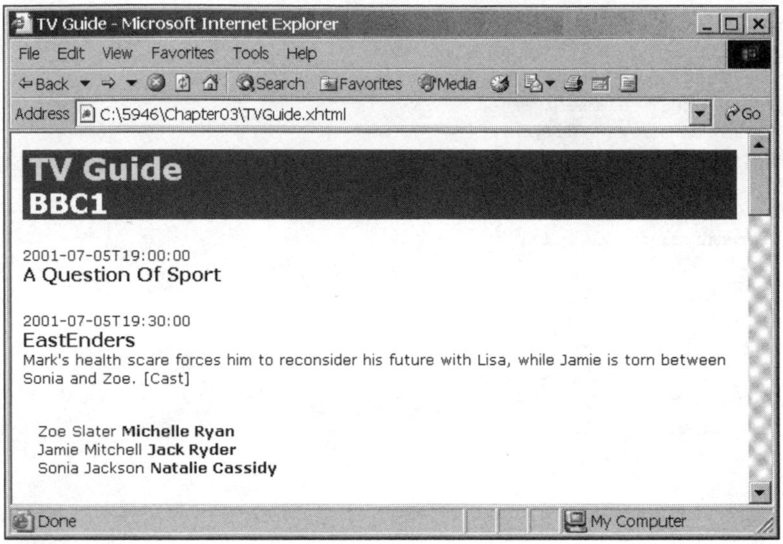

Note that `TVGuide.xhtml` *still links to a CSS stylesheet to make the page look pretty.*

We can use TVGuide.xhtml as the basis of our stylesheet, which we'll call TVGuide.xsl. As you'll remember from the end of the last section, the one necessity in a simplified stylesheet is that the document element (<html> in this case) has an xsl:version attribute on it. The xsl:version attribute is in the XSLT namespace, so the first change from TVGuide.xhtml to TVGuide.xsl is to add these attributes to the <html> element:

```
<?xml version="1.0" encoding="ISO-8859-1"?>
<html xmlns:xsl="http://www.w3.org/1999/XSL/Transform"
      xsl:version="1.0">
   ...
</html>
```

If you transform TVGuide.xml with this stylesheet, you should get a result that looks pretty much identical to TVGuide.xhtml. But not so fast – all of the information about all of the programs is written in to the stylesheet, whereas we want the stylesheet to get that information from TVGuide.xml. So let's look at how to do that in more detail.

Iterating Over Elements

If you examine the content of TVGuide.xhtml in more detail you should be able to relate the content that we have in the HTML that we want to generate to the content that's held in TVGuide.xml. The first thing we can see is that some of the content of TVGuide.xhtml should never change even if the content of TVGuide.xml changes – things like the title, the link to the CSS stylesheet, and the script are just static. The static parts are the parts highlighted in the following:

```
<html>
<head>
  <title>TV Guide</title>
  <link rel="stylesheet" href="TVGuide.css" />
  <script type="text/javascript">
    function toggle(element) {
      if (element.style.display == 'none') {
        element.style.display = 'block';
      }
      else {
        element.style.display = 'none';
      }
    }
  </script>
</head>
<body>
  <h1>TV Guide</h1>
  <h2 class="channel">BBC1</h2>
  <div>
    ...
  </div>
  ...
</body>
</html>
```

The rest of the content is influenced by the content of `TVGuide.xml`. Let's look at `TVGuide.xml` again:

```
<?xml version="1.0" encoding="ISO-8859-1"?>
<TVGuide start="2001-07-05" end="2001-07-05">
  <Channel>
    <Name>BBC1</Name>
    ...
    <Program>
      <Start>2001-07-05T19:30:00</Start>
      <Duration>PT30M</Duration>
      <Series>EastEnders</Series>
      <Title></Title>
      <Description>
        Mark's health scare forces him to reconsider his future with Lisa,
        while Jamie is torn between Sonia and Zoe.
      </Description>
      <CastList>
        <CastMember>
          <Character><Name>Zoe Slater</Name></Character>
          <Actor><Name>Michelle Ryan</Name></Actor>
        </CastMember>
        <CastMember>
          <Character><Name>Jamie Mitchell</Name></Character>
          <Actor><Name>Jack Ryder</Name></Actor>
        </CastMember>
        <CastMember>
          <Character><Name>Sonia Jackson</Name></Character>
          <Actor><Name>Natalie Cassidy</Name></Actor>
        </CastMember>
        ...
      </CastList>
```

```
      <Writers>
        <Writer><Name>Nick Saltrese</Name></Writer>
        <Writer><Name>Julie Wassmer</Name></Writer>
      </Writers>
      <Director><Name>Stewart Edwards</Name></Director>
      <Producer><Name>Emma Turner</Name></Producer>
    </Program>
    ...
  </Channel>
  ...
</TVGuide>
```

In TVGuide.xml, the <TVGuide> element contains a number of <Channel> elements. In the output, for every <Channel> element in TVGuide.xml, we want to have an <h2> element naming the channel, and then some information about each of the programs available on that channel.

The <xsl:for-each> Element

You can go through each of the <Channel> elements one by one using an XSLT instruction – <xsl:for-each>. The <xsl:for-each> element has a select attribute which you use to point to the elements that you want to iterate over. So, you can iterate over each of the <Channel> elements that are children of the <TVGuide> element with the following XSLT instruction:

```
<xsl:for-each select="/TVGuide/Channel">
  ...
</xsl:for-each>
```

The XSLT processor collects all the elements that you point to with the select attribute and goes through them one by one, in the same order that they appear in the XML document. Anything that you put in the content of the <xsl:for-each> instruction gets processed once for each of the elements that you select.

The <xsl:for-each> element iterates over the nodes selected by the XPath specified in its select attribute.

Absolute and Relative Paths

We saw in the 'Hello World' example how to get the value of an element with <xsl:value-of>. In that example, we used an **absolute path** to point to the value of the <greeting> document element. Absolute paths start from the top of the document and work down from there, just like an absolute file path or absolute URL.

But here we want to give the name of each channel, which is contained in the <Name> element under each <Channel> element. To let you point to the name of this particular channel, you can use **relative paths** in the select attribute of <xsl:value-of>. Relative paths don't start with a /, and are similar to relative file paths or relative URLs. In the TV Guide stylesheet, we can give the name of each channel, inside an <h2> element, with the following:

```
<xsl:for-each select="/TVGuide/Channel">
  <h2 class="channel"><xsl:value-of select="Name" /></h2>
</xsl:for-each>
```

Relative paths are always evaluated relative to the **context node**. The context node is the element (or attribute, comment, or processing instruction) that you're currently processing. So when the XSLT processor selects the first `<Channel>` element to process in the above `<xsl:for-each>` instruction, the context node becomes that first `<Channel>` element. When the XSLT processor evaluates the `select` attribute of the `<xsl:value-of>` instruction, it looks for the `<Name>` element under the first `<Channel>` element. When the processor moves on to the second `<Channel>` element, the context node becomes the second `<Channel>` element, so the `<xsl:value-of>` gives the name of the second channel.

> **Absolute paths start with a / and reference nodes starting from the top of the XML document. Relative paths are evaluated starting from the context node, which is whatever node is currently being processed.**

Try It Out – Giving a Title for Every Channel

It's time to try out iterating over all the `<Channel>` elements in `TVGuide.xml` and giving each of their names in the HTML. The stylesheet needs to contain an `<xsl:for-each>` element that selects all the `<Channel>` elements. For each of those, it needs to create an `<h2>` element, and inside it give the name of the channel, which is held in the `<Name>` element under the `<Channel>` element. The stylesheet contains all the static information that it did before, but the main body of the stylesheet outputs the channel names. `TVGuide2.xsl` looks as follows:

```
<html xmlns:xsl="http://www.w3.org/1999/XSL/Transform"
      xsl:version="1.0">
<head>
  <title>TV Guide</title>
  <link rel="stylesheet" href="TVGuide.css" />
  <script type="text/javascript">
    function toggle(element) {
      if (element.style.display == 'none') {
        element.style.display = 'block';
      }
      else {
        element.style.display = 'none';
      }
    }
  </script>
</head>
<body>
  <h1>TV Guide</h1>
  <xsl:for-each select="/TVGuide/Channel">
    <h2 class="channel"><xsl:value-of select="Name" /></h2>
  </xsl:for-each>
</body>
</html>
```

Run an XSLT processor to transform `TVGuide.xml` with `TVGuide2.xsl` as the stylesheet to produce `TVGuide2.html`. For instance, using MSXML use the following at the command prompt:

>msxsl TVGuide.xml TVGuide2.xsl -o TVGuide2.html

The source code of the result of the transformation is:

```
<html>
  <head>
    <link rel="stylesheet" href="TVGuide.css">
    <script type="text/javascript">
      function toggle(element) {
        if (element.style.display == 'none') {
          element.style.display = 'block';
        }
        else {
          element.style.display = 'none';
        }
      }
    </script>
  </head>
  <body>
    <h1>TV Guide</h1>
    <h2 class="channel">BBC1</h2>
    <h2 class="channel">BBC2</h2>
    <h2 class="channel">ITV</h2>
    <h2 class="channel">Channel 4</h2>
    <h2 class="channel">Channel 5</h2>
  </body>
</html>
```

The static parts of the page are added, and for each channel that you've listed in `TVGuide.xml`, you get an `<h2>` element in the result. When you look at this in Internet Explorer, you see:

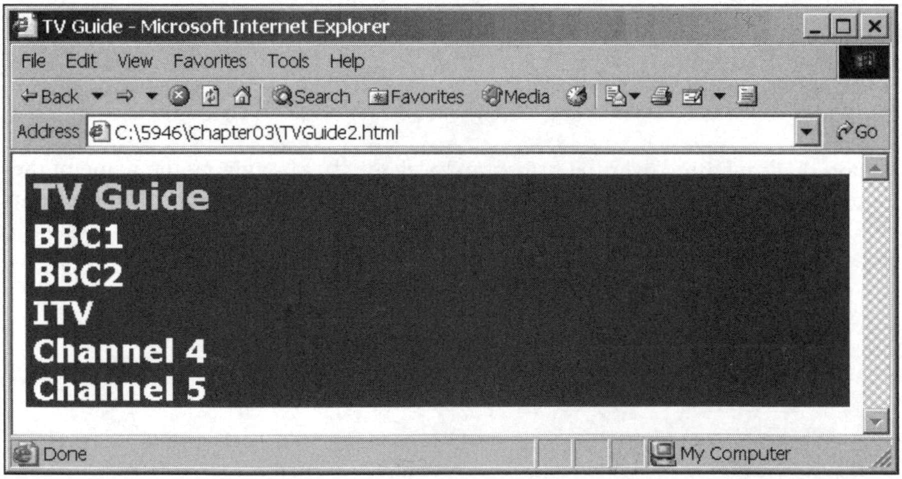

As before, the alternative method is to reference the stylesheet from within the XML document itself. Insert the highlighted line into `TVGuide.xml` to create `TVGuide2.xml`:

```
<?xml version="1.0" encoding="ISO-8859-1"?>
<?xml-stylesheet type="text/xsl" href="TVGuide2.xsl"?>
<TVGuide start="2001-07-05" end="2001-07-05">
  ...
</TVGuide>
```

The output you see in Internet Explorer should be the same as with `TVGuide2.html`.

You can nest `<xsl:for-each>` elements as much as you want. So let's try adding some more information to the output. We'll aim to generate something like the following for each program in `TVGuide.xml`:

```
<div>
  <p>
    <span class="date">2001-07-05T19:30:00</span><br />
    <span class="title">EastEnders</span><br />
    Mark's health scare forces him to reconsider his future with Lisa,
    while Jamie is torn between Sonia and Zoe.
  </p>
  <ul class="castlist">
    <li>
      <span class="character">Zoe Slater</span>
      <span class="actor">Michelle Ryan</span>
    </li>
    <li>
      <span class="character">Jamie Mitchell</span>
      <span class="actor">Jack Ryder</span>
    </li>
    <li>
      <span class="character">Sonia Jackson</span>
      <span class="actor">Natalie Cassidy</span>
    </li>
    ...
  </ul>
</div>
```

Inside the loop that's iterating over the `<Channel>` elements, after giving the name of the channel, we need to loop over each of the `<Program>` elements. As we did when we were giving the name of the channel, we want a relative path to select only the `<Program>` elements that are within this particular `<Channel>` element:

```
<xsl:for-each select="/TVGuide/Channel">
  <h2 class="channel"><xsl:value-of select="Name" /></h2>
  <xsl:for-each select="Program">
    ...
  </xsl:for-each>
</xsl:for-each>
```

For each of the <Program> elements, we create a <div> element. Inside the <div> element we need a <p> element to hold the start date and time, the series name, and the description of the program. Because we're within an <xsl:for-each> instruction that's selected <Program> elements, the current node is a <Program> element, and the paths that we use should be relative to the <Program> element:

```
<xsl:for-each select="/TVGuide/Channel">
  <h2 class="channel"><xsl:value-of select="Name" /></h2>
  <xsl:for-each select="Program">
    <div>
      <p>
        <span class="date"><xsl:value-of select="Start" /></span><br />
        <span class="title"><xsl:value-of select="Series" /></span><br />
        <xsl:value-of select="Description" />
      </p>
      ...
    </div>
  </xsl:for-each>
</xsl:for-each>
```

After the <p> element, we need a <ul> element. To get the contents of the <ul> element, we need to iterate over the <CastMember> elements in the cast list for the program and for each of those give an <li> element containing the value of the <Character> and <Actor> elements from the source, so TVGuide3.xsl contains:

```
<xsl:for-each select="/TVGuide/Channel">
  <h2 class="channel"><xsl:value-of select="Name" /></h2>
  <xsl:for-each select="Program">
    <div>
      <p>
        <span class="date"><xsl:value-of select="Start" /></span><br />
        <span class="title"><xsl:value-of select="Series" /></span><br />
        <xsl:value-of select="Description" />
      </p>
      <ul class="castlist">
        <xsl:for-each select="CastList/CastMember">
          <li>
            <span class="character">
              <xsl:value-of select="Character" />
            </span>
            <span class="actor">
              <xsl:value-of select="Actor" />
            </span>
          </li>
        </xsl:for-each>
      </ul>
    </div>
  </xsl:for-each>
</xsl:for-each>
```

Now create TVGuide3.html by running TVGuide3.xsl against TVGuide.xml, or alternatively, you can generate the same result by amending the href attribute in TVGuide2.xml to reference TVGuide3.xsl thus creating TVGuide3.xml. You'll see roughly the result that we were aiming for, though there are still a few bits that could be neater:

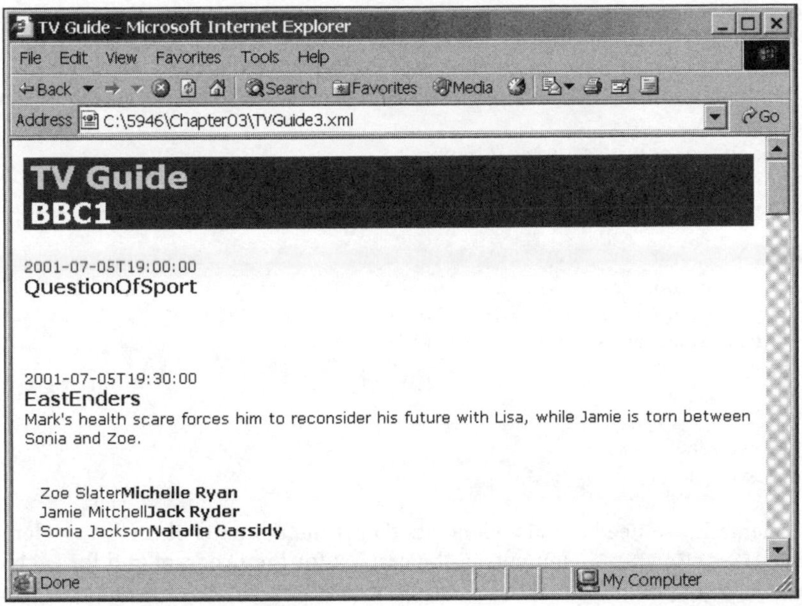

Generating Attribute Values

In the original well-formed HTML that we were aiming for, we had a bit of dynamic HTML so that the end user could show or hide the cast list for a program. For the EastEnders program, the dynamic HTML looked like:

```
<div>
  <p>
    <span class="date">2001-07-05T19:30:00</span><br />
    <span class="title">EastEnders</span><br />
    Mark's health scare forces him to reconsider his future with Lisa,
    while Jamie is torn between Sonia and Zoe.
    <span onclick="toggle(EastEndersCast);">[Cast]</span>
  </p>
  <div id="EastEndersCast" style="display: none;">
    <ul class="castlist">
      ...
    </ul>
  </div>
</div>
```

The `onclick` attribute in the `<span>` element calls the `toggle()` function that we defined in a `<script>` element in the head of the HTML page. It toggles whether the `<div>` element around the cast list is displayed or not.

We've seen that we can add predefined attributes, such as the `style` attribute on the `<div>` element, to the HTML that we generate with our stylesheet just by including them on the literal result elements in the stylesheet. But the dynamic HTML uses attributes that have values that are dependent on the identity of the program. For this program, the `<div>` has an `id` attribute equal to `EastEndersCast`, and the `onclick` attribute of the `<span>` references that `id`. For another program, the `id` would be different, so that clicking on `[Cast]` for different programs would display different cast lists.

Here, we want to make the `id` attribute of the `<div>` around the cast list be dependent on the `<Series>` to which the program belongs. For `<Series>EastEnders</Series>`, we want it to be `EastEndersCast`. For `<Series>Friends</Series>`, we'd want it to be `FriendsCast`.

Attribute Value Templates

You can dynamically generate the value of an attribute using an **attribute value template**. If you put curly brackets (`{}`) in an attribute value, then whatever you have inside the curly brackets is evaluated as if it were in the `select` attribute of an `<xsl:value-of>`, and the result is inserted into the attribute value. For example, if we have:

```
<div id="{Series}Cast" style="display: none;">
  ...
</div>
```

then the `{Series}` part of the `id` attribute value is interpreted by the XSLT processor and it puts the value of the `<Series>` element in its place.

You can insert as many values as you like within an attribute's value with separate pairs of curly brackets. If you want to insert a curly bracket literally into an attribute's value, then double it up – `alt="{{flag}}"` will be output as `alt="{flag}"`.

Not all attributes in a stylesheet are interpreted as attribute value templates, so you can't just use curly brackets in attribute values wherever you like. Most attributes on XSLT elements aren't attribute value templates, so you couldn't dynamically evaluate the value of the `select` attributes of `<xsl:for-each>` or `<xsl:value-of>`, for example.

You can use pairs of curly brackets (`{}`) in attribute values on literal result elements to generate attribute values based on information in the source XML.

Try It Out – Using Attribute Value Templates

Now that you know how to give attributes values based on values from the source XML, let's try adding the dynamic HTML for showing and hiding the cast list. The well-formed HTML we want to generate is:

```
<div>
  <p>
    <span class="date">2001-07-05T19:30:00</span><br />
    <span class="title">EastEnders</span><br />
```

```
        Mark's health scare forces him to reconsider his future with Lisa,
        while Jamie is torn between Sonia and Zoe.
        <span onclick="toggle(EastEndersCast);">[Cast]</span>
      </p>
      <div id="EastEndersCast" style="display: none;">
        <ul class="castlist">
          ...
        </ul>
      </div>
    </div>
```

So in the paragraph describing each program, you need to add a `<span>` element whose `onclick` attribute's value is based on the value of the `<Series>` element under the program. Similarly, you need to generate a `<div>` element with an `id` attribute based on the program's series. You can do both with an attribute value template in `TVGuide4.xsl`, as follows:

```
<xsl:for-each select="Program">
  <div>
    <p>
      <span class="date"><xsl:value-of select="Start" /></span><br />
      <span class="title"><xsl:value-of select="Series" /></span><br />
      <xsl:value-of select="Description" />
      <span onclick="toggle({Series}Cast);">[Cast]</span>
    </p>
    <div id="{Series}Cast" style="display: none;">
      <ul class="castlist">
        ...
      </ul>
    </div>
  </div>
</xsl:for-each>
```

Create `TVGuide4.html` and `TVGuide4.xml` using the same methods as before, and look at the result in a web browser. You should see something like the following:

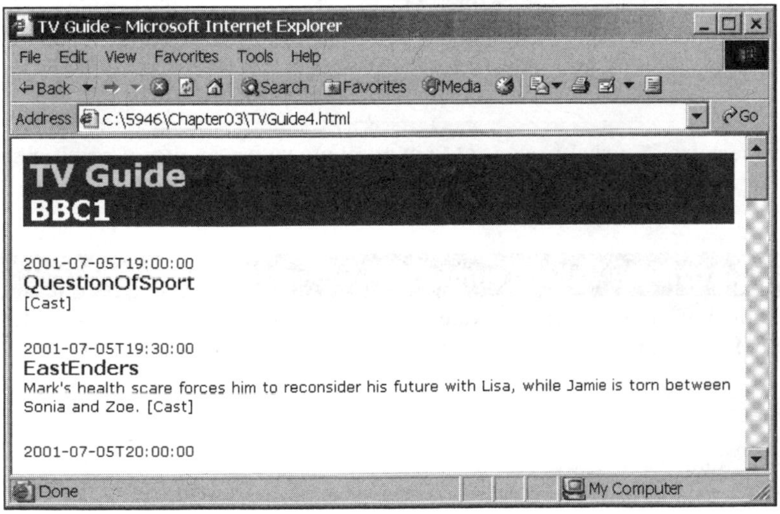

You'll see the information that you've pulled out from `TVGuide.xml`. Try clicking on the [Cast] link for EastEnders and you should see the cast list displayed:

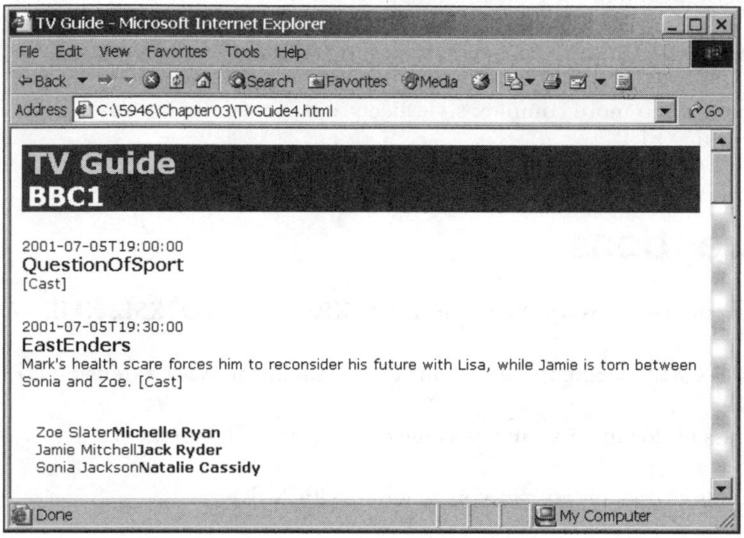

The script that you originally had in the well-formed HTML works just as well when it's generated from a stylesheet.

Summary

This chapter has introduced you to the basic features of XSLT, and it's proved enough to generate quite a nice looking web page. Sure, there are a few things that could be smartened up – it would be good to have the programs given in a table again, and really it would be nice to use a different date format than the one we have at the moment – but all in all, it's not bad for a first shot.

You've learned a bit about the background of XSLT, how it originated as part of a language for styling XML documents, and how it's evolved into something that you can use to generate any text-based format. You've seen how to use XSLT processors embedded in web browsers or run from the command line to run stylesheets; you can use them embedded within other programs as well, but running them like this helps you to test stylesheets.

You've been introduced to the concept of namespaces. Namespaces are really useful in XSLT because they enable XSLT processors to discriminate between literal result elements (which are just added to the output) and XSLT instructions. We're going to return to namespaces in Chapter 7.

You've seen two XSLT instructions in action:

- `<xsl:value-of>` to get the value of an expression
- `<xsl:for-each>` to iterate over a set of nodes

You've also generated attributes with values taken from the XML source using attribute value templates.

But the type of stylesheet that we've seen here is the most basic kind, known as a simplified stylesheet. You can turn any XML document into a simplified stylesheet by adding an `xsl:version` attribute and a namespace declaration for the XSLT namespace to the document element, so they're often a good starting point when you're creating some XSLT. However, they're not very flexible, so in the next chapter, we'll move on to more complex stylesheets and see a different way of approaching transformations with XSLT.

Review Questions

1. What are the relationships between XSLT, XPath, XSL-FO, XSL, XML, DSSSL, and SGML?
2. What are XML documents written in XSLT called, and what extension do they usually use?
3. What class of documents can act as the input to an XSLT processor?
4. What kinds of documents can you generate with XSLT?
5. Name three XSLT processors.
6. Do XSLT processors live on the client or the server in client-server architecture?
7. How can you associate an XML document with an XSLT stylesheet?
8. What is the term for elements that are specified in the stylesheet and output literally in the result?
9. What XSLT instruction can you use to give the value of an element?
10. What is the significance of the URL `http://www.w3.org/1999/XSL/Transform`?
11. Why would you use a namespace declaration?
12. What does an `xmlns` "attribute" do?
13. What namespace prefix is commonly used with XSLT?
14. What attribute must be given on the document element of a simplified stylesheet? What else must be specified on the document element for the attribute to be recognized?
15. What XSLT instruction can you use to iterate over a set of elements?
16. How does an XSLT processor resolve paths that don't begin with `/`?
17. How can you insert a value from your source XML into an attribute value?

Beginning
XSLT

4

Templates

In the last chapter, you saw how to take a well-formed HTML document and turn it into a stylesheet by adding the XSLT elements `<xsl:value-of>` and `<xsl:for-each>` to pick out information from a source XML document and produce an HTML result. The stylesheets that we looked at were **simplified stylesheets**. Simplified stylesheets are good as a starting point when you're creating a stylesheet, and they can be all you need in some cases. However, to utilize the more sophisticated functionality of XSLT, you need to use full stylesheets.

In this chapter, we'll take the simplified stylesheet that we developed during the last chapter and turn it into a full stylesheet. I'll also introduce you to **templates** as a way of breaking up your code and look in a bit more detail at how XSLT processors construct a result from some source XML. You'll learn:

- What full stylesheets look like
- How the XSLT processor navigates the source document to create a result
- How to break up your code into separate templates
- How templates help with document-oriented and unpredictable XML
- How to create tables of contents in your pages using template modes

XSLT Stylesheet Structure

The simplified stylesheets that we used in the last chapter are a specialized form of stylesheet that make a good starting point when we're creating an XSLT stylesheet. Simplified stylesheets aren't all that common in larger applications because they're fairly restricted in what they can do, especially with document-oriented XML.

Technically, simplified stylesheets are defined in the XSLT Recommendation in terms of how they map on to full stylesheets. In the last chapter, we developed the following simplified stylesheet (`HelloWorld.xsl`) to take the Hello World XML document (`HelloWorld.xml`) and convert it to HTML:

```
<?xml version="1.0" encoding="ISO-8859-1"?>
<html xmlns:xsl="http://www.w3.org/1999/XSL/Transform"
      xsl:version="1.0">
  <head><title>Hello World Example</title></head>
  <body>
    <p>
      <xsl:value-of select="/greeting" />
    </p>
  </body>
</html>
```

The equivalent full stylesheet for the simplified stylesheet looks very similar. The content of the simplified stylesheet is wrapped in two elements – `<xsl:template>` and `<xsl:stylesheet>` – to create `HelloWorld2.xsl`. The `<xsl:stylesheet>` element takes the `version` attribute and the XSLT namespace declaration instead of the `<html>` element, giving the following:

```
<?xml version="1.0" encoding="ISO-8859-1"?>
<xsl:stylesheet version="1.0"
                xmlns:xsl="http://www.w3.org/1999/XSL/Transform">
<xsl:template match="/">
  <html>
    <head><title>Hello World Example</title></head>
    <body>
      <p>
        <xsl:value-of select="/greeting" />
      </p>
    </body>
  </html>
</xsl:template>
</xsl:stylesheet>
```

In the next couple of sections, we'll look at what these new XSLT elements do.

Stylesheet Document Elements

The document element of a full stylesheet is `<xsl:stylesheet>` (a `<stylesheet>` element in the namespace `http://www.w3.org/1999/XSL/Transform` – as usual I'm using the prefix `xsl` here but you could use whatever you liked as long as it's associated with the XSLT namespace with a namespace declaration). Like the document element in simplified stylesheets, the `<xsl:stylesheet>` element needs to declare the XSLT namespace and give the version of XSLT that's used in the stylesheet with a `version` attribute. This time, though, the `version` attribute doesn't need to be qualified with the `xsl` prefix because it already lives on an element in the XSLT namespace, so the processor knows it's part of XSLT.

> *You can also use `<xsl:transform>` as the document element in a full stylesheet, rather than `<xsl:stylesheet>`. There is no difference in functionality between the two document elements – they each use exactly the same attributes and do exactly the same thing. Some people prefer to use `<xsl:transform>` when doing transformations that aren't producing presentation-oriented formats such as XSL-FO or XHTML. Personally, I use `<xsl:stylesheet>` all the time.*

Defining Templates

Inside the `<xsl:stylesheet>` document element, XSLT stylesheets are made up of a number of templates, each of which matches a particular part of the source XML document and processes it whatever way you define. The templates are rules that define how a particular part of the source XML document maps on to the result that you want. Thus a full stylesheet has a structure that's quite similar to the structure of CSS stylesheets – a set of rules that match different elements and describe how they should be presented.

> *There are some very fundamental differences between CSS stylesheets and XSLT stylesheets, though. First, while CSS always processes all the elements in a document, you can use XSLT to pick and choose which elements to display. Second, while multiple rules can be applied to style a particular element in CSS, only one template can be applied at a time in XSLT. Third, XSLT templates can match a lot of things that CSS templates can't, such as attributes and comments.*

Templates are defined using the `<xsl:template>` element. The `match` attribute on `<xsl:template>` indicates which parts of the source document should be processed with the particular template and the content of the `<xsl:template>` element dictates what is done with that particular part of the source document. You can use literal result elements, `<xsl:value-of>`, and `<xsl:for-each>` inside a template in exactly the same way as you do within a simplified stylesheet to generate some output.

> **A full XSLT stylesheet has an `<xsl:stylesheet>` document element, which contains a number of `<xsl:template>` elements, each of which defines the processing that should be carried out on a particular part of the source XML.**

Try It Out – Converting a Simplified Stylesheet to a Full Stylesheet

In this section, we'll convert the simplified stylesheet `TVGuide.xsl` that we created in the last chapter into a full stylesheet and test that the full stylesheet gives exactly the same result for `TVGuide.xml` as the simplified stylesheet did.

The simplified stylesheet `TVGuide.xsl` looks as follows:

```
<?xml version="1.0" encoding="ISO-8859-1"?>
<html xmlns:xsl="http://www.w3.org/1999/XSL/Transform"
      xsl:version="1.0">
<head>
  <title>TV Guide</title>
  <link rel="stylesheet" href="TVGuide.css" />
  <script type="text/javascript">
    function toggle(element) {
      if (element.style.display == 'none') {
        element.style.display = 'block';
      } else {
        element.style.display = 'none';
      }
    }
  </script>
```

```
</head>

<body>
  <h1>TV Guide</h1>
  <xsl:for-each select="/TVGuide/Channel">
    <h2 class="channel"><xsl:value-of select="Name" /></h2>
    <xsl:for-each select="Program">
      <div>
        <p>
          <span class="date"><xsl:value-of select="Start" /></span><br />
          <span class="title"><xsl:value-of select="Series" /></span><br />
          <xsl:value-of select="Description" />
          <span onclick="toggle({Series}Cast);">[Cast]</span>
        </p>
        <div id="{Series}Cast" style="display: none;">
          <ul class="castlist">
            <xsl:for-each select="CastList/CastMember">
              <li>
                <span class="character">
                  <xsl:value-of select="Character" />
                </span>
                <span class="actor">
                  <xsl:value-of select="Actor" />
                </span>
              </li>
            </xsl:for-each>
          </ul>
        </div>
      </div>
    </xsl:for-each>
  </xsl:for-each>
</body>
</html>
```

When you use this stylesheet with `TVGuide.xml`, you get the following display:

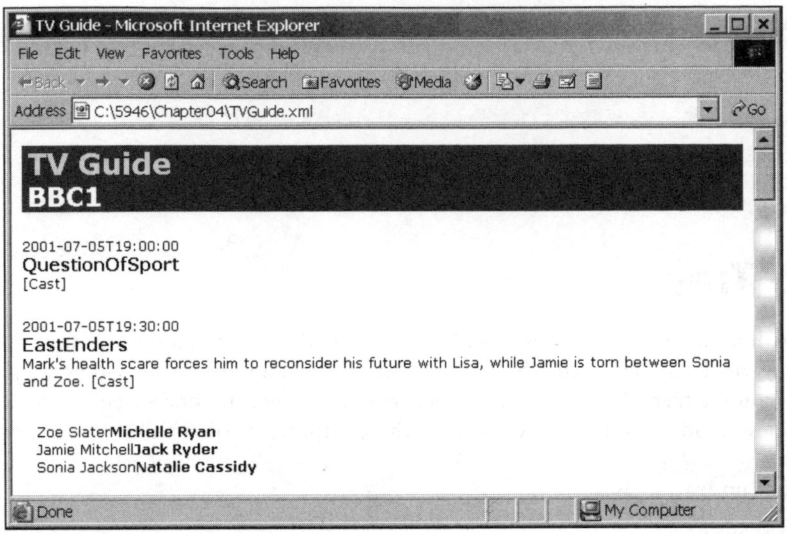

To create a full stylesheet from this simplified stylesheet, you need to do the following:

- Add an `<xsl:template>` element whose `match` attribute has the value `/` around the `<html>` element
- Add an `<xsl:stylesheet>` element around the new `<xsl:template>` element
- Move the XSLT namespace declaration from the `<html>` element to the `<xsl:stylesheet>` element
- Remove the `xsl:version` attribute from the `<html>` element and add an equivalent `version` attribute on the `<xsl:stylesheet>` element

The result of these four steps is `TVGuide2.xsl`, with the following outline:

```
<?xml version="1.0" encoding="ISO-8859-1"?>
<xsl:stylesheet version="1.0"
                xmlns:xsl="http://www.w3.org/1999/XSL/Transform">

<xsl:template match="/">
  <html>
    <head>
      ...
    </head>
    <body>
      ...
    </body>
  </html>
</xsl:template>

</xsl:stylesheet>
```

Now run the transformation with `TVGuide.xml`, this time with the full stylesheet `TVGuide2.xsl`. Do this by amending the `xml-stylesheet` processing instruction in `TVGuide.xml` as follows:

```
<?xml-stylesheet type="text/xsl" href="TVGuide2.xsl"?>
```

You should see exactly the same result as you had before.

The Node Tree

Before we start looking at templates in detail, we first need to look at an XML document in the way that an XSLT processor does. When an XSLT processor reads in a document, it generates a representation of the XML as a **node tree**. As you might expect from its name, the node tree is a bunch of **nodes** arranged in a tree. Nodes are a general term for the components of an XML document, such as:

- element nodes
- attribute nodes
- text nodes
- comment nodes
- processing instruction nodes

The nodes are arranged in a tree such that the tree forms a new branch for every node contained in an element. The relationships between the nodes in the tree are described in terms of familial relationships, so the nodes that an element contains are called its **children** and an element node is its children's **parent**. Similarly, all the children of an element node are **siblings**, and you can also talk about the **descendents** of an element node or a node's **ancestors**.

At the very top of the node tree is the **root node** (for some reason node trees grow down rather than up). You can think of the root node as being equivalent to the XML document itself. The root node's children are the document element and any comments or processing instructions that live outside the document element.

Attribute nodes are a bit special because attributes are not contained in elements in the same way as other elements or text, but they are still associated with particular elements. The element that an attribute is associated with is still known as its parent, but attributes are not their parent element's children, just its attributes.

Note that comments and processing instructions are nodes and part of the node tree, so you need to take them into account if you count nodes or iterate over them. As we'll see in Chapter 7, text nodes that consist purely of whitespace might also be part of the node tree, but you have some control over which are and which aren't.

The view of XML as a node tree is a very natural view because of the way that XML is structured, with elements nesting inside each other. In XML, the relationship between an element and its contents is a one-to-many relationship – each element can only have one parent – which fits the pattern of a tree structure. Processing XML as a tree of nodes is also useful because it means you can focus down on a particular branch of the tree (the content of a particular element) very easily. Other models of XML documents, such as the Document Object Model (DOM) and the XML Infoset, also view XML documents as tree structures, although the models are just slightly different from the node tree that XSLT uses.

You can find out more about the DOM at http://www.w3.org/DOM/Activity.html *and more about the XML Infoset at* http://www.w3.org/TR/xml-infoset/.

XSLT processors treat documents as a node tree in which the contents of an element are represented as its children. Every node in a node tree descends from the root node.

Having a picture of the node tree can be very useful because it lets you view the XML document in the same way as the XSLT processor does. Here's a simplified version of the XML that we're using to hold the information in our TV guide:

```
<?xml version="1.0" encoding="ISO-8859-1"?>
<?xml-stylesheet type="text/xsl" href="TVGuide.xsl"?>
<TVGuide start="2001-07-05" end="2001-07-05">
  <Channel>
    <Name>BBC1</Name>
    ...
    <Program>
      <Start>2001-07-05T19:30:00</Start>
      <Duration>PT30M</Duration>
      <Series>EastEnders</Series>
      ...
    </Program>
    ...
  </Channel>
  ...
</TVGuide>
```

Every node tree starts with the root node, so that's the starting point for our diagram. The root node of the tree is like the document itself. The XML document has two nodes at the top level, the `xml-stylesheet` processing instruction and the document element – the `<TVGuide>` element. The document element is the top-most element in the node tree, but other things (like comments and processing instructions) can occur at the same level. We can also draw the children of the root node in, as follows:

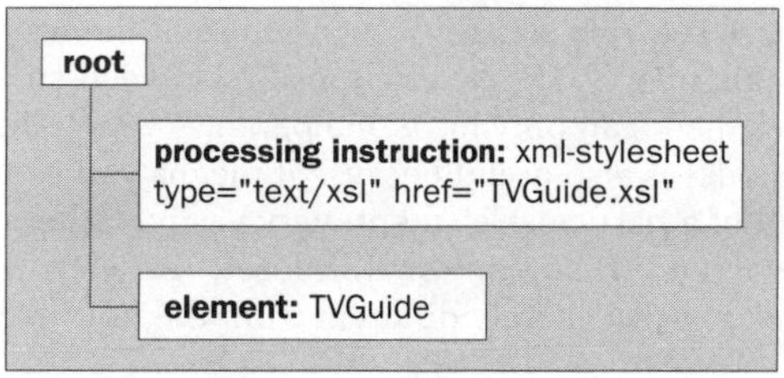

An XSLT processor doesn't see the XML declaration (the first line of an XML file). The information held in the XML declaration relates to how the XML document has been stored, which the XSLT processor doesn't care about. Also, note that the pseudo-attributes in the `xml-stylesheet` *processing instruction aren't nodes (unlike proper attributes), they're just part of the value of the processing instruction.*

Now, the `<TVGuide>` element has a couple of attributes: `start` and `end`. These attributes shouldn't be added to the tree in the same way as the children of the `<TVGuide>` would be, so we'll place them off to one side and use a different kind of line for them, as follows:

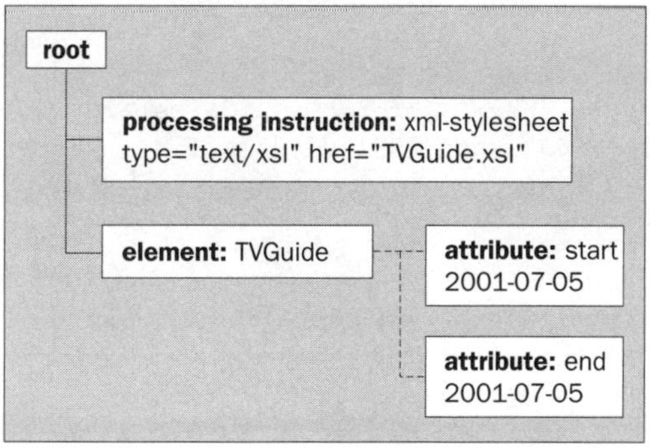

Now let's look at the content of the `<TVGuide>` element. The `<TVGuide>` element contains a `<Channel>` element, which in turn contains a `<Name>` element and a `<Program>` element. The `<Name>` element contains some text. Pieces of text are represented as separate nodes in the node tree, so the `<Name>` element node contains a text node, as shown here:

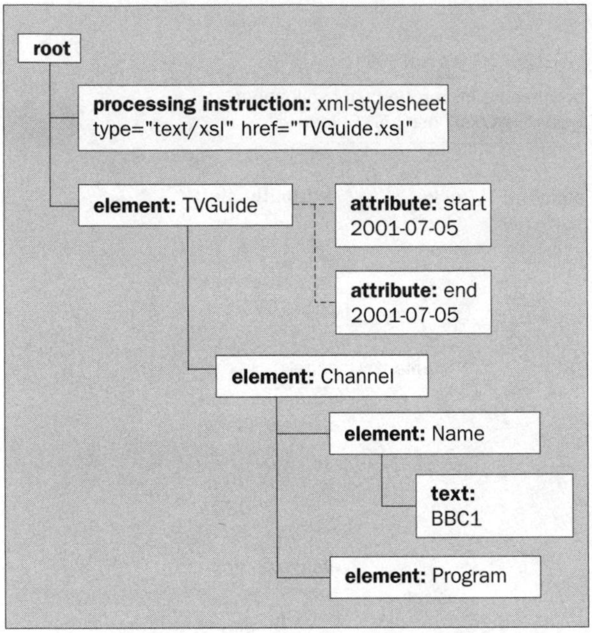

The child elements of the `<Program>` element are treated in the same way – they each have a single text node as a child:

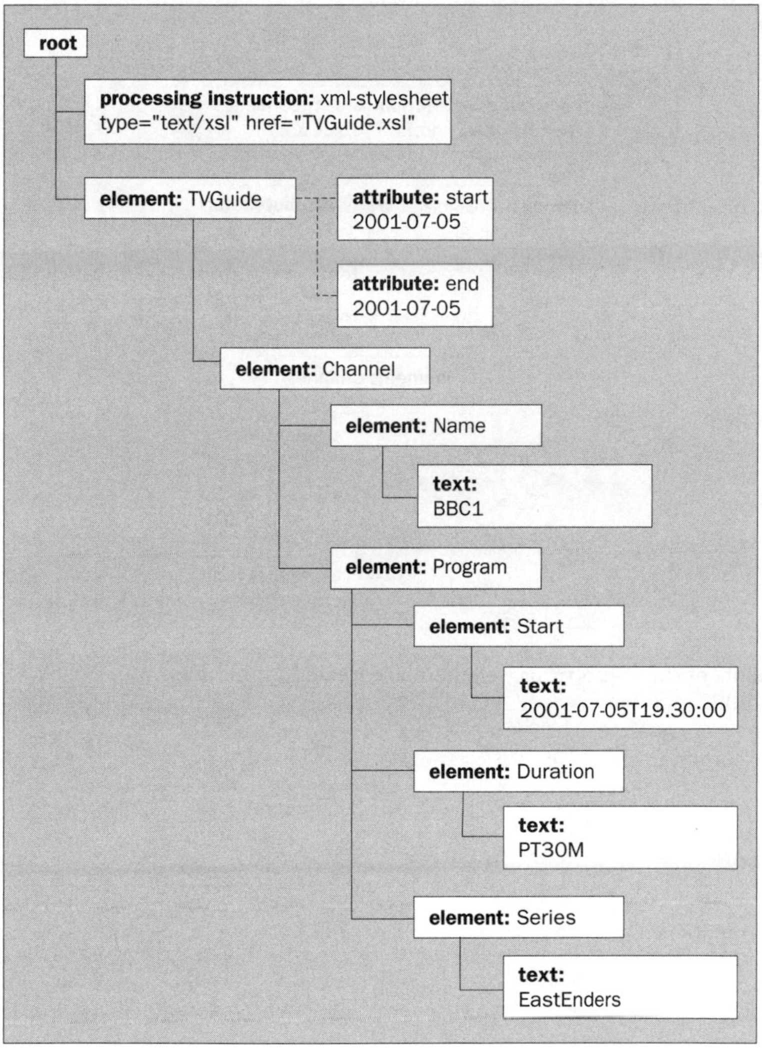

The rest of the tree follows a similar pattern: element nodes having either other elements or text nodes as children. It's often very useful to keep a picture of the node tree of the source document that you're working with close at hand, to help you work out what nodes you're selecting and processing.

Many XSLT editors help with this by providing a simple tree view on a source document. Alternatively, you can use a stand-alone tool such as Mike Brown's Pretty XML Tree Viewer (http://skew.org/xml/stylesheets/treeview/html/).

XSLT Processing Model

Templates in stylesheets each match particular nodes in the node tree. The `match` attribute on a template tells the XSLT processor what kind of nodes they match. In a full stylesheet, you tell the XSLT processor what nodes you want to be processed (using an `<xsl:apply-templates>` instruction, as you'll see later) and the XSLT processor goes through the nodes you've selected one by one trying to find a matching template for each in turn. When it looks for a template, it searches the whole stylesheet, so it doesn't matter where the template is within that stylesheet.

When the XSLT processor finds a matching template, it uses the content of that template to process the matching node and generate some output. The content of the template might include instructions that tell the processor to apply templates to a particular set of nodes, in which case it goes through those nodes finding and processing matching templates, and so on.

In this section, we'll look at the implications of this processing model and the kinds of changes that we can make to our stylesheet to take advantage of templates.

> **XSLT processing involves telling the processor to apply templates to some nodes in the source document. The XSLT processor locates a template that matches the node, and processes its content to generate a result. The location of the template within the stylesheet doesn't matter.**

The Starting Template

This process of applying templates to nodes in the node tree has to start somewhere. In the majority of cases, the input to the stylesheet is an XML document, and the processor starts at the top of the node tree, on the root node. After building the node tree, the XSLT processor takes the root node and tries to find a template that matches it. If the XSLT processor finds one, it processes the content of that template to generate the output.

If you're running a stylesheet from code, then you can make the stylesheet start from a node other than the root node if you want. This is useful if you want to only process a section of a larger document, for example. In these cases, you need templates that match the nodes that you use as the source of the transformation – a template that matches the root node will only be used if you tell the processor to process the root node.

A template that matches the root node has a `match` attribute with a value of `/`, one that looks like:

```
<xsl:template match="/">
  ...
</xsl:template>
```

If you're familiar with programming, you can think of this template as analogous to the `main()` method on a class. Whatever happens, when you process a document with the stylesheet, the XSLT processor will process the contents of this template, so it gives you top-level control over what the stylesheet does.

If you look back at the full stylesheet that you created based on the simplified stylesheet from the last chapter, you'll see that it contains only one template, which matches the root node. The stylesheet works because the XSLT processor always activates that template.

A template that matches the root node acts as high-level control over the result of the stylesheet.

Matching Elements with Templates

At the moment, we use `<xsl:for-each>` to tell the XSLT processor to go through the `<Channel>` elements one by one. That's one place where we could use templates instead. In this section, we'll look at how we can replace this `<xsl:for-each>` with a separate template and an `<xsl:apply-templates>` instruction.

First, we need a template that tells the XSLT processor what to do when it's told to process a `<Channel>` element. You can match an element with a template by giving the name of the element in the `match` attribute of the `<xsl:template>` element. So the following template will match `<Channel>` elements and process them to generate the same result as is currently generated inside `<xsl:for-each>`:

```
<xsl:template match="Channel">
  <h2 class="channel"><xsl:value-of select="Name" /></h2>
  <xsl:for-each select="Program">
    <div>
      <p>
        <span class="date"><xsl:value-of select="Start" /></span><br />
        <span class="title"><xsl:value-of select="Series" /></span><br />
        <xsl:value-of select="Description" />
        <span onclick="toggle({Series}Cast);">[Cast]</span>
      </p>
      <div id="{Series}Cast" style="display: none;">
        <ul class="castlist">
          <xsl:for-each select="CastList/CastMember">
            <li>
              <span class="character">
                <xsl:value-of select="Character" />
              </span>
              <span class="actor">
                <xsl:value-of select="Actor" />
              </span>
            </li>
          </xsl:for-each>
        </ul>
      </div>
    </div>
  </xsl:for-each>
</xsl:template>
```

If a template's `match` attribute gives the name of an element, the XSLT processor will use that template for elements with that name.

You can put this template wherever you like at the top level of the stylesheet (at the same level as the other `<xsl:template>` elements). The XSLT processor will find it and use it whenever it needs to process a `<Channel>` element. In `TVGuide3.xsl`, I've put this template after the template that matches the root node, so the top level of the stylesheet looks like:

```
<?xml version="1.0" encoding="ISO-8859-1"?>
<xsl:stylesheet version="1.0"
                xmlns:xsl="http://www.w3.org/1999/XSL/Transform">

<xsl:template match="/">
  ...
</xsl:template>

<xsl:template match="Channel">
  ...
</xsl:template>

</xsl:stylesheet>
```

I usually order the templates in my stylesheets starting from the template matching the root node and working down the levels of the node tree. But you are free to arrange your templates however you like.

However, the XSLT processor will never use this template unless you tell the processor to process (apply templates to) a `<Channel>` element. You instruct the XSLT processor to apply templates to some nodes using the `<xsl:apply-templates>` instruction. Like `<xsl:for-each>`, the result of the `<xsl:apply-templates>` instruction gets inserted into the result of the transformation at the point where you use the instruction, so while the location of `<xsl:template>` doesn't matter, the positioning of `<xsl:apply-templates>` is very important.

The `<xsl:apply-templates>` instruction has a `select` attribute, which tells the XSLT processor which nodes to apply templates to. The `select` attribute on `<xsl:apply-templates>` works in the same way as the `select` attribute on `<xsl:for-each>` – you give a path that points to the nodes to which you want to apply templates.

We want the result to appear at the same place as the result of the original `<xsl:for-each>`, and we already know the path to those nodes because we're already using it on the `<xsl:for-each>`. So you can apply templates instead by replacing the `<xsl:for-each>` with an `<xsl:apply-templates>` element that has exactly the same `select` attribute. Doing this in `TVGuide4.xsl` gives a template matching the root node as follows:

```
<xsl:template match="/">
  <html>
    <head>
      <title>TV Guide</title>
      ...
```

```
      </head>
      <body>
        <h1>TV Guide</h1>
        <xsl:apply-templates select="/TVGuide/Channel" />
      </body>
    </html>
  </xsl:template>
```

Using templates instead of `<xsl:for-each>` breaks up the stylesheet into manageable chunks in a similar way to functions and methods in standard programming languages. One advantage of this is that you don't have XSLT with lots and lots of indentations, which can really help with readability! A bigger advantage is that you can use the same template for similar nodes in different places or on the same node multiple times, as we'll see later in the chapter. On the down side, the stylesheet no longer looks as similar to the HTML document that we're producing as it used to, and to change the result of the stylesheet, you may have to navigate between multiple templates.

> **You can replace an `<xsl:for-each>` element with a template holding its contents and an `<xsl:apply-templates>` element selecting the nodes you want to process.**

Try It Out – Replacing `<xsl:for-each>` with Templates

We've still used `<xsl:for-each>` in a couple of other places within `TVGuide4.xsl`, so let's convert those instances in the same way as we've done with the one that iterated over `<Channel>` elements.

The next `<xsl:for-each>` is where we iterate over the `<Program>` elements, which is not within the template that matches `<Channel>` elements. We can convert it by first replacing the `<xsl:for-each>` with an `<xsl:apply-templates>` element that has the same value for its `select` attribute:

```
  <xsl:template match="Channel">
    <h2 class="channel"><xsl:value-of select="Name" /></h2>
    <xsl:apply-templates select="Program" />
  </xsl:template>
```

and then creating a template that matches `<Program>` elements. The new template has the same contents as the old `<xsl:for-each>` did:

```
  <xsl:template match="Program">
    <div>
      <p>
        <span class="date"><xsl:value-of select="Start" /></span><br />
        <span class="title"><xsl:value-of select="Series" /></span><br />
        <xsl:value-of select="Description" />
        <span onclick="toggle({Series}Cast);">[Cast]</span>
      </p>
      <div id="{Series}Cast" style="display: none;">
        <ul class="castlist">
          <xsl:for-each select="CastList/CastMember">
            <li>
```

```
            <span class="character">
              <xsl:value-of select="Character" />
            </span>
            <span class="actor">
              <xsl:value-of select="Actor" />
            </span>
          </li>
        </xsl:for-each>
      </ul>
    </div>
  </div>
</xsl:template>
```

This template also contains an `<xsl:for-each>`, one that iterates over the `<CastMember>` element children of `<CastList>` elements. Again, we can replace this `<xsl:for-each>` with an `<xsl:apply-templates>`:

```
<xsl:template match="Program">
  <div>
    <p>
      <span class="date"><xsl:value-of select="Start" /></span><br />
      <span class="title"><xsl:value-of select="Series" /></span><br />
      <xsl:value-of select="Description" />
      <span onclick="toggle({Series}Cast);">[Cast]</span>
    </p>
    <div id="{Series}Cast" style="display: none;">
      <ul class="castlist">
        <xsl:apply-templates select="CastList/CastMember" />
      </ul>
    </div>
  </div>
</xsl:template>
```

and create a separate template that deals with giving output for `<CastMember>` elements:

```
<xsl:template match="CastMember">
  <li>
    <span class="character"><xsl:value-of select="Character" /></span>
    <span class="actor"><xsl:value-of select="Actor" /></span>
  </li>
</xsl:template>
```

We now have four templates in `TVGuide5.xsl`, matching:

- The root node
- `<Channel>` elements
- `<Program>` elements
- `<CastMember>` elements

If you run TVGuide5.xsl with TVGuide.xml, you should get exactly the same result as the original, simplified stylesheet. Splitting up the processing into separate templates hasn't changed the result of the transformation.

The Built-in Templates

We've seen that when you apply templates to a node, the XSLT processor tries to find the template that matches that node. But what happens when there isn't a template that matches a node? For example, if we applied templates to the <Name> child of the <Channel> element, as follows, but didn't have a template to match the <Name> element:

```
<xsl:template match="Channel">
  <h2 class="channel"><xsl:apply-templates select="Name" /></h2>
  <xsl:apply-templates select="Program" />
</xsl:template>
```

When the XSLT processor can't find a template to match the node that it's been told to process, it uses a **built-in template**. If you find that the result of your stylesheet includes text you didn't expect, the chances are that it's due to the built-in templates. Just because there isn't a template for a particular node that doesn't mean that it's not processed.

For elements, the built-in template is as follows:

```
<xsl:template match="*">
  <xsl:apply-templates />
</xsl:template>
```

This template uses two bits of syntax that we haven't seen before:

- The match attribute of the template takes the value *. Templates with a match pattern of * match all elements.
- The <xsl:apply-templates> element doesn't have a select attribute. If you use <xsl:apply-templates> without a select attribute, the XSLT processor collects all the children of the current node (which is the node that the template matches) and applies templates to them.

To see the effect of this, take another look at the part of the node tree containing the <Name> element:

The <Name> element has only one child node, a text node with the value BBC1. When you tell the XSLT processor to apply templates to the <Name> element, it will use the built-in template for elements, and hence apply templates to the text node.

Now, again, we don't have a template that matches text nodes in our stylesheet, so the processor uses a built-in template. The built-in template for text nodes is:

```
<xsl:template match="text()">
  <xsl:value-of select="." />
</xsl:template>
```

Again, this template uses a couple of new bits of syntax:

- The `match` attribute of the `<xsl:template>` element takes the value `text()`. Templates with a match pattern of `text()` match text nodes.
- The `select` attribute of the `<xsl:value-of>` element takes the value `.`. The path `.` selects the context node, so `<xsl:value-of select="." />` gives the value of the context node, in this case the text node.

In combination, these two built-in templates mean that if you apply templates to an element, but don't have a template for that element (or any elements it contains), then you'll get the value of the text held within the element. So applying templates to the `<Name>` element means that you get the value `BBC1` in the result.

> **If a processor can't find a template that matches a node, it uses the built-in template for that node type. In effect, these give the value of the elements to which you apply templates.**

Try It Out – Using the Built-in Templates

There are quite a few places in our stylesheet where we want to just get the value of an element. Rather than using `<xsl:value-of>` to get these values, we could apply templates to the elements and let the built-in templates do their work to give us the element values.

We've already done this with the template for `<Channel>` elements, to get the name of the channel:

```
<xsl:template match="Channel">
  <h2 class="channel"><xsl:apply-templates select="Name" /></h2>
  <xsl:apply-templates select="Program" />
</xsl:template>
```

We can also replace the `<xsl:value-of>` instructions in the template for `<Program>` elements to get the values of the `<Start>`, `<Series>`, and `<Description>` elements:

```
<xsl:template match="Program">
  <div>
    <p>
      <span class="date"><xsl:apply-templates select="Start" /></span>
      <br />
      <span class="title"><xsl:apply-templates select="Series" /></span>
      <br />
      <xsl:apply-templates select="Description" />
```

```
        <span onclick="toggle({Series}Cast);">[Cast]</span>
      </p>
      <div id="{Series}Cast" style="display: none;">
        <ul class="castlist">
          <xsl:apply-templates select="CastList/CastMember" />
        </ul>
      </div>
    </div>
  </xsl:template>
```

and in the template for `<CastMember>` elements, to get the values of the `<Character>` and `<Actor>` elements:

```
  <xsl:template match="CastMember">
    <li>
      <span class="character">
        <xsl:apply-templates select="Character" />
      </span>
      <span class="actor">
        <xsl:apply-templates select="Actor" />
      </span>
    </li>
  </xsl:template>
```

Both the `<Character>` and `<Actor>` elements actually contain `<Name>` elements giving the name of the character or actor. With the built-in templates, you get the value of the text held in these `<Name>` elements.

The stylesheet `TVGuide6.xsl` still contains the same number of templates, but applies templates to all the elements that it processes rather than simply getting their values. If you run `TVGuide6.xsl` with `TVGuide.xml` you should get exactly the same result as you did before. Changing the `<xsl:value-of>` elements to `<xsl:apply-templates>` elements hasn't altered the result of the stylesheet.

Extending Stylesheets

As we've seen in the previous section, the effect of the built-in templates is that if you apply templates to an element, you get all the text that's contained in the element, at any level. This is the same as what you get when you use `<xsl:value-of>` and select the element. In other words, if you don't have a template that matches `<Program>` elements or any of their descendants then the following instructions give you exactly the same result:

```
  <xsl:apply-templates select="Program" />
  <xsl:value-of select="Program" />
```

There are pluses and minuses to using `<xsl:apply-templates>` rather than `<xsl:value-of>`. The biggest downside is that it's less efficient to use `<xsl:apply-templates>` because it forces the XSLT processor to search through the stylesheet for templates that match the node rather than directly giving the value of the node. For this reason, I would generally only apply templates to elements that I know could contain other elements, and not to text nodes, attributes, or elements that I know only have text content.

On the plus side, using `<xsl:apply-templates>` makes it a lot easier to change the format of the value that you get from an element, just by adding a template for that element. For example, if I wanted to change the way I give the name of the series so that it's given as a link to a page on that series instead, I can add a template that matches the `<Series>` element and generates an `<a>` element in the result giving a link to the page.

```
<xsl:template match="Series">
  <a href="{.}.html">
    <xsl:value-of select="." />
  </a>
</xsl:template>
```

This uses an attribute value template (which we met in the last chapter) to give the URL for the page, using the value of the context node (the `<Series>` element) plus the string '`.html`'. For example, the element `<Series>EastEnders</Series>` will result in a link to `EastEnders.html`.

This flexibility is also very useful when the XML format that you're converting from isn't finalized. If we added `<Description>` elements to the `<Character>` and `<Actor>` elements, as in `TVGuide2.xml` in the code download, then we could update the stylesheet to cope with the change by adding templates for these elements so that they only generate the value of the `<Name>` rather than including the description. We do this in `TVGuide7.xsl`, which contains:

```
<xsl:template match="Actor">
  <xsl:apply-templates select="Name" />
</xsl:template>

<xsl:template match="Character">
  <xsl:apply-templates select="Name" />
</xsl:template>
```

If you didn't add these templates, then applying templates to the `<Actor>` or `<Character>` elements would result in text containing both the name and description of the actor or character, concatenated.

Using templates allows you to extend your stylesheet more easily than you can if you use `<xsl:for-each>` and `<xsl:value-of>`.

Templates as Mapping Rules

We've been a little formulaic in our conversion from the simplified stylesheet to the full stylesheet that we have now – we take every `<xsl:for-each>` and `<xsl:value-of>` and turn it into an `<xsl:apply-templates>`. The introduction of templates has really just been a way of modularizing the code.

But there's another way of thinking about templates that can make your stylesheets more elegant and more extensible, and that's to consider them as a mapping rule. Each template describes how to map a particular node in the source XML on to a result that you're after. In this section, we'll first look at using templates with mixed content, and at how using templates as mapping rules is particularly useful when processing document-oriented XML. Then, we'll go on to look at how we could apply the same kind of technique to our stylesheet and the impact of doing so.

Processing Document-Oriented XML

Let's first look at the problem of generating output from document-oriented XML. Document-oriented XML arises when you take a paragraph of text and mark up particular words and phrases within that paragraph, giving mixed content – elements and text intermingled. This is in contrast to data-oriented XML, which is concerned with storing data and usually results in element-only and text-only content.

Take another look at the XML structure that we're using to store information about TV programs:

```
<Program>
  <Start>2001-07-05T19:30:00</Start>
  <Duration>PT30M</Duration>
  <Series>EastEnders</Series>
  <Title></Title>
  <Description>
    Mark's health scare forces him to reconsider his future with Lisa,
    while Jamie is torn between Sonia and Zoe.
  </Description>
  ...
</Program>
```

While most of the XML structure is oriented around providing data, the description of the TV program is more document-oriented. You could imagine wanting to add a bit of document-oriented markup to the <Description> element, perhaps a link to the EastEnders biography for Jamie and highlights around the names of the characters:

```
<Description>
  <Character>Mark</Character>'s health scare forces him to reconsider his
  future with <Character>Lisa</Character>, while
  <Link
    href="http://www.bbc.co.uk/eastenders/characters/jamie_m_biog.shtml">
    <Character>Jamie</Character>
  </Link> is torn between <Character>Sonia</Character> and
  <Character>Zoe</Character>.
</Description>
```

The <Description> element now holds mixed content. Looking at the node tree representation of that piece of XML makes this clearer:

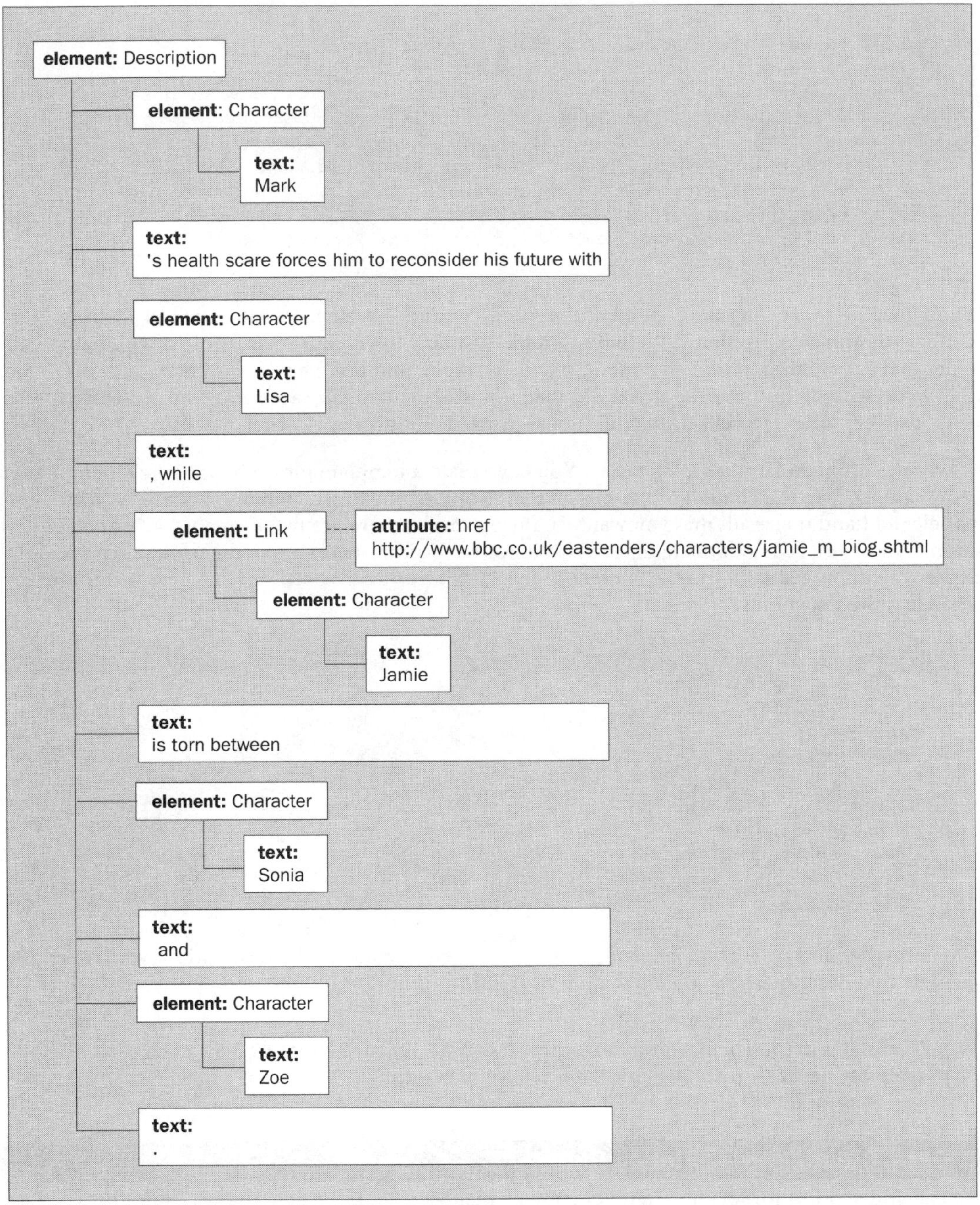

We want the elements that we use in the description to be transformed into HTML elements instead. In the HTML version of the page, we want to use `<span>` elements around the character names, and transform the `<Link>` elements into `<a>` elements, to give:

```
<p>
  <span class="date">2001-07-05T19:30:00</span><br />
  <span class="title">EastEnders</span><br />
  <span class="character">Mark</span>'s health scare forces him to
  reconsider his future with <span class="character">Lisa</span>, while
  <a href="http://www.bbc.co.uk/eastenders/characters/jamie_m_biog.shtml">
  <span class="character">Jamie</span></a> is torn between
  <span class="character">Sonia</span> and
  <span class="character">Zoe</span>.
  <span onclick="toggle(EastEndersCast);">[Cast]</span>
</p>
```

If you imagine processing the content of the `<Description>` element with `<xsl:for-each>`, you'll see that you run into problems. We haven't looked at how to yet, but it's possible to iterate over all the nodes that are children of the `<Description>` element, and test what kind of node they are to decide what to do with them. But even if you did that, you still need to take account of nested elements, so you'd get very long and very deep conditional processing to cover all levels of nesting.

However, with templates it's a lot easier. You can create a template for each kind of element that you know can occur in the content of the `<Description>` element, which describes how to map between that element and the result that you want. In this example, there are two elements, `<Character>` and `<Link>`, so you need a template for each. Within the `<span>` and `<a>` elements that these templates create, you apply templates to the content of the `<Character>` or `<Link>` element to account for possible nested elements:

```
<xsl:template match="Character">
  <span class="character">
    <xsl:apply-templates />
  </span>
</xsl:template>

<xsl:template match="Link">
  <a href="{@href}">
    <xsl:apply-templates />
  </a>
</xsl:template>
```

Whenever you add a new type of element that you might include in the description, you can add a new template that describes how to map that on to HTML.

> **Templates are particularly suited to processing document-oriented XML. Each template acts as a mapping rule from source to result.**

Try It Out – Creating Presentation Rules

We can add support for lots of different elements that we want to be able to use within the `<Description>` element. Highlighting character names and providing links to other web sites is useful, but you might also want to add elements for emphasis, foreign words, names of directors, series, channels, films, and so on – different elements for the different types of words and phrases that can appear in descriptions of TV programs and series.

We'll add just a few of these elements in TVGuide2.xml, to create TVGuide3.xml, which looks as follows:

```
<?xml version="1.0" encoding="ISO-8859-1"?>
<TVGuide start="2001-07-05" end="2001-07-05">

<Channel>
  <Name>BBC1</Name>
  ...
  <Program rating="5" flag="favorite">
    <Start>2001-07-05T19:30:00</Start>
    <Duration>PT30M</Duration>
    <Series>EastEnders</Series>
    <Title></Title>
    <Description>
      <Character>Mark</Character>'s health scare forces him to reconsider
      his future with <Character>Lisa</Character>, while
      <Link
      href="http://www.bbc.co.uk/eastenders/characters/jamie_m_biog.shtml">
        <Character>Jamie</Character>
      </Link> is torn between <Character>Sonia</Character> and
      <Character>Zoe</Character>.
    </Description>
    <CastList>
      <CastMember>
        <Character>
          <Name>Zoe Slater</Name>
          <Description>
            The youngest Slater girl, <Character>Zoe</Character> really
            makes the most of the fact she's the baby of the family.
          </Description>
        </Character>
        <Actor>
          <Name>Michelle Ryan</Name>
          <Description>
            For more details, see
            <Link href="http://www.ajmanagement.co.uk/michelle-ryan.htm">
              <Actor>Michelle Ryan</Actor>'s Agency
            </Link>.
          </Description>
        </Actor>
      </CastMember>
      <CastMember>
        <Character>
          <Name>Jamie Mitchell</Name>
          <Description>
            Jamie's a bit of a heartthrob (who could resist that
            little-boy-lost look?) but until <Character>Janine
            Butcher</Character> came along he'd steered clear of girls.
          </Description>
        </Character>
        <Actor>
          <Name>Jack Ryder</Name>
```

```
            <Description>
              Won Best Newcomer for <Character>Jamie Mitchell</Character>
              in the 1999 TV awards.
            </Description>
          </Actor>
        </CastMember>
        <CastMember>
          ...
        </CastMember>
      </CastList>
      ...
    </Program>
    ...
  </Channel>
  ...
  </TVGuide>
```

Try using TVGuide6.xsl with TVGuide3.xml, which uses <xsl:apply-templates> to apply templates to the <Description> element. There aren't any templates for <Character> or <Link> elements, so the built-in templates are used instead. The result of the transformation of the <Description> element looks just the same as before, because the built-in templates automatically show any text within an element.

We want a new version of the stylesheet (TVGuide8.xsl), which generates HTML where the words and phrases in the description that we've picked out with <Character> and <Link> elements are displayed and behave slightly differently from the rest of the text. Links should *be* links, for example, and character names should be slightly larger than the surrounding text.

To make the marked-up text display and act differently, we need to introduce templates for these new elements: one for the <Link> element, to create a hypertext link with an HTML <a> element:

```
<xsl:template match="Link">
  <a href="{@href}">
    <xsl:apply-templates />
  </a>
</xsl:template>
```

and one for the <Character> element, to create a <span> element with a class of character around the character names:

```
<xsl:template match="Character">
  <span class="character">
    <xsl:apply-templates />
  </span>
</xsl:template>
```

To make the character names slightly bigger, we'll add a rule to TVGuide.css, to create TVGuide2.css, which contains:

```
.character {
  font-size: larger;
}
```

Putting the final touches on TVGuide8.xsl, we need the HTML that it creates to point to TVGuide2.css rather than TVGuide.css, so the <link> element generated in the template matching the root node needs to be altered slightly:

```
<xsl:template match="/">
  <html>
    <head>
      <title>TV Guide</title>
      <link rel="stylesheet" href="TVGuide2.css" />
      ...
    </head>
    ...
  </html>
</xsl:template>
```

Having made this final change, transform TVGuide3.xml with TVGuide8.xsl. The result of the transformation should look something like the following:

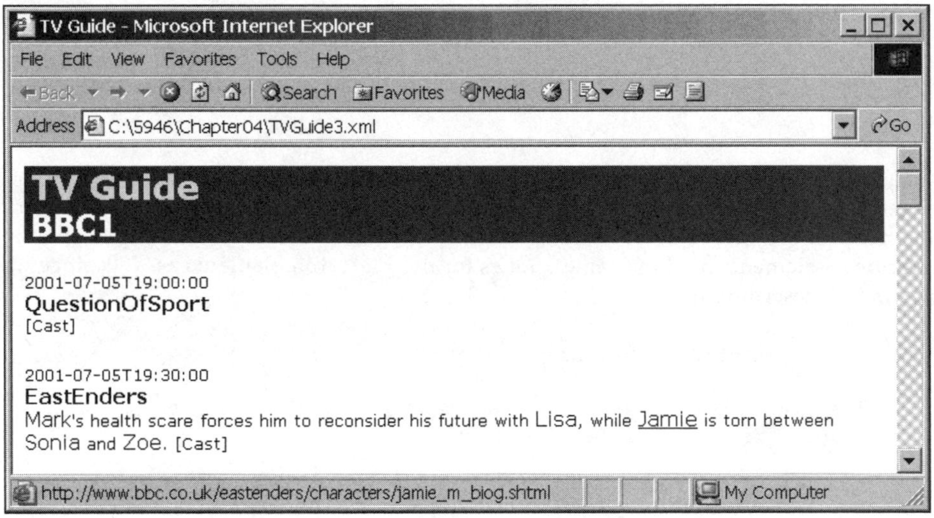

The character names are slightly larger than the rest of the text, and clicking on the word "Jamie" takes you to the EastEnders site with Jamie Mitchell's biography. Feel free to add your own elements to that description, and add your own templates matching them to present the document-oriented XML.

Context-Dependent Processing

We've now introduced a number of elements into our XML structure that we're actually using elsewhere in different ways. For example, we use the <Character> element to indicate the name of a character in a description, and to hold information about a character within the <CastMember> element. The template makes no distinction between these two uses of the <Character> element, and does the same thing for each, making a <span> element with a character class:

```
<xsl:template match="Character">
  <span class="character">
    <xsl:apply-templates />
  </span>
</xsl:template>
```

At the moment, we're also creating a <span> element when we create the cast list, in the template matching the <CastMember> element:

```
<xsl:template match="CastMember">
  <li>
    <span class="character">
      <xsl:apply-templates select="Character" />
    </span>
    <span class="actor">
      <xsl:apply-templates select="Actor" />
    </span>
  </li>
</xsl:template>
```

This means we end up with two <span> elements around the names of the characters in the cast list. We can get rid of the superfluous <span> element either by reverting back to using <xsl:value-of> to get the name of the character, or by removing the <span> element in the template that matches <CastMember> elements (and the same applies for the <Actor> elements as well, since we might name actors in a description):

```
<xsl:template match="CastMember">
  <li>
    <xsl:apply-templates select="Character" />
    <xsl:apply-templates select="Actor" />
  </li>
</xsl:template>
```

So now we have the same template being used to process <Character> elements in different contexts. However, one of the extensions that we made earlier in this chapter was to have the <Character> and <Actor> elements within <CastMember> actually give both a name and a description of the character. When we take this into account, we have a problem because we don't want the <span> element to contain both the name and the description of the character. We need a different template for the <Character> and <Actor> elements when they are children of <CastMember> elements (ones that just apply templates to the <Name> element child of the <Character> or <Actor> element). The new templates for the <Character> elements that occur in <CastMember> elements need to look like:

```
<xsl:template match="Character">
  <span class="character">
    <xsl:apply-templates select="Name" />
  </span>
</xsl:template>
```

But we can't use this template with the <Character> elements that occur in <Description> elements because they don't contain <Name> elements. If we use this template with those elements, the <span> elements won't have any content.

So we need some way of having different templates for the different contexts in which these elements are allowed. We can do this by changing the value of the `match` attribute of <xsl:template>, and this is where we need to use patterns, which are why they are introduced next.

Patterns

So far we've seen four kinds of values for the `match` attribute of <xsl:template>:

- / matches the root node
- * matches any element
- `text()` matches text nodes
- the name of an element matches that element

These values are all examples of **patterns**. An XSLT processor uses the pattern specified in the `match` attribute of <xsl:template> to work out whether it can use a template to process a node to which you've told it to apply templates. In our case, we need one pattern to match <Character> elements that are children of <CastMember> elements, and another pattern to match <Character> elements that appear at any level within <Description> elements. In both cases, we're checking the context in which the <Character> element appears. The two patterns we need are:

- `CastMember/Character` to match <Character> elements that occur within <CastMember> elements
- `Description//Character` to match <Character> elements that occur nested to any level within <Description> elements

These types of patterns are technically known as **location path patterns**. As you can see, location path patterns look a lot like the location paths that we use to select nodes to process in `select` attributes, and it can be easy to get confused between the two. You use location paths to select nodes; they point from the current node to a set of other nodes in the tree, stepping down from element to child. You use location path patterns to match nodes; they test whether a particular node has particular ancestors, looking up the node tree to work out the context of the node.

A location path pattern is made up of a number of **step patterns**, separated by either / or //. If the separator is a /, then the pattern tests a parent-child relationship. For example, the pattern `Description/Character` matches <Character> elements whose *immediate parent* is a <Description> element. If the separator is //, on the other hand, then the pattern tests an ancestor-descendent relationship. For example, the pattern `Description//Character` matches <Character> elements that have a <Description> element as an ancestor at any level.

Location path patterns enable you to match elements according to the context in which they occur.

Identifying Elements in Different Contexts

In our XML document, `TVGuide3.xml`, there are some elements that have different meanings in different contexts. If you remember back that far, it was one of our design decisions when we first put together our XML structure that we would make use of the context an element was in, rather than use different names for elements in different contexts, to work out what an element meant and what we should do with it.

So now we have to deal with that decision by creating different templates with different match patterns for the different contexts in which an element can occur. The contexts within which different elements can occur are shown in the following table:

Element	Contexts
`<Name>`	child of `<Channel>`
	child of `<Character>`
	child of `<Actor>`
`<Description>`	child of `<Program>`
	child of `<Character>`
	child of `<Actor>`
`<Character>`	child of `<CastMember>`
	descendent of `<Description>`
`<Actor>`	child of `<CastMember>`
	descendent of `<Description>`
`<Series>`	child of `<Program>`
	descendent of `<Description>`
`<Program>`	child of `<Channel>`
	descendent of `<Description>`
`<Channel>`	child of `<TVGuide>`
	descendent of `<Description>`

A stylesheet that deals with documents that follow our markup language really needs to have templates that deal with elements occurring in each of these possible contexts, using patterns that include ancestry information.

Try It Out – Creating Templates for Context-Dependent Elements

At this stage, we'll create a new version of the stylesheet, TVGuide9.xsl, which contains separate templates for each of these elements in each of these contexts. You should be able to put together different templates for the elements in their different contexts as mapping rules. For example, the <Name> element can occur in three contexts – <Channel>, <Character>, and <Actor> – so there should be three corresponding templates:

```
<xsl:template match="Channel/Name">...</xsl:template>
<xsl:template match="Character/Name">...</xsl:template>
<xsl:template match="Actor/Name">...</xsl:template>
```

As you add these templates, you should consider whether some of the HTML that you're currently generating in higher-level templates can be generated in lower-level templates instead. For example, my feeling is that the <Name> element in the <Channel> element maps on to the <h2> heading element in the result, so the template should look like:

```
<xsl:template match="Channel/Name">
  <h2 class="channel"><xsl:value-of select="." /></h2>
</xsl:template>
```

But if you create the <h2> element in the above template, you don't need to create it in the template for the <Channel> element. So you need to change that template too, removing the <h2> element that you were creating within it:

```
<xsl:template match="TVGuide/Channel">
  <xsl:apply-templates select="Name" />
  <xsl:apply-templates select="Program" />
</xsl:template>
```

This template only applies to <Channel> elements that are children of the <TVGuide> element, not those that are descendents of <Description> elements.

If you go through this process religiously, you should end up with about 19 different templates, as in TVGuide9.xsl. Using TVGuide9.xsl with TVGuide3.xml results in a page in which both the <Character> elements within the cast list and those within the <Description> are treated properly, so the result looks like the following when you view it in Internet Explorer:

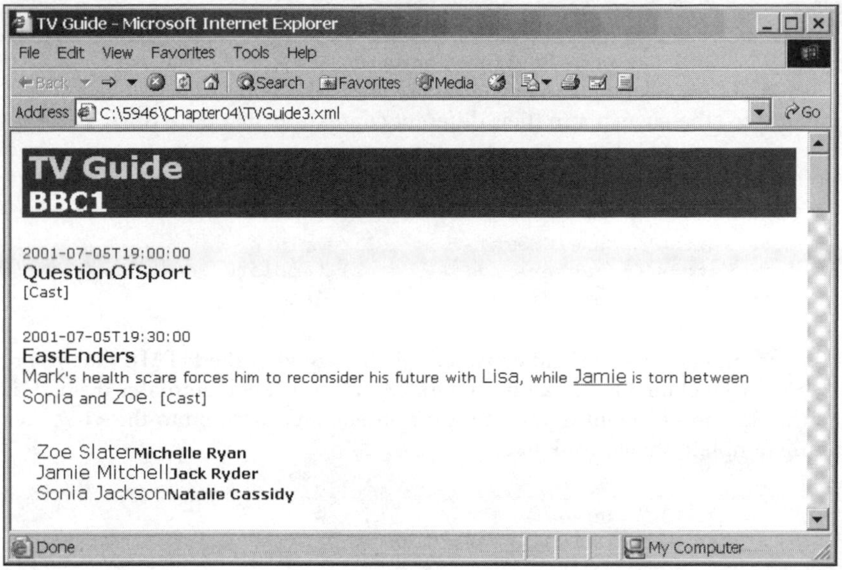

This process of adding templates on an element-by-element basis, taking account of the different contexts in which an element can occur, has left us with a lot of templates, but it has made the stylesheet more robust. We've handled the problem that we had with `<Character>` elements being treated differently in different contexts, and we've included templates to handle the possibility of things that aren't actually present in `TVGuide3.xml`, but which could happen in more complete documents that follow the markup language, such as `<Channel>` elements in `<Description>` elements.

Unnecessary Templates

Adding templates to deal with every kind of element, in every context, within a stylesheet can leave you with a stylesheet that contains lots of templates that actually don't do very much. This makes the stylesheet harder for you to maintain (because it's longer) and it makes more work for the processor when it needs to identify which template to apply in a particular situation. You need to find a judicious balance between the two.

First, you don't need to create a template for every element in every context. Remember that if the XSLT processor can't find a template that matches a node, then it will use a built-in template. If an element (and all its content) gets processed by the built-in templates, then you'll just get the value of the node. So, if you have templates that look like either of the following:

```
<xsl:template match="...">
  <xsl:value-of select="." />
</xsl:template>

<xsl:template match="...">
  <xsl:apply-templates />
</xsl:template>
```

then you may as well get rid of them.

Second, you can get rid of templates that essentially process the children of the element that they match in the order that they appear. For example, the revised template for the <Channel> elements that are children of <TVGuide> elements is like that:

```
<xsl:template match="TVGuide/Channel">
  <xsl:apply-templates select="Name" />
  <xsl:apply-templates select="Program" />
</xsl:template>
```

When a <Channel> element appears as a child of a <TVGuide> element then it can only contain a <Name> element followed by any number of <Program> elements. So telling the processor to apply templates first to the <Name> element and then to the <Program> elements has the same effect as telling the processor to apply templates to all the <Channel> element's children in the order they occur, which would be the template:

```
<xsl:template match="TVGuide/Channel">
  <xsl:apply-templates />
</xsl:template>
```

This template has the same effect as the built-in template for elements, so you can delete it without affecting the result of the stylesheet.

Finally, you can get rid of templates that match elements that are never selected for processing. Remember that a template is never actually used if the processor never gets told to apply templates to a node that matches that template. A template that is never matched will never be used, and can therefore be safely removed.

Try It Out – Removing Unnecessary Templates

TVGuide9.xsl does contain a few templates that aren't really necessary, and to make it easier to understand we could prune it to create TVGuide10.xsl.

There are three templates that do the same thing as the built-in templates, and just contain an <xsl:apply-templates> or an <xsl:value-of> instruction that gives the value of the current node. They are the one matching <Name> element children of <Character> elements, the one matching <Name> element children of <Actor> elements, and the one matching <Description> element children of <Program> elements – you can safely delete them:

```
<xsl:template match="Character/Name">
  <xsl:value-of select="." />
</xsl:template>

<xsl:template match="Actor/Name">
  <xsl:value-of select="." />
</xsl:template>

<xsl:template match="Program/Description">
  <xsl:apply-templates />
</xsl:template>
```

We identified the template matching <Channel> element children of the <TVGuide> element as falling into the second category. It had two <xsl:apply-templates> in it, but these selected nodes in the same order as they occurred in the source document, essentially the same as applying templates to all the children, which again is just what the built-in templates do. So you can safely delete the following template:

```
<xsl:template match="TVGuide/Channel">
  <xsl:apply-templates select="Name" />
  <xsl:apply-templates select="Program" />
</xsl:template>
```

Finally, in TVGuide9.xsl there are two templates that can never be applied – the one matching <Description> elements within <Character> elements, and the one matching <Description> elements within <Actor> elements. These templates will never get activated because the templates that match <Character> and <Actor> elements (within <CastMember> elements) never apply templates to their child <Description> elements. So these two templates can also be deleted:

```
<xsl:template match="Character/Description" />

<xsl:template match="Actor/Description" />
```

Once you've done all that, you should have something like the following stylesheet, TVGuide10.xsl. The ordering of the templates within the stylesheet doesn't matter.

```
<?xml version="1.0" encoding="ISO-8859-1"?>
<xsl:stylesheet version="1.0"
                xmlns:xsl="http://www.w3.org/1999/XSL/Transform">

<xsl:template match="/">
  <html>
    ...
  </html>
</xsl:template>

<xsl:template match="Channel/Name">
  <h2 class="channel"><xsl:value-of select="." /></h2>
</xsl:template>

<xsl:template match="Channel/Program">
  <div>
    ...
  </div>
</xsl:template>

<xsl:template match="Program/Series">
 <span class="title"><xsl:value-of select="." /></span>
</xsl:template>

<xsl:template match="CastMember">
  <li>
    <xsl:apply-templates select="Character" />
    <xsl:apply-templates select="Actor" />
```

```
  </li>
</xsl:template>

<xsl:template match="CastMember/Character">
  <span class="character">
    <xsl:apply-templates select="Name" />
  </span>
</xsl:template>

<xsl:template match="CastMember/Actor">
  <span class="actor">
    <xsl:apply-templates select="Name" />
  </span>
</xsl:template>

<xsl:template match="Description//Character">
  <span class="character">
    <xsl:apply-templates />
  </span>
</xsl:template>

<xsl:template match="Description//Actor">
  <span class="actor">
    <xsl:apply-templates />
  </span>
</xsl:template>

<xsl:template match="Link">
  <a href="{@href}">
    <xsl:apply-templates />
  </a>
</xsl:template>

<xsl:template match="Description//Program">
  <span class="program"><xsl:apply-templates /></span>
</xsl:template>

<xsl:template match="Description//Series">
  <span class="series"><xsl:apply-templates /></span>
</xsl:template>

<xsl:template match="Description//Channel">
  <span class="channel"><xsl:apply-templates /></span>
</xsl:template>

</xsl:stylesheet>
```

Using `TVGuide10.xsl` with `TVGuide3.xml` should give the same result as `TVGuide9.xsl` did.

Resolving Conflicts Between Templates

Whenever you have rules in a language, such as rules in CSS or templates in XSLT, you need some way to resolve conflicts when two of the rules apply to the same situation. What would happen, for example, if you had one template that matched all <Character> elements and another template that matched only those <Character> elements that had <CastMember> as their parent:

```
<xsl:template match="Character">
  <span class="character"><xsl:apply-templates /></span>
</xsl:template>

<xsl:template match="CastMember/Character">
  <span class="character"><xsl:apply-templates select="Name" /></span>
</xsl:template>
```

A <Character> element in a <Description> element only matches one of the templates, because it doesn't have a <CastMember> element as its parent, so obviously the XSLT processor uses that template with it. But what about a <Character> element in a <CastMember> element? It matches both of the template's patterns, so what should the XSLT processor do?

Template Priority

Well, the XSLT processor will only ever process one template when you apply templates to a node, so it has to choose between the two templates that it's presented with in some way. It does this by looking at the template's **priority**. A template with a high priority is chosen over a template with a lower priority.

You can specifically assign a template a priority using the priority attribute on the <xsl:template> element. The priority attribute can be set to any number, including decimal and negative numbers. For example, you can give the two templates different specific priorities, as follows:

```
<xsl:template match="Character" priority="-1">
  <span class="character"><xsl:apply-templates /></span>
</xsl:template>

<xsl:template match="CastMember/Character" priority="2">
  <span class="character"><xsl:apply-templates select="Name" /></span>
</xsl:template>
```

Default Priorities

However, it would be very difficult to assign and keep track of priorities if the priority attribute was your only option. If you don't specify a priority attribute on a template, the XSLT processor assigns it a priority based on how specific its match pattern is. XSLT processors recognize three levels of priority in patterns:

- Patterns that match a class of nodes, such as *, which matches all elements, are assigned an implicit priority of -0.5
- Patterns that match nodes according to their name, such as Character, which matches <Character> elements, are assigned an implicit priority of 0

- Patterns that match nodes according to their context, such as CastMember/Character, which matches <Character> elements whose parent is a <CastMember> element, are assigned an implicit priority of 0.5

When assigning priorities based on patterns, it doesn't matter how specific the context information is: if you specify any context for a node then the template has a priority of 0.5. For example, `Description/Link/Character` *has exactly the same priority as* `Description//Character`.

Technically, it's an error if you have two templates that match the same node and the match patterns for the two templates have the same specificity. However, most processors recover from the error and use the template that you've defined last in the stylesheet. You should try to avoid having templates that have the same priority and can feasibly match the same node; use the `priority` attribute to assign them specific, different priorities.

> **If two templates match the same node, the processor uses the one with the highest priority. Priority can be assigned explicitly with the `priority` attribute or determined implicitly from the template's match pattern. As a last resort, the processor can select the last matching template in the stylesheet.**

Try It Out – Using Priorities

Currently, the templates that our stylesheet contains don't have any conflicts with each other because each of them only matches elements in a fairly specific context. To try out priorities, let's try making some of the templates conflict by removing some of that context information from one of them. For example, in TVGuide11.xsl, let's change the template that matches <Program> elements within <Description> elements to match any <Program> element:

```
<xsl:template match="Program">
  <span class="program"><xsl:apply-templates /></span>
</xsl:template>
```

Now a <Program> element will always be matched by this template, and if it's a child of a <Channel> element then it will also match the following template:

```
<xsl:template match="Channel/Program">
  <div>
    <p>
      <span class="date"><xsl:apply-templates select="Start" /></span>
      <br />
      <xsl:apply-templates select="Series" />
      <br />
      <xsl:apply-templates select="Description" />
      <span onclick="toggle({Series}Cast);">[Cast]</span>
    </p>
    <div id="{Series}Cast" style="display: none;">
      <ul class="castlist">
        <xsl:apply-templates select="CastList/CastMember" />
```

```
      </ul>
    </div>
  </div>
</xsl:template>
```

However, if you run TVGuide11.xsl with TVGuide3.xml, it won't make any difference to the result because the latter template, matching <Program> element children of <Channel> elements, has a higher priority. When the <Program> element that the XSLT processor is trying to process is a child of a <Channel> element, it will use the latter template, with the match pattern of Channel/Program; when it's not (such as when it's a child of a <Description> element), the processor will use the former template, with the match pattern of Program.

But we can change that in two ways. First, we can assign different priorities to the two templates using the priority attribute. Assign the general template a priority of 1, to create TVGuide12.xsl:

```
<xsl:template match="Program" priority="1">
  <span class="program"><xsl:apply-templates /></span>
</xsl:template>
```

This explicit priority is higher than the implicit priority of the second template. If you run TVGuide12.xsl with TVGuide3.xml, you get the following mess:

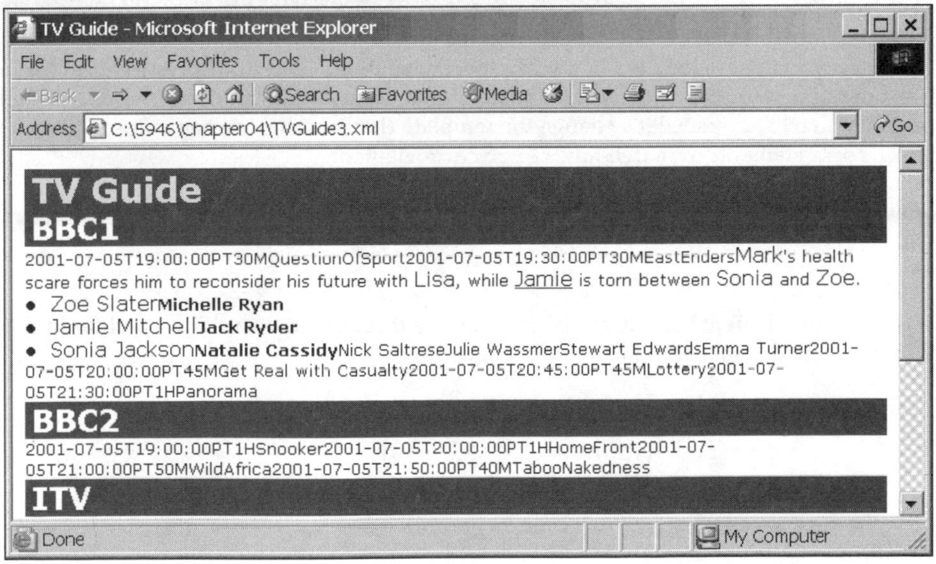

Some of the formatting is still present because the elements inside the <Program> element still get processed by this template. However, the parts of the result that were generated by the second template, such as the <div> and <p> elements, are no longer present. You can get the same effect by removing the priority on the template matching all <Program> elements and giving the template matching <Program> elements within <Channel> elements a priority lower than -0.5.

A second way of manipulating the priority of the templates is to remove the context from the path for the second template (and remove the `priority` attributes that you just added), so the template that's supposed to be used to process `<Program>` elements within `<Channel>` elements looks like:

```
<xsl:template match="Program">
  <div>
    <p>
      <span class="date"><xsl:apply-templates select="Start" /></span>
      <br />
      <xsl:apply-templates select="Series" />
      <br />
      <xsl:apply-templates select="Description" />
      <span onclick="toggle({Series}Cast);">[Cast]</span>
    </p>
    <div id="{Series}Cast" style="display: none;">
      <ul class="castlist">
        <xsl:apply-templates select="CastList/CastMember" />
      </ul>
    </div>
  </div>
</xsl:template>
```

Now the templates both apply to the same `<Program>` elements and have the same priority, which is an error. Move the template that's supposed to be for `<Program>` elements within `<Description>` elements below the above in the stylesheet (if it's not there already), to give `TVGuide13.xsl`. Most likely your processor will use the lower template in the stylesheet to process the `<Program>` elements, and you'll get the same mess as when you changed the priority explicitly. Processors are within their rights to terminate the stylesheet and give you an error, though, and some processors might warn you that there are two templates that match the same node with the same priority. Saxon, for example, gives reams of recoverable error messages, though it produces the result perfectly well:

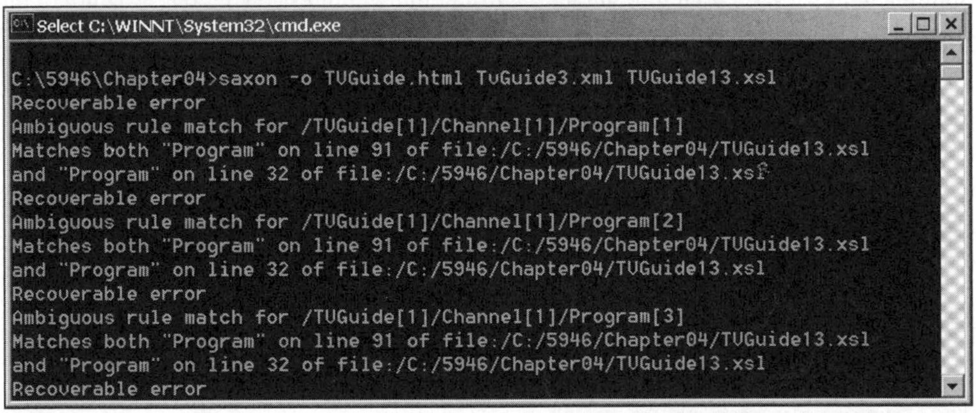

It's often simpler to make templates whose match patterns don't include any information about the ancestry of the element, and it's easier for the processor too, because it doesn't have to check. For our TV guide stylesheet, we could adopt one of two styles to deal with elements that need to be treated differently in different places – add ancestry information for those templates that deal with elements in the descriptions, or add ancestry information to the other templates, those that deal with the bulk of the result. I think it makes more sense to keep ancestry information on the templates that deal with descriptions, because that way it's easy to tell which templates are those that deal with descriptions and which aren't. `TVGuide14.xsl` shows the result of doing that.

Processing with Push and Pull

Using templates as mapping rules really makes explicit the correspondence between a bit of the source XML and the result that you desire from it. As we've seen in `TVGuide14.xsl`, we can adopt this approach in data-oriented XML as well as document-oriented XML – you can have different templates matching different elements, even if those elements follow the traditionally 'data-oriented' pattern of just having element or text children. The approach that we were working with at the start of this chapter was quite different. There, we had very few templates (we started with just one!), and where we did use them it was really to make the stylesheet more manageable and to get reuse.

These two approaches to transformations with XSLT are termed **push** and **pull**.

Processing with Push

In the push approach, templates specify fairly low-level rules and the source XML document gets pushed through the stylesheet to be transformed on the way. Stylesheets that use the push approach tend to have a lot of templates, each containing a snippet of XML with an `<xsl:apply-templates>` instruction that moves the processing down to all an element's children. The final structure of the result is highly determined by the structure of the source.

Here's an example of a stylesheet, `TVGuide15.xsl`, which demonstrates a push approach. You can see how multiple templates are used to build up the result, but without knowing the structure of the source XML document it's hard to tell exactly what result you'll get (I've highlighted the main changes from `TVGuide14.xsl`, though it was actually quite push-like already):

```
<?xml version="1.0" encoding="ISO-8859-1"?>
<xsl:stylesheet version="1.0"
                xmlns:xsl="http://www.w3.org/1999/XSL/Transform">

<xsl:template match="/">
  <html>
    <head>
      ...
    </head>
    <body>
      <h1>TV Guide</h1>
      <xsl:apply-templates />
    </body>
  </html>
</xsl:template>

<xsl:template match="Channel/Name">
```

```
    <h2 class="channel"><xsl:apply-templates /></h2>
  </xsl:template>

  <xsl:template match="Program">
    <div>
      <p>
        <xsl:apply-templates select="Start" /><br />
        <xsl:apply-templates select="Series" /><br />
        <xsl:apply-templates select="Description" />
        <span onclick="toggle({Series}Cast);">[Cast]</span>
      </p>
      <div id="{Series}Cast" style="display: none;">
        <ul class="castlist">
          <xsl:apply-templates select="CastList" />
        </ul>
      </div>
    </div>
  </xsl:template>

  <xsl:template match="Start">
    <span class="date"><xsl:apply-templates /></span>
  </xsl:template>

  <xsl:template match="Series">
   <span class="title"><xsl:apply-templates /></span>
  </xsl:template>

  <xsl:template match="CastMember">
    <li><xsl:apply-templates /></li>
  </xsl:template>

  <xsl:template match="Character">
    <span class="character"><xsl:apply-templates /></span>
  </xsl:template>

  <xsl:template match="Actor">
    <span class="actor"><xsl:apply-templates /></span>
  </xsl:template>

  <xsl:template match="Character/Description" />

  <xsl:template match="Actor/Description" />

  <xsl:template match="Description//Character">
    <span class="character"><xsl:apply-templates /></span>
  </xsl:template>

  <xsl:template match="Description//Actor">
    <span class="actor"><xsl:apply-templates /></span>
  </xsl:template>

  <xsl:template match="Description//Link">
    <a href="{@href}"><xsl:apply-templates /></a>
```

```
</xsl:template>

<xsl:template match="Description//Program">
  <span class="program"><xsl:apply-templates /></span>
</xsl:template>

<xsl:template match="Description//Series">
  <span class="series"><xsl:apply-templates /></span>
</xsl:template>

<xsl:template match="Description//Channel">
  <span class="channel"><xsl:apply-templates /></span>
</xsl:template>

</xsl:stylesheet>
```

Note that in this stylesheet I've used empty templates to do nothing with the `<Description>` *elements within* `<Character>` *and* `<Actor>` *elements within the cast list. I apply templates to both the* `<Name>` *and* `<Description>` *children of these elements, but then ignore the* `<Description>` *element. This contrasts with a pull approach, which would only apply templates to the* `<Name>` *element in the first place.*

Processing with Pull

In the pull approach, the stylesheet pulls in information from the source XML document to populate a template structure. Stylesheets that use the pull approach tend to have only a few templates and to use `<xsl:for-each>` and `<xsl:value-of>` to generate the result. The final structure of the result is mainly determined by the structure of the stylesheet and how the templates fit together.

Here's an example of a stylesheet that demonstrates a pull approach (actually, it's `TVGuide2.xsl` – the first stylesheet we used in this chapter, more or less). As you can see, there's only one template and its content follows the structure of the result that it generates very closely:

```
<?xml version="1.0" encoding="ISO-8859-1"?>
<xsl:stylesheet version="1.0"
                xmlns:xsl="http://www.w3.org/1999/XSL/Transform">

<xsl:template match="/">
  <html>
    <head>
      ...
    </head>
    <body>
      <h1>TV Guide</h1>
      <xsl:for-each select="/TVGuide/Channel">
        <h2 class="channel"><xsl:value-of select="Name" /></h2>
        <xsl:for-each select="Program">
          <div>
            <p>
              <span class="date"><xsl:value-of select="Start" /></span>
              <br />
              <span class="title"><xsl:value-of select="Series" /></span>
```

```
              <br />
              <xsl:value-of select="Description" />
              <span onclick="toggle({Series}Cast);">[Cast]</span>
            </p>
            <div id="{Series}Cast" style="display: none;">
              <ul class="castlist">
                <xsl:for-each select="CastList/CastMember">
                  <li>
                    <span class="character">
                      <xsl:value-of select="Character/Name" />
                    </span>
                    <span class="actor">
                      <xsl:value-of select="Actor/Name" />
                    </span>
                  </li>
                </xsl:for-each>
              </ul>
            </div>
          </div>
        </xsl:for-each>
      </xsl:for-each>
    </body>
  </html>
</xsl:template>

</xsl:stylesheet>
```

If you look carefully, you'll notice that I haven't even tried to style the content of the <Description> element in this stylesheet – it's very hard to process document-oriented XML with a pull style.

When to Use Push and Pull

Push and pull approaches both have their own advantages and disadvantages, and the best stylesheets use both approaches in tandem to process different parts of a particular XML document. You might use pull for the data-oriented parts of the XML and push for the document-oriented parts, for example. Here are some general guidelines about where to use push and where to use pull:

- Use multiple templates, each matching different types of nodes (a push approach) to process document-oriented XML.
- Select the nodes that you specifically want to process (a pull approach) to change the order in which the source is processed or to only process certain portions of the source. This is very common in data-oriented XML where the order in which information is contained in the source is not the same as the order in which it is required in the result.
- Apply templates to nodes, rather than getting their value directly (a push approach) to allow for extensibility in areas where the structure of the source XML, or the result that you want to generate from it, might change in the future.
- Access the values of nodes directly (a pull approach) when the structure of the source XML is fixed and you know exactly what result you want from it.

Taking these guidelines into account, `TVGuide16.xsl` gives a stylesheet that balances the push and pull approaches. It mainly uses a push style, but selects nodes directly for processing in certain places, notably to get only the `<Name>` child of `<Character>` and `<Actor>` elements and ignore the `<Description>`.

> **Using templates to match nodes is a push approach, which is good for document-oriented XML and for extensibility. Selecting nodes to process is a pull approach, which is good for changing the structure of a document.**

Using Moded Templates

We've seen how to use separate templates to process different nodes in different ways. However, one thing that we might lose when we use templates like this is the ability to process the *same* node in different ways in different situations. For example, say we want to create a table of contents for the HTML page that we're generating, giving a list of the channels that the TV guide offers, as shown in the following screenshot:

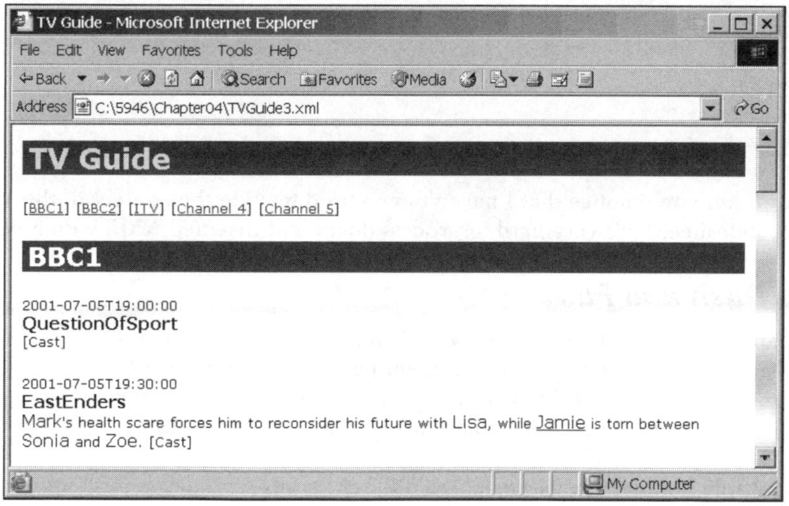

The HTML underlying the above page is as follows:

```
...
<h1>TV Guide</h1>
<p>
  [<a href="#BBC1">BBC1</a>]
  [<a href="#BBC2">BBC2</a>]
  [<a href="#ITV">ITV</a>]
  [<a href="#Channel 4">Channel 4</a>]
  [<a href="#Channel 5">Channel 5</a>]
</p>
<h2 class="channel"><a name="BBC1" id="BBC1">BBC1</a></h2>
...
```

We can get the table of contents by processing the <Channel> elements, but we're already processing the <Channel> elements to get the lists of the programs available on each channel. We want to process the same <Channel> elements twice: once for their entry in the channel list and once to get their details.

This is fairly easy with <xsl:for-each> because the content of the particular <xsl:for-each> determines the result that you get. So we could do:

```
<h1>TV Guide</h1>
<p>
  <xsl:for-each select="TVGuide/Channel">
    [<a href="#{Name}"><xsl:value-of select="Name" /></a>]
  </xsl:for-each>
</p>
<xsl:apply-templates />
```

to get the entries in the channel list, and then either use another <xsl:for-each> or apply templates (as above) to the <Channel> elements to get their content later on.

However, you can also achieve this by using template **modes**. Modes allow you to process the same node with different templates in different situations. You can apply templates in a particular mode using the mode attribute on <xsl:apply-templates>, and you can define the mode for a template with the mode attribute on <xsl:template>. When you apply templates in a particular mode then the XSLT processor will only look at those templates with that mode.

With modes, then, you can apply templates to the same node in different modes to get different results. So in this case, we can use a template in ChannelList mode to generate the result for each channel in the channel list, as follows:

```
<xsl:template match="Channel" mode="ChannelList">
  [<a href="#{Name}"><xsl:value-of select="Name" /></a>]
</xsl:template>
```

This template will only match <Channel> elements if you apply templates in ChannelList mode. So we need to have an <xsl:apply-templates> element in the template for the root node that applies templates in ChannelList mode:

```
<h1>TV Guide</h1>
<p>
  <xsl:apply-templates select="TVGuide/Channel" mode="ChannelList" />
</p>
<xsl:apply-templates />
```

When you apply templates without setting the mode, then the processor uses templates that don't have a mode attribute.

You can use moded templates to get different processing for the same node in different situations.

Built-in Moded Templates

As you'll recall, when an XSLT processor can't find a template that matches a particular node then it will use a built-in template instead. There are similar built-in templates for moded templates, one for elements, which simply applies templates to their content in the same mode:

```
<xsl:template match="*" mode="any-mode">
  <xsl:apply-templates mode="any-mode" />
</xsl:template>
```

and another that matches text nodes in that mode and gives their value:

```
<xsl:template match="text()" mode="any-mode">
  <xsl:value-of select="." />
</xsl:template>
```

These built-in templates mean that you can get rid of superfluous templates and apply templates without explicitly specifying the nodes to which you're applying them in exactly the same way as you can with the default mode.

When applying templates in `ChannelList` mode, then, we don't have to specify the nodes to which we're applying templates and can just use:

```
<h1>TV Guide</h1>
<p>
  <xsl:apply-templates mode="ChannelList" />
</p>
<xsl:apply-templates />
```

The current node in the template (which matches the root node) is the root node, so the `<xsl:apply-templates>` in `ChannelList` mode with no `select` attribute will apply templates to the document element, the `<TVGuide>` element in `ChannelList` mode. There isn't a template for the `<TVGuide>` element in `ChannelList` mode, so the processor will apply the built-in moded template. This template selects the children of the `<TVGuide>` element, the `<Channel>` elements, and applies templates to them in `ChannelList` mode.

> **There are built-in moded templates in the same way as there are built-in normal templates.**

Try It Out – Creating a Channel List

There are three things that we need to do to `TVGuide16.xsl` to create a linked list of channels in our page:

1. Add anchors to the headings for the channels in the main body of the page

2. Create a template in `ChannelList` mode to give the link to each channel

3. Apply templates in `ChannelList` mode at the point at which the channel list should be given on the page

We'll make these three changes to create a new version of our stylesheet, TVGuide17.xsl.

You can add the anchors to the headings by changing the template for the <Name> element child of the <Channel> element to include an <a> element whose name and id attributes give the name of the channel:

```
<xsl:template match="Channel/Name">
  <h2 class="channel">
    <a name="{.}" id="{.}"><xsl:value-of select="." /></a>
  </h2>
</xsl:template>
```

The XHTML Recommendation advises that you use both the name and id attributes when creating anchors for backward and forward compatibility. We're not yet generating proper XHTML, but it's a good guideline to follow, as that's our final goal.

You can create the template for <Channel> elements in ChannelList mode to reference these links, as follows:

```
<xsl:template match="Channel" mode="ChannelList">
  [<a href="#{Name}"><xsl:value-of select="Name" /></a>]
</xsl:template>
```

Finally, you can apply templates in ChannelList mode in the template matching the root node to insert the channel list just under the title. The main content of the page comes after this channel list and is generated by applying templates in the normal mode:

```
<xsl:template match="/">
  <html>
    <head>
      ...
    </head>
    <body>
      <h1>TV Guide</h1>
      <p>
        <xsl:apply-templates mode="ChannelList" />
      </p>
      <xsl:apply-templates />
    </body>
  </html>
</xsl:template>
```

You could repeat the same list again at the bottom of the page very easily, by repeating the same instruction after the <xsl:apply-templates> that generates the main body of the page:

```
<xsl:template match="/">
  <html>
    <head>
      ...
```

```
      </head>
      <body>
        <h1>TV Guide</h1>
        <p>
          <xsl:apply-templates mode="ChannelList" />
        </p>
        <xsl:apply-templates />
        <p>
          <xsl:apply-templates mode="ChannelList" />
        </p>
      </body>
    </html>
  </xsl:template>
```

This demonstrates one of the advantages of using templates over using `<xsl:for-each>` – you can reuse the same code by applying the same template. Transforming `TVGuide3.xml` with `TVGuide17.xsl` gives the display that we were aiming for, with a list of channel names at the top and the bottom of the page. Clicking on the channel name takes you to the program listing for that channel.

Summary

We've covered a lot of ground in this chapter. We've looked at full stylesheets for the first time – XML documents whose primary markup language is XSLT. You've learned how to convert from the starting point of a simplified stylesheet into a full stylesheet, by adding an `<xsl:stylesheet>` document element and an `<xsl:template>` element to give a template for the root node.

You've seen how an XSLT processor sees an XML document, as a node tree, and learned how to make an XSLT processor give you the output you want by telling it to apply templates to a bunch of nodes and providing the templates that it should use with them. You've discovered how to create templates that match various types of nodes:

- The root node
- Text nodes
- All element nodes
- Element nodes with particular names
- Element nodes with particular parents or ancestors

XSLT processors can only use one template to process a node when you apply templates to it. We've talked about how the processor deals with finding more than one template that matches a node by looking at the templates' priorities, and how it handles not finding one at all by using the built-in templates. You've also learned how to use modes to get the XSLT processor to use different templates in different situations.

Templates are the main constituent of a stylesheet, and the templates that you produce and the way you fit them together has a big effect on the stylesheet. You've now experienced the two main approaches used in stylesheets – push and pull – and we discussed the advantages and disadvantages of using each of them.

The XSLT that you've learned in this chapter hasn't much changed what you can generate from a stylesheet, just the way in which you get it. In the next chapter, we'll start looking at how to get a stylesheet to do more complicated processing dependent on the values of elements and attributes.

Review Questions

1. Turn the following simplified stylesheet into a full stylesheet:

```
<?xml version="1.0" encoding="ISO-8859-1"?>
<html xmlns:xsl="http://www.w3.org/1999/XSL/Transform"
      xsl:version="1.0">
  <head><title>Films</title></head>
  <body>
    <ul>
      <xsl:for-each select="/Films/Film">
        <li><xsl:value-of select="Name" /></li>
      </xsl:for-each>
    </ul>
  </body>
</html>
```

2. What is the term for the node at the top of the node tree? What relationship does it have to the document element?

3. Draw a node tree for the following XML document:

```
<?xml version="1.0" encoding="ISO-8859-1"?>
<?xml-stylesheet type="text/xsl" href="Films.xsl"?>
<Films>
  <Film rating="12">
    <Name>Crouching Tiger Hidden Dragon</Name>
    <Notes>
      Directed by <Director>Ang Lee</Director>.
    </Notes>
  </Film>
</Films>
```

4. Which template is the first template to be processed when you use a stylesheet with an entire document?

5. What kind of nodes does the following template process, and what does it do with them?

```
<xsl:template match="Description//Film">
  <a href="http://www.imdb.com/Find?for={.}">
    <xsl:value-of select="." />
  </a>
</xsl:template>
```

6. What will be the result of applying the following stylesheet to a document:

```
<?xml version="1.0" encoding="ISO-8859-1"?>
<xsl:stylesheet version="1.0"
                xmlns:xsl="http://www.w3.org/1999/XSL/Transform">

<xsl:template match="/">
  <xsl:apply-templates />
</xsl:template>

</xsl:stylesheet>
```

7. Which of the following templates will be applied to a `<Film>` element that's a child of a `<Link>` element that's a child of a `<Description>` element:

```
<xsl:template match="Description/Link/Film">...</xsl:template>
<xsl:template match="Film" priority="1">...</xsl:template>
<xsl:template match="Description//Film" priority="-1">...</xsl:template>
<xsl:template match="*">...</xsl:template>
<xsl:template match="Link/Film" mode="Description">...</xsl:template>
```

8. Which of the templates given in the previous question will be applied to the `<Film>` element if it's selected with the instruction:

```
<xsl:apply-templates mode="Description" />
```

Beginning
XSLT

5

Conditions

The last couple of chapters have given us a good foundation in XSLT. You've learned how to generate elements and attributes, and how to use the values of elements in XML as the values of the new nodes you create. You've learned how to iterate over elements in two ways – using `<xsl:for-each>` and using templates – and you've seen how to use patterns and modes to generate different content in different circumstances.

So far, we've been treating the information that's held in the source XML document as precisely the information we want in the result. In the TV Guide example, we've been listing all the programs in all the channels, and if a piece of information is there then we use it (more or less). Normally processing a document is more complex than that – perhaps you want to filter out some information, or only add something to the result if a particular case is true. For these cases, you need **conditional processing**, so you can choose to do something on the basis of an expression that can return either `true` or `false`.

In this chapter, you'll learn a number of ways of carrying out conditional processing in XSLT. Over the course of the chapter, you'll gain an understanding of:

- How to generate content only under certain positive and negative conditions
- How to supply default values when information is missing
- How to test whether an element or attribute is present or not
- How to test the values of elements and attributes
- How to filter a set of elements

Conditional Processing

Conditional processing is all about doing different things in different circumstances, such as only showing a cast list if there is a `<CastList>` element that holds information to present, or only adding a flag image to the description of a program if the `<Program>` element has a `flag` attribute.

In fact, we've already seen a certain amount of conditional processing, so before we move on to the new methods that this chapter introduces, we'll remind ourselves of the kinds of conditional processing we can do already. There are three types of conditional processing that we've encountered from previous chapters:

- Creating different results if an element is present or missing
- Creating different results for elements with different ancestry
- Creating different HTML for the same element in different locations in the result

Processing Optional Elements

The first and most obvious type of conditional content is when we only want to generate a piece of HTML in the result when there is an element in the source. Take the example of the cast list. Here's the XML that we use in `TVGuide.xml` to represent the cast list for a program:

```
<Program>
  ...
  <CastList>
    <CastMember>
      <Character><Name>Zoe Slater</Name>...</Character>
      <Actor><Name>Michelle Ryan</Name>...</Actor>
    </CastMember>
    <CastMember>
      <Character><Name>Jamie Mitchell</Name>...</Character>
      <Actor><Name>Jack Ryder</Name>...</Actor>
    </CastMember>
    <CastMember>
      <Character><Name>Sonia Jackson</Name>...</Character>
      <Actor><Name>Natalie Cassidy</Name>...</Actor>
    </CastMember>
  </CastList>
  ...
</Program>
```

When we generate the HTML for this cast list, we generate one `<li>` element for each `<CastMember>` element in the list. If there are only three cast members, we only generate three items. We make sure we don't generate more (or fewer) list items than we need by telling the processor to collect the `<CastMember>` elements together in a node set and process them, either by iterating over them with `<xsl:for-each>` or by applying templates to them with `<xsl:apply-templates>`.

Some TV programs, such as documentaries, don't have a cast; when we represent the information about these programs in XML, we don't include a `<CastList>` element in the `<Program>` element for the program. Take a look at the XSLT that we're currently using to deal with the `<CastList>` element. In the template for the `<Program>` element, we apply templates to the `<CastList>` element:

```
<xsl:template match="Program">
  <div>
    <p>
      <xsl:apply-templates select="Start" /><br />
```

```
      <xsl:apply-templates select="Series" /><br />
      <xsl:apply-templates select="Description" />
      <span onclick="toggle({Series}Cast);">[Cast]</span>
    </p>
    <div id="{Series}Cast" style="display: none;">
      <xsl:apply-templates select="CastList" />
    </div>
  </div>
</xsl:template>
```

and later on we have a template that matches the <CastList> element. This generates the <ul> element that wraps around the list and populates the <ul> element with the result of transforming the <CastMember> elements that the <CastList> element contains:

```
<xsl:template match="CastList">
  <ul class="castlist"><xsl:apply-templates /></ul>
</xsl:template>
```

If the <CastList> element is missing from the XML, the processor won't find a <CastList> element node to which to apply templates. Without finding a node to process, the XSLT processor won't process any template, so you won't get the <ul> element or any <li> elements added to the result.

If you tell an XSLT processor to apply templates to a type of node, but the node doesn't exist in the source, then the processor will not generate any output at that point.

Using the Ancestry of Source XML

We've used context information from the source XML to generate different results when an element occurs with different parents or ancestors in the last chapter. For example, we had one template to generate the result when a <Character> element occurs as a descendant of a <Description> element:

```
<xsl:template match="Description//Character">
  <span class="character"><xsl:apply-templates /></span>
</xsl:template>
```

and another to generate the result when it occurs as a child of a <CastMember> element:

```
<xsl:template match="Character">
  <span class="character"><xsl:apply-templates select="Name" /></span>
</xsl:template>
```

If you recall, this template doesn't explicitly only match <Character> elements that are children of <CastMember> elements, but it only gets used for those <Character> elements because of the different priority of the different patterns in the match attributes.

Another example is the template that matches <Name> element children of <Channel> elements. This template isn't used, for example, for <Name> elements that are children of the <Character> or <Actor> elements.

```
<xsl:template match="Channel/Name">
  <h2 class="channel">
    <a name="{.}" id="{.}"><xsl:apply-templates /></a>
  </h2>
</xsl:template>
```

You can create different templates for elements with different ancestry by using different location path patterns in the templates' match attributes.

Using the Location of Result XML

We've also seen how to use modes to generate different HTML based on the location at which the HTML is used in the page. So we have one template for <Channel> elements that gives just the name of the channel, for the top of the page:

```
<xsl:template match="Channel" mode="ChannelList">
  [<a href="#{Name}"><xsl:value-of select="Name" /></a>]
</xsl:template>
```

and we use the built-in templates for <Channel> elements when we generate the body of the page:

```
<xsl:template match="*">
  <xsl:apply-templates />
</xsl:template>
```

The <xsl:apply-templates> instruction tells the processor what mode should be used; the location of the <xsl:apply-templates> indicates where on the page it should go. In TVGuide.xsl, for example, we have:

```
<xsl:template match="/">
  <html>
    <head>
     ...
    </head>
    <body>
      <h1>TV Guide</h1>
      <p>
        <xsl:apply-templates mode="ChannelList" />
      </p>
      <xsl:apply-templates />
      <p>
        <xsl:apply-templates mode="ChannelList" />
      </p>
    </body>
```

```
  </html>
</xsl:template>
```

So you get one set of content for the <Channel> elements to create the main listing (when templates are applied without a mode) and a channel list before and after this main listing, generated by applying templates to the same elements, but this time in ChannelList mode.

> **You can create different output for different locations in the result using moded templates.**

Try It Out – Generating Content for an Optional Cast List

We can use the fact that an XSLT processor will not generate a result for elements that don't exist to our advantage. If you take another look at the way we're generating a result for the program in TVGuide.xsl, you'll see that we still get some information that we don't want if the <CastList> element is missing, namely a <div> element around the cast list and a <span> element that acts to show or hide the cast:

```
<xsl:template match="Channel/Program">
  <div>
    <p>
      <xsl:apply-templates select="Series" /><br />
      <xsl:apply-templates select="Description" />
      <span onclick="toggle({Series}Cast);">[Cast]</span>
    </p>
    <div id="{Series}Cast" style="display: none;">
      <xsl:apply-templates select="CastList" />
    </div>
  </div>
</xsl:template>
```

The <div> doesn't matter too much, because it doesn't actually get displayed unless it has some content, but the <span> containing the text [Cast] shows up for programs even when we really don't want it to. Look at the Question of Sport program in the following screenshot – there's no cast, but it still has a [Cast] "button":

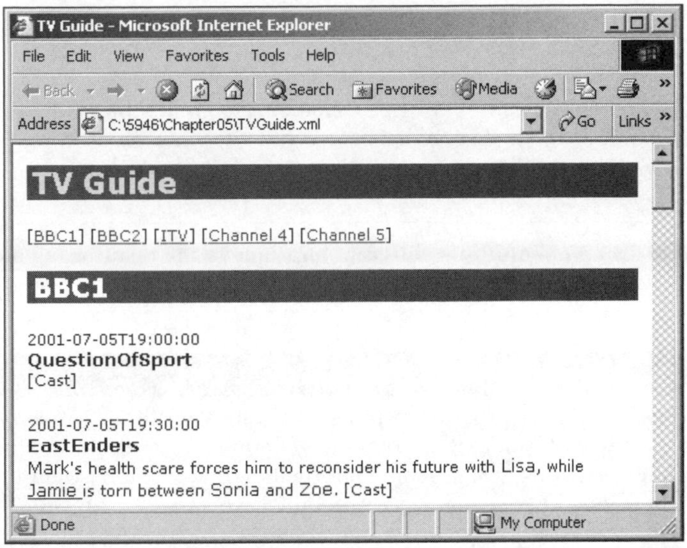

Let's try to get rid of that extra <div> and toggling <span> in the next version of our stylesheet, TVGuide2.xsl.

We can make sure that the <div> element isn't generated if the <CastList> element isn't present by moving the <div> element inside the template for the <CastList> element. That way, if there isn't a <CastList> element to have templates applied to, we won't get the <div> in the result. The new template for <CastList> elements looks as follows:

```
<xsl:template match="CastList">
  <div id="{../Series}Cast" style="display: none;">
    <ul class="castlist"><xsl:apply-templates /></ul>
  </div>
</xsl:template>
```

The attribute value template we use in the id *attribute has to change a little because the current node in this template is the* <CastList> *element, which is a sibling of the* <Series> *element rather than its parent. The new attribute value template uses a path that goes up a level (to the* <Program> *element), before going down again to the* <Series> *element.*

The other piece of content that we don't want to generate if there isn't a <CastList> element is the <span> element that acts as the toggle for displaying or hiding the cast list. We can't move that inside the template for the <CastList> element because it needs to be generated inside the paragraph that holds the title and description of the program.

However, we can still use the same principal of trying to apply templates to a node if we use a moded template. As you'll remember from the last chapter, a moded template allows you to generate different content for the same node in different situations. So in this case we can apply templates to the <CastList> element in a different mode (DisplayToggle, for example) to generate the <span> element. The DisplayToggle mode template for the <CastList> element looks as follows:

```
<xsl:template match="CastList" mode="DisplayToggle">
  <span onclick="toggle({../Series}Cast);">[Cast]</span>
</xsl:template>
```

The template for the <Program> element now just needs to apply templates to the <CastList> element at the relevant places, first in DisplayToggle mode, then in normal mode:

```
<xsl:template match="Program">
  <div>
    <p>
      <xsl:apply-templates select="Start" /><br />
      <xsl:apply-templates select="Series" /><br />
      <xsl:apply-templates select="Description" />
      <xsl:apply-templates select="CastList" mode="DisplayToggle" />
    </p>
    <xsl:apply-templates select="CastList" />
  </div>
</xsl:template>
```

Now transform TVGuide.xml using TVGuide2.xsl. TVGuide.xml includes the following XML for the Question of Sport program:

```
<Program>
  <Start>2001-07-05T19:00:00</Start>
  <Duration>PT30M</Duration>
  <Series>QuestionOfSport</Series>
  <Title></Title>
</Program>
```

This <Program> element doesn't contain a <CastList> element, so it gets transformed to the following HTML:

```
<div>
  <p>
    <span class="date">2001-07-05T19:00:00</span><br>
    <span class="title">QuestionOfSport</span><br>
  </p>
</div>
```

On the other hand, the XML for the EastEnders program contains the extra HTML because it does have a <CastList> element, so it gets transformed into the following HTML:

```
<div>
  <p>
    <span class="date">2001-07-05T19:30:00</span><br>
    <span class="title">EastEnders</span><br>
     ...
    <span onclick="toggle(EastEndersCast);">[Cast]</span>
  </p>
  <div id="EastEndersCast" style="display: none;">
    <ul class="castlist">
```

```
      ...
      </ul>
    </div>
  </div>
```

You can also see the effect if you look at the page in a web browser:

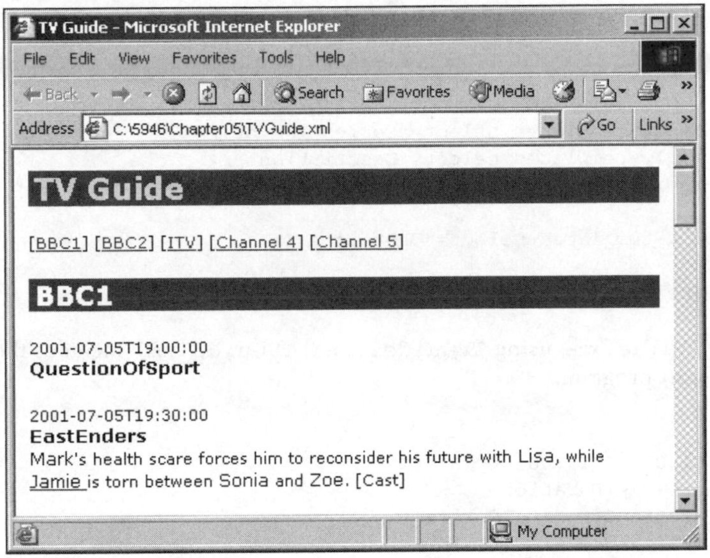

The Question of Sport program (and many other programs) no longer has a toggle "button" for its cast, since the source XML doesn't contain a `<CastList>` element.

Conditional Elements in XSLT

We've seen three situations where we can use what we know already to generate results conditionally:

- Generate content only when an element is present
- Generate content only if an element has a particular ancestry
- Generate content for a particular location in the result

But these three situations are special cases because they can be handled through template processing as we've seen. We can't use these techniques in all cases – what if we want to generate particular content if an element is absent, has a particular child or attribute, or has a particular value? In these cases we need to use a conditional construct. In XSLT there are two conditional constructs, which we'll be looking at in this section: an `if` statement and a `choose` statement.

if Statements

The most basic conditional construct in XSLT is `<xsl:if>`. The `<xsl:if>` element takes a single attribute, `test`, which holds an XPath expression. If the XPath expression evaluates to `true`, then the content of `<xsl:if>` is processed, otherwise nothing happens. The basic form of the `<xsl:if>` element is:

```
<xsl:if test="...">
  ...
</xsl:if>
```

There are all sorts of conditions that you can put in a `test` attribute, as you'll see in the next section. One of the simplest is testing for the presence of an element or attribute, which you do with a path that points to the element or attribute for which you want to test. If the XSLT processor finds any nodes when it evaluates that path, then the condition evaluates to `true`, and the XSLT processor processes the content of the `<xsl:if>` element; if it doesn't find any nodes, the condition evaluates to `false`, and the content of the `<xsl:if>` element is ignored. For example, take the `if` statement:

```
<xsl:if test="Program">
  There are programs showing on this channel.
</xsl:if>
```

The content of the `<xsl:if>` will be processed (and thus the text "There are programs showing on this channel" added to the result) if the current node (a `<Channel>` element) has any `<Program>` element children.

Conditions that consist of a location path actually work because the node set that's returned by the location path is implicitly converted to a boolean value because it's in a `test` attribute. You can also convert a node set to a boolean value explicitly, with the `boolean()` function, as you'll see later in this chapter.

The `<xsl:if>` instruction only generates output if the condition held in its `test` attribute evaluates as true.

Try It Out – Adding Conditional Content

In the previous section, you saw how to use templates and modes to generate the elements associated with a cast list only in cases where there was a `<CastList>` element child of the `<Program>` element that was being processed. Here, we'll look at how to use `<xsl:if>` to achieve the same effect.

The original template, in `TVGuide.xsl`, was as follows; the highlighted `<span>` and `<div>` elements should only be generated if the `<Program>` element has a `<CastList>` element child:

```
<xsl:template match="Program">
  <div>
    <p>
      <xsl:apply-templates select="Start" /><br />
      <xsl:apply-templates select="Series" /><br />
      <xsl:apply-templates select="Description" />
      <span onclick="toggle({Series}Cast);">[Cast]</span>
    </p>
    <div id="{Series}Cast" style="display: none;">
      <xsl:apply-templates select="CastList" />
    </div>
  </div>
```

```
</xsl:template>
```

We can add content under a particular condition using an <xsl:if> element. To test whether the current node has a particular element child, we can just use the name of the element in the test attribute. So, to test whether the <Program> element (which is the current node in a template matching <Program> elements) has a <CastList> child element, and add something to the result if it does, we can use:

```
<xsl:if test="CastList">
  ...
</xsl:if>
```

In this example, we need two <xsl:if> elements – one to wrap around the <span> element and the other to wrap around the <div> element. The amended template for the <Program> element, in TVGuide3.xsl, is as follows:

```
<xsl:template match="Program">
  <div>
    <p>
      <xsl:apply-templates select="Start" /><br />
      <xsl:apply-templates select="Series" /><br />
      <xsl:apply-templates select="Description" />
      <xsl:if test="CastList">
        <span onclick="toggle({Series}Cast);">[Cast]</span>
      </xsl:if>
    </p>
    <xsl:if test="CastList">
      <div id="{Series}Cast" style="display: none;">
        <xsl:apply-templates select="CastList" />
      </div>
    </xsl:if>
  </div>
</xsl:template>
```

Note that unlike <xsl:for-each>, an <xsl:if> does not change the current node – the paths within the <xsl:if> are still evaluated relative to the node that the template matches, rather than the node whose presence you are testing for (for example).

If you run TVGuide3.xsl with the TVGuide.xml document, you'll see that the [Cast] "buttons" do not appear, in just the same way as they weren't generated when we used modes in TVGuide2.xsl:

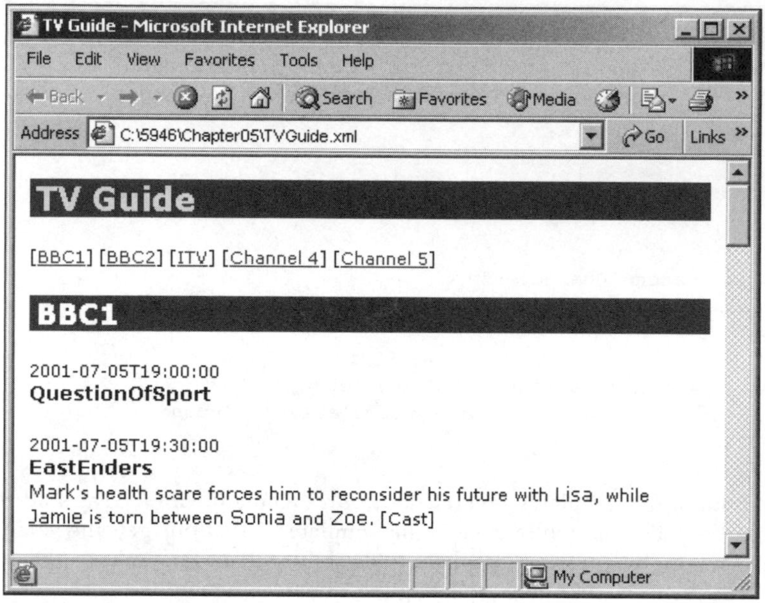

choose Statements

XSLT doesn't have an else-if statement, but instead uses `<xsl:choose>`. The `<xsl:choose>` element contains a number of `<xsl:when>` elements, which can be followed by an `<xsl:otherwise>` element. Each of the `<xsl:when>` elements tests for a particular condition with a `test` attribute that works in exactly the same way as the `test` attribute on `<xsl:if>`. The basic form of the `<xsl:choose>` element is:

```
<xsl:choose>
  <xsl:when test="...">...</xsl:when>
  <xsl:when test="...">...</xsl:when>
  ...
  <xsl:otherwise>...</xsl:otherwise>
</xsl:choose>
```

The XSLT processor works through the `<xsl:when>` elements one at a time. When it comes across an `<xsl:when>` element whose `test` attribute evaluates to `true`, then it processes the content of that `<xsl:when>` element and ignores the rest of the `<xsl:choose>`. If the XSLT processor doesn't find an `<xsl:when>` whose condition is `true`, then it processes the content of the `<xsl:otherwise>` (if there is one).

> **The `<xsl:choose>` instruction gives a choice between different outputs based on different conditions. The content and conditions are defined in separate `<xsl:when>` elements and their `test` attribute. If no condition is true, the XSLT processor processes the content of `<xsl:otherwise>`.**

Try It Out – Merging Templates that Share Content

You've already seen how to use the match patterns of templates to generate different results for elements with different ancestors or parents. Here, we'll look at how to use <xsl:choose> to do the same thing.

In TVGuide3.xsl, we currently have two templates to deal with <Character> elements in different contexts:

```
<xsl:template match="Character">
  <span class="character"><xsl:apply-templates select="Name" /></span>
</xsl:template>

<xsl:template match="Description//Character">
  <span class="character"><xsl:apply-templates /></span>
</xsl:template>
```

As you can see, both of the templates generate a <span> element with a class attribute that's given the value character. The only difference in the templates is that one gets the value of the <Character> element (by applying templates to its children), and the other applies templates only to its child <Name> element. Rather than repeating the <span> element in the two separate templates, we could use a single template with an <xsl:choose> within the <span> element to decide whether to give the value of the <Character> element or apply templates to its child <Name> element.

We haven't yet looked at how to select parents or ancestors of an element (we'll come to that in Chapter 7). However, we know that the only <Character> elements that have a <Name> element child are those in the cast list, so instead of testing whether the parent of the <Character> element is a <CastMember> element, we can test whether it has a <Name> element as a child. The template would look like:

```
<xsl:template match="Character">
  <span class="character">
    <xsl:choose>
      <xsl:when test="Name">
        <xsl:apply-templates select="Name" />
      </xsl:when>
      <xsl:otherwise>
        <xsl:apply-templates />
      </xsl:otherwise>
    </xsl:choose>
  </span>
</xsl:template>
```

This template replaces the two templates in TVGuide3.xsl, to give TVGuide4.xsl. When you transform TVGuide.xml with TVGuide4.xsl, you get the following:

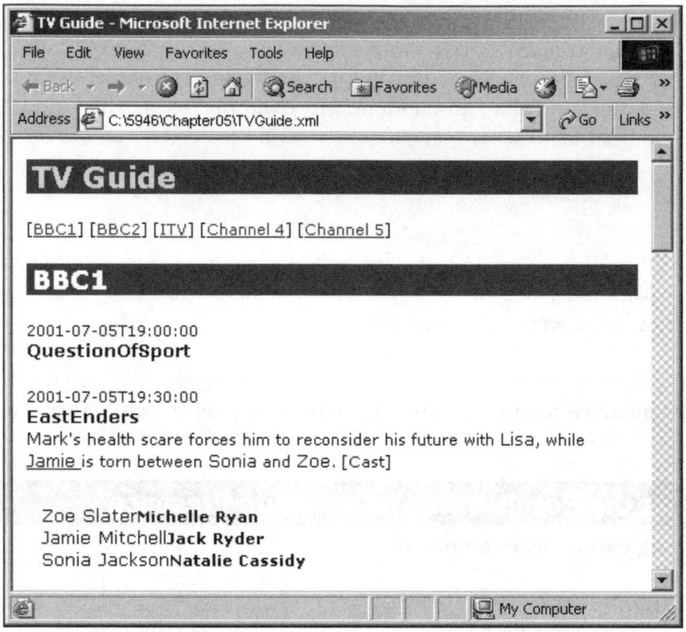

As you can see, the descriptions of the characters are not included in the cast list, and character names in the description of the program are highlighted as usual (by being slightly larger).

Testing Elements and Attributes

The `<xsl:if>` and `<xsl:choose>` constructs are only as powerful as the conditions that you test with them. You've seen how to test whether an element has a particular child element by using the name of the child element in the `test` attribute. In this section, we'll look at the other kinds of tests that you can use there.

Testing for Attributes

You can test for the presence of an attribute in a very similar way to testing for the presence of an element. You use a location path to select the attribute; if the XSLT processor finds an attribute when it evaluates the path, then the condition is `true`, otherwise it's `false`.

You select an attribute on the current element by giving the name of the attribute preceded by an `@` sign. For example, if the current node is the `<TVGuide>` element, you could test whether it has a `start` attribute with the following `<xsl:if>` instruction:

```
<xsl:if test="@start">
  ...
</xsl:if>
```

You can select attributes from further down the node tree, on descendant elements of the current node, by stepping down the node tree in exactly the same way as you do when selecting elements, except that once you get to an attribute there's no further to go. The @ sign in front of the name indicates that you want to select an attribute rather than an element. For example, to get the value of the `start` attribute of the `<TVGuide>` element from wherever you are within the stylesheet, you could do:

```
<xsl:value-of select="/TVGuide/@start" />
```

You can use the attributes you select in just the same way as you can an element – you can get the values of attributes with `<xsl:value-of>`, iterate over them with `<xsl:for-each>`, and apply templates to them with `<xsl:apply-templates>`.

You can select an attribute in a location path by giving an @ sign before its name.

Try It Out – Changing the Result Based on Attribute Presence

Consider the following extract from a node tree:

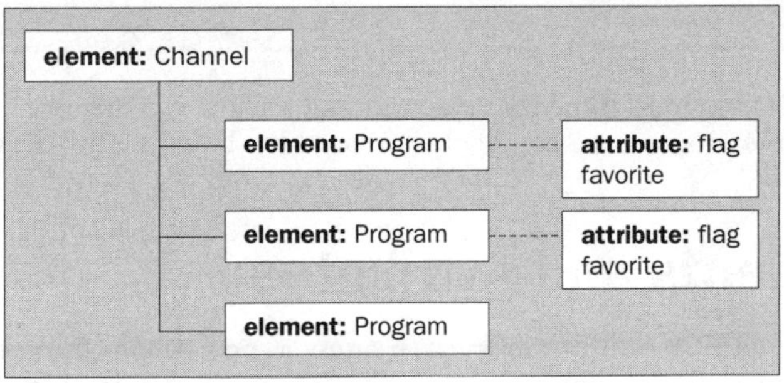

Two of the `<Program>` elements have `flag` attributes. Say that in the next version of our stylesheet, `TVGuide5.xsl`, we don't want to show a channel if it doesn't have any flagged programs. We don't have a specific template for `<Channel>` elements (in default mode) at the moment – we just use the built-in templates to process each `<Channel>` element and all its content. One method of approaching this problem would be to introduce a template for a `<Channel>` element, in which you test the content of the `<Channel>` element to see whether its content should be processed at all, as follows:

```
<xsl:template match="Channel">
  <xsl:if test="...">
    <xsl:apply-templates />
  </xsl:if>
</xsl:template>
```

In this template for the <Channel> element, you could test whether *any* of the <Program> elements have flag attributes by stepping from the current <Channel> element down to the <Program> elements, and then across to their flag attributes. The location path Program/@flag selects the flag attributes that are the children of <Program> elements that are the children of the current (<Channel>) element. As with tests that test for the presence of an element, if the node set contains some flag attributes, then the test evaluates as true; if the processor doesn't manage to find any flag attributes then it evaluates as false. The effect is that we only apply templates to the content of the <Channel> element if we find any flag attributes:

```
<xsl:template match="Channel">
  <xsl:if test="Program/@flag">
    <xsl:apply-templates />
  </xsl:if>
</xsl:template>
```

To prevent frustration, it would probably also be a good idea not to display links in the channel listing at the top and bottom of the page to those channels that are not actually shown within the page. The template for <Channel> elements in ChannelList mode also needs a similar <xsl:if> added, as follows:

```
<xsl:template match="Channel" mode="ChannelList">
  <xsl:if test="Program/@flag">
    [<a href="#{Name}"><xsl:value-of select="Name" /></a>]
  </xsl:if>
</xsl:template>
```

We're still showing all the programs for these channels, but we want the flagged programs to be marked by an image. In the template for the <Program> element, we want to add a flag image before the title of the program if the <Program> element has a flag attribute. Again, we use an <xsl:if> instruction to add the conditional content, as follows:

```
<xsl:template match="Channel/Program">
  <div>
    <p>
      <xsl:if test="@flag">
        <img src="flag.gif" alt="[Flagged]" width="20" height="20" />
      </xsl:if>
      <xsl:apply-templates select="Series" /><br />
      <xsl:apply-templates select="Description" />
      <xsl:apply-templates select="CastList" mode="DisplayToggle" />
    </p>
    <xsl:apply-templates select="CastList" />
  </div>
</xsl:template>
```

Transforming TVGuide.xml with TVGuide5.xsl only shows the channels that have flagged programs, both in the channel list at the top of the page and in the main content of the page. It also adds an image to those programs that are flagged, such as EastEnders, as shown in the following screenshot:

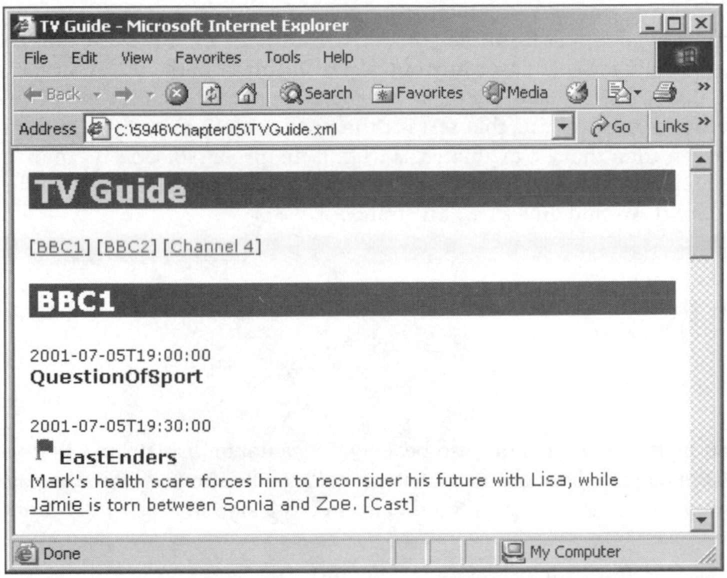

So, in `TVGuide5.xsl` we're both omitting content conditionally and adding content conditionally, based on the presence or absence of attributes.

Comparing Values

XPath has a number of **operators** that allow you to compare the value of an element or attribute to a string or a number. Operators are symbols that sit between two expressions and perform some operation on the results of those expressions. For example, you can test whether the `flag` attribute on the current `<Program>` element is equal to the string `'favorite'` with the following expression, which uses an = (equals) operator:

```
@flag = 'favorite'
```

This is the first time that we've seen a literal string being used in an expression. Note the single quotes around the string `'favorite'`. Putting single or double quotes around a string makes the XPath processor recognize it as a string, as opposed to a location path. If you missed out the quotes (and it's an easy mistake to make!) and did `@flag = favorite` then you'd be testing whether the `flag` attribute has the same value as the `<favorite>` child element of the context node, which isn't what you want at all.

Whether you use single or double quotes is up to you, but XPaths in XSLT are always held within attribute values, so if you use double quotes around an attribute value, and double quotes around a literal string in an XPath, then you have to escape the double quotes in the XPath with `"`. *Similarly, if you use single quotes around an attribute value, and single quotes around a literal string in an XPath, then you have to escape the single quotes in the XPath with* `'`. *I usually use double quotes around attribute values and single quotes around literal strings in XPaths to prevent having to escape too much.*

Like most things in XML, comparisons between strings are case-sensitive. The above expression will only return true if the flag attribute has exactly the value favorite. The comparison will not return true for any of the following <Program> elements:

```
<Program flag="interesting">...</Program>
<Program>...</Program>
<Program flag="Favorite">...</Program>
<Program flag="FAVORITE">...</Program>
<Program flag=" favorite ">...</Program>
```

Comparison Operators

The full set of operators for performing comparisons is as follows:

Name	Operator	Example	Explanation
Equals	=	@flag = 'favorite'	Returns true if the flag attribute is equal to the string 'favorite'.
Not equals	!=	@flag != 'favorite'	Returns true if the flag attribute is not equal to the string 'favorite'.
Less than	<	@rating < 2	Returns true if the rating attribute is less than 2.
Less than or equal to	<=	@rating <= 4	Returns true if the rating attribute is less than or equal to 4.
Greater than	>	@rating > 8	Returns true if the rating attribute is more than 8.
Greater than or equal to	>=	@rating >= 6	Returns true if the rating attribute is more than or equal to 6.

You always have to escape the less-than (<) operator as < and the less-than-or-equal-to (<=) operator as <= when you use them in XSLT because XSLT is XML and less-than signs must always be escaped in XML. For example, if you want to do the test @rating < 2 in an XSLT stylesheet, then you actually need to write:

```
<xsl:if test="@rating &lt; 2">
  ...
</xsl:if>
```

If you want to, you can escape the greater-than (>) operator as > and the greater-than-or-equal-to (>=) operator as >=. However, people often use the fact that the greater-than sign doesn't have to be escaped to prevent any escaping at all. For example, you can turn around the test @rating < 2 to give 2 > @rating, which you could happily write in XSLT without any escaping as:

```
<xsl:if test="2 > @rating">
  ...
</xsl:if>
```

XPath defines these operators and is designed to be used in languages other than XSLT, including text-based languages where you don't need to do this escaping. Fortunately, the less-than and less-than-or-equal-to operators are the only operators that need to be escaped in XSLT.

There are six operators for performing comparisons between values: =, !=, <, <=, > and >=.

Comparing Node Sets and Values

Comparisons between a node set (which you select with a location path) and values work in a special way in XPath. For example, say that the current node is the `<Channel>` element and we want to test the `flag` attributes on its `<Program>` child elements. Look at the following expression:

```
Program/@flag = 'favorite'
```

The path `Program/@flag` evaluates as a node set containing a number of `flag` attributes, namely all the `flag` attributes that were found on `<Program>` element children of the current `<Channel>` element. When you compare this node set to the string `'favorite'`, the XSLT processor goes through each of the `flag` attributes in turn. If it finds *any* `flag` attribute that has the value `favorite`, then the comparison returns `true`. So the above condition is `true` if *any* programs have been flagged as favorite programs.

Now consider the following condition:

```
Program/@flag != 'favorite'
```

As previously, the `Program/@flag` path gives a node set. The XSLT processor goes through each of the `flag` attributes in turn, this time checking whether they are *not* equal to the string `'favorite'`. If it finds *any* `flag` attribute that does not have the value `favorite`, then the comparison returns `true`. So the above condition is `true` if *any* programs have not been flagged as favorite programs.

This is different from testing whether there are *no* programs that have been flagged as favorite programs. Testing whether there are no `flag` attributes that have the value `favorite` is the opposite of testing whether there are *any* `flag` attributes that have the value `favorite`. You can reverse a condition with the `not()` function, as follows:

```
not(Program/@flag = 'favorite')
```

The `not()` function takes a single argument, which is interpreted as a boolean value. Note that all function names in XPath are case-sensitive – in fact they are all lowercase, with hyphens separating words where necessary.

The same technicality applies to the other comparisons. If you compare a node set to a value, then the comparison returns `true` if there are any nodes for which the comparison is `true`. This distinction doesn't matter if you're only picking a single node, but it does if you're selecting more than one. This can be confusing, because it looks like the test works differently in different circumstances. For example, if you have the test:

```
Series != 'EastEnders'
```

then the test returns `true` if the `<Series>` element child of the current `<Program>` element is not equal to the value `'EastEnders'` (if the current program isn't an EastEnders episode). There can only be one `<Series>` element child of the `<Program>` element, so it's a one-to-one comparison, and it works as you expect. On the other hand, with the test:

```
Program/Series != 'EastEnders'
```

you get a `true` result if *any* of the `<Series>` element children of the `<Program>` element children of the current `<Channel>` element are *not* equal to the value `'EastEnders'` (in other words, if any of the programs showing on the channel are not EastEnders episodes). Unless a channel shows EastEnders episodes exclusively, round the clock, the test will return `false`. More than likely, what you're after is actually:

```
not(Program/Series = 'EastEnders')
```

which returns `true` if *none* of the programs showing on the channel are EastEnders episodes.

A comparison between a node set and a value is true if the comparison is true for any node in the node set.

Try It Out – Generating Different Results for Different Attribute Values

In `TVGuide5.xsl`, we use the same kind of flag no matter what the value of the `flag` attribute. But say we have different kinds of flags for favorite programs and interesting programs, and we want those flags to be indicated with different images (`favorite.gif` and `interest.gif`).

Rather than using an `<xsl:if>` as we do in `TVGuide5.xsl`, in `TVGuide6.xsl`, the template for the `<Program>` element can use an `<xsl:choose>` that tests whether the `flag` attribute is equal to the string `'favorite'` or `'interesting'` and gives an appropriate image, as follows:

```
<xsl:template match="Program">
  <div>
    <p>
      <xsl:apply-templates select="Start" /><br />
      <xsl:choose>
        <xsl:when test="@flag = 'favorite'">
          <img src="favorite.gif" alt="[Favorite]" width="20" height="20" />
        </xsl:when>
        <xsl:when test="@flag = 'interesting'">
          <img src="interest.gif" alt="[Interest]" width="20" height="20" />
        </xsl:when>
```

```
          </xsl:choose>
          <xsl:apply-templates select="Series" /><br />
          <xsl:apply-templates select="Description" />
          <xsl:if test="CastList">
            <span onclick="toggle({Series}Cast);">[Cast]</span>
          </xsl:if>
        </p>
        <xsl:if test="CastList">
          <div id="{Series}Cast" style="display: none;">
            <xsl:apply-templates select="CastList" />
          </div>
        </xsl:if>
      </div>
    </xsl:template>
```

The condition `@flag = 'favorite'` will only be `true` if there is a `flag` attribute with the value `favorite`. We use another `<xsl:when>`, rather than an `<xsl:otherwise>`, to make sure we only add an image under those conditions, not if the `flag` attribute is missing. The result of transforming `TVGuide.xml` with `TVGuide6.xsl` is:

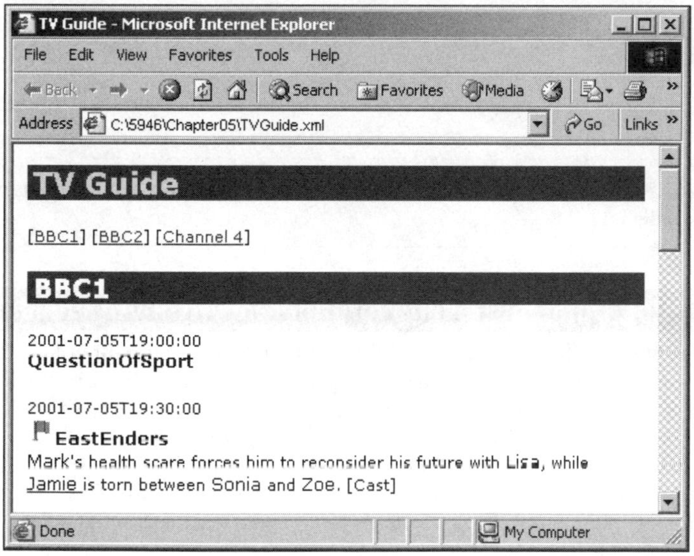

As you can see, EastEnders is flagged with a green flag now, indicating that it's a favorite program (rather than a particularly interesting one). If you scroll down, you'll see blue flags next to some of the other programs, those that have a `flag` attribute with a value of `interesting`.

Testing with Functions

As well as operators, XPath defines a number of **functions** that are particularly useful in tests. Functions are often passed **arguments**, which are listed in brackets after the function name, separated by commas. In this section, we'll have a look at some functions that are particularly useful when testing values; we'll come across a lot more functions as we progress with the rest of the book.

Testing Strings and Numbers

When we first started looking at conditions, we saw how if you use a location path in a `test` attribute, it evaluates to `true` if the location path manages to select any nodes. In more technical terms, the location path evaluates to a **node set** and this node set is converted to a boolean – `true` if the node set contains any nodes and `false` if it doesn't.

XPath defines four value types:

- Booleans
- Numbers
- Strings
- Node sets

XSLT adds another value type to these basic types from XPath: result tree fragments. We'll meet result tree fragments in Chapter 6 when we learn about variables.

Every expression evaluates to one particular type of value. A location path evaluates to a node set; a comparison (with one of the operators that we saw above) evaluates to a boolean value. Different functions evaluate to different kinds of values. In particular, there is a set of functions that convert values to particular value types, namely:

- `boolean()` – converts to a boolean value
- `number()` – converts to a number
- `string()` – converts to a string

The ways in which these functions convert the four value types is shown in the following table:

Value Type	**`boolean()`**	**`number()`**	**`string()`**
boolean	-	`1` if true, `0` if false	`'true'` if true, `'false'` if false
number	`false` if number is `0` or `NaN`, `true` otherwise	-	a string of the number, `'NaN'`, `'Infinity'`, or `'-Infinity'`
string	`false` if the string doesn't contain any characters, `true` otherwise	the number if numeric, `NaN` otherwise; exponents, `'Infinity'`, and `'-Infinity'` aren't recognized	-

Table continued on following page

Value Type	boolean()	number()	string()
node set	`true` if the node set contains any nodes, `false` otherwise	the result of converting the string value of the first node in the node set to a number	the string value of the first node in the node set

If you use `string()` or `number()` without giving an argument, then the functions use the current node as the argument. So the function call:

```
number()
```

returns the result of converting the current node to a number.

> **There are four types of values in XPath: booleans, numbers, strings, and node sets. You can convert between them with the functions `boolean()`, `string()`, and `number()`.**

Try It Out – Testing if an Element Has a Value

We've seen how to test if an element is present, but what if the element is present but doesn't have a value. For example, the EastEnders program is represented by the following XML in `TVGuide.xml`:

```
<Program>
  <Start>2001-07-05T19:30:00</Start>
  <Duration>PT30M</Duration>
  <Series>EastEnders</Series>
  <Title></Title>
  <Description>
    ...
  </Description>
  ...
</Program>
```

The `<Title>` element is empty because EastEnders episodes don't have individual titles. Other programs have individual titles for episodes in a series, and still others aren't part of a series. We've chosen to represent this in our XML by always having a `<Series>` element and a `<Title>` element. If the program isn't part of a series, then the `<Series>` element is empty; if the program hasn't got an individual title, then the `<Title>` element is empty.

When it comes to the HTML, we have the following possibilities:

```
<span class="title">Series</span>
<span class="title">Series - <span class="subtitle">Title</span></span>
<span class="title">Title</span>
```

We're currently only recognizing the first possibility, which is why several of the programs in the program listing haven't got titles at the moment.

Which of these possibilities we use depends on the string values of the `<Series>` and `<Title>` elements. If they don't have a string value, then they are empty. You can convert an element to a string using the `string()` function. If the resulting string has any values in it then it will evaluate as `true` in a `test` attribute; if the element is empty, the string is empty, and the condition will evaluate to `false`. Therefore we can use the following XSLT in the template for the `<Program>` element to insert the correct XML:

```
<xsl:template match="Program">
  ...
  <span class="title">
    <xsl:choose>
      <xsl:when test="string(Series)">
        <xsl:value-of select="Series" />
        <xsl:if test="string(Title)">
        - <span class="subtitle"><xsl:value-of select="Title" /></span>
        </xsl:if>
      </xsl:when>
      <xsl:otherwise>
        <xsl:value-of select="Title" />
      </xsl:otherwise>
    </xsl:choose>
  </span>
  ...
</xsl:template>
```

This version is used in `TVGuide7.xsl`. When you transform `TVGuide.xml` with `TVGuide7.xsl` you should see that every program has a title, and that some of them have subtitles as well. For example, BBC2 is showing four programs, the last of which has a pretty racy subtitle (which may contribute to the fact that it's flagged as interesting!):

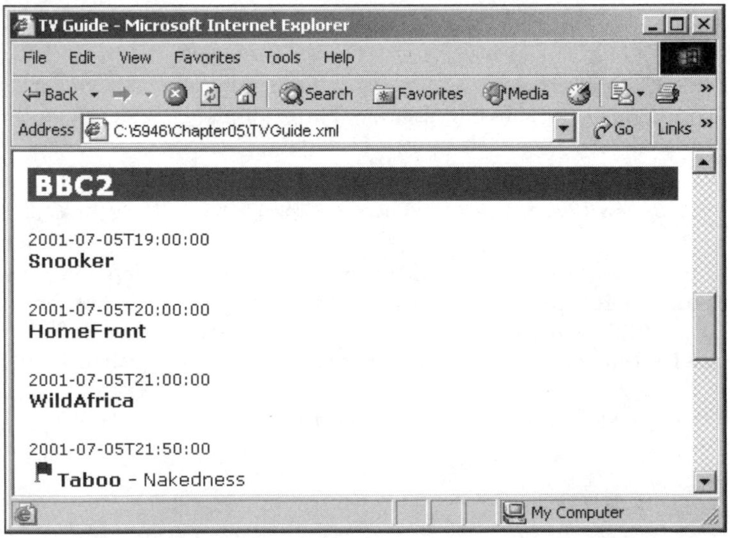

Alternatively, you could use similar conditions within the templates for the `<Series>` and `<Title>` elements. See if you can achieve the same output as shown above using separate templates for `<Series>` and `<Title>` elements instead.

Testing the Contents of Strings

There are two functions that are particularly useful when testing element and attribute values – `starts-with()` and `contains()`.

The `starts-with()` function takes two strings as arguments. The first string is the string to test – usually the value of an attribute or element – and the second string gives the starting string for which you want to test. The function returns `true` if the first string starts with the second string. For example, with the current node being a `<CastMember>` element, the following tests whether the character's first name is Mark:

```
starts-with(Character/Name, 'Mark ')
```

Note that the space at the end of the string `'Mark '` *ensures that we don't select people whose first name is* `'Marko'` *or* `'Markie'` *for example.*

Similarly, the `contains()` function takes two strings as arguments, but this time returns `true` if the first string contains the second string at any point. For example, with the current node being a `<Program>` element, the following tests whether the description of the program contains the word "sport":

```
contains(Description, 'sport')
```

Like the operators that work with strings, these functions are case-sensitive – you need to use the `translate()` *function, which we'll meet in the next chapter. Also note that the above function call would return* `true` *if the description contained words like "sporting", "spoilsport", or "transporter", which may or may not be what you're after.*

These functions don't work in the same way as the operators when it comes to testing whether a bunch of nodes start with or contain a particular string. If you use a location path to give the first argument, then the node set that it returns is converted to a string by taking the first node in the node set (in document order) and testing the value of that node. For example, consider the following expression with the current node being a `<Program>` element:

```
starts-with(CastList/CastMember/Character/Name, 'Mark ')
```

The first argument evaluates to a node set containing all the `<Name>` elements for all the characters in the cast list. That node set gets converted to a string by taking just the first of the `<Name>` elements. The function returns `true` if this string starts with `'Mark'`. So it tests whether the first name of the first character in the cast list is Mark, not whether there are any characters called Mark in the cast list.

We'll see how to get around this limitation a little later on in this chapter, by using predicates.

> **The `starts-with()` function tests whether a string starts with another string, while the `contains()` function tests whether a string contains another string.**

Try It Out – Identifying Elements that Start with a String

A new feature that we'll introduce to our TV guide in `TVGuide8.xsl` is that we use a special icon alongside every Star Trek episode of whichever series (Star Trek, Star Trek The Next Generation, Star Trek Deep Space Nine, Star Trek Voyager, and Star Trek Enterprise). To identify these programs, we can test whether the series starts with the string `'StarTrek'`; if it does, we add the relevant image:

```
<xsl:template match="Program">
  ...
  <xsl:if test="starts-with(Series, 'StarTrek')">
    <img src="StarTrek.gif" alt="[Star Trek]" width="20" height="20" />
  </xsl:if>
  ...
</xsl:template>
```

Add this instruction to the template for the `<Program>` element so that it shows a logo prior to the title for all the Star Trek programs. Actually, `TVGuide.xml` doesn't contain any Star Trek programs, so we'll add a new channel (Sky One) that includes some to create `TVGuide2.xml`, which lets us test out the logo. The new channel includes the following XML:

```
<Channel>
  <Name>Sky One</Name>
  ...
  <Program rating="8">
    <Start>2001-07-05T20:00:00</Start>
    <Duration>PT1H</Duration>
    <Series>StarTrekVoyager</Series>
    <Title>Renaissance Man</Title>
  </Program>
  ...
  <Program flag="favorite">
    <Start>2001-07-05T22:00:00</Start>
    <Duration>PT1H</Duration>
    <Series>StarTrekNextGeneration</Series>
    <Title>The Inner Light</Title>
  </Program>
</Channel>
```

When you transform `TVGuide2.xml`, which includes Star Trek programs, with `TVGuide8.xsl`, which highlights Star Trek programs, you get logos next to the two Star Trek episodes, as follows:

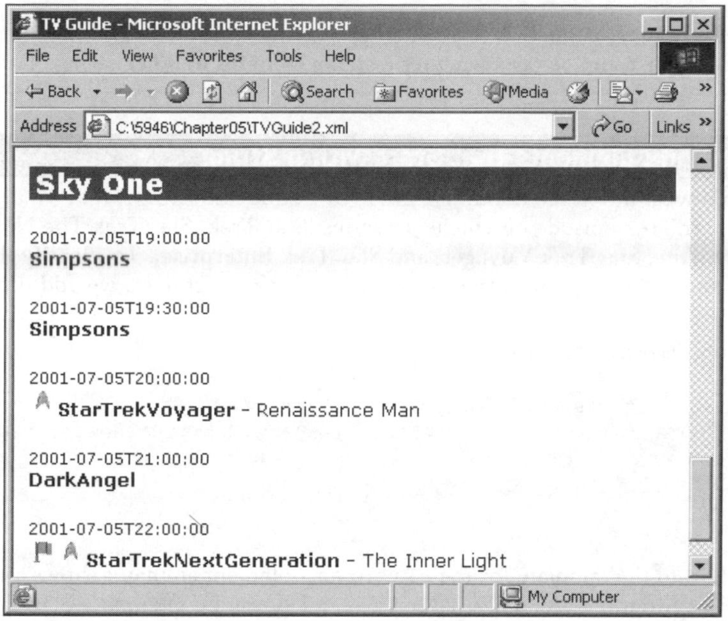

The Star Trek logo only appears when the `<Series>` element starts with the string `'StarTrek'`.

Combining Tests

Often constructing the tests that you want requires you to combine tests together. You can combine tests with the operators `and` and `or` in XPath, and use brackets (`()`) to collect multiple tests together.

> *The main reason that XPath uses* `and` *and* `or` *rather than* `&&` *and* `||` *is that if it used* `&&` *then the ampersands would have to be escaped when XPath was used with XSLT, so you'd end up with* `&&` *all over the place, which is pretty ugly! Like the rest of XPath,* `and` *and* `or` *are case-sensitive, so* `AND` *won't work, for example.*

For example, you could test whether a program both belongs to a series (a non-empty `<Series>` element) and has a title (a non-empty `<Title>` element) with the condition:

```
string(Series) and string(Title)
```

You can test whether a program either is flagged as a favorite (has a `flag` attribute with the value `favorite`) or has a high rating (has a `rating` attribute with a value greater than `6`) with the condition:

```
@flag = 'favorite' or @rating > 6
```

You can combine tests with the operators `and` and `or`.

Try It Out – Using Logical Operators to Highlight Interesting Programs

There are lots of factors that might make a program interesting to a user of the TV guide:

- Being flagged as interesting or a favorite
- Having a high rating
- Containing one of several keywords in its title or description

We can create a new version of the stylesheet, TVGuide9.xsl, which shows all the programs and highlights those interesting programs. If a program isn't interesting, then it is contained in an attribute-less <div> element, as in:

```
<div>
  <p>
    <span class="date">2001-07-05T21:30:00</span><br>
    <span class="title">Panorama</span><br>
  </p>
</div>
```

However, if it is interesting, then the <div> element should take a class attribute with the value interesting, as well as have any other icons attached to it as desired. For example, if "News" is a keyword, then the Channel 4 News should be highlighted with:

```
<div class="interesting">
  <p>
    <span class="date">2001-07-05T19:00:00</span><br>
    <span class="title">Channel4News</span><br>
  </p>
</div>
```

The TVGuide.css CSS stylesheet needs to be updated to pick up on these interesting programs. We'll create a new version, TVGuide2.css, which highlights them by giving them a yellow background, with the following rule:

```
div.interesting {
    background: yellow;
}
```

and remember to change the <link> element generated by TVGuide9.xsl so that it points to TVGuide2.css.

The template for the <Program> element in TVGuide9.xsl needs to test for the various conditions that make a program interesting, and use the relevant <div> element around the HTML for the program:

```
<xsl:template match="Program">
  <xsl:choose>
    <xsl:when test="@flag = 'favorite' or @flag = 'interesting' or
                    @rating > 6 or contains(Series, 'News') or
                    contains(Title, 'News') or
                    contains(Description, 'news')">
```

```
      <div class="interesting">...</div>
    </xsl:when>
    <xsl:otherwise>
      <div>...</div>
    </xsl:otherwise>
  </xsl:choose>
</xsl:template>
```

Adding conditional parent elements is difficult because it requires you to repeat the same content within the XSLT. In the above, the content of both `<div>` elements is the same. For now, we can get around this problem by using a template in `Details` mode that matches all `<Program>` elements and generates the content for them:

```
<xsl:template match="Program" mode="Details">
  <p>
    ...
  </p>
  <xsl:if test="CastList">
    ...
  </xsl:if>
</xsl:template>
```

In the main template for the `<Program>` elements, we can apply templates to the current node (the `<Program>` element) in `Details` mode to get the content of the two `<div>` elements.

```
<xsl:template match="Program">
  <xsl:choose>
    <xsl:when test="@flag = 'favorite' or @flag = 'interesting' or
                    @rating > 6 or contains(Series, 'News') or
                    contains(Title, 'News') or
                    contains(Description, 'news')">
      <div class="interesting">
        <xsl:apply-templates select="." mode="Details" />
      </div>
    </xsl:when>
    <xsl:otherwise>
      <div>
        <xsl:apply-templates select="." mode="Details" />
      </div>
    </xsl:otherwise>
  </xsl:choose>
</xsl:template>
```

We'll see a couple of other ways of handling the same problem in the next few chapters – with variables in Chapter 6 and using instructions that generate attributes independently of elements in Chapter 8. In Chapter 12 and later in Chapter 14, you'll also see how to enable a user to customize these kinds of queries according to their preferences.

The result of applying `TVGuide9.xsl` to `TVGuide2.xml` includes several highlighted programs, including EastEnders:

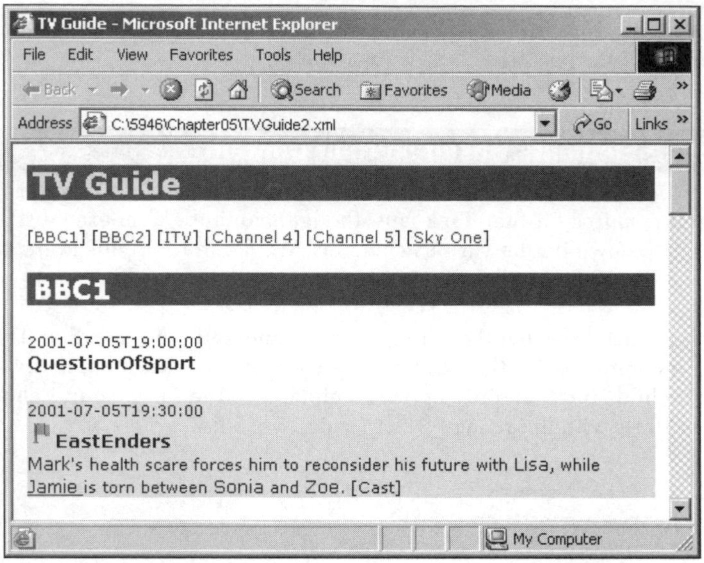

Other programs are highlighted if they're interesting, have a high rating, or if their series, title, or description contains the word "News".

Filtering XML

Thus far, this chapter has focused on using conditions to generate different content in different circumstances. You can also use these tests to only select particular elements and attributes based on their values (for example), so that you can apply templates to them, iterate over them, or get their values. You do this by placing the test in square brackets (`[]`) after the location path. The square brackets and the test inside them are known as a **predicate**.

For example, with the current node being a `<Channel>` element, you can select all `<Program>` elements that have a `flag` attribute with a value of `favorite` using the path:

```
Program[@flag = 'favorite']
```

The component `[@flag = 'favorite']` is a predicate that filters the `<Program>` elements returned by the rest of the path to include only those `<Program>` elements for which the condition is `true`. Without the predicate, the location path `Program` would return *all* the `<Program>` element children of the context node. With the predicate, the location path only returns those `<Program>` elements that have a `flag` attribute whose value is `favorite`. You can apply templates to only this filtered set of `<Program>` elements with the following `<xsl:apply-templates>` instruction:

```
<xsl:apply-templates select="Program[@flag = 'favorite']" />
```

As we'll see in Chapter 7, you can also use predicates in patterns, for example, to make a template match only a particular type of element based on the element's value.

You can filter a node set with a predicate, which is a test in square brackets. Nodes are only selected if the predicate is true for them.

Try It Out – Selecting Elements Based on their Content

In the previous sections, we've highlighted Star Trek episodes within the main program listing using icons. A more useful resource for Star Trek fans, though, would be a separate list including all the Star Trek episodes that are shown on the various channels. We'll aim to do this in the new stylesheet, `StarTrek.xsl`, which is based on `TVGuide9.xsl`.

The first change is to make sure that the listing for a channel only displays Star Trek episodes. We can do that by altering the template for the `<Channel>` elements, so that it explicitly applies templates to its `<Name>` element child, and then only applies templates to the `<Program>` elements whose `<Series>` element starts with the string `'StarTrek'`, as follows:

```
<xsl:template match="Channel">
  <xsl:apply-templates select="Name" />
  <xsl:apply-templates select="Program[starts-with(Series, 'StarTrek')]" />
</xsl:template>
```

The second problem is a bit trickier. In this new stylesheet, we only want to list a channel if any of the programs that it shows are Star Trek episodes. As we saw earlier, with the current node being a `<Channel>` element, the test:

```
starts-with(Program/Series, 'StarTrek')
```

will only test whether the first program showing on the channel is a Star Trek episode – it won't test whether there are *any* programs that are Star Trek episodes.

However, we've seen that we can make a node set made up of `<Program>` elements that represent Star Trek episodes, and we know that an empty node set evaluates as `false` when you use it as a test. Therefore, if we construct a node set containing the Star Trek episodes for a channel, we can find out whether there are any Star Trek episodes on that channel. We can do this inside the template for the `<Channel>` elements, as follows:

```
<xsl:template match="Channel">
  <xsl:if test="Program[starts-with(Series, 'StarTrek')]">
    <xsl:apply-templates select="Name" />
    <xsl:apply-templates
        select="Program[starts-with(Series, 'StarTrek')]" />
  </xsl:if>
</xsl:template>
```

We should make a similar change to the template in `ChannelList` mode, so the channel list at the top and bottom of the page only shows those channels showing Star Trek episodes as well:

```
<xsl:template match="Channel" mode="ChannelList">
  <xsl:if test="Program[starts-with(Series, 'StarTrek')]">
```

```
    [<a href="#{Name}"><xsl:value-of select="Name" /></a>]
  </xsl:if>
</xsl:template>
```

The result of applying `StarTrek.xsl` to `TVGuide2.xml` is shown in the following screenshot:

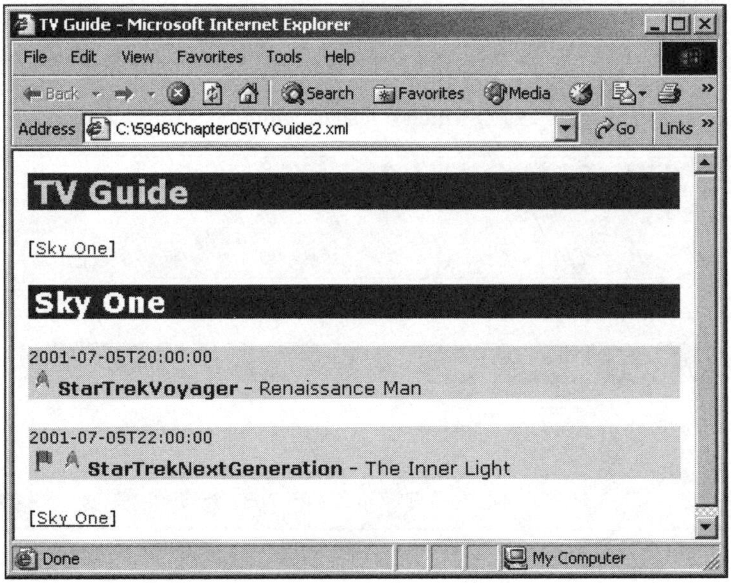

The only channel that's showing any Star Trek episodes is Sky One, so that's the only channel that gets shown in either the channel listing at the top and bottom of the page or the main body of the page.

Both Star Trek episodes are highlighted – the Voyager episode because it has a high rating, the Next Generation episode because it's flagged as a favorite program.

There's no prohibition on nesting predicates. Just as with the `<Program>` elements, rather than apply templates to all channels but only give a result for those that show Star Trek episodes, we could just apply templates to those channels that show Star Trek episodes. You can select the `<Channel>` elements that have a `<Program>` element child whose `<Series>` element child starts with the string `'StarTrek'` with the location path:

```
Channel[Program[starts-with(Series, 'StarTrek')]]
```

So, in another version of the stylesheet, `StarTrek2.xsl`, within a template for the `<TVGuide>` element, you can make sure that you only display information for channels that show Star Trek episodes, and give a message if there are no such channels, with the following:

```
<xsl:template match="TVGuide">
  <xsl:choose>
    <xsl:when test="Channel[Program[starts-with(Series, 'StarTrek')]]">
      <xsl:apply-templates
```

```
        select="Channel[Program[starts-with(Series, 'StarTrek')]]" />
    </xsl:when>
    <xsl:otherwise>
      <p>No Star Trek showing this week!</p>
    </xsl:otherwise>
  </xsl:choose>
</xsl:template>
```

When we use StarTrek2.xsl on TVGuide2.xml, we get exactly the same as we did before – Sky One is showing some Star Trek episodes, so it gets shown. On the other hand, if you try using StarTrek2.xsl with TVGuide.xml, which doesn't include Sky One, you should see the following:

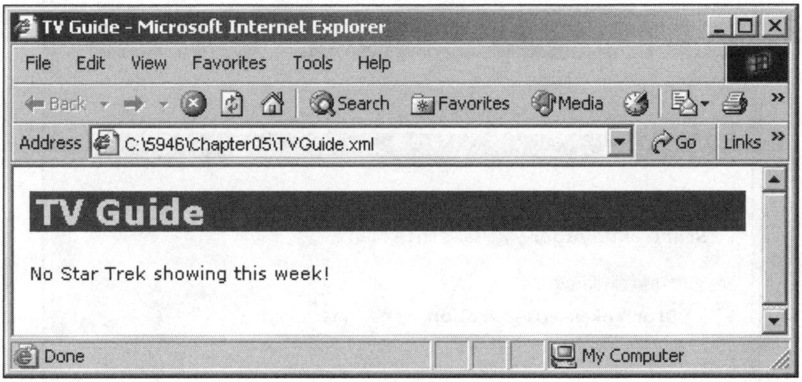

The stylesheet has detected that none of the channels are showing Star Trek episodes, and it's given a different message.

Testing Positions

The predicate can hold any expression, and it's usually evaluated as a boolean, just as if the expression were used in a test attribute. However, if the expression evaluates to a number then it's taken as the position of the node in the node set that you've selected with the beginning bit of the path. Have a look at the following XPath with the current node being a <Channel> element:

```
Program[1]
```

This expression selects just the first <Program> element in the list for the channel. You can use the last() function to get the last element in a list. For example, the following selects the last <CastMember> element in the <CastList>, assuming the current node is the <Program> element:

```
CastList/CastMember[last()]
```

Using a number in a predicate is actually shorthand for testing the number returned by the position() function. The two paths given above are shorthand for:

```
Program[position() = 1]
CastList/CastMember[position() = last()]
```

The `position()` function returns the index of the node you're looking at in the set of nodes that you're selecting. You can test whether the position of a node is in a particular range using less-than and greater-than operators. For example, with the `<TVGuide>` element as the current node, the following XPath applies templates to the third, fourth, and fifth `<Channel>` elements:

```
<xsl:apply-templates select="Channel[position() >= 3 and
                                  position() &lt;= 5]" />
```

You can also test the position of a node outside a predicate, in the `test` attribute of `<xsl:if>` or `<xsl:when>`. If you do so, you test the position of the current node (the node that the template matches) in the set of nodes that have had templates applied to them. We'll look at the implications of this in Chapter 9 when we look at sorting and numbering.

A numerical predicate indicates the position of the selected node; you can use the `last()` function to get the index of the last node in a list. You can also use the `position()` function to test the position of a node explicitly.

Try It Out – Testing the Position of Nodes

When we list the channels that are available in our TV guide, they are given in a line that looks like the following:

[BBC1] [BBC2] [ITV] [Channel 4] [Channel 5] [Sky One]

This formatting is easy because every channel is treated in exactly the same way. Instead, say we wanted to create the links separated by pipe symbols:

BBC1 | BBC2 | ITV | Channel 4 | Channel 5 | Sky One

With this formatting, every channel name has a pipe after it except the last channel, which doesn't have a pipe symbol. To create this format in `TVGuide10.xsl`, we need to add a pipe sign only if the channel isn't the last channel in the list. If you recall, we made this list of channels with a template matching `<Channel>` elements in `ChannelList` mode, which was applied to all `<Channel>` elements at once. In `TVGuide9.xsl`, this template looks like the following:

```
<xsl:template match="Channel" mode="ChannelList">
  [<a href="#{Name}"><xsl:value-of select="Name" /></a>]
</xsl:template>
```

We can change this template to add an `<xsl:if>` that adds a pipe symbol conditional on the position of the `<Channel>` element, as follows:

```
<xsl:template match="Channel" mode="ChannelList">
  <a href="#{Name}"><xsl:value-of select="Name" /></a>
  <xsl:if test="position() != last()"> | </xsl:if>
</xsl:template>
```

If you transform `TVGuide2.xml` with `TVGuide10.xsl`, you should get the following:

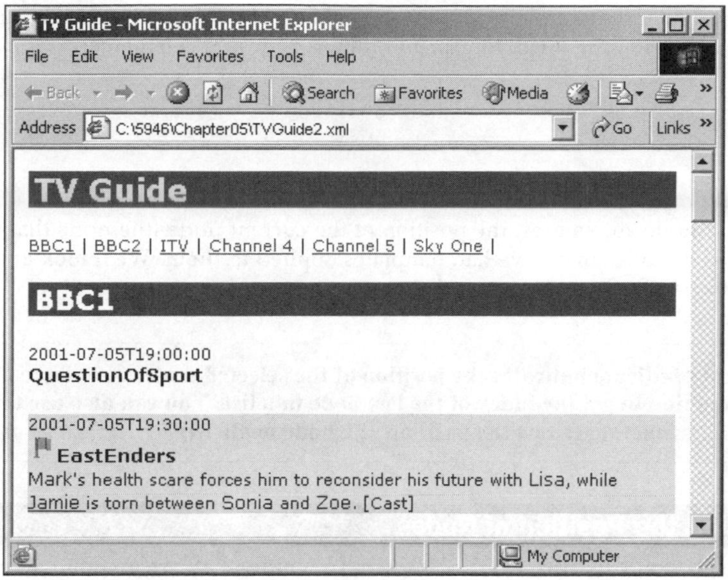

The channel names are separated by pipe symbols. The only channel that doesn't have a pipe symbol after its name is Sky One, because that's the last channel in the list.

> *This technique is often very handy when you're creating comma-separated or space-separated lists of values.*

Summary

This chapter has covered how to generate output conditionally, based on the presence of information in some source XML. You've learned how to generate different HTML dependent on:

- The presence or absence of elements and attributes
- The ancestry of an element or attribute
- The values of elements and attributes

You've seen two new XSLT instructions: `<xsl:if>` to generate optional content and `<xsl:choose>` to generate different content in different situations.

Both `<xsl:if>` and the `<xsl:when>` elements inside `<xsl:choose>` use a `test` attribute to hold an XPath expression that's interpreted as a boolean value. In this chapter, we introduced the four different value types that XPath expressions could evaluate as – booleans, numbers, strings, and node sets – and saw how each is converted to a boolean if you put it in a `test` attribute. You've also seen how to use the `boolean()`, `number()`, and `string()` functions to convert between the different value types.

Many tests involve comparing values, and you've learned about the six operators that enable you to do comparisons: =, !=, <, <=, >, and >=. You've discovered how to combine tests together with `and` and `or`, and negate them with the `not()` function. As well as testing the value of an element or attribute exactly, you've also seen how to test the content of a string using `starts-with()` and `contains()`.

The expressions that we've tried out in this chapter have been more complex than the ones we've looked at before. In particular, we've seen how to use predicates to filter node sets. We'll be looking in more detail at paths in Chapter 7, but in the next chapter we're going to investigate expressions in general more closely, and look at how to use variables and parameters within them.

Review Questions

1. What output do you get when you try to apply templates to a node that doesn't exist?

2. How can you use templates to generate different output for a `<Film>` element that's a descendant of a `<Description>` element and for a `<Film>` element that's a child of a `<Channel>` element?

3. What does the following code do?

```
<div>
  <xsl:apply-templates select="Film" />
  <xsl:if test="not(Film)">No films showing on this channel.</xsl:if>
</div>
```

4. Rewrite the preceding code using an `<xsl:choose>` element. What are the advantages and disadvantages of the two forms?

5. What does the following code do?

```
<xsl:choose>
  <xsl:when test="@flag = 'favorite'">
    <img src="favorite.gif" alt="[Favorite]" width="20" height="20" />
  </xsl:when>
  <xsl:when test="@flag = 'interesting'">
    <img src="interest.gif" alt="[Interest]" width="20" height="20" />
  </xsl:when>
  <xsl:when test="@flag">
    <img src="flag.gif" alt="[Flagged]" width="20" height="20" />
  </xsl:when>
</xsl:choose>
```

6. Rewrite the above code as a sequence of `<xsl:if>` elements. What are the advantages and disadvantages of the two forms?

7. Write an expression that tests whether any `<Film>` element children of the current node have a `year` attribute whose value is greater than `1950`.

8. Write an expression that selects all the `<Film>` element children of the current node whose `<Title>` element child starts with the string `'Romeo'`.

9. Write an expression that tests whether the current node's value is a non-zero number.

10. Write an expression that tests whether the current node's value is a number (including zero).

Beginning
XSLT

6

Variables, Expressions, and Parameters

The last chapter focused on how to create conditional content using XSLT, and along the way we introduced **XPath expressions**. XPath expressions are simple bits of code that a processor evaluates to get a value. XPath expressions are used by XSLT a lot, but other languages such as XPointer also use them. In the last chapter you learned about the four basic data types in XPath: booleans, numbers, strings, and node sets.

When XPath is used in XSLT, XPath expressions always reside in attributes. You've seen three classes of attributes that use XPath expressions so far:

- The `select` attributes of `<xsl:for-each>` and `<xsl:apply-templates>` point to nodes for the XSLT processor to process. The XPath expressions they hold must evaluate to node sets; these expressions are therefore called **node-set expressions**.
- The `select` attribute of `<xsl:value-of>` indicates some text that should be included in the result of the transformation. These XPath expressions are interpreted as strings and are therefore called **string expressions**.
- The `test` attributes of `<xsl:if>` and `<xsl:when>` give a condition that can be true or false. The XPath expressions they hold are interpreted as booleans; these expressions are therefore called **boolean expressions**.

Expressions can be fairly complicated. As you've seen, they can include **location paths** for accessing values from XML documents, **operators** for comparing values, and **functions** for testing values. As you start using more complex expressions, it soon becomes apparent that you need some way of storing the result of intermediate expressions, both to make the code easier to read and to enable you to reuse the same calculated value again and again. As with other programming languages, XSLT allows you to store these values within **variables**, which are the subject of this chapter. In this chapter, you'll learn:

- How to define variables using XSLT
- How to use variables within XPaths
- How to generate snippets of XML to reuse later on

- How to manipulate strings and numbers with new operators and functions
- How to declare and use parameters within templates

Defining Variables

Variables allow you to use a particular name to stand for a value within an expression. You define a variable in XSLT using an `<xsl:variable>` element. Each `<xsl:variable>` element usually has two attributes:

- `name` – specifies the name of the variable
- `select` – holds an expression that specifies the value of the variable

Variable names must follow the same rules as the names of attributes or elements, so they can't start with numbers, for example. The expression that you use in the `select` attribute can evaluate to any type of value. At the simplest level, you can just give a literal string or number, for example:

```
<xsl:variable name="daysInWeek" select="7" />
<xsl:variable name="myName" select="'Jeni Tennison'" />
```

If you set a variable to a string, remember to put either single or double quotes around the string, otherwise the XSLT processor will try to interpret the content of the string as an expression, which may result in an error or (if it's just one word) may be interpreted as a location path and evaluate to an empty node set. For example, `select="Program"` *assigns a node set of* `<Program>` *elements to the variable, whereas* `select="'Program'"` *assigns the string* `'Program'` *to the variable. You don't have to worry with numbers – element names can't start with a number, so XPath processors can tell that when you use a literal number, you mean that number rather than an element.*

In fact, you can use any expression you like to give the value of a variable. For example, you could set a variable to the node set containing all the `<Program>` element children of the current node using a location path, with:

```
<xsl:variable name="programs" select="Program" />
```

Or you could set a variable to a boolean value, `true` if the current program is interesting (has a `flag` attribute or a `rating` attribute with a value over 6), with:

```
<xsl:variable name="isInteresting" select="@flag or (@rating > 6)" />
```

Remember from the last chapter that you can use brackets around subexpressions if you want to make the priority of different operators explicit. In the above expression, the comparison `@rating > 6` *is performed first, and the true or false result is compared with the true or false result of the expression* `@flag` *(which tests whether a* `flag` *attribute is present).*

You can define a variable with the `<xsl:variable>` element; its `name` attribute specifies the name of the variable. The `select` attribute holds an expression that's evaluated to set the value of the variable.

Referring to Variables

Knowing how to set variables isn't much use if you don't know how to use them. Once you've declared a variable with a particular value, you can refer to that variable's value within another XPath expression using the variable's name prefixed with a dollar sign (`$`). Like most things in XML, variable names are case-sensitive.

I'm going to use the same syntax when I talk about variables in the explanatory text in this book. So when I say "`$minRating` has the value `6`" I mean that the variable named `minRating` has the value `6`.

As a simple example, you could use a variable to hold a number that indicates the minimum rating that a program can have for it to count as an interesting program:

```
<xsl:variable name="minRating" select="6" />
```

You can generate some output that gives that number using `<xsl:value-of>`, giving a variable reference in its `select` attribute:

```
Minimum rating: <xsl:value-of select="$minRating" />
```

The result would then be:

```
Minimum rating: 6
```

You could also use the `$minRating` variable within a larger expression, when testing whether a program is interesting or not in order to decide whether or not to generate some HTML for the program:

```
<xsl:if test="@rating > $minRating">
  ...
</xsl:if>
```

You can refer to a variable within an expression by prefixing its name with a dollar sign. Names are case-sensitive as usual. When the expression is evaluated, the processor uses the value of the variable in place of the reference.

Try It Out – Reusing Node Sets

Variables can make your XSLT more efficient if you use them to hold values that you use more than once in your code, especially if those values are time-consuming for the XSLT processor to evaluate, such as complicated location paths. In the last chapter, we looked at filtering `TVGuide.xml` to generate a page that only listed Star Trek programs and the channels that show them with `StarTrek.xsl`.

The template for <Channel> elements in this stylesheet is as follows:

```
<xsl:template match="Channel">
  <xsl:if test="Program[starts-with(Series, 'StarTrek')]">
    <xsl:apply-templates select="Name" />
    <xsl:apply-templates
      select="Program[starts-with(Series, 'StarTrek')]" />
  </xsl:if>
</xsl:template>
```

As you can see, the expression `Program[starts-with(Series, 'Star Trek')]` is used twice in the above template, once to test whether there are any Star Trek programs showing on the channel and once (if there are such) to apply templates to those programs. Evaluating this expression could be fairly time-consuming because the XSLT processor has to go through all the <Program> element children of the <Channel> element to locate the relevant ones. Therefore, you don't want to evaluate this location path twice if you can help it. Instead, you could use a variable to hold the resulting node set and then refer to it in the two different locations. We'll do this in the next version of this stylesheet, in StarTrek2.xsl.

First, you need to set up a $StarTrekPrograms variable to hold all the Star Trek programs that are showing on a particular channel. The select attribute needs to hold a location path that points to all the <Program> element children of the current <Channel> element whose <Series> child starts with the string 'Star Trek', as follows:

```
<xsl:template match="Channel">
  <xsl:variable name="StarTrekPrograms"
                select="Program[starts-with(Series, 'StarTrek')]" />
  ...
</xsl:template>
```

As we'll see in the next section, you'll only be able to use this variable within this template.

Then you need to substitute the path where it's used in the test attribute of the <xsl:if> and in the select attribute of the <xsl:apply-templates> instruction with a reference to the $StarTrekPrograms variable:

```
<xsl:template match="Channel">
  <xsl:variable name="StarTrekPrograms"
                select="Program[starts-with(Series, 'StarTrek')]" />
  <xsl:if test="$StarTrekPrograms">
    <xsl:apply-templates select="Name" />
    <xsl:apply-templates select="$StarTrekPrograms" />
  </xsl:if>
</xsl:template>
```

The result of running StarTrek2.xsl with TVGuide.xml is just the same as the one you get when using StarTrek.xsl:

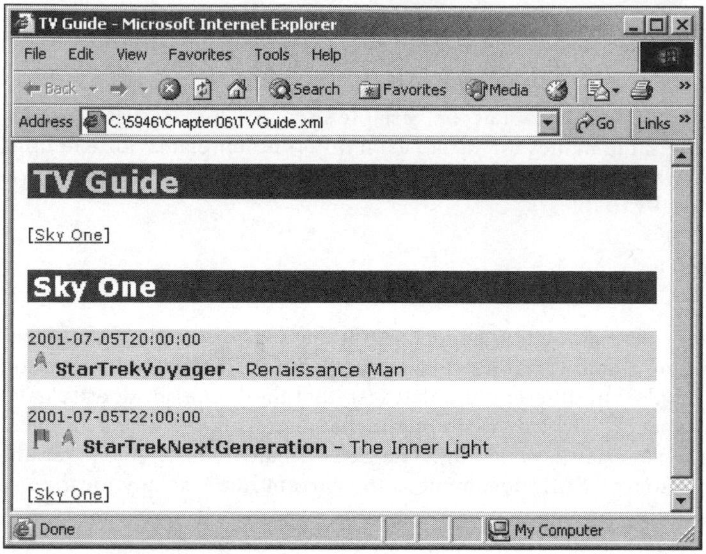

You probably won't notice the difference, but it's likely to run slightly faster. Moreover, making this change has the benefit that you only have to write the complex XPath expression once, which makes it easier to maintain – if you make a mistake in it, or if you want to change it later on, you only have to adjust it in one location rather than two.

You can make the same kind of change to the template for the `<TVGuide>` element where you tell the user when there are no Star Trek programs showing. The next version of the stylesheet, `StarTrek3.xsl`, contains the following:

```
<xsl:template match="TVGuide">
  <xsl:variable name="StarTrekChannels"
    select="Channel[Program[starts-with(Series, 'StarTrek')]]" />
  <xsl:choose>
    <xsl:when test="$StarTrekChannels">
      <xsl:apply-templates select="$StarTrekChannels" />
    </xsl:when>
    <xsl:otherwise>
      <p>No Star Trek showing this week!</p>
    </xsl:otherwise>
  </xsl:choose>
</xsl:template>
```

Again, it generates exactly the same result, but is likely to be fractionally faster, and quite a bit easier to maintain.

Variable Scope

Where you declare a variable determines where you can refer to it. The area of the stylesheet in which a variable can be referred to is known as the variable's **scope**. The fact that variables have different scopes allows you to use the same names for variables in different templates, for example. You can define variables at two levels in XSLT: at the top level of the stylesheet, to give global variables, or within a template, to give local variables.

Global Variables

Variables that you declare at the top level of a stylesheet (as direct children of the `<xsl:stylesheet>` element) are known as **global variables**. Typically, global variables hold either constants or values that are used across a number of different templates (so that the processor doesn't have to evaluate them each time) or constants or values that you might change during the course of developing the stylesheet (to make the stylesheet easier to maintain). The `select` attribute of global variables is interpreted with the root node of the source XML document as the current node, so any location paths that you use should be relative to the root node.

I normally use absolute location paths when I set global variables.

The order in which you declare global variables doesn't matter. For example, in the following code the `$channelsShowingSeries` variable holds those channels that show programs in the series whose name is held in the `$series` variable. The `$channelsShowingSeries` variable can be declared before the `$series` variable despite the fact that it refers to it (although it would be clearer if it weren't).

```
<xsl:variable name="channelsShowingSeries"
  select="/TVGuide/Channel[Program[starts-with(Series, $series)]]" />
<xsl:variable name="series" select="'Star Trek'" />
```

However, you cannot have two global variables with the same name in the same stylesheet (or in included stylesheets, as we'll see in Chapter 12), and you cannot have circular references, where the value of one variable relies on the value of another variable, which relies on the first variable. For example, if you had variables to hold information about the size of a table, it would be an error to have them all depend on each other, as follows:

```
<xsl:variable name="rows" select="$cells div $columns" />
<xsl:variable name="columns" select="$cells div $rows" />
<xsl:variable name="cells" select="$rows * $columns" />
```

Global variables are declared at the top level of the stylesheet and are visible throughout the stylesheet.

Local Variables

Variables that you declare within a template are known as **local variables**. Local variables are only accessible within the template in which they're declared, so you can't declare a variable in one template and then access it from another (you need to use parameters, which we'll come to later in this chapter, if you find yourself needing to do that).

What's more, a local variable is only accessible to the `<xsl:variable>` element's following siblings and their descendants, not to everything within the template. For example, we are currently using the following template to generate HTML for the details of the TV programs in `TVGuide.xsl`:

```
<xsl:template match="Program" mode="Details">
  <p>
    ...
    <xsl:apply-templates select="CastList" mode="DisplayToggle" />
  </p>
  <xsl:apply-templates select="CastList" />
</xsl:template>
```

The `<CastList>` element is referred to twice within the template: once to generate the cast list itself and once to generate a clickable piece of text to toggle the display of the cast list. We could hold the `<CastList>` element child of the `<Program>` element within a variable, as follows:

```
<xsl:variable name="castList" select="CastList" />
```

We would then be able to refer to it in the two `<xsl:apply-templates>` instructions rather than using the path directly. However, we need to position the variable declaration so that both `<xsl:apply-templates>` instructions follow the variable declaration, either as siblings or as children of their siblings. If we put it just before the first `<xsl:apply-templates>`, as in `TVGuide2.xsl`, which contains:

```
<xsl:template match="Program" mode="Details">
  <p>
    ...
    <xsl:variable name="castList" select="CastList" />
    <xsl:apply-templates select="$castList" mode="DisplayToggle" />
  </p>
  <xsl:apply-templates select="$castList" />
</xsl:template>
```

we would run into problems because the second `<xsl:apply-templates>` is at a higher level in the tree than the variable declaration. If you try to run the stylesheet with this template, the XSLT processor should complain that there is no `$castList` variable in scope. For example, when running Saxon, you will see:

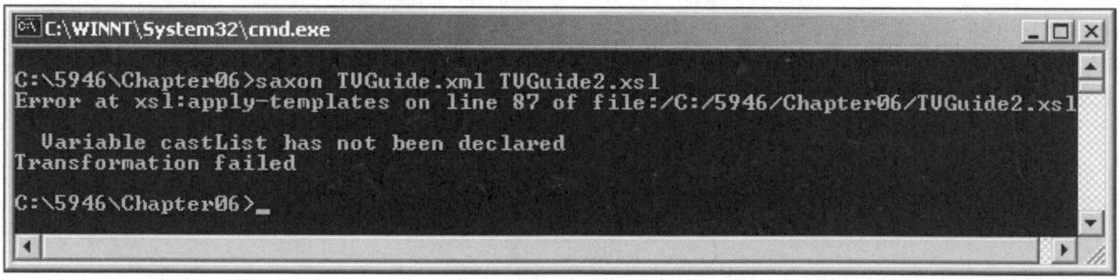
C:\WINNT\System32\cmd.exe
C:\5946\Chapter06>saxon TVGuide.xml TVGuide2.xsl
Error at xsl:apply-templates on line 87 of file:/C:/5946/Chapter06/TVGuide2.xsl
Variable castList has not been declared
Transformation failed
C:\5946\Chapter06>_

There's a bug in MSXML (versions 3 and 4) that prevents it from recognizing this as an error.

The only legal location for the variable declaration to make it visible to both `<xsl:apply-templates>` instructions is just before the `<p>` element, as in `TVGuide3.xsl`, as follows:

```
<xsl:template match="Program" mode="Details">
  <xsl:variable name="castList" select="CastList" />
  <p>
    <xsl:apply-templates select="Series" /><br />
    <xsl:apply-templates select="Description" />
    <xsl:apply-templates select="$castList" mode="DisplayToggle" />
  </p>
  <xsl:apply-templates select="$castList" />
</xsl:template>
```

As with global variables, you cannot declare a variable if a local variable with the same name is in scope, so if you declare the `$castList` local variable at the start of a template, as above, you cannot declare another variable called `$castList` within that template. However, you can declare a local variable that has the same name as an existing global variable; this is known as **shadowing**. Within the scope of the local variable, its value is used instead of the value of the global variable.

> **Local variables are declared within templates and are only visible to their following siblings and their descendants. A local variable can shadow a global variable.**

Try It Out – Declaring Global and Local Variables

To try out the distinction between global and local variables, let's try declaring some variables in `StarTrek4.xsl`. First, we'll create a global variable to hold the name of the series (`'StarTrek'`). This variable declaration goes at the top level of the stylesheet, as a direct child of the `<xsl:stylesheet>` element, as follows:

```
<xsl:stylesheet version="1.0"
                xmlns:xsl="http://www.w3.org/1999/XSL/Transform">

<xsl:variable name="series" select="'StarTrek'" />
...
</xsl:stylesheet>
```

We can use this `$series` variable wherever we want. There are three locations where we need to know the series that we want to look at. The first one is within the template for the `<TVGuide>` element, to identify those channels that show programs from the series. Here, we're putting these channels into a `$StarTrekChannels` variable, which is defined locally within the `<TVGuide>` template:

```
<xsl:template match="TVGuide">
  <xsl:variable name="StarTrekChannels"
                select="Channel[Program[starts-with(Series, $series)]]" />
  <xsl:choose>
    <xsl:when test="$StarTrekChannels">
      <xsl:apply-templates select="$StarTrekChannels" />
    </xsl:when>
```

```
    <xsl:otherwise>
      <p>No Star Trek showing this week!</p>
    </xsl:otherwise>
  </xsl:choose>
</xsl:template>
```

The second is within the template matching the <Channel> elements. We know that this template will only be called if the channel shows programs in the relevant series, so we can get rid of the <xsl:if> that we had before, but we still want to identify those programs so that we only apply templates to the relevant <Program> elements, as follows:

```
<xsl:template match="Channel">
  <xsl:apply-templates select="Name" />
  <xsl:apply-templates select="Program[starts-with(Series, $series)]" />
</xsl:template>
```

The third is within the template matching the <Channel> elements in ChannelList mode, to give the list of channels at the top and bottom of the page:

```
<xsl:template match="Channel" mode="ChannelList">
  <xsl:if test="Program[starts-with(Series, $series)]">
    [<a href="#{Name}"><xsl:value-of select="Name" /></a>]
  </xsl:if>
</xsl:template>
```

All three templates use the value from the global $series variable. Run StarTrek4.xsl, in which the $series variable is set to 'StarTrek', and you'll get a page that shows the Star Trek programs:

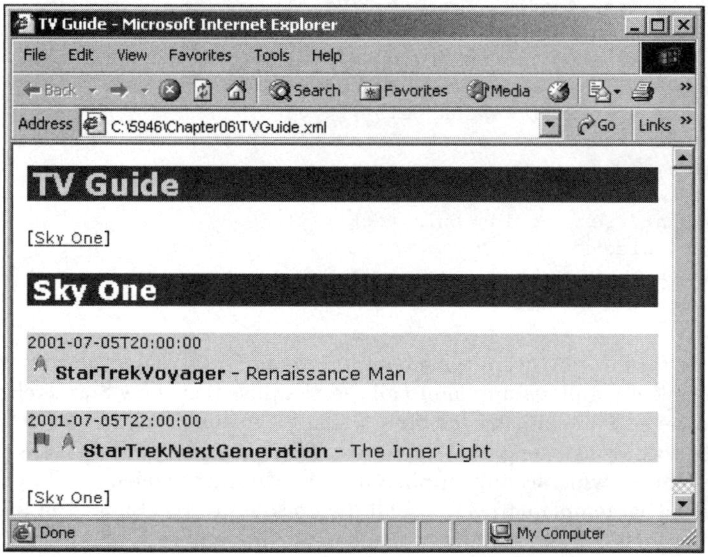

On the other hand, if you make a copy of StarTrek4.xsl, called EastEnders.xsl, in which the $series variable takes the value 'EastEnders', you'll get a page showing only EastEnders episodes:

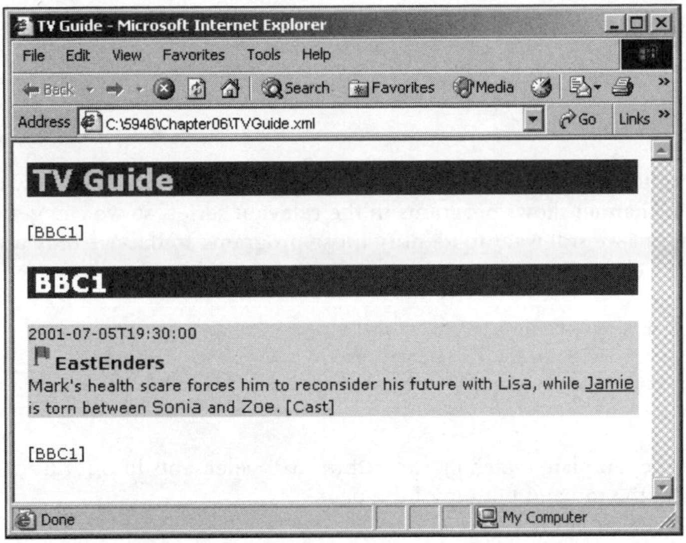

Now we'll shadow the `$series` variable within the template for the `<TVGuide>` element, in `StarTrek5.xsl`. We'll set the global variable to `'EastEnders'` but have a local variable of the same name set to `'StarTrek'` as follows:

```
<xsl:variable name="series" select="'EastEnders'" />

<xsl:template match="TVGuide">
  <xsl:variable name="series" select="'StarTrek'" />
  <xsl:variable name="StarTrekChannels"
                select="Channel[Program[starts-with(Series, $series)]]" />
  <xsl:choose>
    <xsl:when test="$StarTrekChannels">
      <xsl:apply-templates select="$StarTrekChannels" />
    </xsl:when>
    <xsl:otherwise>
      <p>No Star Trek showing this week!</p>
    </xsl:otherwise>
  </xsl:choose>
</xsl:template>
```

Within the template for the `<TVGuide>` element, the `$series` variable is set to the string `'StarTrek'`, so we get templates applied to all the channels that show Star Trek programs, which is only Sky One. However, the templates for the `<Channel>` element don't have local definitions of the `$series` variable, so they use the global definition. The main part of the page is provided by the template in default mode, which is only applied to one `<Channel>` element (Sky One, since it shows Star Trek episodes). That template tries to list all the episodes of EastEnders on the channel. Unfortunately, there aren't any EastEnders episodes showing on Sky One, so we end up with no programs being listed for Sky One. On the other hand, the template in `ChannelList` mode is applied to all the channels, but only provides links to those showing EastEnders episodes, so we get BBC1 listed at the top and bottom of the page. The result is as follows:

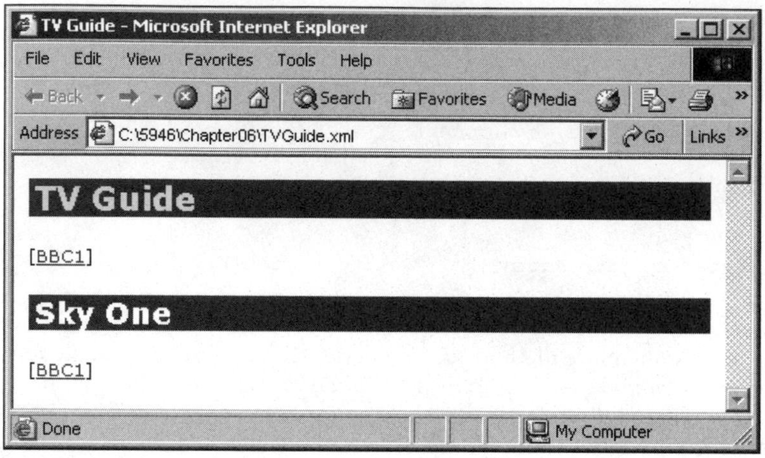

Loops and Counters

XSLT variables have one quite peculiar feature: they can't vary. Once you've set the value of a local variable, it remains the same throughout its scope. This can appear strange, particularly if you're used to programming with procedural languages, such as JavaScript, but it does not limit what you can do with XSLT because there are other methods for achieving the same goals.

A common use of variables in procedural programming languages is in loops that use counters to index into arrays. For example, when programming with a document object model (DOM) in JavaScript we could iterate over the `<Channel>` children of a `<TVGuide>` element with the following code:

```
var TVGuide = document.documentElement;
var Channels = TVGuide.getElementsByTagName('Channel');
for (var i = 0; i < Channels.length; i++) {
  var Channel = Channels.item(i);
  ...
}
```

In XSLT, the `<xsl:for-each>` element is specifically oriented towards iterating over nodes, so the equivalent code in XSLT would look something like the following:

```
<xsl:variable name="TVGuide" select="/TVGuide" />
<xsl:variable name="Channels" select="$TVGuide/Channel" />
<xsl:for-each select="$Channels">
  <xsl:variable name="Channel" select="." />
  ...
</xsl:for-each>
```

Variables that act as counters in procedural programming languages can be useful in numbering the items that they count, and in counting or summing them. For example, in JavaScript we could iterate over the programs shown on a channel, counting them and keeping track of the total rating for the channel as follows:

```
var Programs = Channel.getElementsByTagName('Program');
var count = 0;
var rating = 0;
for (; count < Programs.length; count++) {
  var Program = Programs.item(count);
  rating = rating + parseInt(Program.getAttribute('rating'));
  document.write(count);
  ...
}
document.write('Average Rating: ' + rating / count);
```

You've already seen how to find the number of an item in XSLT using the `position()` function in the last chapter (we'll see some more methods in Chapter 9). XPath also has specific functions for counting the number of nodes in a node set – the `count()` function – and for summing the numeric values of nodes – the `sum()` function. Both functions take a single argument – a node set containing the nodes to count or to sum as appropriate. Here's the equivalent to the above JavaScript, in XSLT:

```
<xsl:variable name="Programs" select="$Channel/Program" />
<xsl:for-each select="$Programs">
  <xsl:variable name="Program" select="." />
  <xsl:value-of select="position()" />
  ...
</xsl:for-each>
Average Rating: <xsl:value-of select="sum($Programs/@rating) div
                                      count($Programs)" />
```

The average is calculated by dividing the sum of the programs' ratings by the number of programs, using the `div` operator, which we'll look at later in this chapter. Note that you can use a node set held in a variable as if that node set was created directly from the original location path: `$Programs/@rating` gives you the `rating` attributes of the nodes held in the `$Programs` variable, in this case exactly the same as `($Channel/Program)/@rating`.

If you've done a lot of procedural programming, you might find the transition to using XSLT a bit confusing because you need to change the way that you think about problems. But you can usually get the result that you're after fairly easily despite the fact that XSLT variables cannot be updated. In more complex cases, you may have to use recursive templates, which is something that we'll look at in Chapter 11.

Once a variable's value is set, it cannot be changed. But you can number nodes using the `position()` function, count nodes with the `count()` function, and sum their values with the `sum()` function.

Try It Out – Counting the Number of Star Trek Episodes

Let's try out counting nodes by providing a count of the number of Star Trek episodes found within `TVGuide.xml`, using a new version of our stylesheet, `StarTrek6.xsl` (based on `StarTrek4.xsl`). When we do find channels showing Star Trek episodes, we'll state how many Star Trek episodes are being shown. For example:

There is 1 Star Trek episode showing this week.
There are 2 Star Trek episodes showing this week.

In the template for the <TVGuide> element, we can find all the Star Trek episodes, no matter what channel they're being shown on, with the following location path:

```
Channel/Program[starts-with(Series, $series)]
```

To count how many episodes there are, we can pass this node set of <Program> elements as the argument to the `count()` variable as follows:

```
count(Channel/Program[starts-with(Series, $series)]
```

Now we need to change the wording slightly depending on whether there's only one Star Trek episode or more than one Star Trek episode, which means using that count at least twice, so we'll store the count in a variable, `$NumberOfStarTrekEpisodes`:

```
<xsl:variable name="NumberOfStarTrekEpisodes"
  select="count(Channel/Program[starts-with(Series, $series)])" />
```

We'll also create another variable, `$Plural`, which will be a boolean – `true` if the number of Star Trek episodes is more than one, `false` otherwise:

```
<xsl:variable name="Plural" select="$NumberOfStarTrekEpisodes > 1" />
```

Now we can create the sentence that we want using a combination of literal text, conditional statements, and <xsl:value-of> instructions. We can use the `$Plural` variable to judge whether we need "are" or "is", and whether we need an "s" at the end of "episodes":

```
<p>
  There
  <xsl:choose>
    <xsl:when test="$Plural">are </xsl:when>
    <xsl:otherwise>is </xsl:otherwise>
  </xsl:choose>
  <xsl:value-of select="$NumberOfStarTrekEpisodes" />
  Star Trek episode<xsl:if test="$Plural">s</xsl:if>
  showing this week.
</p>
```

Putting this all together in the template for the <TVGuide> element in `StarTrek6.xsl`, we get:

```
<xsl:template match="TVGuide">
  <xsl:variable name="StarTrekChannels"
    select="Channel[Program[starts-with(Series, $series)]]" />
  <xsl:choose>
    <xsl:when test="$StarTrekChannels">
      <xsl:variable name="NumberOfStarTrekEpisodes"
        select="count(Channel/Program[starts-with(Series, $series)])" />
      <xsl:variable name="Plural" select="$NumberOfStarTrekEpisodes > 1" />
      <p>
```

```
        There
        <xsl:choose>
          <xsl:when test="$Plural">are </xsl:when>
          <xsl:otherwise>is </xsl:otherwise>
        </xsl:choose>
        <xsl:value-of select="$NumberOfStarTrekEpisodes" />
        Star Trek episode<xsl:if test="$Plural">s</xsl:if>
        showing this week.
      </p>
      <xsl:apply-templates select="$StarTrekChannels" />
    </xsl:when>
    <xsl:otherwise>
      <p>No Star Trek showing this week!</p>
    </xsl:otherwise>
  </xsl:choose>
</xsl:template>
```

The result of transforming `TVGuide.xml` with `StarTrek6.xsl` is as follows:

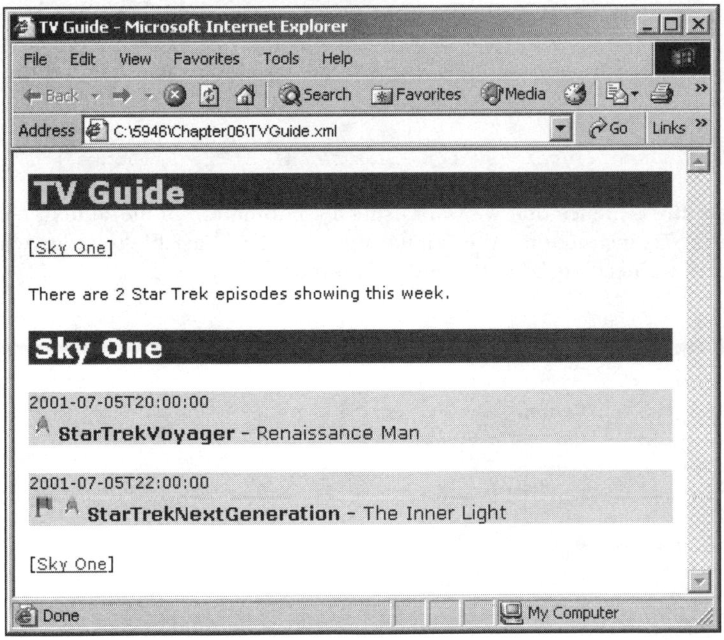

Result Tree Fragments

So far we've looked at how to use `<xsl:variable>` to define variables that have boolean, numeric, string, and node-set values. As you'll remember, these are the only types of values that are defined in XPath. However, XSLT defines another type of value: **result tree fragments**. Result tree fragments are bits of XML that are intended for the result tree. They are much like miniature node trees except for one thing: you can only ever access the root node of that miniature node tree – once you create a result tree fragment, you cannot use a location path to access its root node's descendants. As a result, the main use of result tree fragments is for holding snippets of XML that you want copied into the result tree later on.

You create a variable that holds a result tree fragment by using the content of the `<xsl:variable>` element rather than the `select` attribute. For example, the following variable declaration sets the `$flagImage` variable to a result tree fragment comprising a root node with a single `<img>` element child:

```
<xsl:variable name="flagImage">
  <img src="flag.gif" alt="[Flagged]" width="20" height="20" />
</xsl:variable>
```

The result tree fragment held by the `$flagImage` variable looks like the following:

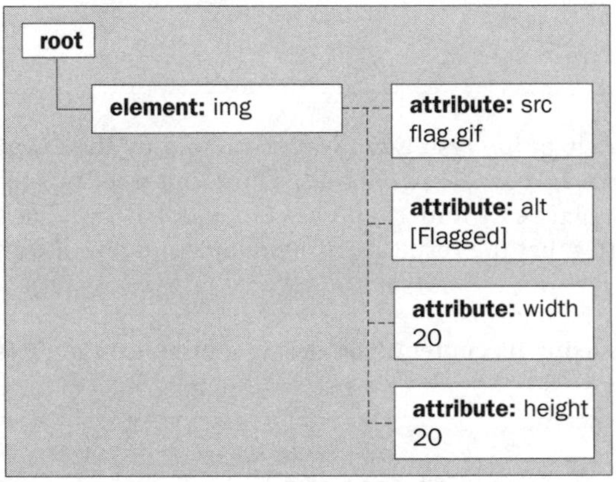

In the node tree that's generated from an XML document, you can only have one element child of the root node, and the root node cannot have any text children or attributes – if you remember from Chapter 2, that's one of the definitions of a well-formed XML document. On the other hand, the root node of a result tree fragment can have as many child elements as you like, and can have text nodes as children, or it can even have no children at all. However, like the root node of the source document, the root node of a result tree fragment cannot have any attributes.

Technically, a result tree fragment, like the full result tree itself, must be a well-formed external parsed entity. This means that the root node's children are limited in exactly the same way as an element's children are limited.

The ability of the root node of a result tree fragment to have multiple element nodes and text nodes as children is very useful. One way in which it's handy is that a result tree fragment can contain some document-oriented XML, containing a mixture of text and elements. For example:

```
<xsl:variable name="copyright">
  Copyright <a href="mailto:jeni@jenitennison.com">Jeni Tennison</a>, 2002
</xsl:variable>
```

The result tree fragment held by the `$copyright` variable looks like the following:

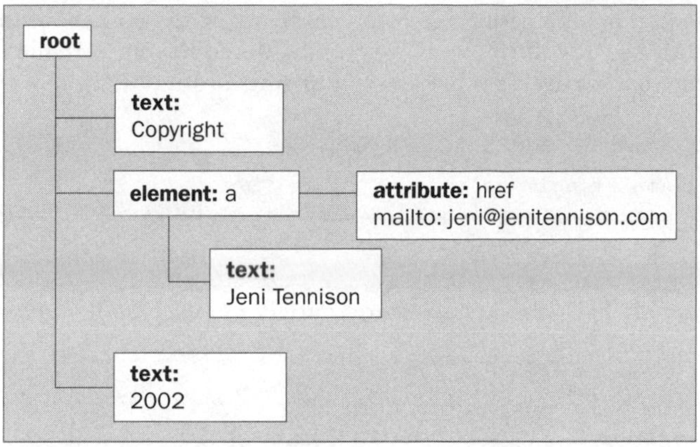

As you can see, the root node of the result tree fragment held by the `$copyright` variable has two text nodes as children, as well as an `<a>` element child. The result tree fragment held by `$copyright` could be copied to several places, or it might be held in a global variable so that it can be altered easily as required. It doesn't matter that the result tree fragment is not a well-formed XML document.

> **If you set a variable using its content, you create a miniature node tree called a "result tree fragment".**

Converting from Result Tree Fragments

When we looked at the basic XPath value types (booleans, numbers, strings, and node sets) in the last chapter, we looked at how each of the types are converted to each of the other types. Knowing how the different value types get converted to each other is useful because XPath is a weakly typed language and you won't get errors if you try to do things which don't make sense; if you're not getting the results that you want, you need to be able to work out what's going on.

When it comes to conversions to the other value types, result tree fragments are treated like a node set consisting of a single root node. Thus you get the following results when converting to the different types:

- Converting to a boolean always gives the value `true`, because the result tree fragment always has a root node
- Converting to a string gives the concatenation of all the text nodes within the result tree fragment (the string value of the root node)
- Converting to a number gives the result of converting the string value of the result tree fragment to a number

You cannot convert a result tree fragment to a node set within XSLT 1.0. However, it turns out that being able to do this is really useful because it allows you to split a transformation into several steps, making complex transformations a lot more straightforward. For this reason, almost every XSLT processor implements an extension function that does the conversion for you; we'll look at these extension functions and how to use them in Chapter 13.

The conversion of a result tree fragment to a node set will almost certainly become automatic in XSLT 2.0. The concept of a result tree fragment was dropped in the XSLT 1.1 Working Draft, and remains absent in the XSLT 2.0 Working Draft as it stands.

These conversions (or lack of conversions) often lead to unexpected errors. For example, imagine if you had the following variable definition:

```
<xsl:variable name="rating">
  <xsl:value-of select="@rating">
</xsl:variable>
```

The `$rating` variable holds a result tree fragment. If the `rating` attribute exists, then the root node of the result tree fragment has a single text node as its child, whose value is the value of the `rating` attribute. If the `rating` attribute is not present, then the root node does not have any children.

What happens if you do the following?

```
<xsl:if test="$rating">
  Rating: <xsl:value-of select="$rating" />
</xsl:if>
```

When you test the value of the `$rating` variable, the result tree fragment gets converted to a boolean value. Since the result tree fragment always holds a root node, the boolean value is always true, and you always get the content of the `<xsl:if>`, even when there was no `rating` attribute. Instead, you need to convert the `$rating` variable to a string, and test whether the string has any characters in it, with:

```
<xsl:if test="string($rating)">
  Rating: <xsl:value-of select="$rating" />
</xsl:if>
```

Or you could change the way the `$rating` variable is defined, using the `select` attribute of `<xsl:variable>` rather than its content:

```
<xsl:variable name="rating" select="@rating" />
```

Now say that the `$rating` variable was defined as follows:

```
<xsl:variable name="rating">
  <span class="rating"><xsl:value-of select="@rating"></span>
</xsl:variable>
```

What happens to the `<span>` element when you do the following?

```
<xsl:value-of select="$rating" />
```

The `<xsl:value-of>` instruction gets the string value of the `$rating` variable, by converting the result tree fragment that it contains to a string. All you get is the string value of the `rating` attribute and the `<span>` element is lost. You need to do a full copy of the `$rating` variable, with the `<xsl:copy-of>` instruction (which we meet in the next section), if you want to keep the `<span>` element:

```
<xsl:copy-of select="$rating" />
```

Finally, what happens if you try to find the `class` of the `<span>` element that you've created with the following?

```
<xsl:value-of select="$rating/span/@class" />
```

Most processors will raise an error if you try to do this, because using the `$rating` variable at the start of a location path means converting the result tree fragment to a node set, and that's not allowed. You need to use an extension function (which we'll look at in Chapter 13).

Processors that do allow you to use result tree fragments at the beginning of a location path are probably implementing the XSLT 1.1 or XSLT 2.0 Working Drafts.

Outputting Result Tree Fragments

One way in which result tree fragments are useful is that you can make a variable that holds a fragment of the result node tree, and then output the same nodes in multiple locations within the output. To use a result tree fragment in this way you have to copy it using the `<xsl:copy-of>` instruction.

The `<xsl:copy-of>` instruction has a single `select` attribute which holds an expression. If the expression evaluates as a node set or as a result tree fragment then the nodes in the node set or result tree fragment are copied to the output.

If the `select` attribute of `<xsl:copy-of>` evaluates to a boolean, number, or string, then the value is converted to a string and is output.

For example, we can set up global variables to hold the `<img>` elements that we want to copy to the output if a program is flagged or is a Star Trek episode:

```
<xsl:variable name="FavoriteFlag">
  <img src="favorite.gif" alt="[Favorite]" width="20" height="20" />
</xsl:variable>

<xsl:variable name="InterestingFlag">
  <img src="interest.gif" alt="[Interest]" width="20" height="20" />
</xsl:variable>

<xsl:variable name="StarTrekLogo">
  <img src="StarTrek.gif" alt="[Star Trek]" width="20" height="20" />
</xsl:variable>
```

These variables are global, so we can refer to them from anywhere within the stylesheet. The template for the `<Program>` element in `TVGuide4.xsl` looks as follows:

```
<xsl:template match="Program" mode="Details">
  <p>
    <xsl:apply-templates select="Start" /><br />
    <xsl:choose>
```

```
        <xsl:when test="@flag = 'favorite'">
          <xsl:copy-of select="$FavoriteFlag" />
        </xsl:when>
        <xsl:when test="@flag = 'interesting'">
          <xsl:copy-of select="$InterestingFlag" />
        </xsl:when>
      </xsl:choose>
      <xsl:if test="starts-with(Series, 'StarTrek')">
        <xsl:copy-of select="$StarTrekLogo" />
      </xsl:if>
      <xsl:apply-templates select="." mode="Title" />
      <br />
      <xsl:apply-templates select="Description" />
      <xsl:apply-templates select="CastList" mode="DisplayToggle" />
    </p>
    <xsl:apply-templates select="CastList" />
  </xsl:template>
```

The content of an `<xsl:variable>` element can contain any instructions, including other `<xsl:variable>` elements; they are evaluated to give the result tree fragment.

> **You can reuse XML from the source document or from a result tree fragment by copying it into the result tree using the `<xsl:copy-of>` instruction.**

Try It Out – Repeating Channel Lists

When we create our TV listing with `TVGuide4.xsl`, we have a list of the channels shown at the top and bottom of the page, to help the person reading the page to navigate to the channel they want to look at. We generate these channel lists by applying templates in `ChannelList` mode in the template for the root node, as follows:

```
<xsl:template match="/">
  <html>
    <head>
      ...
    </head>
    <body>
      <h1>TV Guide</h1>
      <p>
        <xsl:apply-templates mode="ChannelList" />
      </p>
      <xsl:apply-templates />
      <p>
        <xsl:apply-templates mode="ChannelList" />
      </p>
    </body>
  </html>
</xsl:template>
```

Each time the XSLT processor encounters these <xsl:apply-templates> instructions, it navigates the source node tree and constructs a list of channels using the following template:

```
<xsl:template match="Channel" mode="ChannelList">
  <a href="#{Name}"><xsl:value-of select="Name" /></a>
  <xsl:if test="position() != last()"> | </xsl:if>
</xsl:template>
```

Exactly the same HTML is generated each time templates are applied in ChannelList mode – we are performing exactly the same transformation twice over. Instead, we can store the results of doing the transformation in a variable and then copy this result into the HTML page wherever we want.

We'll make this change in TVGuide5.xsl, and make it a global variable because that will enable us to add the same channel list at other locations within our page if we want to later on (such as prior to the program listing for each channel). We want the variable to hold the result of applying templates in ChannelList mode, so we use the content of the <xsl:variable> element to set the variable value:

```
<xsl:variable name="ChannelList">
  <p><xsl:apply-templates mode="ChannelList" /></p>
</xsl:variable>
```

To copy the value of that variable into the result HTML, you need the <xsl:copy-of> instruction. This replaces the original <xsl:apply-templates> elements in the template that matches the root node, as follows:

```
<xsl:template match="/">
  <html>
    <head>
     ...
    </head>
    <body>
      <h1>TV Guide</h1>
      <xsl:copy-of select="$ChannelList" />
      <xsl:apply-templates />
      <xsl:copy-of select="$ChannelList" />
    </body>
  </html>
</xsl:template>
```

Try transforming TVGuide.xml with TVGuide5.xsl. You should get:

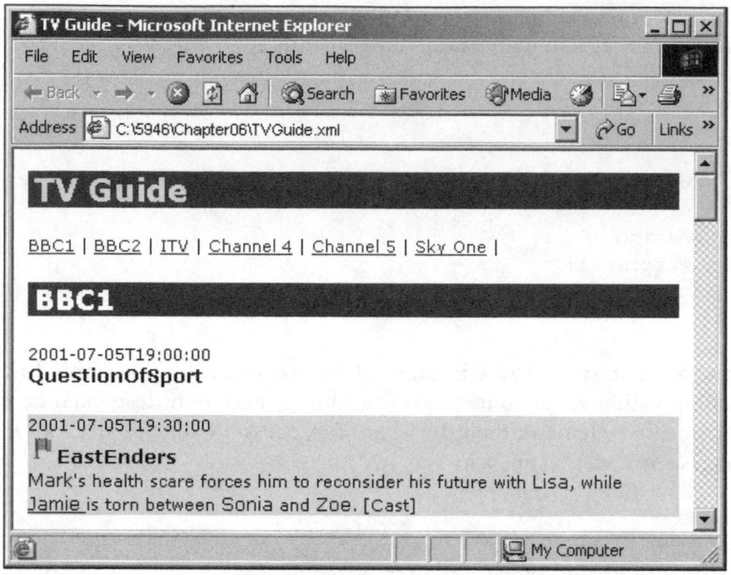

Using a variable has made absolutely no difference to the result you get, and the speed increase is likely to be fractional, but using a variable has made your stylesheet easier to maintain and change later on.

Conditional Variables

In the last chapter, you saw how to generate different kinds of content in different circumstances using <xsl:if> and <xsl:choose>. One of the problems that we looked at was how to add different <img> elements to indicate different types of flags for programs. The solution that we came up with was the following:

```
<xsl:choose>
  <xsl:when test="@flag = 'favorite'">
    <img src="favorite.gif" alt="[Favorite]" width="20" height="20" />
  </xsl:when>
  <xsl:when test="@flag = 'interesting'">
    <img src="interest.gif" alt="[Interest]" width="20" height="20" />
  </xsl:when>
</xsl:choose>
```

The two <img> elements that we're creating here are fairly similar – they both have the same width and height, both refer to GIFs, and both use square brackets around the alternative text. We looked at replacing these <img> elements with global variables in the previous section, but it would be even more maintainable if we could use a variable to hold the image name and the alternative text, and then use attribute value templates to insert the relevant values:

```
<img src="{$image}.gif" alt="[{$alt}]" width="20" height="20" />
```

Remember that the curly braces ({ }) are the only braces that are important in attribute value templates; the string inside them is interpreted as an XPath.

In a procedural programming language, we would be able to set the `$image` and `$alt` variables to different values in a `switch` statement, something like the following JavaScript:

```
switch (Program.getAttribute('flag')) {
  case 'favorite':
    image = 'favorite';
    alt = 'Favorite';
    break;
  case 'interesting':
    image = 'interest';
    alt = 'Interest';
}
```

You cannot follow this pattern in XSLT because of the scoping rules that apply to variables. Remember that a variable is only within scope to its following siblings and their descendants; if you set a variable within an `<xsl:choose>` element, then it will not be accessible outside the `<xsl:choose>`. So trying to do the following, as in `TVGuide6.xsl`:

```
<xsl:choose>
  <xsl:when test="@flag = 'favorite'">
    <xsl:variable name="image" select="'favorite'" />
    <xsl:variable name="alt" select="'Favorite'" />
  </xsl:when>
  <xsl:when test="@flag = 'interesting'">
    <xsl:variable name="image" select="'interest'" />
    <xsl:variable name="alt" select="'Interest'" />
  </xsl:when>
</xsl:choose>
<xsl:if test="@flag">
  <img src="{$image}.gif" alt="[{$alt}]" width="20" height="20" />
</xsl:if>
```

will not work because the `$image` and `$alt` variables will be out of scope when you move outside the `<xsl:choose>` to create the `<img>` element. In Internet Explorer, you get the following error:

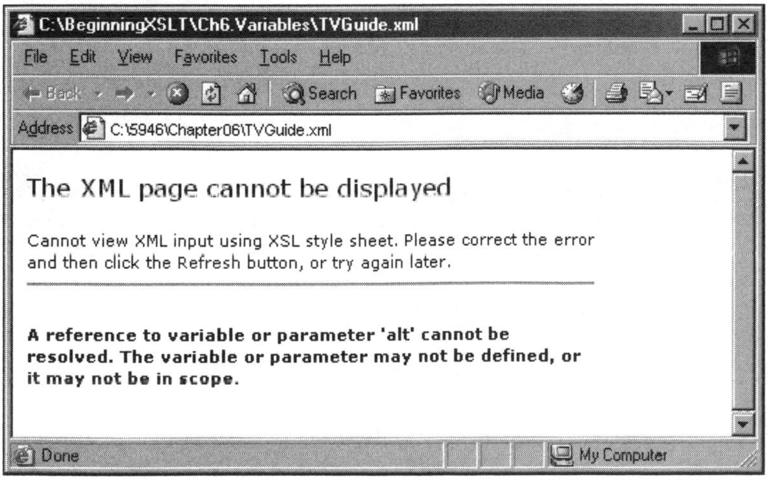

Instead you have to turn the construction round and use the conditional constructs within the `<xsl:variable>` instruction that you use to set the variable, as with the following in `TVGuide7.xsl`:

```
<xsl:variable name="image">
  <xsl:choose>
    <xsl:when test="@flag = 'favorite'">favorite</xsl:when>
    <xsl:when test="@flag = 'interesting'">interest</xsl:when>
  </xsl:choose>
</xsl:variable>
<xsl:variable name="alt">
  <xsl:choose>
    <xsl:when test="@flag = 'favorite'">Favorite</xsl:when>
    <xsl:when test="@flag = 'interesting'">Interest</xsl:when>
  </xsl:choose>
</xsl:variable>
<xsl:if test="@flag">
  <img src="{$image}.gif" alt="[{$alt}]" width="20" height="20" />
</xsl:if>
```

One thing to note when you set variables conditionally in this way is that the variable holds a result tree fragment rather than a string. For example, if the `flag` attribute has the value `'interesting'` then the `$image` variable holds a small result tree fragment that looks like the following:

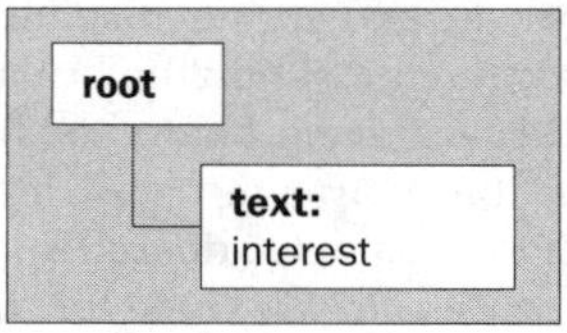

As we explored earlier, this is particularly important if you come to test the value of the `$image` variable; if the `flag` attribute is neither `'interesting'` nor `'favorite'` then the `$image` variable will consist of a single root node with no children. If you just test the value of the `$image` variable as follows:

```
<xsl:if test="$image">
  ...
</xsl:if>
```

then the test will always be `true` because result tree fragments are always converted to boolean `true`. In contrast, if the variable was set with:

```
<xsl:variable name="image" select="''" />
```

then the test would be boolean `false` because an empty string is converted to boolean `false`.

To test whether the result tree fragment holds a value, you need to convert it to a string, as follows:

```
<xsl:if test="string($image)">
  ...
</xsl:if>
```

You can set a variable's value conditionally using `<xsl:choose>` within the `<xsl:variable>` element.

String and Number Expressions

In the last chapter, we looked at several operators and functions that you can use in boolean expressions and in predicates. We've also gone into some detail about how to construct node sets using location paths (we'll be looking at this in more detail in the next chapter as well). In this section, we'll start looking at various other operators and functions that are useful in manipulating strings and numbers.

Manipulating Strings

There are quite a few functions for manipulating strings within XPath, for example, allowing you to break up strings, to combine them together, and to format them to a certain extent. There are some limitations though; in particular XPath doesn't support regular expressions, and there's no native facility for searching and replacing strings.

Splitting and Recombining Strings

The `substring-before()` and `substring-after()` functions are handy for splitting up character-delimited strings. They both take two arguments, the first being the original string and the second being the character or string at which it should be broken. The `substring-before()` function returns the substring of the first argument before the first occurrence of the second argument, while the `substring-after()` function returns the substring of the first argument after the first occurrence of the second argument. If the character doesn't appear in the string then both functions return an empty string. For example, you could use these functions to get someone's forename and surname given just their name:

```
substring-before('Jeni Tennison', ' ')
substring-after('Jeni Tennison', ' ')
```

The `substring()` function is useful when you have strings that follow a fixed-width format. It normally takes three arguments: the original string, the index of the first character in the string that you want (starting from 1), and the number of characters you want to get in the substring. You can omit the third argument to get all the remaining characters in a string. For example, both the following calls return the string `'xyz'`:

```
substring('abcdefghijklmnopqrstuvwxyz', 24, 3)
substring('abcdefghijklmnopqrstuvwxyz', 24)
```

Note that there's no limit in XPath to the number of characters that a string can contain, though it will be limited in particular implementations, or by the memory capacity of the computer on which you're running the transformation. There are limits on the numbers that XPath can handle, since XPath numbers are double-precision 64-bit floating point numbers. I've never seen either limit be a real problem.

When you're trying to get the last part of a string, it's often useful to know the string's length. You can do this with the `string-length()` function. For example, you can get the last letter in a string with:

```
substring($string, string-length($string))
```

Once you've broken up a string, you often want to recombine the component parts in a different way. You can do this with the `concat()` function, which takes two or more string arguments and combines them into a single string. For example, once you've pulled out the forename and surname from a string, you might want to combine them back together in a sortable format, with the surname first:

```
concat($surname, ',', $forename)
```

> **You can split up a string with the `substring()`, `substring-before()`, and `substring-after()` functions and put a string together with the `concat()` function. The `string-length()` function tells you the length of a string.**

Try It Out – Parsing Dates and Times

The TV Guide markup language holds the start date and time of a program in a `<Start>` element which uses the format `YYYY-MM-DDThh:mm:ss`. This format is a good standard format to use, but it isn't very readable. Instead, it would be good to just use a US date format and just give the hours and minutes when the show starts. The start date of `2001-07-05T19:30:00` should be shown as something like:

```
7/5/2001 19:30
```

We'll try to generate this format in the next version of our stylesheet, `TVGuide8.xsl`, which is based on `TVGuide7.xsl`.

The date and time format held in the `<Start>` element is a fixed-width format: the first four characters always give the year and the last eight characters give the time. Therefore we can split the string up with the `substring()` function. First, in the template for the `<Start>` element, let's split the value into the components we're interested in:

```
<xsl:variable name="year" select="substring(., 1, 4)" />
<xsl:variable name="month" select="substring(., 6, 2)" />
<xsl:variable name="day" select="substring(., 9, 2)" />
<xsl:variable name="time" select="substring(., 12, 5)" />
```

Now we can construct the new string by concatenating the various components together in a different order (and inserting two `/`s and a space), to give the template:

```
<xsl:template match="Start">
  <xsl:variable name="year" select="substring(., 1, 4)" />
  <xsl:variable name="month" select="substring(., 6, 2)" />
  <xsl:variable name="day" select="substring(., 9, 2)" />
  <xsl:variable name="time" select="substring(., 12, 5)" />
  <span class="date">
```

```
      <xsl:value-of select="concat($month, '/', $day, '/', $year,
                                   ' ', $time)" />
    </span>
  </xsl:template>
```

This gives a much more readable format to the dates, as you can see:

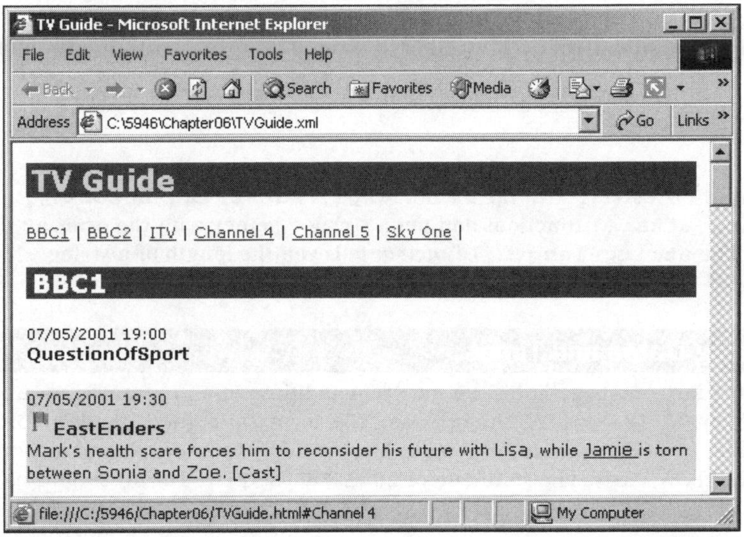

However, all the variables are set to string values, so the `$month` and `$day` variables hold the values `'07'` and `'05'` respectively, giving leading zeros to the resulting format. The neatest way of getting rid of those zeros in the next version, `TVGuide9.xsl`, is to convert the variables into numbers first, using the `number()` function, as follows:

```
  <xsl:variable name="month" select="number(substring(., 6, 2))" />
  <xsl:variable name="day" select="number(substring(., 9, 2))" />
```

With this change made in `TVGuide9.xsl`, the leading zeros on the month and the day disappear:

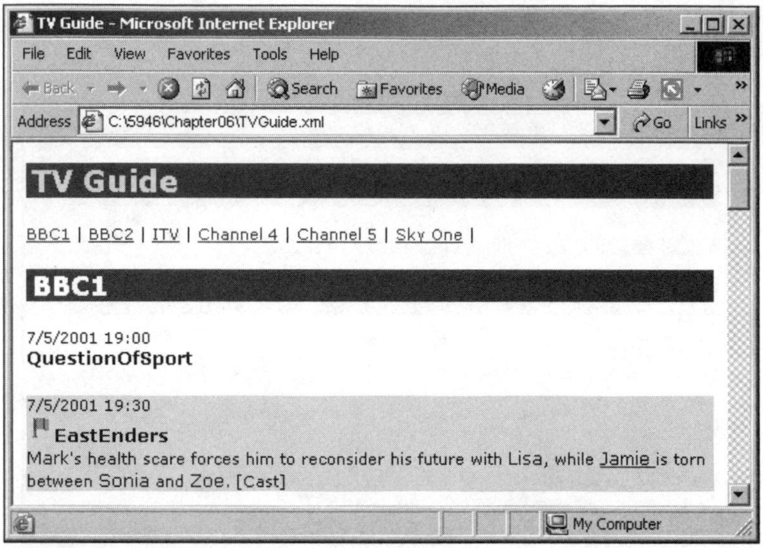

Reformatting Strings

There are two other functions that are mainly useful when formatting strings. The first is `normalize-space()`, which can take a single argument (it defaults to the string value of the context node if you don't give an argument). The `normalize-space()` function strips leading and trailing whitespace from a string and substitutes all the whitespace within the string with single spaces. This is particularly useful when the XML that you're processing has had whitespace added within it to help with readability. For example `TVGuide2.xml` includes elements with a lot of whitespace within them:

```
<Program rating="5" flag="favorite">
  <Start>
    2001-07-05T19:30:00
  </Start>
  <Duration>
    PT30M
  </Duration>
  <Series>
    EastEnders
  </Series>
  ...
</Program>
```

When the values of these elements are accessed as strings, they contain line breaks and tabs where really they should only contain spaces. The actual string value of the `<Start>` element is as follows (`
` is a line break and `	` is a tab):

```
&#xA;&#x9;&#x9;2001-07-05T19:30:00&#xA;&#x9;
```

This means that when you try to extract the year, month, day, and time from the `<Start>` element, you get a different set of characters to the ones that you're expecting. Trying to transform `TVGuide2.xml` with `TVGuide9.xsl`, for example, gives you:

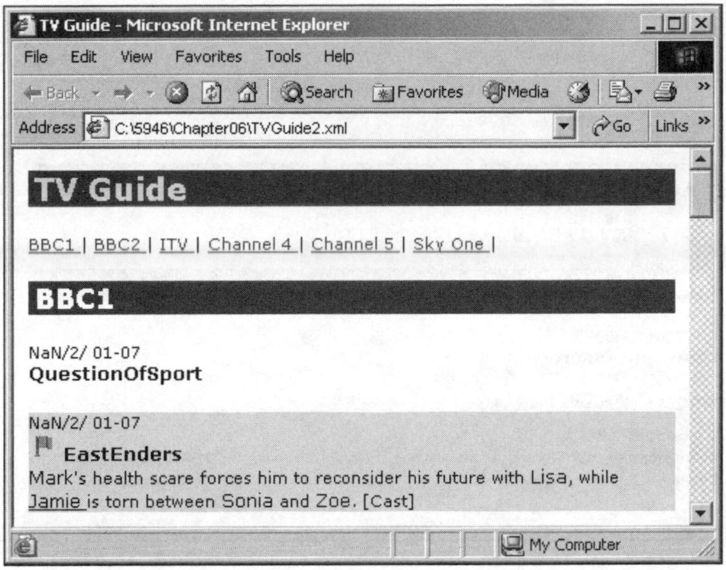

You can get rid of the spurious whitespace in the string by passing the value of the `<Start>` element as the argument to `normalize-space()` as follows in the template for the `<Start>` element:

```
normalize-space(.)
```

If you don't explicitly pass a node as the argument to the `normalize-space()` *function, it assumes that you want the normalized value of the current node. Thus* `normalize-space(.)` *is equivalent to simply* `normalize-space()`.

The result is the following string; all the trailing and leading whitespace is removed. If the string had contained line breaks or tabs, these would be substituted with a single space:

```
2001-07-05T19:30:00
```

You can see the effect of this by looking at `TVGuide10.xsl`, which includes:

```
<xsl:template match="Start">
  <xsl:variable name="dateTime" select="normalize-space()" />
  <xsl:variable name="year" select="substring($dateTime, 1, 4)" />
  <xsl:variable name="month" select="number(substring($dateTime, 6, 2))" />
  <xsl:variable name="day" select="number(substring($dateTime, 9, 2))" />
  <xsl:variable name="time" select="substring($dateTime, 12, 5)" />
  <span class="date">
    <xsl:value-of select="concat($month, '/', $day, '/', $year,
                                  ' ', $time)" />
  </span>
</xsl:template>
```

When `TVGuide2.xml` is transformed using `TVGuide10.xsl`, you get the dates formatted correctly once more.

> **You can normalize a string to get rid of superfluous whitespace using the `normalize-space()` function.**

The second function that's handy in reformatting strings is the `translate()` function. The `translate()` function allows you to delete all occurrences of specific characters in a string or replace them with other single characters. The first argument to the `translate()` function is the string that you want to alter; the second is a string containing the characters to search for in the original string; and the third is a string containing the replacement characters in the equivalent order. The most common use of the `translate()` function is in turning a word into upper- or lowercase, for example:

```
translate('sport', 'abcdefghijklmnopqrstuvwxyz',
                   'ABCDEFGHIJKLMNOPQRSTUVWXYZ')
```

I'm showing my English bias here. You can employ the same method for other languages using the characters you need for those languages, as long as there's a one-to-one correspondence between lowercase and uppercase characters. If there isn't (for example, in German `ß` *should be replaced by* `SS`*) then you need to use a recursive template to do the translation. We'll meet just such a recursive template in Chapter 11.*

The XSLT processor will replace all occurrences of the character `a` with the character `A`, `b` with `B`, `c` with `C`, and so on, so the string `'News'` will be translated into the string `'NEWS'`.

A second use of the `translate()` function is to remove all occurrences of a particular character from a string by not giving an equivalent character in the string given as the third argument. For example, you could remove all line breaks from the string value of the `<Description>` element with:

```
translate(Description, '&#xA;','')
```

Note that the character reference `
` *counts as a single line break character rather than the separate characters* `&`, `#`, `x`, `A`, *and* `;` *because the character reference is substituted with a line break character when the XML that contains it is initially parsed. Also note that when the source XML document is initially parsed, the XML parser automatically converts all combinations of line breaks and carriage returns to single line breaks, so this method works no matter what platform your XML document is saved on.*

> **The `translate()` function replaces single characters with other single characters or nothing at all. You cannot use it to replace words.**

Try It Out – Case-Insensitive Searches

In the last chapter, we created pages that highlighted programs that had particular words in their descriptions or titles. In `TVGuide10.xsl`, we search for the word "News" in the <Series>, <Title>, and <Description> children of the <Program> element and mark the program as interesting if they occur with the following template:

```
<xsl:template match="Program">
  <xsl:choose>
    <xsl:when test="@flag = 'favorite' or @flag = 'interesting' or
                    @rating > 6 or contains(Series, 'News') or
                    contains(Title, 'News') or
                    contains(Description, 'news')">
      <div class="interesting">
        <xsl:apply-templates select="." mode="Details" />
      </div>
    </xsl:when>
    <xsl:otherwise>
      <div>
        <xsl:apply-templates select="." mode="Details" />
      </div>
    </xsl:otherwise>
  </xsl:choose>
</xsl:template>
```

The `contains()` function, like all other functions in XPath, is case-sensitive. A program will only be marked as interesting if the word "News" occurs with a capital 'N' within the program's <Series> or <Title>, or if the word "news" occurs completely in lowercase in the program's <Description>. However, the person reading the page would probably also be interested in the program if it contained "News" or "NEWS" in its description. To highlight those programs as well, we have to do a case-insensitive search.

You can do a case-insensitive search for a word within a string by making sure both strings use the same case throughout. If we changed the series, title, and description of the program to contain only lowercase characters then occurrences of "News" and "NEWS" would both become "news" and therefore match the term for which we're looking.

The first step to support case-insensitive searches in `TVGuide11.xsl` is to set up variables that contain the upper- and lowercase letters in order. I would normally make these global variables in case I wanted to use them elsewhere later on:

```
<xsl:variable name="upper" select="'ABCDEFGHIJKLMNOPQRSTUVWXYZ'" />
<xsl:variable name="lower" select="'abcdefghijklmnopqrstuvwxyz'" />
```

To make it easier to change later on, let's also turn the string `'news'` into a global variable:

```
<xsl:variable name="keyword" select="'news'" />
```

Now in the condition that looks for the keyword, we need to translate the values of the <Description>, <Series>, and <Title> elements into lowercase using the `translate()` function:

```
<xsl:template match="Program">
  <xsl:choose>
    <xsl:when
      test="@flag = 'favorite' or @flag = 'interesting' or @rating > 6 or
            contains(translate(Series, $upper, $lower), $keyword) or
            contains(translate(Title, $upper, $lower), $keyword) or
            contains(translate(Description, $upper, $lower), $keyword)">
      <div class="interesting">
        <xsl:apply-templates select="." mode="Details" />
      </div>
    </xsl:when>
    <xsl:otherwise>
      <div>
        <xsl:apply-templates select="." mode="Details" />
      </div>
    </xsl:otherwise>
  </xsl:choose>
</xsl:template>
```

When you transform `TVGuide.xml` with `TVGuide11.xsl`, programs with the string "News" in their `<Series>` are still highlighted, despite the fact that the keyword held in the `$keyword` variable is all lowercase:

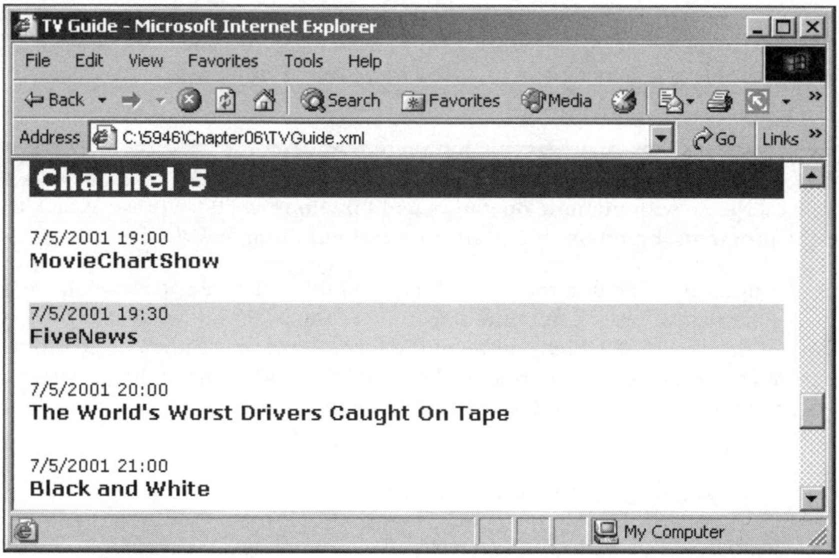

Manipulating Numbers

As you already know, you can convert a value into a number using the `number()` function. XPath has a number of operators that you can use to perform basic mathematics. The operands for these operators are automatically converted into numbers. The operators are:

Name	Operator	Example	Explanation
Plus	+	`2 + 2`	Adds two numbers together
Minus	-	`3 - 2`	Subtracts one number from another
Multiplied by	*	`2 * 2`	Multiplies two numbers together
Divided by	`div`	`3 div 2`	Divides a number by another using floating point division
Mod	`mod`	`3 mod 2`	Gives the remainder after integer division
Unary minus	-	`- 2`	Negates a number

Other than that, functions for numerical manipulation are fairly thin on the ground. XPath offers three functions for rounding numbers in various ways, each of which takes a single argument:

- `floor()` – rounds a number down to the nearest integer
- `ceiling()` – rounds a number up to the nearest integer
- `round()` – rounds a number to the nearest integer, or to the nearest even integer if it is half way between two integers

> **XPath supports the numeric operators +, -, *, `div`, `mod`, and unary -. You can round numbers with the functions `floor()`, `ceiling()`, and `round()`.**

Try It Out – Parsing Durations and Calculating End Times

To gain some experience with numeric operators and functions, we'll try to use XSLT to calculate the end times of the programs, based on their start time and duration, in `TVGuide12.xsl`.

The duration of a program is held in the `<Duration>` child of the `<Program>` element. As with the date and time format that we use to store the start time of the program, we're using a standard format for the duration of the program, which will be of the form `PTnM` or `PTnHnM` or possibly `PTnH`. The interesting part of the duration is the part after the initial `PT`, and to make things easier we'll store that in a variable within the template for the `<Start>` element:

```
<xsl:variable name="duration"
              select="substring(normalize-space(../Duration), 3)" />
```

To find the duration in the template matching the `<Start>` element, we need to go up a level to the `<Program>` element, and then down a level to the `<Duration>` element. We'll use the `normalize-space()` function again, just in case there's whitespace around the duration, as there is in `TVGuide2.xml`.

After the initial `PT`, the format is character-delimited rather than fixed-width, so the best functions to use to break up the string into its components are `substring-before()` and `substring-after()`. First, the number of hours: `0` if the duration doesn't contain an `H` or the number before the `H` if it does:

```
<xsl:variable name="durationHours">
  <xsl:choose>
    <xsl:when test="contains($duration, 'H')">
      <xsl:value-of select="substring-before($duration, 'H')" />
    </xsl:when>
    <xsl:otherwise>0</xsl:otherwise>
  </xsl:choose>
</xsl:variable>
```

Second the number of minutes: `0` if the duration doesn't contain an `M`, the number after the `H` and before the `M` if it contains both an `H` and an `M`, or the number before the `M` if it just contains an `M`:

```
<xsl:variable name="durationMinutes">
  <xsl:choose>
    <xsl:when test="contains($duration, 'M')">
      <xsl:choose>
        <xsl:when test="contains($duration, 'H')">
          <xsl:value-of select="substring-before(
                                     substring-after($duration, 'H'), 'M')" />
        </xsl:when>
        <xsl:otherwise>
          <xsl:value-of select="substring-before($duration, 'M')" />
        </xsl:otherwise>
      </xsl:choose>
    </xsl:when>
    <xsl:otherwise>0</xsl:otherwise>
  </xsl:choose>
</xsl:variable>
```

From these two variables, we can work out the number of minutes that the program lasts – the number of hours multiplied by 60, plus the number of minutes:

```
<xsl:variable name="durationMins"
              select="($durationHours * 60) + $durationMinutes" />
```

We want to use the duration to work out the end time for the program. We've already isolated the start time for the program in the `$time` variable using the `substring()` function. We can use that function again to work out the start hours and minutes for the program:

```
<xsl:variable name="startHours" select="substring($time, 1, 2)" />
<xsl:variable name="startMinutes" select="substring($time, 4, 2)" />
```

We can work out the end time for the program by calculating the end minutes and hours. The end minutes is the start minutes plus the duration minutes, `mod` 60:

```
<xsl:variable name="endMinutes"
              select="($startMinutes + $durationMins) mod 60" />
```

The end hours is the start minutes plus the duration minutes divided by 60, plus the start hours, rounded down (since the hours has to be an integer) and `mod` 24 (in case some programs extend over midnight):

```
<xsl:variable name="endHours"
  select="floor((($startMinutes + $durationMins) div 60) + $startHours)
          mod 24" />
```

We can add this information to the details that we give about the timing of the program as follows:

```
<xsl:template match="Start">
  <xsl:variable name="dateTime" select="normalize-space()" />
  <xsl:variable name="year" select="substring($dateTime, 1, 4)" />
  <xsl:variable name="month" select="number(substring($dateTime, 6, 2))" />
  <xsl:variable name="day" select="number(substring($dateTime, 9, 2))" />
  <xsl:variable name="time" select="substring($dateTime, 12, 5)" />
  <xsl:variable name="duration"
                select="substring(normalize-space(../Duration), 3)" />
  <xsl:variable name="durationHours">...</xsl:variable>
  <xsl:variable name="durationMinutes">...</xsl:variable>
  <xsl:variable name="durationMins"
                select="($durationHours * 60) + $durationMinutes" />
  <xsl:variable name="startHours" select="substring($time, 1, 2)" />
  <xsl:variable name="startMinutes" select="substring($time, 4, 2)" />
  <xsl:variable name="endMinutes"
                select="($startMinutes + $durationMins) mod 60" />
  <xsl:variable name="endHours"
    select="floor((($startMinutes + $durationMins) div 60) + $startHours)
            mod 24" />
  <span class="date">
    <xsl:value-of select="concat($month, '/', $day, '/', $year, ' ', $time,
                                 ' - ', $endHours, ':', $endMinutes)" />
  </span>
</xsl:template>
```

The result of transforming `TVGuide.xml` with `TVGuide12.xsl` is the following:

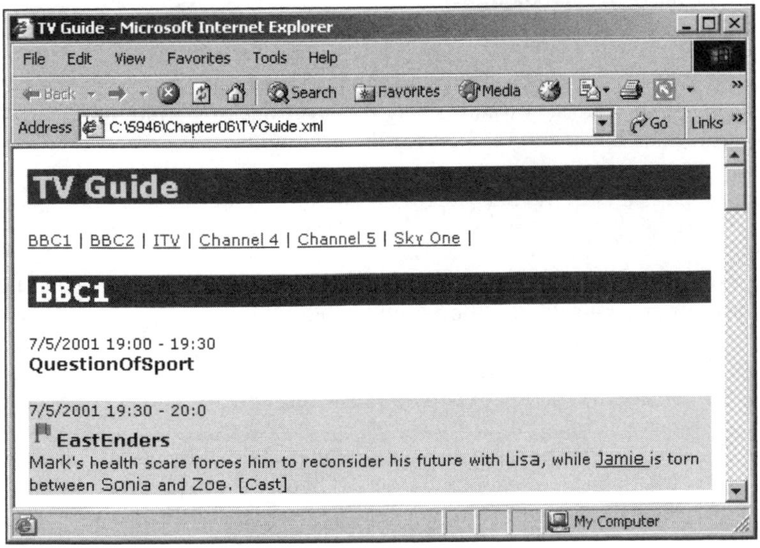

We're getting `20:0` *rather than* `20:00` *in the above because the XSLT processor doesn't know that we expect two digits for the minutes, so it doesn't give a leading* `0` *when it gives the string version of the number. We'll see how to pad numbers in the next section.*

Naturally all these string manipulation and numeric calculations take some time, and you wouldn't want to do them more than you had to, but, in general, working with strings and numbers is a lot more efficient than working with node sets. Nodes are expensive to create, take a lot of memory to store, and take a lot of time to iterate over. So while we're doing a lot more processing in this template than we were, I wouldn't expect a good XSLT processor to suffer much in terms of performance.

Having said that, for most programs – all those aside from the last showing on a particular channel – you could work out the program's end time by looking at the next program's start time, and that's likely to be slightly quicker (and easier to understand) than going through the calculations. We'll see how to use the start time of the next program as the end time of this program in the next chapter.

Formatting Numbers

While XSLT isn't spectacularly easy to use for doing sophisticated math, it has a lot more support for formatting numbers, provided by the `format-number()` function. The `format-number()` function usually takes two arguments: the first argument is the number that you want to format and the second is a pattern that determines the format for the number. For example:

```
format-number(12345.6789, '#,##0.00')
```

will give the string `'12,345.68'`. Or, to get around the problems we've had with the end times missing leading zeros on their hours and minutes, we could use the following, as in `TVGuide13.xsl`:

```
<xsl:value-of select="concat($month, '/', $day, '/', $year, ' ', $time,
                             ' - ', format-number($endHours, '00'),
                             ':', format-number($endMinutes, '00'))" />
```

This means that the end time `20:00` is formatted correctly, as follows:

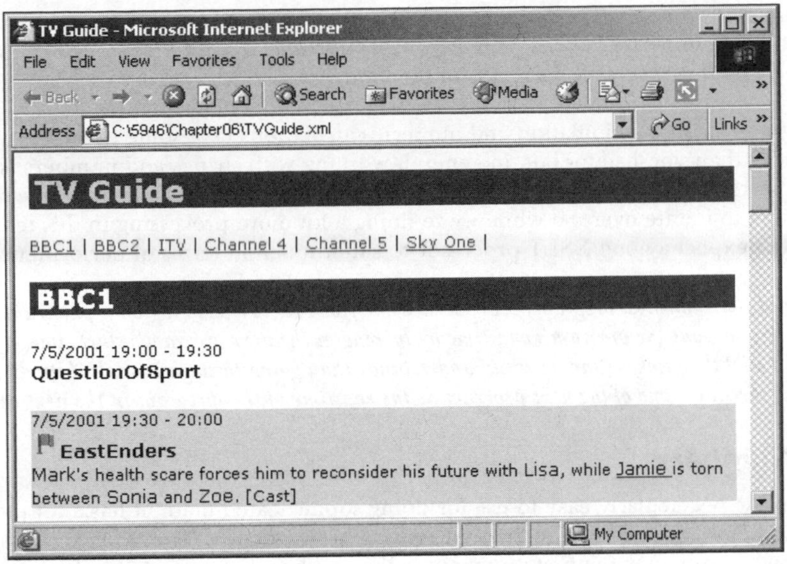

Format Patterns

The following symbols are significant in the pattern string that's passed as the second argument to `format-number()`:

Name	Character	Description
Digit	#	Placeholder for optional digits in the formatted number – indicates the maximum number of fraction digits to be shown.
Zero digit	0	Placeholder for required digits in the formatted number – indicates the minimum number of integer and fraction digits to be shown.
Decimal separator	.	Separates the integer and fraction digit characters.
Grouping separator	,	Indicates the number of digits in a group.
Pattern separator	;	Separates the pattern for positive numbers from that for negative numbers.
Minus sign	-	Shows the location of the minus sign in the negative pattern.
Percent	%	Indicates that the number should be multiplied by 100 and shows the location of the percent sign.
Per-mille	‰	Indicates that the number should be multiplied by 1000 and shows the location of the per-mille sign.

You may have to use the character reference for the per-mille sign, if your editor or character encoding doesn't support it. The character reference you need is `‰`.

If the number that you pass as the first argument to `format-number()` is negative, the XSLT processor will use the negative pattern if you supply one, or prefix a minus sign to the positive pattern if you don't. If the number is not a number, then the `format-number()` function will return the string `'NaN'`. If the number is infinity, then `format-number()` will return the string `'Infinity'`.

The `format-number()` function formats the number passed as its first argument according to the format pattern passed as its second argument.

Localized Numbers

As you can see from looking at the characters that are listed as being significant in the format pattern, the `format-number()` function uses a US numbering scheme by default, with the decimal point indicated by `.` and groups of digits separated by `,`. In other regions, people use different numerical formats. The French, for example, use a comma as the decimal point and a space to separate groups of numbers. However, the XSLT processor does not take the locale into account when it formats numbers. If you tried to format numbers in the French style, with:

```
format-number(12345.6789, '# ##0,00')
```

then you would not get the string `'12 345,67'` even if you ran the stylesheet on a machine set up with a French locale.

What you do *get depends on the processor that you use. MSXML raises an error, saying "The '0' format symbol may not follow the '#' format symbol in this section of a format pattern". Saxon creates the string `'12345.6789 ,'` and Xalan creates the string `'1,23,45'`. These differences probably arise because the way that `format-number()` works is not particularly well specified in the XSLT 1.0 Recommendation.*

To format a number with a different locale, you need to tell the XSLT processor to use a different set of significant characters when interpreting the formatting pattern that you pass as the second argument to `format-number()`. You can do this with a **decimal format**. Decimal formats specify the characters that are significant in a formatting pattern and the special strings that are used when the number is `NaN` or `Infinity`.

You declare a decimal format with the `<xsl:decimal-format>` element, which lives at the top level of the stylesheet. You can name the decimal format using the `name` attribute. If you name a decimal format, then you can tell the XSLT processor to use that decimal format when formatting a specific number by passing that name as a third argument to the `format-number()` function. For example, if you set up a decimal format named `French` then you could format a number in the French style with:

```
format-number(12345.6789, '# ##0,00', 'French')
```

If you don't specify a name for a decimal format in the `<xsl:decimal-format>` element, then that decimal format is the **default decimal format**. This is useful when you format a lot of numbers in exactly the same way, whereas named decimal formats are handy if you want to format different numbers in different ways.

The special characters and strings that you use in particular decimal formats are set using attributes on the `<xsl:decimal-format>` element. The full details of the characters and strings that you can set are given in the *XSLT Quick Reference* in Appendix B at the back of this book, but, for example, you could set up a French decimal format with:

```
<xsl:decimal-format name="French"
                    decimal-separator=","
                    grouping-separator=" "
                    infinity="Infinit&#233;" />
```

If you want to format numbers in non-US styles, you have to declare your own decimal formats that specify the characters used for the decimal point, for grouping separators, and so on.

Using Parameters

As we've seen, variables can hold information within a specific stylesheet or within a specific template. **Parameters** are like variables, but their values can be set from outside their scope, allowing values to be passed in to the stylesheet or to be passed in to a template.

Earlier in this chapter, we looked at how to create a global variable that could hold the string `'Star Trek'` that we then used to create a page dedicated to Star Trek shows. The relevant piece of XSLT is the following from `StarTrek6.xsl`:

```
<xsl:variable name="series" select="'StarTrek'" />

<xsl:template match="TVGuide">
  <xsl:variable name="StarTrekChannels"
    select="Channel[Program[starts-with(Series, $series)]]" />
  <xsl:choose>
    <xsl:when test="$StarTrekChannels">
      <xsl:variable name="NumberOfStarTrekEpisodes"
        select="count(Channel/Program[starts-with(Series, $series)])" />
      <xsl:variable name="Plural" select="$NumberOfStarTrekEpisodes > 1" />
      <p>
        There
        <xsl:choose>
          <xsl:when test="$Plural">are </xsl:when>
          <xsl:otherwise>is </xsl:otherwise>
        </xsl:choose>
        <xsl:value-of select="$NumberOfStarTrekEpisodes" />
        Star Trek episode<xsl:if test="$Plural">s</xsl:if>
        showing this week.
      </p>
      <xsl:apply-templates select="$StarTrekChannels" />
    </xsl:when>
    <xsl:otherwise>
      <p>No Star Trek showing this week!</p>
```

```
      </xsl:otherwise>
    </xsl:choose>
  </xsl:template>

  <xsl:template match="Channel" mode="ChannelList">
    <xsl:if test="Program[starts-with(Series, $series)]">
      [<a href="#{Name}"><xsl:value-of select="Name" /></a>]
    </xsl:if>
  </xsl:template>

  <xsl:template match="Channel">
    <xsl:apply-templates select="Name" />
    <xsl:apply-templates select="Program[starts-with(Series, $series)]" />
  </xsl:template>
```

Despite the naming of the `$StarTrekChannels` and `$NumberOfStarTrekEpisodes` variables, and the messages that get displayed to say how many episodes are showing, if we changed the value of the `$series` variable we could use this same XSLT to create a page dedicated to any series we wanted. Currently, changing the value of the `$series` variable would mean editing the stylesheet itself each time we want to create a different page (for example, we did this to create `EastEnders.xsl` earlier). However, XSLT provides parameters to allow you to change the values of variables on the fly, without editing the stylesheet. In this section, we'll look at how parameters work and how to use them.

Declaring and Referring to Parameters

Parameters are very similar to variables. When you declare a parameter, you do so with an `<xsl:param>` element rather than an `<xsl:variable>` element, but the syntax of the two elements is basically the same. As with variables, every parameter must have a name, defined through the `<xsl:param>` element's `name` attribute, and this is prefixed with a dollar sign (`$`) when it's referred to within an XPath.

You can give parameters values in the same ways as you can with variables, either through the `<xsl:param>` element's `select` attribute or through its content. The main difference between variables and parameters, though, is that the value that you specify for a parameter when you declare it can be overridden from elsewhere – it acts as a default for the parameter.

Like variables, parameters can occur at two levels within a stylesheet – as top-level elements similar to global variables (children of the `<xsl:stylesheet>` element), or within a template similar to local variables. Parameters that are declared at the top level of a stylesheet are known as **stylesheet parameters** while those that are declared within templates are known as **template parameters**.

The scoping rules for parameters are the same as those for variables, and their names are in the same symbol space, so you can't have a variable and a parameter in the same scope with the same name. A local variable can shadow a stylesheet parameter and a template parameter can shadow a global variable.

Parameters are like variables that you can set to different values on the fly.

Stylesheet Parameters

Stylesheet parameters are declared at the top level of the stylesheet. Once you've declared a stylesheet parameter you can use different values for that parameter each time you run a transformation with the stylesheet. For example, you can turn the `$series` global variable into a stylesheet parameter by changing the name of the element from `<xsl:variable>` to `<xsl:param>`:

```
<xsl:param name="series" select="'StarTrek'" />
```

How you pass a value for the parameter into the stylesheet depends on the XSLT processor that you're using and how you're using it. That makes it difficult to state exactly how you do it in general.

If you're using a client-side transformation or if you're running your own script on the server side then you have to use the methods available in the interface to the transformation to set the parameters. Some server-side frameworks, such as Cocoon, AxKit, and XSQL, allow you to pass parameters to a stylesheet using the URL that you use to access the XML document that's transformed with the stylesheet.

> *You can find out more about Cocoon at* http://xml.apache.org/cocoon/; *more about AxKit at* http://axkit.org/; *and more about XSQL at* http://technet.oracle.com/tech/xml/xdk_java/.

For example, you would be able to use the URL:

```
http://www.example.com/TVGuide.xml?series=EastEnders
```

to generate an HTML page that showed only the EastEnders programs. We'll be looking at how to pass parameters into stylesheets from code and using Cocoon in detail in Chapter 14, *Dynamic XSLT.*

You can also pass parameters into stylesheets when you run them from the command line. With MSXML, the syntax is:

```
>msxsl TVGuide.xml Series.xsl -o EastEnders.html series=EastEnders
```

It's similar with (Instant) Saxon:

```
>saxon -o EastEnders.html TVGuide.xml Series.xsl series=EastEnders
```

With Xalan, it's slightly different:

```
>java org.apache.xalan.xslt.Process -IN TVGuide.xml -XSL Series.xsl
-OUT EastEnders.html -PARAM series EastEnders
```

Stylesheet parameters are declared at the top level of the stylesheet. You can use different values for these parameters each time you run the stylesheet.

Try It Out – Creating Series-Specific TV Guides

The easiest way to test stylesheet parameters is to use a command line to run the transformation. First, we'll create a new stylesheet, called `Series.xsl`, in which the `$series` global variable is a stylesheet parameter instead; you could correct the messages generated by the template that matches the `<TVGuide>` element at the same time, so that it isn't specific to Star Trek:

```
<xsl:param name="series" select="'Star Trek'" />

<xsl:template match="TVGuide">
  <xsl:variable name="channels"
                select="Channel[Program[starts-with(Series, $series)]]" />
  <xsl:choose>
    <xsl:when test="$channels">
      <xsl:apply-templates select="$channels" />
    </xsl:when>
    <xsl:otherwise>
      <p>No <xsl:value-of select="$series" /> showing this week!</p>
    </xsl:otherwise>
  </xsl:choose>
</xsl:template>
```

Run the stylesheet as it is, using the normal command line for the processor that you're using. The relevant command lines for MSXML, Saxon, and Xalan are as follows:

>msxsl TVGuide.xml Series.xsl -o StarTrek.html

>saxon -o StarTrek.html TVGuide.xml Series.xsl

>java org.apache.xalan.xslt.Process -IN TVGuide.xml -XSL Series.xsl -OUT StarTrek.html

The `StarTrek.html` page will list any Star Trek programs in the TV Guide XML; the default value for the `$series` parameter is `'StarTrek'` and in the absence of a different value being passed in at the command line, the stylesheet will use this default. When you view it in Internet Explorer, `StarTrek.html` looks like:

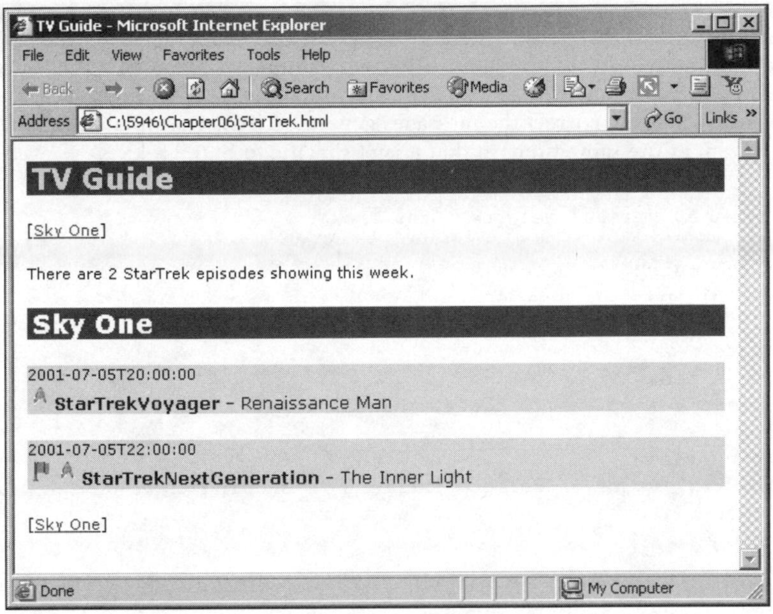

Now try using the same stylesheet to generate an episode listing for EastEnders. To pass the string `'EastEnders'` as the value of the `$series` parameter, you should use the relevant one of the following three command lines:

```
>msxsl TVGuide.xml Series.xsl -o EastEnders.html series=EastEnders
```

```
>saxon -o EastEnders.html TVGuide.xml Series.xsl series=EastEnders
```

```
>java org.apache.xalan.xslt.Process -IN TVGuide.xml -XSL Series.xsl -OUT
  EastEnders.html -PARAM series EastEnders
```

The `EastEnders.html` HTML page looks like the following in Internet Explorer:

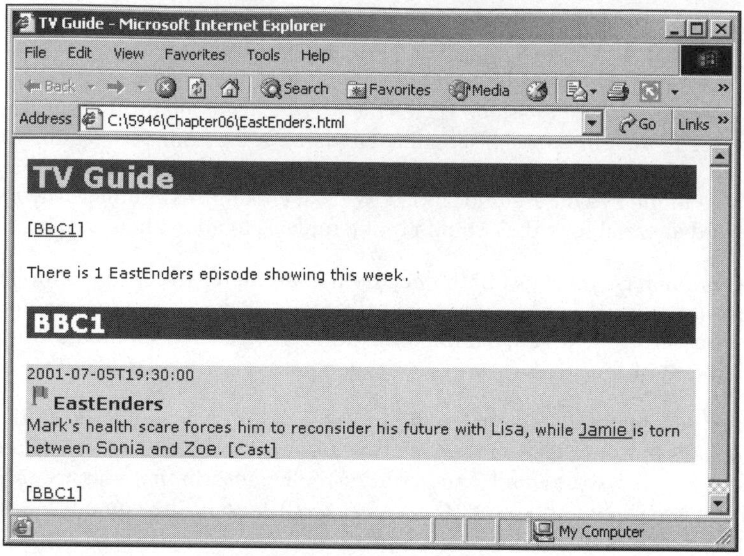

You can do the same for any other series that you like by passing in different values for the `$series` stylesheet parameter. Being able to use the same stylesheet to generate lots of different pages drastically cuts down on the number of stylesheets you need to maintain, and makes it a lot easier to create dynamic applications, as we'll see in Chapter 14.

Template Parameters

You can also pass parameters to templates, which is particularly useful when you start using recursive templates, which we'll come on to in Chapter 11. One place in which they would be useful in our stylesheet is when we create the HTML for the TV programs, specifically for the cast list. If you recall, we're currently applying templates to the `<CastList>` elements twice: once to create the cast list itself and once, in `DisplayToggle` mode, to create a link that shows or hides the cast list. The relevant templates are as follows:

```
<xsl:template match="Program" mode="Details">
  <p>
    ...
    <xsl:apply-templates select="Description" />
    <xsl:apply-templates select="CastList" mode="DisplayToggle" />
  </p>
  <xsl:apply-templates select="CastList" />
</xsl:template>

<xsl:template match="CastList" mode="DisplayToggle">
  <span onclick="toggle({Series}Cast);">[Cast]</span>
</xsl:template>

<xsl:template match="CastList">
  <div id="{Series}Cast" style="display: none;">
    <ul class="castlist"><xsl:apply-templates /></ul>
```

```
  </div>
</xsl:template>
```

Both of the templates need to use the same ID for the <div> that contains the cast list. As it stands, we're creating this ID twice in the same way in separate templates. If the code for creating the <div> and the reference to it were within the same template, we could create the ID once, use a variable to hold it, and refer to that variable in the two different locations. We can create the variable easily enough, but we need to pass the value of that variable to the two different templates to allow them to use it.

To use template parameters, you must both declare the parameter within the template that uses it and pass in values for that parameter when you apply templates to the nodes that are processed with that template. When you declare template parameters, the <xsl:param> elements must be the first elements in the content of the <xsl:template> element.

To pass parameters to a template, you use <xsl:with-param> elements within the <xsl:apply-templates> element that results in the template being processed. The <xsl:with-param> element is a lot like the <xsl:variable> and <xsl:param> elements, in that you use the name attribute to give the name of the parameter and either the select attribute or the content of the <xsl:with-param> element to specify the value for the parameter.

The name that you use when you pass the parameter value into the template has to be the same as the name of the parameter that you've declared in the template; the XSLT processor won't complain if you try to pass a parameter into a template that doesn't declare that parameter or if you don't pass a value for a particular parameter, so missing parameter values can be simply the result of spelling mistakes.

Another problem that sometimes arises with parameters is that they get lost if you rely on the built-in templates to process a particular node. When you pass a parameter with <xsl:apply-templates> make sure that the select attribute of the <xsl:apply-templates> points directly to the node that's matched by the template that accepts the parameter rather than to one of its ancestors. We will see more about this later when we talk about <xsl:call-template>.

> **Template parameters have to be declared as the first thing in a template. You can use them to change what a template generates based on information from the template that causes it to be processed.**

Try It Out – Passing Parameters to Templates

Let's look at how to use parameters so that we only create the ID for the <div> element once in TVGuide14.xsl. There are two templates that use the ID; both need to declare that they accept a parameter (which we'll call $divID) and then use that parameter in the HTML that they create:

```
<xsl:template match="CastList" mode="DisplayToggle">
  <xsl:param name="divID" />
  <span onclick="toggle({$divID});">[Cast]</span>
</xsl:template>

<xsl:template match="CastList">
  <xsl:param name="divID" />
```

```
    <div id="{$divID}" style="display: none;">
      <ul class="castlist"><xsl:apply-templates /></ul>
    </div>
  </xsl:template>
```

In the template that applies templates to the <CastList> elements that these templates match, we need to construct the ID for the <div> element we're creating and then pass that ID into the two templates using <xsl:with-param> within the two <xsl:apply-templates> elements, as follows:

```
  <xsl:template match="Program" mode="Details">
    <xsl:variable name="programID" select="concat(Series, 'Cast')" />
    <p>
      ...
      <xsl:apply-templates select="Description" />
      <xsl:apply-templates select="CastList" mode="DisplayToggle">
        <xsl:with-param name="divID" select="$programID" />
      </xsl:apply-templates>
    </p>
    <xsl:apply-templates select="CastList">
      <xsl:with-param name="divID" select="$programID" />
    </xsl:apply-templates>
  </xsl:template>
```

If you transform TVGuide.xml with TVGuide14.xsl, which uses these template parameters, you get the following page, exactly the same as before:

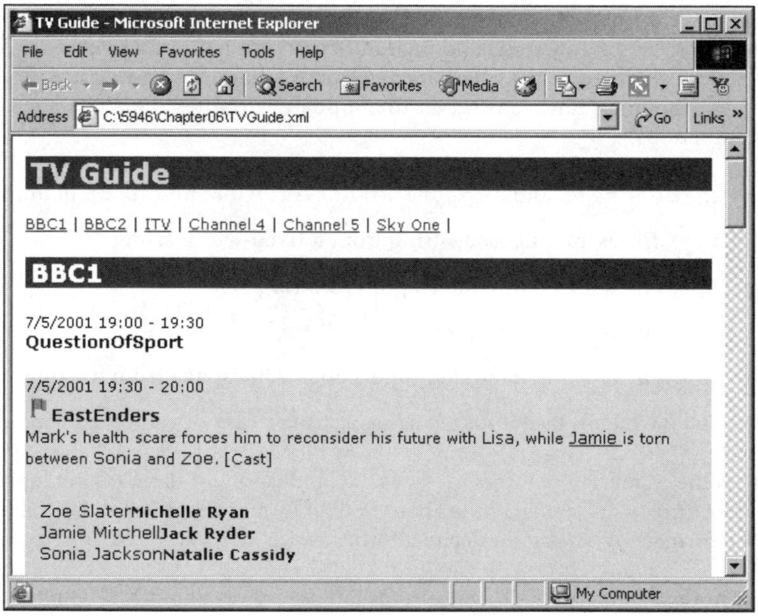

The [Cast] 'button' hides and reveals the list of cast members as it used to, but the stylesheet is easier to maintain because the way in which you identify the relevant <div> element is only defined in one location, rather than in two separate templates.

Summary

The main focus of this chapter has been on setting and using variables and parameters. You've learned how to associate a value with variables and parameters using the three new elements:

- `<xsl:variable>` for setting variables
- `<xsl:param>` for declaring parameters
- `<xsl:with-param>` for passing parameters into templates

You've seen the difference between setting variables and parameters using the `select` attribute and the content of these elements. The `select` attribute sets variables or parameters to the basic XPath value types – booleans, numbers, strings, or node sets – while using the content sets the variable or parameter to a result tree fragment. Result tree fragments are useful for storing snippets of XML that you want to copy into the result at several locations using `<xsl:copy-of>`. You also have to use the content of a variable to set its value if you want to set the value of the variable conditionally.

You've seen how variables are scoped, to allow you to use the same name for different variables in different templates, with global variables being visible throughout the stylesheet and local variables being visible only by their following siblings and their following siblings' descendants. You've also found out about the difference between stylesheet parameters and template parameters and how to use them. We'll look at template parameters in more detail in Chapter 11, when we study recursion, and at stylesheet parameters in Chapter 14, when we create dynamic XSLT applications.

Variables can only hold a value if you can compute that value using XPaths, so we also spent some time in this chapter building on the functions and operators that you learned about in the last chapter. You saw how to use `count()` to count the number of nodes in a node set and `sum()` to add their values together, and how to use these functions rather than update variables. This chapter also introduced a number of string functions:

- `substring-before()` and `substring-after()` for splitting up delimited strings
- `substring()` for extracting a substring from a fixed-width string
- `string-length()` for getting the length of a string
- `concat()` for building new strings
- `normalize-space()` for removing superfluous whitespace from a string
- `translate()` which is useful for changing a string's case or removing characters from a string

We also introduced the numeric operators `+`, `-`, `*`, `div`, and `mod` and the numeric functions `floor()`, `ceiling()`, and `round()`. You saw a little about how to format numbers with `format-number()` and how to localize the formats by setting up decimal formats with `<xsl:decimal-format>`.

As you've seen from this chapter, XPath expressions are used throughout XSLT to pull apart information from an XML document and to use that information to perform calculations or reformat it for display. The most useful feature of XPath expressions is their ability to access nodes in the node tree using location paths; in the next chapter we'll examine how to navigate around the node tree in much more detail.

Review Questions

1. What are the four types of values that XPath expressions can evaluate to, and what fifth value type is used in XSLT?

2. What types of values do the following variables hold?

```
<xsl:variable name="price" select="Price" />
<xsl:variable name="keyword">sport</xsl:variable>
<xsl:variable name="good" select="@rating > 6" />
<xsl:variable name="date" select="substring-before(Start, 'T')" />
<xsl:variable name="duration" select="substring(Duration, 3, 1) * 60" />
```

3. What is the difference between `<xsl:copy-of>` and `<xsl:value-of>`?

4. Correct the error in the following piece of XSLT:

```
<xsl:choose>
  <xsl:when test="@rating > 6">
    <xsl:variable name="rating" select="'high'" />
  </xsl:when>
  <xsl:when test="@rating < 4">
    <xsl:variable name="rating" select="'low'" />
  </xsl:when>
  <xsl:otherwise>
    <xsl:variable name="rating" select="'medium'" />
  </xsl:otherwise>
</xsl:choose>
<xsl:value-of select="$rating" />
```

5. Create a piece of XSLT that will take a date in the US date format `M/D/YYYY` and convert it to the standard date format `YYYY-MM-DD`. The date `9/4/2001` should get converted to `2001-09-04`.

6. Given the following decimal formats, create some XSLT that will output a number formatted in English, French, and German style:

```
<xsl:decimal-format name="French"
                    decimal-separator="," grouping-separator=" " />
<xsl:decimal-format name="German"
                    decimal-separator="," grouping-separator="." />
```

7. What are the differences between a global variable and a stylesheet parameter?

8. What will the following XSLT stylesheet normally output?

```
<xsl:stylesheet version="1.0"
                xmlns:xsl="http://www.w3.org/1999/XSL/Transform">
```

```
<xsl:param name="author" select="$defaultAuthor" />
<xsl:variable name="defaultAuthor" select="'A.N.Other'" />

<xsl:template match="/">
  <xsl:param name="by" />
  <xsl:apply-templates select="." mode="author" />
</xsl:template>

<xsl:template match="/" mode="author">
  <xsl:param name="by" select="$author" />
  Written by: <xsl:value-of select="$by" />
</xsl:template>

</xsl:stylesheet>
```

Beginning
XSLT

7

Paths

As you've learned, the purpose of XSLT is to transform an XML document into something else: text, HTML, or different XML. To do so, XSLT processors accept an XML document as input, known as the **source** of the transformation, and output a different document, known as the **result** of the transformation.

XSLT processors regard both the source and the result of the transformation as **node trees**. You've seen what node trees look like in previous chapters; you've used expressions and patterns to select and match nodes within a node tree and constructed new node trees using literal result elements. Over the next couple of chapters, we're going to look at node trees in more detail. In this chapter, we'll examine how to construct paths to walk around source node trees and to match nodes within them. In the next chapter, we'll look at how to construct a new node tree as the result of the transformation.

The first part of this chapter deals with how a node tree is constructed and looks at what information is stored about each node and how whitespace is treated within the node tree. The second part talks about how to construct paths to navigate the node tree. There are two types of paths that we'll look at in this chapter: **location paths**, which select nodes for the XSLT processor to process, and **location path patterns**, which match nodes so the XSLT processor can tell which template to apply to a particular node. These two types of paths look similar, but they're used in very different ways. We'll look at location path patterns first because they're a bit more restricted about how they match nodes in the node tree.

In this chapter, you'll learn:

- How to get information about the name and namespace of a node
- How to control the whitespace held in a node tree
- How to test for different kinds of nodes
- How to use predicates when matching nodes
- How to construct patterns that match several nodes
- How to select nodes with various tree relationships

Node Trees Revisited

When we first looked at node trees in Chapter 4, we constructed a basic diagram from the following simple piece of XML. To remind you, here's the XML again:

```
<?xml version="1.0" encoding="ISO-8859-1"?>
<?xml-stylesheet type="text/xsl" href="TVGuide.xsl"?>
<TVGuide start="2001-07-05" end="2001-07-05">
  <Channel>
    <Name>BBC1</Name>
    ...
    <Program>
      <Start>2001-07-05T19:30:00</Start>
      <Duration>PT30M</Duration>
      <Series>EastEnders</Series>
      ...
    </Program>
    ...
  </Channel>
  ...
</TVGuide>
```

The node tree that we constructed from this XML document was as follows:

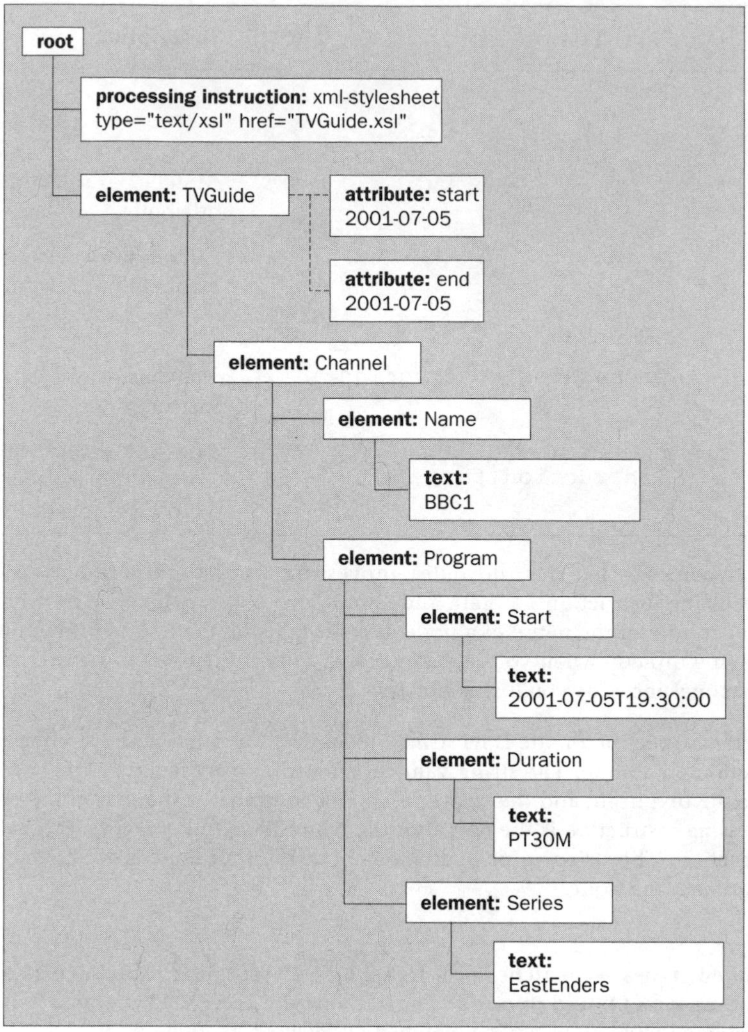

In this section, we're going to revisit this node tree, looking in more detail at how it is constructed. We're going to cover three areas: the information that's stored about each of the nodes within the node tree, how namespaces are handled within the node tree, and finally how to control the whitespace that remained within the node tree.

Accessing Information About Nodes

There are three important aspects of any node in XPath: its **type**, **name**, and **string value**.

The type of a node indicates whether it is an element, attribute, text, or other kind of node. You can't find out the type of a node directly, but you can select nodes of different types using different **node tests**. Node tests are used in location paths and in patterns to identify nodes of different types. The following table lists the node tests that you can use to select or match the different kinds of children of an element:

Node Type	Node Test	Description
Nodes	`node()`	
Text	`text()`	
Elements and attributes	`*`	Matches or selects all elements or attributes.
	`name`	Matches or selects elements or attributes with a particular name.
Comments	`comment()`	
Processing Instructions	`processing-instruction()`	Matches or selects all processing instructions.
	`processing-instruction(`*`target`*`)`	Matches or selects processing instructions with a particular target. The target must be a literal string.

Some nodes have names – elements, attributes, processing instructions (a processing instruction node's name is the processing instruction's target), and namespace nodes (which we'll come on to in a little while). You can get hold of the name of a node as a string using the `name()` function, but you can also use the node's name directly when you select or match nodes. Element and attribute names are a little complicated by namespaces, as you'll see shortly.

The final important aspect of a node is its string value, which is what you get when you call the `string()` function on a node. The string value of an attribute is the attribute's value, the string value of a text node is the text itself, and the string value of a comment is the text of the comment. The string value of a processing instruction is the text after the whitespace following the target (or name) of the processing instruction. The string value of an element or the root node is the concatenation of all the text nodes underneath the node.

> **Different node types are matched or selected by different node tests, such as `node()`, `text()`, `comment()`, and `processing-instruction()`. Elements, attributes, and processing instructions can be matched or selected by name.**

Try It Out – Accessing Node Information

You can now build a node tree for an XML document automatically using XSLT. We'll create a stylesheet called `NodeTree.xsl` that contains the templates for each of the different kinds of nodes and outputs the relevant information about them:

```
<xsl:template match="*">
  element: <xsl:value-of select="name()" />
  <xsl:apply-templates select="@*" />
  <xsl:apply-templates />
</xsl:template>
```

```
<xsl:template match="@*">
  attribute: <xsl:value-of select="name()" />:
             <xsl:value-of select="." />
</xsl:template>

<xsl:template match="text()">
  text: <xsl:value-of select="." />
</xsl:template>

<xsl:template match="processing-instruction()">
  processing instruction: <xsl:value-of select="name()" />:
                          <xsl:value-of select="." />
</xsl:template>

<xsl:template match="comment()">
  comment: <xsl:value-of select="." />
</xsl:template>
```

Running this stylesheet over an XML document will give you a text list of the nodes in the document and their node type. If you use `NodeTree.xsl` with `TVGuide.xml` using MSXSL as follows:

>**msxsl TVGuide.xml NodeTree.xsl -o Output.txt**

then you'll get a document that looks something like:

```
<?xml version="1.0" encoding="UTF-16"?>
  processing instruction: xml-stylesheet:
                          type="text/xsl" href="NodeTree.xsl"
  element: TVGuide
  attribute: start:
             2001-07-05
  attribute: end:
             2001-07-05
  text:

  element: Channel
  text:

  element: Name
  text: BBC1
  text:

  element: Program
  text:

  element: Start
  text: 2001-07-05T19:00:00
  text:

  element: Duration
```

```
text: PT30M
text:

element: Series
text: QuestionOfSport
text:

element: Title
text:

text:

...
```

You'll notice that a lot of the lines that start with `text:` *just have whitespace in them. Later in this chapter, you'll learn where these text nodes come from and how to get rid of them if you want to.*

You can make the result of `NodeTree.xsl` look prettier by outputting HTML rather than text, using `<div>` elements to nest and indent the output that you generate. You could also use parameters to keep track of the location of the nodes in the document if you wanted.

There are several applications around that give you pretty-printed views of XML documents using XSLT. For example, the Pretty XML Tree Viewer by Mike Brown and myself, available from http://skew.org/xml/stylesheets/treeview/html/, uses XSLT to create a view of a node tree. More sophisticated viewers are interactive, allowing you to enter XPaths and highlighting the nodes that they select. See the list available at http://www.xmlsoftware.com/xpath/.

Namespaces in the Node Tree

Now we're looking at the node tree in more detail, let's make the XML a bit more complicated by including a couple of namespace declarations on the `<TVGuide>` element to create `TVGuide2.xml`:

```
<?xml version="1.0" encoding="ISO-8859-1"?>
<?xml-stylesheet type="text/xsl" href="TVGuide.xsl"?>
<TVGuide xmlns="http://www.example.com/TVGuide"
         xmlns:xsi="http://www.w3.org/2001/XMLSchema-instance"
         xsi:schemaLocation="http://www.example.com/TVGuide TVGuide.xsd"
         start="2001-07-05" end="2001-07-05">
  <Channel>
    <Name>BBC1</Name>
    ...
    <Program rating="5" flag="favorite">
      <Start>2001-07-05T19:30:00</Start>
      <Duration>PT30M</Duration>
      <Series>EastEnders</Series>
      ...
    </Program>
    ...
  </Channel>
  ...

</TVGuide>
```

We introduced namespaces in Chapter 3 and you've been using the XSLT namespace in the stylesheets that you've been generating. Introducing namespaces to the source document makes life a bit more complicated.

Let's look at what we've added to the `<TVGuide>` element. First, we've added an `xmlns` attribute:

```
xmlns="http://www.example.com/TVGuide"
```

The `xmlns` attribute is a special attribute that sets the **default namespace** for an element and its content. If an element doesn't have a prefix on its name, then it will be in the default namespace; in our document none of the elements have prefixes, so they will all be in the namespace `http://www.example.com/TVGuide`.

The next attribute we added was an `xmlns:xsi` attribute:

```
xmlns:xsi="http://www.w3.org/2001/XMLSchema-instance"
```

Attributes that start with `xmlns:` are namespace declarations that associate a particular prefix to a namespace URI. This namespace declaration associates the prefix `xsi` with the namespace `http://www.w3.org/2001/XMLSchema-instance` (a namespace used to associate XML documents with XML Schemas). The only node in the document that uses this prefix is the final attribute that we added to the `<TVGuide>` element:

```
xsi:schemaLocation="http://www.example.com/TVGuide TVGuide.xsd"
```

The name of the attribute is `xsi:schemaLocation`, but the part before the colon is a prefix that indicates the namespace to which the attribute belongs – the `XMLSchema-instance` namespace. XML Schema validators use this attribute to work out where to find the schema for an XML document.

Qualified Names

Introducing namespaces means that we have to look at names a bit more carefully. Elements and attributes have **qualified names**, a **namespace URI** that indicates the markup language that the element or attribute belongs to, and a **local name** that indicates the element or attribute's role within that markup language. There are three functions in XPath that enable you to get at the name of an element or attribute:

- `name()` returns the full name of the element or attribute as given in the source document, including the prefix if there is one
- `namespace-uri()` returns the namespace URI of the element's or attribute's namespace
- `local-name()` returns the element's or attribute's local name

The following table gives some examples of the three functions in action. The left column shows the function call in the stylesheet, and the right shows the result of the function call. I've assumed that the namespace URI `http://www.w3.org/2001/XMLSchema` is associated with the prefix `xsi` in the stylesheet, and that the namespace URI `http://www.example.com/TVGuide` is associated with the prefix `tv` in the stylesheet. I've also assumed that the `<TVGuide>` element is the current node:

Function Call	Result
`name(@xsi:schemaLocation)`	`'xsi:schemaLocation'`
`name(tv:Channel)`	`'Channel'`
`namespace-uri(@xsi:schemaLocation)`	`'http://www.w3.org/2001/XMLSchema-instance'`
`namespace-uri(tv:Channel)`	`'http://www.example.com/TVGuide'`
`local-name(@xsi:schemaLocation)`	`'schemaLocation'`
`local-name(tv:Channel)`	`'Channel'`

Note that when you locate a node with a location path in your stylesheet, such as `tv:Channel`*, you need to use the prefixes that are declared in your stylesheet rather than the prefixes that are declared within the source document. We'll look at this in more detail later in the chapter.*

The prefix that you associate with a namespace in a particular document (and therefore the prefixes that you use on the elements and attributes in that document) should not matter to your stylesheet. Therefore, in general you should avoid using the `name()` function on elements or attributes so that you don't inadvertently make your stylesheet dependent on the author of a document using particular prefixes in their namespace declarations. You can generally use a combination of the `local-name()` function and the `namespace-uri()` function instead.

In the node tree, we'll illustrate the namespace URI of a particular node by showing it in `{}`s before the name of the node. The following illustration shows the node tree for the XML document above. Note in particular that the namespace declarations themselves aren't included as attributes on the `<TVGuide>` element within the node tree:

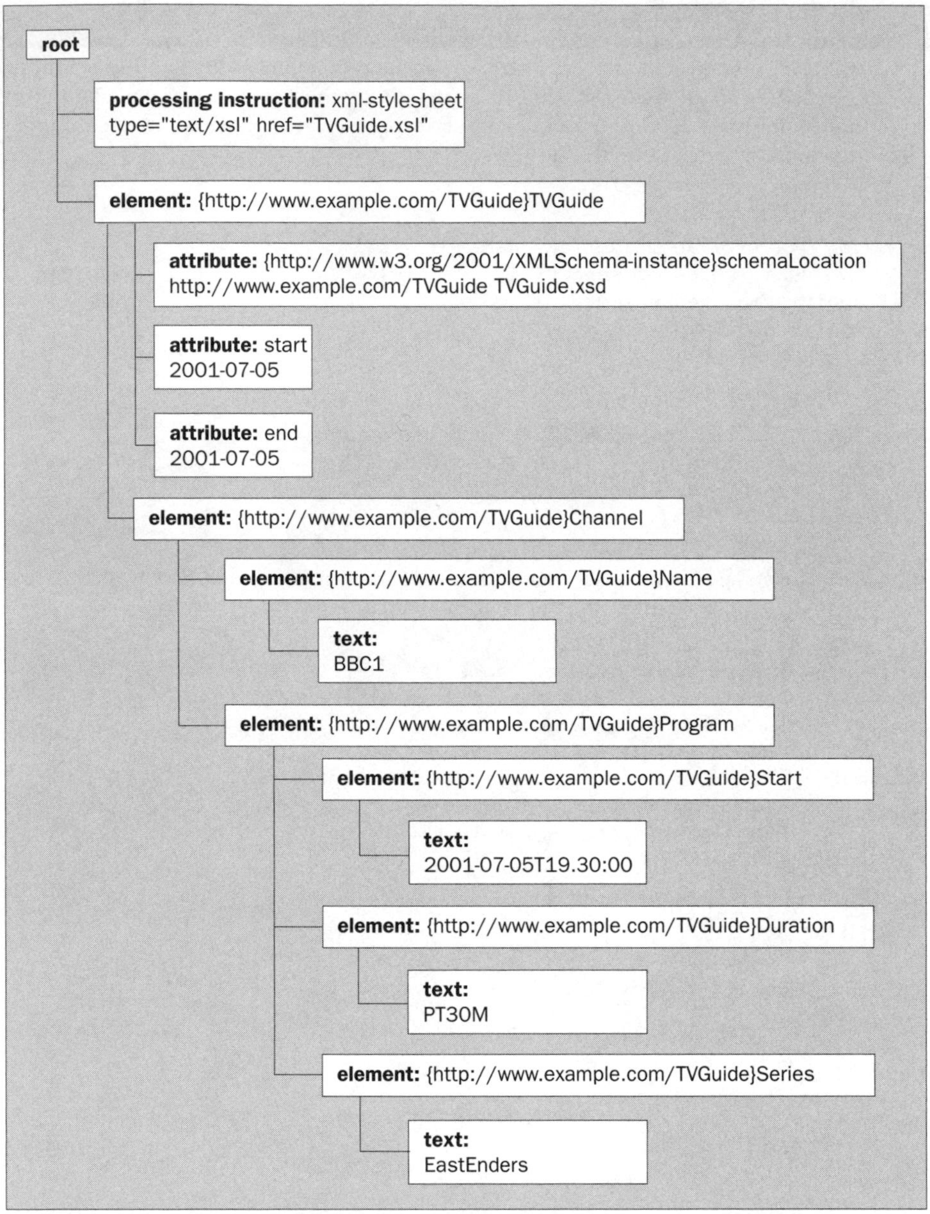

The `name()` function returns the name of an element or attribute including its prefix; the `local-name()` function returns the local part of the node's name; and the `namespace-uri()` function returns the URI of the namespace of which the node is a part.

Try It Out – Displaying Namespace Information

We can make a new version of the `NodeTree.xsl` stylesheet, which adds namespace information to the details of elements and attributes. Rather than just giving the name of elements and attributes, it should give their namespace URI and local name. For `NodeTree2.xsl`, adjust the templates that match elements and attributes to read as follows:

```
<xsl:template match="*">
  element: {<xsl:value-of select="namespace-uri()" />}
           <xsl:value-of select="local-name()" />
  <xsl:apply-templates select="@*" />
  <xsl:apply-templates />
</xsl:template>

<xsl:template match="@*">
  attribute: {<xsl:value-of select="namespace-uri()" />}
             <xsl:value-of select="local-name()" />:
             <xsl:value-of select="." />
</xsl:template>
```

Now try running the stylesheet on a document that uses namespaces, such as `TVGuide2.xml`:

```
<?xml version="1.0" encoding="UTF-16"?>
  processing instruction: xml-stylesheet:
                          type="text/xsl" href="NodeTree2.xsl"
  element: {http://www.example.com/TVGuide}
           TVGuide
  attribute: {http://www.w3.org/2001/XMLSchema-instance}
             schemaLocation:
             http://www.example.com/TVGuide TVGuide.xsd
  attribute: {}
             start:
             2001-07-05
  attribute: {}
             end:
             2001-07-05
  text:

  element: {http://www.example.com/TVGuide}
           Channel
  text:

  element: {http://www.example.com/TVGuide}
           Name
  text: BBC1
  text:

  element: {http://www.example.com/TVGuide}
           Program
  text:
```

```
element: {http://www.example.com/TVGuide}
         Start
text: 2001-07-05T19:00:00
text:

element: {http://www.example.com/TVGuide}
         Duration
text: PT30M
text:

element: {http://www.example.com/TVGuide}
         Series
text: QuestionOfSport
text:

element: {http://www.example.com/TVGuide}
         Title
text:

text:

...
```

The namespace URIs of the elements and attributes are displayed; note that the attributes that don't have a prefix have an empty namespace URI, indicating that they are not in any namespace.

Namespace Nodes

Namespace declarations each have a scope within which the particular prefix/namespace association holds true. The scope of a namespace declaration is the element that the namespace is declared on and all its contents. In terms of the node tree, a **namespace node** is added to every element in the scope of the namespace declaration. The "name" of the namespace node is the prefix that's used for the namespace (an empty string for the default namespace), and its string value is the namespace URI.

Like attributes, namespace nodes live to one side of the main tree, so you can't access them without specifically selecting them. The following diagram shows the namespace nodes within the XML document:

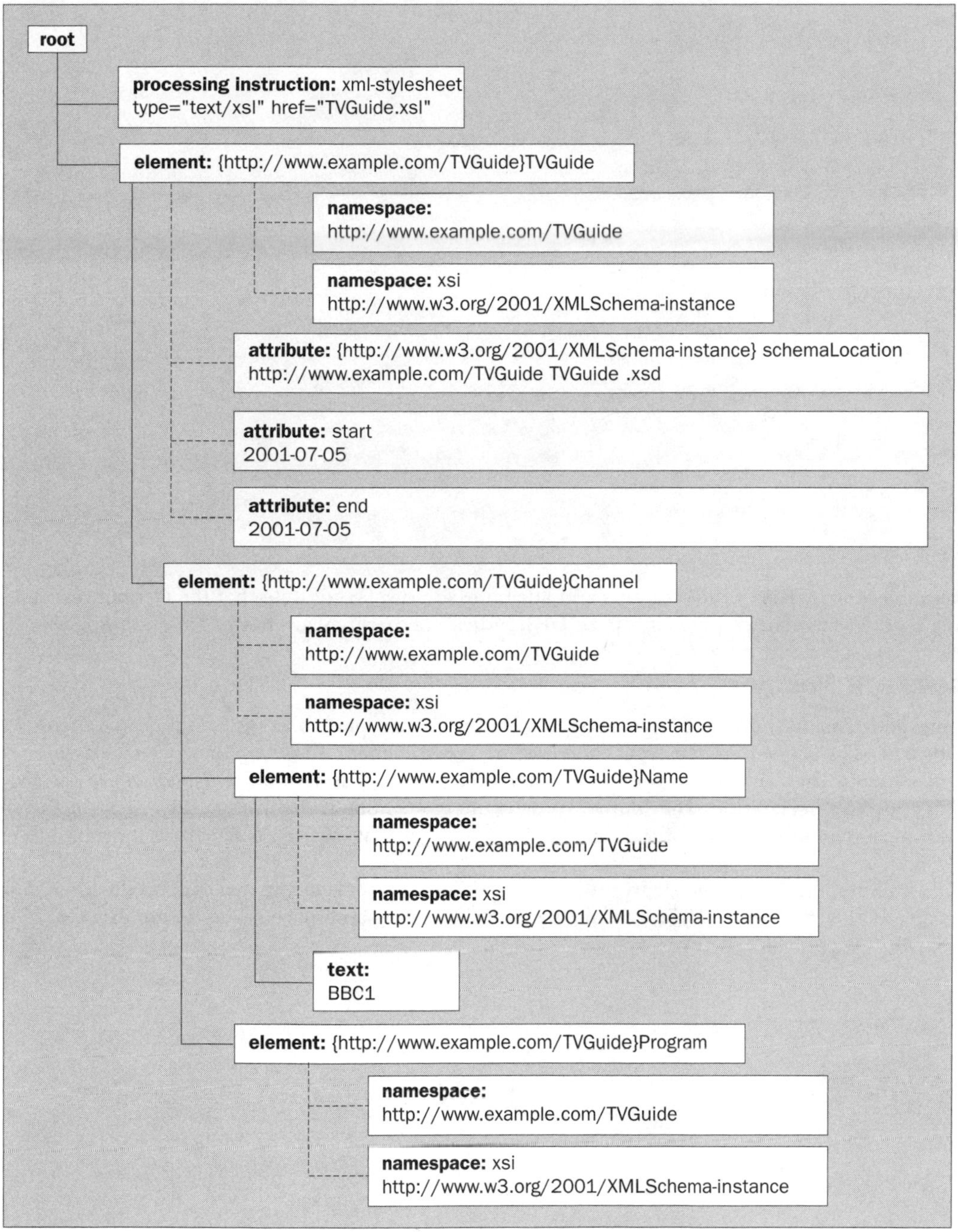
root
processing instruction: xml-stylesheet type="text/xsl" href="TVGuide.xsl"
element: {http://www.example.com/TVGuide}TVGuide
namespace: http://www.example.com/TVGuide
namespace: xsi http://www.w3.org/2001/XMLSchema-instance
attribute: {http://www.w3.org/2001/XMLSchema-instance} schemaLocation http://www.example.com/TVGuide TVGuide .xsd
attribute: start 2001-07-05
attribute: end 2001-07-05
element: {http://www.example.com/TVGuide}Channel
namespace: http://www.example.com/TVGuide
namespace: xsi http://www.w3.org/2001/XMLSchema-instance
element: {http://www.example.com/TVGuide}Name
namespace: http://www.example.com/TVGuide
namespace: xsi http://www.w3.org/2001/XMLSchema-instance
text: BBC1
element: {http://www.example.com/TVGuide}Program
namespace: http://www.example.com/TVGuide
namespace: xsi http://www.w3.org/2001/XMLSchema-instance

Namespace nodes aren't selected very often, and you cannot match namespace nodes, but it's useful to know about them because when you construct a node tree as the result of a transformation, the locations of the namespace nodes within the node tree determines where namespace declarations will be added when the node tree is serialized into another XML document. We'll look at this in detail in the next chapter.

Every element has a number of namespace nodes, one for each of the namespace declarations that are in scope for that element.

Whitespace in Node Trees

When we used the `NodeTree.xsl` stylesheet in the last couple of sections, we noticed that as well as all the nodes that we expected to find within the tree, we also found a bunch of text nodes that didn't seem to have any content. If you take another look at the XML document, you'll see that in order to format it nicely, we've used new lines between elements and indented elements with tabs and spaces to indicate their level within the node tree. This is good practice because it makes XML documents easier to understand, especially if they have lots of levels, but it also introduces **whitespace** (characters that are displayed as white spaces) to the document that really we want to ignore.

XML regards four characters as whitespace characters:

- space (` `)
- tab (`	`)
- newline (`
`)
- carriage return (`
`)

The code held in brackets is the character reference for the whitespace character.

The whitespace that you use within tags, for example, between the element name and attributes, between attributes, or at the end of the tag, doesn't matter, but whitespace that you use in element content, attribute values, comments, and processing instructions is faithfully reported to the XSLT processor by the XML parser, and is included in the node tree that the XSLT processor constructs. We can replace the whitespace in element content and attribute values with the character references for the whitespace characters instead, as in `TVGuide3.xml`, and the XSLT processor will build exactly the same node tree:

```
<?xml version="1.0" encoding="ISO-8859-1"?>
<?xml-stylesheet type="text/xsl" href="TVGuide.xsl"?>
<TVGuide xmlns="http://www.example.com/TVGuide"
         xmlns:xsi="http://www.w3.org/2001/XMLSchema-instance"
         xsi:schemaLocation="http://www.example.com/TVGuide TVGuide.xsd"
         start="2001-07-05" end="2001-07-05"
>&#xA;&#x20;&#x20;<Channel
>&#xA;&#x20;&#x20;&#x20;&#x20;<Name>BBC1</Name
>&#xA;&#x20;&#x20;&#x20;&#x20;<Program rating="5" flag="favorite"
>&#xA;&#x20;&#x20;&#x20;&#x20;&#x20;&#x20;<Start>2001-07-05T19:30:00</Start
```

```
>&#xA;&#x20;&#x20;&#x20;&#x20;&#x20;&#x20;<Duration>PT30M</Duration
>&#xA;&#x20;&#x20;&#x20;&#x20;&#x20;&#x20;<Series>EastEnders</Series
>&#xA;&#x20;&#x20;&#x20;&#x20;&#x20;&#x20;<Title></Title
>&#xA;&#x20;&#x20;&#x20;&#x20;</Program
>&#xA;&#x20;&#x20;</Channel
>&#xA;</TVGuide>
```

If you replace all the literal line breaks with the character reference `
` *then you end up with a file that's pretty unreadable because it's all on one line. I've made this file easier to read by adding line breaks within the element start and end tags (where whitespace doesn't matter) instead, which is why most of the lines start with the greater-than signs that signal the end of the tag started on the previous line.*

The whitespace that you use to indent elements in your file is included in the node tree as text nodes. Looking at the above XML, you can see whitespace between the `<TVGuide>` and the `<Channel>` start tags, between the `<Channel>` start tag and the `<Name>` element, between the `<Name>` and the `<Program>` element, and so on. In fact, the node tree that the XSLT processor constructs for this XML document looks like the one shown in the following diagram:

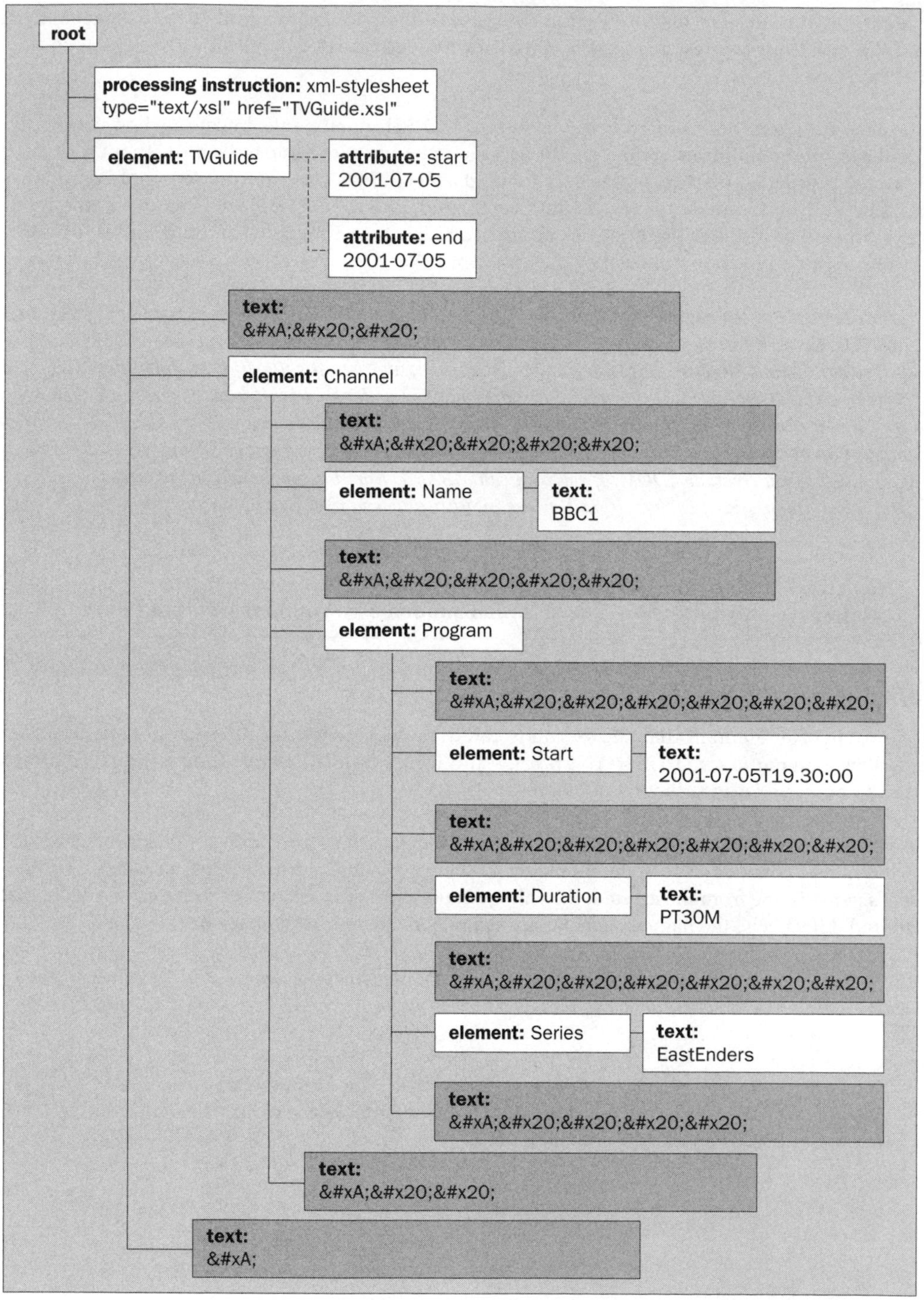
root
processing instruction: xml-stylesheet type="text/xsl" href="TVGuide.xsl"
element: TVGuide
attribute: start 2001-07-05
attribute: end 2001-07-05
text:

element: Channel
text:

element: Name
text: BBC1
text:

element: Program
text:

element: Start
text: 2001-07-05T19.30:00
text:

element: Duration
text: PT30M
text:

element: Series
text: EastEnders
text:

text:

text:

The highlighted nodes are text nodes that consist purely of whitespace, called **whitespace-only text nodes**. We saw these whitespace-only text nodes when we transformed `TVGuide.xml` with `NodeTree.xsl`.

Whitespace-only text nodes often cause problems in XML documents, because when you apply templates to all the children of an element using `<xsl:apply-templates>` without a `select` attribute, whitespace-only text nodes get included as well. What happens if you apply templates to a text node? The built-in template for text nodes is activated, and the whitespace is output to the tree. What's more, if you try to number the nodes using the `position()` function, then the whitespace-only text nodes are included in the numbering.

What I've said in the above paragraph is true for the majority of XSLT processors. However, if you use MSXML through Internet Explorer, you'll find that the node tree actually contains no whitespace-only text nodes. Because Internet Explorer uses the DOM API, which is slightly different from the XSLT view of an XML document, it ignores whitespace-only text nodes by default when it constructs the node tree. If you're running the transformation from code (as in Chapter 14), you can stop this from happening by explicitly setting the property `preserveWhiteSpace` *on the* `Document` *object to* `true` *when you create the DOM. If you then run MSXML from the command line, whitespace-only text nodes are preserved by default, as they are in other conformant XSLT processors.*

Node trees often contain text nodes that contain only whitespace characters (whitespace-only text nodes) due to the indentation used within the XML document.

Stripping Whitespace-Only Text Nodes

XSLT provides an element that allows you to tell the XSLT processor to ignore the whitespace-only text nodes. This element is `<xsl:strip-space>` and it's a top-level element, occurring as a direct child of the `<xsl:stylesheet>` document element.

The `<xsl:strip-space>` element has a single attribute, `elements`, whose value is either an asterisk (*) or a whitespace-separated list of element names. If the `elements` attribute holds an asterisk, or if an element's name is one from those listed, then all the whitespace-only text nodes that are children of that element are ignored. Effectively, the named elements are **stripped** of all their whitespace-only text node children.

Stripping whitespace-only text nodes has no effect at all on whitespace contained in the values of text-only elements or attributes; to control that, you need to use the `normalize-space()` *function.*

You can get rid of whitespace-only text nodes using the `<xsl:strip-space>` element, whose `elements` attribute lists the elements whose child whitespace-only text nodes are stripped from the node tree.

Try It Out – Ignoring Whitespace-Only Text Nodes

Now we'll add an instruction telling the processor to remove all the whitespace-only text nodes from the document. Add an `<xsl:strip-space>` element at the top level of `NodeTree2.xsl` to create a new version, `NodeTree3.xsl`, that strips all the whitespace-only text nodes from the tree, so that the stylesheet reads as follows:

```
<?xml version="1.0" encoding="ISO-8859-1"?>
<xsl:stylesheet version="1.0"
                xmlns:xsl="http://www.w3.org/1999/XSL/Transform">
<xsl:strip-space elements="*" />
...
</xsl:stylesheet>
```

Run `NodeTree3.xsl` on `TVGuide2.xml`, and you should get the following output:

```
<?xml version="1.0" encoding="UTF-16"?>
  processing instruction: xml-stylesheet:
                          type="text/xsl" href="NodeTree3.xsl"
  element: {http://www.example.com/TVGuide}
           TVGuide
  attribute: {http://www.w3.org/2001/XMLSchema-instance}
             schemaLocation:
             http://www.example.com/TVGuide TVGuide.xsd
  attribute: {}
             start:
             2001-07-05
  attribute: {}
             end:
             2001-07-05
  element: {http://www.example.com/TVGuide}
           Channel
  element: {http://www.example.com/TVGuide}
           Name
  text: BBC1
  element: {http://www.example.com/TVGuide}
           Program
  element: {http://www.example.com/TVGuide}
           Start
  text: 2001-07-05T19:00:00
  element: {http://www.example.com/TVGuide}
           Duration
  text: PT30M
  element: {http://www.example.com/TVGuide}
           Series
  text: QuestionOfSport
  element: {http://www.example.com/TVGuide}
           Title
```

The whitespace-only text nodes have been stripped from the tree, so there are no lines that start with `text:` but hold no information.

Preserving Whitespace-Only Text Nodes

In data-oriented XML, all whitespace-only text nodes can usually be safely stripped out of the node tree. In document-oriented XML, on the other hand, you often get whitespace-only text nodes that should be **preserved**. For example, look at the following <Description> element:

```
<Description>
  ...
  <Character>Jamie</Character> <Link href="Mitchells.html">Mitchell</Link>
  ...
</Description>
```

The space between the <Character> element and the <Link> element is part of the description; when we read the description in an HTML page, we want to read Jamie Mitchell, not JamieMitchell. But this space occurs without any non-whitespace characters around it, creating a whitespace-only text node between the <Character> and <Link> elements in the node tree as follows:

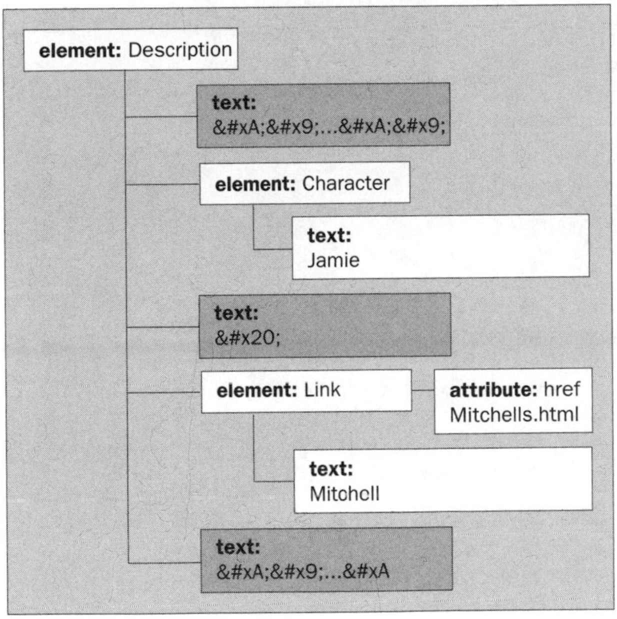

If you used <xsl:strip-space elements="*" /> to strip all the whitespace-only text nodes from the node tree, then this significant whitespace-only text node would be lost as well. On the other hand, if you didn't then you'd have to be aware of the whitespace-only text nodes that occur in the rest of the document, or list all the element names in the elements attribute of <xsl:strip-space>, which would be tedious.

So there are two facilities for preventing whitespace-only text nodes from being stripped.

The first is <xsl:preserve-space>, which is the opposite of <xsl:strip-space>. The <xsl:preserve-space> element is also a top-level element and has an elements attribute that can take the same kind of values as the elements attribute of <xsl:strip-space>. If an element is listed in the elements attribute of <xsl:preserve-space> then the whitespace-only text nodes that it contains are kept in the node tree.

The <xsl:preserve-space> element stops whitespace-only text nodes from being stripped from the elements named in its elements attribute.

The second method of preventing whitespace-only text nodes from being stripped is to use the attribute xml:space with the value preserve in the XML document itself. The xml:space attribute is defined in the XML Recommendation as the way to indicate how whitespace should be treated within a particular element. If you put an xml:space attribute with the value preserve on an element in the source XML document, then no matter what <xsl:strip-space> instruction you have, all the whitespace-only text nodes that descend from that element will be preserved.

You'll notice that the xml:space attribute's name includes a colon, indicating that it's a space attribute in the XML namespace. Unlike other namespaces, however, you don't have to declare the XML namespace with the prefix xml. Namespace-aware applications assume that an element or attribute that has the prefix xml is in the XML namespace automatically.

Putting an xml:space attribute with the value preserve on an element preserves all the whitespace-only text nodes that it contains, at any level.

Matching Nodes

In the first part of this chapter, we've revisited the node tree that is constructed by an XSLT processor when you give it an XML document to process. In this section, we'll look at how to match nodes within that node tree with match patterns.

You've already encountered a number of match patterns, which you've used to create templates that match particular elements in particular contexts. In this section, we'll take a more formal look at the syntax of location path patterns and you'll learn how to construct patterns that match different types of nodes in different contexts and with different values.

Location Path Patterns

In the patterns that we've looked at in previous chapters, we've seen how to select all elements or particular elements by name and by context. You've seen how a template can match all elements of a particular name in a document by simply naming the elements that it matches. For example, the following template matches all <Program> elements:

```
<xsl:template match="Program">
  ...
</xsl:template>
```

You've also seen how you can use location path patterns to match elements that occur in specific contexts. For example, the following template matches only those <Program> elements that occur at some level within <Description> elements:

```
<xsl:template match="Description//Program">
  ...
</xsl:template>
```

You can use a single pattern to match several different particular elements by separating their location path patterns with | characters. For example, the following template matches <Channel>, <Program>, and <Series> elements that occur within <Description> elements:

```
<xsl:template match="Description//Channel | Description//Program |
                     Description//Series">
  ...
</xsl:template>
```

Note that the character |, when used within a pattern (such as the `match` attribute of `<xsl:template>`), separates alternative patterns. As we'll see later, when you use the character | within an expression (such as in the `select` attribute of `<xsl:apply-templates>`) then it acts as the union operator, which creates a node set that contains all the nodes from its two operands.

Each one of the location path patterns, separated by | characters, can consist of a number of **step patterns**, which can be separated by / or //. Separating step patterns using / indicates a parent-child or element-attribute relationship, while separating steps using // indicates an ancestor-descendant relationship. For example, `Description//Program` matches <Program> elements that are descendants of <Description> elements at any level, while `Description/Program` only matches <Program> elements that are direct children of <Description> elements.

Patterns can contain a number of location path patterns, separated by | characters. A node matches the pattern as a whole if it matches any of the location path patterns.

Step Patterns

Each step pattern is actually made up of three parts, though only one, the **node test**, is always required. The three parts are an **axis**, which indicates a *tree relationship* between nodes; the node test, which specifies the *type* of node that the step pattern matches; and the **predicates**, which *test* these nodes further to see if they match the pattern. You've already seen node tests, such as `node()`, `text()`, and `*`, in action; here we'll have a closer look at axes and predicates in step patterns.

Axes in Step Patterns

The axis is separated from the node test with a double-colon (`::`). In patterns, the only kinds of axes you can have are the `child::` axis (to match element content) and the `attribute::` axis (to match attributes). If you don't specify an axis, then it's just the same as specifying the `child::` axis. For example, the following three paths all match <Series> elements that are children of <Program> elements:

```
child::Program/child::Series
Program/child::Series
Program/Series
```

You have to use the `attribute::` axis if you want to match attributes, but you can use an `@` instead of `attribute::` as a shorthand. For example, the following patterns match `start` attributes on `<TVGuide>` elements:

```
child::TVGuide/attribute::start
TVGuide/attribute::start
TVGuide/@start
```

It's rare to actually specify axes in step patterns, but they are very useful when you start selecting nodes by navigating the node tree via different tree relationships, as you'll see later on.

Predicates in Step Patterns

A step pattern can have one or more predicates to further filter the nodes that are matched by the node test. The predicate contains a test; if the test is `true` then the node is matched, and if the test is `false` then the node is not matched. Often a predicate will test the value, children, or attributes of an element. For example, a step pattern that matched `<Program>` elements whose child `<Series>` element started with `'StarTrek'` would be:

```
Program[starts-with(Series, 'StarTrek')]
```

If the expression that you use in the predicate evaluates to a number, then the number is tested against the position of the matched node amongst its siblings that are also matched by the portion of the step pattern prior to the predicate. Most frequently you use this to work out whether the matched element is the first child of its type within its parent. For example, the following pattern matches the first `<Program>` element child of the `<Channel>` element:

```
Program[1]
```

You can have as many predicates as you like after specifying the matched node. The second predicate is used on the result of whatever you get after the first predicate. If you're using several predicates, including one that indicates the position of a node, you need to make sure that they are in the order that you intend. For example, the following matches the `<Program>` element that is the first `<Program>` element child of its parent element, but only if its `<Series>` element child starts with the string `'StarTrek'`; if the first program is not a Star Trek episode, the template will never be used:

```
Program[1][starts-with(Series, 'StarTrek')]
```

On the other hand, the following pattern matches the first `<Program>` element within its parent whose `<Series>` child starts with the string `'StarTrek'`; even if the first episode of Star Trek is the third program shown on the channel, the template with this match pattern will still process it:

```
Program[starts-with(Series, 'StarTrek')][1]
```

Predicates don't always occur at the end of a match pattern. For example, the following pattern matches `<Program>` element children of `<Channel>` elements whose `<Name>` child element starts with the string `'BBC'`, in other words the programs shown by the BBC:

```
Channel[starts-with(Name, 'BBC')]/Program
```

In general, you can convert templates that only contain an `<xsl:if>` or `<xsl:choose>` element into two or more templates, each of which covers one of the possibilities. A template that only contains an `<xsl:if>` as follows:

```
<xsl:template match="pattern">
  <xsl:if test="test">
    instructions
  </xsl:if>
</xsl:template>
```

can be converted into two templates. One of these does nothing and the other has a match pattern with a predicate that holds the test that was used by the `<xsl:if>`, as follows:

```
<xsl:template match="pattern" />
<xsl:template match="pattern[test]">
  instructions
</xsl:template>
```

If you use predicates rather than `<xsl:choose>` or `<xsl:if>`, you have to beware of three pitfalls:

- You cannot use a variable reference within the `match` attribute of `<xsl:template>`, so the predicates cannot be dependent on the values of global variables or parameters.
- Templates that have match patterns that include predicates all have a default priority of 0.5, just like those that include information about the parent or ancestors of the node being matched (you learned about the default priorities of different templates in Chapter 4). You need to either construct match patterns that cannot match the same node or add `priority` attributes to the `<xsl:template>` elements to make sure that the XSLT processor applies the correct template.
- When you test the position of a node, a test within a template relates to its position amongst all the other nodes that are having templates applied to them, in the order in which they are having templates applied (as we'll see when we look at sorting and numbering in Chapter 9). On the other hand, a test within a predicate in the step pattern relates to the position of the node amongst other nodes matched by the preceding portion of the step pattern. These two sets of nodes might not be the same.

As an example of this last point, say that you applied templates to only Star Trek episodes, with the instruction:

```
<xsl:apply-templates select="Program[starts-with(Series, 'StarTrek')]" />
```

and imagine that you had two separate templates – one that matches the first `<Program>` element (and highlights it), and one that matches other `<Program>` elements, as follows:

```
<xsl:template match="Program[1]">
  <div class="highlight">
    <xsl:apply-templates select="." mode="Details" />
  </div>
</xsl:template>

<xsl:template match="Program[position() > 1]">
  <div><xsl:apply-templates select="." mode="Details" /></div>
</xsl:template>
```

In this situation, whether or not the first template is ever used depends on whether the first program within the channel is a Star Trek episode or not. The first template matches only the first `<Program>` element within the `<Channel>`. If the first program is not a Star Trek episode, then even though we're only listing Star Trek episodes, the first template will never get used.

What's probably required is a single template that matches all programs, wherever they are, in which you test the position of the program *amongst the selected programs.* This would give:

```
<xsl:template match="Program">
  <xsl:choose>
    <xsl:when test="position() = 1">
      <div class="highlight">
        <xsl:apply-templates select="." mode="Details" />
      </div>
    </xsl:when>
    <xsl:otherwise>
      <div><xsl:apply-templates select="." mode="Details" /></div>
    </xsl:otherwise>
  </xsl:choose>
</xsl:template>
```

With this, the first selected program will be highlighted no matter where it occurs in the source document. Using the `position()` function tests the position of the node within the list of nodes to which templates are applied; predicates within match patterns test the position of the node amongst its same-named siblings.

> **If you include a predicate in a step, then the step only matches nodes for which the predicate is true. The position of a node is assessed within the list of other nodes that match the part of the step prior to the predicate.**

Try It Out – Positional Predicates in Match Patterns

Let's return to `TVGuide.xsl` to have a look at how predicates work within match patterns. We'll amend the template matching `<Program>` elements in `TVGuide.xsl` so that the first program on each channel (the program that's showing now) is highlighted using the `nowShowing` class, with an additional `<xsl:when>` clause as follows:

```
<xsl:template match="Program">
  <xsl:choose>
    <xsl:when test="position() = 1">
```

```
        <div class="nowShowing">
          <xsl:apply-templates select="." mode="Details" />
        </div>
      </xsl:when>
      <xsl:when test="@flag = 'favorite' or @flag = 'interesting' or
                      @rating > 6 or
                      contains(translate(Series, $upper, $lower), $keyword) or
                      contains(translate(Title, $upper, $lower), $keyword) or
                      contains(translate(Description, $upper, $lower),
                               $keyword)">
        <div class="interesting">
          <xsl:apply-templates select="." mode="Details" />
        </div>
      </xsl:when>
      <xsl:otherwise>
        <div>
          <xsl:apply-templates select="." mode="Details" />
        </div>
      </xsl:otherwise>
    </xsl:choose>
  </xsl:template>
```

We'll add a style to the CSS stylesheet for the TV Guide, to create `TVGuide2.css`, so that the details for the first program showing on each channel are shown with a slightly larger font, as follows:

```
div.nowShowing {
    font-size: 120%;
}
```

The template matching `<Program>` elements is processed when templates are applied to the children of `<Channel>` elements. At the moment, the XSLT processor applies templates to all the children of the `<Channel>` elements at once, including whitespace-only text nodes and the `<Name>` element, as follows:

```
<xsl:template match="Channel">
  <xsl:apply-templates />
</xsl:template>
```

When we use `TVGuide2.xsl` with `TVGuide.xml`, we get the following result:

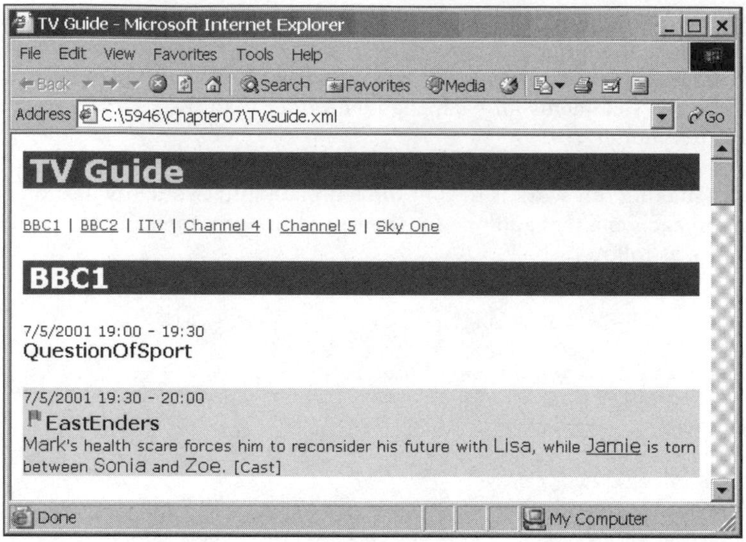

Now let's change the `<xsl:apply-templates>` instruction so that we explicitly select the `<Program>` elements, as follows, in `TVGuide3.xsl`:

```
<xsl:template match="Channel">
  <xsl:apply-templates select="Name" />
  <xsl:apply-templates select="Program" />
</xsl:template>
```

When you use `TVGuide3.xsl` with `TVGuide.xml`, you should get the following result:

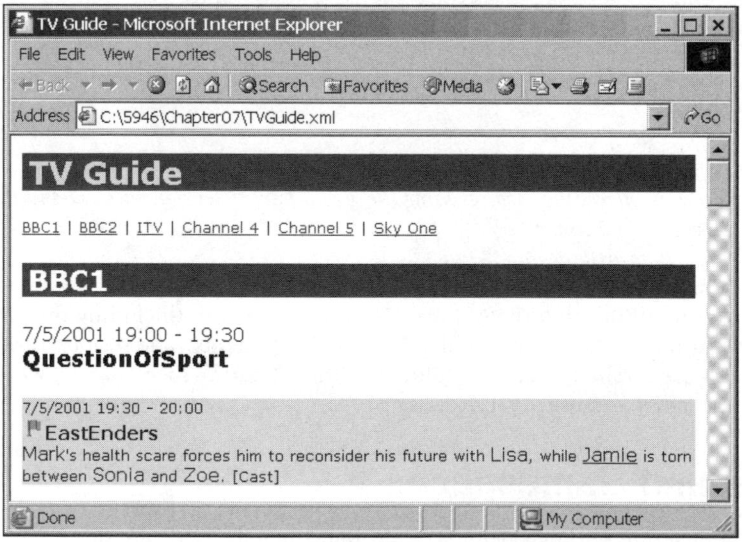

The details for 'Question of Sport', and the other programs that are showing 'now', one per channel, are larger than the details for the other programs. The `position()` function, used within the template for the `<Program>` element, looks at the position of the current node within the current node list, which is now only the `<Program>` elements for each channel, rather than the `<Name>` element and any number of whitespace-only text nodes.

Another method of making this work is to split the template into two templates: one for the first program showing on each channel and one for the rest of the programs. The two templates, in `TVGuide4.xsl`, are as follows:

```
<xsl:template match="Program[1]">
  <div class="nowShowing">
    <xsl:apply-templates select="." mode="Details" />
  </div>
</xsl:template>

<xsl:template match="Program">
  <xsl:choose>
    <xsl:when test="@flag = 'favorite' or @flag = 'interesting' or
                    @rating > 6 or
                    contains(translate(Series, $upper, $lower), $keyword) or
                    contains(translate(Title, $upper, $lower), $keyword) or
                    contains(translate(Description, $upper, $lower),
                             $keyword)">
      <div class="interesting">
        <xsl:apply-templates select="." mode="Details" />
      </div>
    </xsl:when>
    <xsl:otherwise>
      <div>
        <xsl:apply-templates select="." mode="Details" />
      </div>
    </xsl:otherwise>
  </xsl:choose>
</xsl:template>
```

Note that you can't use a separate template to match the "interesting" programs, since testing whether a program is interesting involves using the global parameter `$keyword` and the global variables `$upper` and `$lower`.

The first template matches the first `<Program>` elements within each `<Channel>` element, whether you apply templates to all the children of the `<Channel>` element (including the `<Name>` element and whitespace-only text nodes), or just its child `<Program>` elements. The result of using `TVGuide4.xsl` (in which templates are applied to all the children of the `<Channel>` elements) with `TVGuide.xml` is exactly the same as when you use `TVGuide3.xsl`.

Name Tests and Namespaces

When you use a node test to select an element or attribute, then the node test doesn't just test the type of the node; it also tests its name. These kinds of tests are termed **name tests**. There are four types of name tests:

- `*` – matches any element/attribute
- *`name`* – matches any element/attribute with that name and that isn't in a namespace
- *`prefix`*`:*` – matches any element/attribute in the namespace indicated by the prefix
- *`prefix`*`:`*`name`* – matches any element/attribute with that name and that is in the namespace indicated by the prefix

Matching Elements in Namespaces

The prefixes that you use in paths should be the ones that you use *in the stylesheet*, not the ones that are used in the source XML document. As an example, let's look again at `TVGuide2.xml`, which includes namespaces:

```
<?xml version="1.0" encoding="ISO-8859-1"?>
<?xml-stylesheet type="text/xsl" href="TVGuide4.xsl"?>
<TVGuide xmlns="http://www.example.com/TVGuide"
         xmlns:xsi="http://www.w3.org/2001/XMLSchema-instance"
         xsi:schemaLocation="http://www.example.com/TVGuide TVGuide.xsd"
         start="2001-07-05" end="2001-07-05">
  <Channel>
    <Name>BBC1</Name>
    ...
    <Program>
      <Start>2001-07-05T19:30:00</Start>
      <Duration>PT30M</Duration>
      <Series>EastEnders</Series>
      ...
    </Program>
    ...
  </Channel>
</TVGuide>
```

All the elements in the XML document are in the TV Guide namespace. What would happen if we tried to process `<Channel>` elements with the following template?

```
<xsl:template match="Channel">
   Channel: <xsl:value-of select="Name" />
</xsl:template>
```

The name test (`Channel`) doesn't give a prefix, so the XSLT processor will only match `<Channel>` elements that aren't in a namespace. The `<Channel>` elements in our source XML document are in the `http://www.example.com/TVGuide` namespace, so they won't get matched. You can see this in action if you try to transform `TVGuide2.xml` with `TVGuide4.xsl`. The result of the transformation is as follows:

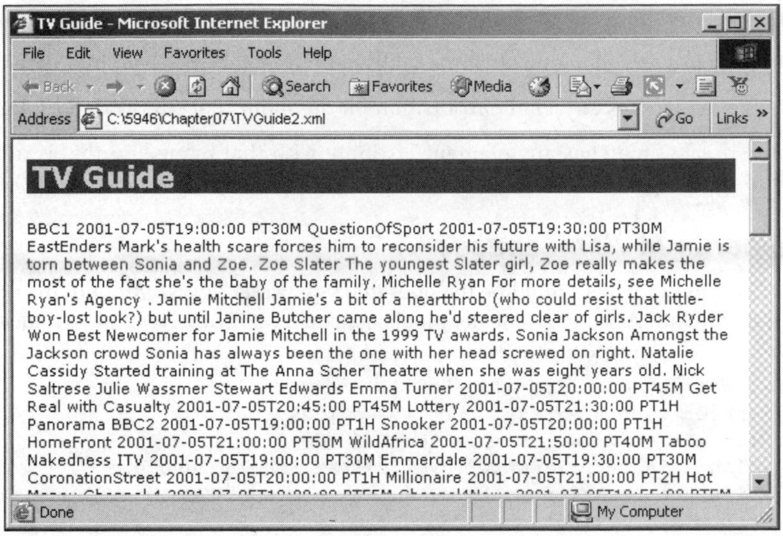

We get three copies of the text within `TVGuide2.xml` – two from applying templates in `ChannelList` mode, and one from applying templates in normal mode. The text is output because none of the templates match the nodes in `TVGuide2.xml`, so the built-in templates (which just output text) are used instead.

To match the elements in the `http://www.example.com/TVGuide` namespace, we have to declare the `http://www.example.com/TVGuide` namespace in the stylesheet, with a prefix, and then use that prefix in the paths throughout the stylesheet. You must use the prefix whenever you specify an element by name, and you can also use it in combination with the wildcard name test. For example, the pattern `tv:*` matches elements in the TV Guide namespace, no matter what their local name is.

> *The pattern * still matches elements in any namespace, so in many cases you don't have to prefix wildcard name tests with the relevant prefix. Matching all elements in a particular namespace is really useful, for example, in transformations where you want to strip all the elements in a particular namespace from a document.*

As a simple example, this stylesheet (`Channels.xsl`) simply lists the names of the channels. The TV Guide namespace is declared in the stylesheet with the prefix `tv`, and that prefix is used both in the pattern used to match the `<Channel>` elements and in the expression used to select the `<Name>` of the channel:

```
<xsl:stylesheet version="1.0"
                xmlns:xsl="http://www.w3.org/1999/XSL/Transform"
                xmlns:tv="http://www.example.com/TVGuide">

<xsl:template match="tv:Channel">
  Channel: <xsl:value-of select="tv:Name" />
</xsl:template>

</xsl:stylesheet>
```

As you can see, adding a default namespace declaration to an XML document makes it impossible to use the same stylesheet with it as you used before – you have to add the namespace to the stylesheet and then go through adding the prefix to all the name tests in all the expressions and patterns in the stylesheet.

> **If an element you want to select or match is in a namespace, you have to use a name test that uses the prefix associated with that namespace within the stylesheet.**

Try It Out – Adding Namespaces to Stylesheets

We've added a default namespace to the `TVGuide2.xml` document. Now it's time to make a new version of our stylesheet (`TVGuide5.xsl`) so that we can display the TV Guide in the way we did before. Adding the default namespace to `TVGuide2.xml` was very easy – we just added an `xmlns` attribute to the document element, as follows:

```
<TVGuide xmlns="http://www.example.com/TVGuide">
  ...
</TVGuide>
```

However, adding this default namespace fundamentally changes the way that the XSLT processor sees the elements in the document. Previously, they've been in no namespace; now they're in the `http://www.example.com/TVGuide` namespace. To match and select them, we have to add a namespace declaration to the `<xsl:stylesheet>` element in `TVGuide5.xsl`, using the same namespace URI but assigning a prefix to it:

```
<xsl:stylesheet version="1.0"
                xmlns:xsl="http://www.w3.org/1999/XSL/Transform"
                xmlns:tv="http://www.example.com/TVGuide">
  ...
</xsl:stylesheet>
```

Then we have to go through all the patterns and expressions in the stylesheet and add the `tv` prefix to the element names that are used within them. For example, here is a converted version of the template for `<Program>` elements in `Details` mode. All the element names used in the template are given a `tv` prefix:

```
<xsl:template match="tv:Program" mode="Details">
  <xsl:variable name="programID" select="concat(tv:Series, 'Cast')" />
  <p>
    <xsl:apply-templates select="tv:Start" /><br />
    <xsl:variable name="image">
      <xsl:choose>
        <xsl:when test="@flag = 'favorite'">favorite</xsl:when>
        <xsl:when test="@flag = 'interesting'">interest</xsl:when>
      </xsl:choose>
    </xsl:variable>
    <xsl:variable name="alt">
      <xsl:choose>
        <xsl:when test="@flag = 'favorite'">Favorite</xsl:when>
        <xsl:when test="@flag = 'interesting'">Interest</xsl:when>
```

```
        </xsl:choose>
      </xsl:variable>
      <xsl:if test="@flag">
        <img src="{$image}.gif" alt="[{$alt}]" width="20" height="20" />
      </xsl:if>
      <xsl:if test="starts-with(tv:Series, 'StarTrek')">
        <xsl:copy-of select="$StarTrekLogo" />
      </xsl:if>
      <xsl:apply-templates select="." mode="Title" />
      <br />
      <xsl:apply-templates select="tv:Description" />
      <xsl:apply-templates select="tv:CastList" mode="DisplayToggle">
        <xsl:with-param name="divID" select="$programID" />
      </xsl:apply-templates>
    </p>
    <xsl:apply-templates select="tv:CastList">
      <xsl:with-param name="divID" select="$programID" />
    </xsl:apply-templates>
  </xsl:template>
```

*Note that you should **not** add the prefix to the names of attributes. Attributes without prefixes are in no namespace, whatever the default namespace, so you must select them using just their name, without a prefix.*

When you have added the `tv` prefix to all the element names in the stylesheet, try transforming `TVGuide2.xml` with `TVGuide5.xsl`. You should see the same result as we had when transforming `TVGuide.xml` with `TVGuide4.xsl`:

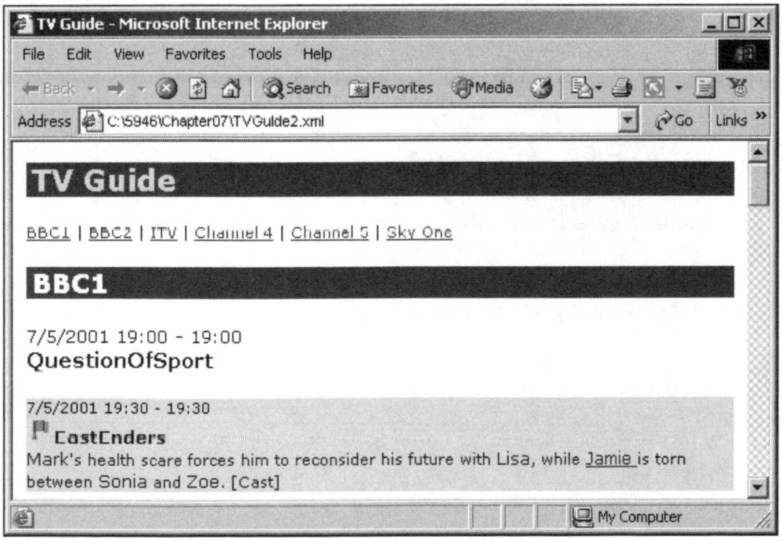

Again, though, if you try transforming `TVGuide.xml`, in which the elements are in no namespace, with `TVGuide5.xsl`, which assumes that the elements are in the TV Guide namespace, you have the same problem as you did when transforming `TVGuide2.xml` with `TVGuide4.xsl`:

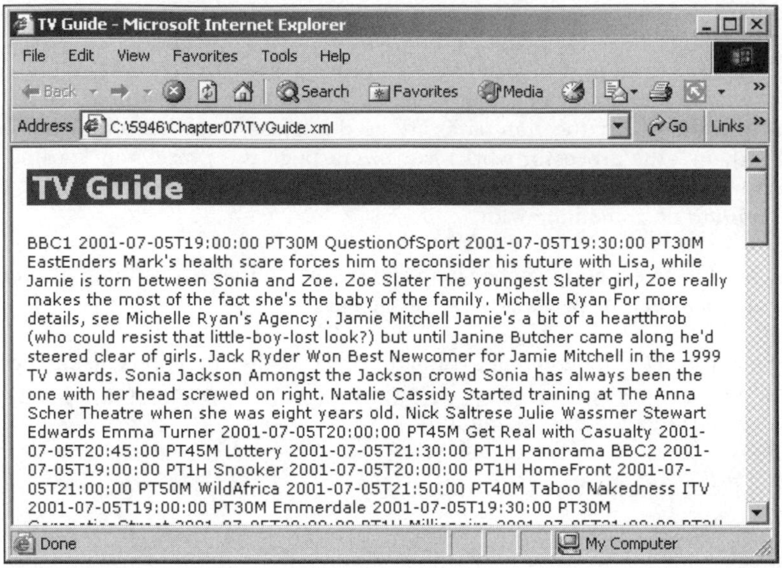

The namespaces that you use in your source XML document must match the namespaces that you use in your XSLT stylesheet to get the result that you require.

Template Priorities

You'll remember from Chapter 4 that the default priority of a template, used if you don't give a `priority` attribute, depends on the pattern that you use in the `match` attribute. In Chapter 4, we saw three priority levels; when you start including patterns that match elements in different namespaces, there are actually four:

- Templates whose match patterns match a class of nodes, such as `*` or `text()`, are assigned a default priority of -0.5
- Templates whose match patterns match elements or attributes in a particular namespace, such as `tv:*` or `xsi:*`, are assigned a default priority of -0.25
- Templates whose match patterns match elements or attributes by name, such as `Channel` or `xsi:schemaLocation`, are assigned a default priority of 0
- Templates whose match patterns contain a number of step patterns or include a predicate, such as `Description//Channel` or `Program[1]`, are assigned a default priority of 0.5

Selecting Nodes

The last section looked at how to indicate what kinds of nodes a template matches, using patterns. In this section, we're going to look at how to select nodes within expressions, using location paths.

The paths that you use to select nodes look very similar to the path patterns that you use to match nodes, and it's easy to get confused between them. Remember that patterns are used to test whether a template should be used for a particular node – the processor works *backwards* through the pattern, checking the parents and ancestors of the node that you've told it to process to see if it complies with the pattern. On the other hand, location paths are used to gather together a bunch of nodes in order to process or query them – the processor works *forwards* through the expression, starting from whatever node you're currently processing, and traveling step by step through the node tree to locate a set of nodes that you want to do something with.

Because they're used to select nodes rather than simply match them, location paths have a syntax that's a lot more flexible than that for patterns, as we'll see later.

Node sets can be constructed by creating a **union** of several other node sets, using the | operator. For example, the following expression selects the `<Writer>`, `<Director>`, and `<Producer>` child elements of the current `<Program>` element:

```
Writer | Director | Producer
```

> **In an expression, the | operator creates a union of a number of node sets.**

Each location path can consist of a number of steps, separated by either a single `/` or a double `//`. In fact, the `//` separator is a shorthand for a more complex step, namely `/descendant-or-self::node()/`. For example, the following two paths both select the `<Link>` element descendants of the `<Description>` child element of the current `<Program>` element:

```
Description//Link
Description/descendant-or-self::node()/Link
```

Steps in location paths themselves comprise the same three components as step patterns in location path patterns: an optional axis, a node test, and any number of predicates. Again, if you don't specify an axis, then the processor uses the `child::` axis, and you can use an `@` as a shorthand for the `attribute::` axis.

You'll recognize that the `descendant-or-self::` part of the expanded step above is a new axis. Location paths can contain a number of axes, which we'll look at in more detail next.

Axes

Axes specify the relationship between the context node and the nodes that each step selects. You've already learned about two axes: the `child::` axis, which selects the children of the context node, and the `attribute::` axis, which selects its attributes. There are several other axes, and they are all shown in the table after the diagram; the example paths all assume that the context node is the `<Program>` element highlighted in the following diagram (note that only the namespace nodes on the `<Program>` element are shown):

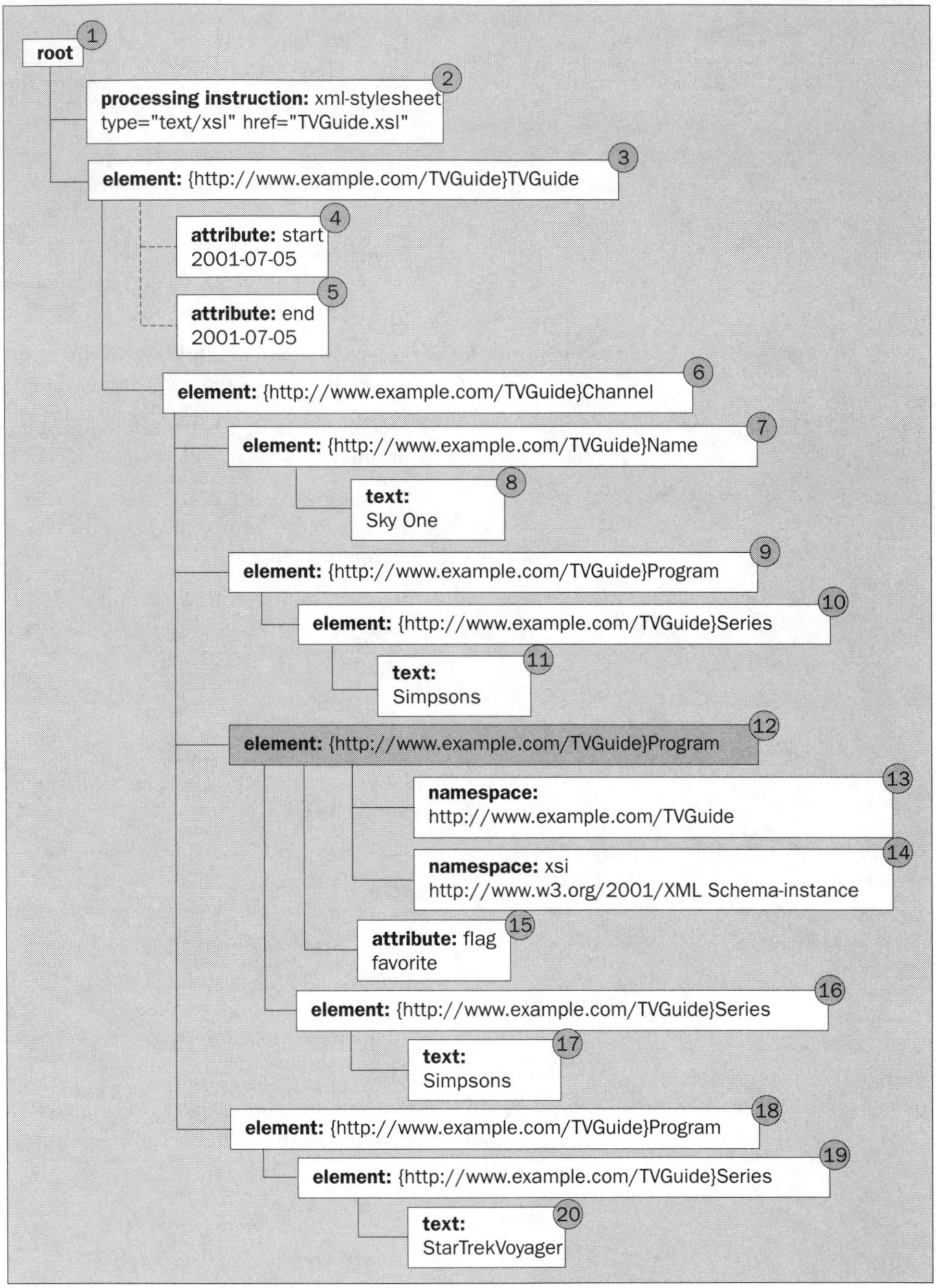

Axes fall into two groups based on the direction in which the XSLT processor goes when it traverses the tree: **forward axes** (indicated by an F in the table) and **reverse axes** (indicated by an R in the table).

Axis	Dir.	Example	Description
`self::`	F	`self::Program`	Selects the node itself (for example, the `<Program>` element, node 12)
`attribute::`	F	`attribute::*`	Selects the node's attributes (for example, any attributes on the `<Program>` element, node 15)
`namespace::`	F	`namespace::*`	Selects the node's namespace nodes (for example, the `TVGuide` and `XMLSchema-instance` namespace nodes, 13 and 14)
`child::`	F	`child::Series`	Selects immediate children of the node (for example, the `<Series>` element, node 16)
`parent::`	R	`parent::Channel`	Selects the node's parent (for example, the parent `<Channel>` element, node 6)
`descendant::`	F	`descendant::text()`	Selects the node's descendants (for example, all text nodes within the `<Program>` element, node 17)
`descendant-or-self::`	F	`descendant-or-self::node()`	Selects the node's descendants and the node itself (for example, all the nodes within the `<Program>` element, including the `<Program>` element itself, nodes 12, 16, and 17)
`ancestor::`	R	`ancestor::*`	Selects the node's ancestors (for example, the `<Channel>` and `<TVGuide>` elements, nodes 6 and 3)
`ancestor-or-self::`	R	`ancestor-or-self::*`	Selects the node's ancestors and the node itself (for example, the `<Program>`, `<Channel>`, and `<TVGuide>` elements, nodes 12, 6, and 3)
`following-sibling::`	F	`following-sibling::Program`	Selects the node's siblings that occur after the node (for example, the later `<Program>` elements in the same `<Channel>`, node 18)
`preceding-sibling::`	R	`preceding-sibling::Name`	Selects the node's siblings that occur before the node (for example, the earlier `<Name>` element in the same `<Channel>`, node 7)

Axis	Dir.	Example	Description
`following::`	F	`following::Series`	Selects nodes that start after the node ends (for example, the `<Series>` elements within all `<Program>` elements in all `<Channel>` elements after this one, node 19)
`preceding::`	R	`preceding::Series`	Selects nodes that end before the node starts (for example, the `<Series>` elements within all the `<Program>` elements in all the `<Channel>` elements before this one, node 10)

When the XSLT processor collects nodes with a forward axis, then the first node it encounters is the first node in that direction in document order, so `child::Program[1]` gives you the first `<Program>` element child of the context node. On the other hand, when an XSLT processor collects nodes with a reverse axis, then the first node it encounters is the last node in that direction in document order, so `ancestor::*[1]` gives you the immediate ancestor of the context node (its parent).

Whether an axis is a forward axis or a reverse axis it only affects predicates based on the position of the node. If you apply templates to the nodes or iterate over them with `<xsl:for-each>`, they will be processed in document order no matter which axis you used to select them.

Some of the location paths that we've seen already have actually been abbreviations of longer paths. Firstly, we've been using the location path `.` to get the value of the context node. This is actually an abbreviation for the longer path:

```
self::node()
```

This selects the context node, whatever type it is or whatever name it has. The `self::` axis is very useful for testing the name of a node. If you want to test whether a node is a `<Program>` element, for example, you can use the test:

```
self::Program
```

It is better to use this kind of test rather than testing the node's name with `name()` because it allows you to deal properly with namespaces.

Similarly, the location path `..` is actually a shorthand for the longer path:

```
parent::node()
```

This selects the parent node, again no matter what type it is or what name it has.

Axes indicate the direction in which nodes are collected in a step.

Evaluating Location Paths

Let's now take a more formal look at how an XSLT processor evaluates a location path.

First, the XSLT processor needs to find a starting point for its journey. Usually, location paths are relative, and start at the **context node**, the node at which the processor is currently looking. When a path is used in a predicate, the context node is the node selected by the portion of the step prior to the predicate. For example, when the XSLT processor evaluates the path `Series` in the following:

```
Program[Series = 'EastEnders']
```

the context node is the `<Program>` element. You can make the XSLT processor start at other points in the XML document, most notably you can start at the root node of the document by starting the path with a `/`. The following path starts from the root node and works from there:

```
/TVGuide/Channel
```

You can also start a path with a variable, as long as that variable has a node set value. For example, the following sets the `$allPrograms` variable to hold the `<Program>` elements under the current node, and the `$allSeries` variable to hold the `<Series>` children of those `<Program>` elements:

```
<xsl:variable name="allPrograms" select="Program" />
<xsl:variable name="allSeries" select="$allPrograms/Series" />
```

Once it has its starting point, the processor evaluates each step in turn, with each node selected by one step becoming a context node for the next step. It's helpful to view this process step by step; take the following path:

```
/node()
  /Channel
    /Program[Series = 'EastEnders']
      /following-sibling::Program[1]
```

The location path starts with a `/` so the starting point is the root node of the document, highlighted in the following diagram:

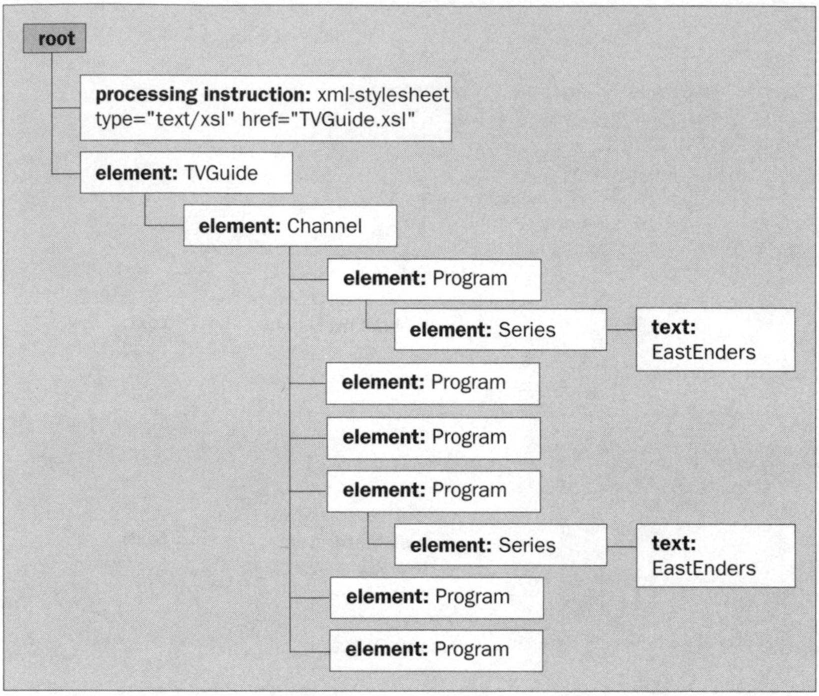

The first step, highlighted in the following, selects all the children of the context node – the processing instruction and the `<TVGuide>` element:

```
/node()
  /Channel
    /Program[Series = 'EastEnders']
      /following-sibling::Program[1]
```

The nodes that are selected are shown in the following diagram:

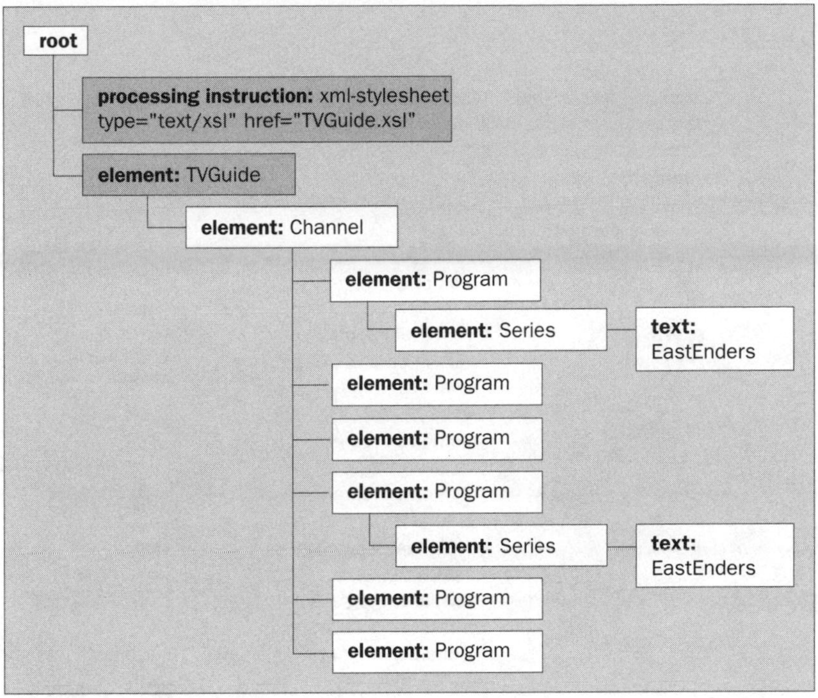

The next step selects all <Channel> children of the context node:

```
/node()
  /Channel
    /Program[Series = 'EastEnders']
      /following-sibling::Program[1]
```

The two context nodes are the processing instruction, which doesn't have any children, and the <TVGuide>, which does have <Channel> element children; these are selected as the result of the second step:

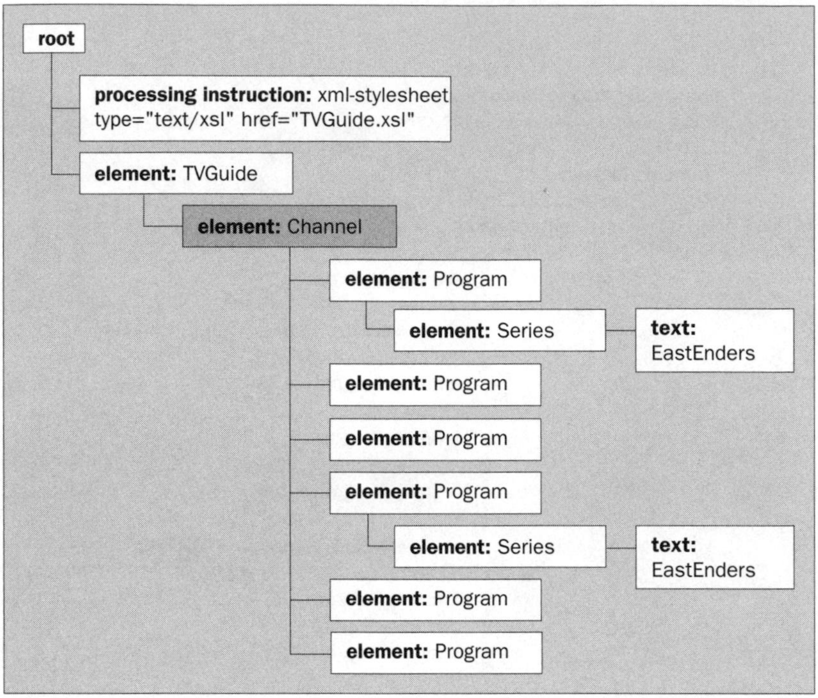

The next step selects the `<Program>` elements whose child `<Series>` element has a string value equal to `'EastEnders'`:

```
/node()
  /Channel
    /Program[Series = 'EastEnders']
      /following-sibling::Program[1]
```

There are two of these `<Program>` elements, so these are selected as the result of the third step:

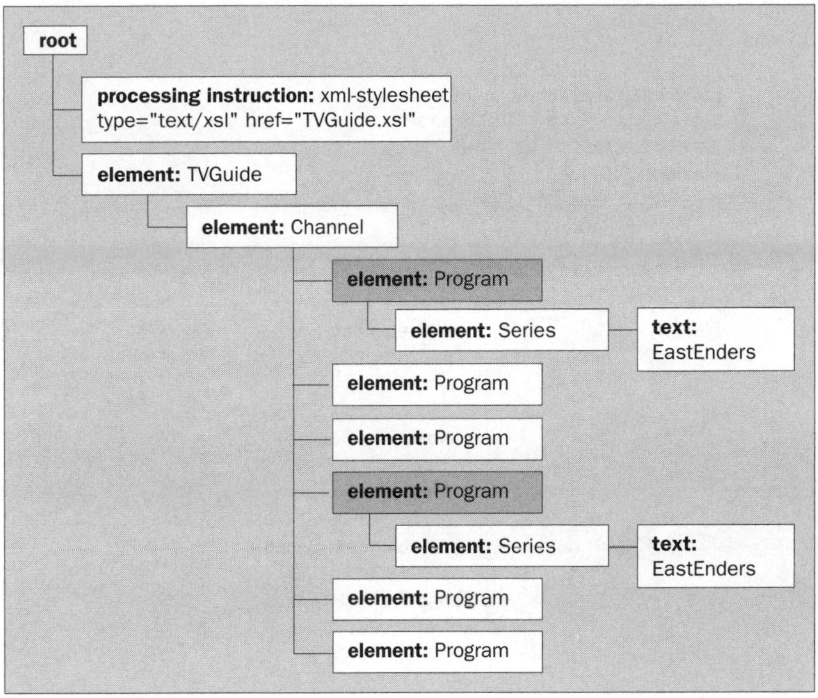

The final step selects the following sibling <Program> elements of the context node, and picks the first of these:

```
/node()
  /Channel
    /Program[Series = 'EastEnders']
      /following-sibling::Program[1]
```

There are two <Program> elements that act as context nodes for this step – the two selected by the previous step. So a single <Program> element is selected for each of these context nodes, and the result of the path as a whole is a node set containing the two <Program> elements that immediately follow the <Program> elements whose <Series> children are equal to 'EastEnders':

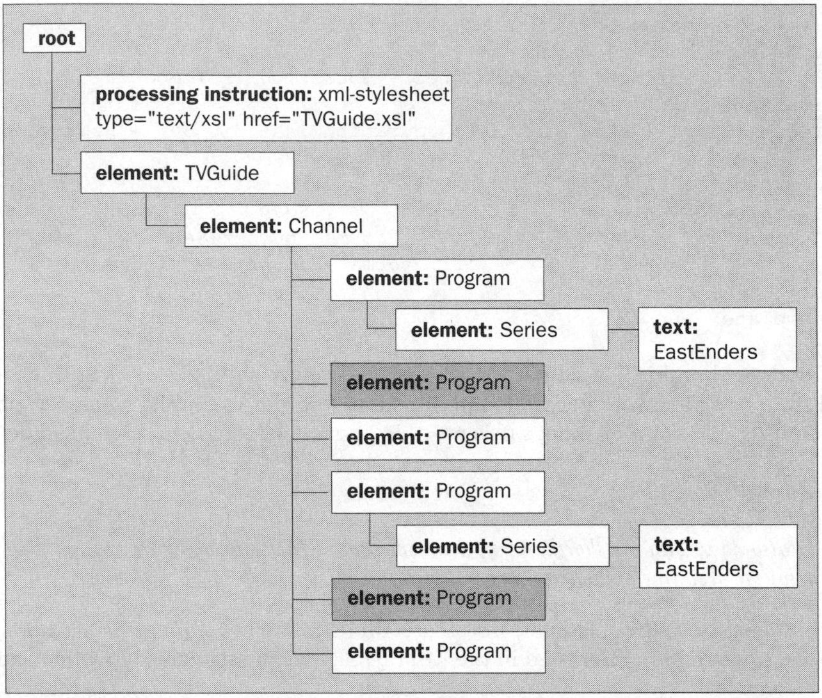

Try It Out – Accessing the Next Program's Start Time

In the last chapter, we went through a lot of work in order to get at the end time for a program – we parsed the start time and the duration of the program, and added the results together to work out the end time. In fact, the end time of one program is the start time of another program, so another way of getting hold of that time would be to look at the `<Start>` element child of the following sibling `<Program>` element within the `<Channel>`. We'll do this in the next version of our stylesheet, `TVGuide6.xsl` (and we'll go back to working with `TVGuide.xml` since that means we don't have to worry about namespaces).

The place where we need to work out the end time for a program is within the template that matches the `<Start>` elements, which currently looks like:

```
<xsl:template match="Start">
  <xsl:variable name="dateTime" select="normalize-space()" />
  <xsl:variable name="year" select="substring($dateTime, 1, 4)" />
  <xsl:variable name="month" select="number(substring($dateTime, 6, 2))" />
  <xsl:variable name="day" select="number(substring($dateTime, 9, 2))" />
  <xsl:variable name="time" select="substring($dateTime, 12, 5)" />
  <xsl:variable name="duration"
                select="substring(normalize-space(../Duration), 3)" />
  <xsl:variable name="durationHours">...</xsl:variable>
  <xsl:variable name="durationMinutes">...</xsl:variable>
  <xsl:variable name="durationMins"
                select="($durationHours * 60) + $durationMinutes" />
  <xsl:variable name="startHours" select="substring($time, 1, 2)" />
```

```
    <xsl:variable name="startMinutes" select="substring($time, 4, 2)" />
    <xsl:variable name="endMinutes"
                  select="($startMinutes + $durationMins) mod 60" />
    <xsl:variable name="endHours"
      select="floor((($startMinutes + $durationMins) div 60) + $startHours)
             mod 24" />
    <span class="date">
      <xsl:value-of select="concat($month, '/', $day, '/', $year, ' ', $time,
                                ' - ', format-number($endHours, '00'),
                                ':', format-number($endMinutes, '00'))" />
    </span>
  </xsl:template>
```

The current node within this template is the `<Start>` element child of the `<Program>` element. We want to find the `<Program>` immediately after this one in order to find its `<Start>` time. Our first step has to be up to this `<Start>` element's parent `<Program>` element, which you can do with:

```
parent::Program
```

You could also do it with the shorthand `..` but sometimes I find that using the `parent::` axis instead helps me keep track of where I am in the document.

Now we're on the `<Program>` element, we can get all its following siblings using the `following-sibling::` axis; we're only interested in the `<Program>` elements that follow this one (not any text nodes), so we can use:

```
parent::Program/following-sibling::Program
```

Now we only want the immediately following sibling of the current `<Program>` element. The `following-sibling::` axis is a forward axis, so if we test the position of the nodes that we're selecting within a predicate, the first will be the earliest `<Program>` element (after this one) in document order, which is exactly what we want:

```
parent::Program/following-sibling::Program[1]
```

Once we've got hold of this `<Program>` element, we want to step down to its child `<Start>` element in order to get its start time:

```
parent::Program/following-sibling::Program[1]/Start
```

We can put this `<Start>` element in a variable so that we can refer to it later on:

```
<xsl:variable name="endDateTime"
   select="parent::Program/following-sibling::Program[1]/Start" />
```

Now there's one program per channel that *doesn't* have a following sibling `<Program>` element, namely the last one. For that program, we're going to have to calculate the end time the old fashioned way, using the program's duration. So we need an `<xsl:choose>` in our template to distinguish the two cases. We can test whether there is a following sibling by looking at the `$endDateTime` variable – if we've managed to find a `<Start>` element with that path, then we can use that; otherwise we have to do the calculations:

```
<xsl:choose>
  <xsl:when test="$endDateTime">
    ...
  </xsl:when>
  <xsl:otherwise>
    <xsl:variable name="duration"
                  select="substring(normalize-space(../Duration), 3)" />
    <xsl:variable name="durationHours">...</xsl:variable>
    <xsl:variable name="durationMinutes">...</xsl:variable>
    <xsl:variable name="durationMins"
                  select="($durationHours * 60) + $durationMinutes" />
    <xsl:variable name="startHours" select="substring($time, 1, 2)" />
    <xsl:variable name="startMinutes" select="substring($time, 4, 2)" />
    <xsl:variable name="endMinutes"
                  select="($startMinutes + $durationMins) mod 60" />
    <xsl:variable name="endHours"
      select="floor((($startMinutes + $durationMins) div 60) + $startHours)
              mod 24" />
    ...
  </xsl:otherwise>
</xsl:choose>
```

The result of the `<xsl:choose>` should be a formatted end time, either from parsing the `<Start>` element held in the `$endDateTime` variable or from the calculated `$endMinutes` and `$endHours`. We'll store this end time in an `$endTime` variable, as follows:

```
<xsl:variable name="endTime">
  <xsl:choose>
    <xsl:when test="$endDateTime">
      <xsl:value-of
        select="substring(normalize-space($endDateTime), 12, 5)" />
    </xsl:when>
    <xsl:otherwise>
      <xsl:variable name="duration"
                    select="substring(normalize-space(../Duration), 3)" />
      <xsl:variable name="durationHours">...</xsl:variable>
      <xsl:variable name="durationMinutes">...</xsl:variable>
      <xsl:variable name="durationMins"
                    select="($durationHours * 60) + $durationMinutes" />
      <xsl:variable name="startHours" select="substring($time, 1, 2)" />
      <xsl:variable name="startMinutes" select="substring($time, 4, 2)" />
      <xsl:variable name="endMinutes"
                    select="($startMinutes + $durationMins) mod 60" />
      <xsl:variable name="endHours"
        select="floor((($startMinutes + $durationMins) div 60) +

                      $startHours) mod 24" />
      <xsl:value-of select="concat(format-number($endHours, '00'), ':',
                                   format-number($endMinutes, '00'))" />
    </xsl:otherwise>
  </xsl:choose>
</xsl:variable>
```

Finally, you can use the value of the `$endTime` variable when you provide the timing information at the end of the template as a whole:

```
<xsl:template match="Start">
  <xsl:variable name="dateTime" select="normalize-space()" />
  <xsl:variable name="year" select="substring($dateTime, 1, 4)" />
  <xsl:variable name="month" select="number(substring($dateTime, 6, 2))" />
  <xsl:variable name="day" select="number(substring($dateTime, 9, 2))" />
  <xsl:variable name="time" select="substring($dateTime, 12, 5)" />
  <xsl:variable name="endDateTime"
    select="parent::Program/following-sibling::Program[1]/Start" />
  <xsl:variable name="endTime">
  ...
  </xsl:variable>
  <span class="date">
    <xsl:value-of select="concat($month, '/', $day, '/', $year, ' ', $time,
                                                   ' - ', $endTime)" />
  </span>
</xsl:template>
```

The result of running `TVGuide6.xsl` over `TVGuide.xml` is as follows:

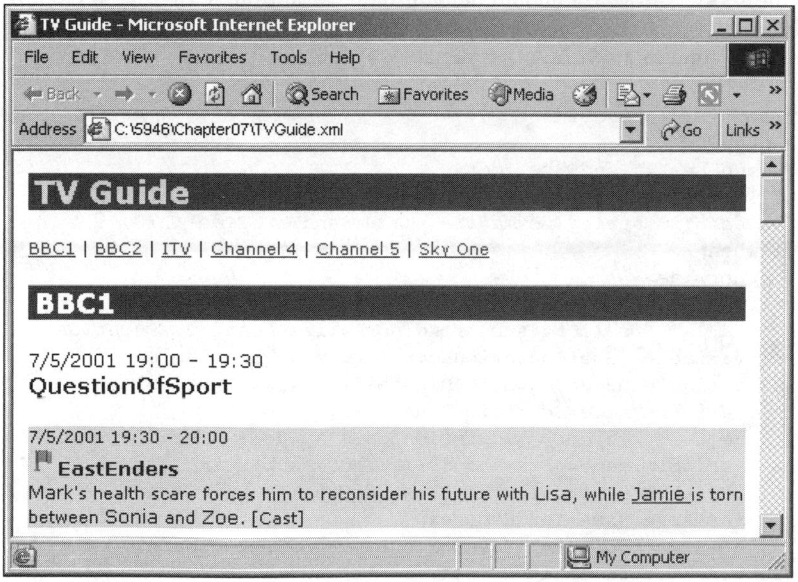

You probably won't notice any particular difference in the speed with which the transformation occurs, but it's likely to be slightly faster because you do not have to do all those calculations each time.

Summary

XSLT is all about querying and constructing node trees, and XPath carries out the querying part of that role. In this chapter, we've looked at node trees in more detail, highlighting some of the aspects that we've glossed over previously, in particular:

- The importance of the namespace of elements and attributes
- The existence of namespace nodes on elements within the node tree
- The presence of whitespace-only text nodes due to indentation in the source XML document

You've learned how to manage whitespace-only text nodes within a node tree that you access as the source of your XSLT transformations, using `<xsl:strip-space>` to get rid of whitespace-only text nodes and `<xsl:preserve-space>` and `xml:space` to retain them. Usually, it's easiest to use `<xsl:strip-space elements="*" />` to remove all whitespace-only text nodes and override the stripping as necessary with `<xsl:preserve-space>` and `xml:space`.

You've also found out more technical details concerning the construction of patterns and expressions. You've seen how to combine several location path patterns into a single pattern with the | operator and learned how to use predicates within step patterns. You've learned how to match nodes of different types, and nodes in different namespaces. You've also been taught how to use the `name()`, `local-name()`, and `namespace-uri()` functions to access the names and namespaces of nodes.

In terms of expressions, you've been shown how to use the | operator to create a union of several node sets. You've been introduced to the full set of axes at your disposal, and we've looked at how the XSLT processor evaluates a location path step by step to create a node set.

This chapter has covered all the technical aspects of how you select and match information from an XML document using XPath. In the next chapter, we'll turn our attention to how to generate a new node tree based on this information.

Review Questions

1. Draw a node tree for the following document, including whitespace-only text nodes, whitespace in text nodes, the namespaces of the elements and attributes, and namespace nodes:

```
<Films xmlns="http://www.example.com/Films">
  <Film year="1994">
    <Name>The Shawshank Redemption</Name>
    <per:Director xmlns:per="http://www.example.com/People">
      Frank Darabont
    </per:Director>

  </Film>
</Films>
```

2. What would the node tree from the previous question look like if you included the following in your XSLT stylesheet?

```
<xsl:strip-space elements="Films" />
```

3. What kinds of nodes do the following patterns match? What are the default priorities of templates that use these patterns?

```
text()
text()[normalize-space()]
Program//comment()
CastMember[1]
CastMember[position() != last()]
tv:Program
@xsi:*
Actor/Name | Character/Name
```

4. Assuming that the prefix `tv` is associated with the namespace `http://www.example.com/TVGuide` within the stylesheet, what kinds of elements do the following expressions select?

```
Program
tv:*
tv:Program
*[name() = 'Program']
*[starts-with(name(), 'tv:')]
*[name() = 'tv:Program']
*[local-name() = 'Program']
*[namespace-uri() = 'http://www.example.com/TVGuide']
*[local-name() = 'Program' and
  namespace-uri() = 'http://www.example.com/TVGuide']
```

5. Add XML comments to the following XSLT extract to explain what it does:

```
<xsl:for-each select="ancestor-or-self::*">
  <xsl:variable name="name" select="name()" />
  /<xsl:value-of select="$name" />
  <xsl:if test="../*[name() = $name]">
    [<xsl:value-of select="count(preceding-sibling::*[name() = $name])" />]
  </xsl:if>
</xsl:for-each>
```

6. Create a location path that selects, from a `<Program>` element, the `<Series>` children of all the preceding `<Program>` elements in the same `<Channel>` element (in other words, siblings of the current `<Program>` element).

7. Based on the answer to the previous question, create an expression that tests whether the current `<Program>` element's `<Series>` child element is the same as the `<Series>` element child of any preceding `<Program>` elements in the same `<Channel>` element.

8. Based on the answer to the previous question, create a location path that selects, from a `<Channel>` element, all those `<Program>` elements whose `<Series>` child element is *not* the same as any `<Series>` element child of the preceding `<Program>` elements in the same `<Channel>` element.

Beginning
XSLT

8

The Result Tree

In the last chapter we looked in detail at how an XSLT processor views an XML document as a node tree and how to access nodes within that node tree using location paths. The source tree isn't the only node tree that the XSLT processor has to deal with, however – it also has to generate a node tree for the output. The node tree that the XSLT processor generates is known as the **result tree**.

The result tree looks very similar to the source tree – it has element and attribute nodes, comments and processing instructions, text nodes (some of which might be whitespace-only text nodes), and namespace nodes. The stylesheet's main job is to build the result tree based on information from the source tree. To do that, it needs to construct all the different types of nodes and fit them together into a tree. You've already seen how to generate elements, attributes, and text nodes. In this chapter, you'll learn how to generate the other kinds of nodes, how to manage whitespace, and how to dynamically name elements and attributes.

Usually, an XSLT processor doesn't just generate a result tree, it also writes the result to a file or sends it to a browser. To write the result tree as output, the XSLT processor needs to serialize the result tree in some way – it needs to output start and end tags and decide what entity reference to use for special characters. As a stylesheet author, you get a fair amount of control about what this serialized output looks like, and in the second part of this chapter we'll look at what you can do to make the output of a transformation readable.

In this chapter, you'll learn:

- How to add nodes to the result tree
- How to create attributes conditionally or create attributes with conditional values
- How to add sets of attributes to elements
- How to create elements and attributes when you don't know their names in advance
- How to generate comments, processing instructions, and whitespace
- How to copy parts of the source tree
- How to generate text, HTML, and XML output

Generating Nodes

The simplest way of adding a node to the result tree is to include it in the body of a template in the stylesheet. Take the following template from TVGuide.xsl as an example:

```
<xsl:template match="/">
  <html>
    <head>
      <title>TV Guide</title>
      <link rel="stylesheet" href="TVGuide.css" />
      <script type="text/javascript">
        <![CDATA[
        function toggle(element) {
          if (element.style.display == 'none') {
            element.style.display = 'block';
          } else {
            element.style.display = 'none';
          }
        }
        ]]>
      </script>
    </head>

    <body>
      <h1>TV Guide</h1>
      <xsl:copy-of select="$ChannelList" />
      <xsl:apply-templates />
      <xsl:copy-of select="$ChannelList" />
    </body>
  </html>
</xsl:template>
```

This template creates the following result tree diagram. The ... at the bottom indicates the part of the result tree that isn't created by this particular template, but rather by the <xsl:copy-of> and <xsl:apply-templates> instructions:

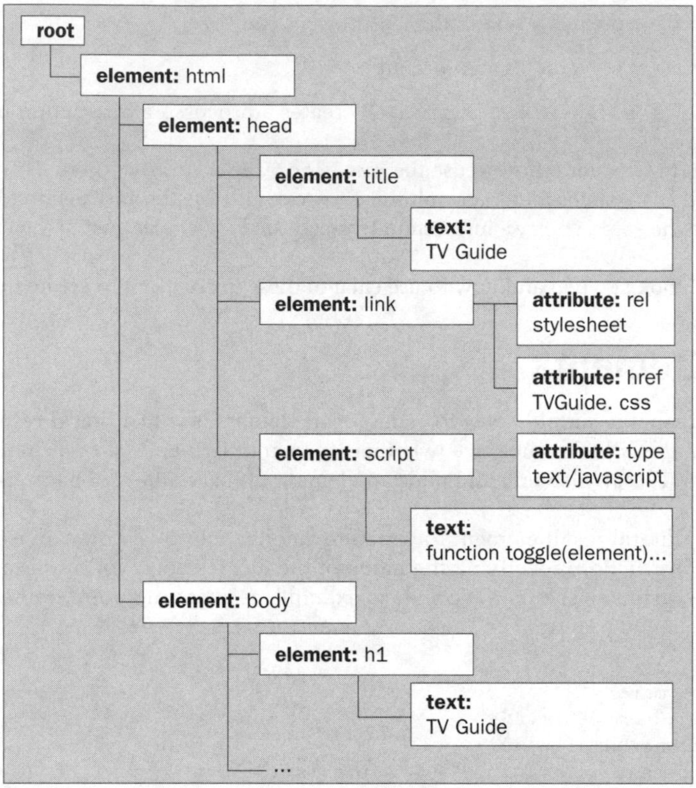

Within the template, all the elements and attributes that aren't in the XSLT namespace (whether they're in no namespace, such as the `<head>` element and the `href` attribute on the `<link>` element, or in a different namespace, as we'll see later) are added to the result tree, and any text that's included in the element (such as "TV Guide") is added to the result tree as a text node. The dynamic content is added using `<xsl:copy-of>` and `<xsl:apply-templates>` instructions.

Note that the CDATA section doesn't become a node in the tree. As described in Chapter 2, unescaped text inside a CDATA section is just the same as escaped text without a CDATA section as far as the XSLT processor is concerned.

The result tree looks a lot like the source tree. The main role of the stylesheet is to construct the result tree.

Mostly, all you need to do in a stylesheet is include the result that you want literally. However, XSLT also provides a set of instructions that allow you to create different types of nodes explicitly. These instructions are:

- `<xsl:element>` – creates an element node
- `<xsl:attribute>` – creates an attribute node

- <xsl:text> – creates a text node
- <xsl:comment> – creates a comment node
- <xsl:processing-instruction> – creates a processing instruction node

You've already seen in Chapter 6 how to use the <xsl:copy-of> instruction to copy result tree fragments that you have stored in variables into the result tree; you can also use this instruction to copy parts of the source tree, and use the <xsl:copy> instruction to create shallow copies, just of the current node.

In this section, we'll look at when and how to use each of these instructions to create nodes in the result tree.

Generating Elements

As you've already seen, the simplest way to generate an element is with a **literal result element**. Any element that isn't in the XSLT namespace (whether it's in another namespace or in no namespace at all) is interpreted as a literal result element, and adds an element of that name and namespace to the result tree.

Rather than using a literal result element to generate an element node, you can use the <xsl:element> instruction, specifying the name of the element that you want to create using the instruction's name attribute. Taking the previous example as a starting point, rather than use literal result elements, we could use <xsl:element>, as in TVGuide2.xsl:

```
<xsl:template match="/">
  <xsl:element name="html">
    <xsl:element name="head">
      <xsl:element name="title">TV Guide</xsl:element>
      <xsl:element name="link">
        <xsl:attribute name="rel">stylesheet</xsl:attribute>
        <xsl:attribute name="href">TVGuide.css</xsl:attribute>
      </xsl:element>
      <xsl:element name="script">
        <xsl:attribute name="type">text/javascript</xsl:attribute>
        <![CDATA[
        ...
        ]]>
      </xsl:element>
    </xsl:element>
    <xsl:element name="body">
      <xsl:element name="h1">TV Guide</xsl:element>
      <xsl:copy-of select="$ChannelList" />
      <xsl:apply-templates />
      <xsl:copy-of select="$ChannelList" />
    </xsl:element>
  </xsl:element>
</xsl:template>
```

Using <xsl:element> makes no difference to the result that's generated – you still get the same HTML, as you can see from the following screenshot, which shows the result of using TVGuide2.xsl with TVGuide.xml:

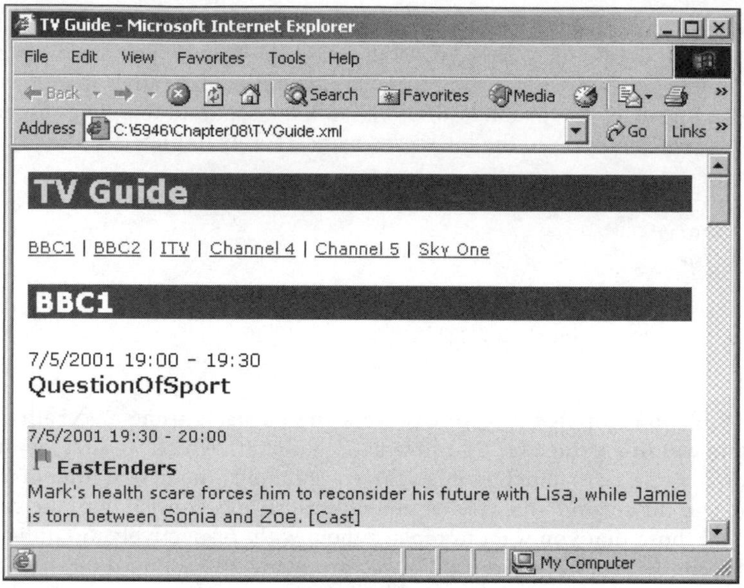

If you take a look at TVGuide2.xsl, you'll see that using <xsl:element> is a lot more verbose than using literal result elements. It also means that you have to use <xsl:attribute> (which we'll look at in detail in the next section) to generate attributes, which again adds to the length of the stylesheet. So why use it? Well, the biggest reason is to decide on the name for the element that you're creating dynamically – we'll see how to do that in the next section.

You can use <xsl:element> as an alternative to literal result elements, to create element nodes in the result tree.

Dynamic Element Names

In previous chapters, we've seen how to use attribute value templates to set the value of an attribute dynamically. The attributes that we've used attribute value templates with have all been on literal result elements – the attributes were added to the result tree with the value that we specified with the attribute value template.

The name attribute of the <xsl:element> element is one of several attributes on XSLT instructions that are also attribute value templates. If you use curly brackets, {}, within the name attribute of <xsl:element> then the content of the brackets is evaluated as an XPath expression and the result is used in the name of the element. For example, in the following the name of the element that's added to the result tree is the value of the class attribute on the current node:

```
<xsl:element name="{@class}">
...
</xsl:element>
```

The main situation in which it's handy to have dynamic element names is when you're transforming from one piece of XML to another similar one. One use case is when you're presented with some HTML that is well-formed XML, but uses uppercase element names rather than lowercase element names. One way to approach the problem would be to have separate templates for each of the elements, mapping the uppercase names on to the lowercase names, for example:

```
<xsl:template match="UL">
  <ul><xsl:apply-templates /></ul>
</xsl:template>

<xsl:template match="LI">
  <li><xsl:apply-templates /></li>
</xsl:template>
```

However, it's possible to compute the lowercase version of a string using an XPath function that replaces characters within a string: the `translate()` function, which we first met in Chapter 6. Just to remind you, the `translate()` function takes three arguments: the first argument is the string that you want to translate, and the second and third arguments are strings consisting of the characters that you want to replace and those that you want to replace them with, respectively. So if the second and third arguments are the alphabet in uppercase and lowercase (which we'll put in `$upper` and `$lower` global variables for ease of use), then you can change all the uppercase characters in the string to lowercase characters, as follows:

```
translate($string, $upper, $lower)
```

We can use this method to change any string to lowercase, so we only need one template to deal with all the elements in the original (uppercase) HTML. The first argument for the `translate()` function is the name of the original element. We can get the name of the current element using the `name()` function, as we saw in the last chapter. Then we can use the new name as the name of the element that we create:

```
<xsl:template match="*">
  <xsl:element name="{translate(name(), $upper, $lower)}">
    <xsl:apply-templates />
  </xsl:element>
</xsl:template>
```

> **The `name` attribute on `<xsl:element>` is an attribute value template, so you can use it to dynamically set the name of an element you generate.**

Try It Out – Generating XML from XHTML

When we first started looking at XML, we generated a well-formed version of our HTML file, which contained `class` attributes that indicated the purpose of different sections in the HTML document. For example, the cast list looked like the following (see `Castlist.html`):

```
<ul class="castlist">
  <li>
    <span class="character">Zoe Slater</span>
```

```
    <span class="actor">Michelle Ryan</span>
  </li>
  <li>
    <span class="character">Jamie Mitchell</span>
    <span class="actor">Jack Ryder</span>
  </li>
  <li>
    <span class="character">Sonia Jackson</span>
    <span class="actor">Natalie Cassidy</span>
  </li>
</ul>
```

We converted this well-formed HTML to an XML structure by hand, but we could have generated at least some of it automatically using the values of the `class` attributes. The XML structure that we created from `CastList.html` was the following (`CastList.xml`):

```
<CastList>
  <CastMember>
    <Character><Name>Zoe Slater</Name></Character>
    <Actor><Name>Michelle Ryan</Name></Actor>
  </CastMember>
  <CastMember>
    <Character><Name>Jamie Mitchell</Name></Character>
    <Actor><Name>Jack Ryder</Name></Actor>
  </CastMember>
  <CastMember>
    <Character><Name>Sonia Jackson</Name></Character>
    <Actor><Name>Natalie Cassidy</Name></Actor>
  </CastMember>
</CastList>
```

The mapping between the two structures in `CastList.xsl` is fairly straightforward: the `<ul>` element transforms into a `<CastList>` element, the `<li>` element transforms into a `<CastMember>` element, and the `<span>` elements transform into `<Character>` or `<Actor>` elements with `<Name>` elements inside them. We may as well do the mappings for the first two types using separate templates:

```
<xsl:template match="ul">
  <CastList><xsl:apply-templates /></CastList>
</xsl:template>

<xsl:template match="li">
  <CastMember><xsl:apply-templates /></CastMember>
</xsl:template>
```

For the mappings involving the `<span>` elements, on the other hand, the name of the element that you want to create is the same as the value of the `class` attribute, but with the first letter capitalized. You can get hold of the first letter of the value of the `class` attribute using the `substring()` function:

```
substring(@class, 1, 1)
```

And you can then capitalize that letter, given an uppercase and lowercase alphabet, using the translate() function. We'll store the upper-and lowercase alphabets in global variables for ease of use:

```
<xsl:variable name="upper" select="'ABCDEFGHIJKLMNOPQRSTUVWXYZ'" />
<xsl:variable name="lower" select="'abcdefghijklmnopqrstuvwxyz'" />
```

The translate() function uses these variables to translate the first character of the name from lowercase to uppercase:

```
translate(substring(@class, 1, 1), $lower, $upper)
```

You can get the rest of the letters in the value of the class attribute using the substring() function again, extracting from the second character to the end of the string:

```
substring(@class, 2)
```

Concatenating these expressions together gets you the name of the element that you want to create. In a template that matches <span> elements, you can hold that name in a $name variable:

```
<xsl:template match="span">
  <xsl:variable name="name"
                select="concat(translate(substring(@class, 1, 1),
                                         $lower, $upper),
                               substring(@class, 2))" />
  ...
</xsl:template>
```

You can then insert the value of this variable into the name attribute of an <xsl:element> that you use to create the new element, using an attribute value template:

```
<xsl:template match="span">
  <xsl:variable name="name"
                select="concat(translate(substring(@class, 1, 1),
                                         $lower, $upper),
                               substring(@class, 2))" />
  <xsl:element name="{$name}">
    <Name><xsl:value-of select="." /></Name>
  </xsl:element>
</xsl:template>
```

If you transform CastList.html using CastList.xsl, you should get the same XML structure as shown in CastList.xml.

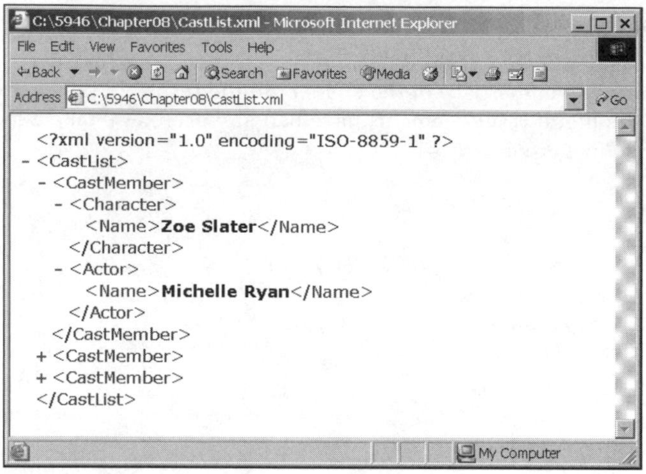

Element Namespaces

Just as in the source tree, the elements and attributes in the result tree all have a namespace and the element nodes that you create with your stylesheet will have namespace nodes associated with them. If and when the result tree is serialized into a file, then the XSLT processor automatically works out where it needs to put namespace declarations to ensure that all the elements are in the desired namespace and have the desired namespace nodes.

In general, any namespace that you declare in the stylesheet will appear in the result of the transformation. If you don't want a namespace to appear, you have to explicitly exclude it using the `exclude-result-prefixes` attribute on the `<xsl:stylesheet>` element. The `exclude-result-prefixes` attribute should hold a whitespace-separated list of the prefixes associated with the namespaces that shouldn't appear in the result of the transformation.

For example, as we saw in the last chapter, you have to declare the TV Guide namespace in the stylesheet so that you can match and select the elements in the TV Guide XML document. However, you don't want its namespace declaration to appear in the output because you're creating HTML, which doesn't include elements in the TV Guide namespace. To prevent the namespace declaration from appearing, you should include the prefix that you've associated with the TV Guide namespace within the `exclude-result-prefixes` attribute as follows:

```
<xsl:stylesheet version="1.0"
                xmlns:xsl="http://www.w3.org/1999/XSL/Transform"
                xmlns:tv="http://www.example.com/TVGuide"
                exclude-result-prefixes="tv">
...
</xsl:stylesheet>
```

The other namespaces that you need to be concerned about are those that you want to appear in the result. The XSLT processor will take care of declaring those namespaces as long as you make sure that the elements that you generate in your stylesheet are in the namespace that you want them to be in. In the rest of this section, we'll look at three ways of creating elements in different namespaces: using literal result elements, using a prefix in the `name` attribute of `<xsl:element>`, and using the `namespace` attribute of `<xsl:element>`.

Namespaces for Literal Result Elements

When you create an element using a literal result element, then the namespace of the element in the stylesheet is the same as the namespace of the element in the result. In the examples that we've been using so far, none of the literal result elements have had any prefixes – take a look again at the template matching the root node in TVGuide.xsl:

```
<xsl:template match="/">
  <html>
    <head>
      <title>TV Guide</title>
      <link rel="stylesheet" href="TVGuide.css" />
      <script type="text/javascript">
        <![CDATA[
        ...
        ]]>
      </script>
    </head>

    <body>
      <h1>TV Guide</h1>
      <xsl:copy-of select="$ChannelList" />
      <xsl:apply-templates />
      <xsl:copy-of select="$ChannelList" />
    </body>
  </html>
</xsl:template>
```

When an element name doesn't have a prefix, the element is assigned to the default namespace. We can't tell from this one template what the default namespace is – we have to look at the document element of TVGuide.xsl, which currently looks like:

```
<xsl:stylesheet version="1.0"
                xmlns:xsl="http://www.w3.org/1999/XSL/Transform">
...
</xsl:stylesheet>
```

The only namespace declaration on the <xsl:stylesheet> element is the one for the XSLT namespace. There's no namespace declaration for the default namespace, so all the literal result elements in the previous template have no namespace. However, we can add a default namespace declaration on the <xsl:stylesheet> element, for the XHTML namespace, as follows:

```
<xsl:stylesheet version="1.0"
                xmlns:xsl="http://www.w3.org/1999/XSL/Transform"
                xmlns="http://www.w3.org/1999/xhtml">
...
</xsl:stylesheet>
```

Now, any literal result elements in the stylesheet that do not have a prefix will be assigned to the XHTML namespace.

Because the default namespace declaration is on the `<xsl:stylesheet>` element, the default namespace is in scope for the entire stylesheet. This way, it doesn't matter in which template the elements are generated; if you don't use a prefix they will be in the XHTML namespace. If you put the default namespace declaration on the `<html>` element within the template, on the other hand, it will only be in scope within the template itself, and only the literal result elements in that template will be in the XHTML namespace. Therefore, I always declare all the namespaces that I want to use on the `<xsl:stylesheet>` element in an XSLT stylesheet.

Similarly, if we wanted to, we could add a namespace declaration for another namespace, for example **MathML**, to the `<xsl:stylesheet>` element:

```
<xsl:stylesheet version="1.0"
                xmlns:xsl="http://www.w3.org/1999/XSL/Transform"
                xmlns="http://www.w3.org/1999/xhtml"
                xmlns:math="http://www.w3.org/1998/Math/MathML">
...
</xsl:stylesheet>
```

With that namespace declaration in place, you can use the `math` prefix on any literal result element, and it will be associated with the MathML namespace.

MathML is a markup language for mathematical expressions, developed by the W3C. You can find out more about MathML at http://www.w3.org/Math/.

The namespace of an element in the result tree is the same as the namespace of the literal result element that generates it.

Try It Out – Generating Elements in the XHTML Namespace

Our stylesheet is supposed to generate XHTML, so the elements that we create with it should be in the XHTML namespace (`http://www.w3.org/1999/xhtml`). The literal result elements that we're using in the stylesheet don't use a prefix, so we can just add a default namespace declaration to the `<xsl:stylesheet>` document element to place the generated elements in the XHTML namespace, as in `TVGuide3.xsl`:

```
<xsl:stylesheet version="1.0"
                xmlns:xsl="http://www.w3.org/1999/XSL/Transform"
                xmlns="http://www.w3.org/1999/xhtml">
...
</xsl:stylesheet>
```

When you do this, the XSLT processor adds a default namespace declaration to the `<html>` element that it generates. Take a look at the result of transforming `TVGuide.xml` with `TVGuide3.xsl`. You should see a namespace declaration for the XHTML namespace in the start tag of the `<html>` element:

```
<html xmlns="http://www.w3.org/1999/xhtml">
  <head>
```

```
    ...
  </head>
  <body>
    ...
  </body>
</html>
```

None of the other elements in the output have a namespace declaration on them because the XSLT processor knows that the namespace declaration it's put on the `<html>` element remains in scope for the rest of the document.

Now try removing the default namespace declaration from the `<xsl:stylesheet>` element and putting it on the `<html>` element where it's generated within the template matching the root node instead, as in `TVGuide4.xsl`:

```
<xsl:template match="/">
  <html xmlns="http://www.w3.org/1999/xhtml">
    <head>
      ...
    </head>

    <body>
      <h1>TV Guide</h1>
      <xsl:copy-of select="$ChannelList" />
      <xsl:apply-templates />
      <xsl:copy-of select="$ChannelList" />
    </body>
  </html>
</xsl:template>
```

Transform `TVGuide.xml` with `TVGuide4.xsl` and take a look at the result. The only literal result elements for which the default namespace declaration is in scope are those within the above template. Elements created in other templates are still in no namespace. The output looks like:

```
<html xmlns="http://www.w3.org/1999/xhtml">
  <head>
  ...
  </head>
  <body>
    <h1>TV Guide</h1>
    <p xmlns=""><a href="#BBC1">BBC1</a>...</p>
    <h2 xmlns="" class="channel"><a name="BBC1" id="BBC1">BBC1</a></h2>
    <div xmlns="" class="nowShowing">...</div>
    ...
  </body>
</html>
```

Because the elements that aren't generated in the template matching the root node are in no namespace, the XSLT processor has to add namespace declarations that reset the default namespace back to no namespace on those elements.

Namespaces for Elements Generated with <xsl:element>

As you've seen, the name attribute of the <xsl:element> element specifies the name of the element that you generate. The name attribute is treated in exactly the same way as the name of a literal result element – if you specify a prefix in the name attribute, then that prefix is resolved according to the namespace declarations in the stylesheet, to tell the XSLT processor to which namespace the element should be assigned; if you don't specify a prefix in the name attribute, then the processor uses the default namespace, if there is one.

For example, if the prefix math is associated with the MathML namespace within the stylesheet, then the following generates a <matrix> element in the MathML namespace (usually with the prefix math):

```
<xsl:element name="math:matrix">
...
</xsl:element>
```

Technically, XSLT processors are allowed to use whatever prefix they like for the elements that they generate, as long as that prefix is associated with the correct namespace in the result document. In practice, processors use the prefix that you provide for the namespace, though if you declare a namespace twice with different prefixes it might choose either of the prefixes you provided.

Including a prefix on the name specified by the <xsl:element> instruction places the generated element in the associated namespace.

Dynamic Element Namespaces

As you've already seen, the name attribute of <xsl:element> is an attribute value template, so you can use {}s to set the name of the element that you create dynamically. This goes for the prefix that you use for the element (and hence its namespace) as well. For example, the following sets the local name of the generated element to the value of the $name variable, and assigns it to the namespace associated with the prefix that's the value of the $prefix variable:

```
<xsl:element name="{$prefix}:{$name}">
...
</xsl:element>
```

You should be careful using this method, however, as you need to make sure that the prefix that you specify for the new element has been declared in the stylesheet. This method also means that you need to know the namespace URI in advance so that you can declare it in your stylesheet, something that isn't always possible in more complex stylesheets. As well as the name attribute, therefore, the <xsl:element> instruction also has a namespace attribute that you can use to set the namespace URI of the element, and which is an attribute value template.

When you create an element using <xsl:element>, then, you can place it in any namespace that you want, even if that namespace can't be hard coded within the stylesheet. The following shows an instruction that generates an element in the namespace specified by the $namespaceURI variable, with a local name held by the $name variable and with a prefix given by the $prefix variable:

```
<xsl:element name="{$prefix}:{$name}" namespace="{$namespaceURI}">
...
</xsl:element>
```

If you specify a prefix in the `name` *attribute as well as a namespace in the* `namespace` *attribute then the prefix is just a hint to the processor about what prefix you'd like it to use. The processor is perfectly free to use whatever prefix it wants, though most honor your intentions and use the prefix that you've specified.*

> **The namespace of an element generated by the `<xsl:element>` instruction can be determined on the fly using an attribute value template in the `namespace` attribute.**

Generating Text Nodes

There are three ways of creating text nodes using a stylesheet, and you've already seen two of them in action. The first, and simplest, method is to include the text that you want within the result tree as text within a template. For example, within a template, the following code:

```
<h1>TV Guide</h1>
```

creates the following branch within the result tree:

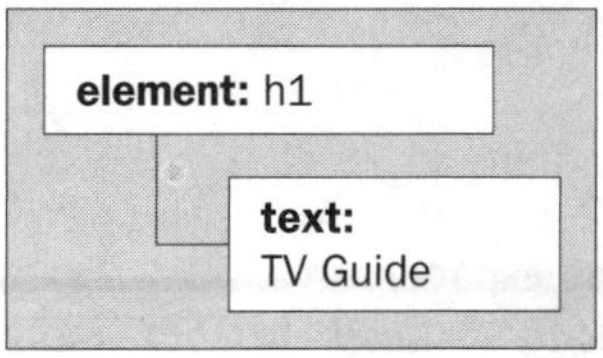

The second method, which you've also seen, is to use `<xsl:value-of>` to insert a text node with a value that's defined through an XPath expression. For example, given that the `$series` variable has the value `'Star Trek'`, the following code:

```
<h1>TV Guide: <xsl:value-of select="$series" /></h1>
```

creates the following branch within the result tree:

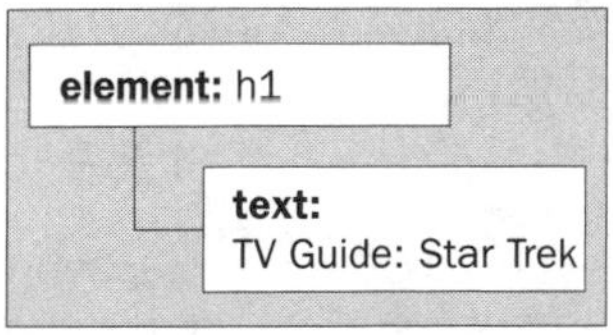

If you create two text nodes next to each other, they get merged into a single text node.

The third method of creating text nodes is to use `<xsl:text>`. The `<xsl:text>` element can only contain literal text, and whatever you put inside it is added to the result as a text node. For example, the following code:

```
<h1><xsl:text>TV Guide</xsl:text></h1>
```

creates the following branch in the result tree:

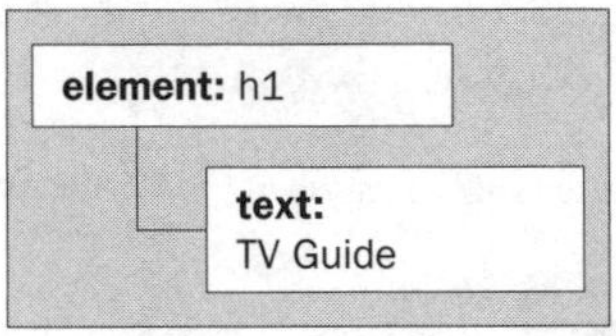

But hang on – that's exactly the same as the branch that we got when we used just literal text in the stylesheet. Why bother using `<xsl:text>`? Well, the reason arises from how XSLT processors handle whitespace, which is what we'll look at next.

> **Text nodes are generated by literal text, `<xsl:value-of>`, and `<xsl:text>`. Text nodes that are generated next to each other are merged into a single text node in the tree.**

Managing Whitespace

In the last chapter, we saw how an XSLT processor builds a node tree from an XML document, and in particular looked at how it treats whitespace within the source document. Of course, stylesheets are XML documents too, and when the XSLT processor is run on a stylesheet, it builds a node tree for the stylesheet as well as the source document. Take the following snippet from a stylesheet as an example:

```
<h1>
  TV Guide:
  <xsl:value-of select="$startDay" />
  <xsl:value-of select="$startMonth" />
</h1>
```

The XSLT processor views this stylesheet as the following node tree (whitespace-only text nodes are highlighted):

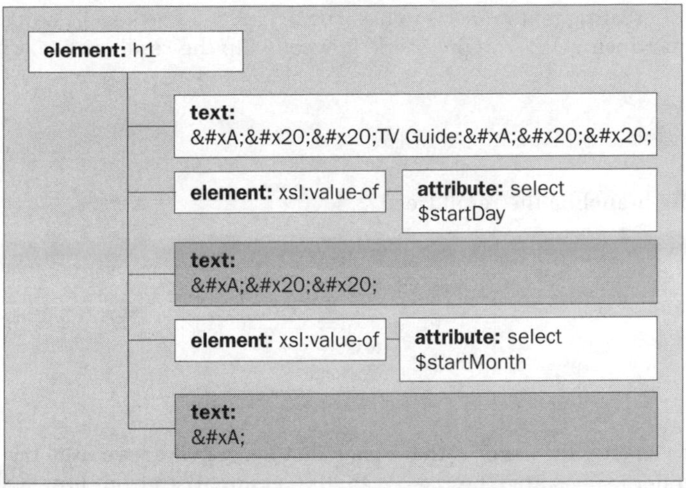

You'll remember from the last chapter how you could use `<xsl:strip-space>` to get rid of whitespace-only text nodes from the node tree of the source document. When an XSLT processor reads the stylesheet, it automatically ignores any whitespace-only text nodes aside from those within `<xsl:text>` elements, so effectively the node tree for this snippet of the stylesheet is in fact:

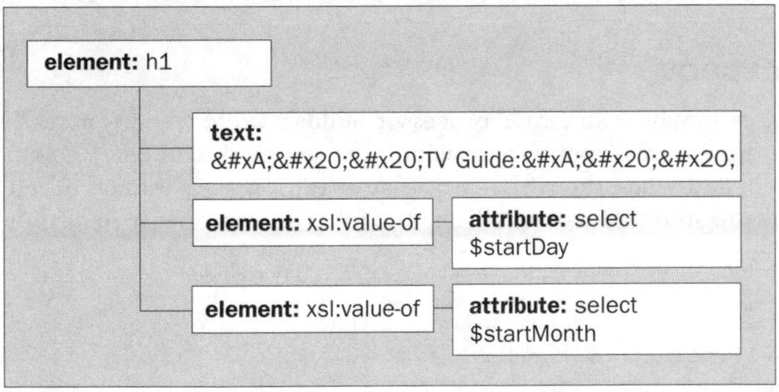

Now there are two problems with this node tree, which we can see if we look at the result that we get when we use the XSLT snippet. Assuming that the `$startDay` variable has the value `'5'` and the `$startMonth` variable has the value `'July'`, the result is:

```
<h1>
  TV Guide:
  5July</h1>
```

Firstly, we have unnecessary whitespace before the content of the `<h1>` element and between the part that we created with literal text and the part we created with `<xsl:value-of>`. That text comes from the original text node in the stylesheet. Secondly, there isn't a space between the day and the month because the whitespace-only text node between the `<xsl:value-of>` elements has been stripped away.

We can use <xsl:text> to solve both these problems. First, you can use <xsl:text> to place boundaries around the text that you actually want to add to the result tree and the whitespace you're just adding to make the stylesheet read better. Second, you can use <xsl:text> to add whitespace between the text created by instructions. In the amended code, we use <xsl:text> around the "TV Guide: " literal text that we want, and between the two <xsl:value-of> instructions to add a space:

```
<h1>
  <xsl:text>TV Guide: </xsl:text>
  <xsl:value-of select="$startDay" />
  <xsl:text> </xsl:text>
  <xsl:value-of select="$startMonth" />
</h1>
```

When the XSLT processor builds a node tree for the stylesheet from this snippet, it sees the following:

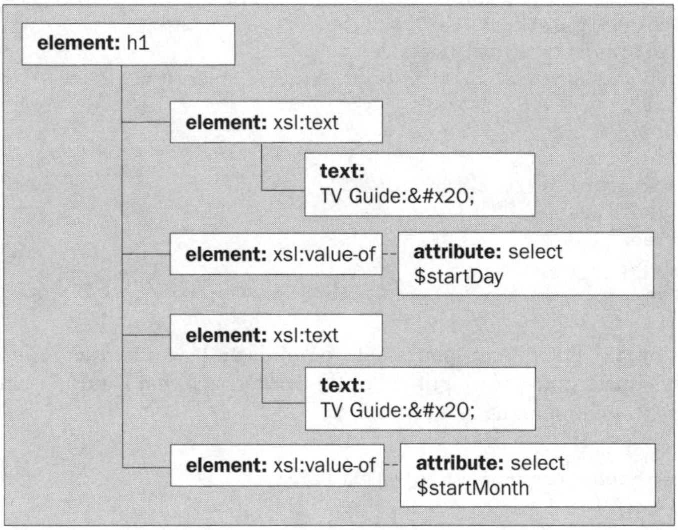

And the result from running the snippet is the following, with all the whitespace that we need:

```
<h1>TV Guide: 5 July</h1>
```

The <xsl:text> element is useful for delimiting the text that should be added to a tree (to omit whitespace) and for adding whitespace-only text nodes to the result tree.

Try It Out – Managing Whitespace in the Result Tree

There are a couple of places where we could improve the result that we're generating with the next version of our stylesheet by controlling the whitespace that we're generating.

Firstly, when we generate the title of a program that has both a series and a title, we're getting a lot of whitespace before the dash that separates them. This whitespace isn't apparent if you look at the page in a browser (because in HTML consecutive spaces are collapsed into a single space for display), but it shows up if you look at the source code. For example, in the result of transforming `TVGuide.xml` with `TVGuide3.xsl`, you'll see:

```
<span class="title">StarTrekVoyager
        - <span class="subtitle">Renaissance Man</span></span><br/>
```

The template that's generating the titles is the following:

```
<xsl:template match="Program" mode="Title">
  <span class="title">
    <xsl:choose>
      <xsl:when test="string(Series)">
       <xsl:value-of select="Series" />
        <xsl:if test="string(Title)">
        - <span class="subtitle"><xsl:value-of select="Title" /></span>
        </xsl:if>
      </xsl:when>
      <xsl:otherwise>
        <xsl:value-of select="Title" />
      </xsl:otherwise>
    </xsl:choose>
  </span>
</xsl:template>
```

We're adding a line break and several spaces before the dash. It would make the file smaller (and more readable, in terms of source code) if we got rid of the whitespace that we don't need by wrapping the dash in an `<xsl:text>` element, as in `TVGuide5.xsl`:

```
<xsl:template match="Program" mode="Title">
  <span class="title">
    <xsl:choose>
      <xsl:when test="string(Series)">
       <xsl:value-of select="Series" />
        <xsl:if test="string(Title)">
          <xsl:text> - </xsl:text>
          <span class="subtitle"><xsl:value-of select="Title" /></span>
        </xsl:if>
      </xsl:when>
      <xsl:otherwise>
        <xsl:value-of select="Title" />
      </xsl:otherwise>
    </xsl:choose>
  </span>
</xsl:template>
```

Another place where there are problems with whitespace is in the generation of the `<span>` elements in the cast list. The template in `TVGuide3.xsl` is:

```
<xsl:template match="CastMember">
  <li>
    <xsl:apply-templates select="Character" />
    <xsl:apply-templates select="Actor" />
  </li>
</xsl:template>
```

But this means that there's no space between the <span> element created to hold the character's name and the one created to hold the actor's name, which means the output looks a little strange, as you can see in the following screenshot:

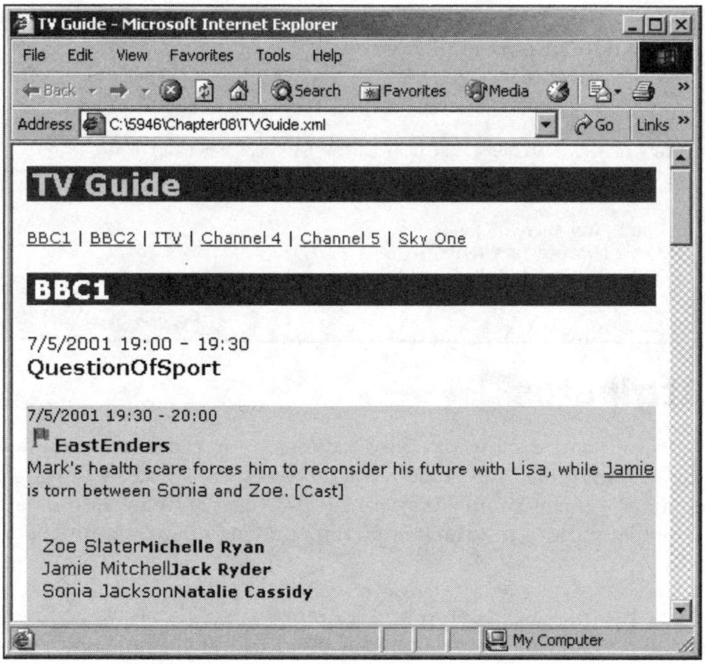

Instead, we should add a space between the two <span> elements, using <xsl:text>, as in TVGuide5.xsl:

```
<xsl:template match="CastMember">
  <li>
    <xsl:apply-templates select="Character" />
    <xsl:text> </xsl:text>
    <xsl:apply-templates select="Actor" />
  </li>
</xsl:template>
```

As you can see from the following screenshot, this makes the cast list a lot more readable:

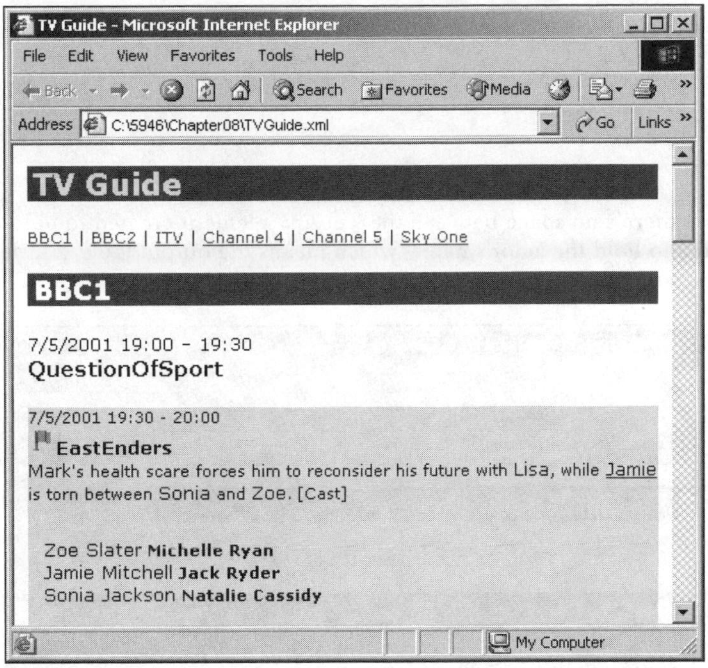

Generating Attributes

You can generate attribute nodes using `<xsl:attribute>` in much the same way as you can create element nodes using `<xsl:element>`. Like `<xsl:element>`, `<xsl:attribute>` has a `name` attribute to set the name of the attribute and a `namespace` attribute to set the namespace of the attribute, both of which are attribute value templates, allowing you to set the name and namespace of an attribute dynamically.

However, `<xsl:attribute>` turns out to be a lot more useful than `<xsl:element>` for two reasons. Firstly, it is an instruction, and therefore can be specified within an `<xsl:if>` or even within a separate template and still be added to the element you're creating. Secondly, the content of the `<xsl:attribute>` element determines the value of the attribute, and the content of `<xsl:attribute>` can include any XSLT instructions you like. As we'll see later, this is especially useful for generating attributes with conditional content.

> *The `<xsl:attribute>` instruction can contain any XSLT instructions, but the only types of nodes that can be generated within it are text nodes, which are then used to give the value of the attribute. In fact, it's usually a good idea to use `<xsl:text>` when generating the text in an attribute value, especially when generating HTML, because new lines in attribute values can prevent web browsers from correctly interpreting attributes.*

Attributes can be added with `<xsl:attribute>` to any result element, whether generated by a literal result element or using `<xsl:element>` (but not to XSLT instructions – remember you're adding attribute nodes to the result tree). In fact, unless you can copy attributes from the original source tree onto the element, you *must* use `<xsl:attribute>` to specify the attributes of elements generated with `<xsl:element>`.

Any attributes that you add to an element with `<xsl:attribute>` instructions have to be added before you add any content to the element that you're generating, so usually `<xsl:attribute>` instructions come immediately after the start tag of the literal result element or the `<xsl:element>` instruction that creates the relevant element. You can use `<xsl:attribute>` to create some attributes, while adding others in the normal way at the same time. For example, the following creates an `<img>` element with `width`, `height`, `src`, and `alt` attributes.

```
<img width="20" height="20">
  <xsl:attribute name="src">favorite.gif</xsl:attribute>
  <xsl:attribute name="alt">[Favorite]</xsl:attribute>
</img>
```

If an attribute you generate using `<xsl:attribute>` has the same name as an attribute that's already on the literal result element, then the `<xsl:attribute>` instruction overrides the existing attribute.

In this section, we'll look at how to use `<xsl:attribute>` for adding optional attributes, attributes with conditional values, and whole sets of attributes at once.

> **You can create attribute nodes using the `<xsl:attribute>` instruction, with the name of the attribute given in the `name` attribute and the value of the attribute specified by the content of the instruction.**

Creating Optional Attributes

When you add an attribute to a literal result element literally, you are forcing the attribute to be present. You can change the value of the literal attribute using an attribute value template, but you can't change whether it's there or not. On the other hand, because the `<xsl:attribute>` element is an instruction, you can put it within `<xsl:if>` or `<xsl:choose>` elements so that an attribute is only added in particular situations, or different attributes are added in different situations. The general patterns are:

```
<elementName>
  <xsl:if test="condition">
    <xsl:attribute name="attributeName">attributeValue</xsl:attribute>
  </xsl:if>
  ...
</elementName>
```

and:

```
<elementName>
  <xsl:choose>
    <xsl:when test="condition1">
      <xsl:attribute name="attributeName1">attributeValue1</xsl:attribute>
    </xsl:when>
    <xsl:when test="condition2">
      <xsl:attribute name="attributeName2">attributeValue2</xsl:attribute>
    </xsl:when>
```

```
    ...
    <xsl:otherwise>
      <xsl:attribute name="defaultAttributeName">
        <xsl:text>defaultAttributeValue</xsl:text>
      </xsl:attribute>
    </xsl:otherwise>
  </xsl:choose>
</elementName>
```

Wrapping `<xsl:attribute>` elements in `<xsl:if>` or `<xsl:choose>` allows you to control which attributes get added to which elements.

Try It Out – Highlighting Interesting Programs (Again)

To illustrate how `<xsl:attribute>` is used to create optional attributes, we'll return to a scenario that we first discussed in Chapter 5: highlighting the interesting programs in our TV Guide. The interesting programs are highlighted in the HTML using CSS – if the `<div>` for the program has a `class` attribute with the value `interesting`, then the program is highlighted.

In the solution that we developed in Chapter 5, and the one we're still using in `TVGuide5.xsl`, we used an `<xsl:choose>` to either create a `<div>` element with a `class` attribute or create one without a `class` attribute, depending on whether the program was interesting. The following code highlights the places where we create the `<div>` element in the template for the `<Program>` element in `TVGuide5.xsl`:

```
<xsl:template match="Program">
  <xsl:choose>
    <xsl:when test="@flag = 'favorite' or @flag = 'interesting' or
                    @rating > 6 or
                    contains(translate(Series, $upper, $lower), $keyword) or
                    contains(translate(Title, $upper, $lower), $keyword) or
                    contains(translate(Description, $upper, $lower),
                             $keyword)">
      <div class="interesting">
        <xsl:apply-templates select="." mode="Details" />
      </div>
    </xsl:when>
    <xsl:otherwise>
      <div>
        <xsl:apply-templates select="." mode="Details" />
      </div>
    </xsl:otherwise>
  </xsl:choose>
</xsl:template>
```

In fact, the only difference between the two `<div>` elements is the `class` attribute – they have the same content and occur in the same place. Rather than repeating the same `<div>` and the same `<xsl:apply-templates>` to get the content of the `<div>`, we can use a single literal result element and add the `class` attribute conditionally, as in `TVGuide6.xsl`:

```
<xsl:template match="Program">
  <div>
    <xsl:if test="@flag = 'favorite' or @flag = 'interesting' or
                  @rating > 6 or
                  contains(translate(Series, $upper, $lower), $keyword) or
                  contains(translate(Title, $upper, $lower), $keyword) or
                  contains(translate(Description, $upper, $lower),
                           $keyword)">
      <xsl:attribute name="class">interesting</xsl:attribute>
    </xsl:if>
    <xsl:apply-templates select="." mode="Details" />
  </div>
</xsl:template>
```

If you transform `TVGuide.xml` with `TVGuide6.xsl`, you'll see the interesting programs highlighted, exactly as they were before:

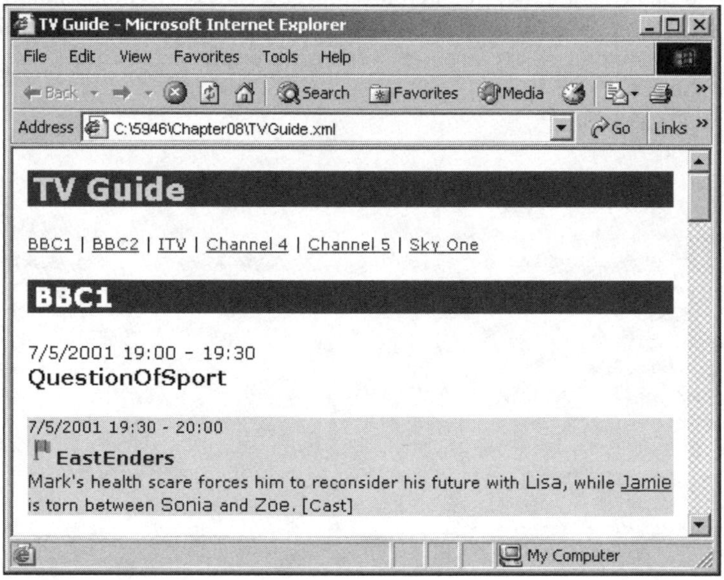

The result of the transformation hasn't changed, but the clarity of the stylesheet has. We could even merge the `Details` mode template back into the main `<Program>` template again if we wanted.

Creating Attributes with Conditional Values

As well as putting `<xsl:if>` and `<xsl:choose>` *around* `<xsl:attribute>` instructions, you can also put them *inside* `<xsl:attribute>` elements in order to give attributes different values in different situations. This is particularly useful for maintenance, to prevent you from repeating the same instructions to create elements whose only difference is an attribute value.

For example, in `TVGuide6.xsl`, we add different flags to programs that have different values for their `flag` attribute with the following code within the template that matches `<Program>` elements in `Detail` mode:

```
<xsl:variable name="image">
  <xsl:choose>
    <xsl:when test="@flag = 'favorite'">favorite</xsl:when>
    <xsl:when test="@flag = 'interesting'">interest</xsl:when>
  </xsl:choose>
</xsl:variable>
<xsl:variable name="alt">
  <xsl:choose>
    <xsl:when test="@flag = 'favorite'">Favorite</xsl:when>
    <xsl:when test="@flag = 'interesting'">Interest</xsl:when>
  </xsl:choose>
</xsl:variable>
<xsl:if test="@flag">
  <img src="{$image}.gif" alt="[{$alt}]" width="20" height="20" />
</xsl:if>
```

The <img> element that is generated by the preceding code always has the same width and height, but it has different `src` and `alt` attributes in the different situations. In an alternative design, you could create these attributes using <xsl:attribute>, giving them different values according to the value of the `flag` attribute, as follows:

```
<xsl:if test="@flag">
  <img width="20" height="20">
    <xsl:attribute name="src">
      <xsl:choose>
        <xsl:when test="@flag = 'favorite'">favorite.gif</xsl:when>
        <xsl:when test="@flag = 'interesting'">interest.gif</xsl:when>
      </xsl:choose>
    </xsl:attribute>
    <xsl:attribute name="alt">
      <xsl:text>[</xsl:text>
      <xsl:choose>
        <xsl:when test="@flag = 'favorite'">Favorite</xsl:when>
        <xsl:when test="@flag = 'interesting'">Interest</xsl:when>
      </xsl:choose>
      <xsl:text>]</xsl:text>
    </xsl:attribute>
  </img>
</xsl:if>
```

When it's used for conditional values, the <xsl:attribute> element saves you the effort of making up variable names.

> **You can put any instructions you like in the content of <xsl:attribute>, as long as they only generate text nodes.**

Attribute Sets

Another aid to maintenance that is offered by XSLT is the ability to define sets of attributes, which you can then apply to elements in different places within your stylesheet. You can define an attribute set using the `<xsl:attribute-set>` element, which lives at the top level of your stylesheet as a direct child of the `<xsl:stylesheet>` document element.

Each `<xsl:attribute-set>` element has a `name` attribute, which specifies the name of the attribute set so that you can refer to it later. Within the `<xsl:attribute-set>` element, you use `<xsl:attribute>` instructions to define the attributes in the set. For example, the following defines an attribute set called `image`, which contains the two attributes `width` and `height`:

```
<xsl:attribute-set name="image">
  <xsl:attribute name="width">20</xsl:attribute>
  <xsl:attribute name="height">20</xsl:attribute>
</xsl:attribute-set>
```

The `<xsl:attribute-set>` element can only have `<xsl:attribute>` elements as children, so you can't create an attribute set to add optional attributes. However, the values of the attributes in the attribute set can be calculated on the fly, based on the current node at the point where the attribute set is used.

You can use an attribute set to add the attributes that it defines to a particular element with the `xsl:use-attribute-sets` attribute on literal result elements or the `use-attribute-sets` attribute on `<xsl:element>` (or `<xsl:copy>`, which we meet later). Each of these attributes takes a whitespace-separated list of the names of attribute sets. For example, both of the following add attributes defined in the `image` and `highlight` attribute sets to newly created `<img>` elements:

```
<img src="flag.gif" xsl:use-attribute-sets="image highlight" />
```

```
<xsl:element name="img" use-attribute-sets="image highlight">
  <xsl:attribute name="src">flag.gif</xsl:attribute>
</xsl:element>
```

You can also use the `use-attribute-sets` attribute on `<xsl:attribute-set>` to include the attributes that you've defined in one attribute set in another, building a hierarchy of attribute sets.

Attribute sets really come into their own as ways of defining styles when you're generating XSL-FO, because XSL-FO uses attributes a great deal to define the look of a formatting object. They are also useful in other XML-to-XML transformations where several elements share the same set of attributes, but tend not to be as useful when you're just creating HTML – it's fairly rare for an HTML page to have the same attributes repeated on elements that are created in different places.

> **You can define sets of attributes using the `<xsl:attribute-set>` top-level element, and add the attributes that they define to literal result elements with the `xsl:use-attribute-sets` attribute or to elements generated with `<xsl:element>` with the `use-attribute-sets` attribute.**

Now you've seen three ways of adding attributes to an element:

- Using attribute sets
- Using literal attributes on literal result elements
- Using `<xsl:attribute>`

It's possible to add an attribute of the same name in all three ways on the same element; if you do so, then the one that you add with `<xsl:attribute>` overrides the one that you add as a literal attribute on the element, which in turn overrides the one that you add using the attribute set. If you add the same attribute from multiple attribute sets, then the definition in the last attribute set that you use is the one that's added to the element.

Generating Comments and Processing Instructions

Unlike elements, attributes, and text, you can't include comments or processing instructions in the output by including them literally within your stylesheet. Instead, you have to use `<xsl:comment>` and `<xsl:processing-instruction>` to create new comment and processing instruction nodes respectively in the result tree.

> *Like other nodes, you can always copy comments or processing instructions from the source document using `<xsl:copy-of>` if they are already around in the correct form.*

The content of an `<xsl:comment>` instruction determines the value of the comment node that you create. You can only create text within an `<xsl:comment>`, but the text can be added literally, with `<xsl:text>` or with `<xsl:value-of>`. For example, the following adds the comment "Generated automatically using XSLT" to the result tree:

```
<xsl:comment>Generated automatically using XSLT</xsl:comment>
```

When serialized, the comment will look like:

```
<!--Generated automatically using XSLT-->
```

> **You can generate comment nodes using `<xsl:comment>`. The content of the `<xsl:comment>` instruction specifies the value of the comment.**

The `<xsl:processing-instruction>` instruction works in a similar way, except that you must give a `name` attribute, holding the name (or target) of the processing instruction. Like the `name` attributes of `<xsl:element>` and `<xsl:attribute>`, the `name` attribute on `<xsl:processing-instruction>` is an attribute value template, so you can create processing instructions whose names are computed on the fly, if you need to. The following example creates an `xml-stylesheet` processing instruction:

```
<xsl:processing-instruction name="xml-stylesheet">
  <xsl:text>type="text/css" href="TVGuide.css"</xsl:text>
</xsl:processing-instruction>
```

When serialized into a file, the processing instruction will look like:

```
<?xml-stylesheet type="text/css" href="TVGuide.css"?>
```

Remember that the content of a processing instruction is just a string as far as an XML application is concerned; the things that look like attributes in the `xml-stylesheet` *processing instruction are just part of the string, so you don't create them with* `<xsl:attribute>`.

> **You can generate processing instruction nodes using `<xsl:processing-instruction>`. The `name` attribute of the `<xsl:processing-instruction>` instruction specifies the name or target of the processing instruction, while its content generates its value.**

Copying Nodes and Branches

You've seen how to create new nodes of various descriptions, but what if you have a description already written in XHTML that you just want replicated in the result?

Well, if you cast your mind back to Chapter 6, you'll remember that when you create a result tree fragment using a variable, you can subsequently add it to the result tree using `<xsl:copy-of>`. You can do the same thing with nodes from the source node tree. Use the `select` attribute to point to the nodes that you want to copy, and the nodes that you select and all their descendants are copied across into the result tree. For example, the following copies the content of the `<Description>` element (without adding the `<Description>` element itself):

```
<xsl:copy-of select="Description/node()" />
```

While `<xsl:copy-of>` is excellent for making copies of entire branches of the source tree, it's often more helpful to use the natural XSLT processing model to traverse the tree, copying the nodes that you encounter as you go, as this enables you to make an exact copy of most of the tree while making small changes at a low level. Rather than using `<xsl:copy-of>`, you can use an **identity template**, which matches any kind of node, copies it to the result, and then recurses down the tree. To create a copy of a node, whatever its type, you can use `<xsl:copy>`, which creates a shallow copy of the node (which doesn't include any attributes or content when you copy an element).

The following identity template matches nodes of any type (including attributes). It uses `<xsl:copy>` to make a copy of the node. Then it applies templates to the attributes and content of the node – if the node isn't an element then it won't have any attributes or content, so the `<xsl:apply-templates>` instruction will do nothing:

```
<xsl:template match="@* | node()">
  <xsl:copy>
    <xsl:apply-templates select="@* | node()" />
  </xsl:copy>
</xsl:template>
```

An identity template is often a useful alternative to the built-in templates – it copies everything exactly as it is by default, and all you have to do is provide templates for the elements and attributes that you want to be treated specially. For example, if you wanted to create a stylesheet that copied most things as is, but changed all the `<Description>` elements to `<Desc>` elements, you could use the identity template coupled with the following template:

```
<xsl:template match="Description">
  <Desc><xsl:apply-templates /></Desc>
</xsl:template>
```

The identity template would copy the majority of the source document, with the template for the `<Description>` element renaming those elements wherever they occurred.

> **The `<xsl:copy-of>` instruction copies an entire branch of the source tree to the result tree. The `<xsl:copy>` instruction is particularly useful within an identity template that copies elements by default.**

Controlling Output

The first part of this chapter looked at how to construct a result tree. Sometimes, that's all an XSLT processor needs to do – another process then takes the result tree and processes it to create a display or add information to a database. However, more often than not, and especially when you're debugging a stylesheet, you'll want the result of the XSLT process to be written to a file so that you can view it.

For the XSLT processor, writing the result tree to a file means that it has to **serialize** the result tree in some way. Serializing involves taking an abstract object (such as a node) that is only held in memory and creating a physical representation of that object. For example, when serializing an element node, a processor will write a start and end tag for that element node. When another processor reads that start and end tag, it will create an element node in memory. Thus serializing is the opposite of parsing; and if you serialize a node tree, and then parse the result, then you should get roughly the same node tree as you started with.

Sometimes an external process might manage this serialization, but XSLT also gives you some control over the serialization from within the stylesheet, using the `<xsl:output>` element. The `<xsl:output>` element resides at the top level of the stylesheet, and holds a number of attributes that give you control over how the XSLT processor outputs the result tree. You can have as many `<xsl:output>` elements as you like within a stylesheet – their attributes are combined (with later `<xsl:output>` elements overriding earlier ones) when the XSLT processor has to decide what to do.

> **The `<xsl:output>` top-level element controls how the result tree is serialized on output.**

Output Methods

The first and most important question that you have to answer when serializing the result tree is what **output method** you want to use. The output method determines the syntax that's used for the various different types of nodes in the result tree. There are three output methods that are built in to XSLT processors: `xml`, `html`, and `text`. You can tell the XSLT processor to use a particular output method with the `method` attribute on `<xsl:output>`. For example, to tell the XSLT processor to use the `text` output method, you should use:

```
<xsl:output method="text" />
```

As we'll see in Chapter 13, some processors support other output methods than the ones mentioned here: for example, methods to allow you to serialize your result according to XHTML rules. You should read your processor's documentation to work out what it supports.

The xml Output Method

The most common output method is `xml`, which serializes the result tree using the standard XML syntax. For example, given a result tree that looks like the following:

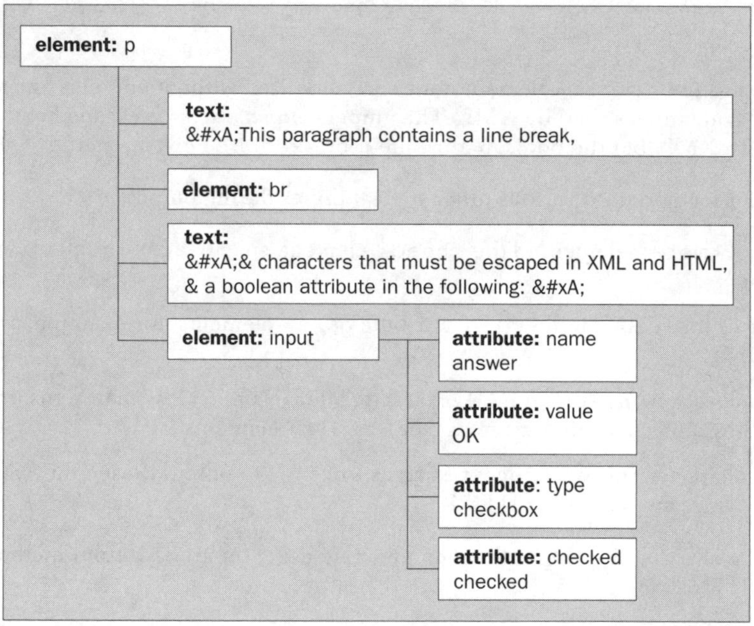

the `xml` output method creates a section in a document that looks something like:

```
<p>
This paragraph contains a line break,<br />
&amp; characters that must be escaped in XML and HTML,
&amp; a boolean attribute in the following:
<input name="answer" value="OK" type="checkbox" checked="checked" />
</p>
```

As you can see, the resulting output follows the XML rules for well-formedness, with end tags for every element, special characters being escaped, and so on.

The html Output Method

The xml output method is the default method if you don't have an <xsl:output> element, unless the document element of the result that you're producing is an <html> element (or an <HTML> element – the name can be in any case) in no namespace. If that's the case, or if you tell the XSLT processor to use it explicitly using the method attribute on <xsl:output>, the XSLT processor will use the html output method.

Under the html output method, elements are serialized according to HTML rules – the XSLT processor recognizes certain elements and attributes as being serialized without end tags, for example, and generates output accordingly. For example, taking the same result tree as we used for the xml output method, the html output method creates a section in a document that looks something like:

```
<p>
This paragraph contains a line break,<br>
&amp; characters that must be escaped in XML and HTML,
&amp; a boolean attribute in the following:
<input name="answer" value="OK" type="checkbox" checked>
</p>
```

Both the <br> and the <input> element nodes are serialized without end tags and without the special empty element syntax that's used by XML. The ampersand character is escaped with a character entity reference, as with XML, but the boolean attribute (checked) isn't given a name.

The html output method does various other special things during output:

- It adds a <meta> element to the <head> element, specifying the content type of the document
- It ensures that URLs, in the href attribute of <a> elements, for example, are escaped correctly
- It doesn't escape the special XML characters (for example, less-than signs or ampersands) when they appear within <script> or <style> elements
- It uses character entity references, such as , to output those non-ASCII characters for which names are defined in HTML

All these steps ensure that the output that you generate using the html output method adheres to the syntax rules of HTML.

The text Output Method

You can use the xml or html output methods to generate a document that holds only text if the result tree that you generate doesn't contain anything other than text nodes. However, as we've seen, if you use these methods the values of the text nodes are escaped – less-than signs become < and ampersands become &. The text method is therefore essential when you're generating plain text, for example, comma-separated files, Java code, or SQL queries, as it prevents the five special XML characters from being escaped with their built-in entity references during serialization.

When you output a result tree using the `text` method, all nodes aside from text nodes are completely ignored. If we take the same tree as we used with the `xml` and `html` output methods, the `text` output method would create the following lines of text:

```
This paragraph contains a line break,
& characters that must be escaped in XML and HTML,
& a boolean attribute in the following:
```

> **There are three built-in output methods: `text` for text outputs, `html` for HTML output, and `xml` for XML-based markup languages. You can tell the processor which output method to use with the `method` attribute on `<xsl:output>`.**

Disabling Output Escaping

In very rare cases, you might want to have the ease of the `xml` output method for creating elements and attributes, combined with the ability of the `text` output method to create strings without the special characters (less-than signs and ampersands in particular) being escaped. This might happen because you want to generate something that isn't quite XML, or because you have a piece of "XML" as a string within a text node rather than as nodes within the node tree (which often occurs when you include XML within a CDATA section). XSLT allows you to indicate whether a piece of text should be escaped or not with the `disable-output-escaping` attribute.

The `disable-output-escaping` attribute can be placed on `<xsl:text>` and `<xsl:value-of>` elements to indicate whether the special characters in the text node that is generated by the instruction should be escaped on output or not. The `disable-output-escaping` attribute's default value is `no`, but if you set it to `yes` then any less-than signs or ampersands that are included within the text node will be output as less-than signs and ampersands rather than as `<` and `&`.

> **If you include a `disable-output-escaping` attribute with a value of `yes` on `<xsl:text>` or `<xsl:value-of>` elements, the text nodes they create might be serialized without special characters being escaped.**

Disabling Output Escaping of Literal Text

The first situation where you might need to disable output escaping is when you are generating something that is not quite XML. For example, Java Server Pages (JSP) includes a special syntax for including scripts within pages. In this special syntax, script is identified with a "scripting element" of the form:

```
<% script %>
```

This isn't valid XML syntax – it's certainly not an element; nor is it a processing instruction or a comment. Thus to generate a JSP page using XSLT, you really should use the `text` output method. However, aside from these "scripting elements", the majority of a JSP page is made up of elements and attributes, so it would be nice to be able to use the `xml` output method for the elements and attributes and the `text` output method for the "scripting elements".

To create a "scripting element", you can use an `<xsl:text>` element with a `disable-output-escaping` attribute with the value `yes`. For example:

```
<xsl:text disable-output-escaping="yes">&lt;% script %></xsl:text>
```

Note that the less-than sign in the stylesheet is still escaped – the stylesheet itself must still be well-formed XML.

When it comes to serialize the result tree, most XSLT processors will recognize the `disable-output-escaping` directive and output the string that you were after.

Disabling Output Escaping of Text from the Source Document

Another situation where using `disable-output-escaping` can be tempting is when the source XML contains some XML that for one reason or another is double-escaped in the source document. This usually occurs when the XML has been placed inside a CDATA section, such as the following:

```
<content>
  <![CDATA[<p>This is well-formed XML.</p>]]>
</content>
```

As you'll recall from Chapter 2, putting XML within a CDATA section has exactly the same effect as escaping the less-than signs that begin the tags using `<`. To the XSLT processor, the above XML is exactly the same as the following:

```
<content>
  &lt;p>This is well-formed XML.&lt;/p>
</content>
```

If you try to output the value of the `<content>` element with a normal `<xsl:value-of>` instruction, then you will get:

```
&lt;p>This is well-formed XML.&lt;/p>
```

To get the value of the `<content>` element *as XML*, you need to add a `disable-output-escaping` attribute with the value `yes` to the `<xsl:value-of>` instruction, as follows:

```
<xsl:value-of select="content" disable-output-escaping="yes" />
```

When the result tree is serialized, you will see the following in the generated XML file:

```
<p>This is well-formed XML.</p>
```

Why Not to Disable Output Escaping

Having described how to disable output escaping, I'm now going to try to persuade you not to use this facility by explaining why disabling output escaping is, in general, a bad idea.

First, and most practically, not all XSLT processors support the disabling of output escaping. According to the XSLT Recommendation, an XSLT processor can ignore the `disable-output-escaping` attribute, and indeed some do ignore it. This is especially the case when an XSLT processor is used to generate a result that is used as the result tree rather than being serialized and re-parsed. It is also quite restricted even in those XSLT processors that do understand it; for example, you can't use `disable-output-escaping` to prevent the special characters in attribute values from being escaped.

Second, there is always the risk when you disable output escaping that the result of the transformation will not be valid, and in particular that it will not be well-formed XML. If you look again at the second example above, if the "XML" value of the `<content>` element were missing the close tag for the `<p>` element, then the result of the transformation as a whole would be a non-well-formed XML document.

Third, there is almost always some other way to achieve what you want to achieve without resorting to disabling output escaping. What's more, the other method of achieving your goal is likely to lead to a more maintainable solution in the long run. For example, rather than using JSP's non-XML "scripting element" syntax, you could use JSP's equivalent `<jsp:scriptlet>` element, which *is* XML; making this change will enable you to process your JSP pages using XSLT or other XML applications. Similarly, rather than embedding XML within a CDATA section, you should use namespaces to distinguish between the wrapper element and the content that you're interested in, so that you have, for example:

```
<content>
  <html:p>This is well-formed XML.</html:p>
</content>
```

This change not only makes it easier to output the embedded XHTML as XHTML, but also makes it possible for you to process the content of the `<html:p>` element using XSLT and other XML applications.

Finally, disabling output escaping often demonstrates underlying misconceptions about how XSLT works. Hopefully, having gone through this book you understand how to wrap an element around the result of processing a set of elements, that you can output a non-breaking space by including ` ` in your stylesheet, and so on. People who don't yet have a good grasp of XSLT often try to disable output escaping to get around the problems that they encounter; the XSLT method always ends up being simpler, more effective, and more maintainable.

Declaring Content Type Information

The `<xsl:output>` element not only determines what kind of output you are creating in general, but also gives you control over a set of features that determine how the content of the output will be interpreted by other applications.

First, and relevant to all output methods, there's the `media-type` attribute, which declares the content type of the output that you're generating. By default, the media type of output produced is `text/xml` with the `xml` output method, `text/html` for the `html` output method, and `text/plain` for the `text` output method. However, you might be generating information with different media types – for example, you might be generating WML using the `xml` output method, and might want to use the media type `text/vnd.wap.wml`. Or you might be generating XHTML using the `xml` output method; if you want XHTML to be read by older browsers, then it can be given a media type of `text/html`:

```
<xsl:output method="xml" media-type="text/html" />
```

The `media-type` attribute of `<xsl:output>` indicates the content type of the output.

Second, applicable to the `xml` and `html` output methods, you can specify a public and/or system identifier to be used in the `DOCTYPE` declaration of the generated file. In Chapter 2, we saw that XHTML 1.0 documents include a `DOCTYPE` declaration of the form:

```
<!DOCTYPE html
      PUBLIC "-//W3C//DTD XHTML 1.0 Strict//EN"
             "DTD/xhtml1-strict.dtd">
```

In this `DOCTYPE` declaration, the public identifier is `-//W3C//DTD XHTML 1.0 Strict//EN` and the system identifier is `DTD/xhtml1-strict.dtd`. These two values can be specified in the `doctype-public` and `doctype-system` attributes on the `<xsl:output>` element, to tell the XSLT processor to include the `DOCTYPE` declaration we need:

```
<xsl:output doctype-public="-//W3C//DTD XHTML 1.0 Strict//EN"
            doctype-system="DTD/xhtml1-strict.dtd" />
```

The `DOCTYPE` declaration also gives the name of the document element in the generated document, but the XSLT processor automatically adds this based on the document element in the result tree that you've constructed.

The `doctype-public` and `doctype-system` attributes of `<xsl:output>` determine what kind of `DOCTYPE` declaration is added to the output in `xml` and `html` output methods.

Controlling Output Formats

The final important group of attributes control how the output looks, and tend to be used most when you're debugging your stylesheet because they allow you to view the output easily.

The first, and most important, of these attributes is the `encoding` attribute, which indicates the character encoding that you'd like the XSLT processor to use when writing the output. If you don't include an `encoding` attribute, then the XSLT processor will output UTF-8 or UTF-16, and you may find that this makes the output from your transformations look strange when you view them in simple text editors such as Notepad. Just as it's often easiest to write XML documents in text editors using ISO-8859-1 (or Windows 1252), it's often easiest to *view* XML documents if they're saved in one of these encodings. For example, to save your document in ISO-8859-1, you should use:

```
<xsl:output encoding="ISO-8859-1" />
```

The `encoding` *attribute applies to all the output methods. If you use it with the* `xml` *output method, then you'll get an XML declaration at the top of the output that specifies the encoding; if you use it with the* `html` *method, then the* `<meta>` *element that the XSLT processor adds will specify this character set. Any characters that aren't available in the encoding that you specify will be replaced with character references when you use the* `xml` *or* `html` *method.*

The `encoding` attribute of `<xsl:output>` indicates the encoding that the processor should use when saving the output.

The second formatting attribute only applies to the `xml` and `html` output methods and controls whether extra indentation is added to the document to make it easier to read. If you specify `yes` for the `indent` attribute, then the XSLT processor is free to add whitespace-only text nodes to the document, to put elements on new lines or indent them (the `indent` attribute defaults to `yes` if you use the `html` output method). This can be very helpful when you need to look at the document that you've just generated, especially if it's highly structured, but of course it adds to the size of the document, so you should only use it if people need to read the document after the transformation. For example:

```
<xsl:output indent="yes" />
```

If the `indent` attribute of `<xsl:output>` has the value `yes`, then the XSLT processor can add whitespace to the output of the transformation to make it more readable.

As we've seen, when an XSLT processor outputs an XML document, it will escape all the markup-significant characters, such as < and `&`, in the document, to create a well-formed XML file. But an alternative method, which is useful when there are a large number of characters that need to be escaped, is to have a `CDATA` section wrapped around the text. If we go back to the example that we looked at earlier, we can see that an alternative XML serialization of the result tree would be:

```
<p><![CDATA[
This paragraph contains a line break,]]><br /><![CDATA[
& characters that must be escaped in XML and HTML,
& a boolean attribute in the following:
]]><input name="answer" value="OK" type="checkbox" checked="checked" />
</p>
```

In the above, the text node children of the `<p>` element are wrapped in the `CDATA` section, so the ampersands that they contain don't have to be escaped with `&`. Normally, an XSLT processor will escape the individual characters rather than use a CDATA section, but you can use the `cdata-section-elements` attribute to tell it to wrap the text node children of particular elements in `CDATA` sections instead. The `cdata-section-elements` attribute lists the elements within which text nodes should be wrapped in `CDATA` sections, separated by spaces. For example, to tell the XSLT processor to wrap the content of `<script>` and `<style>` elements in `CDATA` sections, you should use:

```
<xsl:output cdata-section-elements="script style" />
```

If you have multiple <xsl:output> elements, then all the cdata-section-elements attributes are combined into a single attribute value.

The cdata-section-elements attribute of <xsl:output> lists the elements whose text node children should be wrapped in CDATA sections.

Try It Out – Generating XHTML

Thus far, the XSLT processor has actually been using the html output method when transforming the TV Guide because it's detected that the document element of the result tree that we've produced is an <html> element that isn't in a namespace. To produce XHTML, we need to use the xml output method and should add a few more details to make the XHTML easier to read and to make it comply with the XHTML Recommendation.

Placing the <html> document element of the result tree into the XHTML namespace (which we did earlier in this chapter) will mean that the XSLT processor will use the xml output method rather than the html output method automatically, but it doesn't hurt to add an <xsl:output> element in TVGuide7.xsl to explicitly tell the processor to use the xml output method:

```
<xsl:output method="xml" />
```

The XHTML that you're generating can still be recognized by HTML browsers, so you still want it to use the same content type (text/html rather than text/xml); you need to add a media-type attribute to the <xsl:output> element to tell the XSLT processor to use this MIME type:

```
<xsl:output method="xml"
            media-type="text/html" />
```

To create a compliant XHTML document, you also need to add a DOCTYPE declaration to the output, using the doctype-public and doctype-system attributes on the <xsl:output> element:

```
<xsl:output method="xml"
            mime-type="text/html"
            doctype-public="-//W3C//DTD XHTML 1.0 Strict//EN"
            doctype-system="DTD/xhtml1-strict.dtd" />
```

That's all that you *need* to do to generate XHTML, but you might also find it helpful to tell the XSLT processor to indent the XHTML that you're generating and ask it to use ISO-8859-1 as the character encoding, so that you can open the file easily in your text editor:

```
<xsl:output method="xml"
            media-type="text/html"
            doctype-public="-//W3C//DTD XHTML 1.0 Strict//EN"
            doctype-system="DTD/xhtml1-strict.dtd"
            cdata-section-elements="script style"
            indent="yes"
            encoding="ISO-8859-1" />
```

Having made these changes, when you transform `TVGuide.xml` with `TVGuide7.xsl`, the top level of the resulting document should look something like the following:

```
<?xml version="1.0" encoding="ISO-8859-1"?>
<!DOCTYPE html
  PUBLIC "-//W3C//DTD XHTML 1.0 Strict//EN" "DTD/xhtml1-strict.dtd">
<html xmlns="http://www.w3.org/1999/xhtml">
   <head>
      <title>TV Guide</title>
      <link rel="stylesheet" href="TVGuide.css"/>
      <script type="text/javascript">

        function toggle(element) {
          if (element.style.display == 'none') {
            element.style.display = 'block';
          } else {
            element.style.display = 'none';
          }
        }

      </script>
   </head>
   <body>
      <h1>TV Guide</h1>
      ...
   </body>
</html>
```

Your processor might use different numbers of spaces when it indents your result, or choose different places to add indentation.

This XHTML document will look the same as the HTML document that we were generating earlier in most web browsers. Internet Explorer, for example, displays the following:

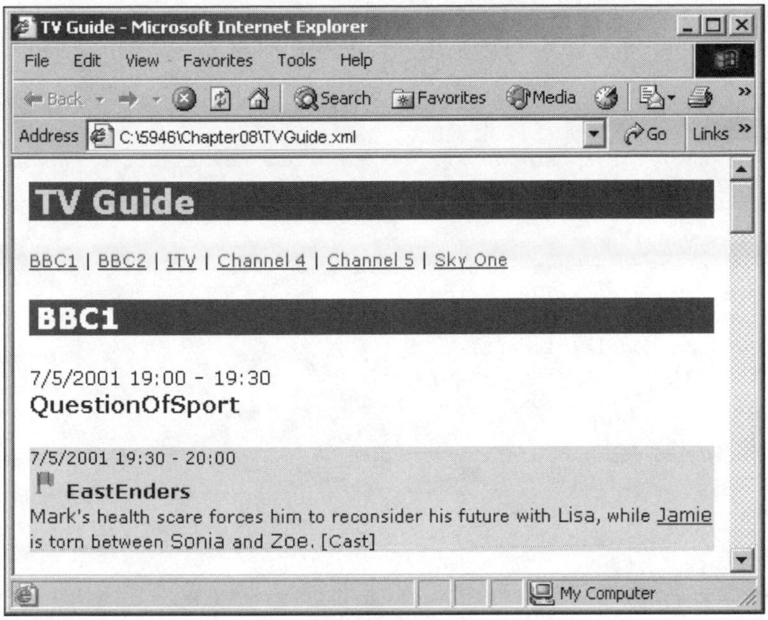

Try removing the indentation (by removing the `indent` attribute or by setting it to `no`) and changing the encoding used to save the file by changing the `encoding` attribute to `UTF-16`, to see how this changes the look of the document in your text editor.

Summary

In this chapter, we've looked at the two components of creating some output from an XSLT process:

- Creating a result tree
- Serializing the result tree

You've learned about several new elements that enable you to generate and add nodes to the result tree. Some of the instructions that you've seen in this chapter simply give an extra bit of functionality over and above the methods you've already seen of creating elements, attributes, and text. Using `<xsl:element>`, `<xsl:attribute>`, and `<xsl:text>` when you don't need to can make your stylesheet longer and (arguably) harder to read, so it's worth thinking about whether you really need to use them before you do so.

However, there are no methods for creating comments and processing instructions aside from using `<xsl:comment>` and `<xsl:processing-instruction>` (unless you've got one that you can copy with `<xsl:copy>` or `<xsl:copy-of>`). You've also seen how to use attribute sets, defined by `<xsl:attribute-set>`, to add several attributes to an element at once, whether it's created with a literal result element or using `<xsl:element>`.

Once you've built a result tree, you'll usually need to output it to a file. This serialization process is governed by the `<xsl:output>` element, and you've learned about several of its attributes:

- `method` – determines whether the output is serialized as XML, HTML, or text
- `media-type` – sets the content type (or `mime-type`) of the output
- `doctype-public` and `doctype-system` – add a `DOCTYPE` declaration to the XML or HTML document
- `encoding` – sets the character encoding of the output
- `indent` – tells the XSLT processor to produce indented output, which makes it more readable
- `cdata-section-elements` – tells the XSLT processor which text nodes to wrap in CDATA sections

These first eight chapters have introduced you to XSLT and shown you the basic principles of constructing transformations and the theory behind querying the source tree and generating the result tree. Thus far, we've been going through the concepts gradually, step by step, giving you a good grounding in the fundamentals of XSLT. The rest of the chapters in this book build on what you've learned up till now, and you can feel free to tackle the next five chapters in any order you want – they each deal with a particular aspect of authoring XSLT stylesheets, but there's no need to go through them in order if one strikes you as particularly interesting.

Review Questions

1. What are the two ways in which you can add an element node to the result tree? What are the advantages and disadvantages of each?

2. What function can you use to change the case of a string?

3. What else do you need to know to work out what namespace the elements generated by the following instructions are in?

```
<html>...</html>
<xsl:element name="html">...</xsl:element>
<xsl:element name="{$prefix}:html">...</xsl:element>
<xsl:element name="html" namespace="{$namespace}">...</xsl:element>
```

4. Write a template that matches any element in the XHTML namespace and generates a copy of that element in no namespace.

5. What are the three ways in which you can add a text node to the result tree?

6. What two reasons might you have for using `<xsl:text>` rather than literal text within a template?

7. In what situations would you use <xsl:attribute> rather than adding an attribute literally to a literal result element?

8. Look at the following piece of XSLT. What value will the class attribute on the <p> element have?

```
<xsl:template match="Program">
  <p xsl:use-attribute-sets="program show"
     class="{local-name()}">
    <xsl:attribute name="class">episode</xsl:attribute>
  </p>
</xsl:template>

<xsl:attribute-set name="program">
  <xsl:attribute name="class">program</xsl:attribute>
</xsl:attribute-set>

<xsl:attribute-set name="show">
  <xsl:attribute name="class">show</xsl:attribute>
</xsl:attribute-set>
```

9. When would you use an identity template to copy a branch of the source tree rather than <xsl:copy-of>?

10. Which output method should you use to generate XHTML? What other attributes do you need to set on <xsl:output> to create a conformant XHTML document?

Beginning
XSLT

9

Sorting and Numbering

Now that you've got a good understanding of the fundamentals of processing XML with XSLT, it's time to move on to look at some of the other XSLT elements that support you in getting the output that you want. In this chapter, we're going to be looking at changing the order in which nodes are processed by sorting them and adding numbers to the output that you generate.

In this chapter, you'll learn:

- How to process node sets in different orders
- How to sort nodes numerically and alphabetically
- How to sort by multiple values
- How to number the items in a list (sorted and unsorted)
- How to number nodes across an entire document
- How to create hierarchical numbers

Sorting

When you use `<xsl:for-each>` or `<xsl:apply-templates>` to process a set of nodes, the nodes are processed in **document order** – the order in which they appear in the source document. So, for example, when we process `TVGuide.xml` with `TVGuide.xsl` we create an XHTML page that lists the channels in the TV guide in the order in which the `<Channel>` elements are listed in the XML document, and lists the programs showing on that channel in the order in which the `<Program>` elements are listed in `TVGuide.xml`.

Often document order is precisely the order that you want, particularly in document-oriented XML where the ordering of sections or paragraphs within a document is important rhetorically. However, in data-oriented XML, the ordering of particular items in the source XML document may very well not be the order in which you want to present them, or you might want to be able to present different orders for different situations. For example, we might want to sort the channels alphabetically by name, or by the ratings of the programs that they show, so that the 'best' channel comes first.

XSLT provides the <xsl:sort> element to allow you to sort nodes in a different order from document order. The <xsl:sort> element can be used within <xsl:for-each> or <xsl:apply-templates> to change the order in which the XSLT processor goes through the nodes that are selected by the instruction. In its basic form (with no attributes), the <xsl:sort> element sorts the nodes in alphabetical order according to their string value. For example, the following will process the <Character> elements in alphabetical order (note that the current node within the <xsl:for-each> will be the <Character> element):

```
<xsl:for-each select="CastMember/Character">
  <xsl:sort />
  ...
</xsl:for-each>
```

In <xsl:for-each> instructions, <xsl:sort> elements must come before the body of the <xsl:for-each>, that is, before the part that indicates what should be generated for each of the nodes being processed.

If you need to sort by something other than the string value of the nodes that you're processing, the <xsl:sort> element can take a select attribute, which contains an XPath expression that's evaluated as a string. For example, the following will apply templates to the <CastMember> elements, sorting them in alphabetical order by their child <Character> element's <Name>:

```
<xsl:apply-templates select="CastMember">
  <xsl:sort select="Character/Name" />
</xsl:apply-templates>
```

Nodes are processed in document order by default. You can process them in a different order using <xsl:sort> within <xsl:for-each> or <xsl:apply-templates>.

Try It Out – Sorting Channels By Name

TVGuide.xsl displays the channels within our TV Guide in two ways – within a list of channels given at the top and bottom of the page, and within the body of the page itself. As you can see from the following screenshot, currently the channels are listed in the same order that they're defined in the XML document.

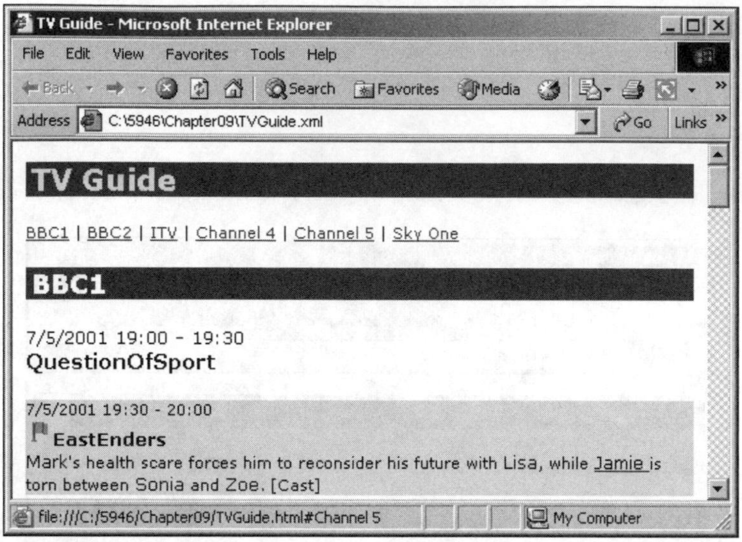

To help people find the channel that they're after, it might be handy to have them sorted by name instead, which we'll do in the next version of our stylesheet, `TVGuide2.xsl`.

The list of `<Channel>` elements that appears at the top and bottom of the page is generated by applying templates to the `<Channel>` elements in `ChannelList` mode, from within a template matching the `<TVGuide>` element in `ChannelList` mode:

```
<xsl:template match="TVGuide" mode="ChannelList">
  <xsl:apply-templates select="Channel" mode="ChannelList" />
</xsl:template>
```

The template that tells the processor to apply templates to the `<Channel>` elements to make up the body of the page is actually a built-in template (since there is no explicit template matching `<TVGuide>` elements in normal mode). To process the `<Channel>` elements in a different order, we need to add a template matching the `<TVGuide>` element, which uses `<xsl:apply-templates>` to process the `<TVGuide>` element's child `<Channel>` elements:

```
<xsl:template match="TVGuide">
  <xsl:apply-templates select="Channel" />
</xsl:template>
```

The `<xsl:apply-templates>` instructions in these two templates process the channels in document order by default. To make them process the channels by name, we need `<xsl:sort>` elements within the `<xsl:apply-templates>` instructions, that use the `<Name>` children of the `<Channel>` elements to sort the `<Channel>` elements alphabetically, as follows:

```
<xsl:template match="TVGuide">
  <xsl:apply-templates select="Channel">
    <xsl:sort select="Name" />
  </xsl:apply-templates>
</xsl:template>
```

```
<xsl:template match="TVGuide" mode="ChannelList">
  <xsl:apply-templates select="Channel" mode="ChannelList">
    <xsl:sort select="Name" />
  </xsl:apply-templates>
</xsl:template>
```

Having made these changes in `TVGuide2.xsl`, the result of the transformation is as follows:

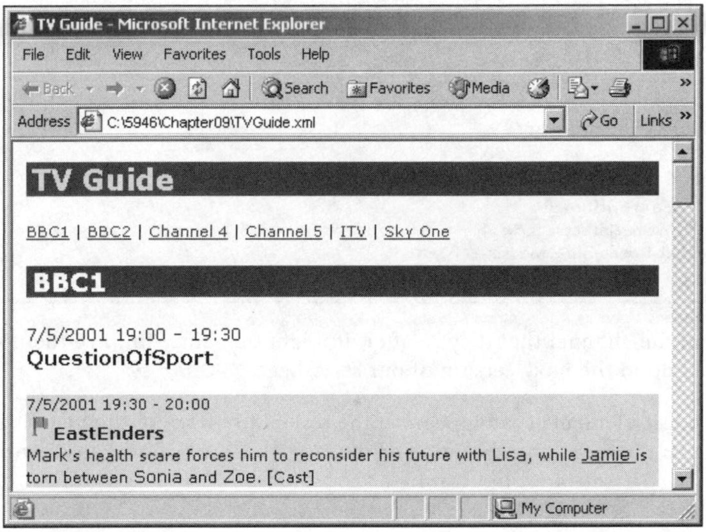

You can see that the order of the channels at the top of the page has changed (the screenshot doesn't show it, but so has the ordering of the channels within the body of the page).

Sorting in Different Orders

By default, `<xsl:sort>` sorts in ascending order, first those that begin with `A`, then those that begin with `B`, and so on. There are three attributes on `<xsl:sort>` that give you control over the precise ordering that the XSLT processor uses:

- `order` – determines whether the values are sorted in `ascending` (the default) or `descending` order.
- `lang` – the code for the language that should be used to sort the values. This defaults to the language that's being used on the system on which the transformation takes place.
- `case-order` – determines whether lowercase letters are sorted before uppercase letters (`lower-first`) or vice versa (`upper-first`). The default depends on the language that's being used.

> **The `order` attribute on `<xsl:sort>` determines whether the nodes are sorted in ascending or descending order. You can fine-tune alphabetical sorts with the `lang` and `case-order` attributes.**

Sorting Numerically

The <xsl:sort> element sorts alphabetically by default. However, if you sort the numbers 1 to 100 alphabetically, you end up with the order 1, 10, 100, 11, 12, ... 2, 20, and so on, which isn't the correct numerical order. If the values that you're sorting by are numbers, then you should use the data-type attribute on <xsl:sort> to tell the XSLT processor to sort numerically rather than alphabetically.

The data-type attribute can take the values text (the default, which gives alphabetical ordering) or number (which gives numerical ordering). Individual XSLT processors may also offer other data types as extensions, but you should check the documentation of your XSLT processor to find out what it supports.

If you need to sort by dates, then using the ISO-8601 date and time formats mean that alphabetical sorting gives you the correct sort order (unless you're using time zones). Other date formats need special handling, as you'll see in the next section.

If the values by which the nodes are being sorted are numeric, you should set the data-type attribute on <xsl:sort> to number.

Try It Out – Sorting by Number

To try out sorting numerically and sorting in different orders, we'll now try to sort the channels in our TV Guide according to the ratings of the programs that they show. Each <Program> element has a rating attribute, ranging from 1 (lousy) to 10 (superb). The channels should be sorted so that the channels that have programs with the highest average rating are sorted first.

Our first problem is working out the average ratings of the programs shown on a particular channel. The average rating is the total of all the ratings divided by the number of programs shown on the channel. You can get the total of all the ratings using the sum() function with an argument of the node set containing all the rating attributes of the <Program> elements:

```
sum(Program/@rating)
```

And you can work out the number of programs shown on the channel using the count() function with an argument of the node set containing all the <Program> elements under the current channel:

```
count(Program)
```

Putting those together, we can enter the expression for calculating the average rating for a channel into the select attribute of the <xsl:sort> in TVGuide3.xsl:

```
<xsl:template match="TVGuide">
  <xsl:apply-templates select="Channel">
    <xsl:sort select="sum(Program/@rating) div count(Program)" />
  </xsl:apply-templates>
</xsl:template>
```

The average rating is a numeric value, so to make sure that the values are sorted correctly, we need to add a `data-type` attribute with the value `number`:

```
<xsl:template match="TVGuide">
  <xsl:apply-templates select="Channel">
    <xsl:sort select="sum(Program/@rating) div count(Program)"
              data-type="number" />
  </xsl:apply-templates>
</xsl:template>
```

And finally, we want the best channels (the ones with the highest program ratings) to come first in our list, so the `<Channel>` elements should be sorted in *descending* order by adding an `order` attribute with the value `descending` to the `<xsl:sort>`:

```
<xsl:template match="TVGuide">
  <xsl:apply-templates select="Channel">
    <xsl:sort select="sum(Program/@rating) div count(Program)"
              data-type="number"
              order="descending" />
  </xsl:apply-templates>
</xsl:template>
```

We also want to display the average rating of the channel underneath the channel's name within the main body of the page. The average rating is a decimal number, which might have lots of decimal places (since we're calculating it through division), so we'll format it using `format-number()` to only show one decimal place when we display it. The template for `<Channel>` elements in `TVGuide3.xsl` is as follows:

```
<xsl:template match="Channel">
  <xsl:apply-templates select="Name" />
  <p class="average">
    <xsl:text>average rating: </xsl:text>
    <xsl:value-of
      select="format-number(sum(Program/@rating) div count(Program),
                            '0.0')" />
  </p>
  <xsl:apply-templates select="Program" />
</xsl:template>
```

And we'll add some styling information for this new paragraph, in `TVGuide2.css`, as follows:

```
p.average {
  font-size: 0.8em;
  margin: 0;
  text-align: right;
}
```

The result of transforming `TVGuide.xml` with `TVGuide3.xsl` is as follows:

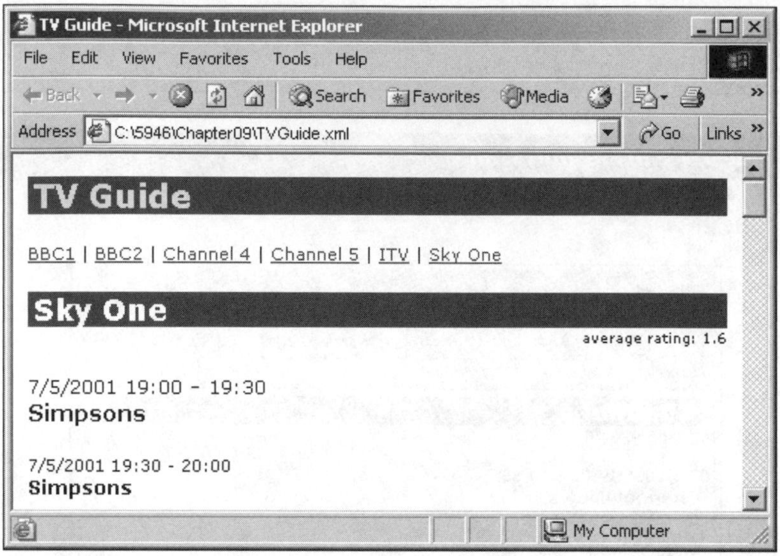

As you can see, Sky One tops the listing; if you take a closer look at `TVGuide.xml`, you'll see why – only Sky One and BBC1 have programs that are rated, and of those Sky One is showing the program with the highest rating. I added some more ratings to `TVGuide2.xml` so that you can see the effect it has; feel free to change them.

Note that the listing at the top of the page is still showing the channels in alphabetical order.

Multiple Sorts

You can use as many `<xsl:sort>` elements as you like within an `<xsl:for-each>` or an `<xsl:apply-templates>`. If two nodes have the same value for the first `<xsl:sort>`, then they're sorted in the order specified by the second `<xsl:sort>`; if they're still the same, they're sorted according to the third `<xsl:sort>`, and so on.

For example, sorting by character name isn't very helpful in our example because the character names are in the form *firstName lastName*, so the character whose first name comes first alphabetically is sorted first. Traditionally in English-speaking countries, names are sorted by last name and then by first name. Assuming that all the character names just consist of a first name and a last name (such that none of the characters have middle names), we can access the last name by taking the substring after the space, and the first name by taking the substring before the space. The first sort needs to select the last name, and the second sort selects the first name:

```
<xsl:for-each select="CastMember">
  <xsl:sort select="substring-after(Character/Name, ' ')" />
  <xsl:sort select="substring-before(Character/Name, ' ')" />
  ...
</xsl:for-each>
```

> **You can have multiple `<xsl:sort>` elements – each subsequent `<xsl:sort>` is a subsort of the previous `<xsl:sort>`.**

Try It Out – Sorting by Rating and Name

Two of the channels in `TVGuide2.xml` turn out to have the same average rating for their programs – Channel 4 and BBC2:

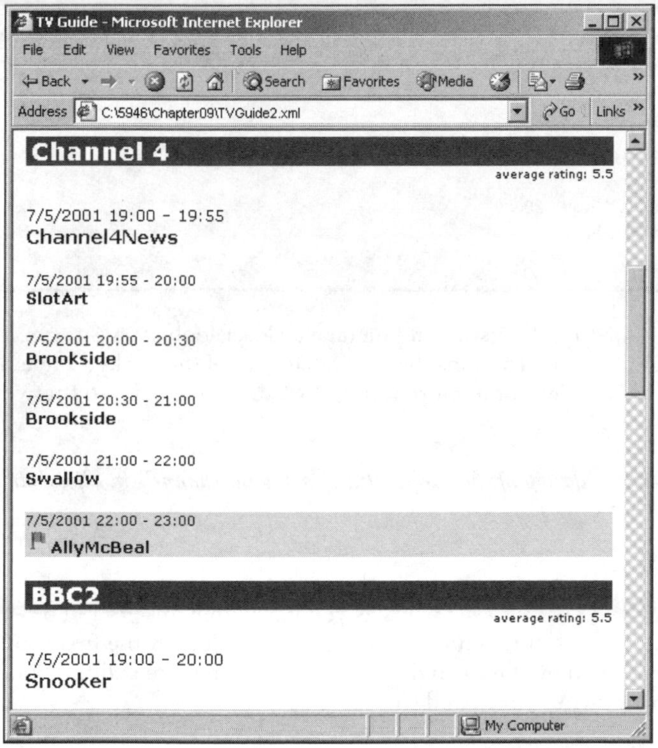

Currently, these channels are listed in reverse document order. When two channels have the same average rating, we'll instead sort them in ascending alphabetical order by their names.

This two-level sort needs two `<xsl:sort>` elements, which are exactly the same as the ones that you developed earlier in this chapter:

```
<xsl:template match="TVGuide">
  <xsl:apply-templates select="Channel">
    <xsl:sort select="sum(Program/@rating) div count(Program)"
              data-type="number"
              order="descending" />
    <xsl:sort select="Name" />
  </xsl:apply-templates>
</xsl:template>
```

This two-level sort is specified in `TVGuide4.xsl`; when you transform `TVGuide2.xml` with `TVGuide4.xsl`, you get the following:

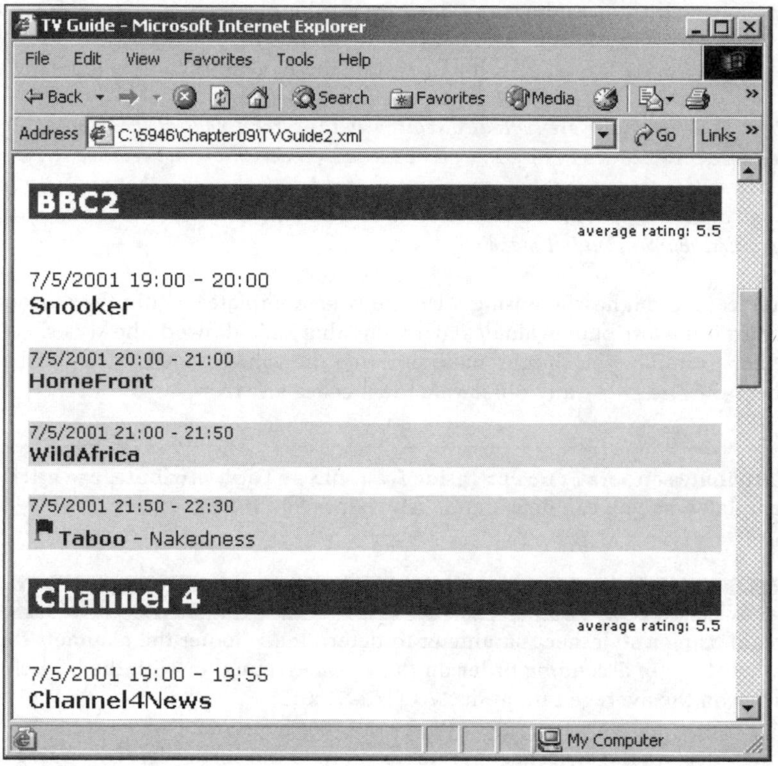

BBC2 now comes before Channel 4 because they have the same rating, but "BBC2" comes before "Channel 4" alphabetically.

Flexible Sorting

Part of the point of using XML and XSLT is that it separates content from presentation. The content part of a page is stored within an XML document, while the stylesheet that you use with that XML document determines the way that the information is presented to the user.

The order in which information is displayed is one of the main ways that you might want to change the presentation of a document. However, while the ordering of the items changes, the way that they're presented and the page around them shouldn't change very much (or at all). In other words, you want to keep the same stylesheet, but use a stylesheet parameter (or other technique) to determine the order in which the items are sorted.

There are two aspects to flexible sorts: changing the **sort order** to ascending or descending and changing the **sort value** so that the items are actually sorted on different things.

Flexible Sort Orders

All the attributes that change the order in which an `<xsl:sort>` arranges nodes (aside from the `select` attribute, which chooses the sort value) are attribute value templates. Most importantly, that includes the `order` attribute and the `data-type` attribute. Anything that you put within `{}`s in the attribute values is interpreted as an XPath expression and evaluated to give the value of the attribute.

The attribute value templates are evaluated relative to the current node at the point of the `<xsl:for-each>` or `<xsl:apply-templates>` instruction, not relative to the nodes that are being sorted; this ensures that the same value is used for all the nodes that are being sorted – otherwise you could end up with some nodes being sorted in ascending order and others in descending order, which wouldn't make any sense.

You should take care, though, when using attribute value templates within the attributes on XSLT elements, because if the attribute evaluates to a value that isn't allowed, the stylesheet will usually halt with an error. For example, you should make sure that the value of the `order` attribute is set to either `ascending` or `descending` – any other value will cause an error.

> **All the attributes on `<xsl:sort>`, aside from the `select` attribute, are attribute value templates, so you can determine their values "on the fly".**

Try It Out – Changing Sort Order with a Parameter

Here we'll look at using a stylesheet parameter to determine whether the channels should be sorted with the worst channels first (in ascending order on the average rating) or with the best channels first (in descending order on the average rating) in `TVGuide5.xsl`.

The first step is to declare the stylesheet parameter to hold the sort order, by adding an `<xsl:param>` element at the top level of the stylesheet. We'll set the parameter to `'descending'` by default, so that unless the parameter is specifically given a value, the sort will give the most highly rated channels first:

```
<xsl:param name="sortOrder" select="'descending'" />
```

In the template that actually sorts the `<Channel>` elements, rather than fix the value of the `order` attribute, you need to calculate it dynamically based on the value of the `$sortOrder` parameter. You can use an attribute value template in the `order` attribute of the first sort to insert the value of the `$sortOrder` parameter:

```
<xsl:template match="TVGuide">
  <xsl:apply-templates select="Channel">
    <xsl:sort select="sum(Program/@rating) div count(Program)"
              data-type="number"
              order="{$sortOrder}" />
    <xsl:sort select="Name" />
  </xsl:apply-templates>
</xsl:template>
```

When you run the stylesheet with `TVGuide2.xml` normally, you'll get the channels sorted in descending order by their average rating, exactly as you did with `TVGuide4.xsl`. However, you can pass the value `ascending` for the `order` attribute instead, using one of the following command lines, and the order will be reversed:

```
>msxsl TVGuide2.xml TVGuide5.xsl -o TVGuide.html sortOrder=ascending

>saxon -o TVGuide.html TVGuide2.xml TVGuide5.xsl sortOrder=ascending

>java org.apache.xalan.xslt.Process -IN TVGuide2.xml -XSL TVGuide5.xsl
-OUT TVGuide.html -PARAM sortOrder ascending
```

The resulting HTML file looks as follows:

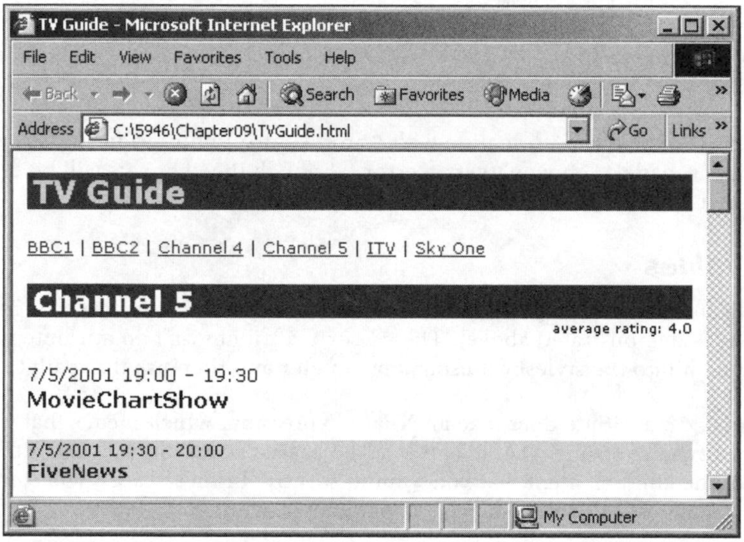

Channel 5 is listed first because it has the lowest average rating; Sky One is listed last because it has the highest average rating.

Now try passing the value `'up'` as the value for the `$sortOrder` parameter. You should get an error from the XSLT processor. For example, with MSXML I get the following:

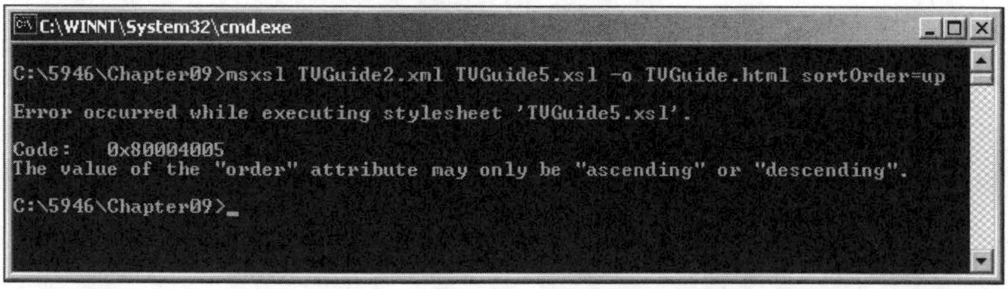

To make your stylesheet more robust, you should watch out for a bad value being passed in to the `$sortOrder` parameter, and make sure that the value that it's set to is either `'ascending'` or `'descending'`. One way to do this is by shadowing the stylesheet parameter with a local variable that sets itself based on the value of the `$sortOrder` parameter, as follows:

```
<xsl:template match="TVGuide">
  <xsl:variable name="sortOrder">
    <xsl:choose>
      <xsl:when test="$sortOrder = 'ascending'">ascending</xsl:when>
      <xsl:otherwise>descending</xsl:otherwise>
    </xsl:choose>
  </xsl:variable>
  <xsl:apply-templates select="Channel">
    <xsl:sort select="sum(Program/@rating) div count(Program)"
              data-type="number"
              order="{$sortOrder}" />
  </xsl:apply-templates>
</xsl:template>
```

If you try running the same transformation with `$sortOrder` set to up (using `TVGuide6.xsl`, in which this change is made), you won't get an error (although the channels will be sorted in descending order, which might not be what's intended by the value up!).

Flexible Sort Values

It's more complicated to change *what* you want to sort on the fly than it is to change *how* that value should be sorted (as demonstrated above). The `select` attribute isn't an attribute value template, so you can't pass a path into the stylesheet using a parameter and then use that path to choose what to sort.

However, the `select` attribute does take an XPath expression, which means that you have a certain amount of flexibility in choosing what to sort by. The easiest situations are where the parameter can hold the name of the child element that you want to sort by. In these cases, you can select the child element whose name has the same value as the parameter, with:

```
<xsl:sort select="*[name() = $sortBy]" />
```

Sometimes the different sort values might come from several locations (rather than all being children of the nodes that are being sorted). For example, if we're sorting `<Program>` elements from `TVGuide.xml`, then `$sortBy` might be `'start'` to get the start time (held in the `<Start>` element child), `'series'` to get the series (held in the `<Series>` element child), or `'channel'` to get the name of the channel it's on (held in its parent `<Channel>` element's child `<Name>` element). In these cases, you can use a predicate to select each possible node only if the `$sortBy` parameter equals the value that's appropriate for that node and then union the results together, as follows:

```
<xsl:sort select="Start[$sortBy = 'start'] |
                  Series[$sortBy = 'series'] |
                  ../Name[$sortBy = 'channel']" />
```

The `select` attribute here holds an expression that evaluates to a node set. The node set is actually the union of three node sets, which contain:

- The <Start> element, but only if the $sortBy parameter has a value of 'start'
- The <Series> element, but only if the $sortBy parameter has a value of 'series'
- The <Name> element child of the parent <Channel>, but only if the $sortBy parameter has a value of 'channel'

Of course, the $sortBy parameter can only have one value – 'start', 'series', or 'channel' – so of these three node sets, only one will actually contain a node. If the $sortBy parameter has a value of 'series', for example, then only the <Series> element will be selected by the expression, and as a result the programs will be sorted by series.

Some processors have an extension function that enables you to evaluate XPath expressions on the fly, which can help in situations like these. We'll be looking at extension functions in Chapter 13.

You can choose what to sort by on the fly by having predicates so that only certain nodes are selected.

Numbering

The first part of this chapter looked at how to reorder items so that they're presented in a different sequence from the one in which they're stored. The second problem that we'll explore in this chapter is how to give these items numbers.

Numbering items is primarily useful in document-oriented XML, particularly when generating XSL-FO: for example, to sequentially number items in a list, to create footnotes, or to give numbers to section headings. In terms of the construction of the result tree, when you generate a number, you're actually generating a text node in the result tree in the same way as you would be with <xsl:value-of>.

There are two stages to numbering items:

- Working out the number for the item
- Formatting the number for different numbering schemas

In this section, we'll look first at three ways of getting the number of an item in a simple list (and introduce <xsl:number>), and then you'll learn how to use <xsl:number> to format the numbers that you get. Then we'll look at two other types of numbering schemes – numbering across an entire document (such as for numbering footnotes) and hierarchical numbering (such as for numbering sections).

Getting the Number of an Item

The most explicit method of getting a number for an item in XSLT is to use the <xsl:number> instruction to generate it for you. The basic form of the <xsl:number> instruction, without any attributes, gives you the number of the current node within the set of similar siblings, counting in document order and starting from 1. So you can number the channels in the TV Guide by adding an empty <xsl:number> element to the template for the <Channel> elements:

```
<xsl:template match="Channel">
  <h2 class="channel">
    <a name="{Name}" id="{Name}">
      <xsl:number />
      <xsl:text> </xsl:text>
      <xsl:value-of select="Name" />
    </a>
  </h2>
  ...
</xsl:template>
```

For example, the result of this template for BBC2, which is the second `<Channel>` element in the document, would be:

```
<h2 class="channel"><a name="BBC2" id="BBC2">2 BBC2</a></h2>
```

> **The `<xsl:number>` instruction creates a number based on the position of the current node in the source tree.**

If you want, you can explicitly state what kind of nodes you want to number using the `count` attribute. The `count` attribute holds a pattern (so shares the same syntax as the `match` attribute of `<xsl:template>`); the processor only counts nodes that match that pattern. For example, you could do the equivalent of the `<xsl:number>` in the above template (which counts `<Channel>` elements) with the following:

```
<xsl:number count="Channel" />
```

If the node that you're currently on doesn't match the `count` pattern, then the processor tries to find an ancestor of the current node that *does* match the pattern, and counts *its* preceding siblings instead. This can be handy because it enables you to insert a number for an element within code that handles one of its descendants. For example, you could number the channels within the template matching their `<Name>` elements, as follows:

```
<xsl:template match="Channel/Name">
  <h2 class="channel">
    <a name="{.}" id="{.}">
      <xsl:number count="Channel" />
      <xsl:value-of select="." />
    </a>
  </h2>
</xsl:template>
```

The `count` attribute is useful when you need to count all the siblings of an element, no matter what kind of node they are, which you can do with:

```
<xsl:number count="node()" />
```

The `count` attribute is also handy if you have different types of elements in a list and want to number them sequentially. For example, if you want to number both `<Program>` and `<Film>` elements in a list in which the two are intermingled, you could use:

```
<xsl:number count="Program | Film" />
```

> **The `count` attribute on `<xsl:number>` holds a pattern that matches the nodes that you want to count when creating the number. It defaults to a pattern that matches nodes of the same type and name as the current node.**

There are two disadvantages with using `<xsl:number>` to give you the number of an item, however. It calculates the number of a node based on the source tree rather than what you're generating in the output and it always starts counting from 1. In the next couple of sections, we'll see ways around these two limitations.

Try It Out – Numbering Cast Members Based on Document Order

To try out numbering with `<xsl:number>`, we'll add numbers to the cast member list that we generate. Of course, because we're generating HTML, the first and easiest method is just to change the numbering scheme used for the `<li>` element using the `list-style-type` property as in `TVGuide3.css`:

```
.castlist li {
  display: list-item;
  list-style-type: decimal;
}
```

When transformed with `TVGuide7.xsl`, which generates XHTML that refers to `TVGuide3.css`, `TVGuide2.xml` displays as follows, with decimal numbering of the cast members:

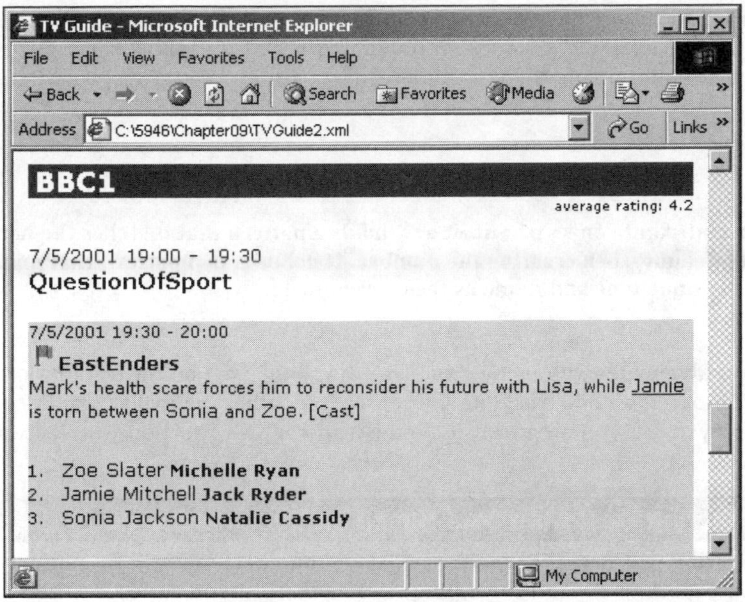

However, CSS does not give full control over the item numbers – for example, you can't make them italic. To do that, you must create the list numbers by hand. So, in `TVGuide8.xsl`, we'll change the template for the `<CastList>` element so that it just creates a `<div>` with a class of `castlist`:

```
<xsl:template match="CastList">
  <xsl:param name="divID" />
  <div id="{$divID}" style="display: none;" class="castlist">
    <xsl:apply-templates />
  </div>
</xsl:template>
```

We'll also change the template for the `<CastMember>` elements to create `<div>` elements in `castmember` style that contain a number (in `number` style) before the content. To begin with, let's number the characters using the basic form of `<xsl:number>`. We'll add a space between the number and the character's name, so that it's more readable:

```
<xsl:template match="CastMember">
  <div class="castmember">
    <span class="number"><xsl:number /></span>
    <xsl:text> </xsl:text>
    <xsl:apply-templates select="Character" />
    <xsl:text> </xsl:text>
    <xsl:apply-templates select="Actor" />
  </div>
</xsl:template>
```

In `TVGuide4.css`, we'll add a style for the `number` class, so that the numbers are italic:

```
.number {
  font-style: italic;
}
```

TVGuide8.xsl makes these changes and creates XHTML that refers to TVGuide4.css. When you use TVGuide8.xsl on the source file TVGuide2.xml, you see the following:

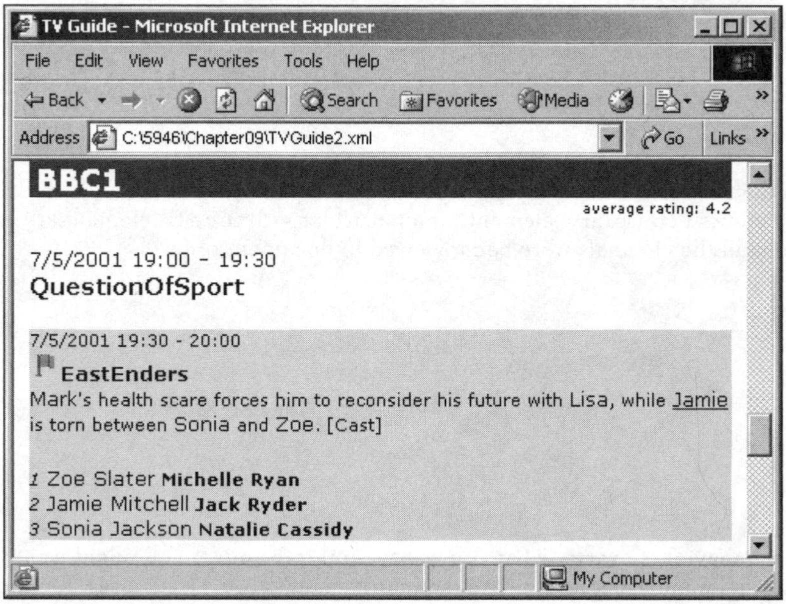

The cast members are numbered in sequence, based on their order in the source XML document.

Numbering Sorted and Filtered Items

The <xsl:number> instruction always gives you the same number for the node, based on its position in the source node tree, and not the position of the node in terms of how and when it's processed. For example, TVGuide2.xml holds details about the following six channels:

1. BBC1
2. BBC2
3. ITV
4. Channel 4
5. Channel 5
6. Sky One

Say that you only want to present information about the channels that show flagged programs, and you want to display them sorted by average rating and channel name as before. The template for the channel name can still provide the number, and the `<xsl:apply-templates>` instruction select the relevant channels and contain an `<xsl:sort>` so that the `<Channel>` elements are sorted in a different order:

```
<xsl:apply-templates
    select="Channel[Program[@flag]]">
    <xsl:sort select="sum(Program/@rating) div count(Program)"
              data-type="number" order="{$sortOrder}" />
    <xsl:sort select="Name" />
</xsl:apply-templates>
```

Only some of the channels are displayed, and in a different order from before, but the numbers generated by the `<xsl:number>` element for a particular `<Channel>` element are exactly the same as they would be if all the channels were being viewed in document order:

6. Sky One

2. BBC2

4. Channel 4

1. BBC1

Sometimes this behavior is exactly what you want – in this example, you might want the channels to retain their original numbering if those are the numbers that your TV set uses. But more often than not, you want the numbers that you generate to be sequential based on the *result* that you're generating rather than the *source* that holds the original information.

The closest that you can get to numbering based on the result is to number nodes in the order that they're processed. When you tell an XSLT processor to process a bunch of nodes with `<xsl:for-each>` or `<xsl:apply-templates>`, those nodes become the current node list and each node that gets processed has a position within it. When you process a particular node, you can get its position in the current node list using the `position()` function. So if you swap the `<xsl:number>` instruction for an `<xsl:value-of>` instruction that selects the current node's position, then the channels will be numbered in the order that they're processed in once more:

```
<xsl:template match="Channel">
  <h2 class="channel">
    <a name="{Name}" id="{Name}">
      <xsl:value-of select="position()" />
      <xsl:value-of select="Name" />
    </a>
  </h2>
</xsl:template>
```

> *Using the position of the current node to number nodes is also more efficient than using `<xsl:number>` because the position of the current node is immediately available to the XSLT processor, whereas each time you use `<xsl:number>` the processor has to check all the preceding siblings of the node that you're processing.*

Something that you have to be careful of when you use the `position()` function to number nodes is that the numbering that you get totally depends on the way in which you apply templates to the nodes. A common trap here is that if you apply templates to all the child nodes of an element, then you often include whitespace-only text nodes in the list, between each of the elements you're actually interested in. This can lead to a sequence of even numbers in the result.

Stripping whitespace-only text nodes using `<xsl:strip-space>` (as we have seen in Chapter 7) can help prevent you getting the wrong numbering in your result. More generally, you should take care to only select the nodes that you're actually interested in when you create a numbered sequence.

> **If nodes are filtered or sorted, you should use the `position()` function to number according to the position of an item in the result.**

Try It Out – Numbering Cast Members Based on Processing Order

In the last Try It Out, we saw how to generate numbers for the members of our cast list using `<xsl:number>`. But what happens when you change the template for the `<CastList>` element, as in `TVGuide9.xsl`, so that the cast is listed in alphabetical order by character name, sorted first on surname then on first name?

```
<xsl:template match="CastList">
  <xsl:param name="divID" />
  <div id="{$divID}" style="display: none;" class="castlist">
    <xsl:apply-templates select="CastMember">
      <xsl:sort select="substring-after(Character/Name, ' ')" />
      <xsl:sort select="substring-before(Character/Name, ' ')" />
    </xsl:apply-templates>
  </div>
</xsl:template>
```

When you transform `TVGuide2.xml` with `TVGuide9.xsl`, you get the following cast list:

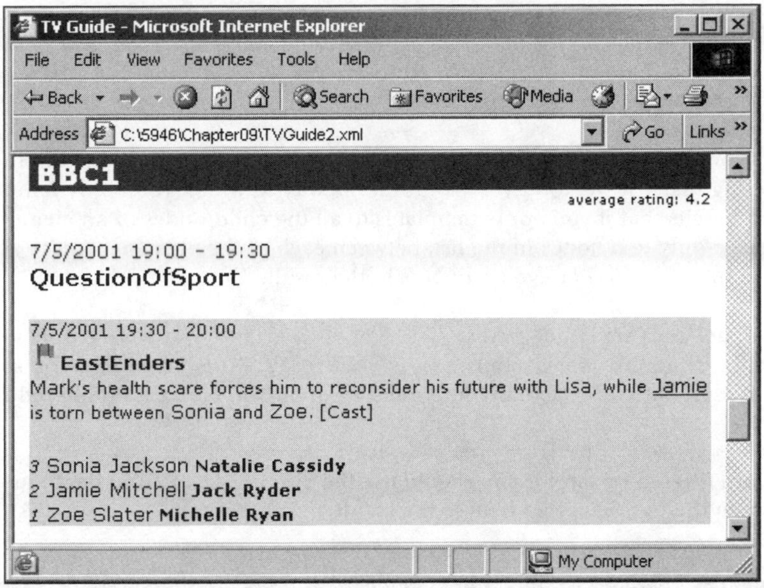

Each cast member is allotted the same number as they were originally, so the numbers in the result are not in sequential order.

To make the numbers sequential, you have to change the way in which the number is generated so that it uses the order in which the nodes are processed rather than the order in which they appear in the source node tree, using `position()`, as in `TVGuide10.xsl` :

```
<xsl:template match="CastMember">
  <div class="castmember">
    <span class="number"><xsl:value-of select="position()" /></span>
    <xsl:text> </xsl:text>
    <xsl:apply-templates select="Character" />
    <xsl:text> </xsl:text>
    <xsl:apply-templates select="Actor" />
  </div>
</xsl:template>
```

When you use `TVGuide10.xsl` with `TVGuide2.xml` you get the following result:

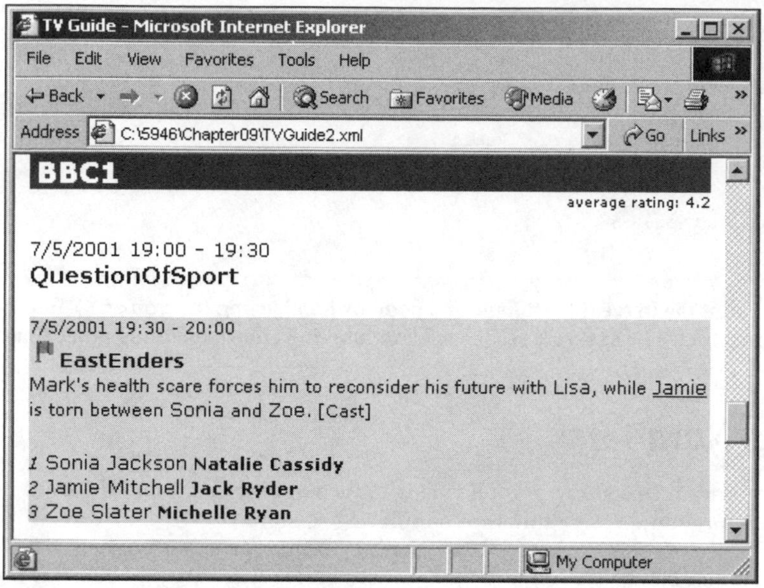

The numbers are sequential again, as they should be. You may also want to compare using `<xsl:number>` with using the `position()` function while timing the transformation, to see whether it has any impact with your XSLT processor.

Changing the Starting Number

The `<xsl:number>` instruction always numbers nodes starting from 1. On new digital boxes, the first channel (BBC1) is numbered 101, the second 102, and so on – the numbering starts from 101 and proceeds from there. Assuming that the channels should be numbered according to this scheme (but we don't want them numbered in the order they're processed in), we need to use something other than `<xsl:number>` to give us the number of each channel.

The solution to this problem is to write an XPath expression that does exactly the same thing as the equivalent `<xsl:number>` instruction in order to calculate the number to use. The number of a channel in this case is the number of sibling `<Channel>` elements that come before it, plus 101 (which is the number we want to get for the first channel). You can get all the `<Channel>` elements that precede the one you're looking at using the `preceding-sibling::` axis:

```
preceding-sibling::Channel
```

This returns an empty node set for the first channel; a node set containing the first channel for the second channel; a node set containing the first two channels for the third channel; and so on. You can find out how many `<Channel>` elements the node set contains using the `count()` function:

```
count(preceding-sibling::Channel)
```

This returns 0 for the first channel, 1 for the second channel, 2 for the third channel, and so on. To get the number that we want to display, add 101:

```
<xsl:template match="Channel">
  <h2 class="channel">
    <a name="{Name}" id="{Name}">
      <xsl:value-of select="count(preceding-sibling::Channel) + 101" />
      <xsl:value-of select="Name" />
    </a>
  </h2>
</xsl:template>
```

You can count the preceding siblings of a node by hand, using the `count()` function and the `preceding-sibling::` axis, to start numbering from something other than 1.

Formatting Numbers

The <xsl:number> instruction's second role is to **format** numbers using different numbering schemes. All XSLT processors support five different numbering schemes:

- Decimal numbering (1, 2, 3, ...), with or without leading zeros (01, 02, 03, ...)
- Lowercase alphabetical numbering (a, b, c, ..., aa, ab, ac, ...)
- Uppercase alphabetical numbering (A, B, C, ..., AA, AB, AC, ...)
- Lowercase Roman numbering (i, ii, iii, iv, v, vi, ...)
- Uppercase Roman numbering (I, II, III, IV, V, VI, ...)

You can tell the XSLT processor which format to use for a particular number using the `format` attribute on <xsl:number>. Including the first token from a numbering scheme in the `format` attribute tells the XSLT processor to use that numbering scheme, but you can also add spaces or punctuation characters to the numbers. For example, to generate numbers consisting of lowercase Roman numerals in brackets, with a space after the close bracket, you should use:

```
<xsl:number format="(i) " />
```

The `format` attribute on <xsl:number> holds a pattern for the number, which must include a number token to give decimal (1, 2, 3), alphabetical (a, b, c), or Roman (i, ii, iii) numbering.

You can use the formatting controls offered by <xsl:number> on numbers that aren't generated by <xsl:number> using the `value` attribute, which takes an XPath expression that's interpreted as a number. For example, if you're generating numbers using the `position()` function, so that items are numbered according to the order in which the nodes are processed rather than the order in which they appear in the source, then you can use <xsl:number> to format and output the number instead of <xsl:value-of>:

```
<xsl:number value="position()" format="A." />
```

The `value` attribute on `<xsl:number>` can specify any XPath expression that evaluates as a number, to be formatted according to the `format` attribute.

The `format` attribute is an attribute value template, so you can decide on the numbering scheme to use on the fly if you want, for example, to use different numbering schemes depending on the depth of a list.

Formatting Large Numbers

If you're numbering lots of items, you may wish to start grouping the digits that make up those numbers so that the numbers can be read more easily. The `<xsl:number>` instruction takes two attributes that allow you to control the grouping of digits in the numbers that you format:

- `grouping-size` – the number of digits in a group (defaults to 3)
- `grouping-separator` – the character used to separate groups of digits (defaults to a comma)

For example, to generate numbers that have pairs of digits separated by spaces, all within square brackets, you could use:

```
<xsl:number format="[1]" grouping-size="2" grouping-separator=" " />
```

Both the attributes are attribute value templates, so again you can decide on their values on the fly to give different types of numbering in different situations or on user request.

The `grouping-size` and `grouping-separator` attributes on `<xsl:number>` specify how the digits in large numbers are grouped together.

Formatting Numbers with Different Alphabets

Some XSLT processors support extra numbering schemes as well as the five that are built in, such as spelt-out numbers (one, two, three, ...) or numbering using different languages (α, β, 6, ...). However, while numbering schemes in some languages (such as Greek) use totally different scripts, those in other languages (such as Finnish) start with the same character as is used in English (a). To allow you to generate numbers in these different languages, `<xsl:number>` has two attributes:

- `lang` – the language code for the language used by the numbering scheme
- `letter-value` – whether to use the normal `alphabetic` numbering scheme of the language or the `traditional` numbering scheme

You should check your XSLT processor's documentation to see which languages it supports and whether there is a traditional variant for that particular language. If you don't specify a language, XSLT processors will always use the English alphabet, with a traditional numbering scheme if you use the letter `i` and an alphabetical numbering scheme if you use the letter `a`.

The `lang` and `letter-value` attributes on `<xsl:number>` give extra control with alphabetical numbering schemes.

Try It Out – Formatting the Numbers for Cast Members

The template that we're currently using, in `TVGuide10.xsl`, for `<CastMember>` elements looks as follows:

```
<xsl:template match="CastMember">
  <div class="castmember">
    <span class="number"><xsl:value-of select="position()" /></span>
    <xsl:text> </xsl:text>
    <xsl:apply-templates select="Character" />
    <xsl:text> </xsl:text>
    <xsl:apply-templates select="Actor" />
  </div>
</xsl:template>
```

The number that you get with this template is just the decimal number showing the position of the `<CastMember>` element amongst its siblings. You can use `<xsl:number>` and its `format` attribute to create a decimal number with curly brackets, but remember that curly brackets are special within attribute value templates, so you have to double them up to get them to appear in the result:

```
<xsl:template match="CastMember">
  <div class="castmember">
    <span class="number">
      <xsl:number value="position()" format="{{1}}" />
    </span>
    <xsl:text> </xsl:text>
    <xsl:apply-templates select="Character" />
    <xsl:text> </xsl:text>
    <xsl:apply-templates select="Actor" />
  </div>
</xsl:template>
```

This change is made in `TVGuide11.xsl`. When you use `TVGuide11.xsl` to transform `TVGuide2.xml`, you should see the following:

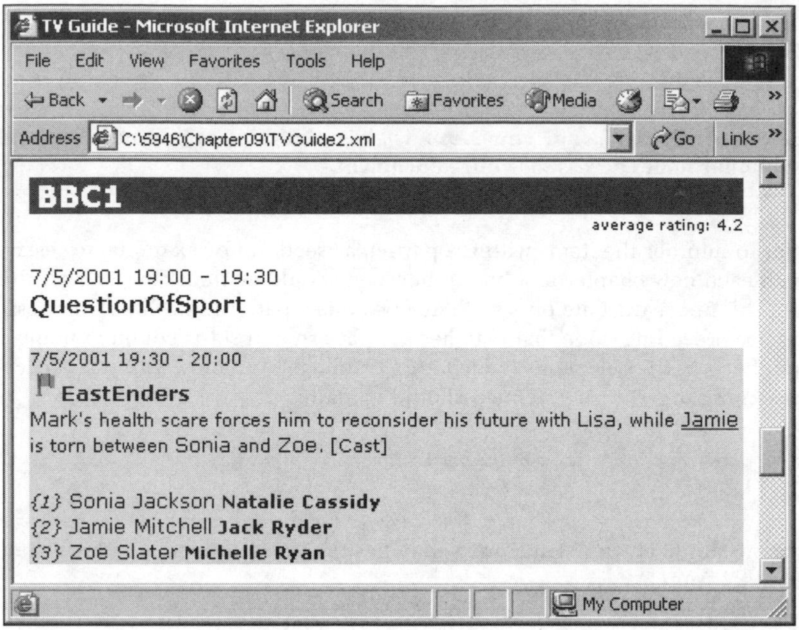

The `format` attribute tells the XSLT processor to format the number that it gets from the `position()` function with curly brackets around it.

Look up the documentation about the numbering schemes supported by the XSLT processor that you're using and try out a few other numbering schemes to experiment with the `grouping-size`, `grouping-separator`, `lang`, and `letter-value` attributes to see their effect.

Numbering Across a Document

The numbering with `<xsl:number>` that we've looked at so far is limited to numbering simple lists where the items that you want to number are all children of the same parent. If you imagine creating numbers for `<ol>` lists, then this simple form of `<xsl:number>` is precisely what you want. On the other hand, imagine that you're trying to number footnotes that are included in paragraphs spread across many sections. The footnotes aren't siblings, but they should still be numbered sequentially.

To do numbering across a document, or at any time where the items that you want to number are not siblings of each other, you need to use the `<xsl:number>` instruction, adding a `level` attribute with the value `any`:

```
<xsl:number level="any" />
```

With this instruction, the XSLT processor doesn't just count the preceding *siblings* that are similar to the current node, it looks at all the ancestors and preceding nodes in the document that are of the same type and have the same name as the current node, and counts how many there are. You can specify exactly the kinds of nodes that you want to count using the `count` attribute as normal, and the number can be formatted with the `format` and other attributes in just the same way as described previously for simple lists.

The `level` attribute has the value `single` by default, which gives numbering of simple lists where all the items are siblings of each other.

If the `level` attribute of `<xsl:number>` is given the value `any`, it numbers nodes amongst similar nodes across the entire document.

If you only want to number the items within a particular section (for example, to restart the numbering of footnotes with each new chapter in a book) then you should combine the `level` attribute with the `from` attribute. The `from` attribute on `<xsl:number>` is a pattern; the XSLT processor finds the nearest ancestor or preceding node that matches the pattern and starts counting nodes from there. For example, to number `<Link>` elements (which aren't siblings), but only within a particular `<Channel>`, the template matching the `<Link>` element should contain:

```
<xsl:number level="any" from="Channel" />
```

The `from` attribute of `<xsl:number>` matches the types of nodes at which counting should restart from 1.

Generating Hierarchical Numbers

The final type of numbering supported by `<xsl:number>` is the numbering of nodes arranged in hierarchies. Hierarchical numbering is often seen in technical documentation, where each part, chapter, section, subsection, or even paragraph, is numbered, with numbers like `B.3.5.iv` indicating the fourth paragraph of the fifth section of the third chapter of the second part of a report.

Hierarchical numbers are supported in XSLT by setting the `level` attribute of `<xsl:number>` to `multiple`. The `count` attribute is particularly useful with hierarchical numbers, since the elements at different levels of the hierarchy tend to be named different things. You should set the `count` attribute to a pattern that matches the types of elements that are significant within the hierarchy. For example, to create a hierarchical number that numbered each `<CastMember>` within each `<Program>` within each `<Channel>`, you could use:

```
<xsl:number level="multiple" count="Channel | Program | CastMember" />
```

The order in which you put the patterns in the `count` attribute has no effect on the way the hierarchical number is constructed, but I find it most intuitive to put them in the order in which they will be used within the number, from the highest to the lowest.

If the `level` attribute of `<xsl:number>` is given the value `multiple`, it generates hierarchical numbers. The `count` attribute is a pattern that matches the elements that should be counted at each level.

When formatting hierarchical numbers, you need a format pattern that is made up of multiple tokens, one for each of the levels in the numbering scheme. If you set the `format` attribute to the number that you'd expect the first item to have, as a kind of template for the others, then you'll get the numbering scheme that you want. So to number the `<CastMember>` elements `1-1.A`, `1-1.B`, ... `1-2.A`, `1-2.B`, ... `2-1.A`, `2-1.B`, and so on, you need to use the following `<xsl:number>` instruction:

```
<xsl:number level="multiple" count="Channel | Program | CastMember"
            format="1-1.A" />
```

The tokens that you can use in these hierarchical numbers are exactly the same as the tokens that you can use in the normal simple lists (for example, `1` for decimal numbering, `I` for uppercase Roman numbering).

Summary

In this chapter, we've looked at two methods of enhancing the presentation of a set of items – by sorting them, and by numbering them.

You've learned about how to use the `<xsl:sort>` element with `<xsl:for-each>` and `<xsl:apply-templates>` to change the order in which nodes are processed. You've seen how to sort in ascending and descending order, how to do numerical sorts by changing the `data-type` attribute, and how to get finer control over alphabetical sorts using the `lang` and `letter-value` attributes.

You've also discovered how to do more sophisticated sorts, either by combining several sorts or by deciding dynamically what to sort a set of items on and in which order. These techniques often come in handy when you're designing dynamic applications such as those that we'll be looking at in Chapter 14.

We've also introduced `<xsl:number>` in this chapter as a method of generating and formatting numbers. The `<xsl:number>` instruction is arguably less useful in the data-oriented XML that we're primarily working with here than it is in document-oriented XML, where you often need to number lists, footnotes, and sections. However, numbering can sometimes come in handy, especially when you're generating IDs for items, which we'll see more of in the next chapter.

You've seen how `<xsl:number>` can be used for three different kinds of numbering: single-level simple lists, numbering items across entire documents or within particular sections, and generating multi-level numbers for hierarchical structures. The `format` attribute controls how these numbers are displayed, allowing you to create numbers from many different numbering schemes. Again, the `format` attribute and the other attributes that control the presentation of the numbers that you generate are all attribute value templates, which means that they can all be set dynamically based on parameters passed into the stylesheet or the individual template.

We've also touched on a couple of other methods of numbering, which you can use to generate numbers even if you still use `<xsl:number>` to format them, namely using `position()` and counting the preceding siblings of the node that you're interested in. The `<xsl:number>` instruction tends to be quite inefficient when it comes to generating numbers, and it always gives you numbers based on the source tree, so it's often better to use the `position()` function to create numbers if you can.

Review Questions

1. Which two XSLT elements can be parents of <xsl:sort> elements?

2. What language is used when you sort alphabetically?

3. What does the following piece of code do?

```
<xsl:apply-templates select="Program">
  <xsl:sort select="position()" data-type="number" order="descending" />
</xsl:apply-templates>
```

4. What order will the <Program> elements be sorted in with the following code?

```
<xsl:variable name="series" select="'Series'" />
<xsl:apply-templates select="Program">
  <xsl:sort select="$series" />
  <xsl:sort select="Title" />
</xsl:apply-templates>
```

5. What does the following piece of code do?

```
<xsl:variable name="sortType">
  <xsl:choose>
    <xsl:when test="$sortBy = 'rating'">number</xsl:when>
    <xsl:otherwise>text</xsl:otherwise>
  </xsl:choose>
</xsl:variable>
<xsl:apply-templates select="Program">
  <xsl:sort select="@rating[$sortBy = 'rating'] |
                    Series[$sortBy = 'series'] |
                    Title[$sortBy = 'title']"
            data-type="{$sortType}" />
</xsl:apply-templates>
```

6. What two ways can you use to generate a number giving the position of a node within the source tree?

7. What's the biggest difference between using position() and using <xsl:number> to number items?

8. What does the following piece of code generate?

```
<xsl:for-each select="Program">
  <xsl:variable name="format">
    <xsl:choose>
      <xsl:when test="position() mod 3 = 1">{1}</xsl:when>
      <xsl:when test="position() mod 3 = 2">[A]</xsl:when>
      <xsl:otherwise>(i)</xsl:when>
```

```
    </xsl:choose>
  </xsl:variable>
  <xsl:number format="{$format}" />
  ...
</xsl:for-each>
```

9. What different values can the `level` attribute on `<xsl:number>` take and how does its value change the numbering of a node?

Beginning
XSLT

10

IDs, Keys, and Groups

One of the big advantages of using XML to hold information is that it is a lot easier to **search** for specific information than it is to store that information in HTML. In the TV Guide example, a simple search on the HTML page would reveal that a particular actor appears in a program that week, but an XML search would give you easy access to find which program that was, when it was showing, on which channel, and who else appeared in it.

This chapter discusses how to search XML documents for information using IDs that are built in to the source XML structure, or those that you generate yourself. You can search based on any combination of information by constructing keys. Defining keys also helps in a common XSLT task, **grouping**, so in addition this chapter looks at how to structure the output that you generate in groups.

In this chapter, you'll learn:

- How to define and use `ID` attributes
- How to create keys to quickly access information
- How to generate IDs to cross-reference in the HTML that you generate
- How to group information

Searching

We've already seen some searches in action in previous chapters where we tried to get hold of all Star Trek programs being shown on a channel with:

```
Program[starts-with(Series, 'StarTrek')]
```

When an XSLT processor evaluates this path, it looks at all the `<Program>` elements in the current channel and filters that set to include only those whose child `<Series>` element starts with the string `'StarTrek'`. The first part of the path indicates the type of node that we're searching for, while the predicate (the part within the `[]`s) indicates what constraints there are on that value.

As you've seen in earlier chapters, there are lots of types of conditions that you can place in a predicate. You can check whether an attribute or element value starts with a particular string using the `starts-with()` function, contains a specific value using the `contains()` function, is equal to something with the equals operator, and so on. You can even combine these tests together using `and` and `or`. So, searching for information within an XML document using predicates is very flexible and very powerful.

However, searching using predicates can also be pretty inefficient. In the example above, the XSLT processor visits every `<Program>` element within a particular `<Channel>` element, and checks each one's `<Series>` element. If there are 100 `<Program>` elements, then the XSLT processor visits 200 nodes (100 `<Program>` elements and 100 `<Series>` elements). If there was another similar path:

```
Program[starts-with(Series, 'EastEnders')]
```

then the XSLT processor would visit those 200 nodes again, despite the fact that it has already had to find out what `<Program>` elements there are and to which series they belong. In this section, we'll examine two ways of increasing the efficiency of searches for specific information within an XML document: using IDs and using keys.

Most processors offer an option that allows you to time how long a transformation takes as a whole. For example, you can use the –t options in Saxon and MSXML and the –DIAG command-line option with Xalan. There is also software available that helps you isolate inefficient parts of your stylesheet, such as CatchXSL! from http://www.xslprofiler.org, which you can use with Saxon or Xalan.

> **You can search an XML document using predicates, which are powerful and flexible, but which can be inefficient.**

IDs

The first type of search that we'll look at is when a particular piece of information can be uniquely identified within a larger set using a **unique identifier**. For example, customers have customer IDs, books have ISBN numbers, and streets have postcodes or zip codes. If you want to reference or retrieve information about a particular customer, book, or street, you can use this unique identifier to do so. XML supports the concept of a unique identifier with **ID attributes**. When you declare an attribute using a DTD, you can state that the attribute holds a value that can be used to uniquely identify the element holding the attribute. When a validating XML parser (such as that used by an XSLT processor) opens a document that uses the markup language defined by the DTD, it checks that no two elements have the same values for their `ID` attributes.

You can also define `ID` attributes using XML Schema, but at the time of writing XSLT processors ignore schemas; DTDs, on the other hand, are commonly accessed and interpreted.

There are some things to watch out for with `ID` attributes, however. In particular, the values of `ID` attributes are fairly tightly constrained – they must be "names" in XML terms. In effect they have to follow the same rules as element and attribute names (starting with a letter, not containing any whitespace, and only holding a restricted set of punctuation characters).

Elements in an XML document can each be assigned a unique identifier within `ID` attributes. The values of `ID` attributes have to follow the same rules as element and attribute names.

Declaring ID Attributes

An `ID` attribute is an attribute that has been declared, within a DTD, as having the type `ID`, using an **ATTLIST declaration**. You cannot specify a default (or fixed) value for an `ID` attribute – it can be either required, in which case it is declared with:

```
<!ATTLIST elementName attributeName ID #REQUIRED>
```

or optional, in which case it is declared with:

```
<!ATTLIST elementName attributeName ID #IMPLIED>
```

Most processors will recognize these `ATTLIST` declarations even if you don't have a corresponding element declaration for that element. However, to work with MSXML, you must have an element declaration as well; `<!ELEMENT elementName (ANY)>` is the simplest of these.

`ID` attributes are declared within an `ATTLIST` declaration.

Try It Out – Uniquely Identifying Series

When we developed the markup language for our TV Guide in Chapter 2, we decided to keep information that applied to all episodes in a series separate from the description of the series and other information about it, such as who its writers, directors, and producers were. We haven't used this information so far, but now we'll include it in the same file as the rest of the TV Guide, after the `<Channel>` elements, as in `TVGuide.xml`:

```
<?xml version="1.0" encoding="ISO-8859-1"?>
<TVGuide start="2001-07-05" end="2001-07-05">
  <Channel>
    <Name>BBC1</Name>
    ...
    <Program rating="5" flag="favorite">
      <Start>2001-07-05T19:30:00</Start>

      <Duration>PT30M</Duration>
      <Series>EastEnders</Series>
      <Title></Title>
      ...
    </Program>
    ...
  </Channel>
  ...
  <Series type="soap">
    <Title>EastEnders</Title>
```

```
    <Description>Soap set in the East End of London.</Description>
  </Series>
  ...
</TVGuide>
```

To make sure that each series is only described once, they should each have their own identifier, which we'll put in an `ID` attribute. Lacking imagination, we'll call this attribute `id`. At the top of `TVGuide2.xml`, we can declare that the `id` attributes of the `<Series>` elements are `ID` attributes with the following `DOCTYPE` declaration:

```
<?xml version="1.0" encoding="ISO-8859-1"?>
<!DOCTYPE TVGuide [
<!ELEMENT Series (Title, Description)>
<!ATTLIST Series id ID #IMPLIED>
]>
<TVGuide start="2001-07-05" end="2001-07-05">
  <Channel>
    <Name>BBC1</Name>
    ...
    <Program rating="5" flag="favorite">
      <Start>2001-07-05T19:30:00</Start>
      <Duration>PT30M</Duration>
      <Series>EastEnders</Series>
      <Title></Title>
      ...
    </Program>
    ...
  </Channel>
  ...
  <Series id="EastEnders" type="soap">
    <Title>EastEnders</Title>
    <Description>Soap set in the East End of London.</Description>
  </Series>
  ...
</TVGuide>
```

The element declaration is included so that this will work with MSXML; other processors don't need it.

Doing this doesn't make the document valid (since the DTD doesn't declare every element in the document) but it does allow an XSLT processor to recognize `ID` attributes. As we'll see in the next section, this enables us to locate the details of a series if we know its ID.

Accessing Elements by ID

`ID` attributes can be treated just like any other attribute, and you can find an element that has a particular value in an attribute you know to be an `ID` attribute using a predicate. For example, to find the description of EastEnders as a series, you can search for the `<Series>` element that has been assigned the value `EastEnders` for its `id` attribute, and go from that `<Series>` element to its child `<Description>` element with:

```
Series[@id = 'EastEnders']/Description
```

However, if you declare that the `id` attribute is an `ID` attribute, then XSLT offers another method of getting hold of the `<Series>` element, using the `id()` function. This function takes a single argument, the `ID` of the element that you want to access, and returns the element node that has that particular `ID`:

```
id('EastEnders')/Description
```

The string `'EastEnders'` could come from anywhere, and typically it would come from an attribute or element elsewhere. In the TV Guide XML, the `<Series>` element within the `<Program>` element holds a reference to the series of which the program is an episode. Within the template for the `<Program>`, you could retrieve and apply templates to the description of the series with the following:

```
<xsl:template match="Program" mode="Details">
  ...
  <xsl:apply-templates select="id(Series)/Description" />
  ...
</xsl:template>
```

The big advantage of using an `ID` attribute and the `id()` function rather than a predicate is that it is more efficient. When an XSLT processor first looks at an XML document, it can build up a table of each element and their unique `ID`s, which it can then use to retrieve the element with a particular `ID`. Whereas with a predicate those elements would have to be visited again and again every time you wanted to find them, with `ID` attributes the elements are visited just once, and the processor generates a table that can retrieve them a lot faster.

> **The `id()` function retrieves the element that has a particular unique identifier within a document.**

Try It Out – Getting Information About TV Series

In the XML for our TV Guide, each program may belong to a particular series. The details about each series are held in `<Series>` elements below the TV listings for each channel, each of which has an `id` attribute that holds a unique identifier for the series. The `<Program>` elements refer to this information with their own child `<Series>` element, whose value is one of these unique identifiers.

In anticipation of using `ID` attributes to refer to the series information, the values of the `<Series>` elements within the `<Program>` elements conform to the rules about the names of IDs; in particular, they don't contain any spaces. So far, we've just presented the value of the `<Series>` element for a `<Program>`, but then the presented information doesn't look very good: rather than "Star Trek: Voyager" we see "StarTrekVoyager" on the HTML page, for example:

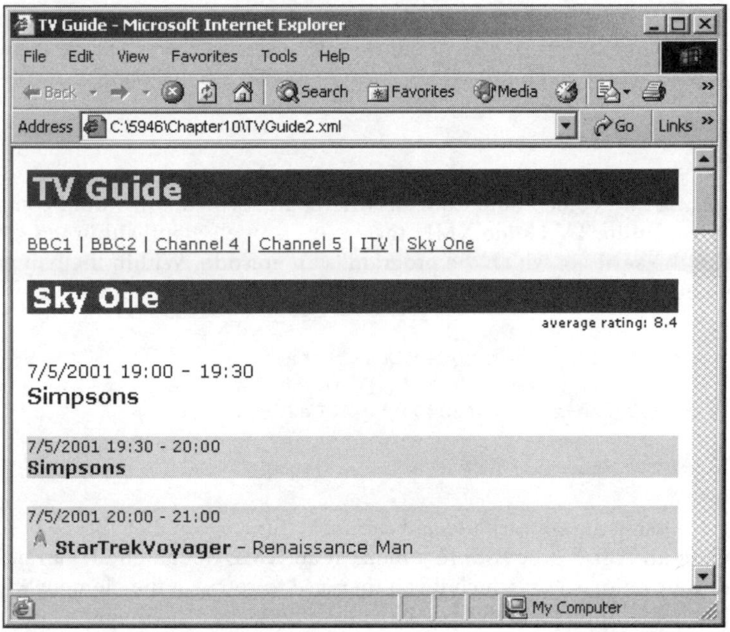

To get a readable name for the series, we need to access the series information that's being pointed to from the <Program> and from there find the <Title> under the referenced <Series> element. Currently, in `TVGuide.xsl`, the template providing the HTML giving details of the series looks as follows:

```
<xsl:template match="Program" mode="Title">
  <span class="title">
    <xsl:choose>
      <xsl:when test="string(Series)">
        <xsl:value-of select="Series" />
        <xsl:if test="string(Title)">
        <xsl:text> - </xsl:text>
        <span class="subtitle"><xsl:value-of select="Title" /></span>
        </xsl:if>
      </xsl:when>
      <xsl:otherwise>
      <xsl:value-of select="Title" />
      </xsl:otherwise>
    </xsl:choose>
  </span>
</xsl:template>
```

Rather than giving the value of that <Series> element, we need to retrieve the <Series> element that has that `ID`, and get its child <Title> element:

```
<xsl:template match="Program" mode="Title">
  <span class="title">
    <xsl:choose>
      <xsl:when test="string(Series)">
```

```
          <xsl:value-of select="id(Series)/Title" />
          <xsl:if test="string(Title)">
            <xsl:text> - </xsl:text>
            <span class="subtitle"><xsl:value-of select="Title" /></span>
          </xsl:if>
        </xsl:when>
        <xsl:otherwise>
          <xsl:value-of select="Title" />
        </xsl:otherwise>
      </xsl:choose>
    </span>
  </xsl:template>
```

With this change made in TVGuide2.xsl, the result of transforming TVGuide2.xml is as follows:

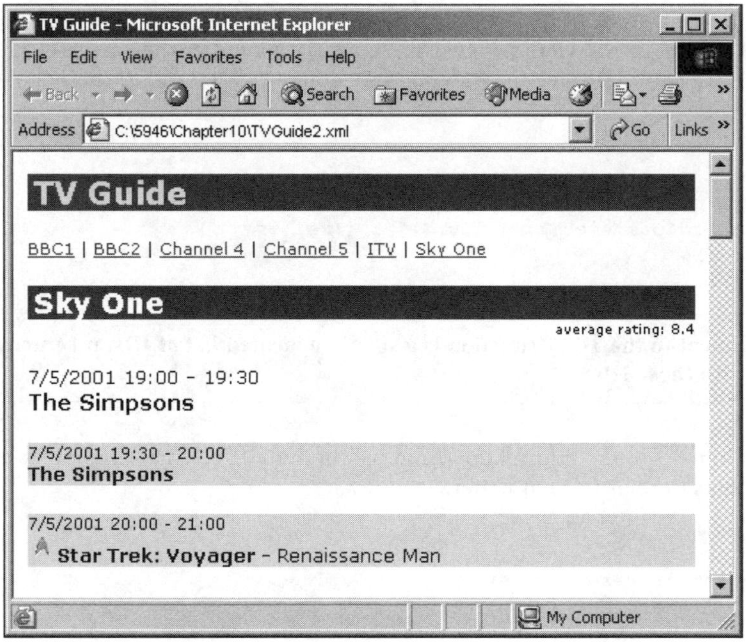

The title of each series is retrieved from the information further down in TVGuide2.xml, using the ID given as the value of the <Series> element within each program and as the value of the id attribute in the series details.

Resolving Multiple References

In the last section, you saw the id() function being passed a single ID and retrieving the single element that had that ID. If you have lots of references, you can also use the id() function to return more than one element at a time. For example, each program and series can have several writers, some of which may work on more than one program or series within the TV Guide. Rather than repeating information about each of the writers, we could also separate the information about writers and store that further down in the TV Guide:

```
<Writer id="NickSaltrese">
  <Name>Nick Saltrese</Name>
  <Bio>...</Bio>
</Writer>
<Writer id="JulieWassmer">
  <Name>Julie Wassmer</Name>
  <Bio>...</Bio>
</Writer>
```

There are two ways to refer to this information from within the `<Program>` element. Firstly, we can use a space-separated list of `ID`s, as follows:

```
<Writers>NickSaltrese JulieWassmer</Writers>
```

When you use a space-separated list of `ID`s as the argument to the `id()` function, it returns a node set containing the elements that have those `ID`s. So, to list the names of the writers (with commas separating them), we could retrieve the `<Writer>` elements with a call to the `id()` function and iterate over them as follows:

```
<xsl:for-each select="id(Writers)">
  <xsl:value-of select="Name" />
  <xsl:if test="position() != last()">, </xsl:if>
</xsl:for-each>
```

If the argument to the `id()` function is a space-separated list of IDs, it returns the elements with those IDs.

The second way to refer to the information from within the `<Program>` element is to use separate `<Writer>` elements to refer to each writer, as follows:

```
<Writers>
  <Writer>NickSaltrese</Writer>
  <Writer>JulieWassmer</Writer>
</Writers>
```

You can also use this structure with the `id()` function. If the argument to the `id()` function is a node set, then the `id()` function takes the values of those nodes and creates a node set comprising the result of using the `id()` function on each of the values. In essence, you get the element(s) referred to by each of the nodes in the node set. With this second representation, the comma-separated list of writer's names could then be generated with the following:

```
<xsl:for-each select="id(Writers/Writer)">
  <xsl:value-of select="Name" />
  <xsl:if test="position() != last()">, </xsl:if>
</xsl:for-each>
```

> **If the argument to the `id()` function is a node set, it returns the elements with the IDs given by the nodes in the node set.**

Keys

As we've seen, the big benefit of using the `id()` function over using a predicate to search a document is the fact that the XSLT processor doesn't have to search through the entire document again and again to find the element with a particular identifier. However, using `ID` attributes can be problematic for the following reasons:

- The `ID` attributes have to be declared within a DTD, but you can't guarantee that a document will reference a DTD, that the DTD will be accessible, or that an XSLT processor will access the DTD. Placing the DTD within the instance document helps, but that is impractical if your markup language contains lots of `ID` attributes on lots of different elements.
- You have to add an `ID` to all the elements to which you want to refer, which adds to the size of the document and means that you have to think of a unique ID for every element in your document.
- The `IDs` must be specified in attributes, but this might not fit in with your preferences when designing your markup language.
- The `IDs` have to follow the rules for XML names, but some `IDs` don't naturally fit with this pattern (for example, ISBNs start with a number and the names of TV series often contain spaces).
- The `IDs` have to be unique within a document, but sometimes you might want to have them scoped to particular element types or to particular sections within a document.

These constraints can make it impractical or inadvisable to rely on `ID` attributes and the `id()` function. XSLT therefore offers an alternative method of assigning identifiers to elements and of accessing elements by those identifiers: **keys**.

> **Using `ID` attributes and the `id()` function can be very limiting. Keys offer a more flexible way of identifying and referencing elements.**

Using Keys Instead of IDs

The first step in using keys is roughly equivalent to declaring an `ID` attribute – you need to tell the XSLT processor that a particular set of elements can be identified by a particular attribute value. It's in declaring keys that we come across the first difference between keys and IDs: you declare keys within the XSLT stylesheet rather than within an XML document. This means you don't have to worry about whether the person authoring the source XML for your transformation has made all the declarations that you need them to have made for the stylesheet to work.

Keys are declared with the `<xsl:key>` element, which is placed at the top level of your stylesheet (the same level as `<xsl:template>` and global variables). As we'll see later in this chapter, you can have several keys within the same document, indexing different elements in different ways, using key values that are arbitrary strings, all while allowing several elements to share the same key value.

XML Schema also allows you to define keys and references to keys within a markup language, but these are somewhat different. Firstly, the key values are sequences of node values rather than arbitrary strings. Secondly, keys are scoped so that they only operate within a certain type of element, rather than across the entire document. Finally, every element within the scope of a key must have a different value for that key (although elements in different scopes can have the same value for the key). In addition, as I said earlier in this chapter, XSLT processors don't have access to information from XML Schema as yet.

The simplest keys are those that are directly equivalent to an `ATTLIST` declaration for an `ID` attribute. These kinds of keys have the following pattern:

```
<xsl:key name="IDs" match="elementName" use="@attributeName" />
```

For example, to declare a key that says that `<Series>` elements can be identified using their `id` attribute, you would use the following key definition:

```
<xsl:key name="IDs" match="Series" use="@id" />
```

If you define one of these keys for each `ID` attribute in your DTD, you'll end up with one key that indexes all the ID'ed elements in your document by their `ID` attribute.

If `<xsl:key>` is equivalent to the `ATTLIST` declaration for `ID` attributes, then you also need something equivalent to the `id()` function to retrieve the element that has a particular `ID`. The equivalent of the `id()` function is the `key()` function, which takes two arguments – the name of the key (as given in the `name` attribute of `<xsl:key>`) and the identifier that's assigned to the element that you want to retrieve. For example, having defined the `IDs` key, to get hold of the `<Series>` element that has the `ID 'EastEnders'`, you would use:

```
key('IDs', 'EastEnders')
```

The second argument to the `key()` function isn't quite as flexible as the argument to the `id()` function, in that it can't take a space-separated list of IDs to return the elements with those IDs (because the identifier itself could have spaces in it), but the second argument can be a node set. For example, if you've set up a key for the `<Writer>` elements:

```
<xsl:key name="IDs" match="Writer" use="@id" />
```

then the references to the `<Writer>` elements must be held in separate elements, as follows:

```
<Writers>
  <Writer>NickSaltrese</Writer>
  <Writer>JulieWassmer</Writer>
</Writers>
```

You could then use the `key()` function to retrieve all the `<Writer>` elements with those IDs with:

```
key('IDs', Writers/Writer)
```

Note that this will also return any <Series> elements whose ID is the same as a writer's ID. In the next section, we'll see how key spaces can be used to focus the search onto particular types of elements.

> **You can declare a key with the `<xsl:key>` element at the top level of the stylesheet, and access elements indexed by the key using the `key()` function.**

Try It Out – Using Keys Instead of IDs

When we looked at IDs, we wrote a template that would insert the name of a series in the details of a program by accessing the relevant <Series> element through its ID. The id attribute of the <Series> element was declared as an ID attribute with the following ATTLIST declaration within the DTD:

```
<!ATTLIST Series id ID #IMPLIED>
```

Try removing the DOCTYPE declaration from TVGuide2.xml so that the XML document no longer references the DTD, to give TVGuide3.xml, and view this using TVGuide2.xsl. You should see the following:

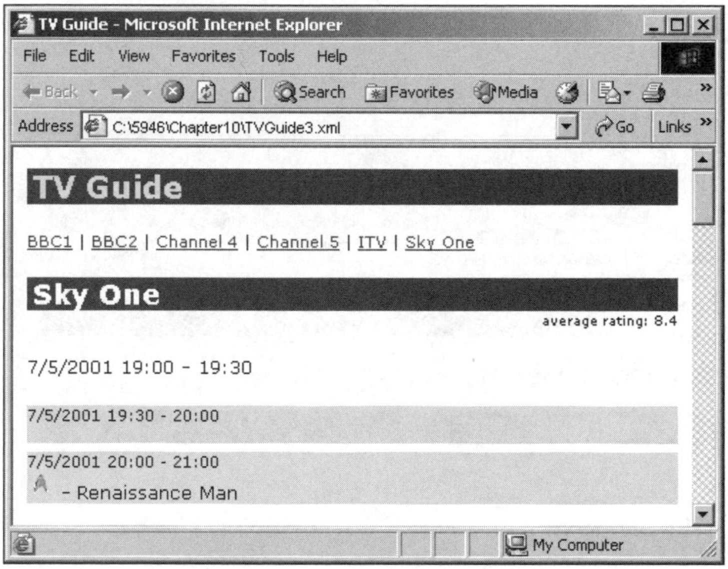

When you remove the DTD, the XSLT processor no longer has access to the fact that the id attribute on the <Series> element is an ID attribute, so it can't retrieve the name of the series for presentation on the page.

This might well happen if an author forgets to include a DOCTYPE declaration in the XML document, or if for some reason the DTD for the XML document is unavailable. To make the stylesheet more robust, you can use a key with the same effect instead. Add an <xsl:key> element to the top level of TVGuide3.xsl to tell the XSLT processor to index all the <Series> elements according to their id attribute, as follows:

```
<xsl:key name="IDs" match="Series" use="@id" />
```

Now change the call to the `id()` function so that you use the key instead. The first argument to the `key()` function is the name of the key (`'IDs'`), and the second argument is the same as the argument you used for the `id()` function – the `ID` that you want to use to retrieve the element:

```
<xsl:template match="Program" mode="Title">
  <span class="title">
    <xsl:choose>
      <xsl:when test="string(Series)">
        <xsl:value-of select="key('IDs', Series)/Title" />
        <xsl:if test="string(Title)">
          <xsl:text> - </xsl:text>
          <span class="subtitle"><xsl:value-of select="Title" /></span>
        </xsl:if>
      </xsl:when>
      <xsl:otherwise>
        <xsl:value-of select="Title" />
      </xsl:otherwise>
    </xsl:choose>

  </span>
</xsl:template>
```

When you run the transformation of `TVGuide3.xml` with `TVGuide3.xsl`, you should see the following:

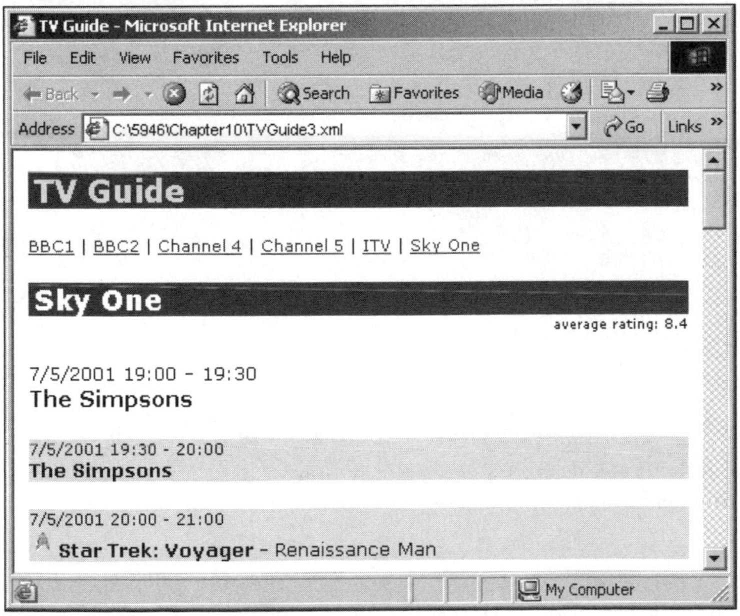

The names of the series appear as they did before you removed the DTD, because keys do not rely on information held within the DTD, only the key definitions in the stylesheet.

Key Spaces

Defining keys rather than ID attributes grants you independence from a DTD, but that's just one of its advantages. As you might guess from the fact that keys have names, you can have several **key spaces**.

With IDs, you could only have one set of IDs throughout the document, so even if you knew that an ID could only refer to a <Series> element, you still had to make sure that it wasn't the same as an ID that you used for a <Writer> element. With keys, you can have separate keys for separate sets of IDs. You can have one key for series:

```
<xsl:key name="series" match="Series" use="@id" />
```

and another key for writers:

```
<xsl:key name="writers" match="Writer" use="@id" />
```

You can have two <xsl:key> elements with the same name attribute, in which case the two indexes created by the <xsl:key> elements are merged into one.

There are two advantages to using different key spaces for different indexes.

First, having several key spaces means two elements can use the same identifier, but you can still retrieve the one that you want. For example, if a series and a writer happened to have the same name, not only could they use the same value for their id attributes, but also you would be able to retrieve the <Series> element when you wanted to retrieve the series, and the <Writer> element when you needed the writer.

Second, the indexes that are built by keys can be much smaller and much more focused than the ones for IDs, which have to cover every element with an ID attribute in the entire document. Using an index is a big advantage over searching through the document multiple times, but likewise the smaller the index, the quicker it is to build and the faster the XSLT processor can retrieve nodes within it.

The name attribute of <xsl:key> defines a key space, which allows several elements to have the same identifier and assists you in focusing the search for them more effectively.

Choosing What to Index

The match attribute on <xsl:key> determines the kinds of nodes that are indexed by the key. As you might expect from its name, the match attribute on <xsl:key> holds the same kinds of values as the match attribute on <xsl:template> – a pattern. The XSLT processor searches through the entire XML document to find all the nodes that match the pattern given in the match attribute, and the index that it creates holds an entry for each of them.

You can tell the XSLT processor to index only text nodes or particular attributes, but most often, the kinds of nodes that you want to retrieve using a key are elements. The main purpose of the match attribute, then, is to limit the kinds of elements that are indexed by the key so that it doesn't hold unnecessary information.

For example, the only `<Series>` elements that we're really interested in indexing are those that are children of the `<TVGuide>` element that is a child of the root node, and not those that are children of the `<Program>` element. So we could change the `match` pattern to only match these kinds of `<Series>` elements, and not those that are held within `<Program>` elements, with:

```
<xsl:key name="series" match="/TVGuide/Series" use="@id" />
```

You can also use the fact that the `match` attribute takes a pattern to create keys that index several different kinds of elements within the same key space. For example, to create a key that indexes `<Writer>`, `<Director>`, and `<Producer>` children of the `<TVGuide>` element by their `id` attributes, you could use:

```
<xsl:key name="productionStaff"
         match="/TVGuide/Writer | /TVGuide/Director | /TVGuide/Producer"
         use="@id" />
```

Using a match pattern of multiple parts has exactly the same effect as if you had several `<xsl:key>` elements, all with the same name, as follows:

```
<xsl:key name="productionStaff" match="/TVGuide/Writer" use="@id" />
<xsl:key name="productionStaff" match="/TVGuide/Director" use="@id" />
<xsl:key name="productionStaff" match="/TVGuide/Producer" use="@id" />
```

> **The `match` attribute of `<xsl:key>` specifies the types of nodes that are indexed by the key. The key indexes all the nodes in a document that match the pattern held in the `match` attribute.**

Indexing by XPaths

With `ID`s, the `ID` of an element has to be stored within an attribute, and has to conform to the rules for XML names. The **key values** used to identify elements indexed by a key are a lot more flexible – they can come from child elements, or any other calculated value, as well as from attributes, and can be in any format at all.

The value that's used to index a particular element is specified with the `use` attribute on `<xsl:key>`. The `use` attribute contains an XPath expression, which means that you can use long and convoluted location paths or call functions to get an identifier for an element. The only limit on what the `use` attribute can contain is that it cannot refer to the values of variables.

When the XSLT processor creates an index for a key, it evaluates the XPath held in the `use` attribute with the node that it's indexing as the current node to give the key value by which the node is indexed. For example, you could use the `<Name>` elements to identify the `<Actor>` elements that contain them as follows:

```
<xsl:key name="actors" match="Actor" use="Name" />
```

Alternatively, you could identify each program based on a combination of the channel on which it's shown (the <Name> child of the <Program> element's parent <Channel>) and the date and time at which it starts (the <Program> element's child <Start> element), by concatenating them together with the concat() function:

```
<xsl:key name="programs" match="Program"
         use="concat(../Name, ' at ', Start)" />
```

With the above key, you could retrieve the program on BBC1 starting at 19:30 on the 5th July 2001 with the following call to the key() function:

```
Key('programs', 'BBC1 at 2001-07-05T19:30:00')
```

The fact that key values can contain spaces is the reason that you can't use space-separated lists of IDs *as the second argument to the* key() *function whereas you can use them as the argument for the* id() *function.*

> **The use attribute of <xsl:key> contains an XPath expression, which specifies the key value used to index an element.**

Multiple Key Values

Keys are not bound by the limitation on IDs that states that there can only be one element with a particular identifier. The same key value can be used to access multiple elements. This is particularly useful when you want to look at reverse relationships, from an element to all the elements that refer to it.

For example, you could set up a key that would allow you to find all the programs that belong to a particular series. The elements that you want to retrieve are <Program> elements, so the match pattern needs to match them, and the key values that they need to be indexed by are the values of their <Series> elements. The key definition looks like:

```
<xsl:key name="programsBySeries" match="Program" use="Series" />
```

It doesn't matter that several programs belong to the same series – all of them are returned by the call to the key() function. For example, the following returns all <Program> elements that are part of the EastEnders series:

```
key('programsBySeries', 'EastEnders')
```

Note that when you use the key() *function, the second argument must match the key value exactly. There's no way to retrieve all the Star Trek episodes (those programs whose series starts with* 'StarTrek'*) using this key, for example, because the programs are indexed by the entirety of their series name.*

What's more, while usually the expression held by the use attribute evaluates to a string, you can also use an expression that evaluates to a node set. If you do, then the indexed node can be retrieved using the value of *any* of the nodes in the node set used for the key, essentially giving the element multiple identifiers. This is particularly useful when you want to access the same element in many different ways.

For example, to enable us to retrieve all the `<Program>` elements that star a particular actor, we could set up a key that again matches `<Program>` elements but this time using the `<Name>` child of the `<Actor>` child of the `<CastMember>` child of the `<CastList>` element, as follows:

```
<xsl:key name="programsByActors" match="Program"
         use="CastList/CastMember/Actor/Name" />
```

When it's evaluated from the context of a `<Program>` element, the path `CastList/CastMember/Actor/Name` returns a node set containing several `<Name>` elements (one for each actor in the program). The values of these `<Name>` elements are used to index the `<Program>` element within the `programsByActors` key. Whichever actor is named by the call to the key, the `<Program>` element will be returned by it. For example, given the following cast list as in `TVGuide3.xml`:

```
<Program>
  ...
  <CastList>
    <CastMember>
      <Character><Name>Zoe Slater</Name>...</Character>
      <Actor><Name>Michelle Ryan</Name>...</Actor>

    </CastMember>
    <CastMember>
      <Character><Name>Jamie Mitchell</Name>...</Character>
      <Actor><Name>Jack Ryder</Name>...</Actor>
    </CastMember>
    <CastMember>
      <Character><Name>Sonia Jackson</Name>...</Character>
      <Actor><Name>Natalie Cassidy</Name>...</Actor>
    </CastMember>
    ...
  </CastList>
  ...
</Program>
```

the following calls to the `key()` function will all return the above `<Program>` element (possibly along with others, if several programs star the same actors):

```
key('programsByActors', 'Michelle Ryan')
key('programsByActors', 'Jack Ryder')
key('programsByActors', 'Natalie Cassidy')
```

A key can assign the same key value to multiple elements (in which case the `key()` function returns all the elements) and can assign multiple key values to the same element (in which case the `key()` function will return the element no matter which value is used).

Try It Out – Creating Lists of Programs in Series

It's easy to tell which series a particular program is an episode of using the XML structure that we've put together, but it's not clear from the XML which episodes of a particular series are being shown. Here, we'll add lists of the episodes showing in each series to the bottom of our TV Guide.

As a first step, we need to add a template that matches the `<Series>` elements that are direct children of the `<TVGuide>` element so that we can create sections that describe each series. The basic template just gives the name of the series as a heading, followed by its description:

```
<xsl:template match="TVGuide/Series">
  <div>
    <h3><xsl:value-of select="Title" /></h3>
    <p>
      <xsl:apply-templates select="Description" />
    </p>
  </div>
</xsl:template>
```

We'll use this template to add information about the series being shown at the bottom of our page, by modifying the template that matches the `<TVGuide>` element. We'll apply templates to the `<Series>` elements in alphabetical order, based on their IDs:

```
<xsl:template match="TVGuide">
  <xsl:variable name="sortOrder">
    <xsl:choose>
      <xsl:when test="$sortOrder = 'ascending'">ascending</xsl:when>
      <xsl:otherwise>descending</xsl:otherwise>
    </xsl:choose>
  </xsl:variable>
  <xsl:apply-templates select="Channel">
    <xsl:sort select="sum(Program/@rating) div count(Program)"
              data-type="number" order="{$sortOrder}" />
    <xsl:sort select="Name" />
  </xsl:apply-templates>
  <h2>Series</h2>
  <xsl:apply-templates select="Series">
    <xsl:sort select="@id" />
  </xsl:apply-templates>
</xsl:template>
```

These two changes have been made in `TVGuide4.xsl`. When you transform `TVGuide3.xml` with `TVGuide4.xsl`, you should see a list of the series at the bottom of the page, as follows:

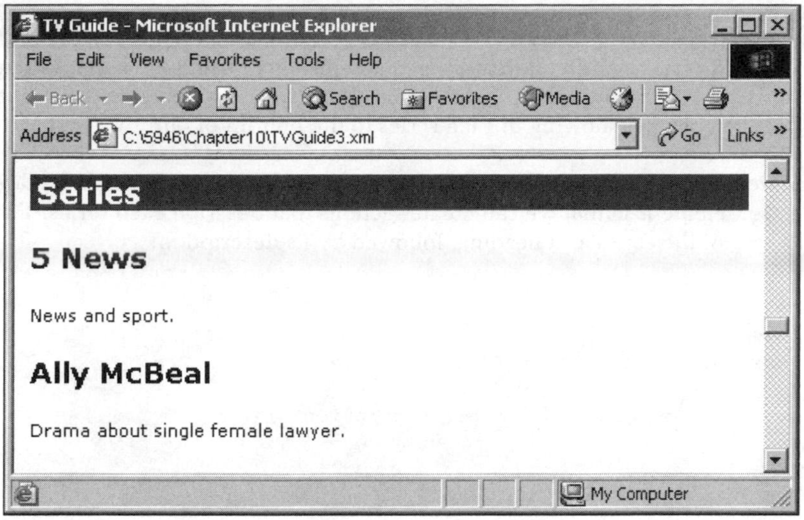

One of the things to add to this description of the series is a list of the programs being shown from the series. To retrieve these programs efficiently, we should set up a key that indexes all the `<Program>` elements within `TVGuide3.xml` by the value of their `<Series>` child element, as follows:

```
<xsl:key name="programsBySeries" match="Program" use="Series" />
```

The values of the `<Series>` element children of the `<Program>` elements tie up with the values of the `id` attributes on the `<Series>` element children of the `<TVGuide>` element. In the template for the latter `<Series>` elements, we can therefore retrieve all the `<Program>` elements that refer to the series using the following:

```
key('programsBySeries', @id)
```

Once we've got hold of the `<Program>` elements using the key, we can iterate over them with an `<xsl:for-each>` as follows:

```
<xsl:template match="TVGuide/Series">
  <div>
    <h3><xsl:value-of select="Title" /></h3>
    <p>
      <xsl:apply-templates select="Description" />
    </p>
    <h4>Episodes</h4>
    <ul>
      <xsl:for-each select="key('programsBySeries', @id)">
        <li>
          <xsl:value-of select="parent::Channel/Name" />
          <xsl:text> at </xsl:text>
          <xsl:value-of select="Start" />
          <xsl:if test="string(Title)">
            <xsl:text>: </xsl:text>
            <xsl:value-of select="Title" />
```

```
          </xsl:if>
        </li>
      </xsl:for-each>
    </ul>
  </div>
</xsl:template>
```

Making these changes in `TVGuide5.xsl` creates the following page when used with `TVGuide3.xml`:

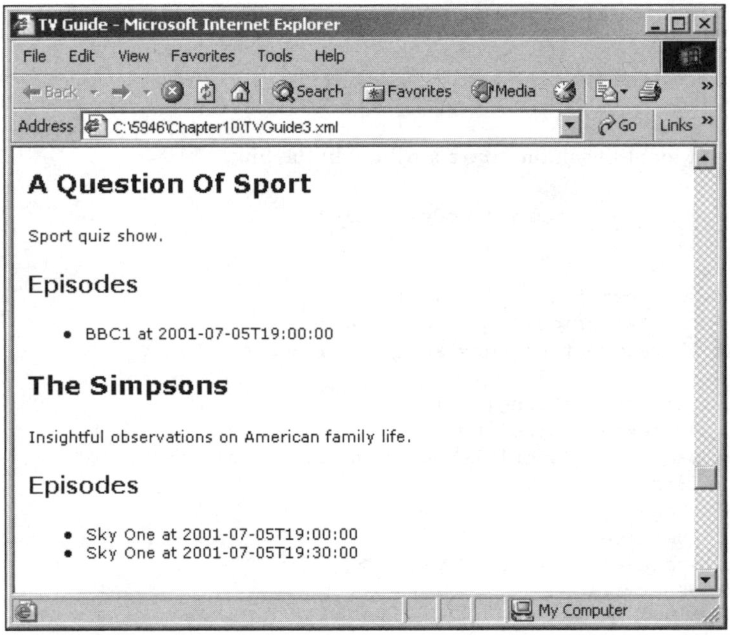

A Question Of Sport has one episode, on BBC1 at 19:00, whereas there are two episodes of The Simpsons showing, at 19:00 and 19:30 on Sky One. The key has indexed each program by its series, and it's used to retrieve all the programs of a particular series.

Generating IDs

If you have an XML structure that contains a lot of cross-references, then you're likely to find it useful to have a presentation format that does the same kind of thing. As an example, the XML for the TV Guide separates the details of TV series off into separate elements, and the HTML presentation follows this format as well, with the descriptions of the series presented after the channel listings.

When you have references within an HTML page, it's helpful to make the references into **hypertext links** so that someone reading the document can jump from place to place. To enable local HTML links, you have to create **anchors** within the HTML document that you generate with the XSLT, and create links that reference these anchors. As you know, you can do this with the <a> element in HTML, using the `name` and `id` attributes to create anchors and the `href` attribute to create a link.

For example, it would be good to link from each program to the series of which it's an episode. To do this, we need to create an anchor when we generate the HTML that describes each series, within the template for the `<Series>` elements within the `<TVGuide>` element, and a link to the anchor from the name of the series when we generate it in the template matching `<Series>` elements within `<Program>` elements. We can use the ID assigned to the series as the basis of the links, as the value of the `name` and `id` attributes in the anchor:

```
<xsl:template match="TVGuide/Series">
  <div>
    <h3><a name="{@id}" id="{@id}"><xsl:value-of select="Title" /></a></h3>
    ...
  </div>
</xsl:template>
```

and as the fragment identifier in the `href` attribute in the link:

```
<xsl:template match="Program" mode="Title">
  <span class="title">
    <xsl:choose>
      <xsl:when test="string(Series)">
        <a href="#{Series}">
          <xsl:value-of select="key('IDs', Series)/Title" />
        </a>
        <xsl:if test="string(Title)">
          <xsl:text> - </xsl:text>
          <span class="subtitle"><xsl:value-of select="Title" /></span>
        </xsl:if>
      </xsl:when>
      <xsl:otherwise>
        <xsl:value-of select="Title" />
      </xsl:otherwise>
    </xsl:choose>
  </span>
</xsl:template>
```

These changes, in `TVGuide6.xsl`, generate a page in which you can navigate from a program to its series by clicking on the name of the series.

Likewise, it would be useful to have links to the programs that are listed in the episode lists for each series. Here, we need an anchor in the result generated from each `<Program>` element and a link in the episode lists generated when we get a description of the series. However, unlike the series, there's no ready-made `ID` that we can use for the anchors.

There are several ways to create unique `ID`s for elements in an XML document, using their name and position within the XML document, a path-like `ID` generated from looking at their ancestors, or information specific to the area that you're looking at (such as the combination of the channel name and the time), but by far the easiest is to use the `generate-id()` function. The `generate-id()` function generates a valid XML `ID` (starting with a letter, not containing any spaces) and is guaranteed to return the same ID for any particular node no matter how many times you call it within a particular run of a stylesheet. If you use the `generate-id()` function without an argument, you get the `ID` of the context node; if you pass an argument, then it must be a node set, and the `generate-id()` function will return an ID for the first node in that node set.

The thing to watch out for when using the generate-id() function is that it is *not* guaranteed to give the same ID on different runs of the same stylesheet, or with different stylesheets operating over the same XML document, let alone across different processors. So, while you can use it to generate IDs that you use locally within a page you can't use it to generate IDs that take you between pages.

Even within a page, it's a little risky since sometimes people record URLs that include the IDs you use. If you were to then regenerate the page, the IDs would change completely.

The generate-id() function generates a unique ID for a node.

Try It Out – Linking from Series to Programs

The <Program> elements don't have any ready-made IDs, so we need to use the generate-id() function to give us anchors, which we can then refer to from within the episode lists for each series. We can use the generate-id() function in attribute value templates for the name and id attributes on an anchor in the template for <Program> elements (and, in fact, this generated ID is much better than the name of the series as a source of the identifier for the cast list):

```
<xsl:template match="Program" mode="Details">
  <xsl:variable name="programID" select="concat(generate-id(), 'Cast')" />
  <p>
    <a name="{generate-id()}" id="{generate-id()}">
      <xsl:apply-templates select="Start" />
    </a>
    ...
    <xsl:apply-templates select="CastList" mode="DisplayToggle">
      <xsl:with-param name="divID" select="$programID" />
    </xsl:apply-templates>
  </p>
  <xsl:apply-templates select="CastList">
    <xsl:with-param name="divID" select="$programID" />
  </xsl:apply-templates>
</xsl:template>
```

And we can use the same function to give an ID to use in the link within the episode lists for each series:

```
<xsl:template match="TVGuide/Series">
  <div>
    <h3><a name="{@id}" id="{@id}"><xsl:value-of select="Title" /></a></h3>
    <p>
      <xsl:apply-templates select="Description" />
    </p>
    <h4>Episodes</h4>
    <ul>
      <xsl:for-each select="key('programsBySeries', @id)">
        <li>
          <a href="#{generate-id()}">
            <xsl:value-of select="parent::Channel/Name" />
            <xsl:text> at </xsl:text>
```

```
            <xsl:value-of select="Start" />
            <xsl:if test="string(Title)">
              <xsl:text>: </xsl:text>
              <xsl:value-of select="Title" />
            </xsl:if>
          </a>
        </li>
      </xsl:for-each>
    </ul>
  </div>
</xsl:template>
```

The ID that you generate with the `generate-id()` function when you process the `<Program>` element to create its details in the main schedule is guaranteed to be the same ID as you get when you process the `<Program>` element in order to describe it in the episode listing. If you use `TVGuide7.xsl`, which uses `generate-id()` in this way, to transform `TVGuide3.xml`, you should find that the episode lists are linked to the program descriptions. For example, if I click on the only EastEnders episode listed, I get the following:

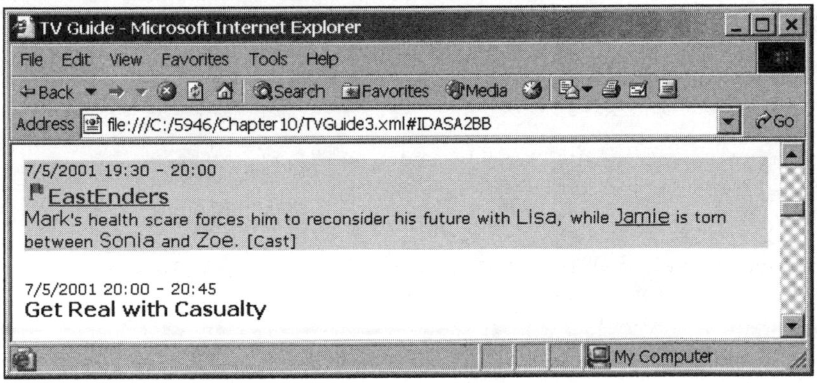

The precise ID that you get (shown after the # in the **Address** bar) will probably be different, but you should be able to navigate from the program to the series description and back again without any difficulties.

Grouping

It might seem a bit strange to cover grouping in this chapter, which is all about quickly accessing elements by some value, but working out which elements belong to a particular group is a lot like working out which element has a particular ID, except that you need to get hold of all the elements in a particular group, whereas you only expect one element to have a particular ID. For example, you might want to group together all the episodes of the same series; in that case, the series that it belongs to is really acting as an identifier for the program.

Grouping is a task that isn't explicitly supported in XSLT 1.0, but it's one of the most common tasks involved in processing data-oriented XML. In this section, we'll look at one particular kind of grouping that uses keys to access all the elements that belong to a particular group.

This kind of grouping is popularly known as Muenchian grouping because it was first described by Steve Muench.

Creating Grouping Keys

As we saw when we looked at defining keys, it's possible to define a key in which several elements have the same value, in effect a group of elements. For example, we defined a key that would return the group of `<Program>` elements that belonged to the same series with:

```
<xsl:key name="programsBySeries" match="Program" use="Series" />
```

You also saw how to define keys that created groups where the same element could belong to multiple groups, such as the `<Program>` elements being grouped by the actors that starred in them:

```
<xsl:key name="programsByActors" match="Program"
         use="CastList/CastMember/Actor/Name" />
```

In both cases, several `<Program>` elements may turn out to have the same value for the key – those that do form a group.

If you look at these keys more closely, you'll see that the attributes follow a set pattern:

- `name` – the name of the grouping scheme
- `match` – a pattern that matches the elements that need to be grouped
- `use` – an expression that gives the grouping value of the element

The first stage in grouping is to set up a key that defines the groups.

Identifying Groups

If you know what groups elements fall into, then you can process the elements that belong to a group by selecting them with the `key()` function, with the first argument being the name of the grouping scheme and the second argument being the grouping value that all the elements have in common. In the episode lists generated for each series, for example, we're really grouping the `<Program>` elements together based on the identifiers of the `<Series>` elements.

More complicated grouping problems arise when you *don't* know in advance what the possible grouping values might be, what groups the elements might fall into. If you didn't have the list of series readily available, for example, if you were using `TVGuide4.xml` rather than `TVGuide3.xml`, how could you tell that you need to create an episode list for EastEnders? Well, you can look at the `<Series>` element children of the `<Program>` elements, and use the value of the `<Series>` elements as the basis of the episode lists. To place this after the channel listings, we can apply templates to all the `<Series>` children of the `<Program>` elements within the `<Channel>` elements in `EpisodeList` mode:

```
<xsl:template match="TVGuide">
  ...
  <h2>Series</h2>
  <xsl:apply-templates select="Channel/Program/Series" mode="EpisodeList">
    <xsl:sort select="." />
  </xsl:apply-templates>
</xsl:template>
```

When we encounter a `<Series>` element in `EpisodeList` mode, we can use the value of the `<Series>` element as the second argument to the `key()` function, to retrieve all the other `<Program>` elements that have the same value for their `<Series>` child:

```
<xsl:template match="Program/Series" mode="EpisodeList">
  <div>
    <h3><a name="{.}" id="{.}"><xsl:value-of select="." /></a></h3>
    <h4>Episodes</h4>
    <ul>
      <xsl:for-each select="key('programsBySeries', .)">
        <li>...</li>
      </xsl:for-each>
    </ul>
  </div>
</xsl:template>
```

This gives us the episode lists for each of the series that are being shown, but it gives us far more episode lists than we want, as you can see from the result of transforming `TVGuide3.xml` with `TVGuide8.xsl`:

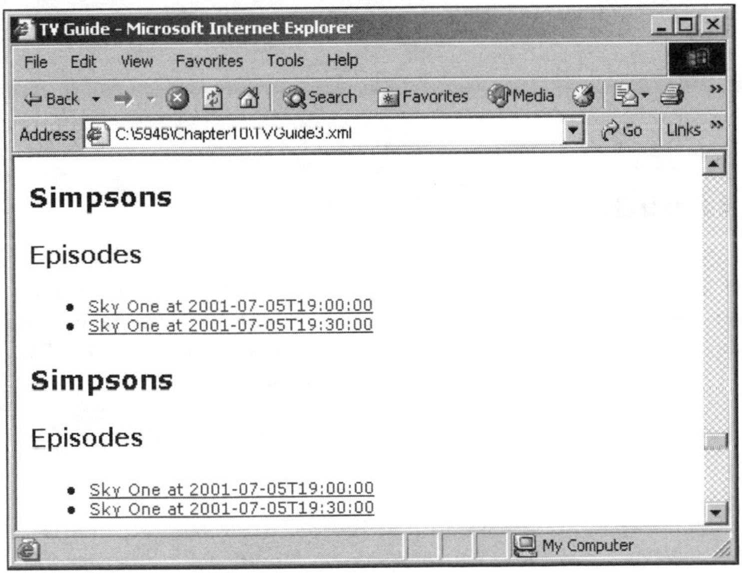

We get one episode list per program – a listing of all the Simpsons episodes for each of the Simpsons episodes. We need to find a way to only show each episode list once.

The answer is to pick on only one of the <Series> elements for each series, and only create the episode list for that <Series> element. For example, we could pick only the first <Series> element that has a particular value.

But how do we identify which <Series> element is the first with a particular value? Well, you can find all the other <Series> elements with the same value, and then see whether the one that you're currently looking at is the same as the first in the list. You can get all the episodes using the key, as usual, and get the first of the episodes by accessing the first of the nodes returned by that key using a positional predicate:

```
<xsl:template match="Program/Series" mode="EpisodeList">
  <xsl:variable name="episodes" select="key('programsBySeries', .)" />
  <xsl:variable name="firstEpisode" select="$episodes[1]" />
  <xsl:if test="...">
    <div>
      <h3><a name="{.}" id="{.}"><xsl:value-of select="." /></a></h3>
      <h4>Episodes</h4>
      <ul>
        <xsl:for-each select="$episodes">
          <li>...</li>
        </xsl:for-each>
      </ul>
    </div>
  </xsl:if>
</xsl:template>
```

OK, so you know the program that the current <Series> element comes from and you've got the first <Program> element from that series. How can you tell whether the two programs are the same? The easiest method is through looking at a unique identifier for the program; as we saw earlier, there isn't a readily accessible unique identifier for <Program> elements, but you can use the `generate-id()` function to get the XSLT processor to make one up for you.

Thus, the test that we need to use to work out whether to create any content for the <Series> element is whether the generated `ID` for the current <Series> element's parent <Program> element is the same as the generated `ID` for the first episode as returned by the key, as follows:

```
<xsl:template match="Program/Series" mode="EpisodeList">
  <xsl:variable name="episodes" select="key('programsBySeries', .)" />
  <xsl:variable name="firstEpisode" select="$episodes[1]" />
  <xsl:if test="generate-id(..) = generate-id($firstEpisode)">
    <div>
      <h3><a name="{.}" id="{.}"><xsl:value-of select="." /></a></h3>
      <h4>Episodes</h4>
      <ul>
        <xsl:for-each select="$episodes">
          <li>...</li>
        </xsl:for-each>
      </ul>
    </div>
  </xsl:if>
</xsl:template>
```

In fact, you can do this same test within a single location path when you apply templates to the <Series> elements to begin with. You want to select only those <Series> elements whose parent <Program> element has the same generated ID as the <Program> element that's first in the list returned when you access the programsBySeries key using that particular series ID:

```
<xsl:template match="TVGuide">
  ...
  <h2>Series</h2>
  <xsl:apply-templates mode="EpisodeList"
    select="Channel/Program
              [generate-id() =
               generate-id(key('programsBySeries', Series)[1])]
              /Series">
    <xsl:sort select="." />
  </xsl:apply-templates>
</xsl:template>
```

This is more efficient because you only apply templates to those <Series> elements in which you're actually interested. It's also more flexible because the position() function will return the position of the <Series> amongst other unique series rather than amongst all programs, so it makes it easier to number the groups that you create.

If you don't know the grouping values for the groups, you can find them out by selecting those elements that are first in the group by comparing each element's ID with the ID of the first element returned for that element's group.

Try It Out – Grouping Programs by Day

In the XML document for the TV Guide, all the programs showing on a particular channel are grouped together. It would make it easier to see what was on at a particular time if the programs were grouped by the hour at which they are being shown and sorted by the precise time at which they're shown.

To achieve this presentation, we need to group the programs (the <Program> elements) according to the time at which they are shown (the 12th and 13th characters of the <Program> element's <Start> element child). A key will help us do the grouping – it needs to match the things we want to group (the <Program> elements) and use the thing we want to group by (the day on which the program is shown). The <xsl:key> element added at the top level of TVGuide10.xsl is as follows:

```
<xsl:key name="programsByHour" match="Program"
         use="substring(Start, 12, 2)" />
```

With this key setup, we can get hold of all the programs that start between 19:00 and 19:59 with:

```
key('programsByHour', '19')
```

And we can get hold of all the programs starting during the same hour as the current program with:

```
key('programsByDay', substring(Start, 12, 2))
```

Given that we want to create a listing of all the programs shown on the same day as the current program, the template that matches the `<Program>` elements should be amended so that it states the hour at which the program is being shown, and then gives the details of all the other programs that are being shown in the same hour (sorted by the time, which is again accessed by taking a substring of the `<Start>` element):

```
<xsl:template match="Program">
  <xsl:variable name="hour" select="substring(Start, 12, 2)" />
  <div class="hour">
    <h2>Showing from <xsl:value-of select="$hour" />:00</h2>
    <xsl:for-each select="key('programsByHour', $hour)">
      <xsl:sort select="substring(Start, 12, 5)" />
      <div>
        ...
        <xsl:apply-templates select="." mode="Details" />
      </div>
    </xsl:for-each>
  </div>
</xsl:template>
```

If we just applied templates to all the `<Program>` elements, then we'd get the same daily listing over and over again, one for each of the programs shown on that day. Instead, we need to pick the first program that starts during a particular hour. The first program that's listed as starting in a particular hour is the first `<Program>` returned by the `programsByHour` key for that hour, and we can compare a given `<Program>` element with this one by looking at the `ID` that's generated for each. In the template for the `<TVGuide>` element that controls what `<Program>` elements get templates applied to them, we can select these using the following expression:

```
Channel/Program
  [generate-id() = generate-id(key('programsByDay',
                                   substring(Start, 1, 10))[1])]
```

The template matching the `<TVGuide>` element should apply templates to these programs, in the order in which they start. The template should look something like the following:

```
<xsl:template match="TVGuide">
  <xsl:apply-templates
    select="Channel/Program
              [generate-id() =
               generate-id(key('programsByHour',
                               substring(Start, 12, 2))[1])]">
    <xsl:sort select="substring(Start, 12, 2)" />
  </xsl:apply-templates>
  <h2>Series</h2>
  <xsl:apply-templates select="Channel/Program/Series" mode="EpisodeList">
    <xsl:sort select="." />
  </xsl:apply-templates>
</xsl:template>
```

This grouping is realized in `TVGuide10.xsl`, and transforming `TVGuide3.xml` with `TVGuide10.xsl` results in the following page:

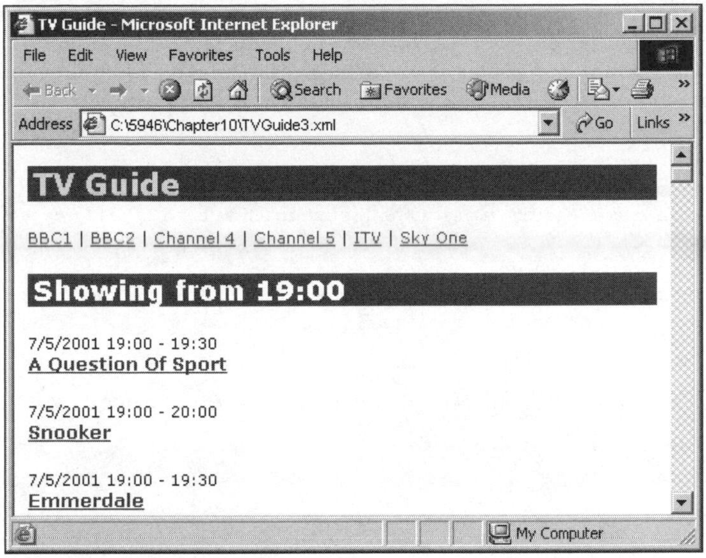

The programs are now sorted according to their start time, with headings indicating each hour.

Multi-level Grouping

The previous section showed you how to group elements by some value at a single level. You can use the same kind of technique to group elements by two things, such as grouping programs by series and channel, but to do so you need to create one key for each level of the grouping. The key for the first level of the grouping is just the same as the kind that you saw in the last section. So to group programs first by series, you need a key that collects all the `<Program>` elements together that have the same value for their child `<Series>` element:

```
<xsl:key name="programsBySeries" match="Program" use="Series" />
```

The key for the second level of the grouping needs to group by *both* the properties by which you're grouping, which is best done by concatenating the values together with some kind of unique separator (I usually use `'+'`). For example, the second-level key when grouping by series and channel needs to combine the identifier for the series (from the `<Series>` child of the `<Program>`) with an identifier for the channel (from the `<Name>` child of the `<Channel>` parent of the `<Program>`), as follows:

```
<xsl:key name="programsBySeriesAndChannel" match="Program"
         use="concat(Series, '+', ../Name)" />
```

This second-level key allows you to get hold of all the programs that have the same name and channel. For example, to get hold of all the Simpsons episodes on Sky One, you could use:

```
key('programsBySeriesAndChannel', 'Simpsons+Sky One')
```

And to get all the programs that are in the same series and on the same channel as the current program, you could use:

```
key('programsBySeriesAndChannel', concat(Series, '+', ../Name))
```

Finding the first element that belongs to the first-level group is done in the same way as when you are grouping with just a single level. For example, finding the first program in each series could be done with the following path from the <TVGuide> element:

```
Channel/Program[generate-id() =
                generate-id(key('programsBySeries', Series)[1])]
```

At the point at which you wish to do the second-level grouping, you are usually processing a particular group from the first-level grouping. For example, when you need to know what channels a particular series is shown on, you already know what series you're talking about. At this point, you can collect all the elements that are in the first-level group, and look amongst them for those that are the first to appear in the second-level group. While processing the first <Program> element in a particular series, the following path would collect the first <Program> elements that are in a particular series on a particular channel:

```
key('programsBySeries', Series)
  [generate-id() =
   generate-id(key('programsBySeriesAndChannel',
                   concat(Series, '+', ../Name))[1])]
```

You can do multi-level grouping by creating a key that matches the things you want to group and using `concat()` to create a value combining the values by which you want to group.

Try It Out – Grouping Programs by Hour and Minute

In the last Try It Out section, we created a stylesheet that grouped programs by the hour at which they started. Now we'll add a second-level group to the stylesheet, so that the programs are grouped both by the hour and the minute at which they are shown.

First, we need to add a key to the next version of our stylesheet, `TVGuide11.xsl`, which groups the programs by hour *and* minute. The key needs to match the <Program> elements just like the first-level key, but this time the key value needs to contain information about both the hour and the minute of the program. In fact, this is quite easy because the <Start> element's date/time format contains both the hour and the minute, so all we need to do is take the five characters starting from the 12th character in the string, which contain both the hour and the minute:

```
<xsl:key name="programsByHourAndMinute" match="Program"
         use="substring(Start, 12, 5)" />
```

For each second-level group, we'll add an <h3> element indicating what the minute is for each of the groups, before going on to list the programs in order. The original template for the <Program> elements, which is used on the first program starting in each hour, is the following:

```
<xsl:template match="Program">
  <xsl:variable name="hour" select="substring(Start, 12, 2)" />
  <div class="hour">
    <h2>Showing from <xsl:value-of select="$hour" />:00</h2>
    <xsl:for-each select="key('programsByHour', $hour)">
      <xsl:sort select="substring(Start, 12, 5)" />
      <div>
        ...
        <xsl:apply-templates select="." mode="Details" />
      </div>
    </xsl:for-each>
  </div>
</xsl:template>
```

Now, rather than iterating over *all* the programs that start during a particular hour, we only want to iterate over the first programs shown in each relevant minute, in order to create the heading for each second-level group. We can get hold of the first programs shown in each relevant minute within the hour with the following path:

```
key('programsByHour', $hour)[generate-id() =
                             generate-id(key('programsByHourAndMinute',
                                             substring(Start, 12, 5))[1])]
```

The template for the `<Program>` elements should therefore look like the following:

```
<xsl:template match="Program">
  <xsl:variable name="hour" select="substring(Start, 12, 2)" />
  <div class="hour">
    <h2>Showing from <xsl:value-of select="$hour" />:00</h2>
    <xsl:for-each
      select="key('programsByHour', $hour)
               [generate-id() =
                generate-id(key('programsByHourAndMinute',
                                substring(Start, 12, 5))[1])]">
      <xsl:sort select="substring(Start, 12, 5)" />
      <xsl:variable name="time" select="substring(Start, 12, 5)" />
      <div class="minute">
        <h3><xsl:value-of select="$time" /></h3>
        ...
      </div>
    </xsl:for-each>
  </div>
</xsl:template>
```

Finally, the template needs to iterate over all the programs that are being shown on the same day and hour as the `<Program>` element that's being processed within the `<xsl:for-each>`. You can use another `<xsl:for-each>` to process them (or apply templates to them directly if you prefer, using a mode), as follows:

```
<xsl:template match="Program">
  <xsl:variable name="hour" select="substring(Start, 12, 2)" />

  <div class="hour">

    <h2>Showing from <xsl:value-of select="$hour" />:00</h2>
    <xsl:for-each
      select="key('programsByHour', $hour)
                [generate-id() =
                 generate-id(key('programsByHourAndMinute',
                                 substring(Start, 12, 5))[1])]">
      <xsl:sort select="substring(Start, 12, 5)" />
      <xsl:variable name="time" select="substring(Start, 12, 5)" />
      <div class="minute">
        <h3><xsl:value-of select="$time" /></h3>
        <xsl:for-each select="key('programsByHourAndMinute', $time)">
          <div>
            ...
            <xsl:apply-templates select="." mode="Details" />
          </div>
        </xsl:for-each>
      </div>
    </xsl:for-each>
  </div>

</xsl:template>
```

The result of applying this stylesheet, TVGuide11.xsl, to TVGuide3.xml is shown in the following screenshot:

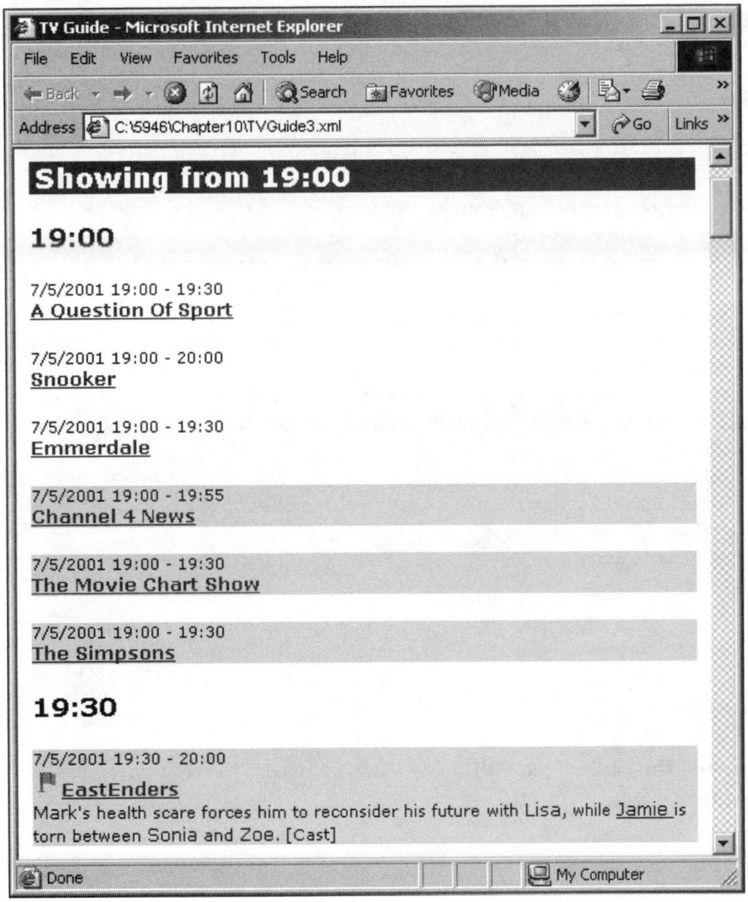

The programs are grouped on two levels – first by the hour during which they are shown, and then by the minute within that hour at which they are shown. You don't get a minute-by-minute report, though; rather, a heading shows the time only if a program actually starts at that time.

Summary

In this chapter, we started off by looking at the ways in which you could search for elements from an XML document that have particular values for their attributes or child elements. While you can use predicates to search for practically anything within an XML document, they can be very inefficient, particularly if you perform the same type of search several times.

To help with this efficiency problem, XPath and XSLT offer two techniques that tell the XSLT processor to index elements within an XML document so that they can be accessed quickly by some value. The first technique is to use `ID` attributes and the `id()` function, but this has several disadvantages such as forcing the identifier to be held within an attribute, constraining the format of the identifier, and allowing only one-to-one mappings between identifiers and elements.

The second technique gets round these problems by giving you full flexibility in the way in which elements, or other nodes, are indexed. With a key, you can state that particular elements should be accessible quickly by key values; these values can be in any format and can come from anywhere. Keys also have the advantage of not making the stylesheet dependent on a DTD being specified for the source XML document, which means that you can rely on the stylesheet having access to the elements through the key in a way that you can't with an ID.

Keys also support many-to-many mappings where the same key value can be used to access many elements and the same element can be accessed with many key values. This facility makes keys very useful for accessing groups of elements having the same value. So, apart from learning how to use keys to get hold of elements with particular identifiers, you also learned in this chapter how to use keys to group elements and how to work out which elements are the first to occur in a document with a particular value.

Review Questions

1. What is the advantage of using `ID` attributes and the `id()` function over using predicates to search for elements?

2. What format can the values of `ID` attributes take?

3. Create an `ATTLIST` declaration to make the required `custNo` attribute of the `<Customer>` element an `ID` attribute.

4. What three types of arguments can the `id()` function take and what does it return from each?

5. What advantages are there for using keys rather than IDs?

6. In what situations might you use the keys defined as follows?

```
<xsl:key name="films" match="Film" use="@id" />
<xsl:key name="filmsByCharacters" match="Film"
         use="CastList/CastMember/Character/Name" />
<xsl:key name="filmsByYear" match="Film" use="Year" />
<xsl:key name="filmsByDirector" match="Film" use="Director/Name" />
<xsl:key name="filmsByYearAndDirector" match="Film"
         use="concat(Year, '::', Director/Name)" />
```

7. Construct a stylesheet that groups `<Film>` elements by their `<Year>` children and by their `rating` attributes.

Beginning
XSLT

11

Named Templates and Recursion

In earlier chapters, you've seen how to use XSLT to iterate over a set of nodes, either using `<xsl:for-each>`, where the instructions on what to do with each node are embedded within the template, or using `<xsl:apply-templates>`, where the instructions are held in a separate block. However, you can't use either of these methods to iterate unless you have a node set that contains the number of nodes you need, for example, to iterate a certain number of times or to process a string by working through it a character at a time.

Most programming languages, such as the scripting languages that you might be familiar with, supply constructs like `for` and `while` loops for iteration. Similarly, in **procedural** programming languages, a variable is initialized and updated to keep track of what iteration the loop is on. XSLT, however, is a **functional** programming language, which means that the same instruction in the same context will always produce the same thing, no matter how many times it's run. So XSLT doesn't have `for` or `while` loops because a variable's value can't change (if it did, the number of times you assigned a new value to a variable would determine what value the variable took).

Therefore, when you're programming with XSLT, you need to use **recursion** to give the same effect as you would get from `for` or `while` loops in procedural languages. In this chapter, you'll learn how to construct recursive templates to carry out common tasks. You'll also learn about **named templates**, which are blocks of code that you can call by name as opposed to templates that apply to specific nodes.

In this chapter, you'll learn:

- How to create and call a named template
- The principles of recursion
- How to write a recursive template
- Recursing with numbers, strings, and nodes
- How to repeat the same thing a number of times
- How to search and replace strings
- How to find maximum or minimum values

Named Templates

Thus far, the templates that you've been writing have all matched a particular node and done something with it. Some of these templates have been moded templates, which enable you to get a different result from the same node, and some of them have used parameters to pass in extra information about how the node should be processed. These templates are the main component of your stylesheets because the main goal of XSLT is to process nodes from a source node tree.

Splitting up your stylesheet into templates actually helps you in two ways. Firstly, it allows you to use the processor's node-matching capabilities to work out what piece of code to use to process a particular node, which is particularly useful when you're processing document-oriented XML or XML whose structure might evolve over time. Secondly, it enables you to break up a stylesheet into reusable portions, which cuts down on the length of the stylesheet (because you don't have to repeat the same code in different places) and makes it easier to author and maintain (because it helps you focus on a particular bit of code at a time). We've used both these aspects of templates in previous chapters, taking advantage of the latter feature when we apply templates to a node in a particular mode to process that node in a particular way.

However, some pieces of processing aren't dependant on what node you're processing, or might need to be carried out when there is no node available on which to hang the process. For example, say that we wanted to provide different images according to the value of the `flag` attribute on the `<Program>` element. We can use a template that matched the `flag` attribute to provide the image, as follows:

```
<xsl:template match="@flag">
  <xsl:variable name="image">
    <xsl:choose>
      <xsl:when test=". = 'favorite'">favorite</xsl:when>
      <xsl:when test=". = 'interesting'">interest</xsl:when>
    </xsl:choose>
  </xsl:variable>
  <xsl:variable name="alt">
    <xsl:choose>
      <xsl:when test=". = 'favorite'">Favorite</xsl:when>
      <xsl:when test=". = 'interesting'">Interest</xsl:when>
    </xsl:choose>
  </xsl:variable>
  <img src="{$image}.gif" alt="[{$alt}]" width="20" height="20" />
</xsl:template>
```

But say that we want to provide a spacer image if the `flag` attribute is missing. However, there's no `flag` attribute node to match on in this case, so the code has to be embedded in the template for the `<Program>` element instead:

```
<xsl:template match="Program" mode="Details">
  ...
  <xsl:variable name="image">
    <xsl:choose>
      <xsl:when test="@flag = 'favorite'">favorite</xsl:when>
      <xsl:when test="@flag = 'interesting'">interest</xsl:when>
      <xsl:otherwise>spacer</xsl:otherwise>
```

```
      </xsl:choose>
    </xsl:variable>
    <xsl:variable name="alt">
      <xsl:choose>
        <xsl:when test="@flag = 'favorite'">Favorite</xsl:when>
        <xsl:when test="@flag = 'interesting'">Interest</xsl:when>
        <xsl:otherwise><xsl:text>  </xsl:text></xsl:otherwise>
      </xsl:choose>
    </xsl:variable>
    <img src="{$image}.gif" alt="[{$alt}]" width="20" height="20" />
    ...
  </xsl:template>
```

While there's nothing wrong with that in terms of the functionality of the code, it does add 15 lines to the `<Program>` element, rather than one line applying the template to the `flag` attribute, and these 15 lines would have to be repeated if the same code were required elsewhere.

What's required in such situations is a way to create a template and call it without applying templates to a particular node. You can do this in XSLT using **named templates**. Every template can be assigned a name with its `name` attribute (including those templates that are already matching templates). Each must have its own distinct name, though it can be the same as the name of a mode. Named templates can take parameters, just like any other template, and indeed since they have no other source of information about what they're supposed to do, it's a rare named template that doesn't have any. In this example, a template named `image` could take a `$flag` parameter, as follows:

```
<xsl:template name="image">
  <xsl:param name="flag" />
  <xsl:variable name="image">
    <xsl:choose>
      <xsl:when test="$flag = 'favorite'">favorite</xsl:when>
      <xsl:when test="$flag = 'interesting'">interest</xsl:when>
      <xsl:otherwise>spacer</xsl:otherwise>
    </xsl:choose>
  </xsl:variable>
  <xsl:variable name="alt">
    <xsl:choose>
      <xsl:when test="$flag = 'favorite'">Favorite</xsl:when>
      <xsl:when test="$flag = 'interesting'">Interest</xsl:when>
      <xsl:otherwise><xsl:text>  </xsl:text></xsl:otherwise>
    </xsl:choose>
  </xsl:variable>
  <img src="{$image}.gif" alt="[{$alt}]" width="20" height="20" />
</xsl:template>
```

You can invoke named templates by calling them with `<xsl:call-template>`. The `<xsl:call-template>` instruction takes a `name` attribute that names the called template. Like `<xsl:apply-templates>`, `<xsl:call-template>` can contain `<xsl:with-param>` elements in order to pass in values for the parameters of the template that it calls.

The current node within a called template is the same as the current node at the point where the template is called. I think that it's bad practice to use the current node within a named template (for example, by using relative location paths), because you have no way of knowing what kind of node it might be. If the current node is important, I use a matching template (which might also be named).

So in the template for the <Program> element, you need an <xsl:call-template> instruction calling the image template. The $flag parameter is assigned the value of the flag attribute of the <Program> element, as follows:

```
<xsl:template match="Program" mode="Details">
  ...
  <xsl:call-template name="image">
    <xsl:with-param name="flag" select="@flag" />
  </xsl:call-template>
  ...
</xsl:template>
```

Named templates are a lot like functions in other programming languages – you call them by name, often passing arguments (parameters) to them, and they return a result. In the case of templates, though, all the results are result tree fragments (though they can be minimal result tree fragments, containing a single text node holding a string or number).

> **Named templates are useful when you want to reuse code that doesn't use the current node. A template is given a name with the <xsl:template> element's name attribute. You can call a named template, with parameters if necessary, using the <xsl:call-template> instruction.**

Try It Out – Creating Links with a Named Template

There are several places within our stylesheet where we need to create a link from a string to a URL. To make the user experience more enthralling, all the <a> elements need to include attributes to change the style of links when you hover over the link with a mouse. The attributes are stored in a linkEvents attribute set which needs to be included on each of the <a> elements that creates a link. The linkEvents attribute set is as follows:

```
<xsl:attribute-set name="linkEvents">
  <xsl:attribute name="style">
    <xsl:text>color: black; border-bottom: 1pt groove #CCC</xsl:text>
  </xsl:attribute>
  <xsl:attribute name="onmouseover">
    <xsl:text>javascript:this.style.background = '#CCC';</xsl:text>
  </xsl:attribute>
  <xsl:attribute name="onmouseout">
    <xsl:text>javascript:this.style.background = 'transparent';</xsl:text>
  </xsl:attribute>
</xsl:attribute-set>
```

Most of the links are generated around the content of nodes, but on occasion the linked text and the URL being linked to can also be partial values or newly-generated text. The links are generated in several templates, for example:

```
<xsl:template match="Channel" mode="ChannelList">
  <a xsl:use-attribute-sets="linkEvents" href="#{Name}">
    <xsl:value-of select="Name" />
  </a>
  <xsl:if test="position() != last()"> | </xsl:if>
</xsl:template>

<xsl:template match="TVGuide/Series">
  <div>
    <h3><a name="{@id}" id="{@id}"><xsl:value-of select="Title" /></a></h3>
    <p>
      <xsl:apply-templates select="Description" />
    </p>
    <h4>Episodes</h4>
    <ul>
      <xsl:for-each select="key('programsBySeries', @id)">
        <li>
          <a xsl:use-attribute-sets="linkEvents" href="#{generate-id()}">
            <xsl:value-of select="parent::Channel/Name" />
            <xsl:text> at </xsl:text>
            <xsl:value-of select="Start" />
            <xsl:if test="string(Title)">
              <xsl:text>: </xsl:text>
              <xsl:value-of select="Title" />
            </xsl:if>
          </a>
        </li>
      </xsl:for-each>
    </ul>
  </div>
</xsl:template>

<xsl:template match="Program" mode="Title">
  <span class="title">
    <xsl:choose>
      <xsl:when test="string(Series)">
        <a xsl:use-attribute-sets="linkEvents" href="#{Series}">
          <xsl:value-of select="key('IDs', Series)/Title" />
        </a>
        <xsl:if test="string(Title)">
          <xsl:text> - </xsl:text>
          <span class="subtitle"><xsl:value-of select="Title" /></span>
        </xsl:if>
      </xsl:when>
      <xsl:otherwise>
        <xsl:value-of select="Title" />
      </xsl:otherwise>
    </xsl:choose>
  </span>
```

```
</xsl:template>

<xsl:template match="Description//Link">
  <a xsl:use-attribute-sets="linkEvents" href="{@href}">
    <xsl:apply-templates />
  </a>
</xsl:template>
```

The result of transforming `TVGuide.xml` with `TVGuide2.xsl`, which contains this code, is a page on which the links are underlined and where, when you hover over a link with the mouse, the link background turns gray. For example, in the following screenshot the mouse is hovering over the link to BBC2 at the top of the page:

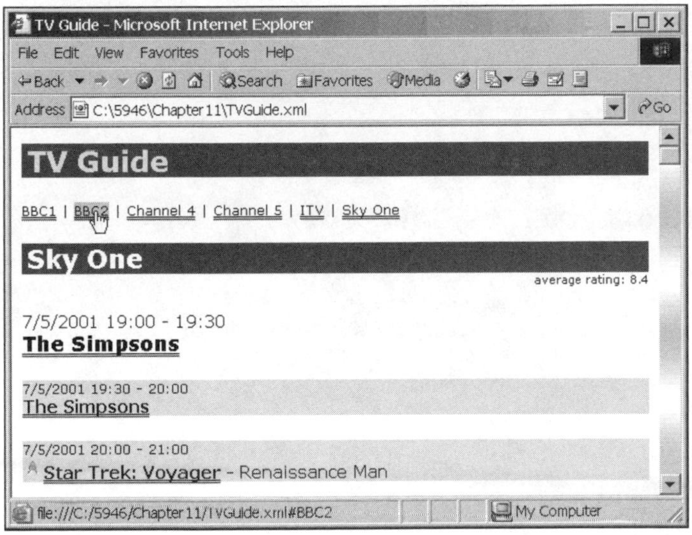

In `TVGuide2.xsl`, roughly the same code is used in multiple different templates to create the same kind of link. In fact, the only things that vary in each place are the URL to which the link is made and the content of the <a> element. However, if you changed your mind about the name of the attribute set, for example, or wanted to add a new set to the <a> elements, then you would have to search through the stylesheet to find each instance and change it.

To make it more maintainable, you can put the link-generating code into a named template that you call on demand. In `TVGuide3.xsl`, the `link` template takes a URL to link to and a value for the content of the <a> element, and creates the required <a> element:

```
<xsl:template name="link">
  <xsl:param name="href" />
  <xsl:param name="content" />
  <a href="{$href}" xsl:use-attribute-sets="linkEvents">
    <xsl:copy-of select="$content" />
  </a>
</xsl:template>
```

The templates that create the <a> elements then need to be changed so that they call this template instead:

```
<xsl:template match="Channel" mode="ChannelList">
  <xsl:call-template name="link">
    <xsl:with-param name="href" select="concat('#', Name)" />
    <xsl:with-param name="content" select="string(Name)" />
  </xsl:call-template>
  <xsl:if test="position() != last()"> | </xsl:if>
</xsl:template>

<xsl:template match="TVGuide/Series">
  <div>
    <h3><a name="{@id}" id="{@id}"><xsl:value-of select="Title" /></a></h3>
    <p>
      <xsl:apply-templates select="Description" />
    </p>
    <h4>Episodes</h4>
    <ul>
      <xsl:for-each select="key('programsBySeries', @id)">
        <li>
          <xsl:call-template name="link">
            <xsl:with-param name="href"
                            select="concat('#', generate-id())" />
            <xsl:with-param name="content">
              <xsl:value-of select="parent::Channel/Name" />
              <xsl:text> at </xsl:text>
              <xsl:value-of select="Start" />
              <xsl:if test="string(Title)">
                <xsl:text>: </xsl:text>
                <xsl:value-of select="Title" />
              </xsl:if>
            </xsl:with-param>
          </xsl:call-template>
        </li>
      </xsl:for-each>
    </ul>
  </div>
</xsl:template>

<xsl:template match="Program" mode="Title">
  <span class="title">
    <xsl:choose>
      <xsl:when test="string(Series)">
        <xsl:call-template name="link">
          <xsl:with-param name="href" select="concat('#', Series)" />
          <xsl:with-param name="content"
                          select="string(key('IDs', Series)/Title)" />
        </xsl:call-template>
        <xsl:if test="string(Title)">
          <xsl:text> - </xsl:text>
          <span class="subtitle"><xsl:value-of select="Title" /></span>
        </xsl:if>
      </xsl:when>
```

```
        <xsl:otherwise>
          <xsl:value-of select="Title" />
        </xsl:otherwise>
      </xsl:choose>
    </span>
  </xsl:template>

  <xsl:template match="Description//Link">
    <xsl:call-template name="link">
      <xsl:with-param name="href" select="@href" />
      <xsl:with-param name="content">
        <xsl:apply-templates />
      </xsl:with-param>
    </xsl:call-template>
  </xsl:template>
```

The result of `TVGuide3.xsl`, which uses the link template, is exactly the same as `TVGuide2.xsl`. Using the named template has unified the way in which links are created throughout the stylesheet, which makes it easier to target changes that need to be made to all the links that get created.

Recursion

When we looked at variables and parameters in Chapter 6, we noted that variables are not available outside their scope, which means that you can't change a variable's value. We looked at how that meant you couldn't use iteration to do things like counting how many nodes there are in a node set. In procedural programming languages, you'd count the nodes in a node set by iterating over those nodes, and keeping a running total in a variable. But because you can't update a variable in XSLT, you can't use iteration.

There are lots of places that you use iteration in procedural programming languages. You use iteration for summing values, for processing strings and numbers, and for doing the same thing a fixed number of times. In XSLT, some of those tasks are supported with purpose-built functions such as `count()` and `sum()`. But in general, rather than using iteration to solve the problem, you have to use **recursion** instead.

> **Because variables can't vary in XSLT, you need to use recursion rather than iteration to do most processing.**

In this section, we're going to look at how to do recursion in XSLT to solve some of the common problems encountered when transforming XML documents. We'll start off with a general description of recursion, and then look at specific types of recursion for processing values of different types.

Recursive Principles

Recursion is a pattern in which a labeled block of code calls itself with different starting conditions. In XSLT, that means having a named template that calls itself with different values for its parameters. These templates are known as **recursive templates**.

The result of a recursive template is some combination of (usually just part of) the values that have been passed through its parameters and the result of calling itself with different values in the parameters. The values passed for these parameters are usually based on the initial parameter value in some way, for example, a substring or the result of subtracting one from the initial parameter value.

Of course, if the template keeps calling itself, and the result of that call is another call to the same template, and so on, the process keeps going forever. This is known as **infinite recursion**, and is something to be avoided! To prevent infinite recursion, the template also has to test whether it's time to stop the recursion, and it should only call itself under certain conditions. The condition that tests when it's time to stop recursing is known as the **stopping condition**, and it involves testing the parameters, usually to see whether they're empty strings or zero or something along those lines. Recursive templates generally use either `<xsl:if>`, as follows:

```
<xsl:template name="templateName">
  <xsl:param name="paramName" select="defaultValue" />
  ...
  <xsl:if test="condition">
    ...
    <xsl:call-template name="templateName">
      <xsl:with-param name="paramName" select="differentValue" />
    </xsl:call-template>
    ...
  </xsl:if>
</xsl:template>
```

or `<xsl:choose>`, as follows:

```
<xsl:template name="templateName">
  <xsl:param name="paramName" select="defaultValue" />
  ...
  <xsl:choose
    <xsl:when test="condition">
      ...
    </xsl:when>
    <xsl:otherwise>
      ...
      <xsl:call-template name="templateName">
        <xsl:with-param name="paramName" select="differentValue" />
      </xsl:call-template>
      ...
    </xsl:otherwise>
  </xsl:choose>
</xsl:template>
```

A recursive template is a named template that calls itself.

Recursing with Numbers

The first type of recursion we'll look at in detail is recursion over a set of numbers. It is useful when you want to generate numeric sequences or when you want to repeat a process a certain number of times. The main parameter for such a template is a counter, which might be set when the template is called (for example, to count down from a certain value) or initialized to a default value.

Within a numeric recursive template, recursion stops when the parameter has reached a certain minimum or maximum value (which itself is sometimes passed as a parameter). The new value for the parameter is based on some numeric manipulation of the counter, such as adding or subtracting a number, dividing the number, or getting the remainder after division.

Repeating

The most common kinds of recursive templates that use numbers are those that repeat exactly the same code multiple times. These templates need a single parameter: a counter that specifies how many times the code needs to be repeated. The template only calls itself if this counter is more than `0`. When the template calls itself, the counter is decreased by one. The general structure for these templates is:

```
<xsl:template name="repeatingTemplate">
  <xsl:param name="repetitions" select="1" />
  <xsl:if test="$repetitions > 0">
    ...
    <xsl:call-template name="repeatingTemplate">
      <xsl:with-param name="repetitions" select="$repetitions - 1" />
    </xsl:call-template>
  </xsl:if>
</xsl:template>
```

If you call this template without explicitly giving a value for the `$repetitions` parameter, then it will only run once, as that's the default value specified in the parameter definition. You can use default values for parameters to give default behavior for the template.

One variation on this template is to pass in strings or result tree fragments to be copied by the template, for example, to create padding of a particular length from a particular character. The following template, given in `pad.xsl`, will repeatedly copy the character you pass as the `$char` parameter, as many times as you tell it to with the `$length` parameter, so that you get a string of `$char` characters, `$length` characters long. You might use it to create indents when creating text output, for example, or to create a string of `0`s that you can use to pad numbers when you use the `format-number()` function. If you don't specify the character that you want, it creates a string that contains spaces:

```
<xsl:template name="pad">
  <xsl:param name="length" select="1" />
  <xsl:param name="char" select="' '" />
  <xsl:if test="$length > 0">
    <xsl:value-of select="$char" />
    <xsl:call-template name="pad">
      <xsl:with-param name="length" select="$length - 1" />
      <xsl:with-param name="char" select="$char" />
    </xsl:call-template>
```

```
  </xsl:if>
</xsl:template>
```

For example, the following call produces a string containing ten `*` characters:

```
<xsl:call-template name="pad">
  <xsl:with-param name="length" select="10" />
  <xsl:with-param name="char" select="'*'" />
</xsl:call-template>
```

You'll also see this template in action later in this chapter, when we look at working out the square root of a number.

Another variation is to subtract more than one from the counter each time, or to vary the amount that is subtracted from the counter based on a feature of the number. For example, the following template would create a "tens" image for every 10 in the passed percentage, and a "ones" image for every 1 in the passed percentage:

```
<xsl:template name="graphPercentage">
  <xsl:param name="percentage" select="0" />
  <xsl:choose>
    <xsl:when test="$percentage >= 10">
      <img src="ten.gif" alt="**********" width="10" height="10" />
      <xsl:call-template name="graphPercentage">
        <xsl:with-param name="percentage" select="$percentage - 10" />
      </xsl:call-template>
    </xsl:when>
    <xsl:when test="$percentage >= 1">
      <img src="one.gif" alt="*" width="1" height="10" />
      <xsl:call-template name="graphPercentage">
        <xsl:with-param name="percentage" select="$percentage - 1" />
      </xsl:call-template>
    </xsl:when>
  </xsl:choose>
</xsl:template>
```

This template should get called with a numeric value as the value of the `$percentage` parameter. If this value is greater than 10, the `graphPercentage` template creates an `<img>` element for the `ten.gif` image, then calls itself with a new value, ten less than the first. It keeps doing this until the remainder is less than 10; at that point it starts generating `<img>` elements for the `one.gif` image, calling itself with a value one less than the one it has been called with, until there's nothing left.

The `graphPercentage.xsl` stylesheet uses this template to create a graph from a set of values. The source document, `graphPercentage.xml` looks like the following:

```
<values>
  <value>52</value>
  <value>13</value>
  <value>74</value>
  <value>38</value>
</values>
```

Within the `graphPercentage.xsl` stylesheet, the template that matches the `<value>` elements calls the `graphPercentage` template to generate a graphic for the value, as follows:

```
<xsl:template match="value">
  <xsl:value-of select="." />
  <xsl:text>: </xsl:text>
  <xsl:call-template name="graphPercentage">
    <xsl:with-param name="percentage" select="." />
  </xsl:call-template>
  <br />
</xsl:template>
```

The result of using `graphPercentage.xsl` with `graphPercentage.xml` is the following:

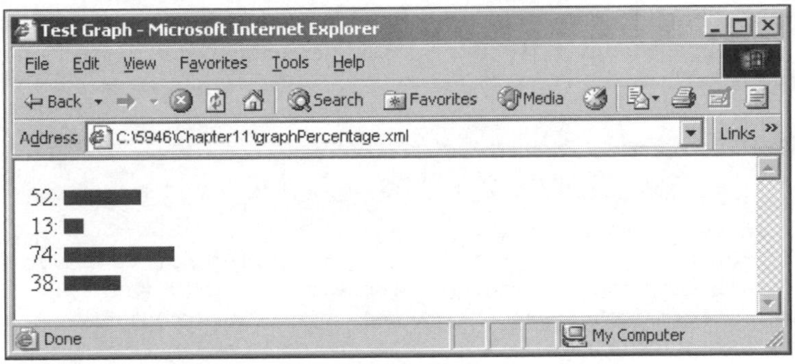

If you look at the source of the resulting HTML, you'll see that the following `<img>` elements are created for the first `<value>` element:

```
<img src="ten.gif" alt="**********" width="10" height="10">
<img src="ten.gif" alt="**********" width="10" height="10">
<img src="ten.gif" alt="**********" width="10" height="10">
<img src="ten.gif" alt="**********" width="10" height="10">
<img src="ten.gif" alt="**********" width="10" height="10">
<img src="one.gif" alt="*" width="1" height="10">
<img src="one.gif" alt="*" width="1" height="10">
```

You can repeat the same content multiple times with a recursive template that decrements a counter by one on each recursion.

Try It Out – Repeating Images to Display Ratings

In the TV Guide, each program is given a rating through its `rating` attribute, which can be any integer from 1 to 10. Rather than displaying this rating as a number, we'll show a number of stars equal to the rating. To do this, we need a repeating template that generates an image on each recursion.

We'll name the template generateStars and use a parameter called $rating to keep track of how many stars the template should produce. To make it easier to call, we'll also make this template match <Program> elements in generateStars mode, and initialize the $rating parameter to the value of the rating attribute.

The body of the template follows the pattern shown above, but includes the code for generating the image:

```
<xsl:template match="Program" mode="generateStars" name="generateStars">
  <xsl:param name="rating" select="@rating" />
  <xsl:if test="$rating > 0">
    <img src="star.gif" alt="*" height="15" width="15" />
    <xsl:call-template name="generateStars">
      <xsl:with-param name="rating" select="$rating - 1" />
    </xsl:call-template>
  </xsl:if>
</xsl:template>
```

In the template for the <Program> element in Details mode, we can then generate the stars by applying templates to the current <Program> element in generateStars mode, as follows:

```
<xsl:template match="Program" mode="Details">
  <xsl:variable name="programID" select="concat(generate-id(), 'Cast')" />
  <p>
    <a name="{generate-id()}" id="{generate-id()}">
      <xsl:apply-templates select="Start" />
    </a>
    <br />
    <xsl:apply-templates select="." mode="generateStars" />
    <br />
    <xsl:apply-templates select="@flag" />
    ...
  </p>
  ...
</xsl:template>
```

These changes are made in TVGuide4.xsl. When you use TVGuide4.xsl to transform TVGuide.xml, you should see the following result:

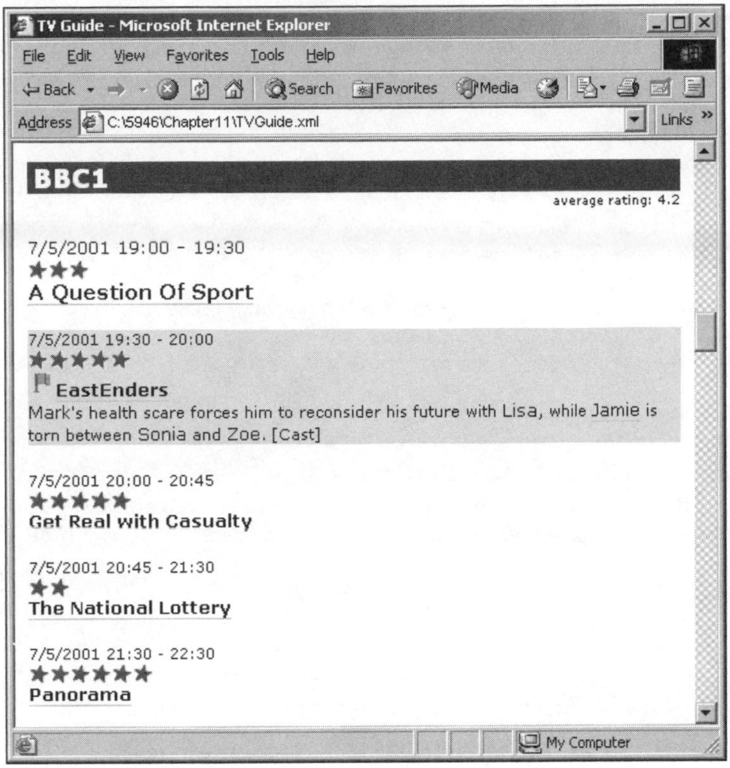

When the details of each program are displayed, the `generateStars` template is called, with the `$rating` parameter set to the value of the `rating` attribute on the `<Program>` element. As long as the `$rating` parameter is one or more, the `generateStars` template creates an `<img>` element for a star, and then calls itself to create a number of stars equal to the `$rating` parameter minus one. For A Question of Sport, which has a rating of 3, the template gets called once with a `$rating` parameter equal to 3, then with `$rating` equal to 2, then with `$rating` equal to 1, and finally with `$rating` equal to 0. The last call doesn't generate a star – it's at that point that the recursion stops.

Numbering

You've already seen how to create numbers for elements or attributes in Chapter 9, using `<xsl:number>` to number nodes according to their position within the source tree and the `position()` function to number them according to the order in which they're processed by the stylesheet. If you need to number nodes, then you should use these techniques to do so.

However, sometimes you need to create numbers that aren't based on the existence of nodes, but are simply sequences that you want to display. To do this, you need a template that keeps track of the number that you're currently on and the maximum number that you want to repeat until. The recursive call adds one to the counter, while the maximum remains the same. The value of the counter is used to generate the number that's displayed. The basic form of these templates is:

```
<xsl:template name="numberingTemplate">
  <xsl:param name="number" select="1" />
  <xsl:param name="maximum" select="1" />
  ...
  <xsl:if test="$number &lt; $maximum">
    <xsl:call-template name="numberingTemplate">
      <xsl:with-param name="number" select="$number + 1" />
      <xsl:with-param name="maximum" select="$maximum" />
    </xsl:call-template>
  </xsl:if>
</xsl:template>
```

You'll usually have to format the number in some way, using either the formatting features of `<xsl:number>` or the `format-number()` function, before you output it.

> **You can create numbers by having two parameters, one that stores the current number and one that stores the maximum the number can reach. The number is incremented on each recursion.**

Try It Out – Numbering Using Recursion

One use for numbering stylesheets is in generating a timeline. Here, we'll try adding a summary table at the top of the page, with columns indicating the time and rows indicating channels. The table goes before the main listings of the channels (and the programs showing on those channels) and the series and episode listings at the bottom of the page, so it's generated in the template for the `<TVGuide>` element:

```
<xsl:template match="TVGuide">
  <table>
    ...
  </table>
  ...
</xsl:template>
```

The first row holds a title for the column holding the channel name, and then times showing every half hour during the day. To get the layout working properly, so that programs can start at times other than on the half hour, each five minute timespan is represented by one column width, so the timeline columns each take up six column widths:

```
<tr>
  <th colspan="6">Channel</th>
  <th colspan="6">19:00</th><th colspan="6">19:30</th>
  <th colspan="6">20:00</th><th colspan="6">20:30</th>
  <th colspan="6">21:00</th><th colspan="6">21:30</th>
  <th colspan="6">22:00</th>
</tr>
```

To generate this timeline, we need to use a recursive template that generates the <th> elements. The recursion needs to keep track of and update two numbers – the hours and the minutes – with hours increasing from 0 to 23 and minutes oscillating between 0 and 30. The template needs to stop when the hours value is 23 and the minutes value is 30. The template is as follows:

```
<xsl:template name="generateTimeline">
  <xsl:param name="startHours" select="0" />
  <xsl:param name="startMinutes" select="0" />
  <xsl:param name="endHours" select="23" />
  <xsl:param name="endMinutes" select="30" />

  <th colspan="6">
    <xsl:value-of select="format-number($startHours, '00')" />
    <xsl:text>:</xsl:text>
    <xsl:value-of select="format-number($startMinutes, '00')" />
  </th>

  <xsl:if test="$startHours &lt; $endHours or
                $startMinutes != $endMinutes">
    <xsl:call-template name="generateTimeline">
      <xsl:with-param name="startHours">
        <xsl:choose>
          <xsl:when test="$startMinutes = 0">
            <xsl:value-of select="$startHours" />
          </xsl:when>
          <xsl:otherwise>
            <xsl:value-of select="$startHours + 1" />
          </xsl:otherwise>
        </xsl:choose>
      </xsl:with-param>
      <xsl:with-param name="startMinutes">
        <xsl:choose>
          <xsl:when test="$startMinutes = 0">30</xsl:when>
          <xsl:otherwise>0</xsl:otherwise>
        </xsl:choose>
      </xsl:with-param>
      <xsl:with-param name="endHours" select="$endHours" />
      <xsl:with-param name="endMinutes" select="$endMinutes" />
    </xsl:call-template>
  </xsl:if>
</xsl:template>
```

Our timeline is going from 19:00 to 22:30, so in the call to the `generateTimeline` template, we need `$startHours` to be 19 and `$endHours` to be 22. `$startMinutes` and `$endMinutes` are the same as the default values in the `generateTimeline` template, but we'll include them in the call in any case, to make things clearer:

```
<xsl:template match="TVGuide">
  <table>
    <tr>
      <th colspan="6">Channel</th>
      <xsl:call-template name="generateTimeline">
```

```
        <xsl:with-param name="startHours" select="19" />
        <xsl:with-param name="startMinutes" select="00" />
        <xsl:with-param name="endHours" select="22" />
        <xsl:with-param name="endMinutes" select="30" />
      </xsl:call-template>
    </tr>
    ...
  </table>
  ...
</xsl:template>
```

We'll generate the remaining rows in the table by applying templates to the `<Channel>` elements in `Table` mode:

```
<xsl:template match="TVGuide">
  <table>
    <tr>
      <th colspan="6">Channel</th>
      <xsl:call-template name="generateTimeline">
        <xsl:with-param name="startHours" select="19" />
        <xsl:with-param name="startMinutes" select="00" />
        <xsl:with-param name="endHours" select="22" />
        <xsl:with-param name="endMinutes" select="30" />
      </xsl:call-template>
    </tr>
    <xsl:apply-templates select="Channel" mode="Table" />
  </table>
  ...
</xsl:template>
```

The template for the `<Channel>` element in `Table` mode creates a row in which the first cell is the name of the channel and the rest of the cells are generated by applying templates to the `<Program>` elements held within the `<Channel>` (as usual we'll assume that the `<Program>` elements are in the correct order; we're also assuming here that the first program on each channel starts at 19:00):

```
<xsl:template match="Channel" mode="Table">
  <tr>
    <th colspan="6"><xsl:value-of select="Name" /></th>
    <xsl:apply-templates select="Program" mode="Table" />
  </tr>
</xsl:template>
```

The template for the `<Program>` elements in `Table` mode needs to create a cell that spans a certain width. The width depends on the duration of the program – it needs to be the duration of the program in minutes divided by 5 (and rounded to the nearest integer, although usually programs are a multiple of 5 minutes long). We created some XSLT for working out the duration of a program in Chapter 6. Here, we want to reuse that code, so we'll create a named template that parses a duration in the format PT*n*H*m*M to give you a number of minutes:

```
<xsl:template name="durationMins">
  <xsl:param name="duration" select="'PT0H0M'" />
  <xsl:variable name="d"
              select="substring(normalize-space($duration), 3)" />
  <xsl:variable name="durationHours">
    <xsl:choose>
      <xsl:when test="contains($d, 'H')">
        <xsl:value-of select="substring-before($d, 'H')" />
      </xsl:when>
      <xsl:otherwise>0</xsl:otherwise>
    </xsl:choose>
  </xsl:variable>
  <xsl:variable name="durationMinutes">
    <xsl:choose>
      <xsl:when test="contains($d, 'M')">
        <xsl:choose>
          <xsl:when test="contains($d, 'H')">
            <xsl:value-of select="substring-before(
                                  substring-after($d, 'H'), 'M')" />
          </xsl:when>
          <xsl:otherwise>
            <xsl:value-of select="substring-before($d, 'M')" />
          </xsl:otherwise>
        </xsl:choose>
      </xsl:when>
      <xsl:otherwise>0</xsl:otherwise>
    </xsl:choose>
  </xsl:variable>
  <xsl:value-of select="($durationHours * 60) + $durationMinutes" />
</xsl:template>
```

We can call this template both from the template matching a program's `<Start>` element (where the code originally comes from) and from our new template matching `<Program>` elements in `Table` mode. In the latter template, the resulting duration in minutes is divided by 5 and rounded to the nearest integer using the `round()` function, to give the column span for the cell. Applying templates to the `<Program>` element in `TableTitle` mode generates the content of the cell:

```
<xsl:template match="Program" mode="Table">
  <td>
    <xsl:attribute name="colspan">
      <xsl:variable name="durationMins">
        <xsl:call-template name="durationMins">
          <xsl:with-param name="duration" select="Duration" />
        </xsl:call-template>
      </xsl:variable>
      <xsl:value-of select="round($durationMins div 5)" />
    </xsl:attribute>
    <xsl:apply-templates select="." mode="TableTitle" />
  </td>
</xsl:template>
```

The template that matches the <Program> elements in TableTitle mode is very similar to the template that matches them in Title mode, except this time the entire series name and episode title is linked to the detailed description of the program further down the page. The linking is done via the link template that we created earlier, so the <a> element and all the special attributes are created automatically:

```
<xsl:template match="Program" mode="TableTitle">
  <xsl:call-template name="link">
    <xsl:with-param name="href" select="concat('#', generate-id())" />
    <xsl:with-param name="content">
      <span class="title">
        <xsl:choose>
          <xsl:when test="string(Series)">
            <xsl:value-of select="key('IDs', Series)/Title" />
            <xsl:if test="string(Title)">
              <xsl:text> - </xsl:text>
              <span class="subtitle"><xsl:value-of select="Title" /></span>
            </xsl:if>
          </xsl:when>
          <xsl:otherwise>
            <xsl:value-of select="Title" />
          </xsl:otherwise>
        </xsl:choose>
      </span>
    </xsl:with-param>
  </xsl:call-template>
</xsl:template>
```

That's it for the XSLT code, but we do need to update the CSS stylesheet to make this table look pretty. The most important thing is to use a fixed table layout, so that all the columns are forced to be the same width; the other things just make it look pleasant:

```
table {
  table-layout: fixed;
  font-size: 1em;
  margin-bottom: 2em;
}
td, th {
  text-align: left;
  vertical-align: top;
  border-left: 1pt solid #C00;
  border-top: 1pt solid black;
  padding: 0.1em;
}
td .title {
  font-size: 1em;
  font-weight: normal;
}
td .subtitle {
  font-style: italic;
}
```

With all these changes made, in `TVGuide5.xsl` and `TVGuide2.css`, we're ready to look at the resulting table. The result of transforming `TVGuide.xml` with `TVGuide5.xsl` is as follows:

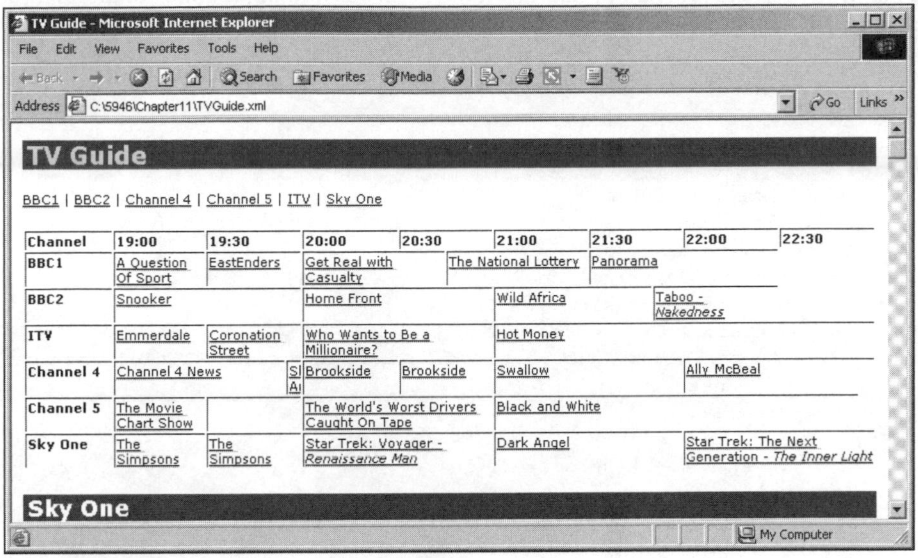

You've used named templates a lot to create this table – for calculating the column span for each of the programs, and for generating the link from the program's name to the program's details further down the page. The most important use, though, has been in creating the timeline shown in the first row of the table, starting from 19:00 and going on up to 22:30. This timeline was created with a recursive template, and you could use it to create timelines for any time span you wanted.

Calculating

The third kind of numeric recursion occurs when you need to calculate a value using recursion. XPath provides operators and functions for some numeric calculations, but not all of them. For example, XPath doesn't offer functions for getting the square root of a number or getting the power of a number.

> *Writing templates for these functions can be quite tricky; usually you can use an extension function instead, as you'll see in Chapter 13, or you can reuse utility templates such as those from EXSLT (http://www.exslt.org/math). I'm really including these templates here as additional examples of recursion.*

In these kinds of templates, you use a parameter to keep track of the value attained so far, and only emit that value when you come to the end of the recursion. This parameter is only ever used within the recursion, it's not passed as a value when the template is first called.

For example, the following template gives the square root of a number by repeatedly adjusting an estimate of the square root by half of the difference between the square of the estimate and the number of which you're attempting to find the square root. We prevent infinite recursion by only using a certain precision, passed in as a parameter. The `$precision` parameter is used to create a decimal format pattern, using the `pad` template that we saw earlier in this chapter. If the current estimate is the same as the next estimate, to the specified precision, then you've found the square root of the number, at least to the desired precision:

```
<xsl:template name="squareRoot">
  <xsl:param name="number" select="0" />
  <xsl:param name="precision" select="4" />
  <xsl:param name="estimate" select="1" />
  <xsl:param name="format">
    <xsl:text>0.</xsl:text>
    <xsl:call-template name="pad">
      <xsl:with-param name="length" select="$precision" />
      <xsl:with-param name="char" select="'0'" />
    </xsl:call-template>
  </xsl:param>
  <xsl:variable name="nextEstimate"
    select="format-number($estimate + (($number - $estimate * $estimate)
                                      div (2 * $estimate)), $format)" />
  <xsl:choose>
    <xsl:when test="number($estimate) = number($nextEstimate)">
      <xsl:value-of select="number($estimate)"/>
    </xsl:when>
    <xsl:otherwise>
      <xsl:call-template name="squareRoot">
        <xsl:with-param name="number" select="$number"/>
        <xsl:with-param name="estimate" select="$nextEstimate" />
        <xsl:with-param name="format" select="$format" />
      </xsl:call-template>
    </xsl:otherwise>
  </xsl:choose>
</xsl:template>
```

For example, you could call the `squareRoot` template with the following call:

```
<xsl:call-template name="squareRoot">
  <xsl:with-param name="number" select="10" />
</xsl:call-template>
```

And it would return the square root of 10 to 4 decimal places (since that's the default precision) – 3.1623.

In other calculating templates, the solution is adjusted a particular number of times. In a template to work out the power of a number, for example, the number needs to be multiplied by itself a certain number of times. In the next template, the `$result` parameter keeps track of the result and is adjusted by being multiplied by the same number (held in the `$number` parameter) the number of times specified by the `$power` parameter:

```
<xsl:template name="power">
  <xsl:param name="number" select="1" />
  <xsl:param name="power" select="1" />
  <xsl:param name="result" select="1" />
  <xsl:choose>
    <xsl:when test="$power = 0">
      <xsl:value-of select="$result"/>
    </xsl:when>
    <xsl:otherwise>
      <xsl:call-template name="power">
```

```
          <xsl:with-param name="number" select="$number" />
          <xsl:with-param name="power" select="$power - 1" />
          <xsl:with-param name="result" select="$result * $number" />
        </xsl:call-template>
      </xsl:otherwise>
    </xsl:choose>
  </xsl:template>
```

For example, you could call the `power` template with the following call:

```
<xsl:call-template name="power">
  <xsl:with-param name="number" select="2" />
  <xsl:with-param name="power" select="8" />
</xsl:call-template>
```

This would return 2 to the power of 8 – 256.

These templates give surprisingly good performance, even with quite large numbers, and especially with processors that optimize tail-recursive templates (which we'll talk about in more detail later in this chapter). However, they will never be as fast as built-in functions, so if your processor supports extension functions for performing these calculations, and performance is an issue, you should use the extensions.

To perform calculations with recursive templates, you need a parameter that is only used for the recursion, to keep track of the result so far.

Recursing with Strings

Recursive templates that deal with strings usually perform some function on the first part of a string and then move on to the rest of the string. There are two ways of splitting a string into the "first" and the "rest":

- Use `substring-before()` to get the first part before a particular character or substring, and `substring-after()` to get the rest, after the same character or substring.
- Use `substring()` to get the first character(s) in the string and to get the remaining characters in the string.

The next few sections describe several situations in which recursive templates are useful: splitting strings up into tokens, searching and replacing words and phrases, iterating over the alphabet, and creating summary statistics about strings.

Splitting Strings

Non-XML methods of encoding repeated information often use strings that contain characters that separate the items of a list. For example, a poem might be represented as a number of lines separated by newline characters; a list of coordinates might be separated by spaces; or you might have comma-delimited data.

XML documents usually place individual items within their own elements, such that it's easy to iterate over them using `<xsl:for-each>` or `<xsl:apply-templates>`. However, if there is a lot of data then using elements can add significantly to the size of the XML (by at least seven characters per item), so XML documents do on occasion contain element or attribute values that hold lists of items separated by characters or delimiting strings.

> *XML Schema standardizes on using whitespace to delimit items in a list, although other languages (notably SVG) use commas instead.*

You frequently need, therefore, to have a template that can iterate over the items in a list that is delimited by a particular character or string. These templates take a string and a delimiter as parameters. The first item in the string is found using the `substring-before()` function and processed; the rest of the string, passed on to the next recursion, is identified with the `substring-after()` function. If the string doesn't contain the delimiter, then the template is processing the last item in the list and so doesn't have to recurse any more.

There are two patterns that these templates can follow. The first uses an `<xsl:choose>` to test whether the string contains the delimiter, with separate actions if it does or doesn't. This method repeats the code for what to do with each item, so it works best when the processing of each item is fairly simple or is done in another template. For example, the following template splits a delimited string into `<token>` elements:

```
<xsl:template name="tokenize">
  <xsl:param name="string" />
  <xsl:param name="delimiter" select="' '" />
  <xsl:choose>
    <xsl:when test="$delimiter and contains($string, $delimiter)">
      <token>
        <xsl:value-of select="substring-before($string, $delimiter)" />
      </token>
      <xsl:call-template name="tokenize">
        <xsl:with-param name="string"
                        select="substring-after($string, $delimiter)" />
        <xsl:with-param name="delimiter" select="$delimiter" />
      </xsl:call-template>
    </xsl:when>
    <xsl:otherwise>
      <token><xsl:value-of select="$string" /></token>
    </xsl:otherwise>
  </xsl:choose>
</xsl:template>
```

The second pattern for templates that work over character or string-delimited items sets a variable to hold the value of the item (whether it is the entire string or part of the string accessed with `substring-before()`), and then goes on to recurse on the rest of the string. This pattern keeps the code that deals with the item in one place, so it's useful if the code for generating the element is more complicated and you don't want to repeat it. The following template does the same as the previous one, but uses the alternative pattern:

```
<xsl:template name="tokenize">
  <xsl:param name="string" />
  <xsl:param name="delimiter" select="' '" />
```

```
    <xsl:variable name="contained"
                  select="$delimiter and contains($string, $delimiter)" />
    <xsl:variable name="item">
      <xsl:choose>
        <xsl:when test="$contained">
          <xsl:value-of select="substring-before($string, $delimiter)" />
        </xsl:when>
        <xsl:otherwise><xsl:value-of select="$string" /></xsl:otherwise>
      </xsl:choose>
    </xsl:variable>

    <token><xsl:value-of select="$item" /></token>

    <xsl:if test="$contained">
      <xsl:call-template name="tokenize">
        <xsl:with-param name="string"
                        select="substring-after($string, $delimiter)" />
        <xsl:with-param name="delimiter" select="$delimiter" />
      </xsl:call-template>
    </xsl:if>
  </xsl:template>
```

You can work through a character-delimited list by recursion using `substring-before()` to get the first item and `substring-after()` to get the rest of the list.

Searching and Replacing

In Chapter 8, you saw how to replace characters with a string using the `translate()` function. Unfortunately, the `translate()` function can only replace characters with other characters, so you can't use it to replace characters or strings with another string, let alone an element, and XPath doesn't offer any functions supporting regular expressions.

Thus, to search and replace throughout a string, you need to use a recursive template to work through the string, finding the character or string to be replaced and inserting in its place the string or element that you want instead. This recursive template breaks the string at the point where the search string appears, emits the string up to that point followed by a copy of whatever has been supplied to replace it, and then moves on to recurse on the rest of the string. Like the templates for splitting strings, this one ends when the string doesn't contain the search string. The following template is set up to replace new lines with `<br>` elements by default:

```
<xsl:template name="replace">
  <xsl:param name="string" />
  <xsl:param name="search" select="'&#xA;'" />
  <xsl:param name="replace"><br /></xsl:param>
  <xsl:choose>
    <xsl:when test="$search and contains($string, $search)">
      <xsl:value-of select="substring-before($string, $search)" />
      <xsl:copy-of select="$replace" />
      <xsl:call-template name="replace">
```

```
          <xsl:with-param name="string"
                    select="substring-after($string, $search)" />
          <xsl:with-param name="search" select="$search" />
          <xsl:with-param name="replace" select="$replace" />
        </xsl:call-template>
      </xsl:when>
      <xsl:otherwise>
        <xsl:value-of select="$string" />
      </xsl:otherwise>
    </xsl:choose>
  </xsl:template>
```

To replace a search string, you need a recursive template that outputs the substring before the search string followed by the replacement value, and then recurses on the substring after the search string.

The preceding template has one limitation, however; it can only carry out replacements for one character or string at a time. If you wanted to replace all newline characters (`
`) with `'\n'`, all carriage returns (`
`) with `'\r'`, and all tab characters (`	`) with `'\t'`, for example, you would have to call the template three times, each time using the result of applying the previous replacements, as follows:

```
<!-- replace tabs with \t -->
<xsl:call-template name="replace">
  <xsl:with-param name="search" select="'&#x9;'" />
  <xsl:with-param name="replace" select="'\t'" />
  <xsl:with-param name="string">
    <!-- replace carriage returns with \r -->
    <xsl:call-template name="replace">
      <xsl:with-param name="search" select="'&#xD;'" />
      <xsl:with-param name="replace" select="'\r'" />
      <xsl:with-param name="string">
        <!-- replace new lines with \n -->
        <xsl:call-template name="replace">
          <xsl:with-param name="search" select="'&#xA;'" />
          <xsl:with-param name="replace" select="'\n'" />
          <xsl:with-param name="string" select="$string" />
        </xsl:call-template>
      </xsl:with-param>
    </xsl:call-template>
  </xsl:with-param>
</xsl:call-template>
```

This is impractical for large numbers of replacements, and will not work if you want some of the characters to be replaced by elements rather than strings. To support multiple searches and replacements, you need a template that does recursion in two places: once on the string before the search string, and once on the string after the search string. For example, the following template replaces tabs (`	`) with three spaces, deletes carriage returns (`
`) by replacing them with nothing, and substitutes newline characters (`
`) with `
` elements:

```
<xsl:template name="replaceWhitespace">
  <xsl:param name="string" />
  <xsl:choose>
    <!-- replacing tabs -->
    <xsl:when test="contains($string, '&#x9;')">
      <xsl:call-template name="replaceWhitespace">
        <xsl:with-param name="string"
                        select="substring-before($string, '&#x9;')" />
      </xsl:call-template>
      <xsl:text>   </xsl:text>
      <xsl:call-template name="replaceWhitespace">
        <xsl:with-param name="string"
                        select="substring-after($string, '&#x9;')" />
      </xsl:call-template>
    </xsl:when>
    <!-- replacing carriage returns -->
    <xsl:when test="contains($string, '&#xD;')">
      <xsl:call-template name="replaceWhitespace">
        <xsl:with-param name="string"
                        select="substring-before($string, '&#xD;')" />
      </xsl:call-template>
      <xsl:call-template name="replaceWhitespace">
        <xsl:with-param name="string"
                        select="substring-after($string, '&#xD;')" />
      </xsl:call-template>
    </xsl:when>
    <!-- replacing new lines -->
    <xsl:when test="contains($string, '&#xA;')">
      <xsl:call-template name="replaceWhitespace">
        <xsl:with-param name="string"
                        select="substring-before($string, '&#xA;')" />
      </xsl:call-template>
      <br />
      <xsl:call-template name="replaceWhitespace">
        <xsl:with-param name="string"
                        select="substring-after($string, '&#xA;')" />
      </xsl:call-template>
    </xsl:when>
    <xsl:otherwise>
      <xsl:value-of select="$string" />
    </xsl:otherwise>
  </xsl:choose>
</xsl:template>
```

You can simplify this kind of search and replace template by having the search and replace strings or nodes held within an XML structure to which you then refer. You'll see this technique in action in the next chapter.

To replace multiple search strings, you need to recurse on both the substring before the search string and the substring after the search string.

Try It Out – Highlighting Keywords in a Description

Every program and series in the XML for the TV Guide has got a description within it. One of the ways in which people viewing the TV Guide can tell whether a program is interesting to them is by highlighting keywords that they've chosen. For example, if a particular user is interested in science fiction, current affairs, and ecology then they might choose keywords like "Sci-fi", "news", "Earth", and so on.

For now, we'll store the information about keywords within the XML for the TV Guide itself, although in the next chapter you'll see how to put it in a separate document to get at later. `TVGuide2.xml` has the following structure:

```
<TVGuide>
  <Channel>...</Channel>
  ...
  <Series>...</Series>
  ...
  <Keywords>
    <Keyword>Sci-fi</Keyword>
    <Keyword>news</Keyword>
    <Keyword>Earth</Keyword>
  </Keywords>
</TVGuide>
```

You can get at a list of the keywords that should be highlighted in a description with the following XPath expression:

```
/TVGuide/Keywords/Keyword
```

Now, whenever you come across text within a `<Description>` element, it should be processed to search for any of the keywords. If one is found, it should be highlighted with a `<span>` element with a `class` attribute equal to `keyword`. For example, take the following `<Series>` element:

```
<Series id="StarTrekVoyager" type="drama">
  <Title>Star Trek: Voyager</Title>
  <Description>
    Sci-fi series set on a space ship stranded far from Earth.
  </Description>
</Series>
```

The HTML paragraph that results from the `<Description>` element should include `<span>` elements to highlight the words `Sci-fi` and `Earth`, since they are in the list of keywords, as follows:

```
<p>
  <span class="keyword">Sci-fi</span> series set on a space ship stranded
  far from <span class="keyword">Earth</span>.
</p>
```

We need a recursive template that's able to take a string and recurse over it, testing if the string contains a keyword and if it does splitting the string at that keyword and inserting a `<span>` element around the keyword in its place. We'll call this template `highlightKeywords`. Obviously it needs to take the string in which the keywords are to be highlighted as a parameter. The keywords themselves can also be passed in as a parameter, to make the template more flexible, although the value of the parameter doesn't change from one recursion to the next. The outline of the template is as follows:

```
<xsl:template name="highlightKeywords">
  <xsl:param name="string" />
  <xsl:param name="keywords" select="/TVGuide/Keywords/Keyword" />
  ...
</xsl:template>
```

The first task is to find a keyword that the string contains. You can do this by finding the first `<Keyword>` element in the list held by the `$keywords` parameter whose value is contained in the string held in the `$string` parameter. This keyword is held in the `$keyword` variable:

```
<xsl:template name="highlightKeywords">
  <xsl:param name="string" />
  <xsl:param name="keywords" select="/TVGuide/Keywords/Keyword" />
  <xsl:variable name="keyword"
                select="$keywords[contains($string, .)][1]" />
  ...
</xsl:template>
```

If there isn't such a keyword, then you can just return the string. If there is, on the other hand, you need to recurse both over the part of the string before the keyword and over the part of the string after the keyword. Between the results of these two parts of the recursion, you need to create the `<span>` element that holds the keyword. The complete template is as follows:

```
<xsl:template name="highlightKeywords">
  <xsl:param name="string" />
  <xsl:param name="keywords" select="/TVGuide/Keywords/Keyword" />
  <xsl:variable name="keyword"
                select="$keywords[contains($string, .)][1]" />
  <xsl:choose>
    <xsl:when test="$keyword">
      <xsl:call-template name="highlightKeywords">
        <xsl:with-param name="string"
                        select="substring-before($string, $keyword)" />
        <xsl:with-param name="keywords" select="$keywords" />
      </xsl:call-template>
      <span class="keyword">
        <xsl:value-of select="$keyword" />
      </span>
      <xsl:call-template name="highlightKeywords">
        <xsl:with-param name="string"
                        select="substring-after($string, $keyword)" />
        <xsl:with-param name="keywords" select="$keywords" />
      </xsl:call-template>
    </xsl:when>
```

```
      <xsl:otherwise>
        <xsl:value-of select="$string" />
      </xsl:otherwise>
    </xsl:choose>
  </xsl:template>
```

We'll call this template whenever we find any text within a <Description> element. The easiest way to identify this text is to have a template that matches text nodes within <Description> elements, as follows:

```
<xsl:template match="Description//text()">
  <xsl:call-template name="highlightKeywords">
    <xsl:with-param name="string" select="." />
  </xsl:call-template>
</xsl:template>
```

And to make the keywords stand out in the resulting HTML page, we need to add a style for them in the CSS stylesheet:

```
.keyword {
  background: #C00;
  color: white;
}
```

With these changes in place in TVGuide6.xsl and TVGuide3.css, transform TVGuide2.xml with TVGuide6.xsl. You should see the following result for the description of Star Trek Voyager:

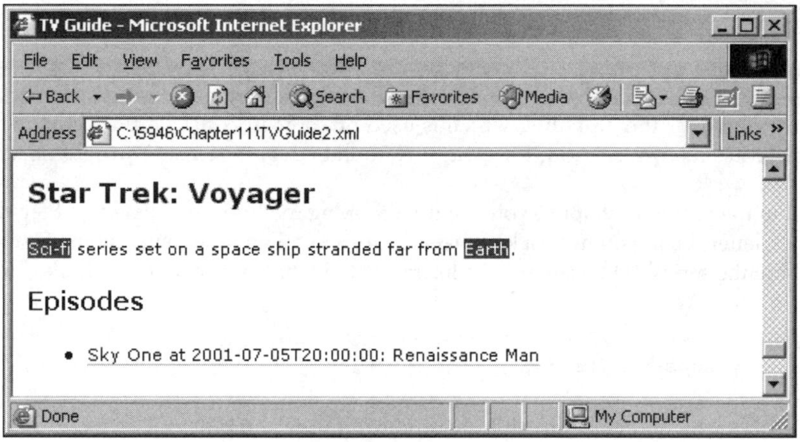

The keywords "Sci-fi" and "Earth" have been highlighted. A further challenge, if you feel like it, is to alter highlightKeywords so that it is case-insensitive.

Iterating Over the Alphabet

The previous couple of sections have both dealt with recursion over strings where the string is split at a particular character or word using substring-before() and substring-after(). A second form of recursion that you might need to carry out with strings is recursion that takes a number of characters from the start of a string (often just one character) and then moves on to the next characters.

A typical use of recursing using `substring()` is recursion that steps over the alphabet. In English, you can represent the alphabet as a single string of 26 characters:

```
'ABCDEFGHIJKLMNOPQRSTUVWXYZ'
```

To recurse over the alphabet, you need to take the first letter from the alphabet string and do something with it, then, if there are any letters left, move on to the rest of the alphabet (the string from the second character on). The pattern for these templates is thus as follows:

```
<xsl:template name="alphabetTemplate">
  <xsl:param name="alphabet" select="'ABCDEFGHIJKLMNOPQRSTUVWXYZ'" />
  <xsl:variable name="letter" select="substring($alphabet, 1, 1)" />
  <xsl:variable name="remainder" select="substring($alphabet, 2)" />
  ...
  <xsl:if test="$remainder">
    <xsl:call-template name="alphabetTemplate">
      <xsl:with-param name="alphabet" select="$remainder" />
    </xsl:call-template>
  </xsl:if>
</xsl:template>
```

You can iterate over the letters of the alphabet by creating a string of the letters and processing the first letter (as revealed by the `substring()` function) and recursing on the rest of the alphabet (again using the `substring()` function).

Try It Out – Iterating Over the Alphabet to Create Alphabetical Indexes

One way of working over the alphabet, which is used often, is in constructing alphabetical indexes where each letter has its own section, for example, alphabetical indexes of programs and series.

As you learned in the previous chapter, you can use grouping methods to collect together all the series with the same starting letter. First, you need a key that indexes `<Series>` elements by the first letter in their `id` attribute (we'll use the series' ID because that's likely not to include irrelevant words like "A" or "The":

```
<xsl:key name="seriesByFirstLetter" match="Series"
         use="substring(@id, 1, 1)" />
```

Now, you could find the letters of the alphabet by examining the indexed `<Series>` elements to find those that are listed first within the key for a particular letter, as you would with any grouping. However, since you know what letters these can be, it's a lot easier and most importantly more efficient to recurse over the alphabet to go through the letters one by one.

The following `alphabeticalSeriesList` template takes the (portion of the) alphabet as a parameter and identifies the first letter. It then accesses all the `<Series>` elements whose IDs start with that letter (using the key defined above). If there are any, it creates a heading (which includes an anchor point for the heading, so that you can link to it) and applies templates to `<Series>` elements. It then goes on to call itself with the remainder of the alphabet, if there is any left:

```
<xsl:template name="alphabeticalSeriesList">
  <xsl:param name="alphabet" select="'ABCDEFGHIJKLMNOPQRSTUVWXYZ'" />
  <xsl:variable name="letter" select="substring($alphabet, 1, 1)" />
  <xsl:variable name="remainder" select="substring($alphabet, 2)" />

  <xsl:variable name="series"
                select="key('seriesByFirstLetter', $letter)" />
  <xsl:if test="$series">
    <h3>
      <a id="series{$letter}" name="series{$letter}">
        <xsl:value-of select="$letter" />
      </a>
    </h3>
    <xsl:apply-templates select="$series">
      <xsl:sort select="@id" />
    </xsl:apply-templates>
  </xsl:if>

  <xsl:if test="$remainder">
    <xsl:call-template name="alphabeticalSeriesList">
      <xsl:with-param name="alphabet" select="$remainder" />
    </xsl:call-template>
  </xsl:if>
</xsl:template>
```

Another template also works through the alphabet to create a list of letters that can link to the alphabetical headings created by the `alphabeticalSeriesList` template. This template works in exactly the same way as far as the recursion is concerned; it's just that it creates a set of links rather than descriptions of the series:

```
<xsl:template name="alphabetList">
  <xsl:param name="alphabet" select="'ABCDEFGHIJKLMNOPQRSTUVWXYZ'" />
  <xsl:variable name="letter" select="substring($alphabet, 1, 1)" />
  <xsl:variable name="remainder" select="substring($alphabet, 2)" />

  <xsl:variable name="series"
                select="key('seriesByFirstLetter', $letter)" />
  <xsl:choose>
    <xsl:when test="$series">
      <xsl:call-template name="link">
        <xsl:with-param name="href" select="concat('#series', $letter)" />
        <xsl:with-param name="content" select="$letter" />
      </xsl:call-template>
    </xsl:when>
    <xsl:otherwise>
      <xsl:value-of select="$letter" />
    </xsl:otherwise>
  </xsl:choose>

  <xsl:if test="$remainder">
```

```
      <xsl:text> . </xsl:text>
      <xsl:call-template name="alphabetList">
        <xsl:with-param name="alphabet" select="$remainder" />
      </xsl:call-template>
    </xsl:if>
  </xsl:template>
```

The two templates are called from within the template matching the <TVGuide> element, replacing the current code, which simply applies templates to all the <Series> elements in ID order:

```
  <xsl:template match="TVGuide">
    ...
    <h2>Series</h2>
    <xsl:call-template name="alphabetList" />
    <xsl:call-template name="alphabeticalSeriesList" />
  </xsl:template>
```

TVGuide7.xsl contains these changes, and also changes the level of the headings produced by the <Series> elements, so that the structure of the document is clearer. The result of transforming TVGuide2.xml with TVGuide7.xsl is as follows:

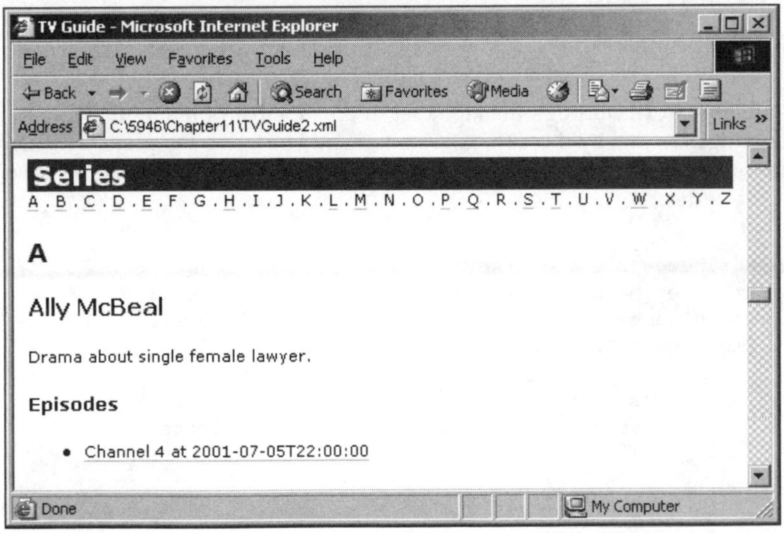

The alphabet just underneath the Series heading gives links to the alphabetically-ordered series further down the page. Both of the alphabetical orderings have been created by recursing, letter by letter, through a string containing the alphabet, rather than by looking to see what the first letters of each series are.

Summarizing Strings

In the previous sections, the result of the recursive template is a result tree fragment that is constructed in the body of the template. Sometimes, though, you need to create summaries of strings, which means that the result of a template that recurses over a string needs to be stored and passed on to the next recursion. This pattern is similar to the calculating templates that we saw when we discussed recursion based on numbers.

Templates that summarize strings not only take the string itself as a parameter, but also keep track of the current result in a parameter that is used purely within the recursion. The following template, for example, counts the number of items in a delimiter-separated list, and keeps track of how many have been found so far within a `$count` parameter. If the string doesn't contain the delimiter, then the template returns the count so far plus one (for the remaining string). If the string *does* contain the delimiter, then it calls itself on the remaining string, adding one to the count:

```
<xsl:template name="countItems">
  <xsl:param name="string" />
  <xsl:param name="delimiter" select="' '" />
  <xsl:param name="count" select="0" />
  <xsl:choose>
    <xsl:when test="contains($string, $delimiter)">
      <xsl:call-template name="countItems">
        <xsl:with-param name="string"
                        select="substring-after($string, $delimiter)" />
        <xsl:with-param name="delimiter" select="$delimiter" />
        <xsl:with-param name="count" select="$count + 1" />
      </xsl:call-template>
    </xsl:when>
    <xsl:otherwise>
      <xsl:value-of select="$count + 1" />
    </xsl:otherwise>
  </xsl:choose>
</xsl:template>
```

You can get summary statistics of strings by keeping track of the result-so-far in a parameter that you pass through to the next recursive call.

Recursing with Nodes

Unlike strings or numbers, XSLT has built-in support for iterating over node sets using either `<xsl:for-each>` or `<xsl:apply-templates>`. If you need to iterate over a set of nodes, you should use one of these instructions rather than create a complicated recursive template. XPath also offers support for the kinds of things that you would otherwise need to do using recursion. Three functions in particular are helpful in reducing the requirement for recursive templates:

- `position()` – gives you a counter
- `count()` – counts how many nodes there are in a node set
- `sum()` – sums the values of all the nodes in a node set

However, there are times when you do need to use recursion with node sets, in particular when you need to perform a calculation over a whole node set, such as working out minima or maxima or when summing things other than the values held directly in nodes.

A template that works over a node set using recursion, then, will usually have at least two parameters: one to hold the node set that is being iterated over and another, used purely within the recursion itself, to hold the result thus far. The first node can be accessed using a numeric predicate, while the "rest" of the nodes are those whose position in the node list is more than one. The recursion should stop when the node set is empty and there are no more nodes to process. Thus, the basic outline for one of these templates is the following:

```
<xsl:template name="nodeRecursionTemplate">
  <xsl:param name="nodes" select="/.." />
  <xsl:param name="current" select="..." />
  <xsl:choose>
    <xsl:when test="$nodes">
      ...
      <xsl:call-template name="nodeRecursionTemplate">
        <xsl:with-param name="nodes" select="$nodes[position > 1]" />
        <xsl:with-param name="current" select="..." />
      </xsl:call-template>
    </xsl:when>
    <xsl:otherwise>
      <xsl:value-of select="$current" />
    </xsl:otherwise>
  </xsl:choose>
</xsl:template>
```

Note that the location path `/..` selects an empty node set, by going to the root node (/) and finding its parent (`..`). The root node by definition cannot have a parent, so the path always returns an empty node set. This is a good default value to use for parameters that are expected to take node sets, since it prevents the processor from complaining about you using node set operations on parameters that have not been passed values when the template is called.

One example of such a template is a template to work out the minimum value of a set of nodes. Here, the value that you must keep track of is the minimum of the nodes so far (which can be safely defaulted to the value of the first node in the node set, to start off with). The new minimum is the smaller of the minimum passed into the template and the value of the first node in the node set. A recursive template to find the minimum value from a set of nodes is as follows:

```
<xsl:template name="minimum">
  <xsl:param name="nodes" select="/.." />
  <xsl:param name="minimum" select="number($nodes[1])" />
  <xsl:choose>
    <xsl:when test="$nodes">
      <xsl:variable name="value" select="number($nodes[1])" />
      <xsl:call-template name="minimum">
        <xsl:with-param name="nodes" select="$nodes[position() > 1]" />
        <xsl:with-param name="minimum">
          <xsl:choose>
            <xsl:when test="$minimum &lt;= $value">
              <xsl:value-of select="$minimum" />
            </xsl:when>
            <xsl:otherwise>
              <xsl:value-of select="$value" />
            </xsl:otherwise>
```

```
          </xsl:choose>
        </xsl:with-param>
      </xsl:call-template>
    </xsl:when>
    <xsl:otherwise>
      <xsl:value-of select="$minimum" />
    </xsl:otherwise>
  </xsl:choose>
</xsl:template>
```

For example, if you have an XML file containing a number of `<value>` elements, as follows:

```
<values>
  <value>52</value>
  <value>13</value>
  <value>74</value>
  <value>38</value>
</values>
```

then you can get the minimum numeric value for these `<value>` elements with the following call:

```
  <xsl:call-template name="minimum">
    <xsl:with-param name="nodes" select="values/value" />
  </xsl:call-template>
```

The result in this case will be `13`.

XSLT and XPath have good support for operations that would usually involve iteration over a node set. Where an operation is not supported, you can use a recursive template that uses the position of a node in a node set to pull out the first node on which to operate and the rest of the nodes on which to recurse.

Try It Out – Calculating the Total Duration of a Set of Programs

Another example of where a template that recurses over nodes can be handy is when calculating a sum of values, where the values are formed by calculation based on several aspects of a node or when the nodes have formats that can't be summed within XPaths. For example, in the TV Guide, the durations of programs are stored in the format of `xs:duration` from XML Schema (such as `PT1H30M` for 1 hour, 30 minutes). These durations cannot be summed in XPath because they're not numbers; in order to work out the total duration of a set of programs, you need a recursive template.

The durations of programs are specified in hours and minutes. Rather than combine hours and minutes as it goes along, the recursive template can keep track of these two things separately and then combine them when it comes to output the final result. There are thus three parameters: the node set of `<Program>` elements, the subtotal of hours, and the subtotal of minutes. What the template does with these parameters depends on whether there are any more programs to process or not:

```
<xsl:template name="totalDuration">
  <xsl:param name="programs" select="/.." />
  <xsl:param name="totalHours" select="0" />
  <xsl:param name="totalMinutes" select="0" />
  <xsl:choose>
    <xsl:when test="$programs">
      ...
    </xsl:when>
    <xsl:otherwise>
      ...
    </xsl:otherwise>
  </xsl:choose>
</xsl:template>
```

If there are programs left to process, then the template needs to look at the first program and work out how many hours and how many minutes it lasts for. The duration is stored in the `<Duration>` child of the `<Program>` element (which should be normalized, in case there's any whitespace around it):

```
<xsl:variable name="duration"
              select="normalize-space($programs[1]/Duration)" />
```

The number of hours is the string after the `'PT'` and before the `'H'`, if the duration contains an `H`, or 0 if it doesn't:

```
<xsl:variable name="hours">
  <xsl:choose>
    <xsl:when test="contains($duration, 'H')">
      <xsl:value-of select="substring-before(
                              substring-after($duration, 'PT'), 'H')" />
    </xsl:when>
    <xsl:otherwise>0</xsl:otherwise>
  </xsl:choose>
</xsl:variable>
```

The number of hours is the string after the `'PT'` and before the `'M'`, if the duration contains an `M` and doesn't contain an `H`. If the duration contains an `H` then it's the string between the `H` and the `M`; if the string doesn't contain an `M` then it's `0`:

```
<xsl:variable name="minutes">
  <xsl:choose>
    <xsl:when test="contains($duration, 'M')">
      <xsl:choose>
        <xsl:when test="contains($duration, 'H')">
          <xsl:value-of select="substring-before(
                                  substring-after($duration, 'H'), 'M')" />
        </xsl:when>
        <xsl:otherwise>
          <xsl:value-of select="substring-before(
                                  substring-after($duration, 'PT'), 'M')" />
        </xsl:otherwise>
      </xsl:choose>
```

```
      </xsl:when>
      <xsl:otherwise>0</xsl:otherwise>
    </xsl:choose>
  </xsl:variable>
```

The `$hours` and `$minutes` variables can be added to the current totals held in the `$totalHours` and `$totalMinutes` parameters. You need to pass the new totals to the next recursion for the template, along with the rest of the nodes in the node set:

```
<xsl:template name="totalDuration">
  <xsl:param name="programs" select="/.." />
  <xsl:param name="totalHours" select="0" />
  <xsl:param name="totalMinutes" select="0" />
  <xsl:choose>
    <xsl:when test="$programs">
      <xsl:variable name="duration"
                    select="normalize-space($programs[1]/Duration)" />
      <xsl:variable name="hours">...</xsl:variable>
      <xsl:variable name="minutes">...</xsl:variable>
      <xsl:call-template name="totalDuration">
        <xsl:with-param name="programs"
                        select="$programs[position() > 1]" />
        <xsl:with-param name="totalHours" select="$totalHours + $hours" />
        <xsl:with-param name="totalMinutes"
                        select="$totalMinutes + $minutes" />
      </xsl:call-template>
    </xsl:when>
    <xsl:otherwise>
      ...
    </xsl:otherwise>
  </xsl:choose>
</xsl:template>
```

The final task for the template is to construct a string showing the hours and minutes taken up in total by the programs. We'll make this a decimal string, so 14 hours and 30 minutes is output as `14.5 hours`. The number of hours to be output is the value given by the `$totalHours` parameter plus the number of minutes given by the `$totalMinutes` parameter divided by 60 and rounded down. The fraction for the number of minutes is `$totalMinutes` mod 60, divided by 60. These can be added together and then formatted with `format-number()` to get the decimal display, as follows:

```
<xsl:template name="totalDuration">
  <xsl:param name="programs" select="/.." />
  <xsl:param name="totalHours" select="0" />
  <xsl:param name="totalMinutes" select="0" />
  <xsl:choose>
    <xsl:when test="$programs">
      <xsl:variable name="duration"
                    select="normalize-space($programs[1]/Duration)" />
      <xsl:variable name="hours">...</xsl:variable>
      <xsl:variable name="minutes">...</xsl:variable>
      <xsl:call-template name="totalDuration">
        <xsl:with-param name="programs"
```

```
                          select="$programs[position() > 1]" />
          <xsl:with-param name="totalHours" select="$totalHours + $hours" />
          <xsl:with-param name="totalMinutes"
                          select="$totalMinutes + $minutes" />
        </xsl:call-template>
      </xsl:when>
      <xsl:otherwise>
        <xsl:variable name="finalHours"
                      select="$totalHours + floor($totalMinutes div 60)" />
        <xsl:variable name="finalMinutes"
                      select="($totalMinutes mod 60) div 60" />
        <xsl:value-of
          select="format-number($finalHours + $finalMinutes, '0.00')" />
      </xsl:otherwise>
    </xsl:choose>
  </xsl:template>
```

We'll use this template to show another statistic for each channel – the total amount of time that it spends showing good programs – those rated above 5. The template for the `<Channel>` elements calls the `totalDuration` template, passing it a node set of `<Program>` elements whose `rating` attribute has a value greater than 5, as follows:

```
  <xsl:template match="Channel">
    <xsl:apply-templates select="Name" />
    <p class="average">
      <xsl:text>average rating: </xsl:text>
      <xsl:value-of select="format-number(sum(Program/@rating) div
                                          count(Program), '0.0')" />
      <br />
      <xsl:text>good programs for: </xsl:text>
      <xsl:call-template name="totalDuration">
        <xsl:with-param name="programs" select="Program[@rating > 5]" />
      </xsl:call-template>
      <xsl:text>hrs</xsl:text>
    </p>
    <xsl:apply-templates select="Program" />
  </xsl:template>
```

When you transform `TVGuide2.xml` with `TVGuide8.xsl`, in which these changes have been made, you should see the following:

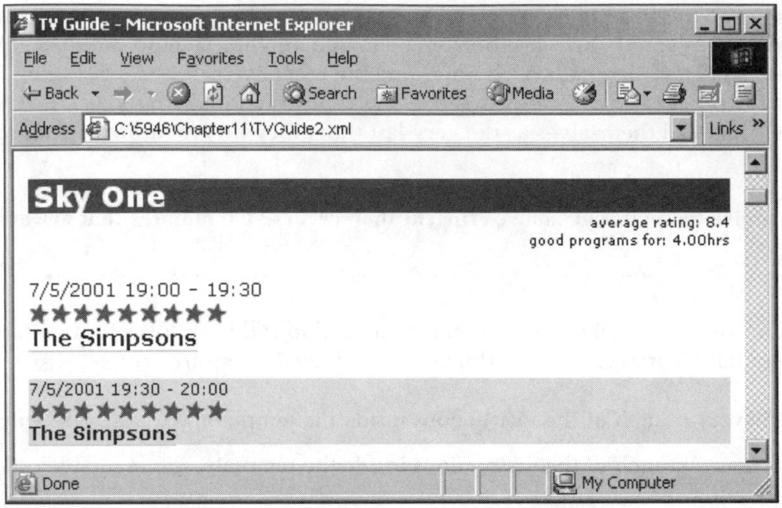

The total duration of the programs with ratings greater than 5 is 4 hours for Sky One. This total is arrived at through a recursive template that sums the durations of a set of `<Program>` *elements; the* `sum()` *function wouldn't work here because the durations of programs are not stored as numbers.*

Tail Recursion

Recursion can be computationally expensive. When a processor comes across a loop in procedural programming languages, it can assign a particular set of resources to hold the values of the variables that are updated within the loop. However, with a recursive process, the processor may have to assign different resources to hold the values of the parameters each time the template is called.

For example, when working through the alphabet, the processor might have to assign one byte for every letter in the alphabet, so 26 bytes for the alphabet to start with. With a loop, those same 26 bytes can be reused again and again. However, with a template the parameter has different resources assigned to it each time, so the total memory consumption is more like 26 + 25 + 24 + ... + 3 + 2 + 1 = 351 bytes.

The fact that a processor has to assign new resources on each recursion means that it has to keep track of where it is within the program by recording which function called this function, and which function called that function, and so on up to the very first call that started the program running. This record of functions calling other functions is known as the **stack**. When you use recursive templates, the stack can get very large; each time a template calls itself it adds another level to the stack. So in the example of working through the alphabet letter by letter, on the last recursion you're 26 levels deeper than you were in the first recursion.

All processors have a limit to the size of the stack, and therefore a limit to the depth that the recursion can reach. If you have a template that has to call itself a lot of times, you might reach the stack limit; at that point the process stops altogether, and the stylesheet generates an error.

Fortunately, most processors are clever enough to recognize when they can reuse the resources that are assigned to a recursive template and so don't need to add another level to the stack. In particular, if you write a template so that it only calls itself once, and the recursive call is the last thing that's done by a template, then the processor can interpret the recursive instructions exactly as if they were specified in a loop. Templates that call themselves as the very last thing they do are known as **tail recursive**.

> **Tail recursive templates are more efficient than recursive templates that are not tail recursive.**

When you are writing a recursive template that will need to call itself lots of times, then it is worthwhile trying to make it tail recursive. The two things that you need to ensure are:

- Within every branch of the instructions inside the template, the template only calls itself once
- Within every branch of the instructions inside the template, the recursive call is the last thing the processor needs to do

We'll look at an alternative design for a template working out a minimum value from a set of nodes to illustrate these issues. Firstly, look at the template from the last section (the recursive call is highlighted):

```
<xsl:template name="minimum">
  <xsl:param name="nodes" select="/.." />
  <xsl:param name="minimum" select="number($nodes[1])" />
  <xsl:choose>
    <xsl:when test="$nodes">
      <xsl:variable name="value" select="number($nodes[1])" />
      <xsl:call-template name="minimum">
        <xsl:with-param name="nodes" select="$nodes[position() > 1]" />
        <xsl:with-param name="minimum">
          <xsl:choose>
            <xsl:when test="$minimum &lt;= $value">
              <xsl:value-of select="$minimum" />
            </xsl:when>
            <xsl:otherwise>
              <xsl:value-of select="$value" />
            </xsl:otherwise>
          </xsl:choose>
        </xsl:with-param>
      </xsl:call-template>
    </xsl:when>
    <xsl:otherwise>
      <xsl:value-of select="$minimum" />
    </xsl:otherwise>
  </xsl:choose>
</xsl:template>
```

There's only one recursive call within this template (the one that's highlighted) and it occurs as the last thing within an `<xsl:when>` that is in an `<xsl:choose>` that is the last thing in the template. If the recursive call happens at all, then it's the last thing that happens.

Now consider the following template, which performs the same calculation, but this time by getting the minimum from the "rest" of the nodes, and then comparing that minimum with the minimum of the first node:

```
<xsl:template name="minimum">
  <xsl:param name="nodes" select="/.." />
  <xsl:variable name="value" select="number($nodes[1])" />
  <xsl:choose>
    <xsl:when test="count($nodes) > 1">
      <xsl:variable name="minimum">
        <xsl:call-template name="minimum">
          <xsl:with-param name="nodes" select="$nodes[position() > 1]" />
        </xsl:call-template>
      </xsl:variable>
      <xsl:choose>
        <xsl:when test="$minimum &lt;= $value">
          <xsl:value-of select="$minimum" />
        </xsl:when>
        <xsl:otherwise>
          <xsl:value-of select="$value" />
        </xsl:otherwise>
      </xsl:choose>
    </xsl:when>
    <xsl:otherwise>
      <xsl:value-of select="$value" />
    </xsl:otherwise>
  </xsl:choose>
</xsl:template>
```

In this template, there's still only one recursive call to the `minimum` template, but it is not the last thing that happens when the template is processed. After working out the minimum of the rest of the nodes, the template goes on to use that minimum to work out what value to give as the result. So the above template is not tail recursive.

> **A tail recursive template is a template that only calls itself once, as the last thing it does during its instantiation.**

Most of the templates that we've looked at in this chapter have been tail recursive. The only one that hasn't been is the one for searching and replacing multiple strings. This template cannot be tail recursive because you need to recurse in two places: on the part of the string before the search string and on the part of the string after it.

Different processors are built in different ways and optimize different aspects of XSLT and XPath. If you need to improve the speed of your stylesheet, then you should try out different ways of solving the same problem to see which one gives you the best performance with your data and your processor.

Summary

This chapter has introduced you to named templates, in particular so that you can use them to create recursive templates.

You can name any template (including those that match nodes) using the `name` attribute on `<xsl:template>`. Every template's name must be different, so that the processor can identify it when you call it with the `<xsl:call-template>` instruction. Like normal templates, you can pass parameters into named templates with `<xsl:with-param>` elements within `<xsl:call-template>`.

The only kinds of sequences of which XSLT and XPath 1.0 are aware are node sets. XSLT supports iteration over a node set with `<xsl:for-each>` and `<xsl:apply-templates>`. XPath supports counters with the `position()` function and has a couple of aggregating functions in `count()` and `sum()`. To iterate over the character-delimited items in a list, or to perform calculations (including getting the minimum or maximum value from a node set), you need recursive templates.

Recursive templates call themselves, and you should design them so that they're tail recursive as this allows processors to enact them without assigning lots of unnecessary resources to them. A tail recursive template calls itself once only, and it's the last thing that it does during a single instantiation of the template. Recursive templates are typically used to do things like:

- Repeating the same thing multiple times
- Numbering items sequentially when it can't be achieved with `<xsl:number>` or the `position()` function
- Performing numeric calculations, particularly calculating statistics on lists held in strings or node sets
- Splitting up character-delimited strings
- Searching and replacing
- Working through the alphabet letter by letter

In this chapter, you've seen how to create recursive templates to handle each of these tasks.

There are many different ways of using XSLT. At the beginning of this book, you learned how to use XSLT as a designer – creating a template of a page and then populating it with information from an XML document. In the previous several chapters, you've become an XSLT author, which has enabled you to create more sophisticated pages. Now, knowing how to design and use recursive templates, you are on your way to becoming an XSLT programmer, someone who can use XSLT to perform just about any task that involves manipulating XML.

Review Questions

1. How do you assign a name to a template?

2. What are the two situations in which the instructions held in a template might be enacted?

3. When should you use named templates rather than matching templates?

4. What is the defining feature of a recursive template? What's special about a tail recursive template?

5. In general, how many parameters are different in a recursive call than in the call to the original template?

6. Create recursive templates to generate a table containing the times tables, up to 12, which should look like the following:

	1	2	3	4	5	6	7	8	9	10	11	12
1	1	-	-	-	-	-	-	-	-	-	-	-
2	2	4	-	-	-	-	-	-	-	-	-	-
3	3	6	9	-	-	-	-	-	-	-	-	-
4	4	8	12	16	-	-	-	-	-	-	-	-
5	5	10	15	20	25	-	-	-	-	-	-	-
6	6	12	18	24	30	36	-	-	-	-	-	-
7	7	14	21	28	35	42	49	-	-	-	-	-
8	8	16	24	32	40	48	56	64	-	-	-	-
9	9	18	27	36	45	54	63	72	81	-	-	-
10	10	20	30	40	50	60	70	80	90	100	-	-
11	11	22	33	44	55	66	77	88	99	110	121	-
12	12	24	36	48	60	72	84	96	108	120	132	144

7. Create a recursive template that goes through a string and substitutes every occurrence of a keyword from a comma-delimited list of keywords with an <em> element holding that keyword. For example, the template call:

```
<xsl:template name="emphasizeKeywords">
  <xsl:with-param name="string">
    Documentary series that examines various cultures' construction of
    pyramidal monuments, from Egypt and Iraq to Central America.
  </xsl:with-param>
```

```
  <xsl:with-param name="keywords" select="Egypt, pyramid, mummies" />
</xsl:template>
```

should result in the following result tree fragment:

```
Documentary series that examines various cultures' construction of
<em>pyramid</em>al monuments, from <em>Egypt</em> and Iraq to Central America.
```

8. Create a recursive template that calculates the average word length in a string. You'll need to keep track of two things in this template: the number of words and the total length of the words. The final result will be the total length divided by the number of words.

9. When can you use the `sum()` function to calculate a sum, and when do you need to use a recursive template?

10. Create a tail recursive template for calculating the maximum value from a set of nodes.

Beginning
XSLT

12

Building XSLT Applications

In all the transformations that you've carried out so far, there's been a single stylesheet operating on a single source document. In this chapter, you'll see how to split a single stylesheet into multiple physical files, and how to access multiple XML documents to get hold of extra information.

There are two reasons why you might want to split up your stylesheet into separate physical documents. Firstly, it helps with **maintenance** if you can focus on a particular file to find the code that you need, rather than searching through one big stylesheet. Secondly, if templates or other declarations are housed in a separate file, you can **reuse** them in multiple XSLT applications.

There are also two ways in which being able to access other source documents is useful. Firstly, external documents can hold extra data that the stylesheet can use, for example, lookup tables to hold names of months or search and replace strings. Secondly, the source document for the transformation might not hold all the information that you need to be present; if this information is spread over several separate files, then you need to be able to access them as well – for example, the information about TV series could be kept in a separate document from the main TV listing.

In this chapter, you'll learn:

- How to split and then include stylesheets with `<xsl:include>`
- How to import stylesheets with `<xsl:import>`
- How to override components from an imported stylesheet
- How to access external documents with the `document()` function
- How to hold data within the stylesheet itself
- How to retrieve referenced information

Splitting Up Stylesheets

The first aspect of larger XSLT applications that we'll look at is how to divide or split up a stylesheet into several separate files using `<xsl:include>`. As your XSLT applications get larger, the files start to become unwieldy – you have to scroll through lots of templates and other declarations to find the piece of code that you want. While authoring tools can help with managing stylesheets, they can also suffer when trying to cope with large documents. Therefore, it helps you manage and maintain your XSLT applications if you can split up your stylesheet into multiple parts.

XSLT allows you to split up your stylesheet into multiple files and then **include** the information from one stylesheet in another with the `<xsl:include>` element. The `<xsl:include>` element sits at the top level of the stylesheet, as a child of the `<xsl:stylesheet>` document element. It takes a single attribute – `href` – which holds the URL of the stylesheet that you want to include, relative to the including stylesheet. For example, the following `<xsl:include>` element includes the `descriptions.xsl` stylesheet:

```
<xsl:include href="descriptions.xsl" />
```

When an XSLT processor comes across an `<xsl:include>` element, it accesses the referenced stylesheet and essentially copies all the contents of that stylesheet (all the components declared within the `<xsl:stylesheet>` element) into the including stylesheet.

> *The inclusion process isn't a textual copy. Instead, it copies the logical components from the included stylesheet. In particular, it's a namespace-aware copy, so you can use different prefixes for different namespaces in the separate stylesheets if you want to.*

To the XSLT processor, the resulting stylesheet is just the same as a stylesheet where all the components from the included stylesheet were defined within the including stylesheet at the point where the `<xsl:include>` element appears. This process is shown in the following diagram:

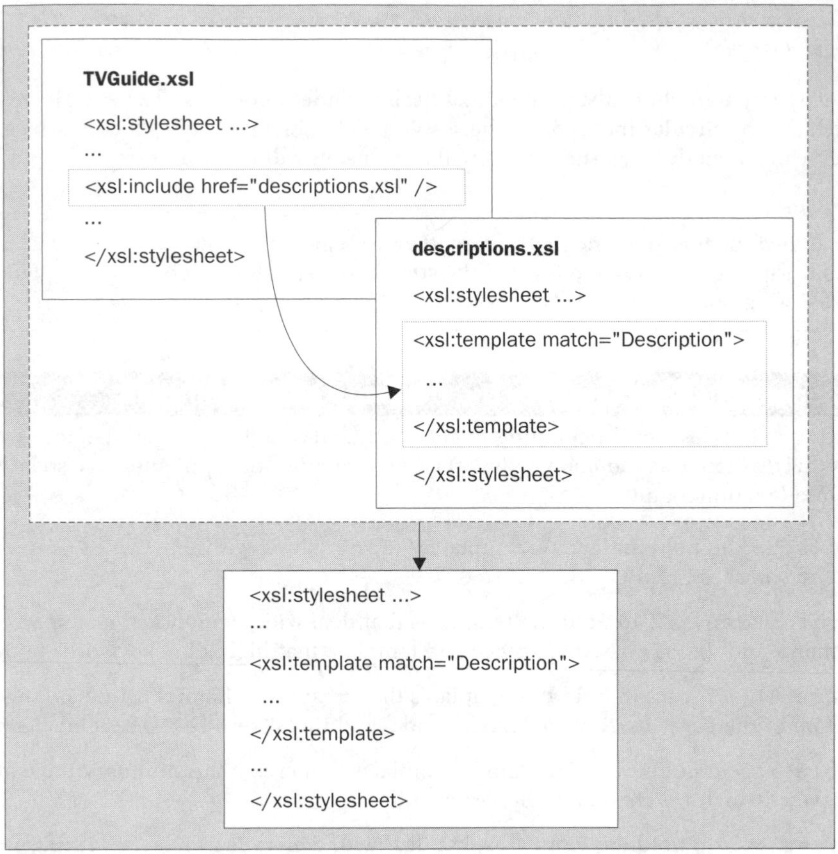

The fact that the contents of the included template are in effect included at the location of the `<xsl:include>` element has two implications:

- The names of components in the included and including stylesheet can clash, so, for example, the included stylesheet must not contain any named templates that have the same name as a named template in the including stylesheet.

- When an XSLT processor needs to decide between two components, it uses the last one in the stylesheet (as long as it doesn't halt with an error), so the position of the `<xsl:include>` matters. For example, consider the situation where you have two templates that match the same element in the same mode with the same priority, one in the included stylesheet and one in the including stylesheet. If the `<xsl:include>` is placed *after* the template in the including stylesheet then the template from the included stylesheet will be used, whereas if the `<xsl:include>` is placed *before* the template in the including stylesheet then the template from the included stylesheet will not be used.

You therefore have to be careful when you're using `<xsl:include>` to include stylesheets. In particular, if a stylesheet contains named templates then you have to make sure that you don't include them twice.

As you'll see in the next section, you're usually safer using `<xsl:import>` to use a stylesheet that holds named templates.

You're perfectly free to include a stylesheet that itself includes another stylesheet. However, you do have to watch out for circular inclusions, where stylesheet A includes stylesheet B, which includes stylesheet C, which includes stylesheet A. Circular inclusion will cause an error.

> **You can include the components from another stylesheet with the `<xsl:include>` element, which goes at the top level of the stylesheet and whose `href` attribute holds a URL pointing to the included stylesheet.**

Try It Out – Separating Templates for the Contents of Descriptions

The `TVGuide.xsl` stylesheet is beginning to get a little bulky so to ease maintenance we'll split it into two files: `TVGuide2.xsl` as the main stylesheet, and a number of supplementary stylesheets, roughly divided up into functional units:

- `utils.xsl` to hold the named templates – `link` (along with the `linkEvents` attribute set), `durationMins`, and `totalDuration`
- `description.xsl` to hold the templates that deal with elements in `<Description>` elements and the `highlightKeywords` template that highlights keywords in descriptions
- `channelList.xsl` to hold the templates that create the channel listing at the top and bottom of the page (in `ChannelList` mode) and the `$ChannelList` global variable
- `table.xsl` to hold the `Table` mode templates that create the summary table at the top of the page (which we created in the last chapter)
- `series.xsl` to hold the templates that deal with generating the series listings, which we've put at the bottom of the page

Each of these stylesheets looks just like normal stylesheets – you don't have to put any special declarations in it to state that it's going to be included elsewhere. For example, `description.xsl` holds all the templates that match elements within `<Description>` elements, and also the `highlightKeywords` template that we created in the last chapter. The `descriptions.xsl` stylesheet looks as follows:

```
<xsl:stylesheet version="1.0"
                xmlns:xsl="http://www.w3.org/1999/XSL/Transform"
                xmlns="http://www.w3.org/1999/xhtml">

  <xsl:template match="Description//Actor">...</xsl:template>
  <xsl:template match="Description//Link">...</xsl:template>
  <xsl:template match="Description//Program">...</xsl:template>
  <xsl:template match="Description//Series">...</xsl:template>
  <xsl:template match="Description//Channel">...</xsl:template>

  <xsl:template name="highlightKeywords">...</xsl:template>

</xsl:stylesheet>
```

Don't forget the namespace declaration for the XHTML namespace, otherwise the literal result elements that you generate in the included stylesheets will be in no namespace, rather than the XHTML namespace.

Once you've moved the various templates, attribute sets, keys, and global variables to their separate stylesheets, you can remove them from `TVGuide2.xsl`. In their place, add `<xsl:include>` elements whose `href` attributes point to the stylesheet modules:

```
<xsl:stylesheet version="1.0"
                xmlns:xsl="http://www.w3.org/1999/XSL/Transform"
                xmlns="http://www.w3.org/1999/xhtml">

...
<xsl:include href="utils.xsl" />

<xsl:include href="description.xsl" />

<xsl:include href="channelList.xsl" />
<xsl:include href="table.xsl" />
<xsl:include href="series.xsl" />
...
</xsl:stylesheet>
```

Now transform `TVGuide.xml` with `TVGuide2.xsl`. You should get just the same result as before:

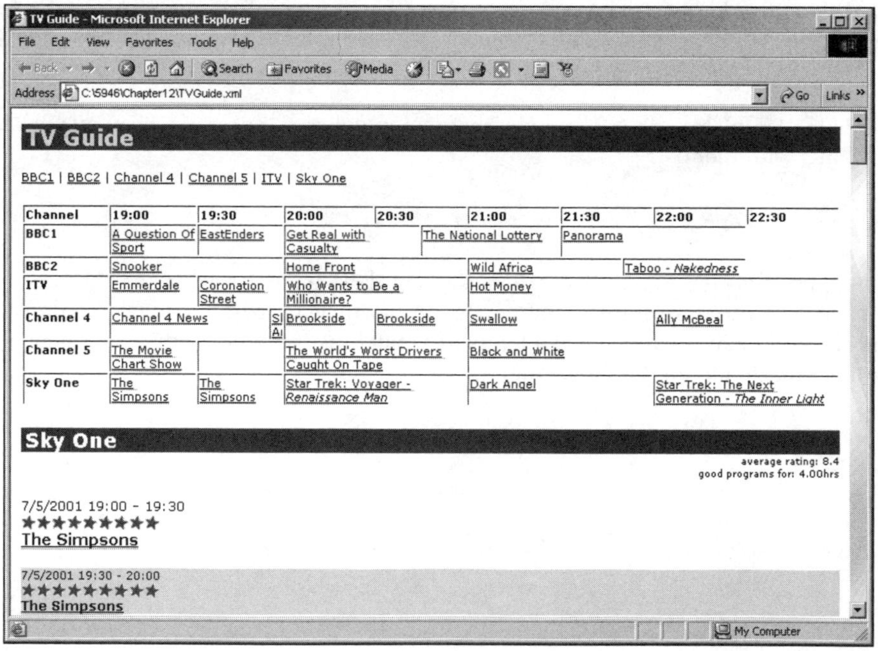

The global variable and templates that create the channel listing are located in `channelList.xsl`; the named and matching templates that create the table are located in `table.xsl`; the templates that provide the main listing are in the stylesheet that's actually referenced, `TVGuide2.xsl`. It doesn't matter where the components come from; they are all combined when the processor uses `TVGuide2.xsl` to transform `TVGuide.xml`.

To see the conflicts that can occur when including stylesheets, we'll try a couple of variations.

First, we'll copy the `highlightKeywords` template from `description.xsl` into `TVGuide3.xsl`, so that there's one copy in each stylesheet. If you try transforming `TVGuide.xml` with `TVGuide3.xsl`, you should see something like the following error:

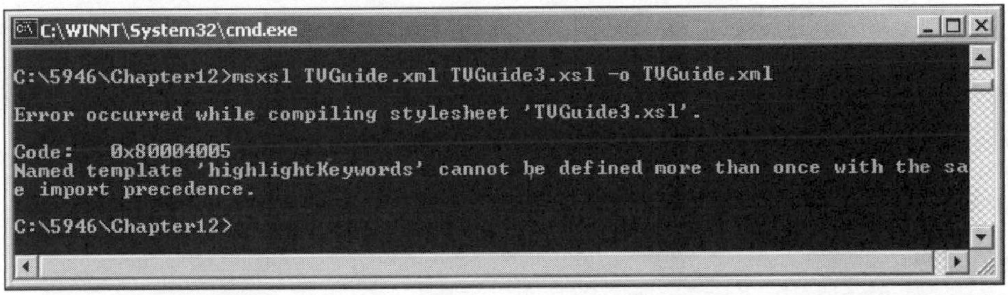

The XSLT processor reports an error because there are two templates with the same name, even though they are in different stylesheets. The same kind of error will occur if you try copying the definition of the global variable `$ChannelList` into `TVGuide3.xsl` because you can't have two global variables that have the same name.

Now try adding a template to the main stylesheet that matches `<Channel>` elements in `Table` mode but does nothing with them:

```
<xsl:template match="Channel" mode="Table" />
```

Place this template *after* the `<xsl:include>` element that includes `table.xsl`, as in `TVGuide4.xsl`, and try transforming `TVGuide.xml` with `TVGuide4.xsl`. If you don't get an error (processors can complain if you have two templates matching the same node in the same mode at the same priority), you should get the following:

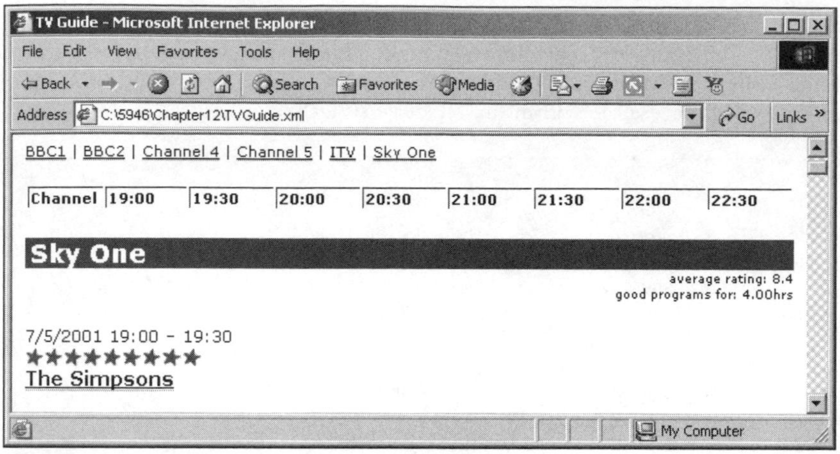

The body of the table is omitted, because the empty template in `TVGuide4.xsl` has been used in preference to the template in `table.xsl`.

If you move the template so that it is placed *before* the `<xsl:include>` element that includes `table.xsl`, then the template from `table.xsl` will be used and you'll get the same result as you did with `TVGuide2.xsl` originally.

Reusing Stylesheets

Dividing a stylesheet for manageability is helpful, but the real win of splitting up a stylesheet is that it allows you to reuse code in multiple XSLT applications. This is particularly helpful when you create named templates to carry out utility functions, for example, getting the square root of a number, working out the minimum value of a set of nodes, or something that's more specific to your application domain. However, often some of the named templates in the reusable stylesheet don't do *exactly* what you want them to do, because they've been designed with different applications in mind, and you need to override them to get precisely the behavior that you desire.

> *There are a growing number of resources on the Web that provide utility templates to do things like finding the maximum or minimum from a set of nodes or formatting dates. In particular, have a look at http://xsltsl.sourceforge.net, http://www.exslt.org, and http://www.topxml.com/xsl/articles/fp/.*

To reuse most of the templates in another stylesheet, but override some of them, you need to **import** the stylesheet rather than include it. You can import a stylesheet using the `<xsl:import>` element, which is very similar to the `<xsl:include>` element in that it occurs at the top level of the stylesheet and it takes an `href` attribute that points to the stylesheet you want to import. The major difference is that any `<xsl:import>` elements in your stylesheet must be the very first elements in the stylesheet, the first children of the `<xsl:stylesheet>` document element.

For example, the following `<xsl:import>` element imports the `utils.xsl` stylesheet:

```
<xsl:import href="utils.xsl" />
```

If there aren't any conflicts between the importing and imported stylesheet, importing a stylesheet has much the same effect in terms of what the processor does as including that stylesheet would, as illustrated in the following diagram. `TVGuide.xsl` imports `utils.xsl`, and this makes the `link` template that it contains accessible within the effective stylesheet:

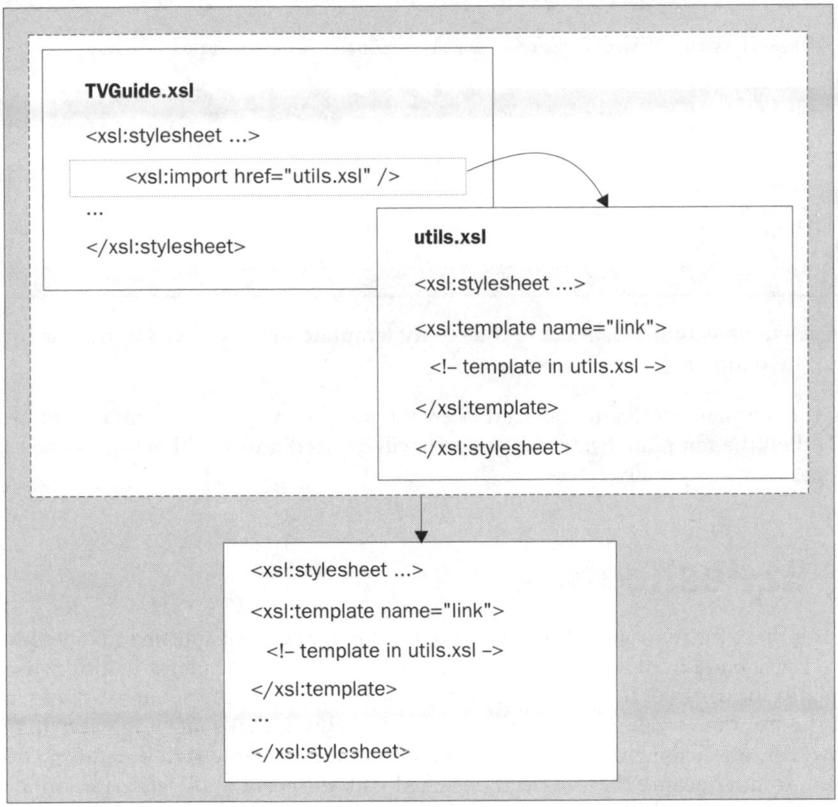

However, when you import a stylesheet, any templates or other components that are defined within the imported stylesheet can be **overridden** by their equivalents in the importing stylesheet. This is handy because it allows you to customize the behavior of the components in the imported stylesheet to the requirements of your particular application, for example, to change the way that the imported stylesheet calculates the value for a node when finding the minimum. In a way, this is similar to creating a subclass (your stylesheet) that overrides methods (templates) on its superclass (the imported stylesheet). This overriding behavior is illustrated in the following diagram; this time `TVGuide.xsl` and `utils.xsl` both have a `link` template; it's the `link` template from `TVGuide.xsl` that gets used:

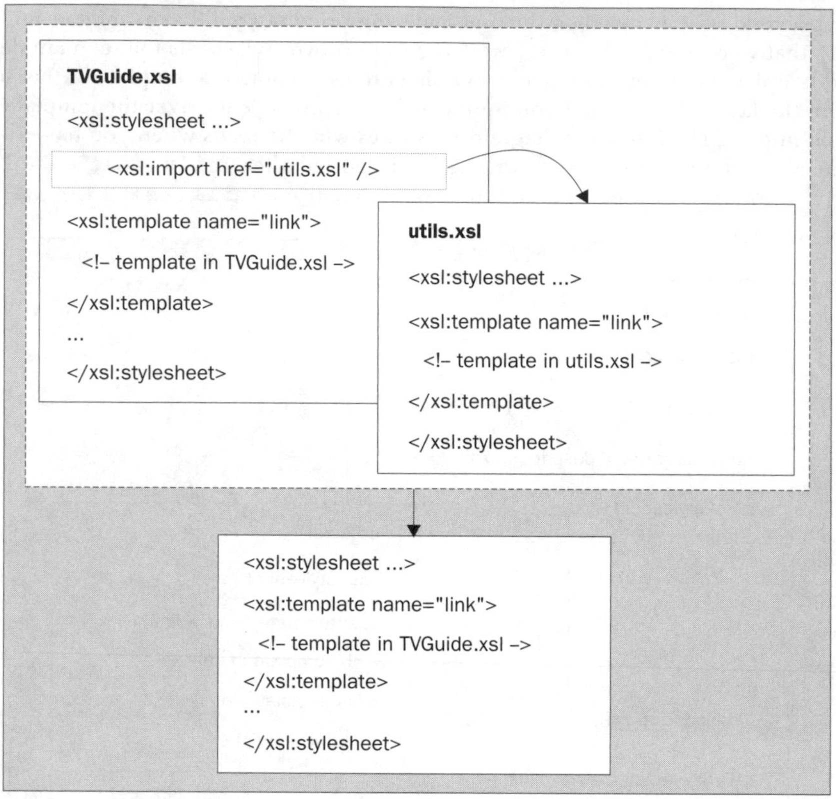

The reason that the components in the importing stylesheet override those in the imported stylesheet is that they have higher **import precedence**. The import precedence of a stylesheet comes into affect when the processor has multiple components to choose from, either because they have the same name or because they match the same node. The kinds of things that you can override in an importing stylesheet are:

- Global variable and parameter definitions
- Key definitions
- Named templates
- Matching templates

The way these matching templates are overridden deserves a bit of explanation. Basically, if a template in an importing template can match a node, then it will. It doesn't matter how high a priority a template in an imported stylesheet has, it won't be used if there's a template in the importing stylesheet that can be applied to the node. Thus, if you want to use some matching templates from an imported stylesheet, you need to make sure that you don't have a template that could match the same kind of nodes (in the same mode) in your importing stylesheet.

If you import several stylesheets, then the one that's imported last will have a higher import precedence than the ones that were imported earlier. So if you import two stylesheets that contain definitions for the same named template (and your importing stylesheet doesn't contain a template of that name), then the template from the last stylesheet that you import will have precedence over the template from the first stylesheet you import. The following diagram illustrates what happens when you have two stylesheets imported one after another; `description.xsl` is imported after `utils.xsl`, so the `link` template from `description.xsl` is used in preference to the one from `utils.xsl`:

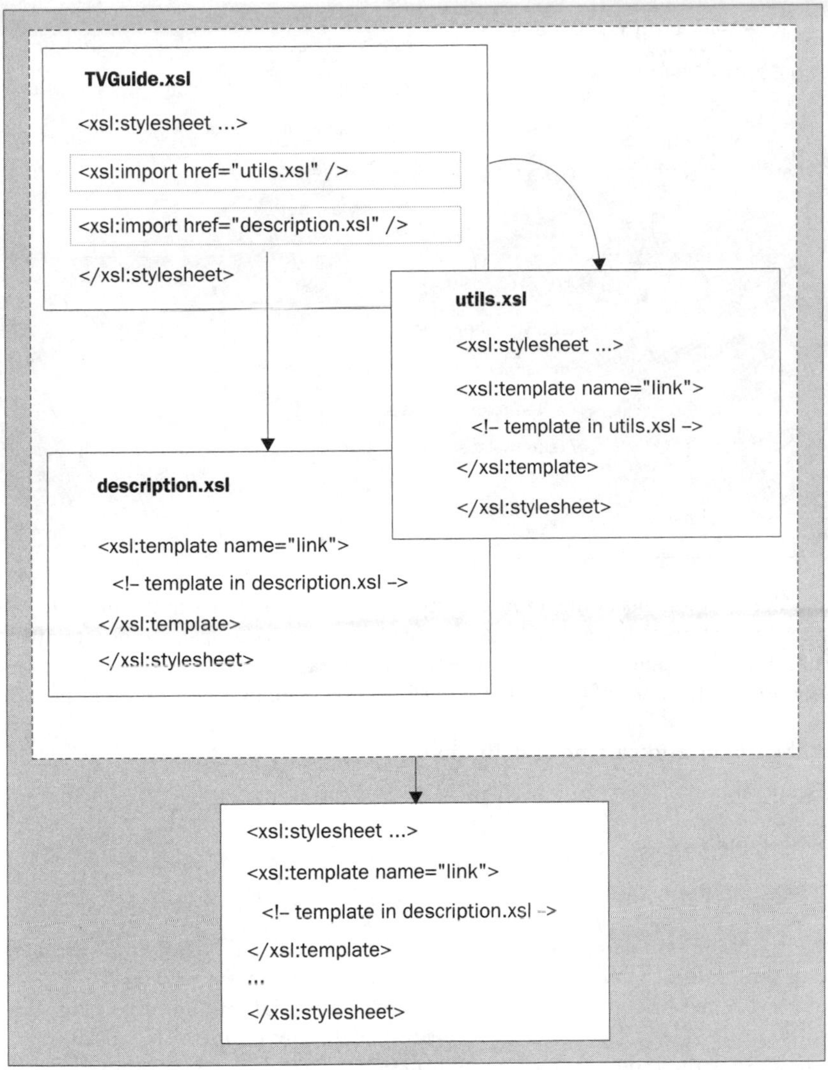

> **When you import a stylesheet, you can override the declarations that it contains from within your stylesheet. You can import stylesheets with `<xsl:import>` elements, which must be the first elements in a stylesheet and which take `href` attributes to indicate the imported stylesheet.**

Try It Out – Overriding Named Templates

The `utils.xsl` stylesheet is quite useful for other stylesheets that we might develop, such as those showing only interesting programs or programs in particular series. All these stylesheets would benefit from having a simple template named `link` that generates a link as follows:

```
<xsl:template name="link">
  <xsl:param name="href" />
  <xsl:param name="content" />
  <a href="{$href}"><xsl:copy-of select="$content" /></a>
</xsl:template>
```

However, in the main TV Guide, the links are a bit more exotic – the style of the links change when you move the mouse over them. This is controlled by three attributes on the `<a>` elements, which are held in the `linkEvents` attribute set so that they can be reused in several situations:

```
<xsl:attribute-set name="linkEvents">
  <xsl:attribute name="style">
    <xsl:text>color: black; border-bottom: 1pt groove #CCC</xsl:text>
  </xsl:attribute>
  <xsl:attribute name="onmouseover">
    <xsl:text>javascript:this.style.background = '#CCC';</xsl:text>
  </xsl:attribute>
  <xsl:attribute name="onmouseout">
    <xsl:text>javascript:this.style.background = 'transparent';</xsl:text>
  </xsl:attribute>
</xsl:attribute-set>
```

So the more general-purpose `link` template isn't quite right because it doesn't add the `linkEvents` attribute set. Since the stylesheet we're working on is the exception to the general rule, it makes sense to change the `link` template in `utils2.xsl` to the simple version above. But then we need to override the `link` template in `TVGuide5.xsl`, so that it produces the links including the `linkEvents` attributes there (and move the `linkEvents` attribute set back into `TVGuide5.xsl`).

As you've seen, you can't override the `link` template if you *include* `utils2.xsl` so you have to import it by removing the `<xsl:include>` that's currently including `utils.xsl` and adding an `<xsl:import>` element instead, right at the top of the stylesheet, just under the start tag for the `<xsl:stylesheet>` element, as in `TVGuide5.xsl`:

```
<xsl:stylesheet version="1.0"
                xmlns:xsl="http://www.w3.org/1999/XSL/Transform"
                xmlns="http://www.w3.org/1999/xhtml">
```

```
<xsl:import href="utils2.xsl" />
...
</xsl:stylesheet>
```

Now, to override the `link` template from the `utils.xsl` stylesheet, all you need to do is add a `link` template to `TVGuide5.xsl` that does what you want it to do, along with the `linkEvents` attributes that it's referring to:

```
<xsl:stylesheet version="1.0"
                xmlns:xsl="http://www.w3.org/1999/XSL/Transform"
                xmlns="http://www.w3.org/1999/xhtml">

<xsl:import href="utils2.xsl" />
...
<xsl:attribute-set name="linkEvents">
  <xsl:attribute name="style">
    <xsl:text>color: black; border-bottom: 1pt groove #CCC</xsl:text>
  </xsl:attribute>
  <xsl:attribute name="onmouseover">
    <xsl:text>javascript:this.style.background = '#CCC';</xsl:text>
  </xsl:attribute>
  <xsl:attribute name="onmouseout">
    <xsl:text>javascript:this.style.background = 'transparent';</xsl:text>
  </xsl:attribute>
</xsl:attribute-set>

<xsl:template name="link">
  <xsl:param name="href" />
  <xsl:param name="content" />
  <a href="{$href}" xsl:use-attribute-sets="linkEvents">
    <xsl:copy-of select="$content" />
  </a>
</xsl:template>
...

</xsl:stylesheet>
```

When you transform `TVGuide.xml` with `TVGuide5.xsl`, you should see the following:

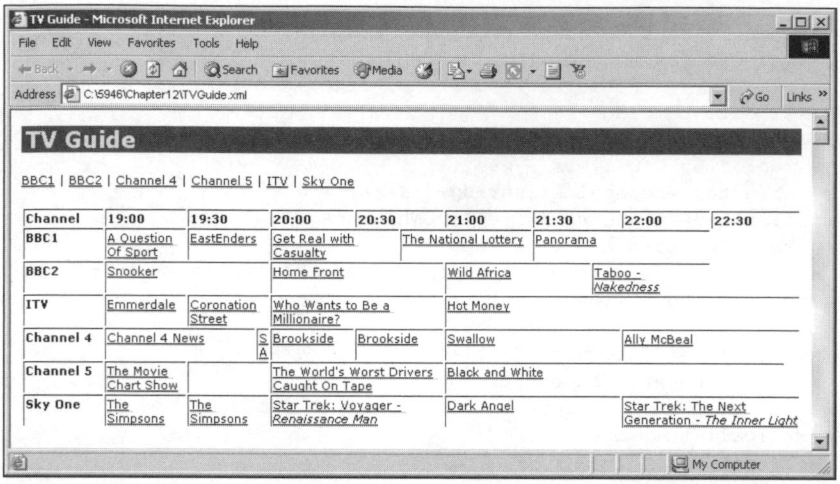

The links are still in the original style, with a gray underline, and react when you place the mouse over them. The `link` template in `TVGuide5.xsl` is used instead of the `link` template in `utils2.xsl`, even if it's called from templates within `utils2.xsl` or any of the stylesheets included in `TVGuide5.xsl`.

Accessing XML Data

In the last chapter, we looked at a template that would search and replace characters, words, and phrases within a string; in the example we looked at, tabs were replaced by three spaces, carriage returns were deleted, and line breaks were replaced by `<br>` elements with the following template:

```
<xsl:template name="replaceWhitespace">
  <xsl:param name="string" />
  <xsl:choose>
    <!-- replacing tabs -->
    <xsl:when test="contains($string, '&#x9;')">
      <xsl:call-template name="replaceWhitespace">
        <xsl:with-param name="string"
                        select="substring-before($string, '&#x9;')" />
      </xsl:call-template>
      <xsl:text>   </xsl:text>
      <xsl:call-template name="replaceWhitespace">
        <xsl:with-param name="string"
                        select="substring-after($string, '&#x9;')" />
      </xsl:call-template>
    </xsl:when>
    <!-- replacing carriage returns -->
    <xsl:when test="contains($string, '&#xD;')">
      <xsl:call-template name="replaceWhitespace">
        <xsl:with-param name="string"
                        select="substring-before($string, '&#xD;')" />
      </xsl:call-template>
```

```
        <xsl:call-template name="replaceWhitespace">
          <xsl:with-param name="string"
                          select="substring-after($string, '&#xD;')" />
        </xsl:call-template>
      </xsl:when>
      <!-- replacing new lines -->
      <xsl:when test="contains($string, '&#xA;')">
        <xsl:call-template name="replaceWhitespace">
          <xsl:with-param name="string"
                          select="substring-before($string, '&#xA;')" />
        </xsl:call-template>
        <br />
        <xsl:call-template name="replaceWhitespace">
          <xsl:with-param name="string"
                          select="substring-after($string, '&#xA;')" />
        </xsl:call-template>
      </xsl:when>
      <xsl:otherwise>
        <xsl:value-of select="$string" />
      </xsl:otherwise>
    </xsl:choose>
  </xsl:template>
```

While this template does the job, it's not very easy to change or extend. If we wanted to change it so that we could use it to replace other characters, words, or phrases, then we would have to alter the template, probably adding even more to it – and it's long enough as it is!

Really, we want to be able to define somewhere which strings should be replaced and with what they should be replaced. Since we know that XML is a good way of representing information, we could store the mappings in an XML structure, and then use that XML to guide the replacements that we need to carry out:

```
<replacements xml:space="preserve">
  <search>&#x9;</search><replace>    </replace>
  <search>&#xD;</search><replace />
  <search>&#xA;</search><replace><br /></replace>
</replacements>
```

The `xml:space` attribute on the `<replacements>` element ensures that the whitespace characters in the XML (the spaces, tabs, new lines, and carriage returns) are always seen by an application, rather than discarded as whitespace-only text nodes.

We could place this XML within the source document for the stylesheet, `TVGuide.xml`, but that would mix the content (the programs and so on) and the presentation of the content in the same document, which is precisely what we moved to XML to avoid. So these replacements need to go in a separate document (`replacements.xml`) and we need a way of getting hold of them.

Accessing External Documents

You can access an external XML document with the `document()` function. The first argument to the `document()` function is the URL for the document that you want to access, relative to the stylesheet itself, and it returns the root node of the node tree from that document, which is built in just the same way as the node tree for the source document (which you learned about in Chapter 7).

For example, to get hold of the root node of `replacements.xml`, you can use the following path:

```
document('replacements.xml')
```

Note that the first argument is a URL rather than a file path. This means that you should use forward slashes to separate directories, and if you want to access a file on your local machine you should prefix the filename with `file:///`. For example, if I wanted to use an absolute path to `replacements.xml`, which is held in the directory `C:\5946\Chapter12\` on my local Windows machine, I would have to use the URL `file:///C:/5946/Chapter12/replacements.xml`.

> *You could use any URL that returns an XML document. The document doesn't have to be a whole file – you can use fragment identifiers to retrieve parts of an external document (as long as they're identified with ID attributes). Also, the document could be generated on the fly on the server (for example, from a database).*

Because the `document()` function returns a root node, you can use it at the beginning of a location path and then step down further into the document. For example, to find the second `<search>` element in the `replacements.xml` document, you could use:

```
document('replacements.xml')/replacements/search[2]
```

The documents that you access with the `document()` function must be well-formed XML documents, just the same as the source XML document, and have to have a single document element. You cannot use the `document()` function to access plain text documents, for example.

If the processor has any problems locating the document that you've specified, or if it turns out not to be an XML document, then the processor can either return an empty node set or halt the transformation altogether. Most processors do the latter, so you have to be quite careful that the file paths that you use do actually point to an existing XML document.

> *Unfortunately, there's no way to test whether a document exists before you try to access it with the `document()` function, at least not without resorting to extension functions.*

When you access an external document within your stylesheet, it's good practice to create global variables that hold the root nodes of both the external document and the source document, so that you can easily switch between the two documents if necessary. For example, if I were using `replacements.xml`, I would usually include the following variable definitions in my stylesheet:

```
<xsl:variable name="data" select="/" />
<xsl:variable name="replacements" select="document('replacements.xml')" />
```

You can use the `document()` function to access information from an external XML document as if it were the source document for the stylesheet. The first argument is the location of the XML document.

Try It Out – Using Information from an External XML Document

To test out using information from external XML documents, we'll create a general template for replacing characters, words, and phrases, and use it to format the dates that are displayed when we list the episodes showing for each series in our TV Guide. Currently (with `TVGuide5.xsl`), the dates are rather difficult to read, as you can see:

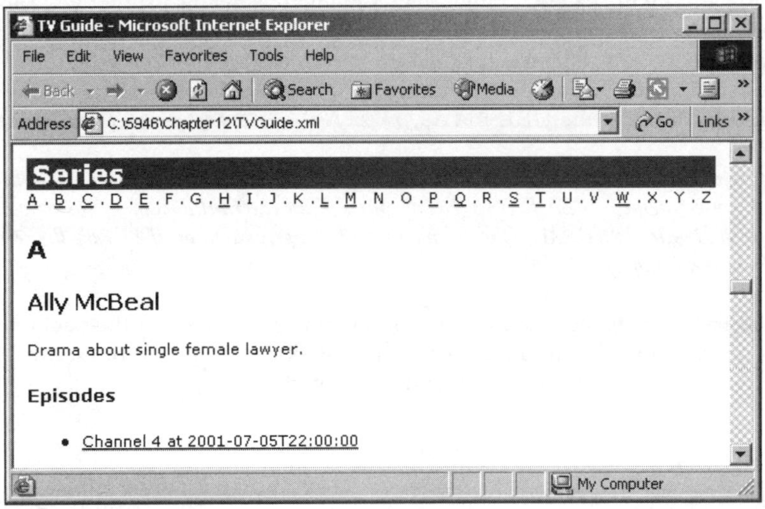

We could make these dates easier to read by replacing `"-01-"` with `" Jan "`, `"-02-"` with `" Feb "`, and so on, and the `T` with a space.

The first step is to create a `replacements.xml` file that holds an XML specification of the replacements that we want to make:

```
<replacements xml:space="preserve">
  <search>-01-</search><replace> Jan </replace>
  <search>-02-</search><replace> Feb </replace>
  ...
  <search>T</search><replace> </replace>
</replacements>
```

Next, we need to edit the `replaceWhitespace` template so that rather than doing a fixed set of replacements, it can use a set of `<search>` elements to work out which strings need to be replaced and with what. Of course, since it replaces more than just whitespace now, we should also change its name, to simply `replace`. The template just needs to be passed the string in which it needs to do the replacements and the first of the `<search>` elements that should be used to do the replacements:

```
<xsl:template name="replace">
  <xsl:param name="string" />
  <xsl:param name="search" select="/.." />
  ...
</xsl:template>
```

Next, we need to think about the stopping condition. The template can stop trying to replace strings if there isn't a string left for it to replace things in (the `$string` parameter is an empty string) or if there are no more replacements to be made (the `$search` parameter is an empty node set):

```
<xsl:template name="replace">
  <xsl:param name="string" />
  <xsl:param name="search" select="/.." />
  <xsl:choose>
    <xsl:when test="$string and $search">
      ...
    </xsl:when>
    <xsl:otherwise>
      <xsl:value-of select="$string" />
    </xsl:otherwise>
  </xsl:choose>
</xsl:template>
```

Now, if the template manages to find the search string (`$search`) in the string, then it needs to recurse on the part before this search string, with the next `<search>` element, and the part after the search string, with the same `<search>` element (in case that same search string occurs twice). Between the results of the two recursions, we need to copy the content of the `<replace>` element that immediately follows the `<search>` element. If the string doesn't contain the search string, then we need to try the replacement on the same string with the next `<search>` element. If there isn't a `<search>` element, or the string's empty, then we can just return the string as it is:

```
<xsl:template name="replace">
  <xsl:param name="string" />
  <xsl:param name="search" select="/.." />
  <xsl:choose>
    <xsl:when test="$string and $search">
      <xsl:variable name="nextSearch"
                    select="$search/following-sibling::search[1]" />
      <xsl:choose>
        <xsl:when test="contains($string, $search)">
          <xsl:call-template name="replace">
            <xsl:with-param name="string"
                            select="substring-before($string, $search)" />
            <xsl:with-param name="search"
                            select="$nextSearch" />
          </xsl:call-template>
          <xsl:copy-of
            select="$search/following-sibling::replace[1]/node()" />
          <xsl:call-template name="replace">
            <xsl:with-param name="string"
                            select="substring-after($string, $search)" />
```

```
            <xsl:with-param name="search" select="$search" />
          </xsl:call-template>
        </xsl:when>
        <xsl:otherwise>
          <xsl:call-template name="replace">
            <xsl:with-param name="string" select="$string" />
            <xsl:with-param name="search" select="$nextSearch" />
          </xsl:call-template>
        </xsl:otherwise>
      </xsl:choose>
    </xsl:when>
    <xsl:otherwise>
      <xsl:value-of select="$string" />
    </xsl:otherwise>
  </xsl:choose>
</xsl:template>
```

This `replace` template is a utility template, so its proper home is `utils3.xsl`.

Now we have to think about calling the `replace` template in order to format the dates that we're using. The template that displays the dates in the episode listing is in `series.xsl` – it's the template that matches `<Series>` elements:

```
<xsl:template match="TVGuide/Series">
  <div>
    ...
    <h5>Episodes</h5>
    <ul>
      <xsl:for-each select="key('programsBySeries', @id)">
        <li>
          <xsl:call-template name="link">
            <xsl:with-param name="href"
                            select="concat('#', generate-id())" />
            <xsl:with-param name="content">
              <xsl:value-of select="parent::Channel/Name" />
              <xsl:text> at </xsl:text>
              <xsl:value-of select="Start" />
              <xsl:if test="string(Title)">
                <xsl:text>: </xsl:text>
                <xsl:value-of select="Title" />
              </xsl:if>
            </xsl:with-param>
          </xsl:call-template>
        </li>
      </xsl:for-each>
    </ul>
  </div>
</xsl:template>
```

We need to replace the instruction that just inserts the value of the `<Start>` element with a call to the `replace` template. The `$string` parameter needs to be the value of the `<Start>` element. The `$search` parameter needs to be the first `<search>` element in our `replacements.xml` document.

We can access the `replacements.xml` document with the `document()` function, as follows:

```
document('replacements.xml')
```

That will get us the root node of `replacements.xml`. We need to step down from there through the `<replacements>` element to the first `<search>` element:

```
document('replacements.xml')/replacements/search[1]
```

That's the `<search>` element that we need to pass to the `replace` template, so the call, in `series2.xsl`, is as follows:

```
<xsl:template match="TVGuide/Series">
  <div>
    ...
    <h5>Episodes</h5>
    <ul>
      <xsl:for-each select="key('programsBySeries', @id)">
        <li>
          <xsl:call-template name="link">
            <xsl:with-param name="href"
                            select="concat('#', generate-id())" />
            <xsl:with-param name="content">
              <xsl:value-of select="parent::Channel/Name" />
              <xsl:text> at </xsl:text>
              <xsl:call-template name="replace">
                <xsl:with-param name="string" select="Start" />
                <xsl:with-param name="search"
                                select="document('replacements.xml')
                                        /replacements/search[1]" />
              </xsl:call-template>
              <xsl:if test="string(Title)">
                <xsl:text>: </xsl:text>
                <xsl:value-of select="Title" />
              </xsl:if>
            </xsl:with-param>
          </xsl:call-template>
        </li>
      </xsl:for-each>
    </ul>
  </div>
</xsl:template>
```

We've amended two of the modules of our stylesheet to create `utils3.xsl` and `series2.xsl`. These need to be imported and included into `TVGuide6.xsl`. When you transform `TVGuide.xml` with `TVGuide6.xsl`, you should see the dates formatted correctly:

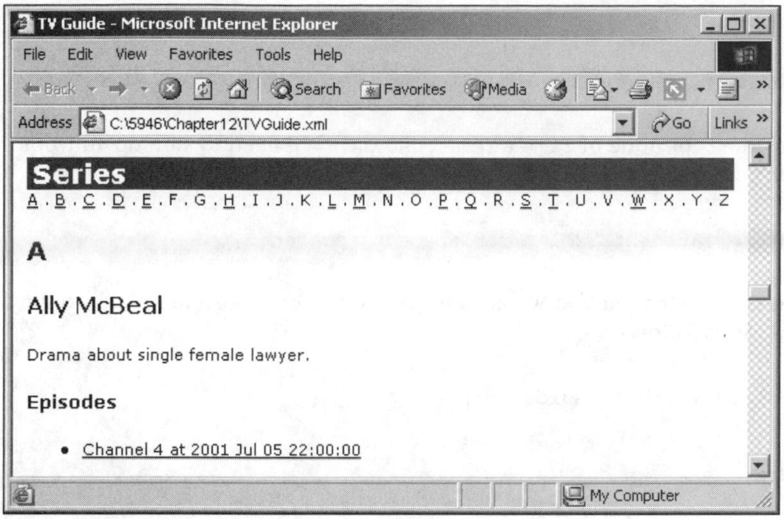

The dates are being formatted via a generic `replace` template. The information about what replacements should take place is held in an external document that acts as an adjunct to the file, in `replacements.xml`. You could edit `replacements.xml` to change what was replaced with what – to give the full names of the months, for example, or to replace the year 2001 with an empty string and thus delete it.

Putting Data in Stylesheets

Sometimes it's convenient to hold the XML data that you want to use in a particular template in the stylesheet holding the template itself. This can ease maintenance because you don't have to create separate files for each bit of XML data, and you can see immediately what information is being used in a particular template.

You can include any XML data you want at the top level of the stylesheet, in elements that are direct children of the `<xsl:stylesheet>` document element, as long as they are in a namespace other than the XSLT namespace. These elements are known as **data elements**.

Normally you should use a prefix for the namespace that you use for the data elements, rather than use the default namespace, as otherwise any un-prefixed literal result elements that you include in your stylesheet will be placed in that namespace as well (which is rarely what you want). In addition, if you ever need to get hold of the data elements by name, you have to use a prefix anyway, because prefixes are always required when naming elements in XPath expressions. To prevent the namespace for the data elements being declared in the result document, you should list the prefix in the `exclude-result-prefixes` attribute that you first saw in Chapter 8. So the general pattern for including data elements in a stylesheet is:

```
<xsl:stylesheet version="1.0"
                xmlns:xsl="http://www.w3.org/1999/XSL/Transform"
                xmlns:data="http://www.example.com/data"
                exclude-result-prefixes="data">
...
```

```
<data:element>
...
</data:element>
...
</xsl:stylesheet>
```

Once you've placed your data in the stylesheet, you can get at it by accessing the stylesheet itself as a node tree using the `document()` function. To access the stylesheet itself, you can use an empty string as the single argument, as follows:

```
document('')
```

This empty string is interpreted as a relative URL to the stylesheet, and so the `document()` function returns the root node of a node tree constructed from the stylesheet in the same way as an XSLT processor creates a node tree for a source XML document. From there, you need to navigate down through the document element (`<xsl:stylesheet>`) and then down to the data that you've included in the stylesheet. For example:

```
document('')/xsl:stylesheet/data:element
```

You can also use the `document()` function on the stylesheet to get at any other information you have within it, such as the global parameters that are defined within it or the names of the templates or attribute sets that are available.

If the only argument to the `document()` function is an empty string, it returns the root node of the stylesheet itself.

Try It Out – Storing Data in the Stylesheet

In the last Try It Out section, we created a `replace` template that could take a set of replacements defined by `<search>` elements and use them to search and replace words in a string.

Rather than holding the XML defining the replacements in a separate file, you could place them in the stylesheet itself (in this case, in `series3.xsl`). To do so, at least the top-most element of the included data needs to be in a namespace, so you also need to declare a namespace (for example, `http://www.example.com/replacements`) within the stylesheet:

```
<xsl:stylesheet version="1.0"
                xmlns:xsl="http://www.w3.org/1999/XSL/Transform"
                xmlns:html="http://www.w3.org/1999/xhtml"
                xmlns:rep="http://www.example.com/replacements"
                exclude-result-prefixes="rep">
...
<rep:replacements xml:space="preserve" xmlns="">
<search>-01-</search><replace> Jan </replace>
<search>-02-</search><replace> Feb </replace>
...
<search>T</search><replace> </replace>
```

```
</rep:replacements>
...
</xsl:stylesheet>
```

I've included a default namespace declaration on the `<replacements>` element so that the `<search>` and `<replace>` elements are in no namespace, just as they were before. Without the default namespace declaration on the `<replacements>` element, the `<search>` and `<replace>` elements would be in the XHTML namespace declared as the default namespace on the `<xsl:stylesheet>` element.

The path to the `<search>` elements that we use when calling the `replace` template needs to change to reflect the facts that:

- The XML is now in the stylesheet rather than `replacements.xml`
- The `<replacements>` element is in a namespace

The new call uses `document('')` to access the root node of the stylesheet, and adds the `rep` prefix to the name of the `<replacements>` element:

```
<xsl:template match="TVGuide/Series">
  <div>
    ...
    <h5>Episodes</h5>
    <ul>
      <xsl:for-each select="key('programsBySeries', @id)">
        <li>
          <xsl:call-template name="link">
            <xsl:with-param name="href"
                            select="concat('#', generate-id())" />
            <xsl:with-param name="content">
              <xsl:value-of select="parent::Channel/Name" />
              <xsl:text> at </xsl:text>
              <xsl:call-template name="replace">
                <xsl:with-param name="string" select="Start" />
                <xsl:with-param name="search"
                                select="document('')/xsl:stylesheet
                                        /rep:replacements/search[1]" />
              </xsl:call-template>
              <xsl:if test="string(Title)">
                <xsl:text>: </xsl:text>
                <xsl:value-of select="Title" />
              </xsl:if>
            </xsl:with-param>
          </xsl:call-template>
        </li>
      </xsl:for-each>
    </ul>
  </div>
</xsl:template>
```

Otherwise everything stays the same – the only difference is where the definitions of the search and replace terms come from. `TVGuide7.xsl` includes `series3.xsl`, in which these changes have been made. When you transform `TVGuide.xml` with `TVGuide7.xsl`, you should find the dates being formatted nicely as they were before:

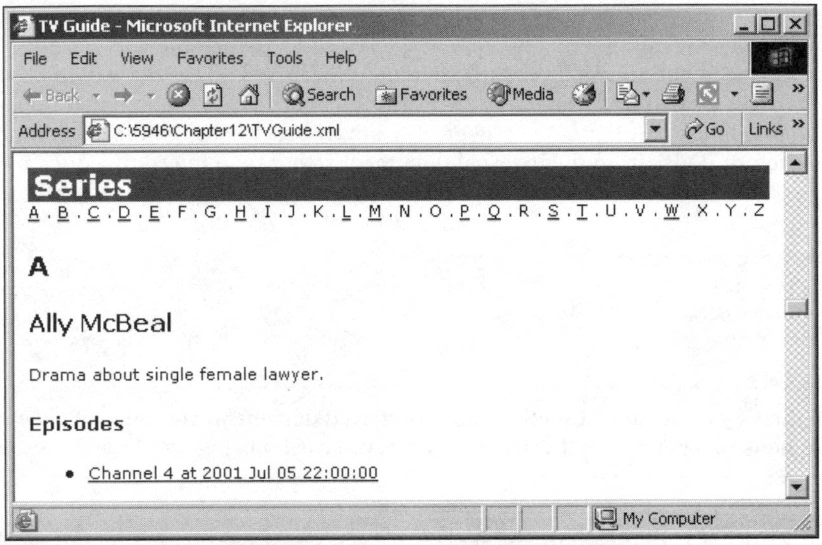

The dates are being formatted in exactly the same way as before, through the `replace` template. But this time the `<search>` and `<replace>` elements that define the replacements are in `series3.xsl` rather than being in an external document.

Using Keys in External Documents

One of the main ways in which you can use external documents to augment your stylesheet is to provide **lookup tables**. Lookup tables encode the mapping between an identifier and a piece of information. They are used to do things like:

- Give translations for a term in different languages
- Provide the labels used for different codes
- Hold the mapping between abbreviations and full names
- Specify the ordering of a set of strings (the position of the node acts as its identifier)

Often the set of mappings held in the XML lookup table will be quite large, or you will want to access it many times. As you learned in Chapter 10, the quickest way of accessing information by the value of one of its attributes or descendants is using a key, defined with an `<xsl:key>` element and accessed using the `key()` function.

However, the `key()` function (and the `id()` function) both only search for the relevant element within the document that holds the context node. As we've seen, the lookup tables are often held in other documents – in the stylesheet itself or another external document. If you try to use the key while processing an element in the source document, then the XSLT processor will only look in the source document for the elements that match the key.

Therefore, to use a key on an external document, you need to change the context node from the source document to the document in which the lookup table is located. The easiest way to do this is with an `<xsl:for-each>` instruction that iterates over just one node within the external document (the root node is a good one to use). The `<xsl:for-each>` simply acts to change the current node, and thus makes the key return nodes from the external document rather than the source document. The code to access nodes in an external document using a key therefore usually looks like the following:

```
<xsl:variable name="keyValue" select="..." />
<xsl:for-each select="document('externalDocument.xml')">
  ... key('keyName', $keyValue) ...
</xsl:for-each>
```

> **To use the `key()` or `id()` functions on an external document, you must change the current node to a node in that external document, usually using `<xsl:for-each>`.**

Try It Out – Decoding Dates

In the last couple of Try It Out sections, we made the dates of the programs more readable by searching and replacing. Here, we'll format them differently, in the format:

```
19:00 on 5 Jul 2001
```

We'll do this in a separate `formatDate` function that we'll put in `utils4.xsl`. Getting hold of the numerical values of the time, day, month, and year is easy using the `substring()` function, and outputting the day and year is straightforward as well, because they're just numbers:

```
<xsl:template name="formatDate">
  <xsl:param name="date" select="." />
  <xsl:variable name="year" select="substring($date, 1, 4)" />
  <xsl:variable name="month" select="substring($date, 6, 2)" />
  <xsl:variable name="day" select="substring($date, 9, 2)" />
  <xsl:variable name="time" select="substring($date, 12, 5)" />
  <xsl:value-of select="$time" />
  <xsl:text> on </xsl:text>
  <xsl:value-of select="number($day)" />
  <xsl:text> </xsl:text>
  ...
  <xsl:text> </xsl:text>
  <xsl:value-of select="$year" />
</xsl:template>
```

The more tricky part is getting hold of the abbreviation for the month. You could use a big `<xsl:choose>` to work it out, but it's easier to create a set of XML that stores all sorts of information about each month – month numbers, names, abbreviations, and days in the month – as follows:

```
<months>
  <month num="1"  abbr="Jan" days="31">January</month>
  <month num="2"  abbr="Feb" days="28">February</month>
  <month num="3"  abbr="Mar" days="31">March</month>
  <month num="4"  abbr="Apr" days="30">April</month>
  <month num="5"  abbr="May" days="31">May</month>
  <month num="6"  abbr="Jun" days="30">June</month>
  <month num="7"  abbr="Jul" days="31">July</month>
  <month num="8"  abbr="Aug" days="31">August</month>
  <month num="9"  abbr="Sep" days="30">September</month>
  <month num="10" abbr="Oct" days="31">October</month>
  <month num="11" abbr="Nov" days="30">November</month>
  <month num="12" abbr="Dec" days="31">December</month>
</months>
```

You can store this in `months.xml`.

To quickly access the `<month>` elements by their month number, you could first define a `months` key that indexed the `<month>` elements by their `num` attribute:

```
<xsl:key name="months" match="month" use="@num" />
```

and then use the `key()` function to retrieve the `<month>` element associated with a particular number. For example, to get the abbreviation for the fourth month in the year, you could use:

```
key('months', 4)/@abbr
```

If you used this key directly within the `formatDate` template, the XSLT processor would search the TV Guide for `<month>` elements (and it won't find any). To use this key on the `months.xml` document, you need to change the context to the `months.xml` document using `<xsl:for-each>` and search within it for the relevant `<month>` element:

```
<xsl:template name="formatDate">
  <xsl:param name="date" select="." />
  <xsl:variable name="year" select="substring($date, 1, 4)" />
  <xsl:variable name="month" select="substring($date, 6, 2)" />
  <xsl:variable name="day" select="substring($date, 9, 2)" />
  <xsl:variable name="time" select="substring($date, 12, 5)" />
  <xsl:value-of select="$time" />
  <xsl:text> on </xsl:text>
  <xsl:value-of select="number($day)" />
  <xsl:text> </xsl:text>
  <xsl:for-each select="document('months.xml')">
    <xsl:value-of select="key('months', number($month))/@abbr" />
  </xsl:for-each>
  <xsl:text> </xsl:text>
  <xsl:value-of select="$year" />
</xsl:template>
```

We'll call this from the template matching `<Series>` elements in `series4.xsl`, at the point where we were using the `replace` template previously:

```
<xsl:template match="TVGuide/Series">
  <div>
    ...
    <h5>Episodes</h5>
    <ul>
      <xsl:for-each select="key('programsBySeries', @id)">
        <li>
          <xsl:call-template name="link">
            <xsl:with-param name="href"
                            select="concat('#', generate-id())" />
            <xsl:with-param name="content">
              <xsl:value-of select="parent::Channel/Name" />
              <xsl:text> at </xsl:text>
              <xsl:call-template name="formatDate">
                <xsl:with-param name="date" select="Start" />
              </xsl:call-template>
              <xsl:if test="string(Title)">
                <xsl:text>: </xsl:text>
                <xsl:value-of select="Title" />
              </xsl:if>
            </xsl:with-param>
          </xsl:call-template>
        </li>
      </xsl:for-each>
    </ul>
  </div>
</xsl:template>
```

`TVGuide8.xsl` imports `utils4.xsl` (which contains the `formatDate` template) and includes `series4.xsl` (which calls the `formatDate` template). When you transform `TVGuide.xml` with `TVGuide8.xsl`, you should see the following:

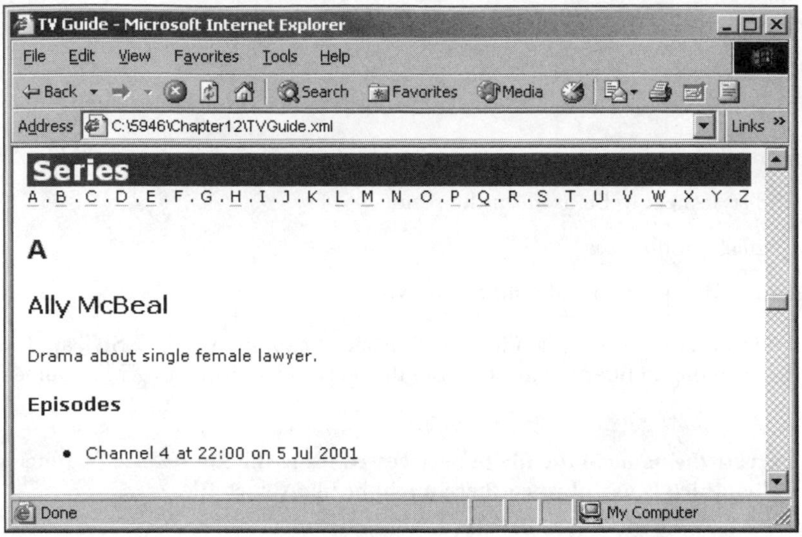

The dates are formatted with the month abbreviations by the template `formatDate`. The month abbreviations come from `months.xml` originally, and are retrieved using the `months` key defined in `utils4.xsl`. If you needed to make the same information available in a different country, you could edit `months.xml` so that you used that country's language for the month abbreviations.

Accessing Customization Information

A second common reason for accessing external documents is to get hold of information that enables you to customize the presentation of the XML source document according to the requirements of the user. One method of organizing customization information is to have separate XML documents available for each user of the system, and name them according to a unique identifier for the user. For example, `JeniT.xml` could hold extra information about how I want the TV Guide to be displayed.

The identifier for the user can be passed into the stylesheet as a global parameter; you have to define the parameter at the top level of the stylesheet. For example, to define the `$userID` parameter, you could use:

```
<xsl:param name="userID" select="'default'" />
```

You learned about defining and using global parameters in Chapter 6. You'll see more about using them in dynamic XSLT applications in Chapter 14. Remember that the single quotes in the `select` attribute set the value to a string and prevent it from being interpreted as a location path.

This user ID parameter can be used as the basis of the string passed to the `document()` function – concatenate the user ID with the string `'.xml'` and you have a reference for the appropriate file. The document element of this preferences document can be stored in its own variable to make it easier to access later on:

```
<xsl:variable name="prefs"
              select="document(concat($userID, '.xml'))/Prefs" />
```

The user preferences that you store in these customization files can include things like:

- The user's name, so that they can be greeted
- The CSS stylesheet to be used on the result
- The language of the user
- The areas of the page that should be shown or hidden

User customization files can also contain information specific to the type of XSLT application that you're constructing, for example, to filter the information that gets shown from an XML source document.

> **You can create the name of the file to be accessed using the `document()` function dynamically, which is useful when there might be many such files.**

Try It Out – Creating XML for User Preferences

There are quite a few user preferences that are currently either built in to the XML for the TV Guide or built in to the XSLT stylesheet. For example:

- Which programs should be flagged?
- Which series should be flagged?
- Which keywords should be highlighted in descriptions?

Rather than having this information built in to either the XML document or the XSLT stylesheet, it should be separated out into a document for each user. That way the same TV Guide XML document can be used for multiple users with different interests. The preferences documents need to contain:

- A list of flagged programs, which can be identified by their channel and start time
- A list of favorite series, which can be identified through their `id` attribute
- A list of keywords

My preferences XML document (`JeniT.xml`) might look like the following:

```
<Prefs>
  <Programs>
    <Program channel="BBC2" start="2001-07-05T21:50:00" />
  </Programs>
  <Series>
    <Series ref="EastEnders" />
    <Series ref="AllyMcBeal" />
    <Series ref="StarTrekNextGeneration" />
  </Series>
  <Keywords>
```

```
    <Keyword>Sci-fi</Keyword>
    <Keyword>news</Keyword>
    <Keyword>Earth</Keyword>
  </Keywords>
</Prefs>
```

The stylesheet needs to be able to accept a parameter that points to the file that holds the user preferences. We'll define this through the `$userID` parameter in `TVGuide9.xsl`:

```
<xsl:param name="userID" select="'default'" />
```

and then get the preferences by concatenating this user ID with the extension `.xml`:

```
<xsl:variable name="prefs"
              select="document(concat($userID, '.xml'))/Prefs" />
```

We'd better create an empty `default.xml` preferences file, so that the XSLT processor finds a document when it tries to look for the preferences. It's very simple:

```
<?xml version="1.0"?>
<Prefs />
```

Now let's look at how to change the XSLT so that it looks at the preferences in the referenced preferences file rather than in the TV Guide XML document.

Rather than looking at a `flag` attribute on the `<Program>` element, a program might now be marked as a favorite (with an image) if the program's series is listed within the preferences document, and marked as interesting if the program itself is listed specifically. We'll work all this out within a template that matches the `<Program>` element in `flag` mode (based on the previous template that was applied to the `flag` attribute):

```
<xsl:template match="Program" mode="flag">
  <xsl:variable name="favorite"
                select="$prefs/Series/Series/@ref = Series" />
  <xsl:variable name="channel" select="parent::Channel/Name" />
  <xsl:variable name="start" select="Start" />
  <xsl:variable name="interesting"
                select="$prefs/Programs/Program[@channel = $channel and
                                                @start = $start]" />
  <xsl:if test="$favorite or $interesting">
    <xsl:variable name="image">
      <xsl:choose>
        <xsl:when test="$favorite">favorite</xsl:when>
        <xsl:when test="$interesting">interest</xsl:when>
      </xsl:choose>
    </xsl:variable>
    <xsl:variable name="alt">
      <xsl:choose>
        <xsl:when test="$favorite">Favorite</xsl:when>
```

```
        <xsl:when test="$interesting">Interest</xsl:when>
      </xsl:choose>
    </xsl:variable>
    <img src="{$image}.gif" alt="[{$alt}]" width="20" height="20" />
  </xsl:if>
</xsl:template>
```

This template is 'called' from the template matching `<Program>` elements in `Details` mode:

```
<xsl:template match="Program" mode="Details">
  ...
  <p>
    <a name="{generate-id()}" id="{generate-id()}">
      <xsl:apply-templates select="Start" />
    </a>
    <br />
    <xsl:apply-templates select="." mode="generateStars" />
    <br />
    <xsl:apply-templates select="." mode="flag" />
    ...
  </p>
  ...
</xsl:template>
```

In the same way, the keywords that are highlighted in description text should come from the preferences document rather than from the TV Guide:

```
<xsl:template match="Description//text()">
  <xsl:call-template name="highlightKeywords">
    <xsl:with-param name="string" select="." />
    <xsl:with-param name="keywords" select="$prefs/Keywords/Keyword" />
  </xsl:call-template>
</xsl:template>
```

Now that `TVGuide9.xsl` is set up properly (and references the altered `description2.xsl`), we can change the TV Guide XML so that it doesn't include all the preferences information that it did before. The ratings are still the same, but the `flag` attributes and keyword list at the bottom of the file can be removed, to create `TVGuide2.xml`.

When you transform `TVGuide2.xml` with `TVGuide9.xsl`, you should see the following:

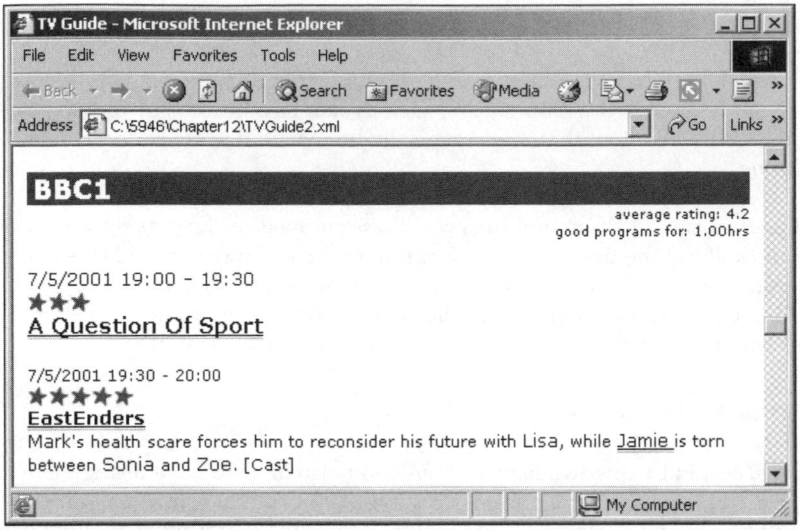

Some programs are still highlighted, because they've got good ratings (which isn't a matter of personal preference), but the TV listing doesn't contain any flags. Currently, the stylesheet is using `default.xml` to provide the preferences information, and it doesn't contain much!

Now try transforming `TVGuide2.xml` with `TVGuide9.xsl` and pass in the value `"JeniT.xml"` as the value of the `$userID` parameter. You should see the following:

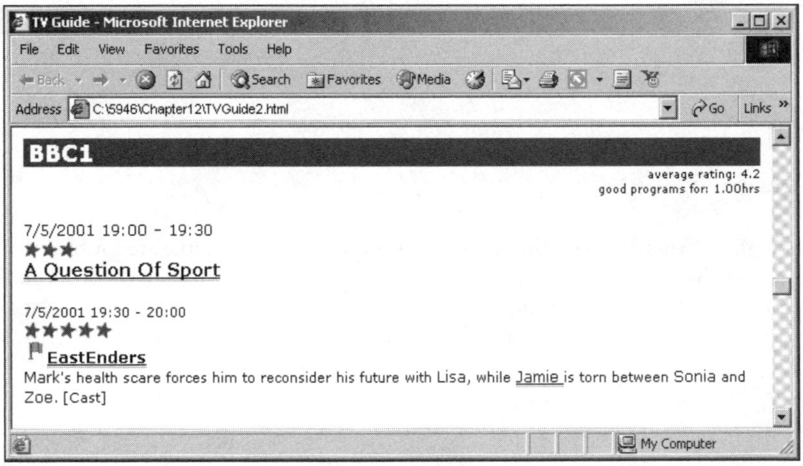

A green flag (for favorite) has been added to the EastEnders listing, because it's one of my favorite programs. Elsewhere, you should see specific words being highlighted in descriptions, and flags being added to other programs.

You can make your own user preferences file to indicate the programs that you like to watch, or the keywords that you want to highlight, and pass your user ID into the stylesheet to see how it changes the presentation of the same TV listing.

Including Content from External Documents

A third way in which external documents can be useful within a stylesheet is in holding snippets of content that should be included within a page, such as standard headers or footers, banner ads, menus, and images – the kind of content that might typically be included using server-side includes in an HTML application.

You can use the `document()` function to access these snippets, as long as they are well-formed XML documents. You can't use the `document()` function to include any old HTML fragment, because the `document()` function always interprets the document as an XML document, and will not be able to parse the HTML. To insert a document into the result, simply copy it into the result tree. For example, to include `header.html` (which is a well-formed XHTML document) use:

```
<xsl:copy-of select="document('header.html')" />
```

The documents accessed by the `document()` function also have to have a single document element. So you could store a table in a document and access it, but you couldn't store a number of rows. To get around this, it's often handy to store the XHTML snippets that you want to include within a larger resources document, for example:

```
<Resources>
  <Menu>...<Menu>
  <Banners>
    <Banner id="...">...</Banner>
    ...
  </Banners>
  <Icons>
    <Icon id="...">...</Icon>
    ...
  </Icons>
  ...
</Resources>
```

You can create a global variable to hold all your resources, or create separate global variables for each type. You can access them through normal XPaths or using keys, as described earlier in this chapter. Once you've got hold of the XML representing the relevant resource, you can copy its content exactly as it stands, which is useful for images, for example, if you store them as well-formed HTML to start with:

```
<xsl:copy-of select="$icon/node()" />
```

Alternatively, you could apply templates to the content of the XML representing the relevant resource – this approach is better for resources that you don't want to store explicitly in HTML, such as menus:

```
<xsl:apply-templates select="$menu" />
```

The biggest advantage of storing resources in a separate file, rather than including them directly within the stylesheet, is that it allows designers to modify the resources without understanding the XSLT. It also means that you can easily reuse the same set of resources across a set of stylesheets.

You can use the `document()` function to retrieve resources and insert them into the HTML page using `<xsl:copy-of>`.

Retrieving Referenced Information

In the last section you saw how to use the `document()` function to access documents holding additional information that can be used by the stylesheet as lookup tables, as user preferences, or as standard headers and footers. All these kinds of documents give further information about how the source XML document should be *presented*. Whatever XML document is accessed, and wherever that XML document is, the same presentation information should be used. Therefore these types of documents are accessed relative to the stylesheet itself.

A second class of document is one that provides additional *content*. The source information for the stylesheet might be split over several XML documents, to make the authoring of the XML document more manageable (for example, splitting the XML for a book into one file per chapter) or to allow the reuse of information from several XML documents (for example, holding the descriptions of TV series in a separate file from the weekly TV guides).

Whatever XSLT stylesheet accesses the source XML document, and wherever that stylesheet is, the same content should be used. Therefore these types of documents need to be accessed relative to the source document rather than relative to the stylesheet.

Resolving Relative URLs

Say that our site houses TV guides for several different countries. Each set of TV guides is stored in its own directory – `usa` for the USA TV guides, `uk` for the UK TV guides, and so on. Each set of TV guides has its own `series.xml` document that lists the series that are shown in that country and a description of each of them. There's one `series.xml` document in the `usa` directory, another in the `uk` directory, and so on.

When the stylesheet comes to display a particular TV guide, it needs to look at the `series.xml` document that's in the same directory as the TV guide at which it's looking. If the `TVGuide.xml` document is in the `usa` directory, then it needs to look at `usa/series.xml`, and if it's in the `uk` directory the processor needs to access `uk/series.xml`.

You don't have explicit access within the stylesheet to the directory in which the source document resides and by default, as we've seen, the `document()` function accesses documents based on their location relative to the stylesheet. However, when you use the `document()` function, you can tell the XSLT processor to resolve a relative URL based on the location of a particular document by passing it a second argument – a node in that document.

So to get hold of the `series.xml` document in the same directory as the `TVGuide.xml` document (which is the source document for the stylesheet), you could use the following global variable:

```
<xsl:variable name="series"
              select="document('series.xml', /)" />
```

The second argument to the `document()` function is the root node of the source `TVGuide.xml` document (in whichever directory that document is located). Passing that as the second argument means that the `'series.xml'` path is resolved relative to the URL of the source document, in other words in the same directory as the `TVGuide.xml` document.

> **The URL passed as the first argument to the `document()` function is usually resolved relative to the stylesheet's location. If you pass a node as the second argument, the processor uses the location of the document that holds that node to resolve the URL.**

Try It Out – Accessing Series Information

Our TV Guide XML document describes the programs on particular channels over a certain period (actually only one day in our example). The descriptions of series are relevant for longer than that period, and could be used by several program listings, so rather than holding the series information in `TVGuide2.xml`, it should be stored in a separate document, `series.xml`:

```
<SeriesList>
  <Series id="EastEnders" type="soap">
    <Title>EastEnders</Title>
    <Description>Soap set in the East End of London.</Description>
  </Series>
  <Series id="BBCNews" type="news">
    <Title>BBC News</Title>
    <Description>Daily news and sport.</Description>
  </Series>
  ...
</SeriesList>
```

This document needs to be accessed relative to the program listing that's acting as the source document for the transformation.

We'll store the `<Series>` document element of `series.xml` in a `$series` global variable in `TVGuide10.xsl`, so that we can access it later on. The call to the `document()` function needs to take two arguments – `'series.xml'` as the relative URL to the series document, and a node from the program listing document (which may as well be the root node) to ensure that the URL is resolved relative to the program listing rather than the stylesheet:

```
<xsl:variable name="series"
              select="document('series.xml', /)/SeriesList" />
```

Whenever you deal with two documents like this, and particularly when you're going to need to jump back and forth between them, it's handy to hold the document element of the source document in a global variable as well:

```
<xsl:variable name="listing"
              select="/TVGuide" />
```

The series information is used in a couple of places within the stylesheet. Firstly, it's used to insert the title of the series (rather than its identifier) in the program description, currently with the following template:

```
<xsl:template match="Program" mode="Title">
  <span class="title">
    <xsl:choose>
      <xsl:when test="string(Series)">
        <xsl:call-template name="link">
          <xsl:with-param name="href" select="concat('#', Series)" />
          <xsl:with-param name="content"
                          select="string(key('IDs', Series)/Title)" />
        </xsl:call-template>
        <xsl:if test="string(Title)">
          <xsl:text> - </xsl:text>
          <span class="subtitle"><xsl:value-of select="Title" /></span>
        </xsl:if>
      </xsl:when>
      <xsl:otherwise>
        <xsl:value-of select="Title" />
      </xsl:otherwise>
    </xsl:choose>
  </span>
</xsl:template>
```

This template uses a key to access the `<Series>` element with a particular ID. As you saw earlier in this chapter, keys will only search in the document holding the context node, whereas we need the key to search in `series.xml`. You can use `<xsl:for-each>` to change the context node to one in `series.xml`; remember to hold the value of the program's `<Series>` element in a variable so that you can use it within the `<xsl:for-each>`, as follows:

```
<xsl:template match="Program" mode="Title">
  <span class="title">
    <xsl:choose>
      <xsl:when test="string(Series)">
        <xsl:call-template name="link">
          <xsl:with-param name="href" select="concat('#', Series)" />
          <xsl:with-param name="content">
            <xsl:variable name="seriesID" select="Series" />
            <xsl:for-each select="$series">
              <xsl:value-of select="key('IDs', $seriesID)/Title" />
            </xsl:for-each>
          </xsl:with-param>
        </xsl:call-template>
        <xsl:if test="string(Title)">
          <xsl:text> - </xsl:text>
          <span class="subtitle"><xsl:value-of select="Title" /></span>
        </xsl:if>
      </xsl:when>
      <xsl:otherwise>
        <xsl:value-of select="Title" />
      </xsl:otherwise>
```

```
      </xsl:choose>
    </span>
  </xsl:template>
```

A similar change is needed to create `table2.xsl`, in which the title of a program is accessed in the same kind of way within the template matching `<Program>` elements in `TableTitle` mode:

```
<xsl:template match="Program" mode="TableTitle">
  <xsl:call-template name="link">
    <xsl:with-param name="href" select="concat('#', generate-id())" />
    <xsl:with-param name="content">
      <span class="title">
        <xsl:choose>
          <xsl:when test="string(Series)">
            <xsl:variable name="seriesID" select="Series" />
            <xsl:for-each select="$series">
              <xsl:value-of select="key('IDs', $seriesID)/Title" />
            </xsl:for-each>
            <xsl:if test="string(Title)">
              <xsl:text> - </xsl:text>
              <span class="subtitle"><xsl:value-of select="Title" /></span>
            </xsl:if>
          </xsl:when>
          <xsl:otherwise>
            <xsl:value-of select="Title" />
          </xsl:otherwise>
        </xsl:choose>
      </span>
    </xsl:with-param>
  </xsl:call-template>
</xsl:template>
```

Another place in which information from `series.xml` is used is in creating a list of programs in each series. The alphabetical listing and the links at the top of the series listing are created with keys. So again, to get this listing to work, you need to change the current node used for these templates so that they look for keys in `series.xml`. You can do this at the point where the templates are called, in the template matching the `<TVGuide>` element within `TVGuide10.xsl`:

```
<xsl:template match="TVGuide">
  ...
  <h2>Series</h2>
  <xsl:for-each select="$series">
    <xsl:call-template name="alphabetList" />
    <xsl:call-template name="alphabeticalSeriesList" />
  </xsl:for-each>
</xsl:template>
```

The template that deals with these `<Series>` elements must also change because it too uses a key to quickly access information, this time from the program listing document. Again, you can use `<xsl:for-each>` to change the context node so that the key searches `TVGuide3.xml` rather than `series.xml`. Also, don't forget to change the `match` attribute of the template, since the `<Series>` elements are now within a `<SeriesList>` element rather than the `<TVGuide>` element as they were before:

```
<xsl:template match="SeriesList/Series">
  <div>
    ...
    <h5>Episodes</h5>
    <ul>
      <xsl:variable name="seriesID" select="@id" />
      <xsl:for-each select="$listing">
        <xsl:for-each select="key('programsBySeries', $seriesID)">
          <li>...</li>
        </xsl:for-each>
      </xsl:for-each>
    </ul>
  </div>
</xsl:template>
```

To sum up, we have two source documents: `series.xml` and `TVGuide3.xml`, with series information and listing information respectively. We've got `TVGuide10.xsl`, which holds the document elements of these two files in the global variables `$series` and `$listing` respectively, and these global variables are used in `TVGuide10.xsl`, in `series5.xsl`, and in `table2.xsl` to jump between documents to ensure that the correct context node is used when we use keys.

If you transform `TVGuide3.xml` with `TVGuide10.xsl`, you should see the following:

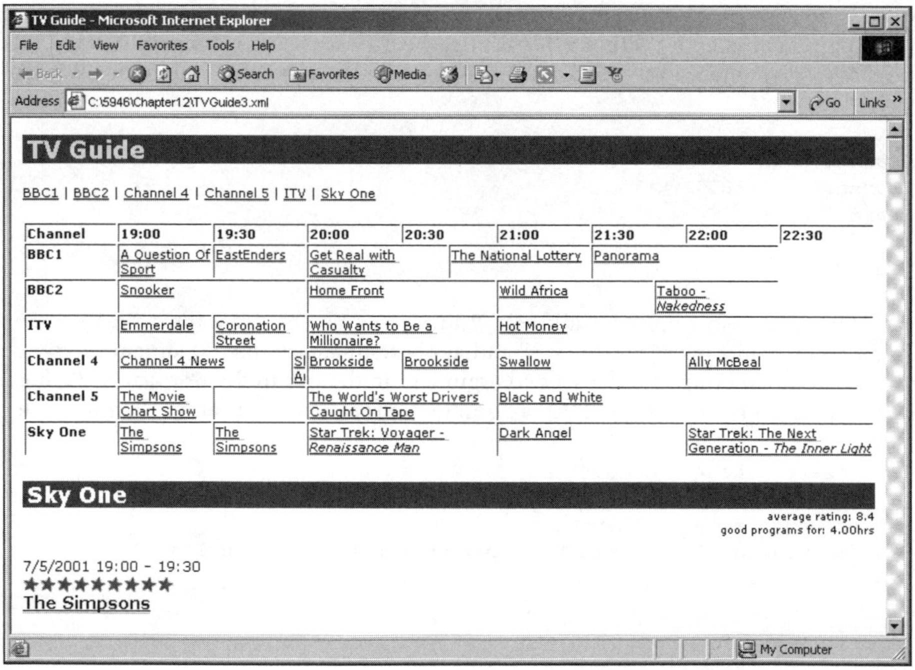

The series information is all present and correct, just as it was when it was embedded within the TV Guide listing. The series titles are retrieved from `series.xml`, which means that the same source of information can be used when the TV listing changes.

Accessing Multiple Documents

A TV listing is likely to be quite a large document, especially when you have lots of channels. Having a big source document is both unwieldy for an author and unwieldy for a stylesheet – the larger a source document, the more information the XSLT processor has to hold. Therefore, it's a good idea to split large XML documents into several smaller ones, such as one per channel. For example `BBC1.xml` might look like:

```
<Channel>
  <Name>BBC1</Name>
  <Program>
    <Start>2001-07-05T19:30:00</Start>
    <Duration>PT30M</Duration>
    <Series>EastEnders</Series>
    <Title></Title>
    <Description>
      Mark's health scare forces him to reconsider his future with Lisa,
      while Jamie is torn between Sonia and Zoe.
    </Description>
    ...
  </Program>
  ...
</Channel>
```

To include a particular channel within a TV listing, the `TVGuide.xml` document could refer to them with `<Channel>` elements whose `href` attribute points to the XML document for the channel:

```
<TVGuide>
  <Channel href="BBC1.xml" />
  <Channel href="BBC2.xml" />
  <Channel href="ITV.xml" />
  ...
</TVGuide>
```

You already know one way to process all the `<Channel>` elements from these files: iterate over each of the `<Channel>` elements in `TVGuide.xml` and apply templates to the document referenced in the `href` attribute (remembering to use a second argument in the call to the `document()` function so that the URLs are resolved relative to the `TVGuide.xml` source document rather than the stylesheet:

```
<xsl:template match="TVGuide">
  ...
  <xsl:for-each select="Channel">
    <xsl:apply-templates select="document(@href, .)/Channel" />
  </xsl:for-each>
  ...
</xsl:template>
```

There's another way to do this, however. Rather than being a string, the first argument to the `document()` function can be a node set. If it is a node set, then the `document()` function returns a node set of the root nodes of *all* the documents referred to by the URLs held by the nodes in the node set. So rather than iterating over all the `<Channel>` elements by hand, you could use the following call:

```
<xsl:template match="TVGuide">
  ...
  <xsl:apply-templates select="document(Channel/@href, .)/Channel" />
  ...
</xsl:template>
```

The XSLT processor takes each href attribute in turn, resolves the URL, and accesses the XML document.

Remember, though, that the more documents you have, the more you have to worry about which document you are in if you use things like keys.

If the first argument to the document() function is a node set, it returns the root nodes of all the documents referenced by the node set.

Summary

As you create larger XSLT applications, both the stylesheet and the source document can become very large and unwieldy. This chapter looked at two main ways of making XSLT applications more modular.

In the first part of the chapter, you saw how to use <xsl:include> and <xsl:import> to split up a stylesheet into several stylesheets. There are two main advantages of splitting up a stylesheet:

- It makes it easier to maintain
- It allows you to reuse the same templates and other components in several stylesheets

Importing stylesheets into each other is often more useful than including them, particularly when it comes to reusing the same utility stylesheet in several XSLT applications, because it allows you to override the templates, global variables and parameters, keys, and so on that the imported stylesheet contains.

In the second part of this chapter, you learned how to use the document() function to access information from documents other than the source of the transformation. These documents still need to be well-formed XML documents, but they can hold very useful information, for example:

- Data for performing operations like searching and replacing
- Lookup tables of various sorts
- User preferences and customization information
- Snippets of XHTML to be included in the result
- Additional information referenced by the source document

In its basic form, with one argument, the `document()` function retrieves documents relative to the stylesheet. These documents should affect how the source XML is presented. When passed a second argument, it's used to retrieve documents relative to documents other than the stylesheet. These documents should hold additional content. In either case, the first argument to the `document()` function can be a node set, in which case the values of all the nodes are used to retrieve external documents.

Review Questions

1. What difference does it make if you move an `<xsl:include>` up or down a stylesheet?

2. Name two things that an included stylesheet must not contain.

3. Can you use `<xsl:include>` within templates?

4. What differences are there between `<xsl:include>` and `<xsl:import>`?

5. Where must you place `<xsl:import>` within a stylesheet?

6. How does the XSLT processor decide which template to use if the main stylesheet and an imported stylesheet both contain templates that match the same node?

7. Is it possible to include or import different stylesheets based on the value of a parameter?

8. What function allows you to access external documents from the stylesheet?

9. Given that the stylesheet is in the `xslt` directory and the current node comes from the source document, which is in the `xml` directory, what documents do the following calls access?

```
document('extra.xml')
document('extra.xml', /)
document('extra.xml', .)
document('extra.xml', document(''))
```

10. Create some XSLT to search `films.xml` for `<Film>` elements whose `<Director>` element child has the value `'James Cameron'`. (The current document is `TVGuide.xml`.)

11. Given that the current node has several `<Reference>` element children, each of whose values is a URL, what do the following calls access?

```
document(Reference)
document(Reference, .)
document(concat('http://www.example.com/', Reference))
```

Beginning
XSLT

13

Extensions

While XSLT 1.0 and XPath 1.0 are quite powerful languages for transforming and querying XML respectively, there are some tasks that are difficult or impossible to achieve using them. For example, you've seen the hoops that you have to jump through to group elements using XSLT, and while it's possible to write recursive templates to calculate the minimum and maximum values from a set of nodes, it's very tedious to use them compared to using a function to do the same thing.

Naturally, as XSLT and XPath develop they will come to include instructions and functions that enable users to do the things that they need to do quickly and easily. However, in the meantime implementers are bound to respond to pressure from users for additional features, just as Netscape and Microsoft did within their respective web browsers during the development of HTML. In these situations, with different applications supporting different features, it can be hard to recognize when a particular feature is part of the standard language and when it is something defined in a particular implementation. Eventually, as with HTML, this leads to the implementations leading the standardization process rather than the other way around.

To prevent the confusion that could arise from implementers extending XSLT and XPath, both languages have a standard way of dealing with extensions, so that you can easily tell which instructions and functions are part of the XSLT and XPath standards and which are implementer-defined extensions. In this chapter, you'll see how to use the extensions that are offered by your XSLT processor and learn about a few extensions that are offered by XSLT processors in particular.

In this chapter, you'll learn:

- The different types of extensions implementations can make to XSLT and XPath
- How to detect whether an extension function or instruction is available
- How to recover when an extension instruction is not available
- How to use extension functions to convert result tree fragments to node sets
- How to use extension elements to create multiple result documents
- How to write your own extension functions with MSXML
- How to write your own extension functions with XSLT

Extensions to XSLT and XPath

The XSLT Recommendation defines precisely what kinds of extensions implementers are allowed to make to XSLT and XPath. In this section, we'll look at the kinds of things that extensions are allowed to do, before going on to look at how to use them. The four kinds of extensions that we'll look at are:

- Extension functions
- Extension attribute values
- Extension attributes
- Extension elements

Extension Functions

The first, and most common, way in which implementers can extend the utility of XSLT and XPath is by adding to the functionality of expressions and patterns. The only way in which implementers are allowed to extend XPath is by adding **extension functions** – they can't, for example, add a new operator or change the way in which their processor 'sees' XML documents.

More drastic changes are reserved for changes to the XPath standard itself. The XPath 2.0 Working Draft (http://www.w3.org/TR/xpath20/) defines a number of new operators and is built on a new data model, described in a second Working Draft (http://www.w3.org/TR/query-datamodel/). XPath 2.0 will also include many functions that are currently implemented as extensions; see http://www.w3.org/TR/query-operators/ for more details.

Most extension functions enable you to do things with expressions that you can't normally do in XPath 1.0. There are lots of things that XPath 1.0 can't do, although many of these things can be done using XSLT templates instead. However, XSLT templates are very verbose and they can't be called from within expressions or patterns. You can't, for example, sort `<Channel>` elements based on the average duration of the programs that they show because the average duration cannot be calculated with an XPath, and XSLT templates cannot be called from within the `<xsl:sort>` element's `select` attribute.

The majority of extension functions enable you to do things that you could do in XSLT, but that would be *incredibly* tedious to implement, such as:

- Evaluating strings as XPath expressions
- Matching strings against regular expressions
- Formatting dates and times
- Parsing formatted strings

Other functions are simply impossible to do from within XSLT at all, because of the limited access that a stylesheet has to its environment or because of the data model that XPath and XSLT 1.0 use, for example:

- Converting result tree fragments into node sets (see later in this chapter)
- Getting the current date and time
- Finding out whether a document already exists

The third class of extension functions is simply shortcuts for things that are already fairly easy to do within XPath 1.0. For example, a `math:avg()` extension function that gives the average value of the nodes in a node set is just a shortcut for dividing the sum (from the `sum()` function) by the count of nodes (from the `count()` function).

> *As you'll see later in this chapter, some XSLT processors allow you to construct your own extension functions, using either XSLT or other programming languages.*

Different XSLT processors support different extension functions; indeed different versions of the *same processor* often support different functions. In general, therefore, you should only use extension functions when you really need to, as the more you use, the harder it becomes to swap to another XSLT processor should you need to in the future.

> *The EXSLT initiative (http://www.exslt.org/) tries to standardize extension functions that are common across processors, to increase portability. However, not all processors implement EXSLT functions, so portability is always an issue, whoever defines the extension function.*

Identifying Extension Functions

Extension functions must have qualified names, which means they must have a prefix. The namespace URI associated with the prefix usually indicates which implementer came up with the function and which XSLT processors support the function. For example, the extension functions supported by MSXML all have the namespace `urn:schemas-microsoft-com:xslt` whereas most of the extension functions supported by Xalan have the namespace `http://xml.apache.org/xalan`.

To use an extension function, you must first declare the namespace for the extension function within the stylesheet, usually in the `<xsl:stylesheet>` document element. This means that you can use the extension function with a particular prefix throughout the stylesheet. For example, you could use the extension functions supported by Xalan if you declared the Xalan namespace within your stylesheet as follows:

```
<xsl:stylesheet version="1.0"
                xmlns:xsl="http://www.w3.org/1999/XSL/Transform"
                xmlns:xalan="http://xml.apache.org/xalan"
                exclude-result-prefixes="xalan">
  ...
</xsl:stylesheet>
```

> *I've added an `exclude-result-prefixes` attribute to the `<xsl:stylesheet>` element so that the Xalan namespace doesn't get added to the result document that we're generating. The `exclude-result-prefixes` attribute stops the namespaces with the listed prefixes from being declared in the result document unless it's necessary. As you'll see later in this chapter, you can also use `extension-element-prefixes` to achieve the same effect.*

Once you've declared the prefix `xalan` as being associated with the namespace `http://xml.apache.org/xalan` in your stylesheet, Xalan will recognize any function that starts with that prefix as being an extension function that it should be able to understand. For example, you could use the `xalan:tokenize()` function to split a date into its constituent parts to format it better. The `xalan:tokenize()` extension function takes two arguments – the string to be tokenized, and a string containing the characters that are delimiters within that string.

The following template uses `xalan:tokenize()` to parse a date and time in ISO 8601 format (for example, `2001-07-05T19:00:00`). The first argument is the date to be broken up, and the second is the characters that are used as delimiters within the date format – hyphens separate the year, month, and day, while a `T` separates the date from the time. The result of the function call is a node set of text nodes, the first holding the year, the second the month, the third the day, and the fourth the time:

```
<xsl:template name="formatDate">
  <xsl:param name="date" select="." />
  <xsl:variable name="d" select="xalan:tokenize($date, '-T')" />
  <xsl:variable name="year" select="$d[1]" />
  <xsl:variable name="month" select="$d[2]" />
  <xsl:variable name="day" select="$d[3]" />
  <xsl:variable name="time" select="substring($d[4], 1, 5)" />
  <xsl:value-of select="$time" />
  <xsl:text> on </xsl:text>
  <xsl:value-of select="number($day)" />
  <xsl:text> </xsl:text>
  <xsl:for-each select="document('months.xml')">
    <xsl:value-of select="key('months', number($month))/@abbr" />
  </xsl:for-each>
  <xsl:text> </xsl:text>
  <xsl:value-of select="$year" />
</xsl:template>
```

Extension functions have a prefix that indicates the namespace to which they belong. You must declare the namespace to use the extension functions in that namespace.

Try It Out – Working Out a Maximum Value

One useful extension function is the `math:max()` extension function in the `http://exslt.org/math` namespace, which takes a single node set argument. The `math:max()` function works out the maximum value for the nodes in a node set. If we wanted to add the highest rating of the programs shown on a channel to the statistics that we display about a channel, for example, we could use this function. The statistics about a channel are included in a page with the following template in `TVGuide.xsl`:

```
<xsl:template match="Channel">
  <xsl:apply-templates select="Name" />
  <p class="average">
    <xsl:text>average rating: </xsl:text>
    <xsl:value-of select="format-number(sum(Program/@rating) div
                                        count(Program), '0.0')" />
```

```
      <br />
      <xsl:text>good programs for: </xsl:text>
      <xsl:call-template name="totalDuration">
        <xsl:with-param name="programs" select="Program[@rating > 5]" />
      </xsl:call-template>
      <xsl:text>hrs</xsl:text>
    </p>
    <xsl:apply-templates select="Program" />
  </xsl:template>
```

To use the `math:max()` extension function in our stylesheet, we first need to declare the `http://exslt.org/math` namespace with a prefix (`math`, by convention) on the `<xsl:stylesheet>` document element within the stylesheet module in which we want to use the extension function. In our case, we want to use it in `TVGuide2.xsl`:

```
<xsl:stylesheet version="1.0"
                xmlns:xsl="http://www.w3.org/1999/XSL/Transform"
                xmlns="http://www.w3.org/1999/xhtml"
                xmlns:math="http://exslt.org/math"
                exclude-result-prefixes="math">
  ...
</xsl:stylesheet>
```

You can then use the `math:max()` function in the template matching `<Channel>` elements within `TVGuide2.xsl`:

```
<xsl:template match="Channel">
  <xsl:apply-templates select="Name" />
  <p class="average">
    <xsl:text>average rating: </xsl:text>
    <xsl:value-of select="format-number(sum(Program/@rating) div
                                        count(Program), '0.0')" />
    <br />
    <xsl:text>good programs for: </xsl:text>
    <xsl:call-template name="totalDuration">
      <xsl:with-param name="programs" select="Program[@rating > 5]" />
    </xsl:call-template>
    <xsl:text>hrs</xsl:text>
    <br />
    <xsl:text>highest rating:</xsl:text>
    <xsl:value-of select="math:max(Program/@rating)" />
  </p>
  <xsl:apply-templates select="Program" />
</xsl:template>
```

The `math:max()` function is defined by the EXSLT initiative, at http://www.exslt.org/math/functions/max/. Several processors implement `math:max()` (Saxon, 4XSLT, jd.xslt, and libxslt) but neither Xalan nor MSXML do. Obviously, you need to use a processor that implements `math:max()`, or it won't work!

If you transform `TVGuide.xml` with `TVGuide2.xsl` to produce `TVGuide2.html` using Saxon (which does support `math:max()` from version 6.4), you should see the maximum rating of the programs shown on each channel, as follows:

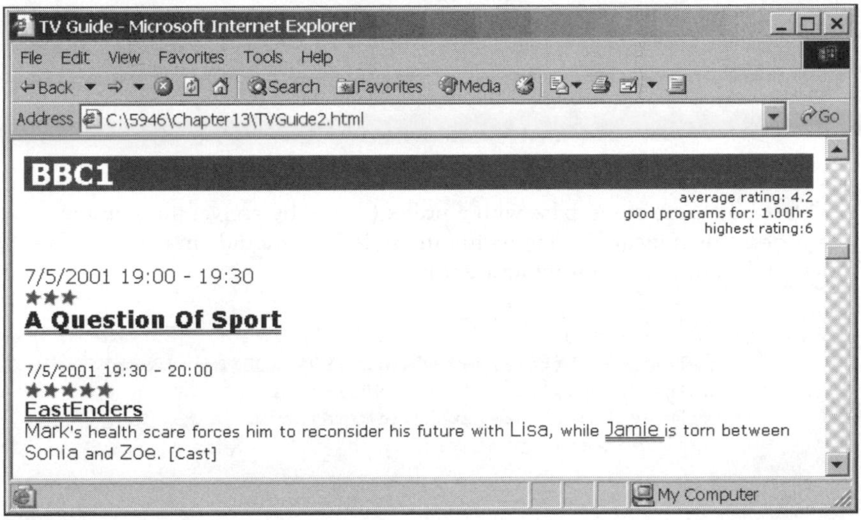

On the other hand, if you try to transform `TVGuide.xml` with `TVGuide2.xsl` with a processor that does not support `math:max()`, then you will get an error. For example, using MSXML gives the following error:

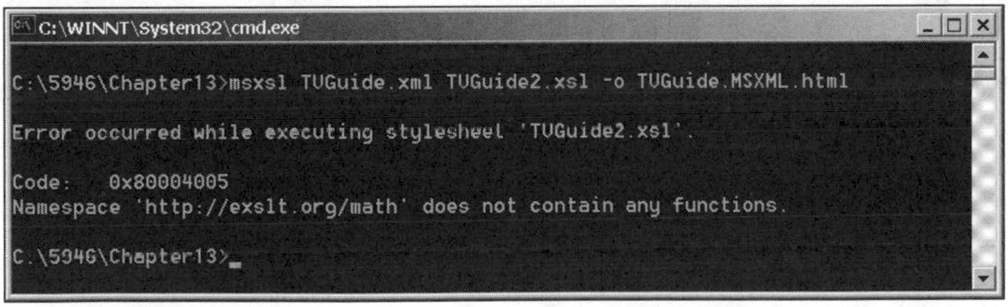

Testing Function Availability

Different processors support different extension functions. If you try to use an extension function with a processor that doesn't support it, the processor will stop the transformation with an error. Often, as we've already noted, the operation that you want to carry out could be done with an XSLT template instead, or even an alternative XPath. In these cases, rather than stopping the transformation altogether, you usually want processors that don't support the extension function to go through the longer or more complicated procedure.

But how do you work out whether the processor that's being used to run the stylesheet supports the extension function that you want to use? Well, you can use the `function-available()` function (which is a standard XPath 1.0 function – you can tell because it doesn't have a prefix) to find out. The `function-available()` function takes the name of a function as an argument and returns `true` if the processor supports the function and `false` if the processor doesn't support the function. So, for example, you could work out whether the processor that's being used with the stylesheet supports the `math:avg()` function with:

```
function-available('math:avg')
```

You can use `function-available()` within a `test` attribute within an `<xsl:choose>` to give an alternative calculation. For example, the average could be calculated by dividing the sum by the count instead. The following code tries to use the `math:avg()` function to work out the average rating of the programs shown on a channel if the extension function is available, but if it isn't it uses the `sum()` and `count()` functions to do the same calculation:

```
<xsl:variable name="ratings" select="Program/@rating" />
<xsl:choose>
  <xsl:when test="function-available('math:avg')">
    <xsl:value-of select="math:avg($ratings)" />
  </xsl:when>
  <xsl:otherwise>
    <xsl:value-of select="sum($ratings) div count($ratings)" />
  </xsl:otherwise>
</xsl:choose>
```

You can use the `function-available()` function within an `<xsl:choose>` whenever you use it in a template or to set a global variable. However, if you use an extension function at the top level of the stylesheet, for example in the `match` attribute of an `<xsl:template>` or the `use` attribute of an `<xsl:key>`, then you can't provide an alternative procedure. Therefore you should try to avoid using extension functions in the expressions and patterns used in top-level elements.

Where possible, the EXSLT initiative provides equivalent XSLT templates for the extension functions that it defines. This enables you to provide the equivalent functionality of the extension functions through portable XSLT code.

You can use the `function-available()` function to test whether the XSLT processor being used supports a particular extension function.

Try It Out – Testing Function Availability

In `TVGuide2.xsl`, we used `math:max()` to work out the highest rating of a program for a particular channel. But when we use `TVGuide2.xsl` with a processor that doesn't support `math:max()`, such as Xalan or MSXML, we get an error.

It's possible for you to come up with some XSLT code that does the same thing as `math:max()`. First, you need to get hold of the maximum value of a set of nodes, which you can do with a recursive template. The recursive template needs to recurse over the set of nodes passed as the parameter, keeping track of the highest value, and then, when there are no nodes left to look at, return that value:

```
<xsl:template name="maximum">
  <xsl:param name="nodes" select="/.." />
  <xsl:param name="maximum" select="$nodes[1]" />
  <xsl:choose>
    <xsl:when test="$nodes">
      <xsl:call-template name="maximum">
        <xsl:with-param name="nodes" select="$nodes[position() > 1]" />
        <xsl:with-param name="maximum">
          <xsl:choose>
            <xsl:when test="$nodes[1] > $maximum">
              <xsl:value-of select="$nodes[1]" />
            </xsl:when>
            <xsl:otherwise>
              <xsl:value-of select="$maximum" />
            </xsl:otherwise>
          </xsl:choose>
        </xsl:with-param>
      </xsl:call-template>
    </xsl:when>
    <xsl:otherwise>
      <xsl:value-of select="$maximum" />
    </xsl:otherwise>
  </xsl:choose>
</xsl:template>
```

Since this is a fairly useful template, we'll add it to the `utils.xsl` stylesheets that we've been using to create `utils2.xsl`.

It's likely, though, that an internal implementation of `math:max()` is going to be faster than using this template, so we may as well use it when we can. We need, then, to choose between using `math:max()`, if it's available, or using the template, if the extension function is not available. You can do this by testing whether the extension function is available with the `function-available()` function:

```
<xsl:template match="Channel">
  <xsl:apply-templates select="Name" />
  <p class="average">
    <xsl:text>average rating: </xsl:text>
    <xsl:value-of select="format-number(sum(Program/@rating) div
                                        count(Program), '0.0')" />
    <br />
    <xsl:text>good programs for: </xsl:text>
    <xsl:call-template name="totalDuration">
      <xsl:with-param name="programs" select="Program[@rating > 5]" />
    </xsl:call-template>
    <xsl:text>hrs</xsl:text>
    <br />
    <xsl:text>highest rating:</xsl:text>
    <xsl:choose>
      <xsl:when test="function-available('math:max')">
        <xsl:value-of select="math:max(Program/@rating)" />
      </xsl:when>
      <xsl:otherwise>
```

```
          <xsl:call-template name="maximum">
            <xsl:with-param name="nodes" select="Program/@rating" />
          </xsl:call-template>
        </xsl:otherwise>
      </xsl:choose>
    </p>
    <xsl:apply-templates select="Program" />
  </xsl:template>
```

These changes have been made in `TVGuide3.xsl`. When you transform `TVGuide.xml` with `TVGuide3.xsl` with a processor that doesn't support `math:max()`, then you should no longer get an error. With MSXML, for example, you should see the following:

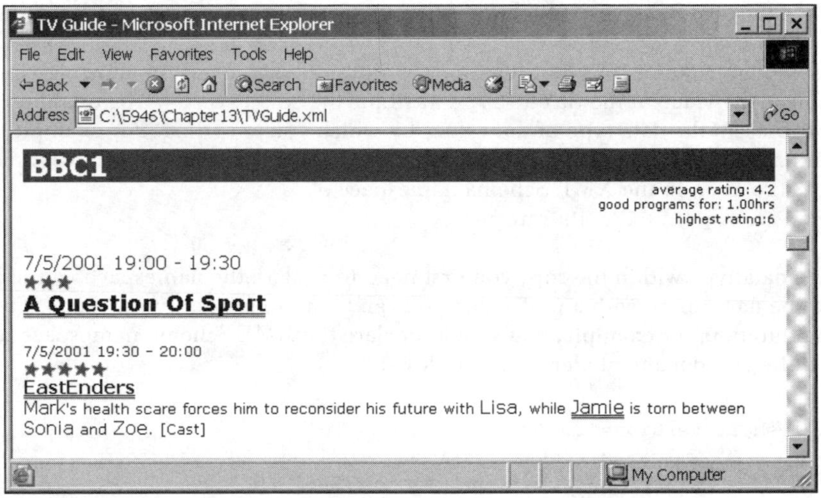

The stylesheet tests whether the `math:max()` function is implemented by a processor before trying to use it; if the extension function isn't implemented, some XSLT code does the job instead.

Extensions to Attribute Values

As well as XPath, implementers also have a fair degree of control over the functionality of XSLT. The first set of extensions that an implementer can make is to extend the set of acceptable values of certain attributes in XSLT instructions. For certain attributes, XSLT defines a list of literal values that are allowed for the attribute, but then allows a processor to accept certain types of values from outside that list. There are two attributes that this affects:

- The `data-type` attribute of `<xsl:sort>`
- The `method` attribute of `<xsl:output>`

The Working Draft of XSLT 2.0 (http://www.w3.org/TR/xslt20) introduces new possible values for these and other attributes.

Extending Sort Data Types

As you'll remember from Chapter 9, when you sort a set of nodes they are usually sorted alphabetically by the value that you select with the `select` attribute on `<xsl:sort>`. This causes problems for numbers (because numbers sort alphabetically in the order `1`, `10`, `100`, and so on rather than `1`, `2`, `3`). You can use the `data-type` attribute to change the sort so that the processor sorts numerically rather than alphabetically. Set to `number`, the `data-type` attribute gives numeric sorts; set to `text` (which is the default), the `data-type` attribute gives alphabetic sorts.

Other data types also need to be sorted non-alphabetically. For example, the `duration` data type from XML Schema, which describes durations in years, months, days, hours, minutes, and seconds and has the syntax `P`*n*`Y`*n*`M`*n*`DT`*n*`H`*n*`M`*n*`S`, needs to be sorted according to the length of time that it represents, rather than alphabetically or numerically. If you sorted alphabetically in ascending order, one hour (`PT1H`) would be sorted before thirty minutes (`PT30M`), but thirty minutes is a shorter duration than one hour.

XSLT allows implementations to support sorting by different data types by allowing you to specify a qualified name as the value of the `data-type` attribute of `<xsl:sort>`. The qualified name that you use needs to represent the data type of the values by which you're sorting. For example, to sort by durations from XML Schema, you should use a qualified name that represents XML Schema durations, for example, `duration` in the XML Schema namespace of `http://www.w3.org/2001/XMLSchema`.

To specify this data type within the sort, you first need to declare the namespace within the stylesheet, and associate the namespace with a prefix that you can then use to qualify the name. To sort by an XML Schema duration, for example, you should declare the XML Schema namespace in the `<xsl:stylesheet>` document element, as follows:

```
<xsl:stylesheet version="1.0"
                xmlns:xsl="http://www.w3.org/1999/XSL/Transform"
                xmlns:xs="http://www.w3.org/2001/XMLSchema"
                exclude-result-prefixes="xs">
  ...
</xsl:stylesheet>
```

The `data-type` attribute of the `<xsl:sort>` element then takes a qualified name, using the prefix that you've assigned to the namespace. For example, to sort `<Program>` elements by their `<Duration>` child (whose value is in an XML Schema duration format), you would use the following:

```
<xsl:apply-templates select="Program">
  <xsl:sort select="Duration" data-type="xs:duration" />
</xsl:apply-templates>
```

Unfortunately, XSLT 1.0 processors in general do not support additional values for the `data-type` attribute, so you are generally stuck with sorting either alphabetically or numerically (or a combination of the two if you have several `<xsl:sort>` elements). However, if you are prepared to write some Java code, some processors allow you to create your own "collations", which determine how values are sorted. In addition, based on the Working Draft, XSLT 2.0 processors are likely to understand what you mean if you specify an XML Schema primitive type in the `data-type` attribute.

> **If a value should not be sorted alphabetically or numerically, the `data-type` attribute of `<xsl:sort>` can take a qualified name to indicate the type of value to be sorted. Different processors support different sort data types.**

Additional Output Methods

A second attribute that accepts a qualified name is the `method` attribute of `<xsl:output>`, which determines the serialization method that's used when the result tree is output by the stylesheet, to file or to another application. The three built-in methods, which you learned about in Chapter 8, are `html`, `xml`, and `text`. The method that you use controls things like:

- The syntax for elements, especially empty elements
- Which characters are escaped, if any, and how
- Whether extra information is added to indicate the encoding of the document
- How boolean attributes are output
- What defaults are used for other attributes on `<xsl:output>`

The HTML output method in particular does a lot behind the scenes because the processor is aware of some of the semantics of HTML elements and attributes, for example:

- The `href` attribute on the `<a>` element is a URI and non-ASCII characters within it should therefore be escaped
- The `<br>` element cannot take any content and should be output without an end tag
- The character `é` can be represented with the character entity reference `é`

Often other XML-based markup languages assign special semantics to particular element or attribute values. Some elements should contain CDATA sections, for example, or some attributes should have their values normalized when they are output. Many markup languages have their own sets of character entity references that should be used in the place of numeric character references to aid the readability of the resulting document. However, an XSLT processor is unable to take advantage of that knowledge because it has no way of knowing which markup language you are generating with the XSLT stylesheet.

In theory, the result tree could even be written using a completely different syntax from XML. For example, rather than indicating elements with start and end tags, you could use a syntax where the name of the element is followed with its content held within curly brackets, for example:

```
p{This is a paragraph containing em{emphasised text}.}
```

The way in which the result tree is written to a file is known as its **serialization**. Different processors support different types of serialization by extending the set of values that they accept in the `method` attribute of `<xsl:output>`. Like the `data-type` attribute of `<xsl:sort>`, the additional acceptable values must be qualified names; usually the namespace of these qualified names will be one based on the implementation itself. For example, Saxon would define its own set of output methods using the Saxon namespace (`http://icl.com/saxon`).

One good example of an extension output method is the XHTML output method that's supported by Saxon. When you use the XHTML output method, Saxon serializes the result tree according to XML rules but takes into account some of the semantics of HTML, namely:

- Elements that can't take any content (such as `<br>` or `<img>`) are output using empty element syntax, with a space before the / (as `<br />` or `<img />`)
- Elements that can take content (such as `<p>`) but happen to be empty are output with a start and end tag (as `<p></p>`)

You can use the XHTML output method if you use Saxon by specifying a qualified name in the `method` attribute of `<xsl:output>` whose namespace URI is `http://icl.com/saxon` and whose local name is `xhtml`. You need to declare the namespace with a prefix, usually in the `<xsl:stylesheet>` document element, and then use that prefix within the value of the `method` attribute of `<xsl:output>`, as follows:

```
<xsl:stylesheet version="1.0"
                xmlns:xsl="http://www.w3.org/1999/XSL/Transform"
                xmlns:saxon="http://icl.com/saxon"
                exclude-result-prefixes="saxon">
<xsl:output method="saxon:xhtml" />
...
</xsl:stylesheet>
```

Other XSLT processors support other output methods; as with all extensions, you should check the documentation of the processor that you're using to see which ones it supports. In some processors, you can even write your own external code (in Java, for example) for serializing the result tree, and you can refer to that through the `method` attribute of `<xsl:output>` to get the output to look the way you want it to look. This can be very useful if you need to write certain characters using entity references, or if you want to generate files in a non-XML format, such as CSS or comma-delimited files, but take advantage of the ease with which an XSLT stylesheet generates elements and attributes compared to the difficulties with managing text output.

There's no way to work out what output methods a processor supports from within an XSLT stylesheet.

There are lots of ways to serialize a result tree. The `method` attribute of `<xsl:output>` can be given a qualified name to allow you to use an extension output method supported by the XSLT processor you're using.

Try It Out – Outputting XML, HTML, and XHTML with Saxon

To illustrate the effect of the output method that you use, we'll create a simple XSLT stylesheet (`outputMethod.xsl`) that creates a basic HTML document as follows:

```
<xsl:stylesheet version="1.0"
                xmlns:xsl="http://www.w3.org/1999/XSL/Transform">
<xsl:output method="html" indent="yes" />
```

```
<xsl:template match="/">
  <html>
    <head><title>Sample HTML Document</title></head>
    <body>
      <!-- an empty paragraph -->
      <p />
      <!-- a line break -->
      <br />
    </body>
  </html>
</xsl:template>
</xsl:stylesheet>
```

Run this stylesheet on itself with Saxon using the following command:

>saxon -o outputMethod.out.html outputMethod.xsl outputMethod.xsl

and you'll get the following HTML file:

```
<html>
  <head>
    <meta http-equiv="Content-Type" content="text/html; charset=utf-8">
    <title>Sample HTML Document</title>
  </head>
  <body>
    <p></p><br></body>
</html>
```

You can see the effect of the HTML output method in this document – a `<meta>` element has been added, the empty `<p>` element is shown as a start tag immediately followed by an end tag, while the `<br>` element has only a start tag.

Now change the output method to XML by changing the `method` attribute of `<xsl:output>`, to create `outputMethod2.xsl`:

```
<xsl:output method="xml" indent="yes" />
```

When you run `outputMethod2.xsl` on itself using the following command:

>saxon -o outputMethod2.out.xml outputMethod2.xsl outputMethod2.xsl

you get the following XML file:

```
<?xml version="1.0" encoding="utf-8"?>
<html>
  <head>
    <title>Sample HTML Document</title>
  </head>
  <body>
    <p/>
    <br/>
```

```
  </body>
</html>
```

The <p> and <br> elements are output in exactly the same way. Note also that there's no space between the name of the <br> element and the / in the empty element.

Finally, change the output to use the saxon:xhtml method (which we can only use because we're using Saxon). To use this method, you must declare the Saxon namespace of http://icl.com/saxon in the <xsl:stylesheet> document element as well, as in outputMethod3.xsl:

```
<xsl:stylesheet version="1.0"
                xmlns:xsl="http://www.w3.org/1999/XSL/Transform"
                xmlns:saxon="http://icl.com/saxon"
                exclude-result-prefixes="saxon">

<xsl:output method="saxon:xhtml" indent="yes" />
  ...
</xsl:stylesheet>
```

When you run outputMethod3.xsl on itself as follows:

>saxon -o outputMethod3.out.xhtml outputMethod3.xsl outputMethod3.xsl

you should get something like the following XHTML document:

```
<?xml version="1.0" encoding="utf-8"?><html>
  <head>
    <title>Sample HTML Document</title>
  </head>
  <body>
    <p></p><br /></body>
</html>
```

The important things to note here are that the <p> element has a start and end tag, as in the HTML output method. The <br> element, though, uses the empty element syntax, but has a space between the element name and the /. This improves compatibility with legacy web browsers, some of which don't recognize <br> elements without a space before the / and some of which interpret <p/> as the start tag of a paragraph rather than a complete paragraph.

Extension Attributes

The attributes of XSLT elements give fine control over the way in which the element operates. To allow XSLT implementers to give you more control over the behavior of an element, every XSLT element can take **extension attributes**. Extension attributes are attributes that are in a namespace (and therefore must have a prefix), but not in the XSLT namespace (and therefore must not have the prefix that you've associated with the XSLT namespace, which is usually xsl).

Each XSLT processor has its own set of extension attributes, some of which might be allowed on any element and others that are permitted on specific elements. One set of extension attributes that's particularly useful is the set allowed on `<xsl:output>` for giving you finer control over the way in which the result of the XSLT transformation is serialized on output.

Both Saxon and Xalan support a number of extension attributes on `<xsl:output>`, which are listed in the following table:

Saxon	Xalan	Description
`saxon:indent-spaces`	`xalan:indent-amount`	Determines the number of spaces that are used to indent elements in the output (if `indent` is `yes`)
`saxon:omit-meta-tag`	`xalan:omit-meta-tag`	If `yes`, doesn't output the `<meta>` element in the `<head>` when using the HTML output method
`saxon:character-representation`	-	Gives you control over the way that characters are output: as character entity references or as numeric character references, with decimal or hexadecimal numbers
-	`xalan:entities`	Points to a file that describes the character entity references that should be used to escape characters on output
-	`xalan:use-url-escaping`	If `no`, doesn't escape URI attribute values when using the HTML output method

To use any extension, a namespace must be declared that associates the namespace for the extension with a prefix. So to use the Saxon extension attributes, you have to declare the Saxon namespace of `http://icl.com/saxon` within the XSLT stylesheet. Similarly, to use the Xalan extension attributes, you have to declare the Xalan namespace of `http://xml.apache.org/xalan` within the XSLT stylesheet.

There's nothing stopping you from using both sets of extension attributes – a processor will ignore extension attributes that aren't in a namespace that it recognizes. Indeed, using both means that you'll be able to get similar behavior whether using Saxon or Xalan as your XSLT processor and allows you to swap between the two processors as desired. For example, the following sets the indentation to be used when the result tree is serialized to two spaces:

```
<xsl:stylesheet version="1.0"
                xmlns:xsl="http://www.w3.org/1999/XSL/Transform"
                xmlns:saxon="http://icl.com/saxon"
                xmlns:xalan="http://xml.apache.org/xalan"
```

```
                    exclude-result-prefixes="saxon xalan">
   <xsl:output indent="yes" saxon:indent-spaces="2" xalan:indent-amount="2" />
   ...
   </xsl:stylesheet>
```

XSLT processors can define their own extension attributes to alter the behavior of XSLT elements.

Extension Elements

As well as changing the fine detail of how an XSLT element works, XSLT processors are also able to define their own new XSLT instructions, known as **extension elements**. Like extension attributes, extension elements have to be in a namespace, and the namespace that they're in cannot be the XSLT namespace.

We'll look at one set of extension elements, those that you can use to create multiple output documents from the same stylesheet, later in this chapter. Before we come on to that, though, we'll look at the general principles behind using extension elements, which you can use with any extension elements supported by your XSLT processor.

Identifying Extension Elements

There's one aspect of using extension elements that's a bit more complex than using extension attributes. To illustrate it, consider the following XSLT stylesheet:

```
<xsl:stylesheet version="1.0"
                xmlns:xsl="http://www.w3.org/1999/XSL/Transform"
                xmlns:ext="http://www.example.com/XSLT/extensions">

<xsl:template match="Channel">
  <ext:group select="Program" by="Series">...</ext:group>
</xsl:template>

</xsl:stylesheet>
```

When an XSLT processor comes across an element that isn't in the XSLT namespace (such as the `<ext:group>` element), what does it do? It thinks that the element is a literal result element, so it adds the element to the result tree. In the above, however, we intend the processor to try to follow the instruction, to look at the `<ext:group>` element and process the `<Program>` elements that it's selecting as a group.

The XSLT processor needs some way of telling the difference between an element that isn't in the XSLT namespace and that's intended to be added to the result tree as a literal result element, and an element that isn't in the XSLT namespace and that's intended to be understood by the XSLT processor as an instruction.

To enable the XSLT processor to make that distinction, you need to declare that the namespace used for the extension element (in this case `http://www.example.com/XSLT/extensions`) is a namespace for extension elements. You can do this by giving the prefix associated with that namespace within the `extension-element-prefixes` attribute on the `<xsl:stylesheet>` document element, as follows:

```
<xsl:stylesheet version="1.0"
                xmlns:xsl="http://www.w3.org/1999/XSL/Transform"
                xmlns:ext="http://www.example.com/XSLT/extensions"
                extension-element-prefixes="ext">

<xsl:template match="Channel">
  <ext:group select="Program" by="Series">...</ext:group>
</xsl:template>

</xsl:stylesheet>
```

Now, when the XSLT processor comes across the `<ext:group>` element, it knows that it needs to do something with that element, that it's an instruction rather than a literal result element.

The `extension-element-prefixes` attribute can have as many prefixes listed within it as you like, separated by spaces, and if you have several namespaces that you use for extension elements you'll have to list them all here. This happens particularly when you have different extension elements doing the same kind of thing in different XSLT processors.

The `document` extension element, which we'll come on to later in this chapter, is a good example of extension elements from multiple namespaces that do the same kind of thing.

You can also use the `extension-element-prefixes` attribute to exclude the namespaces that you use for extensions from the result document. The elements in the result tree won't have namespace nodes for the namespaces listed in the `extension-element-prefixes` attribute unless they have to (because one of their attributes is in that namespace), which means that they won't have namespace declarations in the output. Therefore, it's good practice to include all the namespaces that you're using for extensions (whether they're extension attribute values, extension attributes, extension elements, extension functions, or extension top-level elements) in the `extension-element-prefixes` list.

The `exclude-result-prefixes` attribute does the same thing – excluding namespaces from the result tree unless they're needed. You should use it for namespaces that you only need because they're used in the source document.

You need to list the prefix associated with an extension namespace in the `extension-element-prefixes` attribute on `<xsl:stylesheet>` so that the XSLT processor recognizes extension elements as being instructions, rather than literal result elements.

Try It Out – Recognizing Extension Elements

To try out extension elements, we'll use an extension element called `<saxon:group>` in the namespace `http://icl.com/saxon`. This extension element only works with Saxon. It groups the nodes that you select with the `select` attribute by the result of applying the expression held in the `group-by` attribute. Within `<saxon:group>`, `<saxon:item>` essentially iterates over each of the items in the group.

Currently, we're grouping `<Series>` elements by the first letter of their ID by recursing over a string holding the alphabet within the `alphabeticalSeriesList` template in `series.xsl`. We could use `<saxon:group>` to do this instead. The `alphabeticalSeriesList` template becomes:

```
<xsl:template name="alphabeticalSeriesList">
  <saxon:group select="/SeriesList/Series" group-by="substring(@id, 1, 1)">
    <xsl:variable name="letter" select="substring(@id, 1, 1)" />
    <h3>
      <a id="series{$letter}" name="series{$letter}">
        <xsl:value-of select="$letter" />
      </a>
    </h3>
    <saxon:item>
      <xsl:apply-templates select="." />
    </saxon:item>
  </saxon:group>
</xsl:template>
```

This change is made in `series2.xsl`, with a namespace declaration added for the `saxon` namespace, but without the `saxon` namespace in the list of extension element namespaces. The `<xsl:stylesheet>` element looks like the following:

```
<xsl:stylesheet version="1.0"
                xmlns:xsl="http://www.w3.org/1999/XSL/Transform"
                xmlns="http://www.w3.org/1999/xhtml"
                xmlns:saxon="http://icl.com/saxon">
...
</xsl:stylesheet>
```

If you run `TVGuide4.xsl` (which uses `series2.xsl`) on `TVGuide.xml` using Saxon and look at the source of the result of the transformation, you should see the following:

```
<saxon:group xmlns:saxon="http://icl.com/saxon"
             select="/SeriesList/Series" group-by="substring(@id, 1, 1)">
  <h3>
    <a id="series" name="series"/>
  </h3>
  <saxon:item>
    <div>
      <h4>
        <a name="EastEnders" id="EastEnders">EastEnders</a>
      </h4>
```

```
      ...
    </div>
    ...
  </saxon:item>
</saxon:group>
```

Despite the fact that the element is in the Saxon namespace, Saxon treats `<saxon:group>` as a literal result element and adds it and its content to the result tree, just as if it were a normal element.

Now add an `extension-element-prefixes` attribute to the `<xsl:stylesheet>` element to specify that the Saxon namespace is a namespace for extension elements, as in `series3.xsl`:

```
<xsl:stylesheet version="1.0"
                xmlns:xsl="http://www.w3.org/1999/XSL/Transform"
                xmlns:saxon="http://icl.com/saxon"
                extension-element-prefixes="saxon">
  ...
</xsl:stylesheet>
```

Run `TVGuide5.xsl` (which includes `series3.xsl`) with `TVGuide.xml` to see the difference. This time you should find that the `<saxon:group>` element generates the alphabetical groups, and when you view the resulting HTML page you should see:

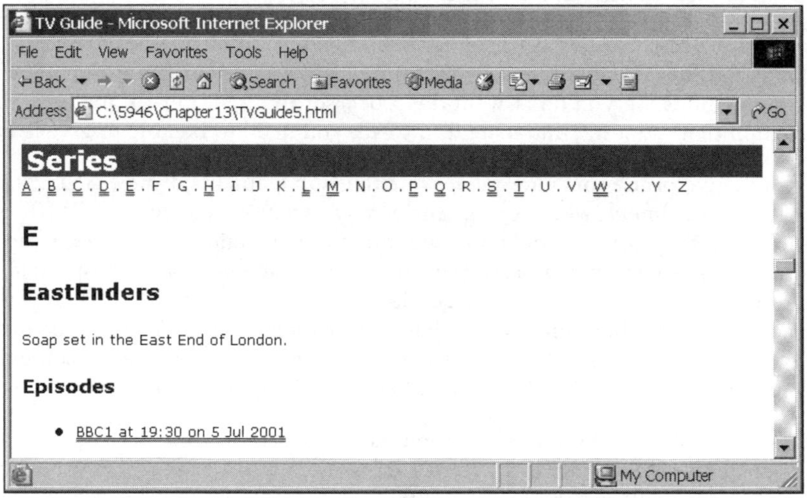

The `<saxon:group>` and `<saxon:item>` elements are being recognized as extension elements, and Saxon is processing them rather than outputting them as literal result elements. It's still not perfect, because the `<Series>` elements are being grouped in the order in which they appear within `series.xml`; to sort them alphabetically, you need to add an `<xsl:sort>` element just after the `<saxon:group>` element, as follows:

```
<xsl:template name="alphabeticalSeriesList">
  <saxon:group select="/SeriesList/Series" group-by="substring(@id, 1, 1)">
    <xsl:sort select="@id" />
    <xsl:variable name="letter" select="substring(@id, 1, 1)" />
```

```
      <h3>
        <a id="series{$letter}" name="series{$letter}">
          <xsl:value-of select="$letter" />
        </a>
      </h3>
      <saxon:item>
        <xsl:apply-templates select="." />
      </saxon:item>
    </saxon:group>
  </xsl:template>
```

With this change made in `series4.xsl`, and with `TVGuide6.xsl` including `series4.xsl`, the result of transforming `TVGuide.xml` with `TVGuide6.XSL` has the series displayed in alphabetical order.

Preventing Errors with Extension Elements

As you've already seen, different XSLT processors support different extension elements. This means that if you try using an extension element with a processor that doesn't recognize that instruction then the processor will halt and give you an error. The same applies to new instructions that are added in later versions of XSLT, such as XSLT 2.0.

You can see what new instructions are likely to be added to XSLT 2.0 by looking at the XSLT 2.0 Working Draft at http://www.w3.org/TR/xslt20.

However, often two processors have very similar sets of extension elements, just in different namespaces. Or sometimes it's possible to do the same processing as an extension element with set of existing XSLT instructions. So you don't want the processor to just stop working as soon as it comes across an instruction that it doesn't understand; instead, you need to be able to give it an alternative.

XSLT allows you to give processors alternatives to extension elements or new XSLT instructions with the `<xsl:fallback>` element, which can go inside any extension element or XSLT instruction. XSLT processors know when they come across an element that they should treat as an instruction, because it's either in the XSLT namespace or in a namespace that's been labeled as a namespace for extension elements using the `extension-element-prefixes` attribute on `<xsl:stylesheet>`. If they come across an instruction element but don't know what to do with it, they look inside the instruction element. If they find an `<xsl:fallback>` element in the instruction element's content, then they process the content of that `<xsl:fallback>` rather than giving an error.

For example, the XSLT 2.0 Working Draft introduces an `<xsl:for-each-group>` instruction for grouping nodes. When an XSLT processor comes across the `<xsl:for-each-group>` element in the following piece of code, it will run the content of the `<xsl:fallback>` element inside the `<xsl:for-each-group>` element rather than complaining that it doesn't understand the `<xsl:for-each-group>` element:

```
<xsl:stylesheet version="2.0"
                xmlns:xsl="http://www.w3.org/1999/XSL/Transform"
                xmlns="http://www.w3.org/1999/xhtml">
...
<xsl:template name="alphabeticalSeriesList">
  <xsl:for-each-group select="/SeriesList/Series"
                      group-by="substring(@id, 1, 1)">
```

```
      <xsl:sort select="@id" />
      <xsl:variable name="letter" select="substring(@id, 1, 1)" />
      <h3>
        <a id="series{$letter}" name="series{$letter}">
          <xsl:value-of select="$letter" />
        </a>
      </h3>
      <xsl:apply-templates select="current-group()">
        <xsl:sort select="@id" />
      </xsl:apply-templates>
      <xsl:fallback>
        ...
      </xsl:fallback>
    </xsl:for-each-group>
  </xsl:template>
  ...
  </xsl:stylesheet>
```

Note that the `version` *attribute in the above stylesheet is* `2.0` *rather than* `1.0`*, reflecting the fact that it contains instructions from XSLT 2.0. At the time of writing, the only processor that implements any of the XSLT 2.0 Working Draft is Saxon version 7.0.*

Of course you might *want* the processing to stop if the processor doesn't recognize the extension element – the fact that it doesn't recognize the element might mean that the stylesheet can't be used with that particular processor. In that case, you can use `<xsl:message>` within the `<xsl:fallback>` element, setting its `terminate` attribute to `yes` to tell the processor to stop processing, and using the content of the `<xsl:message>` to give a more user-friendly error than the one the processor is likely to give on its own. For example:

```
<xsl:stylesheet version="2.0"
                xmlns:xsl="http://www.w3.org/1999/XSL/Transform"
                xmlns="http://www.w3.org/1999/xhtml">
...
<xsl:template name="alphabeticalSeriesList">
  <xsl:for-each-group select="/SeriesList/Series"
                      group-by="substring(@id, 1, 1)">
    <xsl:sort select="@id" />
    <xsl:variable name="letter" select="substring(@id, 1, 1)" />
    <h3>
      <a id="series{$letter}" name="series{$letter}">
        <xsl:value-of select="$letter" />
      </a>
    </h3>
    <xsl:apply-templates select="current-group()">
      <xsl:sort select="@id" />
    </xsl:apply-templates>
    <xsl:fallback>
      <xsl:message terminate="yes">
        ERROR: This stylesheet requires support for XSLT 2.0.
      </xsl:message>
    </xsl:fallback>
```

```
  </xsl:for-each-group>
</xsl:template>
...
</xsl:stylesheet>
```

An XSLT processor will process the contents of an `<xsl:fallback>` element within an extension element if the processor doesn't understand the element.

Try It Out – Supplying Alternative Instructions

`TVGuide6.xsl` includes `series4.xsl`, which uses `<saxon:group>`. If you try transforming `TVGuide.xml` with `TVGuide6.xsl` with a processor other than Saxon, you should get an error because the XSLT processor knows that it should treat `<saxon:group>` as an instruction (since the prefix `saxon` has been listed as an extension element prefix), but doesn't recognize it. For example, with MSXML, you will see the following error:

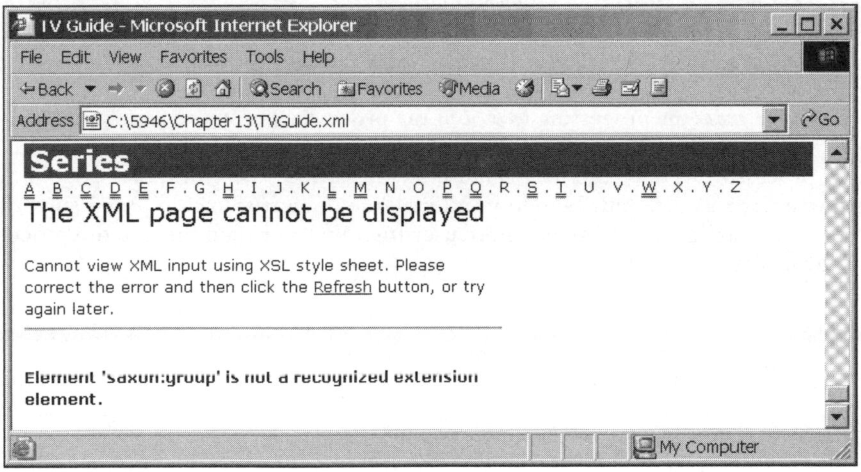

Rather than give an obscure error, you could use `<xsl:fallback>` to call a template that will do the grouping by recursion. Add the `<xsl:fallback>` element within `<saxon:group>`. It doesn't matter where you put the `<xsl:fallback>`, but putting it at the beginning or the end will make it clearer:

```
<xsl:template name="alphabeticalSeriesList">
  <saxon:group select="/SeriesList/Series" group-by="substring(@id, 1, 1)">
    <xsl:sort select="@id" />
    <xsl:variable name="letter" select="substring(@id, 1, 1)" />
    <h3>
      <a id="series{$letter}" name="series{$letter}">
        <xsl:value-of select="$letter" />
      </a>
    </h3>
    <saxon:item>
      <xsl:apply-templates select="." />
```

```
    </saxon:item>
    <xsl:fallback>
      <xsl:call-template name="alphabeticalSeriesListByRecursion" />
    </xsl:fallback>
  </saxon:group>
</xsl:template>
```

The `alphabeticalSeriesListByRecursion` template is just the same as the original `alphabeticalSeriesList` template, before we started using `<saxon:group>`. The only difference is the name of the template (remember to change it in the recursive call!):

```
<xsl:template name="alphabeticalSeriesListByRecursion">
  <xsl:param name="alphabet" select="'ABCDEFGHIJKLMNOPQRSTUVWXYZ'" />
  <xsl:variable name="letter" select="substring($alphabet, 1, 1)" />
  <xsl:variable name="remainder" select="substring($alphabet, 2)" />

  <xsl:variable name="series"
                select="key('seriesByFirstLetter', $letter)" />
  <xsl:if test="$series">
    <h3>
      <a id="series{$letter}" name="series{$letter}">
        <xsl:value-of select="$letter" />
      </a>
    </h3>
    <xsl:apply-templates select="$series">
      <xsl:sort select="@id" />
    </xsl:apply-templates>
  </xsl:if>

  <xsl:if test="$remainder">
    <xsl:call-template name="alphabeticalSeriesListByRecursion">
      <xsl:with-param name="alphabet" select="$remainder" />
    </xsl:call-template>
  </xsl:if>
</xsl:template>
```

If you run `TVGuide7.xsl` now, which includes `series5.xsl` in which these changes have been made, you should get roughly the same result whichever processor you use. For example, with MSXML in Internet Explorer, you should get the following:

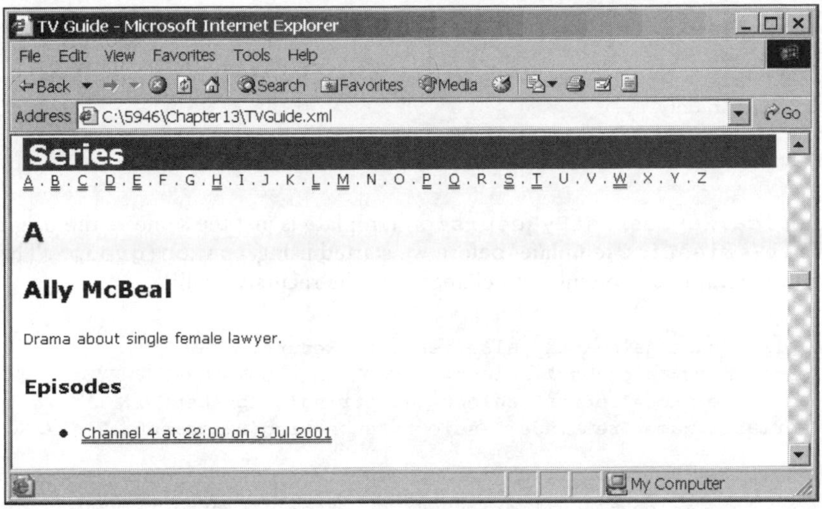

The XSLT processor will use <saxon:group> if it supports the extension element, but it will use the recursive template if it doesn't. Either way, the series get grouped by their first letter.

Testing Element Availability

Another method of preventing errors when a stylesheet that uses a particular extension element is used on a processor that doesn't support that extension element is to test whether the extension element is available before you use it. Using the `element-available()` function you can test whether the extension element is supported by the processor that's being used.

The `element-available()` function takes a single argument – the name of the extension element that you are interested in. If the processor supports the extension element then it returns `true`; if it doesn't support the extension element then it returns `false`. For example, to test whether the processor supports the <xsl:for-each-group> instruction from XSLT 2.0, you could use:

```
element-available('xsl:for-each-group')
```

The `element-available()` function tests what instructions an XSLT processor supports; it doesn't test whether an element is present within an XML document or stylesheet.

You can use the `element-available()` function to give you the same kind of alternative processing as <xsl:fallback>. For example, rather than using <xsl:fallback> to generate a message when the processor doesn't support <xsl:for-each-group>, you could use:

```
<xsl:template name="alphabeticalSeriesList">
  <xsl:choose>
    <xsl:when test="element-available('xsl:for-each-group')">
      <xsl:for-each-group select="/SeriesList/Series"
                          group-by="substring(@id, 1, 1)">
        <xsl:sort select="@id" />
        <xsl:variable name="letter" select="substring(@id, 1, 1)" />
```

```
        <h3>
          <a id="series{$letter}" name="series{$letter}">
            <xsl:value-of select="$letter" />
          </a>
        </h3>
        <xsl:apply-templates select="current-group()">
          <xsl:sort select="@id" />
        </xsl:apply-templates>
      </xsl:for-each-group>
    </xsl:when>
    <xsl:otherwise>
      <xsl:message terminate="yes">
        ERROR: This stylesheet requires support for XSLT 2.0.
      </xsl:message>
    </xsl:otherwise>
  </xsl:choose>
</xsl:template>
```

The `element-available()` function is more useful than `<xsl:fallback>` if you want to test for the availability of a series of extension elements – you can use a big `<xsl:choose>` rather than having very deep nesting of elements inside `<xsl:fallback>`. It's also handy if you want to test whether an extension element is available early on in the stylesheet rather than waiting until you need to use the extension element.

> **The `element-available()` function returns `true` if the element whose name is passed as the argument to the function is supported by the XSLT processor.**

Try It Out – Checking Element Availability

Rather than using `<xsl:fallback>` as we did last time, this time we'll use an `<xsl:choose>` to decide whether to use `<saxon:group>` to group the series or whether to use the recursive template. The `test` attribute of `<xsl:when>` calls the `element-available()` function, which only returns `true` if the named extension element is supported by the processor. The new version of the `alphabeticalSeriesList` template looks like the following:

```
<xsl:template name="alphabeticalSeriesList">
  <xsl:choose>
    <xsl:when test="element-available('saxon:group')">
      <saxon:group select="/SeriesList/Series"
                   group-by="substring(@id, 1, 1)">
        <xsl:sort select="@id" />
        <xsl:variable name="letter" select="substring(@id, 1, 1)" />
        <h3>
          <a id="series{$letter}" name="series{$letter}">
            <xsl:value-of select="$letter" />
          </a>
        </h3>
        <saxon:item>
          <xsl:apply-templates select="." />
        </saxon:item>
```

```
        </saxon:group>
      </xsl:when>
      <xsl:otherwise>
        <xsl:call-template name="alphabeticalSeriesListByRecursion" />
      </xsl:otherwise>
    </xsl:choose>
  </xsl:template>
```

If you try running `TVGuide8.xsl` (which includes `series6.xsl`, in which these changes have been made) in any processor, you'll see the alphabetical list of series as before. This time the choice about what code to use is being made through an explicit `<xsl:choose>` rather than an `<xsl:fallback>` element.

Top-Level Elements

You can place any non-XSLT elements you like at the top level of an XSLT document (as direct children of `<xsl:stylesheet>`). Like extension elements, these top-level elements must be in a namespace and the namespace must not be the XSLT namespace. However, unlike extension elements, XSLT processors effectively ignore top-level elements, so you can't use `<xsl:fallback>` or `element-available()` to make sure that you can use them.

You may remember that we used top-level elements in the last chapter to store XML data within the stylesheet itself.

Top-level elements are generally used in XSLT to affect the way in which the whole stylesheet works. A typical use of a top-level element is to define your own extension functions, as you'll see later in this chapter.

If a processor doesn't recognize the namespace of a top-level element, it ignores the element.

Example Extensions

Now that you've seen the basics of how extensions of various kinds work, we'll look at three extensions in particular in more detail. I've primarily picked out these extensions to concentrate on because they're useful, there are similar ones across several XSLT processors, and they or something like them are likely to make it into the next version of XSLT.

Using the three extensions that we'll look at here, you'll learn:

- How to turn result tree fragments into node sets so that you can process them further
- How to create multiple result documents from a single stylesheet
- How to define your own extension functions using XSLT or another programming language

Turning Result Tree Fragments into Node Sets

The first extension that we'll look at is an extension function that allows you to turn result tree fragments into node sets. If you cast your mind back to Chapter 6, when we first looked at variables and parameters, you'll remember that variables and parameters can be set in two ways:

- Using the `select` attribute, which sets the variable or parameter to one of the basic XPath types (boolean, number, string, or node set)
- Using the content of the `<xsl:variable>`, `<xsl:param>`, or `<xsl:with-param>` element, which sets the variable or parameter to a result tree fragment

Result tree fragments are like small node trees – they have their own root node and the rest of the content of the `<xsl:variable>`, `<xsl:param>`, or `<xsl:with-param>` element forms the rest of the node tree. Having a variable or parameter set to a result tree fragment is like having a variable or parameter whose value is a node set containing just the root node of a node tree.

However, result tree fragments differ from node sets in one major way. You can't use paths with a result tree fragment – once you construct a result tree fragment, that's it. All it's really useful for is copying (with `<xsl:copy-of>`) or getting its string value (with `<xsl:value-of>` or within an expression).

This is a shame because being able to construct a node set and then process that node set is actually really useful. Processing result tree fragments allows you to break down a complicated process into several smaller, simpler steps. Often it means that you don't have to use recursive templates to do something, but can use a two-step process instead. For example, instead of using a recursive template to calculate the total duration of a set of programs, you could iterate over them to create a node set on which you could then use the `sum()` function. This might end up taking more time, since it involves visiting twice the number of nodes than a recursive template (once to compute their values, once to calculate the sum), but the code to do it is a lot simpler to read and maintain.

Most XSLT processor implementers responded to this requirement by creating extension functions to turn result tree fragments into node sets. These extension functions are all named similarly:

- `exsl:node-set` – namespace `http://exslt.org/common`; supported by Saxon, 4XSLT, jd.xslt, and libxslt
- `msxsl:node-set` – namespace `urn:schemas-microsoft-com:xslt`; supported by MSXML
- `xalan:nodeset` – namespace `http://xml.apache.org/xalan`; supported by Xalan

Other processors may have their own similar extension functions; check the documentation of your processor to find out what it supports.

All these extension functions take a result tree fragment as an argument and turn the result tree fragment into a node set, returning the root node of the result tree fragment.

In XSLT 2.0, it's likely that you'll be able to use a result tree fragment as a node set without explicitly converting it using a function.

> **Most XSLT processors have a `node-set()` extension function to allow you to convert from a result tree fragment to a node set.**

Try It Out – Summing Durations Using Intermediate Node Sets

In Chapter 11, we used the following `totalDuration` recursive template, which is in `utils2.xsl`, to work out the total duration of a set of programs:

```
<xsl:template name="totalDuration">
  <xsl:param name="programs" select="/.." />
  <xsl:param name="totalHours" select="0" />
  <xsl:param name="totalMinutes" select="0" />
  <xsl:choose>
    <xsl:when test="$programs">
      <xsl:variable name="duration"
                    select="normalize-space($programs[1]/Duration)" />
      <xsl:variable name="hours">
        <xsl:choose>
          <xsl:when test="contains($duration, 'H')">
            <xsl:value-of select="substring-before(
                                    substring-after($duration, 'PT'),
                                    'H')" />
          </xsl:when>
          <xsl:otherwise>0</xsl:otherwise>
        </xsl:choose>
      </xsl:variable>
      <xsl:variable name="minutes">
        <xsl:choose>
          <xsl:when test="contains($duration, 'M')">
            <xsl:choose>
              <xsl:when test="contains($duration, 'H')">
                <xsl:value-of select="substring-before(
                                        substring-after($duration, 'H'),
                                        'M')" />
              </xsl:when>
              <xsl:otherwise>
                <xsl:value-of select="substring-before(
                                        substring-after($duration, 'PT'),
                                        'M')" />
              </xsl:otherwise>
            </xsl:choose>
          </xsl:when>
          <xsl:otherwise>0</xsl:otherwise>
        </xsl:choose>
      </xsl:variable>
      <xsl:call-template name="totalDuration">
        <xsl:with-param name="programs"
                        select="$programs[position() > 1]" />
        <xsl:with-param name="totalHours"
                        select="$totalHours + $hours" />
```

```
          <xsl:with-param name="totalMinutes"
                          select="$totalMinutes + $minutes" />
        </xsl:call-template>
      </xsl:when>
      <xsl:otherwise>
        <xsl:variable name="finalHours"
                      select="$totalHours + floor($totalMinutes div 60)" />
        <xsl:variable name="finalMinutes"
                      select="($totalMinutes mod 60) div 60" />
        <xsl:value-of
          select="format-number($finalHours + $finalMinutes, '0.00')" />
      </xsl:otherwise>
    </xsl:choose>
  </xsl:template>
```

Rather than using recursion, we could create a result tree fragment of `<Duration>` elements, each holding a number of minutes duration, by calling the `durationMins` template (which is also in `utils2.xsl`) on each of the `<Program>` elements in turn, creating a `<Duration>` element for each one:

```
<xsl:template name="totalDuration">
  <xsl:param name="programs" select="/.." />
  <xsl:variable name="durations">
    <xsl:for-each select="$programs">
      <Duration xmlns="">
        <xsl:call-template name="durationMins">
          <xsl:with-param name="duration" select="Duration" />
        </xsl:call-template>
      </Duration>
    </xsl:for-each>
  </xsl:variable>
  ...
</xsl:template>
```

Note that the default namespace is reset for the `<Duration>` element. This prevents the `<Duration>` element from being placed in the XHTML namespace, which is the default namespace for the stylesheet as a whole.

If the `<Duration>` elements held within the `$durations` variable were a node set, we could use the `sum()` function to sum their values and get a total duration for the programs in minutes. To convert the result tree fragment to a node set, you need to use a `node-set()` extension function.

Choose the appropriate extension function for the processor that you're using and declare the namespace in the `<xsl:stylesheet>` document element. For example, if you're using MSXML, then you need to use the `msxsl:node-set()` extension function, which means declaring the `urn:schemas-microsoft-com:xslt` namespace:

```
<xsl:stylesheet version="1.0"
                xmlns:xsl="http://www.w3.org/1999/XSL/Transform"
                xmlns:msxsl="urn:schemas-microsoft-com:xslt"
                extension-element-prefixes="msxsl">
  ...
</xsl:stylesheet>
```

You can convert the `$durations` result tree fragment to a node set by passing it as the argument to your selected `node-set()` function. For example, to use the `msxsl:node-set()` function you would use:

```
msxsl:node-set($durations)
```

Remember that this gives you the root node of the result tree fragment; you want to sum the `<Duration>` children of that root node, so you need to step down to the `<Duration>` elements and sum them as follows:

```
sum(msxsl:node-set($durations)/Duration)
```

The rest of the code within the template works out how many hours and minutes the total number of minutes is equivalent to, and returns a decimal number of hours:

```
<xsl:template name="totalDuration">
  <xsl:param name="programs" select="/.." />
  <xsl:variable name="durations">
    <xsl:apply-templates select="$programs" mode="duration" />
  </xsl:variable>
  <xsl:variable name="totalMinutes"
                select="sum(exsl:node-set($durations)/Duration)" />
  <xsl:value-of select="format-number($totalMinutes div 60, '0.00')" />
</xsl:template>
```

When you transform `TVGuide.xml` with `TVGuide8a.xsl`, which imports `utils3.xsl` in which these changes have been made, you should see the total duration of 'good' programs shown for each channel, as in the following:

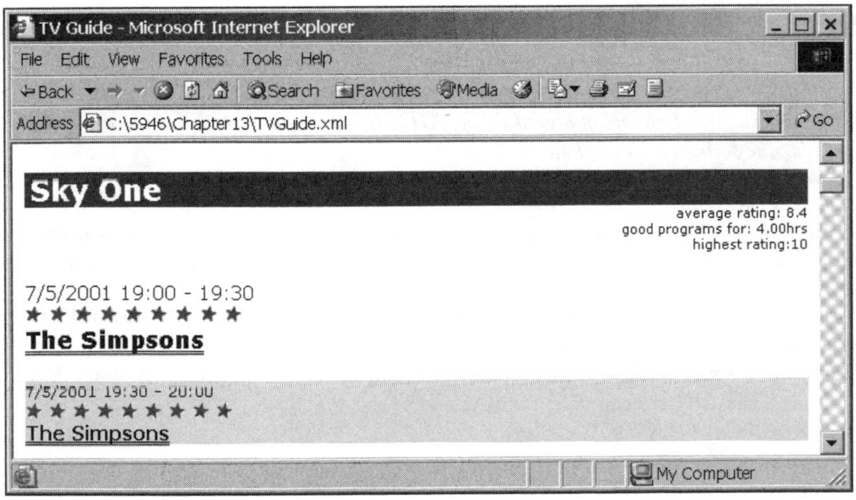

This stylesheet will only work if the extension function that you've chosen to use is supported by the XSLT processor that you use with the stylesheet. To make the template portable, so that you can use it with other XSLT processors, you should choose the `node-set()` extension function to be used based on the one that is available. You can test which function is available using the `function-available()` function and choose what to do on that basis with an `<xsl:choose>`, as we saw earlier in this chapter. If none of the ones that you know about is available, then you could make the template terminate the transformation and generate an error message, or use a recursive template like the original `totalDuration` template as a substitute.

Creating Multiple Result Documents

A second set of extensions that have proved popular are those that enable you to create multiple result documents from the same stylesheet. This facility is particularly useful when doing batch processing, when you take a single XML document and use that document to create multiple HTML files. You could imagine doing it with our TV Guide, to create separate pages for:

- The summary table currently at the top of the page
- A program listing for each channel
- A page listing the series

There are a couple of advantages to creating all these pages from the same process.

Firstly, creating all the pages at once makes it easier to do linking between the pages. As you'll remember from Chapter 10, you can use the `generate-id()` function to generate a unique ID for a node, which you can use to create anchors within a page. But the `generate-id()` function can produce different IDs during different runs of the same stylesheet, even on the same source document, so it's not usually useful for linking between pages. If all the pages are generated during the same process, however, the IDs will be the same.

Secondly, having a single process for creating all the pages means that the source document (`TVGuide.xml`), which could be very large, only needs to be parsed once rather than multiple times. Parsing big documents and creating node trees for them takes a long time, so being able to do it once rather than hundreds of times can give big savings.

Stylesheets that support a range of types of result document can get pretty large; you should use the methods that we saw in Chapter 11 to break them up into separate modules that could be used as standalone stylesheets or within the larger application.

Several processors support different extension elements that enable you to create several documents from the same stylesheet, although they work slightly differently. The XSLT 1.1 Working Draft included an `<xsl:document>` element and the XSLT 2.0 Working Draft includes an `<xsl:result-document>` element, both of which do the same kind of thing. We're going to look at the support within Saxon and Xalan; MSXML does not support an extension element for creating multiple output documents.

Creating Multiple Output Documents with Saxon

In Saxon, you can use `<saxon:output>` to create a new output document. Of course, you can use whatever prefix you like for the element name, but whatever you use it must be associated with the namespace `http://icl.com/saxon`. Also, you must identify the namespace as being a namespace for extension elements using the `extension-element-prefixes` attribute on the `<xsl:stylesheet>` document element.

The `<saxon:output>` extension element is an instruction, so it goes inside a template (unlike `<xsl:output>`, which lives at the top level of the stylesheet). The content of `<saxon:output>` forms the content of the output document, and the `href` attribute indicates the name of the new document. The `href` attribute is an attribute value template, so you can use `{}`s to calculate the name of the document on the fly. For example, the following template generates a page for each channel, using the name of the `<Channel>` element (with spaces replaced by underscores) as the name of the page:

```
<xsl:stylesheet version="1.0"
                xmlns:xsl="http://www.w3.org/1999/XSL/Transform"
                xmlns="http://www.w3.org/1999/xhtml"
                xmlns:math="http://exslt.org/math"
                xmlns:saxon="http://icl.com/saxon"
                extension-element-prefixes="math saxon">

...
<xsl:template match="TVGuide">
  ...
  <xsl:for-each select="Channel">
    <saxon:output href="{translate(Name, ' ', '_')}.html">
      <html>
        <head>
          <title><xsl:value-of select="Name" /></title>
          <link rel="stylesheet" href="TVGuide.css" />
          <script type="text/javascript">
            ...
          </script>
        </head>
        <body>
          <xsl:apply-templates select="." />
        </body>
      </html>
    </saxon:output>
  </xsl:for-each>
  ...
</xsl:template>
...
</xsl:stylesheet>
```

Other attributes are also allowed on `<saxon:output>` – the same attributes that are allowed on `<xsl:output>` which we saw in Chapter 8, although on `<saxon:output>` they can be set dynamically using attribute value templates.

The <saxon:output> extension element allows you to create multiple output documents if you use Saxon.

Creating Multiple Output Documents with Xalan

In Xalan, you can use <redirect:write> to create a new output document, where the redirect prefix is associated with the namespace org.apache.xalan.xslt.extensions.Redirect. As usual for extension elements, you must list the redirect prefix in the extension-element-prefixes attribute on the <xsl:stylesheet> document element so that it's recognized as being an extension element.

You can set the location of the new document using two attributes on the <redirect:write> extension element: file to give the literal file for the document or select to give an expression that evaluates to the filename. If the select attribute isn't present, or if it results in an empty string, then the file attribute is used for the filename instead. So to create an HTML file for each <Channel> element using the name of the element as the name of the file, you would use:

```
<xsl:stylesheet version="1.0"
                xmlns:xsl="http://www.w3.org/1999/XSL/Transform"
                xmlns="http://www.w3.org/1999/xhtml"
                xmlns:math="http://exslt.org/math"
                xmlns:redirect="org.apache.xalan.xslt.extensions.Redirect"
                extension-element-prefixes="math redirect">
...
<xsl:template match="TVGuide">
  ...
  <xsl:for-each select="Channel">
    <redirect:write select="concat(translate(Name, ' ', '_'), '.html')">
      <html>
        <head>
          <title><xsl:value-of select="Name" /></title>
          <link rel="stylesheet" href="TVGuide.css" />
          <script type="text/javascript">
            ...
          </script>
        </head>
        <body>
          <xsl:apply-templates select="." />
        </body>
      </html>
    </redirect:write>
  </xsl:for-each>
  ...
</xsl:template>
...
</xsl:stylesheet>
```

The <redirect:write> extension element allows you to create multiple output documents if you use Xalan.

Try It Out – Creating a Page Per Channel

To try out creating multiple output documents, we'll try to create one HTML page per channel listed within TVGuide.xml. To do this, you have to be using Saxon, Xalan, or another XSLT processor that has an extension element for outputting multiple documents.

MSXML doesn't have an extension element for outputting multiple documents.

To use an extension element, you have to declare the namespace for the extension element in the <xsl:stylesheet> document element, and list its prefix in the extension-element-prefixes attribute on <xsl:stylesheet>. For example, if you're using <saxon:output> and <redirect:write>, the <xsl:stylesheet> document element should look like the following:

```
<xsl:stylesheet version="1.0"
                xmlns:xsl="http://www.w3.org/1999/XSL/Transform"
                xmlns="http://www.w3.org/1999/xhtml"
                xmlns:math="http://exslt.org/math"
                xmlns:saxon="http://icl.com/saxon"
                xmlns:redirect="org.apache.xalan.xslt.extensions.Redirect"
                extension-element-prefixes="math saxon redirect">
  ...
</xsl:stylesheet>
```

Since we're using two different extension elements, we'll add a template that matches <Channel> elements in page mode to create the page, as follows:

```
<xsl:template match="Channel" mode="page">
  <html>
    <head>
      <title><xsl:value-of select="Name" /></title>
      <link rel="stylesheet" href="TVGuide.css" />
      <script type="text/javascript">
        ...
      </script>
    </head>
    <body>
      <xsl:apply-templates select="." />
    </body>
  </html>
</xsl:template>
```

We'll actually create these pages, using the relevant extension element, from within the template matching the <TVGuide> element. This template has to decide which extension element to use based on which extension element is supported by the current processor, which you can find out using the element-available() function, as follows:

```
<xsl:template match="TVGuide">
  <table>
    <tr>
      <th colspan="6">Channel</th>
      <xsl:call-template name="generateTimeline">
        <xsl:with-param name="startHours" select="19" />
        <xsl:with-param name="startMinutes" select="00" />
        <xsl:with-param name="endHours" select="22" />
        <xsl:with-param name="endMinutes" select="30" />
      </xsl:call-template>
    </tr>
    <xsl:apply-templates select="Channel" mode="Table" />
  </table>
  <xsl:choose>
    <xsl:when test="element-available('saxon:output')">
      <xsl:for-each select="Channel">
        <saxon:output href="{translate(Name, ' ', '_')}.html">
          <xsl:apply-templates select="." mode="page" />
        </saxon:output>
      </xsl:for-each>
    </xsl:when>
    <xsl:when test="element-available('redirect:write')">
      <xsl:for-each select="Channel">
       <redirect:write select="concat(translate(Name, ' ', '_'), '.html')">
         <xsl:apply-templates select="." mode="page" />
       </redirect:write>
      </xsl:for-each>
    </xsl:when>
    <xsl:otherwise>
      <xsl:apply-templates select="Channel" />
    </xsl:otherwise>
  </xsl:choose>
  <h2>Series</h2>
  <xsl:for-each select="$series">
    <xsl:call-template name="alphabetList" />
    <xsl:call-template name="alphabeticalSeriesList" />
  </xsl:for-each>
</xsl:template>
```

Try running `TVGuide9.xsl` (in which these changes have been made) over `TVGuide.xml` using either Saxon or Xalan. For example:

```
>Saxon -o TVGuide9.html TVGuide.xml TVGuide9.xsl
```

In both cases, you should get not only `TVGuide9.html` but also a bunch of other HTML files, one per channel, displaying the programs showing on that channel. For example, `BBC1.html` looks like:

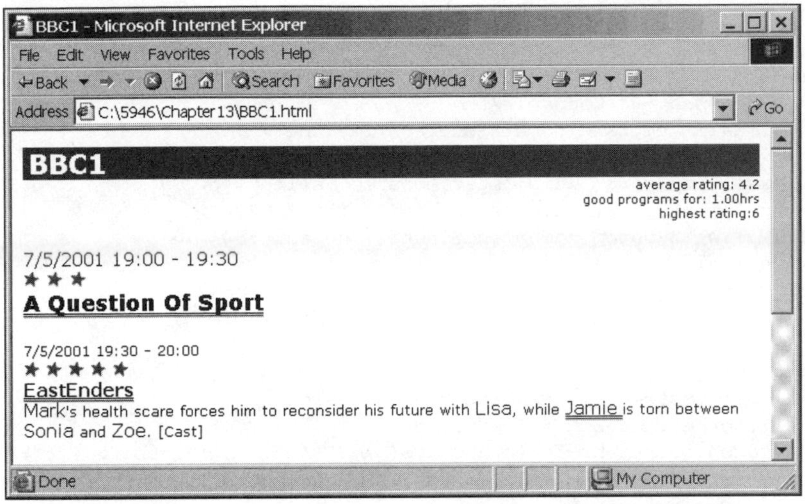

Writing Your Own Extension Functions

The final class of extensions that we'll look at in this chapter is the class that allows you to create your own extension functions. Updating an XSLT processor is hard work, and implementers can never anticipate all the requirements of their users, so most processors have some facilities that allow you to define your own extension functions instead.

I'll concentrate here on methods of creating your own functions in which the code is embedded within the stylesheet. Java-based processors (Saxon and Xalan) also enable you to reference Java classes available outside the stylesheet.

Defining Extension Functions in Scripting Languages

Both MSXML and Xalan support you defining your own extension functions in scripting languages such as JavaScript, MSXML through its built-in understanding of scripting languages and Xalan through the Java Bean Scripting Framework (BSF).

Defining Extension Functions with MSXML

If you're using MSXML, you can define your own extension functions using the `<msxsl:script>` element at the top level of the stylesheet. You must declare the `msxsl` prefix to be associated with the `urn:schemas-microsoft-com:xslt` namespace so that MSXML recognizes the element. You can define extension functions in the same range of languages that you can use within the HTML `<script>` element, including VBScript and JScript. If you're not using JScript, you should specify the language that you use in the `language` attribute on `<msxsl:script>`.

Usually it makes sense to use a CDATA section within the `<msxsl:script>` element to save you from escaping any `<` and `&` characters that you need to use in the code.

Like all extension functions, the functions that you define using `<msxsl:script>` must be placed in a namespace that is associated with a prefix. You need to declare the namespace that you want to put your extension functions in within the `<xsl:stylesheet>` document element. You then use the `implements-prefix` attribute on `<msxsl:script>` to indicate the namespace to which the extension functions belong.

For example, to define a `math:avg()` function in the namespace `http://www.example.com/math`, you could use the following:

```
<xsl:stylesheet version="1.0"
                xmlns:xsl="http://www.w3.org/1999/XSL/Transform"
                xmlns:msxsl="urn:schemas-microsoft-com:xslt"
                xmlns:math="http://www.example.com/math"
                extension-element-prefixes="msxsl math">
  ...
<msxsl:script implements-prefix="math" language="javascript">
  <![CDATA[
    function avg(nodeSet) {
      ...
    }
  ]]>
</msxsl:script>
  ...
</xsl:stylesheet>
```

> **MSXML allows you to define your own extension functions using the `<msxsl:script>` top-level element.**

Defining Extension Functions with Xalan

Xalan's method is a little bit different and uses two elements, both in the `http://xml.apache.org/xslt` namespace, which is associated with the prefix `lxslt` by convention. The `<lxslt:component>` element has a `prefix` attribute that indicates the namespace of the extension functions that you're defining (which works in the same way as the `implements-prefix` attribute on `<msxsl:script>`). The `<lxslt:component>` element also has a `functions` attribute, which holds a space-separated list of functions that the component defines.

Within the `<lxslt:component>` are any number of `<lxslt:script>` elements, each of which defines a set of functions using a particular language. The language of the functions contained in an `<lxslt:script>` element is specified with the `lang` attribute. This arrangement allows you to define the same set of functions (as listed by the `functions` attribute on `<lxslt:component>`) in a number of different languages, with one `<lxslt:script>` per language.

To define the `math:avg()` function in Xalan, you would use the following:

```
<xsl:stylesheet version="1.0"
                xmlns:xsl="http://www.w3.org/1999/XSL/Transform"
                xmlns:lxslt="http://xml.apache.org/xslt"
                xmlns:math="http://www.example.com/math"
```

```
                    exclude-result-prefixes="lxslt"
                    extension-element-prefixes="math">
...
<lxslt:component prefix="math" functions="avg">
  <lxslt:script lang="javascript">
    <![CDATA[
      function avg(nodeSet) {
        ...
      }
    ]]>
  </lxslt:script>
</lxslt:component>
...
</xsl:stylesheet>
```

Xalan will raise an error if you indicate that the `http://xml.apache.org/xslt` *namespace is an extension element namespace by listing the prefix* `lxslt` *in the* `extension-element-prefixes` *attribute.*

Xalan supports you writing extension functions in a wide range of languages, but to do so you usually have to download extra Java files and add them to your classpath. For example, to implement extension functions with Xalan using JavaScript, you need to get hold of `js.jar` from http://www.mozilla.org/rhino/ and make sure that both `js.jar` and `bsf.jar` (which comes with Xalan) are in your classpath.

> **Xalan allows you to define your own extension functions using the `<xalan:component>` and `<xalan:script>` elements.**

Argument Types

There are a couple of things that you need to be a little careful of when you define your own extension functions with MSXML or Xalan. When people use XPath, they tend to get used to the fact that it often automatically turns nodes and numbers into strings or uses the first node in a node set. This doesn't happen within your extension functions unless you program them to accept different kinds of values.

When a node set gets passed into a function, it gets converted into a DOM `NodeList` object, which you need to manipulate within the function using the standard DOM methods and properties. Remember that even if you select one node as the argument for the function, you'll still be passing in a `NodeList`; usually you'll want the function to get the first node from the `NodeList` using the `item()` method. Similarly, if you return a DOM `Node` or `NodeList` from the function, it gets turned into a node set and can be used as such within further XPath functions.

You can find out more about the DOM methods and properties from http://www.w3.org/TR/DOM-Level-2-Core/. *For programming with MSXML, I also find the MSXML SDK documentation, available from* http://msdn.microsoft.com/, *very useful.*

In addition, arguments to user-defined extension functions are never automatically converted to numbers or strings. If you create a function whose argument is supposed to be a string, then you need to be careful to always call it with a string, using the `string()` function to do the conversion within the XPath expression that calls the function. Similarly, you need to use the `number()` function to convert the argument to a number, if that's what the function expects to be dealing with. Alternatively, you can put the conversion code within the definition of the extension function. If you don't do the conversion at all, then the extension function will often generate an error because it expects to be dealing with a different type from the type it receives.

> **Remember to convert the arguments of functions into the correct type, either within the function definition or within the XPath expression that calls the function.**

Try It Out – Creating a Function to Calculate Durations Using JavaScript

We'll try out extension functions by creating a function that works out how many minutes a duration (in hours and minutes) represents. The function that we'll use is the following, which uses a regular expression to pull apart a duration string and work out how many minutes it represents:

```
function minutes(duration) {
  durationRE = new RegExp('^PT(([0-9]+)H)?(([0-9]+)M)?$');
  if (parts = durationRE.exec(duration)) {
    return (parts[1] ? parts[2] * 60 : 0) + (parts[3] ? parts[4] * 1 : 0);
  } else {
    return 0;
  }
}
```

To define this function using JavaScript, you must either use MSXML (which has support for defining JavaScript functions built in) or Xalan (which uses BSF to access Java implementations of the scripting languages).

> *If you use Xalan, you must make sure that your classpath contains* js.jar *from* http://www.mozilla.org/rhino/.

We'll place this extension function in `utils5.xsl`, and in the namespace `http://www.example.com/extensions`, which we'll declare with the `ext` prefix in the `<xsl:stylesheet>` document element. You also need to declare the namespace for whatever processor you're using to define the function, `urn:schemas-microsoft-com:xslt` if you're using MSXML or `http://xml.apache.org/xslt` if you're using Xalan. The `<xsl:stylesheet>` document element in `utils5.xsl` should look something like the following:

```
<xsl:stylesheet version="1.0"
                xmlns:xsl="http://www.w3.org/1999/XSL/Transform"
                xmlns="http://www.w3.org/1999/xhtml"
                xmlns:ext="http://www.example.com/extensions"
                xmlns:msxsl="urn:schemas-microsoft-com:xslt"
                xmlns:lxslt="http://xml.apache.org/xslt"
                xmlns:xalan="http://xml.apache.org/xalan"
                xmlns:exsl="http://exslt.org/common"
```

```
                    exclude-result-prefixes="lxslt"
                    extension-element-prefixes="ext msxsl xalan exsl">
  ...
</xsl:stylesheet>
```

Now you need to define the extension function, either using MSXML or using Xalan, or with both. With MSXML, you need an `<msxsl:script>` element at the top level of the stylesheet, which should look like:

```
<msxsl:script implements-prefix="ext" language="javascript">
  function minutes(duration) {
    durationRE = new RegExp('^PT(([0-9]+)H)?(([0-9]+)M)?$');
    if (parts = durationRE.exec(duration)) {
      return (parts[1] ? parts[2] * 60 : 0) + (parts[3] ? parts[4] * 1 : 0);
    } else {
      return 0;
    }
  }
</msxsl:script>
```

If you're using Xalan, you need an `<lxslt:component>` element with an `<lxslt:script>` element inside it holding the function itself. This should look like the following:

```
<lxslt:component prefix="ext" functions="minutes">
  <lxslt:script lang="javascript">
  function minutes(duration) {
    durationRE = new RegExp('^PT(([0-9]+)H)?(([0-9]+)M)?$');
    if (parts = durationRE.exec(duration)) {
      return (parts[1] ? parts[2] * 60 : 0) + (parts[3] ? parts[4] * 1 : 0);
    } else {
      return 0;
    }
  }
  </lxslt:script>
</lxslt:component>
```

You can add both definitions in the same stylesheet. MSXML will pick up on the `<msxsl:script>` element while Xalan uses the `<lxslt:component>` element.

We'll use this extension function rather than the XSLT code that we're using in the `durationMins` template, if it's available. We can check whether the extension function is available using the `function-available()` function, and use the XSLT code if not:

```
<xsl:template name="durationMins">
  <xsl:param name="duration" select="'PT0H0M'" />
  <xsl:choose>
    <xsl:when test="function-available('ext:minutes')">
      <xsl:value-of select="ext:minutes(string($duration))" />
    </xsl:when>
    <xsl:otherwise>
```

```
        <xsl:variable name="d"
                      select="substring(normalize-space($duration), 3)" />
        <xsl:variable name="durationHours">
          <xsl:choose>
            <xsl:when test="contains($d, 'H')">
              <xsl:value-of select="substring-before($d, 'H')" />
            </xsl:when>
            <xsl:otherwise>0</xsl:otherwise>
          </xsl:choose>
        </xsl:variable>
        <xsl:variable name="durationMinutes">
          <xsl:choose>
            <xsl:when test="contains($d, 'M')">
              <xsl:choose>
                <xsl:when test="contains($d, 'H')">
                  <xsl:value-of select="substring-before(
                                        substring-after($d, 'H'), 'M')" />
                </xsl:when>
                <xsl:otherwise>
                  <xsl:value-of select="substring-before($d, 'M')" />
                </xsl:otherwise>
              </xsl:choose>
            </xsl:when>
            <xsl:otherwise>0</xsl:otherwise>
          </xsl:choose>
        </xsl:variable>
        <xsl:value-of select="($durationHours * 60) + $durationMinutes" />
      </xsl:otherwise>
    </xsl:choose>
  </xsl:template>
```

If you transform `TVGuide.xml` with `TVGuide10.xsl`, which imports `utils5.xsl` in which these changes are made, you should see the correct durations whatever processor you use. The `durationMins` template is used to work out the column span of the cells in the table at the top of the page, and to supply the duration in minutes that's used to work out the total duration for the statistic about how long "good" programs are shown for, displayed for each channel. You can tell that the extension function is working properly if the table looks as follows:

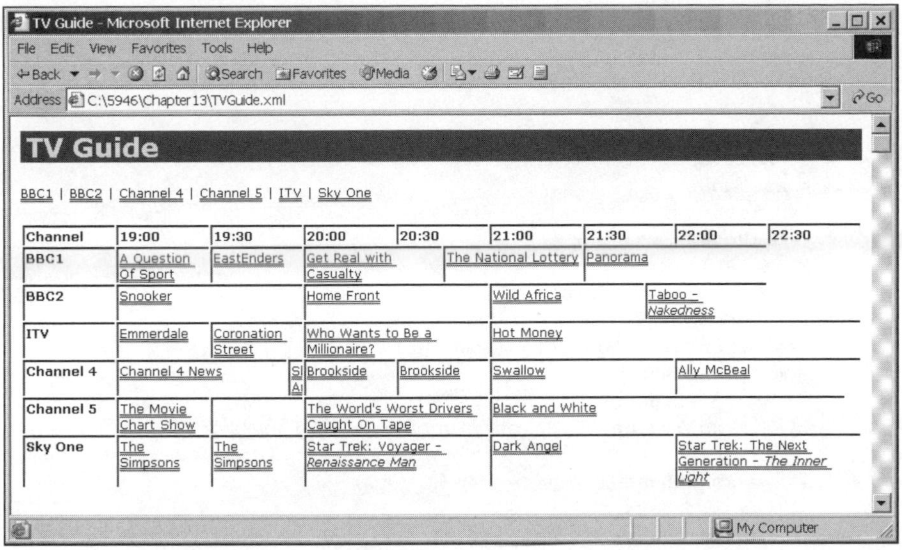

Defining Extension Functions in XSLT

A second method of defining extension functions is defined by the EXSLT initiative at http://www.exslt.org/func/. This method is supported by Saxon, 4XSLT, and libxslt, but not by other processors. A similar method is likely to be available in XSLT 2.0, according to the current Working Draft. Rather than defining extension functions using a scripting language, in many cases you can define the extension function using XSLT.

Now this doesn't work with all the things that you might want to do with an extension function – XSLT is still limited by the facilities available within XPath, and in particular it's impossible to write extension functions in XSLT that gain access to system information and very difficult to write extension functions that use regular expressions. However, in many cases, you can write the functions that you want in XSLT, and then use them elsewhere in your stylesheet.

Based on the method defined by the EXSLT initiative, you can define extension functions using XSLT with the `<func:function>` top-level element, which is in the `http://exslt.org/functions` namespace. The `<func:function>` element has a `name` attribute, which specifies the name of the extension function, including a prefix indicating the namespace of the extension function.

The arguments to the function are defined by `<xsl:param>` elements, in the same way as you define parameters for templates. The order of the `<xsl:param>` elements is significant, however – the first parameter gets assigned the value of the first argument, the second parameter is assigned the value of the second argument, and so on.

For example, to define the `math:avg()` extension function, you would use something like the following:

```
<xsl:stylesheet version="1.0"
                xmlns:xsl="http://www.w3.org/1999/XSL/Transform"
                xmlns:func="http://exslt.org/functions"
                xmlns:math="http://www.example.com/math"
                extension-element-prefixes="func math">
```

```
...
<func:function name="math:avg">
  <xsl:param name="nodeSet" select="/.." />
  ...
</func:function>
...
</xsl:stylesheet>
```

The result of the function is specified using a <func:result> element within the function. The <func:result> element works in much the same way as <xsl:variable> or <xsl:param>. You can either use its select attribute to return booleans, numbers, strings, and node sets or use its body to return a result tree fragment. For example, to give the result of the math:avg() extension function as the sum of the node set divided by the count of nodes in the node set, you would use the following <func:function> element:

```
<func:function name="math:avg">
  <xsl:param name="nodeSet" select="/.." />
  <func:result select="sum($nodeSet) div count($nodeSet)" />
</func:function>
```

You can use the <func:result> element several times within the function body, as long as it's only ever possible for a processor to encounter one <func:result> when it processes the function definition. For example, you can have a <func:result> within each <xsl:when> and <xsl:otherwise> within an <xsl:choose>, but you can't have a <func:result> within an <xsl:if> and a <func:result> outside that <xsl:if>, unless the <xsl:if> is never true. Similarly, you can have a <func:result> within an <xsl:for-each>, but only if the <xsl:for-each> only processes a single node, or the <func:result> is within an <xsl:if> such that it can only ever get used once.

For example, the problem with the above definition of the math:avg() function is that if there aren't any nodes in the node set that's passed as the argument to the function then the function returns Infinity, which is a rather high average for an empty node set! To return 0 if the node set is empty, you need to use an <xsl:choose> to test the node set. You can have a separate <func:result> within each branch of the <xsl:choose>, as follows:

```
<func:function name="math:avg">
  <xsl:param name="nodeSet" select="/.." />
  <xsl:choose>
    <xsl:when test="$nodeSet">
      <func:result select="sum($nodeSet) div count($nodeSet)" />
    </xsl:when>
    <xsl:otherwise>
      <func:result select="0" />
    </xsl:otherwise>
  </xsl:choose>
</func:function>
```

You can define functions using XSLT with the `<func:function>` top-level element. The arguments to the function are defined with `<xsl:param>` elements, and the result of the function is specified using a `<func:result>` instruction.

Try It Out – Creating a Function to Calculate Durations Using XSLT

It's not difficult to write an XSLT version of the `ext:minutes()` function that we defined using JavaScript before. In fact, we're doing it currently within the `durationMins` template, as highlighted in the following:

```
<xsl:template name="durationMins">
  <xsl:param name="duration" select="'PT0H0M'" />
  <xsl:choose>
    <xsl:when test="function-available('ext:minutes')">
      <xsl:value-of select="ext:minutes(string($duration))" />
    </xsl:when>
    <xsl:otherwise>
      <xsl:variable name="d"
                    select="substring(normalize-space($duration), 3)" />
      <xsl:variable name="durationHours">
        <xsl:choose>
          <xsl:when test="contains($d, 'H')">
            <xsl:value-of select="substring-before($d, 'H')" />
          </xsl:when>
          <xsl:otherwise>0</xsl:otherwise>
        </xsl:choose>
      </xsl:variable>
      <xsl:variable name="durationMinutes">
        <xsl:choose>
          <xsl:when test="contains($d, 'M')">
            <xsl:choose>
              <xsl:when test="contains($d, 'H')">
                <xsl:value-of select="substring-before(
                                        substring-after($d, 'H'), 'M')" />
              </xsl:when>
              <xsl:otherwise>
                <xsl:value-of select="substring-before($d, 'M')" />
              </xsl:otherwise>
            </xsl:choose>
          </xsl:when>
          <xsl:otherwise>0</xsl:otherwise>
        </xsl:choose>
      </xsl:variable>
      <xsl:value-of select="($durationHours * 60) + $durationMinutes" />
    </xsl:otherwise>
  </xsl:choose>
</xsl:template>
```

We can turn this code into a function very easily. We need to use `<func:function>` to define the function and we need to accept the duration as an argument. To return a *number* from the function, we need to use the `select` attribute of `<func:result>`. If we used the content of `<func:result>` we'd return a result tree fragment rather than a number. The function definition therefore looks like the following:

```
<func:function name="ext:minutes">
  <xsl:param name="duration" />
  <xsl:variable name="d"
                select="substring(normalize-space($duration), 3)" />
  <xsl:variable name="durationHours">
    <xsl:choose>
      <xsl:when test="contains($d, 'H')">
        <xsl:value-of select="substring-before($d, 'H')" />
      </xsl:when>
      <xsl:otherwise>0</xsl:otherwise>
    </xsl:choose>
  </xsl:variable>
  <xsl:variable name="durationMinutes">
    <xsl:choose>
      <xsl:when test="contains($d, 'M')">
        <xsl:choose>
          <xsl:when test="contains($d, 'H')">
            <xsl:value-of select="substring-before(
                                    substring-after($d, 'H'), 'M')" />
          </xsl:when>
          <xsl:otherwise>
            <xsl:value-of select="substring-before($d, 'M')" />
          </xsl:otherwise>
        </xsl:choose>
      </xsl:when>
      <xsl:otherwise>0</xsl:otherwise>
    </xsl:choose>
  </xsl:variable>
  <func:result select="($durationHours * 60) + $durationMinutes" />
</func:function>
```

You can now use the `ext:minutes()` function in Saxon, 4XSLT, and libxslt as well as MSXML and Xalan, although it's still best to test whether it's available before you use it, in case someone uses the stylesheet with another processor, such as Sablotron. In `utils6.xsl`, the `durationMins` template is as follows:

```
<xsl:template name="durationMins">
  <xsl:param name="duration" select="'PT0H0M'" />
  <xsl:choose>
    <xsl:when test="function-available('ext:minutes')">
      <xsl:value-of select="ext:minutes(string($duration))" />
    </xsl:when>
    <xsl:otherwise>
      <xsl:message terminate="yes">
        ERROR: ext:minutes() is not supported.
      </xsl:message>
    </xsl:otherwise>
```

```
    </xsl:choose>
  </xsl:template>
```

As long as you use a processor that supports `<func:function>`, `<msxsl:script>`, or `<lxslt:component>`, you should see the same table of programs displayed when you transform `TVGuide.xml` with `TVGuide11.xsl` (which imports `utils6.xsl`) as you did with `TVGuide10.xsl`.

Summary

The extensibility of XSLT and XPath is one of their strengths. Firstly, it means that if XSLT or XPath doesn't currently enable you to do something, then it's likely that an implementer will be able to put something together that will. Secondly, it means that implementers don't change XSLT, so you can tell exactly what's standard and what isn't. Finally, it enables users to try out new elements and functions before they get added to the language, which helps make XSLT usable and stable. Many functions that are implementer-specific extensions in XPath 1.0 are specified in the XPath 2.0 Working Draft, and many extension elements have been moved into the XSLT namespace in the XSLT 2.0 Working Draft.

In this chapter, you've learned about several different ways in which implementers can extend XSLT and XPath:

- Extension functions that can be used in XPath expressions and patterns
- Additional attribute values for changing the data type of a sort or the output method used when serializing the result tree
- Extension attributes that alter the behavior of existing XSLT elements
- Extension elements that add to the set of instructions that you can use
- Top-level elements that enable you to define your own constructs

You've seen how to use each of these different kinds of extensions, and how to stop XSLT processors that don't understand them from trying to use them, using `function-available()` to test for the availability of extension functions, `extension-available()` to test for the availability of extension elements and new instructions, or `<xsl:fallback>` to give alternative behavior if an extension element or new instruction isn't supported.

You've also learned about three important extensions that greatly add to the amount that you can do with XSLT, and the ease with which you can do it. These extensions are:

- The `node-set()` extension functions, which turn result tree fragments into node sets so that you can continue to process them
- Extension elements that enable you to create additional result documents
- Top-level elements that allow you to define your own extension functions

These extensions to XSLT and XPath 1.0 are likely to be standard in XSLT 2.0 and XPath 2.0 and are implemented across a range of processors, so they are worthwhile learning and using.

This chapter is the last in this part of the book. You've learned about pretty much all the elements and attributes that are available in XSLT, and the functions and operators that are available in XPath, and in this chapter you've learned how to add to what XSLT and XPath offer as standard. In the next part of the book, we'll turn our attention to some practical uses of XSLT and XPath so that you can see how it all fits together in the real world.

Review Questions

1. What is the main difference between an extension function and an XPath function?

2. How can you test whether the XSLT processor that's running the stylesheet supports an extension function?

3. What does an XSLT processor do if it finds an `<xsl:sort>` element whose `data-type` attribute contains a qualified name?

4. What are the main differences between the `html`, `xml`, and `saxon:xhtml` output methods?

5. Which extension attributes does your XSLT processor support and what do they do?

6. How does an XSLT processor tell the difference between a literal result element and an extension element?

7. What two ways are there of detecting when an XSLT processor doesn't support an extension element, and when is it appropriate to use them?

8. Write a template that uses an intermediate node set to create a four-column table listing cast members in alphabetical order by the surname of their character. It should look like:

Character	Actor	Character	Actor
Ian Beale	Adam Woodyatt	Laura Beale	Hannah Waterman
Janine Butcher	Charlie Brooks	Peggy Butcher	Barbara Windsor
...	...	...	...

9. Create a stylesheet that processes `series.xml` and produces a page for each series, giving the title of the series, a description of the series, and a list of the programs in that series, from `TVGuide.xml`.

10. Write an extension function that you can use with MSXML or Xalan to give you the current date, and use it to add a footer to the page generated by `TVGuide.xsl`.

Beginning
XSLT

14

Dynamic XSLT

So far, we have mainly transformed XML in a batch process from the command line. Using a command-line processor is very useful when first developing a stylesheet for several reasons. Firstly, it tends to be easier and quicker to debug stylesheets when using a processor from the command line rather than using it in a more dynamic environment. Secondly, there are lots of processors that you can use from the command line, so you can often work out what's going wrong by trying to use several different ones on the same transformation. Thirdly, command lines often give you access to additional information about the performance of the stylesheet, such as timing information or trace reports that you can use to perfect the stylesheet.

However, batch processing is seldom the best approach in real-world architectures. The result of a transformation can change for several reasons – amendments to the stylesheet, changes to the source document (perhaps because it is itself generated dynamically), alterations to the supplementary documents that you're using, and so on – and with batch processing you need to run the transformation each time one of these documents changes. This can easily lead to the transformed documents being out of step with the original documents.

If you can use a dynamic process to perform the transformation and display the results, then you don't have to worry about the source document changing later on – any changes will be automatically reflected in the newly transformed result. In this chapter, we'll look at how to carry out transformations dynamically and at two applications that support dynamic XSLT.

In this chapter, you'll learn:

- How to run dynamic transformations
- The advantages and disadvantages of client and server side transformations
- How to set up and use Cocoon 2
- How to manage client side transformations using MSXML
- How to pass parameters to create dynamic applications

Dynamic Transformations

Dynamic XSLT transformations can take place in two locations – **server side** or **client side**. Server side transformations are run on the server in response to the client's request for a particular page. Client side transformations are run on the client when it receives a particular page.

This chapter focuses on transforming XML for presentation, but the same distinction between server side and client side transformations can be made for XML-to-XML transformations as well – the XML is transformed into the desired format either in the application that is the source of the XML or in the application that receives the XML.

Server Side Transformations

With server side transformations, the client makes a single request for a page and the server returns a single page to the client. When the server receives a request, it identifies the XML that holds the data for the page to use and what XSLT stylesheet to use with it. The server then performs the transformation and returns the result of the transformation to the client. This process is illustrated in the following diagram:

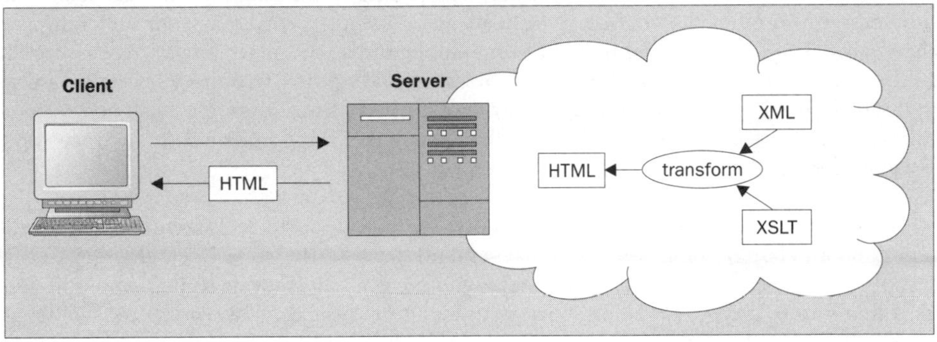

Assuming that the standard web protocol (HTTP) is being used, the server can work out what information the client should receive by looking at the **headers** of the request, which include the URL that's being requested and information about the client that's making the request. Based on this, the server can deliver different information according to the client – different HTML for different web browsers, WML for mobile phones, even XML if the client is one that can carry out client side transformations. The server, and therefore the developer of the application, is in control of what stylesheet is used and what kind of result the client sees. As far as the client is concerned, the server is just like any other – the client can't tell what's going on behind the scenes and doesn't know that the page is automatically generated.

Server side transformations have the disadvantage that they place a heavy load on the server. If 100 clients request XML pages in a minute, then the server has to perform those 100 transformations itself, and deliver the results, within a reasonable timeframe. While each individual transformation might be manageable, 100 transformations might not be, especially if those transformations take a long time or more importantly involve high memory use.

On the plus side, server side transformations can make sensible use of caches, to enable the server to store the results of common transformations so that it doesn't have to run them afresh each time a particular XML document is requested. However, this is only beneficial when you have XML pages that are relatively long lived (and that are requested more than once before being changed) and if the transformations that you carry out with them don't rely on changeable information such as user preferences or other display information.

You can write server side scripts (in Perl or ASP, for example) to support server side transformations yourself, or you can often use XSLT processors as Java servlets with your HTTP server. However, there are several sophisticated XML frameworks that incorporate server side transformations, and it's worth having a look at them before you launch into your own. For example:

- AxKit – an Apache module, implemented in Perl, that uses libxslt, Sablotron, or XML::XSLT for its transformations (http://www.axkit.org/)
- Cocoon – a Java servlet that uses Xalan (by default) to transform XML documents which may be generated on the fly (http://xml.apache.org/cocoon)
- XSQL – a Java servlet that generates XML from a database and uses Oracle's XSLT processor to transform it (http://technet.oracle.com/)

Of these three, Cocoon is arguably the most advanced, and is the one that we will look at in detail later on in this chapter.

Client Side Transformations

With client side transformations, the page that the client requests from the server includes instructions that tell the client how to transform the XML. The client performs the transformation, and displays the results.

There are two main models for client side transformations. The first and simplest is when the client requests an XML document and you tell the client what XSLT stylesheet to use with that XML document using the `xml-stylesheet` processing instruction. This approach is illustrated in the following diagram:

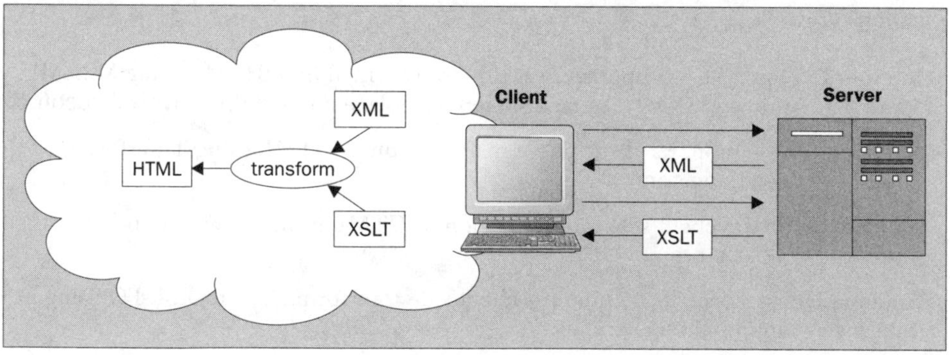

The `xml-stylesheet` processing instruction has two main pseudo-attributes: `href`, which points to the stylesheet that should be used with the XML document, and `type`, which states the content type of the stylesheet (`text/xsl`, by convention, for XSLT documents). You can have multiple `xml-stylesheet` processing instructions within a document, in which case the client should choose which one to use based on the other pseudo-attributes. In particular, the `media` pseudo-attribute should contain the type of client that the stylesheet should be used with – for example, `screen`, `handheld`, or `print`. However, these additional pseudo-attributes are not well supported in current clients.

The simple automatic transformation using the `xml-stylesheet` processing instruction is often all that you need. However, if you want to do more sophisticated things on the client, such as cache the XML or XSLT documents or pass parameters into the stylesheet, then you need to control the client side transformation somehow. These kinds of dynamic transformations are essential when creating pages that provide different views of the same XML document, such as tables that you can sort dynamically or applications where you can page through information.

Most usually you control the transformation with a script within an HTML page – it is this HTML page that the client first requests, and this HTML page that contains the instructions about which XML document and which XSLT stylesheet to use. This pattern is illustrated in the following diagram:

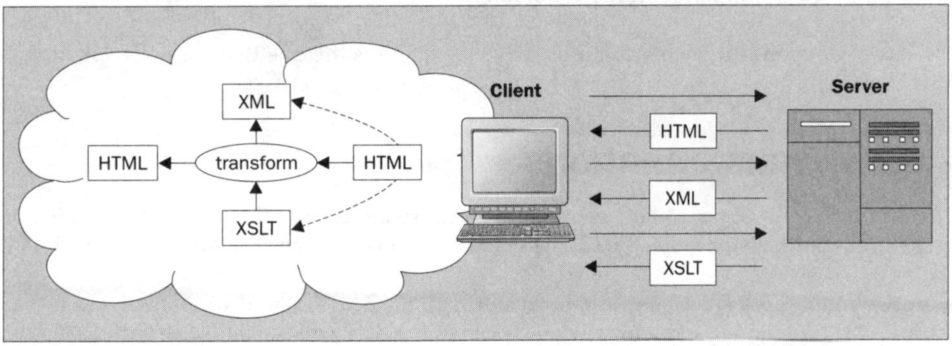

The biggest drawback with designing applications around client side transformations is that there are relatively few clients that support XSLT. The five browsers that currently support client side transformations are:

- Internet Explorer 5+ – supports client side transformation to HTML using MSXML; versions 5 and 5.5 requires MSXML3 to be installed in replace mode (http://www.microsoft.com/ie)
- Netscape 6.1+ – supports client side transformation to HTML using Transformiix (http://www.netscape.com)
- Mozilla – supports client side transformation to HTML using Transformiix (http://www.mozilla.org)
- Antenna House Formatter – supports client side transformations to XSL-FO using MSXML3 (http://www.antennahouse.com)
- XSmiles – supports client side transformations to XSL-FO using Xalan (http://www.xsmiles.org)

Of these, Internet Explorer provides the best support for XSLT, in particular providing good support for running transformations using scripts, as we will see later on.

The advantage of using client side transformations is in the lighter load that it places on the server. Rather than having to transform every file that's requested itself, the server can offload this processing onto the client, where it's much more likely that there will be sufficient resources for the processing to be carried out quickly.

In some applications, client side transformations can be particularly beneficial in reducing the number of requests that are made to the server as well. For example, imagine an application that involves transforming the same XML page with the same XSLT stylesheet again and again using different parameters each time. With a server side transformation, the XML page would be requested, and the resulting HTML file returned to the client each time a change was made to a parameter. With a client side transformation, the XML and XSLT files are requested just once, and can then be reused again and again, just with different parameters. This can make XSLT applications involving client side transformations very responsive.

Client Side or Server Side?

XSLT is now a fairly stable technology and there are a number of good XSLT processor implementations. However, neither client side nor server side transformations are particularly mature as yet. Aside from the basic method of associating a set of stylesheets to an XML document, there is no standard API for running either type of transformation. Whichever method you use, it will involve configuring your application with implementation-specific details. Hopefully this situation will improve as time goes on.

Whether you should use client side or server side transformations generally comes down to whether you can guarantee that the users accessing your site will be using browsers that can carry out client side transformations. If you can't, then delivering XML rather than HTML will exclude a significant number of people from your site. On the other hand, if you're limited in the control you have over your web server then you might not have a choice.

However, the decision between client side or server side transformation is not necessarily an either/or selection. Even if you opt for a server side transformation for the majority of browsers, you can still use client side transformations on those clients that can manage it, sending them the XML that you want them to use and letting them identify the XSLT to use with it. This gives you the benefits of offloading as much work as possible to the clients, while retaining the ability to supply usable content to other browsers.

Server Side Transformations Using Cocoon

In this section, we'll look at how to use Cocoon 2 to automatically transform XML pages into various formats using XSLT. First, we'll go through how to install Cocoon 2 with Jakarta Tomcat as the Java servlet engine, then look at how Cocoon works, and finally see how to configure Cocoon to carry out various dynamic transformations, including:

- Simple transformations of an XML document with an XSLT stylesheet
- Providing different results depending on which browser is being used
- Providing different results based on parameters passed to the stylesheet

Installing Cocoon

Cocoon needs a Java servlet engine to run. A servlet engine accepts the requests made by your browser and routes them to Java code that generates responses. The first step towards using Cocoon is to set up a Java servlet engine to run Cocoon. There are a variety of servlet engines that you could use, including:

- Jakarta Tomcat from Apache (http://jakarta.apache.org/tomcat/)
- WebLogic from BEA (http://www.bea.com/)
- ServletExec from New Atlanta Communications (http://www.newatlanta.com)
- Resin from Caucho Technology (http://www.caucho.com)
- HP-AS from Hewlett Packard (http://www.hpmiddleware.com)
- JRun from Macromedia (http://www.macromedia.com/software/jrun/)

Some of these work standalone while others are plug-ins for web servers. If you just want to install Cocoon to have a look at how it works, I recommend that you install Jakarta Tomcat 4. It works standalone (such that you don't have to worry about installing a web server) and it comes from Apache, so there's a lot more support for using Cocoon (which also comes from Apache) with Jakarta Tomcat than there is for most of the other servlet engines.

To use Jakarta Tomcat 4, you must first install a Java Software Development Kit (SDK). To get Cocoon working with my setup, I installed the SDK for Java 2 Standard Edition (J2SE) version 1.4.0. You can get hold of J2SE version 1.4.0 from http://java.sun.com/j2se/1.4/. I installed my copy in the directory `C:\Java\j2sdk1.4.0`.

Once you have installed the Java SDK, you need to set the `JAVA_HOME` environment variable to the directory in which you've installed it, in my case `C:\Java\j2sdk1.4.0`. You can set the `JAVA_HOME` environment variable through the System control panel in Windows.

Next download the binary release of the latest version of Jakarta Tomcat 4 from http://jakarta.apache.org/site/binindex.html and unzip its contents into a directory on your computer. I downloaded version 4.0.3 and installed my copy in the directory `C:\jakarta-tomcat`.

To start Jakarta Tomcat, run the `startup` program in the `bin` directory:

```
>C:\jakarta-tomcat\bin\>startup
```

If all goes well, you should see the Jakarta Tomcat Project page if you point your browser to http://localhost:8080/, as follows:

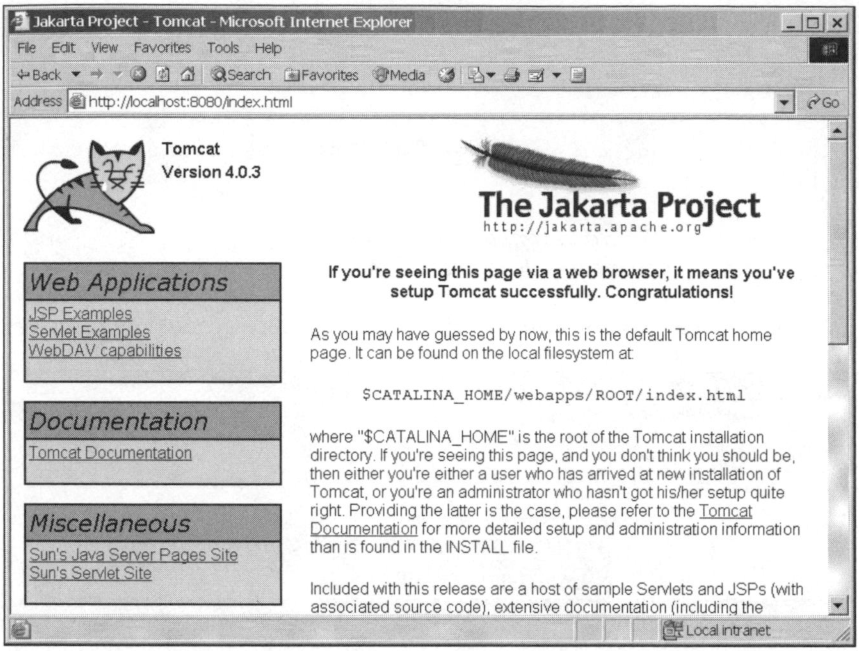

The second step for installing Cocoon is to download the binary distribution of Cocoon from http://xml.apache.org/cocoon/dist/. Unzip the contents of the distribution; I put my copy into `C:\cocoon`.

Within the Cocoon distribution is a file called `cocoon.war`. This file contains all of the information that the servlet engine needs to know in order to run Cocoon. For Jakarta Tomcat, you need to copy this file into the `webapps` directory of the Jakarta Tomcat installation, and restart the servlet engine:

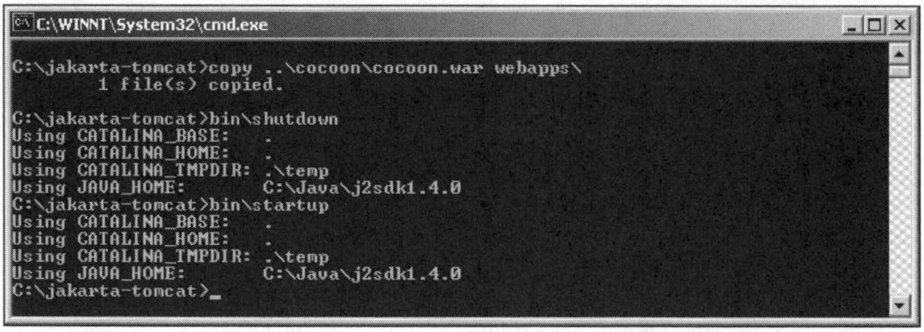

Jakarta Tomcat will take a little time to start up this time, because Cocoon has to create various directory structures when it's first used. Once it's started, if you look in the Jakarta Tomcat `webapps` directory, you should now see a `cocoon` subdirectory with a number of subdirectories of its own.

If you're using Cocoon 2.0.1 with Java 1.4 (as I am), you now need to do a little tweaking with the newly created Jar files in `C:\jakarta-tomcat\webapps\cocoon\WEB-INF\lib` to get things to work properly. This is because some of the Java files that are provided with Cocoon are actually already available within Java 1.4. Doing the following seems to work:

- Move batik-libs-1.1.1.jar and xml-apis.jar into C:\Java\j2sdk1.4.0\jre\lib\ext.
- Delete javac.jar.

When you've made those changes, restart Jakarta Tomcat using the shutdown and startup scripts that you used before.

> *Detailed instructions for other servlet engines are available at http://xml.apache.org/cocoon/installing/index.html.*

Once the setup has completed, try navigating to http://localhost:8080/cocoon. You should see the following:

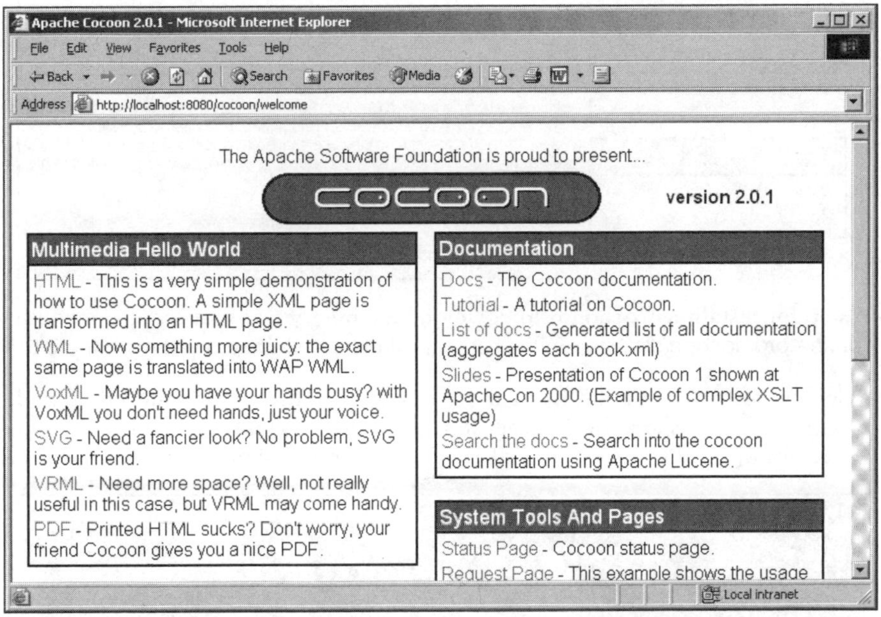

This page, like the rest of the pages accessible through http://localhost:8080/cocoon, is generated dynamically by transforming some XML with XSLT. You can view the source for the welcome page at C:\jakarta-tomcat\webapps\cocoon\docs\samples\samples.xml and the stylesheet at C:\jakarta-tomcat\webapps\cocoon\stylesheets\simple-samples2html.xsl.

You can read more about Cocoon and how it works by following the Docs link to http://localhost:8080/cocoon/documents/, which gives you the same information as can be found on the main Cocoon site at http://xml.apache.org/cocoon/.

> *We're just going to be trying things out with Cocoon on a local server, so all the URLs that we'll be using will start with http://localhost:8080/cocoon/. If you want your application to appear under a different URL, you need to configure your web server to redirect URLs so that requests to your web server are redirected to Cocoon. See the Cocoon FAQ at http://xml.apache.org/cocoon/faq.html#faq-20 for more details.*

Pipelines

Conceptually, all the pages that you access using Cocoon go through a **pipeline**, which is a three-stage process:

- Generating
- Transforming
- Serializing

Pipelines are called pipelines because they are like pipes that you fit together in order to route water (information) from one place to another. The generating process creates some information – it's like the tap at the beginning of a pipe. The transforming process transforms that information into another format. There can be several transformations, each working on the result of the previous one – they're like the pieces of pipe that can be fitted together. Finally, the serializing process takes the result of the last transformation and writes it out into a series of bytes – that's the faucet right at the end of the pipe.

The details of an individual pipeline – what gets generated, how it's transformed, and how it's serialized (or in plumbing terms, which faucet to attach the pipe to, what pipes to use, and what kind of faucet to fit at the end) – depend on the request that's made to Cocoon. Cocoon works out what you want to do by matching and selecting various aspects of the request, most importantly the URL. The processes that do the matching and selecting are like robots that fit the pipeline together – it's up to you, as the plumber, to make sure that those robots create the correct pipeline for the job.

Before we leap into using Cocoon, we'll take a little time to look at the components of the pipeline that are available to you in a bit more detail, and how matching and selecting works within Cocoon.

Generating

The generation step generates the XML content of a page. The simplest and most useful kind of **generator** is the File Generator, which just accesses an XML file that exists within the file system on your computer. For example, when you access http://localhost:8080/cocoon, the generator is a File Generator that accesses the file at C:\jakarta-tomcat\webapps\cocoon\docs\samples\samples.xml.

Cocoon also supports other types of generators, for example:

- Directory Generator – generates an XML page that describes the content of a directory
- Request Generator – generates an XML page that represents the information held in the original page request
- HTML Generator – generates an XHTML page from an HTML page

With these generators, you can create pages for navigating through your directory structure, or use information about the browser that requested the page. See http://localhost:8080/cocoon/request for an example of the XML that gets generated by the Request Generator.

Transforming

The transformation step transforms the XML that's been generated by applying a series of **transformers**. The most common kind of transformer, and the kind that we'll be using, is an XSLT Transformer, which transforms the generated XML using an XSLT stylesheet. For example, when you access http://localhost:8080/cocoon, the transformer is an XSLT Transformer that uses the XSLT stylesheet at C:\jakarta-tomcat\webapps\cocoon\stylesheets\simple-samples2html.xsl.

Other useful transformers are XInclude Transformers, which resolve XInclude elements within the generated XML, and Filter Transformers, which group a set of records in the generated XML according to their position.

You can have several transformers in a pipeline, each of them providing the input to the next transformer or (in the case of the last one) to the serializer. This enables you to split transformations into multiple steps, which makes each individual transformation easier to write and means that you can reuse them as necessary.

Serializing

The final step in a pipeline is serialization, which is carried out by a **serializer**. The default kind of serializer is the HTML Serializer, which serializes the result of the transformations as HTML. The HTML Serializer is the one that's used for the page http://localhost:8080/cocoon; if you look at the source code of the page, you'll see that it's an HTML page rather than well-formed XHTML.

Other useful serializers are:

- XML Serializer – serializes the result as XML
- Text Serializer – serializes the result as text
- PDF Serializer – serializes the XSL-FO result as PDF
- SVG Serializer – converts the SVG result to JPEG or PNG graphics

Note that the fact that serializers are a distinct step within the pipeline means that it doesn't matter what output instructions you include within your XSLT stylesheet using `<xsl:output>`, these will be overridden by the instructions supplied by the serializer that you use within the pipeline.

Matching and Selecting Pipelines

The generator, transformer, and serializer that are to be used to give the result of a particular request are determined by **matchers** and **selectors**. Matchers try to match a particular aspect of the request against a pattern string, which might contain wildcards or a regular expression. Selectors choose between multiple distinct possibilities.

The most frequently used matcher in Cocoon is the Wildcard URI Matcher, which matches the URI requested by the client against a pattern that can contain the wildcards * (which means any individual part of a URI, any characters not including the / character) or ** (which means any path within a URI, any characters including the / character). For example, when you access the page http://localhost:8080/cocoon, it gets picked up by a matcher that matches nothing (since there's nothing after the 'cocoon') and redirects you to the page http://localhost:8080/cocoon/welcome. Then there's another matcher that matches the pattern `welcome` from this URL and decides to create a page based on the `samples.xml` document because of that.

You can also match URIs against regular expressions with the Regular Expression URI Matcher, or you can match against the presence and values of request parameters with the Request Parameter Matcher and the Wildcard Request Parameter Matcher.

Selectors tend to be used to test other aspects of the request. The most common kind of selector is the Browser Selector, which determines what to do based on the identity of the browser that's being used to access the page. You can also use selectors to determine what to do based on the values of request headers and parameters, the host of the page, or the referring page.

Cocoon serves information by activating a pipeline in response to a request. The pipeline generates, transforms, and serializes XML. Cocoon comes with a set of generators, transformers, serializers, matchers, and selectors built in.

Configuring Cocoon

Cocoon is configured using **sitemaps** that describe the way the web site is arranged, just like a sitemap on a web site. You can change what Cocoon does when it receives a particular request by editing the sitemap. The main sitemap for the Cocoon site as a whole is the `sitemap.xmap` file within the `cocoon` directory (in my setup, at `C:\jakarta-tomcat\webapps\cocoon\sitemap.xmap`).

Sitemaps are XML documents; the document element is a `<map:sitemap>` element (where the prefix `map` is associated with the namespace URI `http://apache.org/cocoon/sitemap/1.0`). You can describe the whole site within that one sitemap or, as we'll see later in this section, you can define sitemaps for subdirectories individually.

Sitemaps have two roles: defining the various generators, transformers, serializers, matchers, and selectors that you can use, and defining the pipelines that are used for the various requests you might make. In terms of the plumbing analogy, they describe what kind of faucets and pipes you have available and the rules used by the robots to fit the pipes to faucets and to each other.

The structure of the sitemap XML document has two parts, following this division. Within the `<map:sitemap>` document element are two child elements: `<map:components>`, in which the various components are defined, and `<map:pipelines>`, in which the pipelines are defined by bringing together those components. Thus the basic outline of a sitemap file is as follows:

```
<map:sitemap xmlns:map="http://apache.org/cocoon/sitemap/1.0">

<map:components>
  <map:generators default="file">...</map:generators>
```

```
    <map:transformers default="xslt">...</map:transformers>
    <map:readers default="resource">...</map:readers>
    <map:serializers default="html">...</map:serializers>
    <map:selectors default="browser">...</map:selectors>
    <map:matchers default="wildcard">...</map:matchers>
  </map:components>

  <map:pipelines>
    <map:pipeline>...</map:pipeline>
    ...
  </map:pipelines>

  </map:sitemap>
```

As you can see from this outline, sitemaps can define other components aside from generators, transformers, serializers, selectors, and matchers, but these are the ones that we'll be using.

Defining Components

You probably won't need to edit the component definitions in your sitemaps, because Cocoon comes with them all set up nicely. This section just briefly explains how the component definitions work, so that you know how you can use them later on.

Each of the children of the `<map:components>` element is a wrapper for a series of component definitions. For example, the `<map:components>` element holds a `<map:generators>` child that contains any number of `<map:generator>` elements, each of which defines a type of generator that you can use.

Each of the component definitions follows the same basic format: it has a `name` attribute that gives the name of the component and a `src` attribute that points to the Java class that implements that component type, and it may have a number of child elements, each of which configures the component in some way. This basic outline for a component definition is shown below:

```
<map:component name="name" src="javaClass">
  <parameter>parameterValue</parameter>
  ...
</map:component>
```

As an example, the `sitemap.xmap` that comes with Cocoon uses the following component definition to define the XSLT Transformer:

```
<map:transformer name="xslt"
                 src="org.apache.cocoon.transformation.TraxTransformer">
  <use-request-parameters>false</use-request-parameters>
  <use-browser-capabilities-db>false</use-browser-capabilities-db>
</map:transformer>
```

This means that you can use the name `xslt` to refer to a **TraxTransformer** (TrAX is an API for running XML transformations used by Xalan and Saxon). Request parameters and information from the browser capabilities database are not passed into the stylesheet by default.

When you define pipelines, you can choose which generator, transformer, serializer, matcher, or selector to use by referring to them by the name that's used to define them in this section of the sitemap. To make life easier, you can also set up a default component that will be used if you don't refer to one specifically by name. You state what component should be used by default using the `default` attribute on the wrapper element that contains the component definitions.

For example, the following XML is used in the root `sitemap.xmap` file that comes with Cocoon to define the matchers that you can use:

```
<map:matchers default="wildcard">
  <map:matcher name="wildcard"
               src="org.apache.cocoon.matching.WildcardURIMatcher"/>
  <map:matcher name="regexp"
               src="org.apache.cocoon.matching.RegexpURIMatcher"/>
  <map:matcher name="request"
               src="org.apache.cocoon.matching.RequestParamMatcher"/>
  ...
</map:matchers>
```

This allows you to explicitly use the Wildcard URI Matcher by referring to it by the name `wildcard`, the Regular Expression URI Matcher using the name `regexp`, the Request Parameter Matcher using the name `request`, and so on. If you don't explicitly say which matcher you want to use when you match within a pipeline, it will assume that you're matching the URI using a wildcard pattern, because the `default` value on the `<map:matchers>` element is `wildcard`.

Defining Pipelines

The main part of configuring Cocoon is defining the pipelines that should be used. Each pipeline is defined within the `<map:pipelines>` element with its own `<map:pipeline>` element. You can use separate `<map:pipeline>` elements to have different error handling in different cases, but mainly you just need to have one `<map:pipeline>` element containing several `<map:match>` elements, each of which specifies a different request or class of requests and how to deal with it.

Each `<map:match>` element has an optional `type` attribute, which specifies the kind of matcher that should be used. If you don't give the `type` attribute specifically, then you'll use the default matcher, which is set when you define the matchers (in the `default` attribute of the `<map:matchers>` element). The URI (or whatever the matcher tests against) is matched against the pattern held in the `pattern` attribute. For example, to define a pipeline that should be used when someone requests `TVGuide.html`, you can use the following:

```
<map:pipeline>
  <map:match pattern="TVGuide.html">
    ...
  </map:match>
</map:pipeline>
```

Within the `<map:match>` element, you put the definition of the generator, transformers, and serializer that you want to use when that request is received. You specify the generator with a `<map:generate>` element, the transformers with `<map:transform>` elements, and the serializer with a `<map:serialize>` element. Each of these elements can take a `type` attribute if you want to specifically select a particular generator, transformer, or serializer for the content.

When we receive a request for `TVGuide.html`, for example, we want to use the XML from `TVGuide.xml`, transformed with the stylesheet from `TVGuide.xsl`, and serialized as HTML. The File Generator, XSLT Transformer, and HTML Serializer are the defaults in the basic Cocoon setup, so you can simply use:

```
<map:pipeline>
  <map:match pattern="TVGuide.html">
    <map:generate src="TVGuide.xml" />
    <map:transform src="TVGuide.xsl" />
    <map:serialize />
  </map:match>
</map:pipeline>
```

Creating Sub-sitemaps

The main sitemap, found in the `cocoon` directory, contains the definitions of many of the components that are available within Cocoon, as described above. Each directory can also have its own sub-sitemap, which deals with the requests for that directory and its subdirectories (unless they too have their own sub-sitemap). These can provide their own component definitions, but often will just contain some pipeline definitions dealing with the requests that are made for files in that directory.

To use one of these sub-sitemaps, you must **mount** the sitemap within the parent sitemap. You do this by defining a simple pipeline that matches paths that start with the directory name. For example, to create a `user` subdirectory, you need a pipeline that matches paths starting with `user/`, as follows:

```
<map:pipeline>
  <map:match pattern="user/**">
    ...
  </map:match>
</map:pipeline>
```

The `**` ensures that requests made for files or directories at whatever level below the `user` subdirectory are passed on to the sitemap for the `user` subdirectory.

Within the pipeline for the subdirectory, you need to mount the sub-sitemap using a `<map:mount>` element. The `<map:mount>` element has two important attributes: the `src` attribute that specifies the subdirectory (don't forget to end it with a trailing `/`), and the `uri-prefix` that specifies the string that's taken off the beginning of the URI when it is passed through to the sitemap in that directory (which again is usually the same as the name of the directory). So, to mount the `user` subdirectory, which contains its own sitemap in `sitemap.xmap`, you can use the following:

```
<map:pipeline>
  <map:match pattern="user/**">
    <map:mount src="user/" uri-prefix="user/" />
  </map:match>
</map:pipeline>
```

You can configure Cocoon through sitemaps. You can set up components and define pipelines within a sitemap. Each sitemap can mount other sitemaps, usually from other directories.

Try It Out – Creating a Sitemap for a Subdirectory

To try out what you've learned about sitemaps in Cocoon, we'll create a directory called `TVGuide` that holds the various XML and XSLT files that we've been using and configure Cocoon so that the URL http://localhost:8080/cocoon/TVGuide/listing returns the result of applying the `TVGuide.xsl` stylesheet to the `TVGuide.xml` file.

First, create a subdirectory of the `C:\jakarta-tomcat\webapps\cocoon` directory, called `TVGuide`, and put all the files that we've been using – `TVGuide.xml`, `series.xml`, `months.xml`, `default.xml`, `JeniT.xml`, `TVGuide.xsl`, `channelList.xsl`, `table.xsl`, `series.xsl`, `description.xsl`, and `utils.xsl` – within this directory.

If you try accessing these files directly at the URL http://localhost:8080/cocoon/TVGuide/TVGuide.xml, you'll get a 404 error because Cocoon hasn't been configured yet to accept that as a URL:

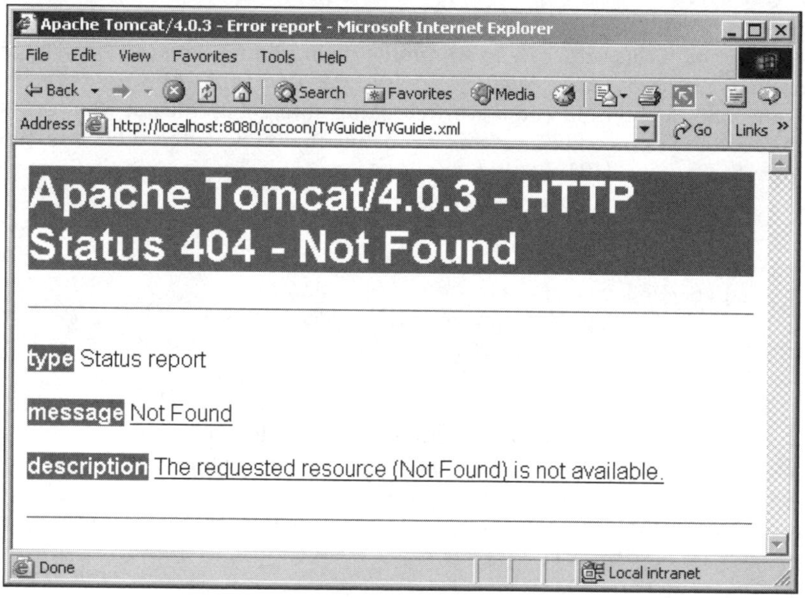

Next, we'll make a sitemap for the `TVGuide` directory. This sitemap is really just the bare bones of a sitemap – it will use the components that are defined in the root sitemap that comes with Cocoon. For now it will just contain one pipeline – when the client requests the URL http://localhost:8080/cocoon/TVGuide/listing, it will "generate" XML from `TVGuide.xml` (which actually just involves reading that file), transform it using `TVGuide.xsl`, and serialize the result as HTML. The sitemap for the `TVGuide` directory, held in `C:\jakarta-tomcat\webapps\cocoon\TVGuide\sitemap.xmap`, looks like the following:

```
<map:sitemap xmlns:map="http://apache.org/cocoon/sitemap/1.0">

<map:components>
  <map:generators default="file" />
  <map:transformers default="xslt" />
  <map:readers default="resource" />
  <map:serializers default="html" />
  <map:selectors default="browser" />
  <map:matchers default="wildcard" />
</map:components>

<map:pipelines>
  <map:pipeline>
    <map:match pattern="listing">
      <map:generate src="TVGuide.xml" />
      <map:transform src="TVGuide.xsl" />
      <map:serialize />
    </map:match>
  </map:pipeline>
</map:pipelines>

</map:sitemap>
```

Finally, we need to mount this sub-sitemap within the main sitemap for Cocoon. The main sitemap for Cocoon is found at `sitemap.xmap` within `C:\jakarta-tomcat\webapps\cocoon`. It has a lot of configuration information within it, and is worth looking at to get an idea of what can be achieved with Cocoon, but for now all you need to do is add a pipeline that mounts the sub-sitemap we've just created for use when people request a URI that begins with `TVGuide`. The pipeline that you need to add within the `<map:pipelines>` element is as follows:

```
<map:pipeline>
  <map:match pattern="TVGuide/**">
    <map:mount src="TVGuide/" uri-prefix="TVGuide/" />
  </map:match>
</map:pipeline>
```

Now restart Cocoon by shutting down and starting up the servlet engine that you're using (for example, Jakarta Tomcat), to make sure that it reads in the changes to the main `sitemap.xmap` and the new `sitemap.xmap` that you've added. When you access the URL http://localhost:8080/cocoon/TVGuide/listing, you should see the results of transforming `TVGuide.xml` with `TVGuide.xsl`:

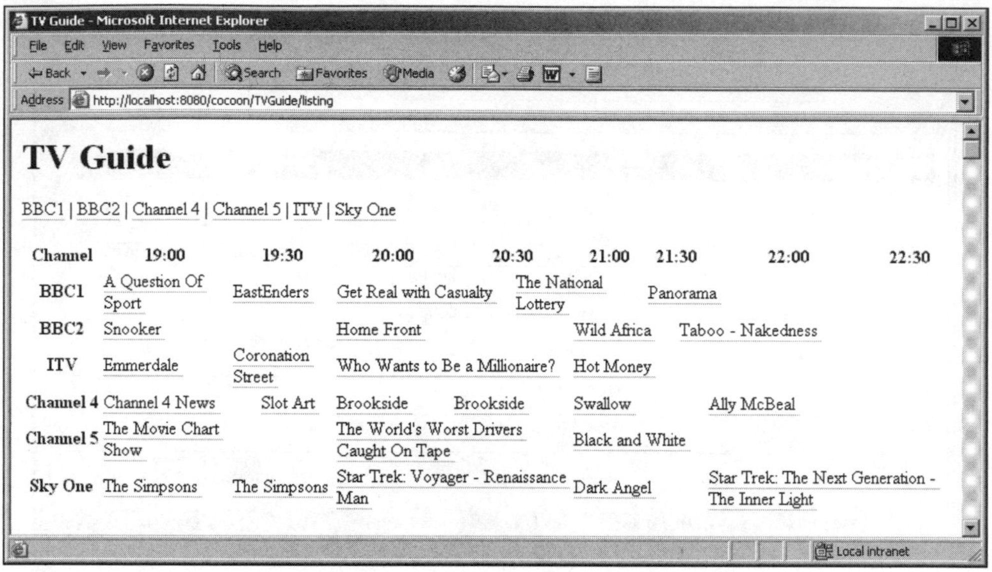

The result doesn't look quite right because the generated HTML page includes references to various other files (the CSS stylesheet and various images). You can configure Cocoon so that requests for CSS files and GIFs within the `TVGuide` subdirectory simply result in returning those files by adding a couple more `<map:match>` elements to the `sitemap.xmap` for the `TVGuide` subdirectory, as follows:

```
<map:pipelines>
  <map:pipeline>

    <map:match pattern="listing">
      <map:generate src="TVGuide.xml" />
      <map:transform src="TVGuide.xsl" />
      <map:serialize />
    </map:match>

    <map:match pattern="**.css">
      <map:read src="{1}.css" mime-type="text/css" />
    </map:match>

    <map:match pattern="**.gif">
      <map:read src="{1}.gif" mime-type="image/gif" />
    </map:match>

  </map:pipeline>
</map:pipelines>
```

If you make these changes, so that your `sitemap.xmap` is the same as `sitemap2.xmap`, viewing http://localhost:8080/cocoon/TVGuide/listing should give you the properly formatted page:

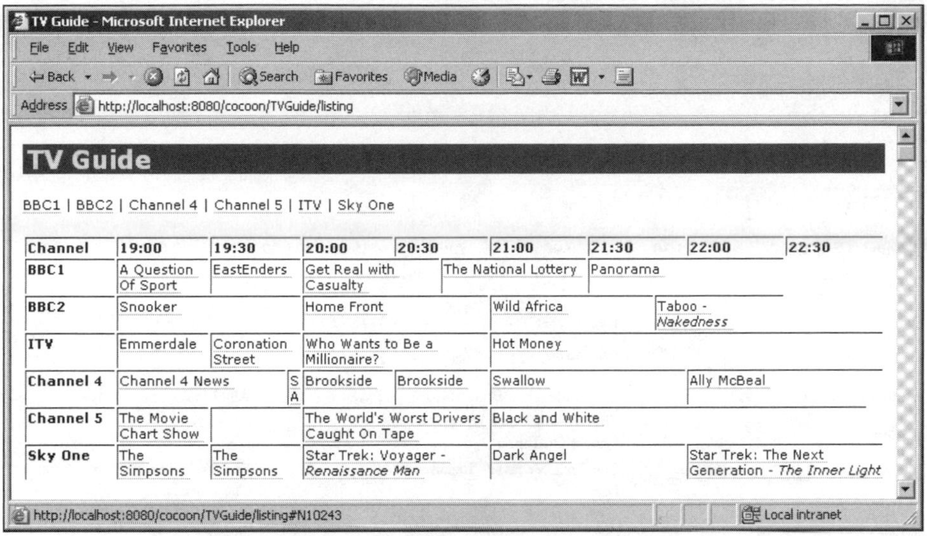

Different Stylesheets for Different Browsers

You can configure Cocoon to use different stylesheets for different browsers using a Browser Selector. These give the same kind of effect as HTML pages containing "sniffer" scripts that test what kind of browser you're using and create different pages as a result.

The Browser Selector named `browser` is the default selector in the usual Cocoon setup, and it defines the identifiers for the browsers that can be discriminated within the sitemap. The selector named `browser` is set up as follows in the main `sitemap.xmap`:

```
<map:selector name="browser"
              src="org.apache.cocoon.selection.BrowserSelector">
  <!-- # NOTE: The appearance indicates the search order. This is very
       # important since some words may be found in more than one browser
       # description. (MSIE is presented as "Mozilla/4.0 (Compatible; MSIE
       # 4.01; ...")
  -->
  <browser name="explorer" useragent="MSIE"/>
  <browser name="pocketexplorer" useragent="MSPIE"/>
  <browser name="handweb" useragent="HandHTTP"/>
  <browser name="avantgo" useragent="AvantGo"/>
  <browser name="imode" useragent="DoCoMo"/>
  <browser name="opera" useragent="Opera"/>
  <browser name="lynx" useragent="Lynx"/>
  <browser name="java" useragent="Java"/>
  <browser name="wap" useragent="Nokia"/>
  <browser name="wap" useragent="UP"/>
  <browser name="wap" useragent="Wapalizer"/>
  <browser name="mozilla5" useragent="Mozilla/5"/>
  <browser name="mozilla5" useragent="Netscape6/"/>
  <browser name="netscape" useragent="Mozilla"/>
</map:selector>
```

You can set up your own Browser Selectors if you want to, with different names, for example, to group all the desktop browsers together or to distinguish more precisely between different versions of browsers. The Browser Selector is set up using `<browser>` child elements, each of which gives the identifier for a browser in the `name` attribute and the string that appears within the **User-Agent** HTTP header when that browser is used to request a file in the `useragent` attribute.

Once a selector has been set up, you can use it within a pipeline with the `<map:select>` element. The `<map:select>` element takes an optional `type` attribute, which specifies the name of the selector component that you want to use (and usually defaults to `browser`, the Browser Selector as shown above).

The content of the `<map:select>` element is similar to the content of the `<xsl:choose>` element and works in roughly the same way. Within the `<map:select>` element are a number of `<map:when>` elements, each with a `test` attribute. The content of a `<map:when>` element is used if its `test` attribute holds the selected value (in this case, the name of the browser). The `<map:select>` element may also have a `<map:otherwise>` child, which is used if none of the `<map:when>` elements hold the relevant value.

For example, to use `TVGuide.ie.xsl` to transform `TVGuide.xml` if the browser is Internet Explorer or Pocket Internet Explorer, and the normal `TVGuide.xsl` otherwise, you could use the following:

```
<map:pipeline>
  <map:match pattern="listing">
    <map:generate src="TVGuide.xml" />
    <map:select>
      <map:when test="explorer">
        <map:transform src="TVGuide.ie.xsl" />
      </map:when>
      <map:when test="pocketexplorer">
        <map:transform src="TVGuide.ie.xsl" />
      </map:when>
      <map:otherwise>
        <map:transform src="TVGuide.xsl" />
      </map:otherwise>
    </map:select>
    <map:serialize />
  </map:match>
</map:pipeline>
```

Sometimes the serialization of the transformed XML should vary according to the browser that's used, perhaps at the same time as the method of transformation. For example, if you have `TVGuide.wap.xsl` that transforms to WML for WAP phones, then you should have the `<map:serialize>` element within the `<map:select>` as well, this time using an XML Serializer configured so that it outputs WML properly:

```
<map:pipeline>
  <map:match pattern="listing">
    <map:generate src="TVGuide.xml" />
    <map:select>
      <map:when test="wap">
        <map:transform src="TVGuide.wap.xsl" />
```

```
      <map:serialize type="wap" />
    </map:when>
    <map:otherwise>
      <map:transform src="TVGuide.xsl" />
      <map:serialize />
    </map:otherwise>
  </map:select>
</map:match>
</map:pipeline>
```

You can nest selectors and matches inside each other as much as you like in order to configure the pipeline.

> **You can change the stylesheet that you use according to the client requesting the file using the `browser` selector.**

Try It Out – Sending XML to Internet Explorer 6

As we explored earlier, it can be beneficial to send raw XML to those browsers that support it, and let the client perform the transformation rather than adding to the server load. To do this with Cocoon, you have to configure Cocoon so that it recognizes those browsers that can do client side transformations.

First, we need to work out the strings that are contained in the User-Agent HTTP header that identifies which browser is being used. Fortunately, Cocoon provides a page that allows you to see what headers are being used by a browser – go to http://localhost:8080/cocoon/request and have a look at the `<header>` element whose `name` attribute is `user-agent`. If you're using Internet Explorer 6, you should see something like:

```
<header name="user-agent">
  Mozilla/4.0 (compatible; MSIE 6.0; Windows NT 5.0)
</header>
```

As you can see, Internet Explorer 6 can be identified because it contains the string `MSIE 6`. We can add a browser entitled `explorer6` to the list of browsers defined for the `browser` selector within the main `sitemap.xmap` document, `C:\jakarta-tomcat\webapps\cocoon\sitemap.xmap`, before the other browsers that include the string `MSIE`, as follows:

```
<map:selector name="browser"
              src="org.apache.cocoon.selection.BrowserSelector">
  ...
  <browser name="explorer6" useragent="MSIE 6"/>
  <browser name="explorer" useragent="MSIE"/>
  ...
</map:selector>
```

Once you've defined Internet Explorer 6 as a browser you can get it to perform the transformation of the XML by sending it the XML without performing any transformations on it. We need to adjust the pipeline that we've defined for the URL http://localhost:8080/cocoon/TVGuide/listing so that it doesn't perform any transformations. It just serializes using the XML Serializer if the browser is Internet Explorer 6, and otherwise it uses `TVGuide.xsl` to run the transformation on the server and returns the result serialized as HTML, as follows:

```
<map:match pattern="listing">
  <map:generate src="TVGuide.xml" />
  <map:select>
    <map:when test="explorer6">
      <map:serialize type="xml" />
    </map:when>
    <map:otherwise>
      <map:transform src="TVGuide.xsl" />
      <map:serialize />
    </map:otherwise>
  </map:select>
</map:match>
```

Make these changes so that `C:\jakarta-tomcat\webapps\cocoon\TVGuide\sitemap.xmap` is the same as `sitemap3.xmap`.

If you try to access http://localhost:8080/cocoon/TVGuide/listing using a version of Internet Explorer other than version 6, or a different web browser, you'll see the HTML generated by applying `TVGuide.xsl` to `TVGuide.xml`. For example, with Netscape, the page looks like:

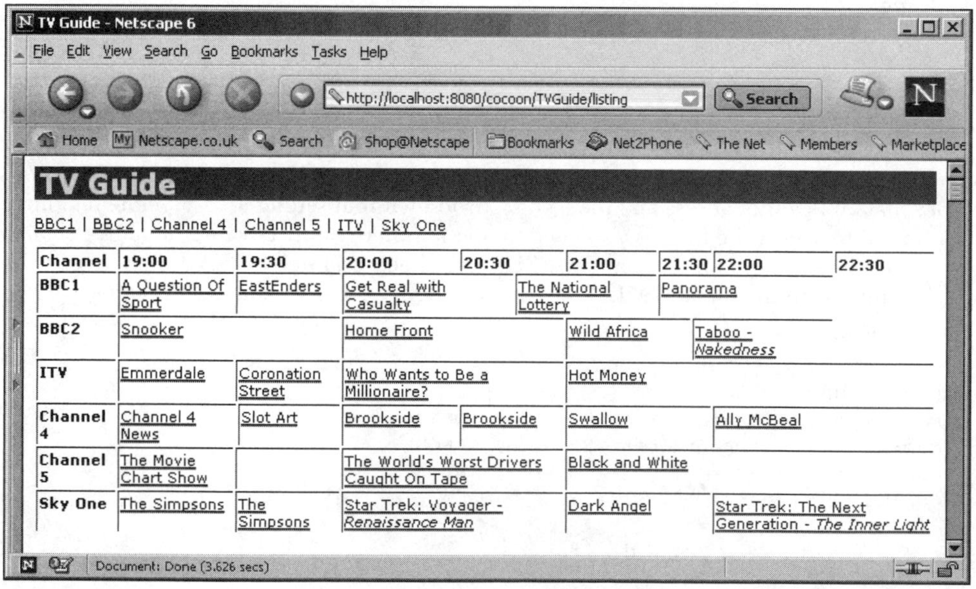

If you try using Internet Explorer 6 to access the same URL, you should see a tree view of the XML source document:

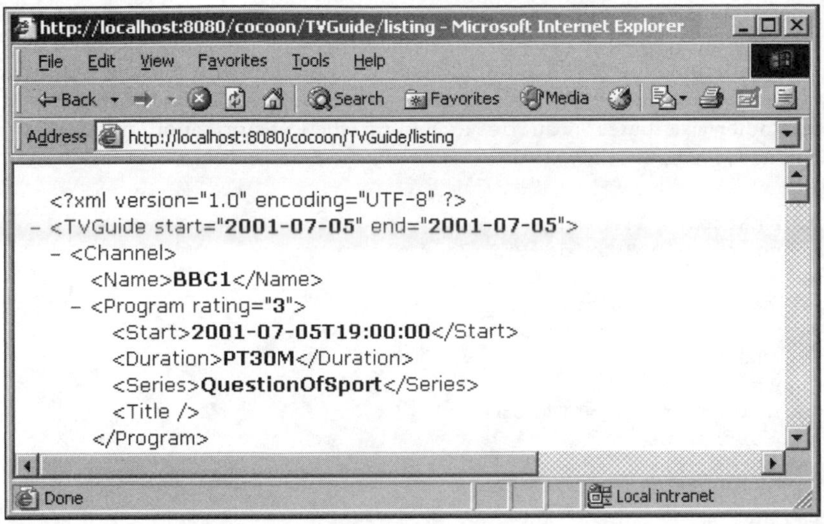

To get this XML source to be transformed by Internet Explorer, we need to do two things. Firstly, we need to add an `xml-stylesheet` processing instruction at the top of `TVGuide.xml`, right after the XML declaration on the first line, pointing to `TVGuide.xsl`, the stylesheet that we want to apply, as in `TVGuide2.xml`:

```
<?xml version="1.0"?>
<?xml-stylesheet type="text/xsl" href="TVGuide.xsl"?>
<TVGuide>
  ...
</TVGuide>
```

Now, when Internet Explorer 6 accesses the XML page, it will determine that it needs to apply `TVGuide.xsl` to the XML in order to create some HTML to view the page. Internet Explorer will try to go and get `TVGuide.xsl` and various other stylesheets and XML documents from Cocoon, but remember that you cannot access any file using Cocoon without setting up a pipeline that matches the URI that's used to access the file. So you need to add another couple of `<map:match>` elements in the `sitemap.xmap` configuration file, one for XSLT stylesheets and one for XML files, that say that these requests should return the file as XML. Edit your `sitemap.xmap` so that it's the same as `sitemap4.xmap`:

```
<map:pipeline>
  <map:match pattern="listing">...</map:match>
  <map:match pattern="**.css">...</map:match>
  <map:match pattern="**.gif">...</map:match>
  <map:match pattern="**.xsl">
    <map:generate src="{1}.xsl" />
    <map:serialize type="xml" />
  </map:match>
  <map:match pattern="**.xml">
    <map:generate src="**.xml" />
```

```
      <map:serialize type="xml" />
    </map:match>
  </map:pipeline>
```

If you now access http://localhost:8080/cocoon/TVGuide/listing using Internet Explorer 6, the browser will perform the XSLT transformation client side; if you access it with a different browser, Cocoon will perform the XSLT transformation server side. Either way, you should get the same result.

Using Parameters

The great advantage of using dynamic transformations rather than static batch transformations is that you can create HTML pages that rely on user input, passed into the stylesheet using parameters. As you'll recall from Chapter 6, you can make a stylesheet accept a parameter by declaring the parameter at the top level of the stylesheet. In Chapter 12, we created a stylesheet that customized the TV listing by adding flags to programs and series that users had selected as being interesting. The user ID is held in the `$userID` parameter, which is declared in `TVGuide.xsl` using:

```
<xsl:param name="userID" select="'default.xml'" />
```

You can pass parameters into a stylesheet that you access using Cocoon in two main ways: by setting the parameter from within the sitemap or by passing through parameters from the URL of the request. These two methods can be combined for any particular request, but we'll look at how to use them individually in the next two sections.

Setting Parameters in the Sitemap

The first way of passing parameters into a transformation is to use <map:parameter> within the <map:transform> element that runs the transformation in the sitemap. This technique is most useful if you want to pass in a parameter that's fixed based on one of the headers used in the request or the path of the request URL itself – for example, if you wanted to pass a different value for a parameter based on the web browser that's being used or based on the 'directory' named in the URL.

One of the things about Cocoon that can take some getting used to is the fact that the URL used to access a page can bear little or no relation to the actual location of the documents used to generate the page.

You pass parameters in to the transformation using the <map:parameter> element, with a `name` attribute giving the name of the parameter (the name that's used in the <xsl:param> definition within the stylesheet) and a `value` attribute specifying the string value of the parameter, as follows:

```
<map:transform src="stylesheet.xsl">
  <map:parameter name="parameterName" value="parameterValue" />
</map:transform>
```

For example, you could use the same stylesheet, `TVGuide.xsl`, to transform `TVGuide.xml` to either produce a listing of the programs grouped by what channel they're on or produce a listing based on what time the programs are showing. The grouping that was used could depend on the `$group` parameter, which takes a value of either `'channels'` or `'startTimes'`, with a default of `'channels'`. The parameter would be declared in `TVGuide.xsl` as follows:

```
<xsl:param name="group" select="'channels'" />
```

In the sitemap, the group that's used depends on the URL that's used to access the information. The URL http://localhost:8080/cocoon/TVGuide/listing/channels shows the listings by channel, whereas the URL http://localhost:8080/cocoon/TVGuide/listing/startTimes shows the listings by start time. To define the different treatment of the two URLs, we could use two separate pipelines:

```
<map:pipeline>
  <map:match pattern="listing">
    <map:generate src="TVGuide.xml" />

    <map:match pattern="listing/channels">
      <map:transform src="TVGuide.xsl">
        <map:parameter name="group" value="channels" />
      </map:transform>
    </map:match>

    <map:match pattern="listing/startTimes">
      <map:transform src="TVGuide.xsl">
        <map:parameter name="group" value="startTimes" />
      </map:transform>
    </map:match>

    <map:serialize />
  </map:match>
</map:pipeline>
```

If the value of the parameter links up with the value used in the URL, as it does here, it's also possible to use wildcards to set the value of the parameter. Any `*` or `**` used in the pattern of a `<map:match>` within the sitemap is assigned to implicit variables, named 1, 2, 3, and so on. You can refer to these variables within the `value` attribute of `<map:parameter>` using `{}`s around the number. So for example, to insert the value matched by the first `*` in the pattern, you would use `{1}`.

In this case, the string after the listing/ part of the URL is the value that we want to pass as the parameter. So, we can use a wildcard as follows:

```
<map:pipeline>
  <map:match pattern="listing/*">
    <map:generate src="TVGuide.xml" />
    <map:transform src="TVGuide.xsl">
      <map:parameter name="group" value="{1}" />
    </map:transform>
    <map:serialize />
  </map:match>
</map:pipeline>
```

You can also use parameters from the match pattern in various other places, including the `src` attributes of `<map:generate>` and `<map:transform>`. We used them earlier in this section when we configured Cocoon to return CSS, GIF, XSLT, and XML files that were requested explicitly.

You can pass parameters in to stylesheets using the `<map:parameter>` element within a `<map:transform>` in the sitemap. The value of the parameter can be based on the URL using wildcards.

Try It Out – Passing Parameters to the Stylesheet

The parameter that we'll pass in to the stylesheet is the `$userID` parameter, which identifies the user configuration file that lists things like keywords and interesting programs. We'll try to set up Cocoon so that the URL http://localhost:8080/cocoon/TVGuide/JeniT/listing/ uses the `TVGuide.xsl` stylesheet on `TVGuide.xml` with the `$userID` parameter set to `'JeniT'`, and the URL http://localhost:8080/cocoon/TVGuide/DavidC/listing `performs` a transformation with the same source and stylesheet, but this time with the `$userID` parameter set to `'DavidC'`.

The general pattern for the URLs is `*/listing`, where the `*` represents the user ID and the value for the `$userID` parameter. URLs of this form should cause `TVGuide.xml` to be transformed using `TVGuide.xsl` and then serialized using the default HTML Serializer. You can therefore include the following `<map:match>` within the pipeline for the site:

```
<map:match pattern="*/listing">
  <map:generate src="TVGuide.xml" />
  <map:transform src="TVGuide.xsl" />
  <map:serialize />
</map:match>
```

Now we can add the passing of a value for the `$userID` parameter in to the stylesheet. The `<map:transform>` element needs a `<map:parameter>` child element whose `name` attribute has the value `userID` and whose `value` attribute refers to the part of the URL matching the first `*` in the pattern, as follows:

```
<map:match pattern="*/listing">
  <map:generate src="TVGuide.xml" />
  <map:transform src="TVGuide.xsl">
    <map:parameter name="userID" value="{1}" />
  </map:transform>
  <map:serialize />
</map:match>
```

Since the URL used to access the listing is different, the browser will also request CSS files and GIFs from that same directory. Therefore you also need to include some `<map:match>` elements to deal with these requests:

```
<map:match pattern="*/**.css">
  <map:read src="{2}.css" mime-type="text/css" />
</map:match>
<map:match pattern="*/**.gif">
  <map:read src="{2}.gif" mime-type="image/gif" />
</map:match>
```

With these changes, your sitemap.xmap should look the same as sitemap5.xmap.

Now try accessing http://localhost:8080/cocoon/TVGuide/JeniT/listing. The result of the transformation should include flags on various TV programs, such as EastEnders, as follows:

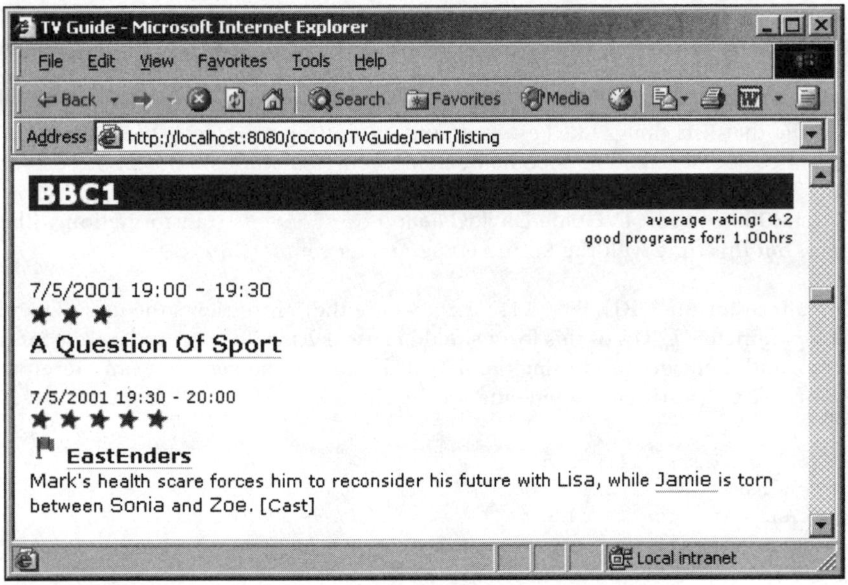

These flags are being added to the page because of the information in JeniT.xml, which is accessed when the $userID parameter is 'JeniT'. If you try the URL http://localhost:8080/cocoon/TVGuide/default/listing then the flags will disappear, because default.xml doesn't hold any information about favorite programs.

Passing Parameters from the URL

Using a part of the main URL as the value for a parameter is often very handy, but when you want more flexibility you should use **request parameters**. The request parameters of a URL are the name-value pairs that are placed in the URL after the ?. For example, in the following URL there are two request parameters: user with the value JeniT and sortOrder with the value descending:

http://localhost:8080/cocoon/TVGuide/listing?user=JeniT&sortOrder=descending

Request parameters can be added to a URL manually by the user or automatically by submitting a form, as well as being hard coded into a particular link. This is more flexible than using the main part of the URL because the user could type anything into an input field in a form and see the result of the transformation with that value being used.

In the default setup of Cocoon 2, request parameters do not get passed through to the stylesheet, so to get the user and group parameters to be passed through to TVGuide.xsl, we need to explicitly tell Cocoon to use the request parameters. This is simple to do using <map:parameter> inside the <map:transform>, this time with the special name use-request-parameters and the value set to true as follows:

```
<map:pipeline>
  <map:match pattern="listing">
    <map:generate src="TVGuide.xml" />
    <map:transform src="TVGuide.xsl">
      <map:parameter name="use-request-parameters" value="true" />
    </map:transform>
    <map:serialize />
  </map:match>
</map:pipeline>
```

All the request parameters are now passed through to `TVGuide.xsl` as stylesheet parameters of the same name, with the string value specified within the URL.

> **Request parameters are passed through to the stylesheet if you set the `use-request-parameters` parameter for a particular `<map:transform>` to `true` within the sitemap.**

Try It Out – Passing Request Parameters to the Stylesheet

To test out the request parameters, we'll make a very simple HTML page that invites the user to enter their user ID, and uses the value that they type as the value of the `$userID` parameter when the form is submitted. The HTML page, `user.html`, should look something like:

```
<html>
  <head><title>User Logon</title></head>
  <body>
    <form action="listing">
      <p>
        Enter your user ID:
        <input name="userID" />
      </p>
    </form>
  </body>
</html>
```

We have to set up the sitemap to deliver `user.html` as an HTML page, when it is requested using the URL http://localhost:8080/cocoon/TVGuide/user.html, with the following `<map:match>` element:

```
<map:match pattern="user.html">
  <map:generate type="html" src="user.html" />
  <map:serialize />
</map:match>
```

Note that the generator is of type `html`. This converts the HTML source document into well-formed XHTML using HTMLTidy (see http://www.w3.org/People/Raggett/tidy/). The XHTML is then serialized using the normal HTML Serializer, and gets turned back into HTML again.

The existing `<map:match>` for viewing the listing needs to be modified slightly. Firstly, we can't do this client side, so the browser that's accessing the page doesn't matter any more. Secondly, the `<map:parameter>` within the `<map:transform>` needs to set the value of the `use-request-parameters` special parameter to `true`, as follows:

```
<map:match pattern="listing">
  <map:generate src="TVGuide.xml" />
  <map:transform src="TVGuide.xsl">
    <map:parameter name="use-request-parameters" value="true" />
  </map:transform>
  <map:serialize />
</map:match>
```

Once you've made these changes, your `sitemap.xmap` should look the same as `sitemap6.xmap`.

Try requesting the HTML file at http://localhost:8080/cocoon/TVGuide/user.html. You should see the following:

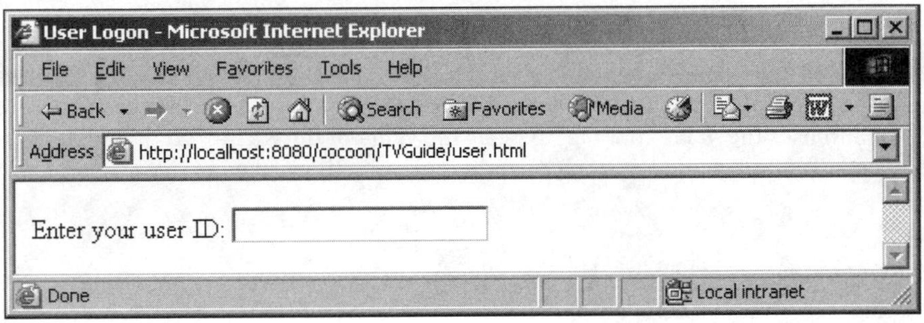

Fill in the ID of a user for whom there's a preferences file, such as `JeniT`, and submit the form by pressing return. The request URL is in the form http://localhost:8080/cocoon/TVGuide/listing?userID=JeniT, and the `userID` request parameter gets passed through to `TVGuide.xsl` as the `$userID` stylesheet parameter. The resulting page should contain flagged programs, such as EastEnders, as before:

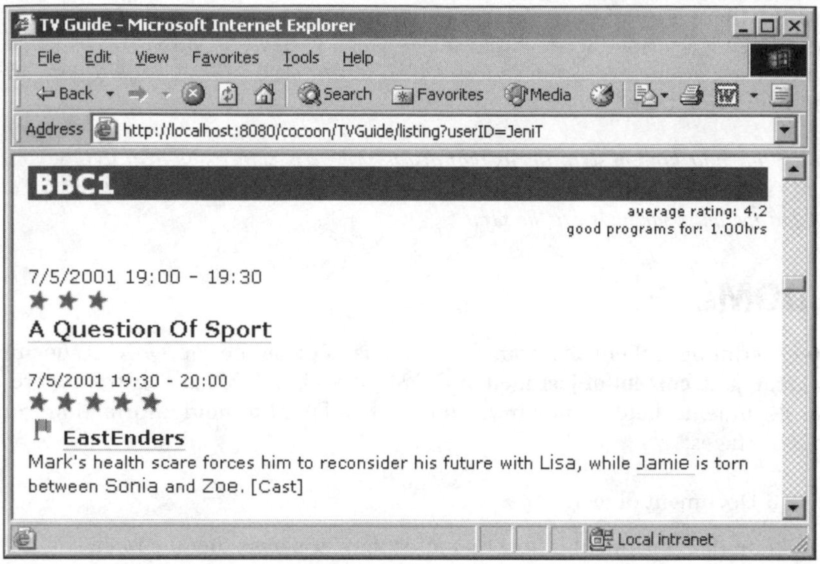

Client Side Transformations Using MSXML

We'll now turn our attention to transformations managed on the client side using MSXML in Internet Explorer.

If you're working with MSXML, it's worth having the MSXML SDK documentation, which comes with MSXML (from http://msdn.microsoft.com/xml*), close at hand. There are also lots of good examples of client side MSXML at Chris Bayes's site at* http://www.bayes.co.uk/xml.

The easiest way of using a client side transformation is to let the browser pick up on which stylesheet to use from the `xml-stylesheet` processing instruction at the top of the XML document. For example, including the following `xml-stylesheet` processing instruction at the top of `TVGuide.xml` tells the browser to use `TVGuide.xsl` to transform the XML document:

```
<?xml-stylesheet type="text/xsl" href="TVGuide.xsl"?>
```

When Internet Explorer 5 or above sees the `xml-stylesheet` processing instruction, it tries to locate the referenced stylesheet and applies it using MSXML automatically, displaying the result of the transformation viewed as an HTML page.

However, as we saw in Chapter 3, there are several versions of MSXML. You can only rely on your audience having automatic client side transformations using XSLT if they have MSXML3 installed in replace mode or if you are using Internet Explorer 6.

You can install MSXML3 on your audience's machines automatically if necessary; see http://www.netcrucible.com/xslt/msxml-faq.htm#Q5 *for more details about installing MSXML3.*

As we saw earlier, there is another method of managing client side transformations, using a script within an HTML page. Using a script allows you to select which version of MSXML should be used, and it allows you to pass in parameters to the stylesheet, so in this section we'll look at how to access MSXML using scripted client side transformations.

> *You can use the same kind of scripting as that discussed here in server side ASP scripts, since these also use MSXML. Some of the details, such as how to access documents and how to return them, are different, but the main methods are the same.*

Creating DOMs

The first step in scripting a client side transformation is to parse the source XML document and the stylesheet to create a **document object model** (DOM) of each. DOMs are abstract representations of the node trees for documents, held in memory. You create a DOM to hold information from an XML document in four stages:

- Create a Document object
- Set flags on the Document object that affect how it parses the document
- Load the XML document into the Document object
- Check that the XML document has loaded properly

Creating Document Objects

The method of creating Document objects varies a little depending on what programming language you're using in your script. In JScript or JavaScript, you need to create it using an `ActiveXObject` constructor, with the line:

```
var xmlDOM = new ActiveXObject(ObjectID);
```

whereas in VBScript, you can use the `CreateObject()` method, with the line:

```
Set xmlDOM = CreateObject(ObjectID)
```

In either case, the object ID that you use determines the version of MSXML that is used to create the DOM, and therefore the version of MSXML that's used when the DOM is used in the transformation.

To use XSLT, you must use either MSXML3 or MSXML4, and therefore should use one of the following object IDs:

- `'MSXML2.FreeThreadedDOMDocument'` – uses the later of MSXML3 or MSXML4, whichever is installed
- `'MSXML2.FreeThreadedDOMDocument.3.0'` – uses MSXML3
- `'MSXML2.FreeThreadedDOMDocument.4.0'` – uses MSXML4

Do not use `'MSXML.Document'` or `'Microsoft.XMLDOM'` as these object IDs use MSXML2 to create the DOM, and therefore the DOMs will not be usable with XSLT. If you're wondering about other object IDs that you may have seen (`'MSXML2.DOMDocument'`, `'MSXML2.DOMDocument.3.0'`, and `'MSXML2.DOMDocument.4.0'`), you can use them, but only for the DOM that you create for the source XML document, not for the XSLT stylesheet.

In JavaScript, for example, you could create a Document object, assigned to the `xmlDOM` variable, as follows:

```
var xmlDOM = new ActiveXObject('MSXML2.FreeThreadedDOMDocument');
```

You create a Document object by creating a new object of type `'MSXML2.FreeThreadedDOMDocument'`.

Setting Flags on the Document Object

There are several flags that control how the parsing of an XML document into the Document object takes place:

- `async` – determines whether the script waits for the XML document to be completely downloaded before continuing. The default is `true`, which means that it doesn't, but you almost always need this to be `false` so that it does.
- `preserveWhiteSpace` – determines whether whitespace-only text nodes in the XML document are represented within the DOM. The default is `false`, which means that they aren't, but since you have a lot finer control over the management of whitespace in the stylesheet, you would usually want this to be set to `true`.
- `resolveExternals` – determines whether references to external DTDs or entities are resolved. The default is `true`, which is what you would usually want.
- `validateOnParse` – determines whether MSXML automatically checks that the document adheres to the rules held in the DTD or schema with which it's associated. The default is `true`, but if you don't care about validation (which usually you won't and most other processors don't) then you should set it to `false`.

The flags are each properties on the Document object, so once you've created the Document object you can set the flags by assigning new values to these properties. For example, in JavaScript you could make sure that the DOM resolves external references, retains whitespace-only text nodes, doesn't validate the XML document, and doesn't continue with the rest of the code until the document is fully loaded by using the following:

```
var xmlDOM = new ActiveXObject('MSXML2.FreeThreadedDOMDocument');
xmlDOM.resolveExternals = true;
xmlDOM.preserveWhiteSpace = true;
xmlDOM.validateOnParse = false;
xmlDOM.async = false;
```

> **You should set the `async` property to `false`, the `preseveWhiteSpace` property to `true`, and the `validateOnParse` property to `false` when creating DOMs for use with XSLT.**

Loading the XML Document

Loading an XML document into the Document object that you've created is simply a matter of calling the `load()` method on the Document object. The `load()` method takes a single argument – the location of the file that you want to load into the Document object.

For example, to load the file `TVGuide.xml` into the new Document object (assuming that `TVGuide.xml` was in the same directory as the script), you would use the following JavaScript:

```
xmlDOM.load('TVGuide.xml');
```

> **You can load a document into the Document object using the `load()` method.**

Checking for Parse Errors

There are several things that can go wrong during loading. For example, the document might not be accessible or it might not be well-formed. Errors in the loading of an XML document don't generate exceptions – instead, you need to look at the `parseError` property of the Document object to see if the document has been loaded properly.

The `parseError` property returns a **ParseError object**, which has the following properties:

- `errorCode` – a number representing the error; `0` indicates that there's no parse error
- `reason` – a string description of the error
- `url` – the location of the file that caused the error
- `filepos` – the index of the position within the file at which the error occurred
- `line` – the line within the file at which the error occurred
- `linepos` – the index of the character within the line at which the error occurred
- `srcText` – the full text of the line at which the error occurred

You can check whether a parse error has occurred during the parsing of a document by testing the value of the `errorCode` property on the ParseError object to see if it is equal to `0`. If it is equal to `0` then everything is OK, otherwise you need to do some error handling:

```
if (xmlDOM.parseError.errorCode != 0) {
  /* parse error */
  ...
}
```

What you do in this case is up to you, but it's usually helpful to display an error message. For example, you could construct a pop-up error message that described the location and cause of the parse error with something like the following:

```
if (xmlDOM.parseError.errorCode != 0) {
  /* parse error */
  var error = xmlDOM.parseError;
  alert('Error parsing ' + error.url +
        ' at ' + error.line + ':' + error.linepos +
        ':\n' + error.reason);
}
```

> **You can get details of any well-formedness errors in the documents you load by checking the `parseError` property of the Document object.**

Try It Out – Creating Document Objects for XML and XSLT Files

Our first task is to create an HTML document that simply creates Document objects for the XML file `TVGuide.xml` and the XSLT file `TVGuide.xsl`. We'll call this HTML document `TVGuide.html`. It should contain a `<script>` element that contains the JavaScript functions that we're defining. `TVGuide.html` should also give an `id` to the `<body>` element so that we can easily display the results of the transformation.

The main function that we'll use is the `displayTransformedXML()` function, which we'll call automatically when the HTML document is loaded. The `TVGuide.html` file therefore looks like the following:

```
<html>
  <head>
    <title>TV Guide</title>
    <script type="text/javascript">
      function displayTransformedXML() {
        ...
      }
    </script>
  </head>
  <body id="result" onload="displayTransformedXML()">
  </body>
</html>
```

The body of the `displayTransformedXML()` function needs to create Document objects for both `TVGuide.xml` and `TVGuide.xsl`. Since creating and setting the flags on both these Document objects is the same, we'll define a function called `createDocumentObject()` to create a new Document object, set the relevant flags, and return the Document object:

```
function createDocumentObject() {
  var DOM = new ActiveXObject('MSXML2.FreeThreadedDOMDocument');
  DOM.async = false;
```

```
    DOM.validateOnParse = false;
    DOM.preserveWhiteSpace = true;
    return DOM;
  }
```

The `displayTransformedXML()` function needs to create two of these Document objects, loading `TVGuide.xml` into one and `TVGuide.xsl` into the other:

```
  function displayTransformedXML() {
    // Create Document objects
    var xmlDOM = createDocumentObject();
    var xslDOM = createDocumentObject();

    // Load XML and stylesheet documents
    xmlDOM.load('TVGuide.xml');
    xslDOM.load('TVGuide.xsl');
    ...
  }
```

The `TVGuide.xml` and `TVGuide.xsl` documents should be well-formed, so we need to check whether either Document object has a parse error after loading the file:

```
  function displayTransformedXML() {
    // Create Document objects
    ...
    // Load XML and stylesheet documents
    ...

    // Check for parse errors
    if (xmlDOM.parseError.errorCode != 0) {
      ...
    }
    if (xslDOM.parseError.errorCode != 0) {
      ...
    }
    ...
  }
```

Again, the reporting of the parse error is the same for both Document objects, so we can create a function that will take care of that for us:

```
  function reportParseError( error ) {
    alert('Error parsing ' + error.url +
          ' at ' + error.line + ':' + error.linepos +
          ':\n' + error.reason);
    return;
  }
```

This function can be called within both `if` statements:

```
function displayTransformedXML() {
  // Create Document objects
  ...
  // Load XML and stylesheet documents
  ...

  // Check for parse errors
  if (xmlDOM.parseError.errorCode != 0) {
    reportParseError(xmlDOM.parseError);
    return;
  }
  if (xslDOM.parseError.errorCode != 0) {
    reportParseError(xslDOM.parseError);
    return;
  }
  ...
}
```

To check that the documents have been loaded in properly and that everything is working OK, we'll make a quick query into the Document objects to pull out the name of the document element, which should be `'TVGuide'` in the case of `TVGuide.xml` and `'xsl:stylesheet'` in the case of `TVGuide.xsl`. The name of the document element of a particular document can be found with the following code:

```
xmlDOM.documentElement.tagName
```

So the following is the completed `displayTransformedXML()` function (for now):

```
function displayTransformedXML() {
  // Create Document objects
  ...
  // Load XML and stylesheet documents
  ...
  // Check for parse errors
  ...

  // Display document element names
  xmlDocEleName = xmlDOM.documentElement.tagName;
  xslDocEleName = xslDOM.documentElement.tagName;
  result.innerHTML =
    ('<p>XML Document Element: ' + xmlDocEleName + '</p>' +
     '<p>XSLT Document Element: ' + xslDocEleName + '</p>');
}
```

When you open `TVGuide.html` with Internet Explorer, you should see the following:

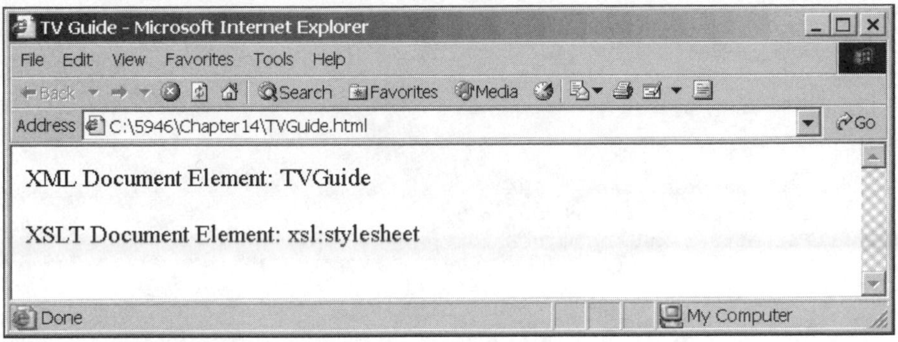

This shows that both the XML document and the stylesheet have loaded properly.

To see what happens when things *don't* run smoothly, try editing `TVGuide.xml` so that it is not well-formed, for example, by deleting the `<TVGuide>` element so that the document has more than one top-level element, as in `TVGuide3.xml`. `TVGuide2.html` points to `TVGuide3.xml`; when you try loading it, you get the following error:

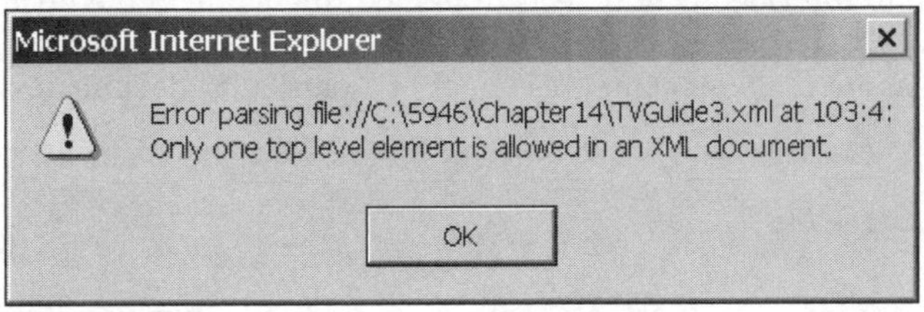

Performing Transformations

Having a Document object for the stylesheet does not immediately enable you to transform the XML document using the stylesheet. Creating the Document object for the stylesheet has read in the stylesheet as an XML document like any other. Now you need to tell MSXML to consider the stylesheet as an XSLT stylesheet, to compile it to create some runnable code that can be used against the XML document to create a result.

Creating a Compiled Stylesheet

In MSXML, **Template objects** hold the result of compiling a stylesheet DOM. You need to create a Template object in much the same way as you created the Document objects for the XML and stylesheet DOMs, by constructing a new `ActiveXObject` in JavaScript or using the `CreateObject()` method in VBScript. This time, though, the ID of the object is `'MSXML2.XSLTemplate'`:

```
var xslTemplate = new ActiveXObject('MSXML2.XSLTemplate');
```

You can use the identifier `'MSXML2.XSLTemplate.3.0'` to force the use of the Template object from MSXML3, or the identifier `'MSXML2.XSLTemplate.4.0'` to force the use of MSXML4. Note that if you are forcing the Document object to be either version 3 or 4 then you should also force the Template object to be the same version.

There's only one thing you need to do to configure the Template object, and that's to set its `stylesheet` property to the stylesheet DOM:

```
xslTemplate.stylesheet = xslDOM;
```

When you set the `stylesheet` property of the Template object, MSXML checks the stylesheet to make sure that it's valid. For example, it checks that all the XSLT elements are arranged in the way that they should be and that the XPaths that you use follow the XPath syntax. If there's anything wrong with the way that your stylesheet is constructed, setting the `stylesheet` property raises an exception, which will be displayed to the user if it's not caught.

You can catch this error using a `try catch` statement around the part of your code where you set the `stylesheet` property of the Template object. If you wish, you can display the cause of the exception using the `description` property of the exception. For example:

```
try {
  var xslTemplate = new ActiveXObject('MSXML2.Template');
  xslTemplate.stylesheet = xslDOM;
} catch (exception) {
  alert(exception.description);
}
```

The Template object represents a compiled stylesheet, which could be used for multiple transformations. To actually run the stylesheet, you need a separate object – a **Processor object**.

You can create a Processor object for a particular stylesheet using the `createProcessor()` method on the Template object for that stylesheet, as follows:

```
xslProcessor = xslTemplate.createProcessor();
```

> **To run a stylesheet, you need to create a Template object, set its `stylesheet` property, and then create a Processor object from that Template object using the `createProcessor()` method.**

Doing the Transformation

Once you've created the Processor object, you need to tell the processor what to use as its source document, by setting the `input` property to hold the DOM of the XML document, as follows:

```
xslProcessor.input = xmlDOM;
```

By calling the `transform()` method on the Processor object, transformation of this source document by the stylesheet is enacted, like this:

```
xslProcessor.transform();
```

Following the transformation, the result of the transformation is available as a string from the `output` property. You can write this string to the document, for example, to replace the HTML document that contains the script with the result of the transformation:

```
document.write(xslProcessor.output);
```

Running the transformation can also cause exceptions to be raised, if, for example, you try within the stylesheet to treat a string as a node set or to access an inaccessible document using the `document()` function. Again, then, you should wrap the code enacting the transformation within a `try catch` statement, which could be the same as the one that you use when setting the stylesheet for the Template object:

```
try {
  ...
  xslProcessor.transform();
  document.write(xslProcessor.output);
} catch (exception) {
  alert(exception.description);
}
```

> **To run a transformation, set the `input` property of the Processor object to the Document object for the source XML, activate the `transform()` method, and collect the results from the `output` property.**

Try It Out – Performing a Transformation

We've created the Document objects for the stylesheet `TVGuide.xsl` and the XML document `TVGuide.xml`. Now we need to create the Template and Processor objects for the stylesheet.

First, we need to create the Template object:

```
function displayTransformedXML() {
  // Create Document objects
  ...
  // Load XML and stylesheet documents
  ...
  // Check for parse errors
  ...
  // Create Template object
  xslTemplate = new ActiveXObject('MSXML2.XSLTemplate');
  ...
}
```

Then we need to set the `stylesheet` property of the Template object to the Document object representing the stylesheet. Doing this might cause errors, if there are problems with the stylesheet, so the line setting the property should be held within a `try catch` statement:

```
function displayTransformedXML() {
  // Create Document objects
  ...
  // Load XML and stylesheet documents
  ...
  // Check for parse errors
  ...

  try {
    // Create Template object
    xslTemplate = new ActiveXObject('MSXML2.XSLTemplate');

    // Compile the stylesheet into the Template object
    xslTemplate.stylesheet = xslDOM;
    ...
  }
  catch (exception) {
    alert(exception.description);
  }
}
```

Now we're on the home straight. Time to create a processor and set its `input` to the XML DOM:

```
function displayTransformedXML() {
  // Create Document objects
  ...
  // Load XML and stylesheet documents
  ...
  // Check for parse errors
  ...

  try {
    // Create Template object
    ...
    // Compile the stylesheet into the Template object
    ...
    // Create a Processor object
    var xslProcessor = xslTemplate.createProcessor();

    // Set the processor input
    xslProcessor.input = xmlDOM;
    ...
  }
  catch (exception) {
    alert(exception.description);
  }
}
```

Now all that's left is to run the transformation and display the results. For our purposes, we can just display the results in place of the HTML page itself, using `document.write()` as follows:

```
function displayTransformedXML() {
  // Create Document objects
  ...
  // Load XML and stylesheet documents
  ...
  // Check for parse errors
  ...

  try {
    // Create Template object
    ...
    // Compile the stylesheet into the Template object
    ...
    // Create a Processor object
    ...
    // Set the processor input
    ...
    // Run the transformation
    xslProcessor.transform();
    document.write(xslProcessor.output);
  }
  catch (exception) {
    alert(exception.description);
  }
}
```

Open TVGuide3.html, which contains this code, in Internet Explorer, and you should see the results of the transformation:

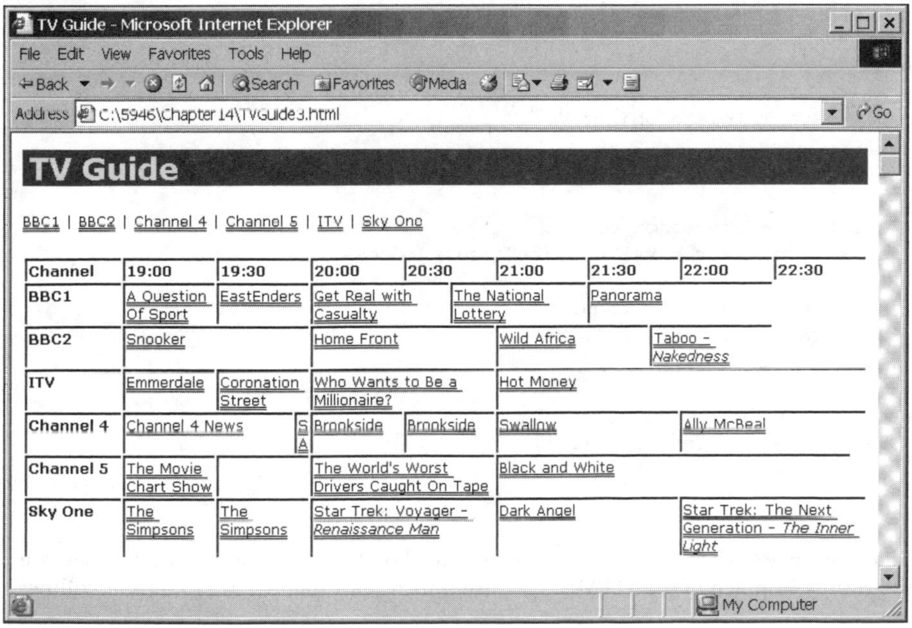

If you don't, you should get an alert that tells you what's wrong with the XML file or with the stylesheet. For example, if you delete the `version` attribute from the `<xsl:stylesheet>` element, as in `TVGuide2.xsl`, then the stylesheet is still a well-formed XML, document, but no longer a valid stylesheet. If you try transforming `TVGuide.xml` with `TVGuide2.xsl`, as in `TVGuide4.html`, then you should get an alert about the structure of the stylesheet:

Handling Output

The way that we're handling output at the moment, just replacing the content of the page with the result of the transformation, is a straightforward way of seeing what the stylesheet has produced. In this section, we'll look at a couple of other ways of handling the output of the transformation from code.

Replacing Part of the Page

It's often handy to only replace a part of the HTML with the result of the transformation, in particular because this allows you to reuse the same Document, Template, and Processor objects multiple times.

You can replace the content of a particular element with some HTML by setting its `innerHTML` property, in the way we did earlier when displaying the names of the document elements of the XML and stylesheet documents:

```
result.innerHTML = xslProcessor.output;
```

If you use this method, remember to make sure that the stylesheet generates something that can be placed in the content of the element that you're using. For example, the stylesheet shouldn't generate an `<html>` element if you're replacing the content of the `<body>` element.

> **You can set the `innerHTML` property of an element in the HTML page to display the result of the transformation in part of the page.**

Continuing Processing

When we looked at Cocoon, we saw that multiple transformations could be joined together in a pipeline, with each transformation using the result of the previous transformation as the source for its own transformation, until finally the result of the last transformation was serialized.

You can pipeline the results of a transformation to another stylesheet using code by setting the `output` property of the Processor object to a DOM *before* running the transformation, as follows:

```
var resultDOM = new ActiveXObject('MSXML2.FreeThreadedDOMDocument');
resultDOM.async = false;
resultDOM.validateOnParse = false;
resultDOM.preserveWhiteSpace = true;

var xslProcessor = xslTemplate.createProcessor();
xslProcessor.input = xmlDOM;
xslProcessor.output = resultDOM;

xslProcessor.transform();
```

Rather than being generated by loading a document into the DOM, the result DOM is generated by the stylesheet. You can use this DOM exactly as you could any other – you can use it as the source of another transformation, or as a stylesheet DOM that you use as the stylesheet for a new Template object, if you want to. For example, to use `resultDOM` as the source of another transformation, and display the result of that, you could do the following:

```
var secondXSLProcessor = secondXSLTemplate.createProcessor();
secondXSLProcessor.input = resultDOM;
secondXSLProcessor.transform();
document.write(secondXSLProcessor.output);
```

You can use the result of one transformation as the source (or stylesheet) for another by setting the `output` property of the Processor object to a newly created DOM before running the transformation.

Passing Parameters

The fact that you're running the transformation from code rather than letting Internet Explorer do it automatically hasn't gained you much so far, since all you're doing is exactly what Internet Explorer would do – displaying the results of the basic transformation of `TVGuide.xml` with `TVGuide.xsl`.

One of the benefits of using code, however, is the fact that you can pass parameters in to the stylesheet. Once you've generated a Processor object, and before you run the transformation, you can set the values of parameters using the `addParameter()` method. The `addParameter()` method usually takes two arguments: the name of the parameter and the value of the parameter. For example, to set the `$userID` parameter to `'JeniT'`, you could use:

```
xslProcessor.addParameter('userID', 'JeniT');
```

You also have a lot of flexibility about the kind of values that you pass in to the stylesheet using `addParameter()`. The second argument to the `addParameter()` method can be a number or a boolean value rather than a string, and can even be a Node or NodeList object, which means that the parameter is set to a node set. This latter method allows you to pass DOMs in to the stylesheet.

> **You can pass a parameter in to the stylesheet using the `addParameter()` method on the Processor object.**

Try It Out – Displaying Results With Parameters

We'll use `TVGuide.xsl` again as the basis of a stylesheet for our parameterized transformation. The `TVGuide.xsl` stylesheet declares a `$sortOrder` parameter that controls whether the channels are listed in ascending or descending order based on the average rating of the programs that they show. The `$sortOrder` parameter needs to be set to either `'ascending'` or `'descending'`.

To arrange this, we'll show the results in a specific area of an otherwise static page, within a `<div>`. We need to make sure that this version of the stylesheet, `TVGuide3.xsl`, generates something that can go within a `<div>` element. Currently, the template that matches the root node generates a whole page, so we need to amend this so that it only generates the important information. The original `<head>` that's generated by `TVGuide.xsl` can go into the `TVGuide5.html` page, as can the `<h1>` title. The root node template therefore simply looks like the following:

```
<xsl:template match="/">
  <xsl:copy-of select="$ChannelList" />
  <xsl:apply-templates />
  <xsl:copy-of select="$ChannelList" />
</xsl:template>
```

`TVGuide5.html`, on the other hand, looks something like the following, with a `<div>` element with an `id` attribute that will allow us to direct the result of the transformation:

```
<html>
  <head>
    <title>TV Guide</title>
    <link rel="stylesheet" href="TVGuide.css" />
    <script type="text/javascript">
      function toggle(element) {
        if (element.style.display == 'none') {
          element.style.display = 'block';
        } else {
          element.style.display = 'none';
        }
      }
    </script>
    <script type="text/javascript">
      function displayTransformedXML() { ... }
      function createDocumentObject() { ... }
      function reportParseError( error ) { ... }
    </script>
  </head>
  <body onload="displayTransformedXML()">
    <h1>TV Guide</h1>
    <div id="result">
    </div>
  </body>
</html>
```

We need to make several changes to the content of the <script> element in TVGuide5.html that deals with transforming the XML document. Firstly, we're going to run several transformations with the same Processor object, so all the code that went towards setting up the processor could be placed outside the function definition, to create global variables, as follows:

```
<script type="text/javascript">
  // Create Document objects
  var xmlDOM = createDocumentObject();
  var xslDOM = createDocumentObject();

  // Load XML and stylesheet documents
  xmlDOM.load('TVGuide.xml');
  xslDOM.load('TVGuide3.xsl');

  // Check for parse errors
  if (xmlDOM.parseError.errorCode != 0) {
    reportParseError(xmlDOM.parseError);
  }
  if (xslDOM.parseError.errorCode != 0) {
    reportParseError(xslDOM.parseError);
  }

  try {
    // Create a template for the processor
    var xslTemplate = new ActiveXObject('MSXML2.XSLTemplate');
// Compile the stylesheet into the Template object
    xslTemplate.stylesheet = xslDOM;
    // Create a Processor object
    var xslProcessor = xslTemplate.createProcessor();
    // Set the processor input
    xslProcessor.input = xmlDOM;
  } catch (exception) {
    alert(exception.description);
  }
  function displayTransformedXML() { ... }
  function createDocumentObject() { ... }
  function reportParseError(error) { ... }
</script>
```

The displayTransformedXML() function is still the function called to do the transformation, but this time we'll call it with a single argument – the value of the $sortOrder parameter that should be passed to the stylesheet. It also doesn't need to contain any of the code to set up the Document, Template, or Processor objects, since that's all done at a global level. All it needs to do is set the parameter on the Processor object, run the transformation, and display the results within the <div>:

```
function displayTransformedXML(sortOrder) {
  try {
    xslProcessor.addParameter('sortOrder', sortOrder);
    xslProcessor.transform();
    result.innerHTML = xslProcessor.output;
```

```
    } catch (exception) {
      alert(exception.description);
    }
  }
```

You can see that this works by passing a value to the `displayTransformedXML()` function when the document is first loaded, within the call in the `onload` attribute on the <body> element within `TVGuide5.html`:

```
<body onload="displayTransformedXML('ascending')">
  ...
</body>
```

When you load `TVGuide5.html`, it loads `TVGuide.xml` and `TVGuide3.xsl` into Document objects and creates a Template and then a Processor object for transforming `TVGuide.xml` using `TVGuide3.xsl`. Then `TVGuide.xml` is transformed with `TVGuide3.xsl`, with the `$sortOrder` parameter set to `'ascending'`, and the channels are listed sorted by the average rating of their programs, in ascending order, such that ITV appears before BBC2 in the listing:

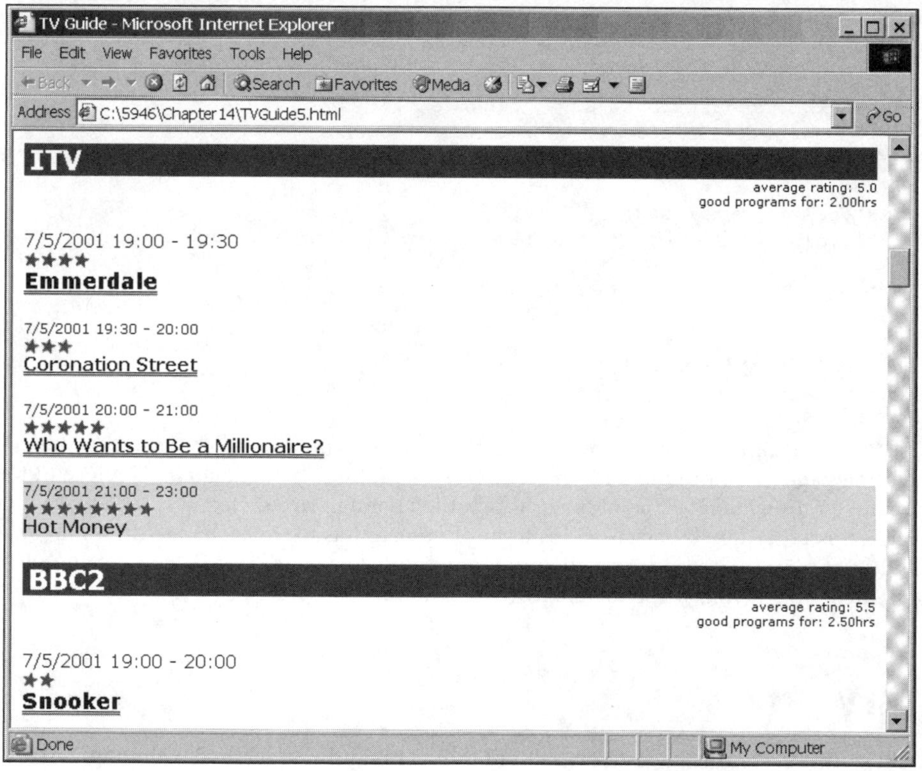

You can make this more interactive by making the text "average rating" clickable so that the order changes when you click on it. When the `$sortOrder` parameter is `'ascending'`, the HTML should look like:

```
<span ... onclick="displayTransformedXML('descending')">
  average rating
</span>
```

When the `$sortOrder` parameter is `'descending'`, the HTML should look like:

```
<span ... onclick="displayTransformedXML('ascending')">
  average rating
</span>
```

You can make this change in the template for the `<Channel>` elements, by testing the value of `$sortOrder` and using that to work out the new sort order (held in the `$newSortOrder` variable), which is used in the `onclick` attribute as follows:

```
<xsl:template match="Channel">
  <xsl:apply-templates select="Name" />
  <p class="average">
<xsl:variable name="newSortOrder">
      <xsl:choose>
        <xsl:when test="$sortOrder = 'ascending'">descending</xsl:when>
        <xsl:otherwise>ascending</xsl:otherwise>
      </xsl:choose>
    </xsl:variable>
    <span xsl:use-attribute-sets="linkEvents"
          onclick="displayTransformedXML('{$newSortOrder}')">
      <xsl:text>average rating</xsl:text>
    </span>
    <xsl:text>: </xsl:text>
    <xsl:value-of select="format-number(sum(Program/@rating) div
                                         count(Program), '0.0')" />
    <br />
    ...
  </p>
  <xsl:apply-templates select="Program" />
</xsl:template>
```

Opening `TVGuide6.html`, which uses `TVGuide4.xsl` in which these changes have been made, will show the same page as before but with the text "average rating" being a clickable piece of text. Clicking on the "average rating" toggles the order in which the channels are sorted and redisplays the page. The transformation is fairly quick because all Internet Explorer has to do is change the value of the `$sortOrder` parameter and perform the transformation. The source XML document and the compiled XSLT stylesheet are cached while the HTML document is displayed.

Summary

Although it's useful to run transformations from the command line while developing XSLT stylesheets, most XSLT applications use either server side or client side processing (or both). Client side and server side processing allow you to create dynamic applications that react to updates in the source XML or in the stylesheet, and also allow the user to pass in parameters to stylesheets to create different pages in different circumstances.

You've learned in this chapter about two applications that support dynamic transformations: Cocoon for server side transformations and Internet Explorer 6 for client side transformations. These aren't the only applications that are available to you – there are other servlets that you can use on the server side, such as AxKit and XSQL, and other browsers that you can use on the client side, such as Netscape 6, Mozilla, the Antenna House Formatter, and XSmiles – but they are the two that are best developed and most widely used.

You've learned the principles underlying Cocoon's treatment of HTTP requests, and seen how to configure it for common tasks, such as delivering HTML documents, automatically transforming XML, delivering different results to different browsers, and using parameters. If you continue working with Cocoon, you will learn about the different types of generators, transformers, serializers, matchers, and selectors that you can use with it. The user documentation on Cocoon, at http://xml.apache.org/cocoon/userdocs/index.html, contains further details about each of these, and if you get into the details, you'll probably find the API documentation at http://xml.apache.org/cocoon/apidocs/ handy.

You have also been shown how to script transformations using MSXML, which could be carried out either client side or server side (using ASP). We've looked at the necessary objects, properties, and methods for running transformations, how to pass parameters in to those transformations, and a couple of ways of using the result of the transformations. If you continue working with MSXML, you will come to be familiar with manipulating DOMs. You can find details about the API offered by MSXML in the MSXML Software Development Kit documentation, which you can get from http://msdn.microsoft.com/xml.

Review Questions

1. What are the advantages and disadvantages of using server side or client side transformations?

2. Which three steps are involved in a pipeline in Cocoon?

3. What file do you have to edit to configure Cocoon?

4. How does Cocoon choose which pipeline to use given a particular HTTP request?

5. Introduce a new subdirectory called `Films`, with its own sitemap, to your local version of Cocoon.

6. Add directives such that when you view http://localhost:8080/cocoon/Films/index you get a list of the films held in `Films.xml`, transformed using `Films.xsl`.

7. Add instructions so that when Internet Explorer 6 requests http://localhost:8080/cocoon/Films/index, Cocoon delivers the raw XML of `Films.xml` rather than running the transformation on the server side.

8. Edit `Films.xsl` so that it accepts a `$film` parameter and displays only those films that start with the string held by the `$film` parameter. Use Cocoon to enable users to pass in the parameter in two ways:

   a. Using part of the URL: http://localhost:8080/cocoon/Films/Leon
   b. Using a request parameter: http://localhost:8080/cocoon/Films?film=Leon

9. Which versions of MSXML do you need to use to transform XML with XSLT? Which versions of Internet Explorer do you need to use to automatically transform XML with XSLT?

10. Write a utility function called `parseXMLDocument()` that returns a Document object for an XML file when passed a filename. If the file is inaccessible or not well-formed, the function should create an alert giving details of the error and return null.

11. Write a utility function called `createXSLTProcessor()` that returns a Processor object for an XSLT stylesheet and an XML document. If the stylesheet isn't a valid stylesheet then the function should create an alert giving details of the error and return null.

12. Write a utility function called `performTransformation()` that returns the result of a transformation run with a particular Processor given an array of pairs of parameter names and values.

13. Use your utility functions in an HTML page that you can use with Internet Explorer 6 where you enter the start of a name of a film in an input field and it displays a list of all the films in `Films.xml` that start with that string, by transforming using a suitably modified `Films.xsl`. Remember to do as much as you can at a global level in the script, so that you cache the Document and Processor objects.

Beginning
XSLT

15

Creating SVG

SVG stands for **Scalable Vector Graphics**, and is a markup language for describing images. SVG is an important markup language for use with XSLT because it allows you to use XSLT to create graphics from XML data – something that XSLT would normally struggle to do due to the fact that most graphic formats are binary formats.

In most uses of SVG, graphics are embedded within an HTML page. You might create a menu list, a graph, a pie chart, a tree, animations, or buttons using SVG. In some cases, where you need a great amount of control over the look of a page, you could even create the entire page using SVG. SVG can be used in many cases where you include graphics in your page, as well as those that use Flash to create dynamic and reactive graphics.

In this chapter, you'll learn:

- How to write a simple SVG document
- How to create simple graphics
- How to link from SVG to other documents
- How to use XSLT to generate SVG
- How to embed SVG within an HTML page

Introducing SVG

SVG is a markup language dedicated to expressing the appearance, animation, and interactivity of images. SVG documents define graphics as **vector graphics** rather than a bitmap, for example, which means that you can scale and zoom in and out of SVG graphics without losing detail.

> *For further information about SVG, the SVG Recommendation is available at* *http://www.w3.org/TR/svg*.

To view SVG, you need to download an application that understands and renders SVG. A good application is the SVG Viewer from Adobe, which can act as a browser plug-in and is available at http://www.adobe.com/svg/viewer/install. When you open an SVG document, your browser should activate the SVG Viewer, so that the SVG is displayed within the browser window.

A full list of SVG implementations is available from the W3C pages at http://www.w3.org/Graphics/SVG/SVG-Implementations.htm8.

For example, try viewing the following simple SVG graphic (`circle.svg`) after installing SVG Viewer:

```
<svg width="12cm" height="4cm" viewBox="0 0 1200 400"
     xmlns="http://www.w3.org/2000/svg">
  <circle r="100" cx="600" cy="200"
          fill="#C00" stroke="black" stroke-width="10"  />
</svg>
```

You should see a red circle with a black border in the browser window, as follows:

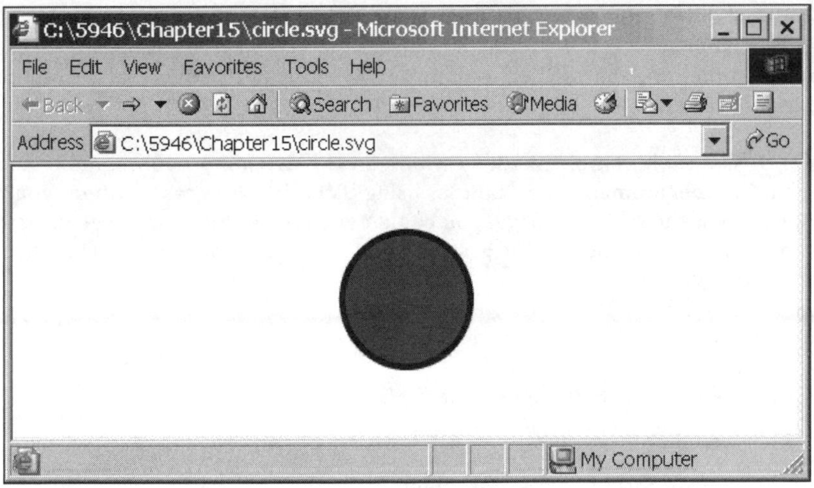

This looks just the same as a bitmap image. For example, here is `circle.bmp` in Microsoft Paint at a normal zoom:

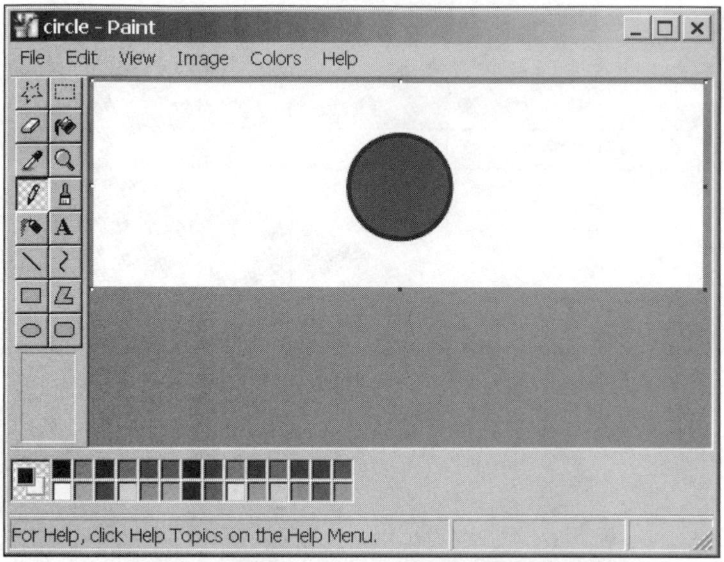

The bitmap circle looks smooth at this resolution, but when you zoom in to the circle's edge, you start to see the pixels that make up the picture:

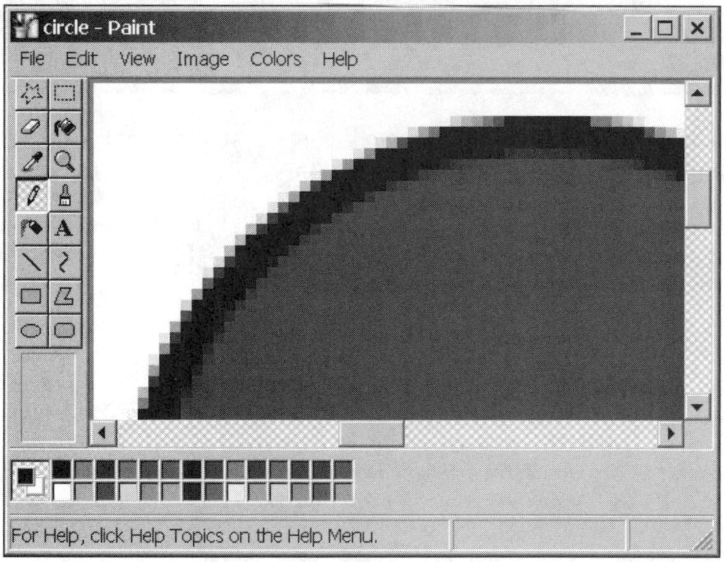

If you bring up the context menu for the SVG graphic (right mouse click on the picture), then you'll see various useful options, including the ability to zoom in to the image. You can use this context menu to zoom in to the edge of the circle:

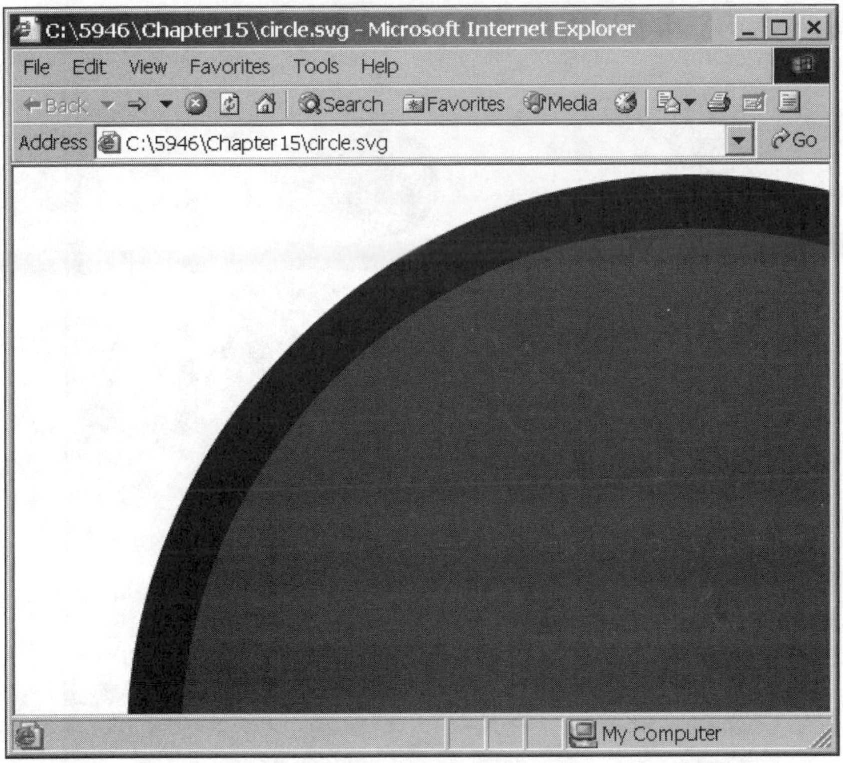

Notice that no matter how closely you zoom in to the image, the edge never becomes pixilated. This demonstrates the advantage of vector graphics over bitmaps.

Like a markup language, SVG uses namespaces to distinguish between elements that are part of SVG and elements that are part of other markup languages (which might be included in the SVG graphic, such as XHTML or XLink). The namespace for SVG elements is:

```
http://www.w3.org/2000/svg
```

You may notice that some SVG graphics don't include a namespace declaration for this namespace. That's because the DTD for SVG includes an attribute declaration for the `xmlns` *attribute that declares the default namespace. I recommend that you always include the namespace declaration explicitly, so that the SVG graphic is readable even if the DTD isn't available for some reason.*

The document element of an SVG document is an `<svg>` element. Inside the `<svg>` element are the elements used to construct the image. But before we start looking at how graphics are drawn, it's worth having a quick look at how coordinates work within SVG.

Lengths and Coordinates

Aside from the namespace declaration, the <svg> element can define the size of the SVG graphic using the `height` and `width` attributes. These attributes describe the default size of the **canvas**, which is the area in which the graphic is displayed. These values may be overridden when the SVG graphic is embedded within an HTML page (or even within another SVG graphic).

You can also specify a `viewBox` attribute on the <svg> element, which holds four numbers separated by spaces: minimum x-coordinate, minimum y-coordinate, width, and height. The `viewBox` attribute defines a coordinate system used when defining lengths within the graphic and defines the size of a **user unit**. For example, in `circle.svg` the `viewBox` attribute defined a coordinate system starting at (0, 0), spanning 1200 user units in width and 400 user units in height. This sets up a grid as follows:

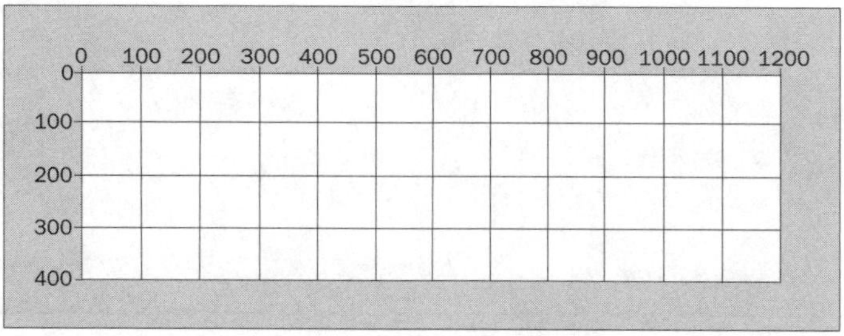

The graphic as a whole has a width of 12 cm and a height of 4 cm, corresponding to the width of 1200 user units and the height of 400 user units. Thus 100 user units on the grid correspond to 1 cm in the page. If the width had instead been set to 24 cm and the height to 8 cm, then 100 user units on the grid would correspond to 2 cm in the page; if the width had been set to 600 mm and the height to 200 mm, then 100 user units would correspond to 50 mm.

In the rest of the image, most lengths and coordinates are described relative to this grid. For example, take another look at the definition of the circle:

```
<circle r="100" cx="600" cy="200"
        fill="#C00" stroke="black" stroke-width="10" />
```

The radius of the circle (specified with the `r` attribute) is defined as 100 user units and the center of the circle (specified with the `cx` and `cy` attributes) is at the coordinate (600, 200), which is the center of the grid. When displayed in the page, the circle should have a 1 cm radius and be placed 6 cm across and 2 cm down the page, because 100 user units is equivalent to 1 cm.

If the width of the image is 12 cm and the height 8 cm (such that the ratio of units to length on the width is different from the ratio of units to length on the height), then the `preserveAspectRatio` attribute comes into play. Usually one user unit will be the same distance horizontally and vertically, with the grid aligned in the center of the image, as in the following:

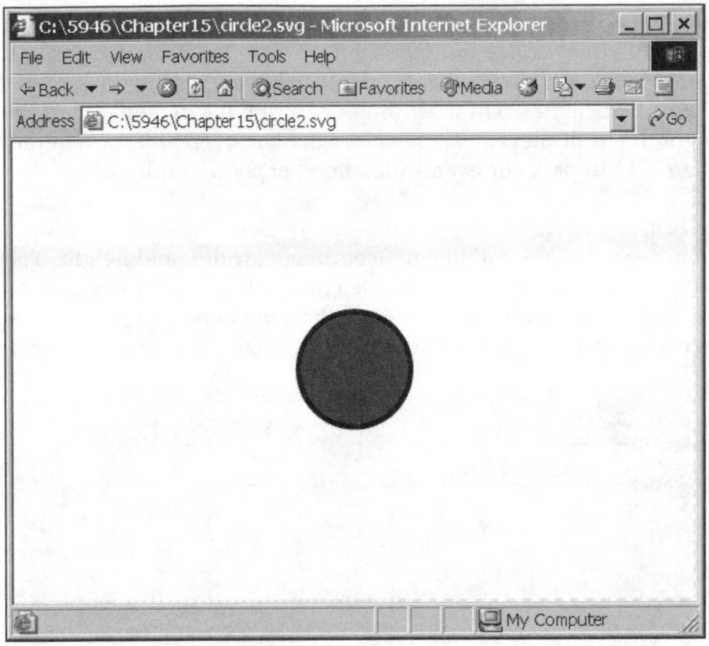

However, if you set `preserveAspectRatio` on the `<svg>` element to `none` then the actual size of the horizontal and vertical user units can be different, and the circle will be stretched as required to fill the image area on the page:

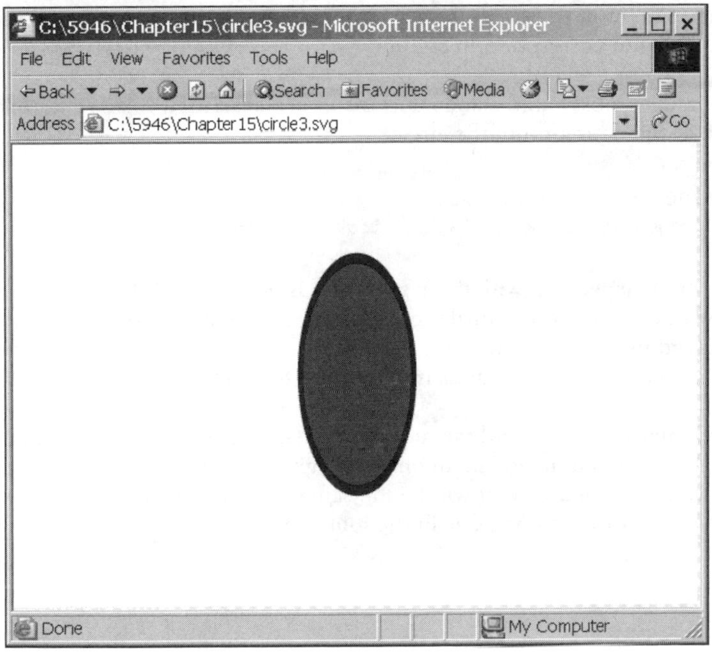

You can use other units of length within SVG. One useful type of length is a percentage length, which calculates a length based on the width or height of the image. For example, the radius and center of the circle could be specified with the following:

```
<svg width="12cm" height="4cm" viewBox="0 0 1200 400"
     xmlns="http://www.w3.org/2000/svg">
  <circle r="11.18%" cx="50%" cy="50%"
          fill="#C00" stroke="black" stroke-width="1.118%"  />
</svg>
```

Percentages other than for x, y coordinates are worked out relative to a combination of the number of units making up the height and width of the image, which is why 100 units corresponds to 11.18%.

Other units look like absolute units, but when they are used within the SVG graphic (rather than being used to set the height and width of the SVG graphic), they are actually calculated based on user units. These units are:

- px – 1 px is equivalent to 1 user unit
- pt – 1 pt is equivalent to 1.25 user units
- pc – 1 pc is equivalent to 15 user units
- in – 1 in is equivalent to 90 user units
- mm – 1 mm is equivalent to 3.543307 user units
- cm – 1 cm is equivalent to 35.43307 user units

When you use text within an SVG graphic, it's also handy to be able to specify lengths relative to the size of the text that you're using. You can do this with the following units:

- em – 1 em is equivalent to the size of the current font
- ex – 1 ex is equivalent to the x-height of the current font

Graphic Elements

The most important elements held within an SVG document are **graphic elements**, which draw shapes on the screen. The graphic elements in SVG are:

- <line> – draws a straight line
- <polyline> – draws a line made up of multiple straight segments
- <rect> – draws a rectangle (or square)
- <circle> – draws a circle
- <ellipse> – draws an ellipse
- <polygon> – draws a shape whose outline can be described by multiple contiguous straight lines, such as triangles or stars

- <path> – used to draw any line or the outline of any shape, including shapes with holes in the middle, for example
- <text> – adds some text to the graphic
- <image> – adds a PNG, JPEG, or SVG image to the graphic
- <use> – refers to and includes other elements from the SVG document

The last of these, the <use> graphic elements reuses graphic elements that you've used elsewhere. We're not going to go into the <use> element here, but you can read more about it in the SVG Recommendation at http://www.w3.org/TR/SVG/struct.html#UseElement.

The order in which you include graphic elements is important, as later graphics are overlaid on earlier graphics. For example, the following SVG graphic contains two <circle> elements, 2circles.svg:

```
<svg width="12cm" height="4cm" viewBox="0 0 1200 400"
     xmlns="http://www.w3.org/2000/svg">
  <circle r="100" cx="550" cy="200"
          fill="#C00" stroke="black" stroke-width="10"  />
  <circle r="100" cx="650" cy="200"
          fill="#C00" stroke="black" stroke-width="10" />
</svg>
```

The second circle is displayed over the first circle, giving the following graphic:

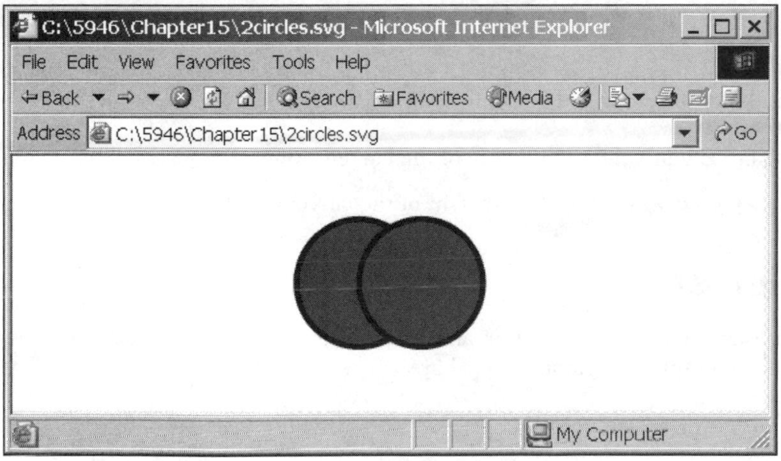

Each of the graphic elements has attributes that position the graphic and control its precise size, shape, and color. Now we'll quickly go through each of the graphic elements to describe how their position, size, shape, and appearance are determined.

Lines

Lines are the simplest of the graphical elements. They start at one point on the canvas and end up at another point. The `<line>` element has two pairs of attributes to describe the start point and the end point of the line:

- `x1` and `y1` specify the coordinate of the start of the line
- `x2` and `y2` specify the coordinate of the end of the line

All these attributes default to 0 (the top/left of the image) if you don't specify them explicitly.

The style of the line is determined by the **stroke properties** of the line, which are a set of attributes as follows:

- `stroke` – the color of the line, which can be a keyword, a color specification (as in CSS or a reference to a color), or a gradient defined earlier in the graphic or in a separate file
- `stroke-opacity` – the opacity of the line; a number between 0 (transparent) and 1 (opaque)
- `stroke-width` – the width of the line
- `stroke-linecap` – how the end of the line is drawn; one of `butt` (square, stopping at the end of the line, the default), `round`, or `square` (square, stopping half the `stroke-width` over the end of the line)
- `stroke-dasharray` – defines the pattern of dashes and spaces that are used to draw the line as a series of comma-separated values giving, alternately, the length of dashes and spaces
- `stroke-dashoffset` – defines the point within the dash array at which the line starts

To demonstrate these attributes in action, look at the following `<line>` element in `line.svg`:

```
<svg width="12cm" height="4cm" viewBox="0 0 1200 400"
     xmlns="http://www.w3.org/2000/svg">
  <line x1="400" y1="200" x2="800" y2="200"
        stroke="red" stroke-opacity="0.25"
        stroke-width="25" stroke-linecap="round"
        stroke-dasharray="25,50,75,50" stroke-dashoffset="50" />
</svg>
```

The line starts at (400, 200) and ends at (800, 200) within the image. It's red, but has an opacity of 0.25, which means it's fairly transparent. The width of the line is 25 user units, and its ends are rounded, which means that the end of the line actually extends 12.5 user units (half the width of the line) past the end coordinate. The line is dashed, the pattern being a dash 25 user units long followed by a space 50 user units long, followed by a dash 75 user units long, followed by a space 50 user units long (this pattern is repeated for the length of the line). The line starts 50 user units into this dash pattern – half way through the first space – so it begins with the rest of the space (25 user units), and the first dash that's drawn is 75 user units long. The line looks as follows:

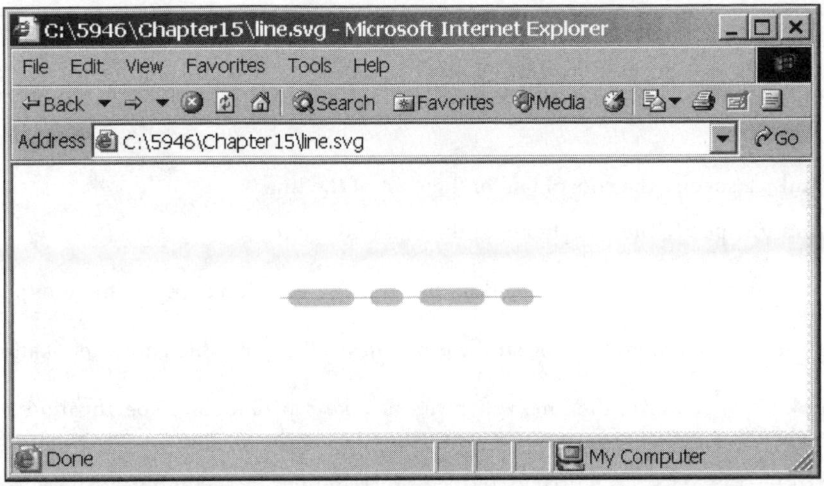

The stroke properties are used with other elements (including polylines and paths), specifically when drawing the outlines of shapes like rectangles and circles.

Polylines

The `<polyline>` element gives a line made up of multiple straight lines. The coordinates of the points along the line are specified within the `points` attribute, which holds space-separated pairs of numbers representing x, y coordinates.

All the stroke properties that could be used with `<line>` can also be used with the `<polyline>` element to give different colors, widths, dash patterns, and so on in the line. Another stroke property is applicable to polylines, specifically the `stroke-linejoin` property, which determines how corners are drawn. The default value is `miter`, which means that the corner is drawn as an angle; the other permissible values are `round`, which rounds the corners, and `bevel`, which chops off the corners.

To see polylines in practice and the difference between the different `stroke-linejoin` attributes, try the following SVG elements, `polyline.svg`:

```
<svg width="12cm" height="4cm" viewBox="0 0 1200 400"
     xmlns="http://www.w3.org/2000/svg">
  <polyline points="200,300 300,100 400,300" fill="none"
            stroke="black" stroke-width="25"
            stroke-linecap="butt" stroke-linejoin="miter" />
  <polyline points="500,300 600,100 700,300" fill="none"
            stroke="black" stroke-width="25"
            stroke-linecap="round" stroke-linejoin="round" />
  <polyline points="800,300 900,100 1000,300" fill="none"
            stroke="black" stroke-width="25"
            stroke-linecap="square" stroke-linejoin="bevel" />
</svg>
```

All the lines are stroked in black, 25 user units in width. The first polyline goes from the coordinate (200, 300) to (300, 100) to (400, 300) and the other polylines follow the same kind of pattern, but offset across the image. The first polyline uses the default line cap and line join values of `butt` and `miter`, giving square ends at the point where the line ends and an angular join. The second polyline has rounded line ends and a rounded corner. The third polyline has square ends (if you look carefully, you can see that they extend a little further than the `butt` ends of the first polyline) and a cut off (`bevel`) corner. The lines look as follows:

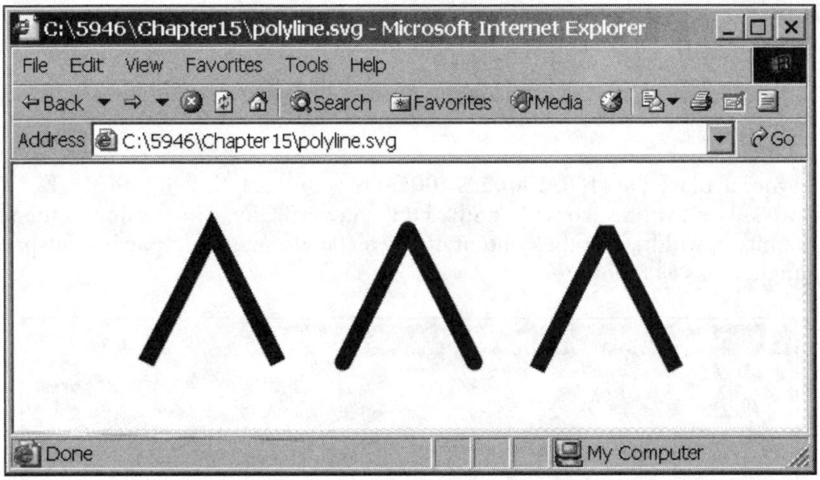

You'll note that each of the `<line>` elements given above had a `fill` attribute with a value of `none`. A polyline can be used like a polygon (which we come on to later), to give any shape whose outline can be described by straight lines, but it is not automatically closed, so is generally used for open lines, and usually the `fill` attribute should take the value `none`.

Rectangles

Rectangles (and squares) are drawn using the `<rect>` element. The size and shape of the rectangle are determined by three pairs of attributes:

- `x` and `y` specify the coordinate of the top left corner of the rectangle
- `width` and `height` specify the width and height of the rectangle and are required
- For rounded rectangles, `rx` and `ry` specify the horizontal and vertical radii of the ellipse used on the corners

If you don't give an x, y coordinate, the rectangle is placed in the top left corner of the canvas. A rectangle will only have rounded corners if you specify one of `rx` or `ry`; if you only specify one of this pair then the other of the pair defaults to the value of the first, and you get circular corners.

As well as the stroke properties (including `stroke-linejoin`) that we've already seen, rectangles and other similar graphics all have **fill properties** that describe the color of the content of the shape. There are two fill properties:

- `fill` – specifies the color of the body of the shape, which again can be a keyword, a hexadecimal color, or a reference to a color or gradient defined elsewhere
- `fill-opacity` – indicates the opacity of the fill; a number between 0 (transparent) and 1 (opaque)

For example, try the rectangle in `rectangle.svg`:

```
<svg width="12cm" height="4cm" viewBox="0 0 1200 400"
    xmlns="http://www.w3.org/2000/svg">
  <rect x="400" y="100" width="400" height="200" rx="50" ry="25"
        fill="red" fill-opacity="0.5" stroke="black" stroke-width="10" />
</svg>
```

The top left corner is placed at (400, 100), it's 400 units wide, and it's 200 units high. The rounding of the corners starts 50 units in horizontally and 25 units in vertically. The outline of the rectangle is in black, 10 user units in width, with the content of the rectangle shaded in partly-transparent red. The resulting rectangle looks as follows:

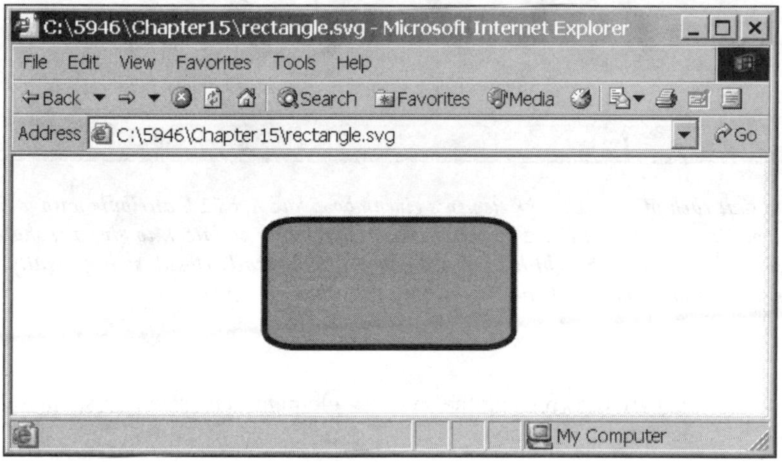

Circles

You've already seen circles in action in `circle.svg` and `2circles.svg`. The `<circle>` element has three attributes that determine its location:

- `cx` and `cy` give the coordinates for the center of the circle
- `r` specifies the radius of the circle and is required

If you don't give an x, y coordinate for the center of the circle, then it will be drawn with its center being the top left corner of the canvas. As with rectangles, you can specify stroke and fill properties to determine the look of the circle.

Ellipses

Ellipses are very similar to circles aside from the fact that you need two radii to describe them – a horizontal radius and a vertical radius. The `<ellipse>` element therefore has two pairs of attributes to determine its location and size:

- `cx` and `cy` give the coordinates for the center of the ellipse
- `rx` and `ry` specify the horizontal and vertical radius of the ellipse respectively and are required

Again, if you don't specify an x, y coordinate for the center of the ellipse then it is drawn with its center in the top left corner of the canvas. For example, try the following ellipse in `ellipse.svg`:

```
<svg width="12cm" height="4cm" viewBox="0 0 1200 400"
     xmlns="http://www.w3.org/2000/svg">
  <ellipse cx="600" cy="200" rx="200" ry="100"
           fill="#C00" stroke="black" stroke-width="10" />
</svg>
```

This ellipse is centered within the canvas and has a radius of 200 units horizontally, a radius of 100 units vertically, a black outline, and a red body. It is rendered as follows:

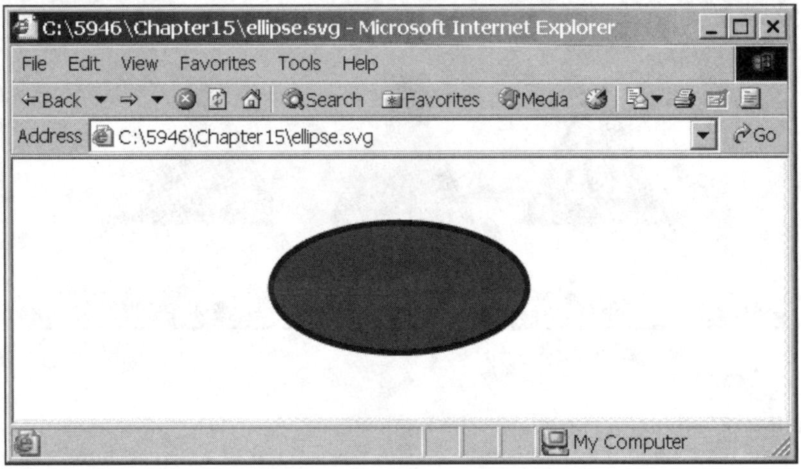

Polygons

Polygons are much like polylines, except that they are automatically closed to create a shape. They have a `points` attribute to specify the corners of the shape as pairs of coordinates, and they can take stroke properties to describe the line and fill properties to describe the interior of the shape.

Automatically closing the polygon means that the lines link up properly. You can make a polyline end at the same place that it begins, so that it describes the same shape as a polygon, but the start/end corner will be rendered in the end-of-line style rather than the corner style.

We can amend the <polyline> elements that we used earlier to give red triangles, for example, polygon.svg:

```
<svg width="12cm" height="4cm" viewBox="0 0 1200 400"
     xmlns="http://www.w3.org/2000/svg">
  <polygon points="200,300 300,100 400,300" fill="red"
           stroke="black" stroke-width="25"
           stroke-linecap="butt" stroke-linejoin="miter" />
  <polygon points="500,300 600,100 700,300" fill="red"
           stroke="black" stroke-width="25"
           stroke-linecap="round" stroke-linejoin="round" />
  <polygon points="800,300 900,100 1000,300" fill="red"
           stroke="black" stroke-width="25"
           stroke-linecap="square" stroke-linejoin="bevel" />
</svg>
```

These three <polygon> elements are rendered as follows:

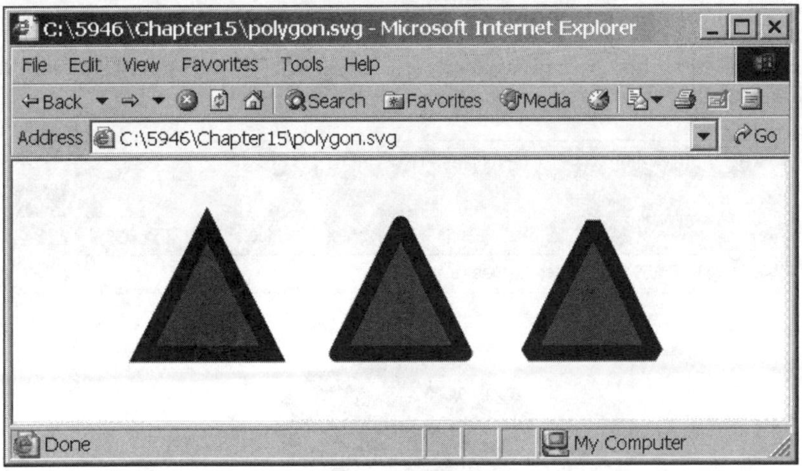

Paths

Paths are a little like polylines, except that the segments in a path are not necessarily straight and are not necessarily stroked when the path is drawn. The description of a path is known as **path data** and is given in the d (data) attribute of the <path> element. Path data has a special syntax that is also used elsewhere in SVG.

Each SVG path consists of a number of **subpaths**, each describing a line. Each subpath consists of a number of **commands**, each of which is identified by a letter, often followed by parameters for the command. The letters that are used for the commands can be either uppercase or lowercase; uppercase indicates that absolute coordinates are used within the parameters for the command, while lowercase indicates that the coordinates are relative to the current location within the path. The basic commands available in SVG are:

- M (absolute) or m (relative) – moveto – "lifts the pen off the paper" and moves to the specified point on the canvas without drawing a line

- `Z` or `z` – closepath – draws a line from the current point to the point at which the path started, closing the path
- `L` (absolute) or `l` (relative) – lineto – draws to the point specified
- `H` (absolute) or `h` (relative) – horizontal lineto – draws a horizontal line to the x-coordinate specified
- `V` (absolute) or `v` (relative) – vertical lineto – draws a vertical line to the y-coordinate specified

Each subpath starts with a moveto command and they often end with a closepath command. For example, the following path consists of two subpaths. The first subpath starts at (600, 50), draws a line to a point 200 units right and 300 units down from there (which is (800, 350)), then draws a line 400 units left horizontally (in other words to (400, 350)), before closing the path (drawing a line back to (600, 50)). The second subpath begins at (600, 150), draws a line to the point (700, 300), and then draws a line to (500, 300) using the horizontal lineto command, before closing the path:

```
M 600,50  l 200,300 h -400 Z
M 600,150 L 700,300 H  500 Z
```

The result of this path is two triangles set inside each other – one from the first subpath and one from the second subpath. The stroke and fill of the two triangles are the same, because they're both specified with the same path. However, you can make the 'interior' of the shape include only the part between the two triangles by setting the `fill-rule` attribute to `evenodd` (which means that a point is 'inside' the shape if drawing a line from that point to a point outside the canvas involves crossing an odd number of lines), as follows, `paths.svg`:

```
<path d="M 600,50  l 200,300 h -400 Z
         M 600,150 L 700,300 H 500 Z"
      fill="red" fill-rule="evenodd"
      stroke="black" stroke-width="25"
      stroke-linecap="round" stroke-linejoin="round" />
```

When you view the SVG containing this path, you see the following:

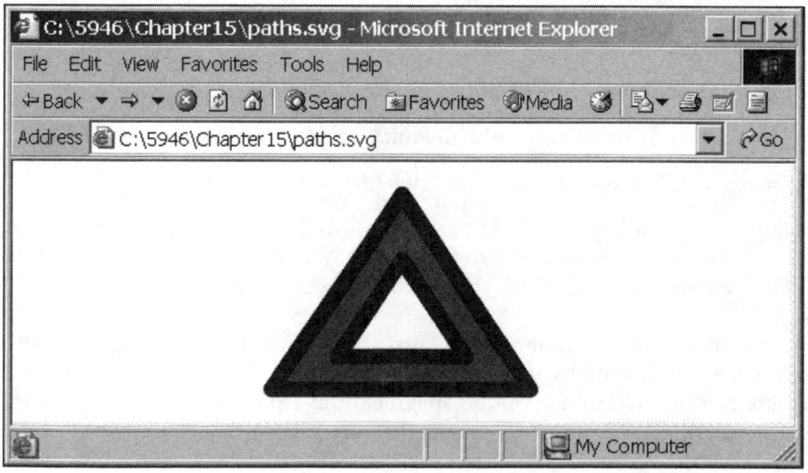

Being able to draw 'hollow' shapes is one of the main advantages of paths over polygons. The other advantage that paths have over polygons and polylines is the ability to have some or all segments in the path curved. There are three types of curve that are supported by SVG:

- Cubic Bézier curves, defined by a start point, an end point, and two control points
- Quadratic Bézier curves, defined by a start point, an end point, and a control point
- Elliptical arcs, defined by a start point, an end point, x and y radii, rotation, and flags indicating whether to use a long or short arc that proceeds with a positive or negative angle

These commands are beyond the scope of this book, but the SVG Recommendation has a detailed description of each of them at http://www.w3.org/TR/SVG/paths.html#PathDataCurveCommands.

Text

You can include text within an SVG image using the `<text>` element. The text itself is the content of the `<text>` element. The `x` and `y` attributes of the `<text>` element indicate the point at which the text is anchored. The `text-anchor` property determines how that point affects the position of the text; `start` (the default) indicates that the text starts at that point (giving left alignment), `end` that the text ends at that point (giving right alignment), and `middle` that the middle of the text is aligned at that point (giving center alignment).

The fill properties that you've already seen determine the color and opacity of the letters, while the stroke properties add an outline around the letters.

Selecting Fonts

As you might expect, `<text>` elements can also specify the kind of font that's used for the text using **font selection properties**. These properties mirror the properties that are available in CSS, but are represented as separate attributes on `<text>` elements:

- `font-family` – the name of the font that should be used, or the generic font family such as `serif`, `sans-serif`, or `monospace`
- `font-size` – an absolute or relative size, based on user units as usual
- `font-weight` – a keyword (`normal`, the default, or `bold`), a relative weight (`bolder` or `lighter`), or a number (one of `100`, `200`, `300`, `400`, `500`, `600`, `700`, `800`, or `900`)
- `font-style` – one of `normal` (the default), `italic`, or `oblique`
- `font-variant` – one of `normal` (the default) or `small-caps`
- `font-stretch` – a keyword (`ultra-condensed`, `extra-condensed`, `condensed`, `semi-condensed`, `normal` (the default), `semi-expanded`, `expanded`, `extra-expanded`, or `ultra-expanded`) or a relative stretch (`narrower` or `wider`)

Many of these properties can be summarized in a single `font` attribute comprising any definitions of style, variant, or weight, followed by the font size, optionally followed by the font family. Alternatively, the `font` attribute can be used to derive font specifications from the viewer's environment by specifying the keywords `caption`, `small-caption`, `menu`, `icon`, `message-box`, or `status-bar`.

Highlighting Phrases

Text often contains phrases, words, or characters that should be rendered differently from the rest of the text. To support this in SVG, the `<text>` element can contain `<tspan>` elements, each of which has its own set of font selection properties. Each `<tspan>` element can have an explicit start point, specified through its `x` and `y` attributes, or be offset from the surrounding text using `dx` and `dy` attributes.

For example, try the following `<text>` element with internal `<tspan>` element, in `text.svg`:

```
<svg width="12cm" height="4cm" viewBox="0 0 1200 400"
     xmlns="http://www.w3.org/2000/svg">
  <text x="600" y="250" text-anchor="middle" font-size="150" fill="black">
    Learning
    <tspan stroke-width="5" font-weight="bold" fill="red"
           stroke="black" stroke-linejoin="round">SVG</tspan>
  </text>
</svg>
```

The `<text>` element contains the text "Learning SVG". The text is anchored with its middle at the point (600, 250). Note that the glyphs are rendered above this point vertically, so the value 250 indicates the vertical position of the baseline of the text. The "Learning" part of the text is in black, and the "SVG" part of the text is bold and in red with a black outline. When rendered, the SVG looks as follows:

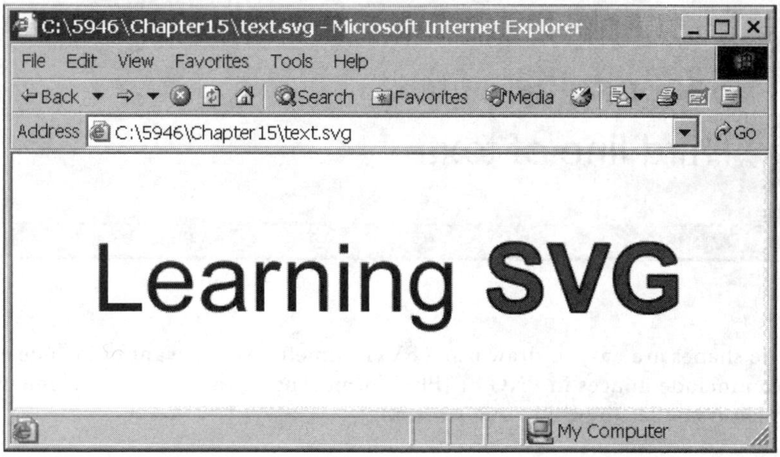

One of the benefits of using SVG to render text rather than a binary image format like JPEG or GIF is that you can actually select the text in the image. Try selecting the string "Learning SVG" from the SVG image. To copy it in Adobe's SVG Viewer, you need to use the context menu and select the option Copy Selected Text; you can then paste it into other applications.

Creating Lines

You have to be careful using text within SVG because SVG does not include any automated word wrapping – it assumes that each `<text>` element represents a separate line of text, and clips any text that goes over the boundary. If you want a single `<text>` element to contain several lines of text, you can use `<tspan>` elements to represent each line.

For example, the following `<text>` element contains three `<tspan>` elements. The first `<tspan>` element starts at the coordinate (50, 120), the second `<tspan>` has the same x-coordinate but starts 100 user units below the first `<tspan>`, and the third `<tspan>` starts 100 user units below the second. See `textlines.svg`:

```
<svg width="12cm" height="4cm" viewBox="0 0 1200 400"
     xmlns="http://www.w3.org/2000/svg">
  <text fill="black" font-size="70">
    <tspan x="50" y="120">First line of text.</tspan>
    <tspan x="50" dy="100">Second line of text.</tspan>
    <tspan x="50" dy="100">Third line of text.</tspan>
  </text>
</svg>
```

When you view `textlines.svg`, you should see the following:

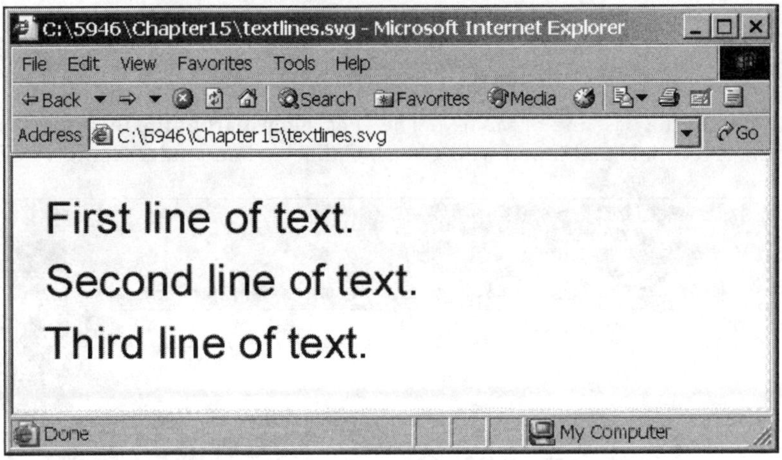

Images

While geometric shapes are easy to draw using SVG, sometimes you want to include a picture in a graphic. You can include images in PNG or JPEG formats using the `<image>` element. Positioning the `<image>` element is similar to positioning a rectangle:

- `x` and `y` specify the coordinate of the top left corner
- `width` and `height` specify the width and height of the image

The location of the image is indicated with the `xlink:href` attribute, where `xlink` is the prefix associated with the namespace `http://www.w3.org/1999/xlink`.

Container Elements

As well as graphic elements, SVG defines a number of elements that are used as containers for other elements, either grouping them together so that they can be referenced and used as a single graphic or bestowing a common behavior on all the elements in the container.

We'll have a quick look at two useful container elements: <g>, which groups graphics together, and <a>, which creates links from a graphic.

Grouping Graphics

You can group sets of graphics together by placing them within a <g> element. The <g> element can hold any graphic elements and/or other container elements (you can nest <g> elements inside each other).

The <g> element is useful in two primary ways; it enables you to apply the same presentational graphics to a set of graphics, and it enables you to move, rotate, and skew a set of graphics together.

Inheriting Presentational Attributes

Being able to inherit presentational attributes from a group can cut down on the size of an SVG document, and makes it easier to see how the document is constructed. For example, in `polygon.svg` we used three <polygon> elements to generate three triangles:

```
<polygon points="200,300 300,100 400,300" fill="red"
         stroke="black" stroke-width="25"
         stroke-linecap="butt" stroke-linejoin="miter" />
<polygon points="500,300 600,100 700,300" fill="red"
         stroke="black" stroke-width="25"
         stroke-linecap="round" stroke-linejoin="round" />
<polygon points="800,300 900,100 1000,300" fill="red"
         stroke="black" stroke-width="25"
         stroke-linecap="square" stroke-linejoin="bevel" />
```

All these <polygon> elements have the same values for the `fill`, `stroke`, and `stroke-width` attributes. Rather than repeating them on each <polygon>, we can use a <g> element to hold these attributes and they will be inherited by the polygons, as in `polygongroup.svg`:

```
<g fill="red" stroke="black" stroke-width="25">
  <polygon points="200,300 300,100 400,300"
           stroke-linecap="butt" stroke-linejoin="miter" />
  <polygon points="500,300 600,100 700,300"
           stroke-linecap="round" stroke-linejoin="round" />
  <polygon points="800,300 900,100 1000,300"
           stroke-linecap="square" stroke-linejoin="bevel" />
</g>
```

Each of the polygons are filled in red and have a black border 25 user units thick because each <polygon> inherits the `fill`, `stroke`, and `stroke-width` attributes from the surrounding group. `polygongroup.svg` will be rendered in exactly the same way as `polygon.svg`.

Transforming

The second helpful feature of <g> elements is that they enable you to move, rotate, or skew a set of graphic elements together through the `transform` attribute. You can use the `transform` attribute on any of the graphic elements individually, but it's generally more useful on the <g> element, where it can be applied to a set of graphic elements together.

The `transform` attribute is a space-separated list of **transform definitions**. Each transform definition looks like a function – a name followed by a comma-separated list of arguments in brackets. The principal transformation definitions are:

- `translate(`*`tx`*`, `*`ty`*`?)` – moves the graphic *`tx`* right and *`ty`* down (*`ty`* is assumed to be 0 if it is not specified)
- `scale(`*`sx`*`, `*`sy`*`?)` – multiplies the width of the graphic by *`sx`* and the height of the graphic by *`sy`* (*`sy`* is assumed to be the same as *`sx`* if it is not specified)
- `rotate(`*`angle`*`, [`*`cx`*`, `*`cy`*`]?)` – rotates the graphic by *`angle`* degrees around the coordinate specified by (*`cx`*, *`cy`*) (the center of the rotation is assumed to be the origin (0, 0) if *`cx`* and *`cy`* are not specified)
- `skewX(`*`angle`*`)` – skews the graphic by *`angle`* degrees, such that y-coordinates stay the same but x-coordinates are changed
- `skewY(`*`angle`*`)` – skews the graphic by *`angle`* degrees, such that x-coordinates stay the same but y-coordinates are changed

Each transformation is applied in turn on the result of running the rest of the transformations on the graphic. For example, in the following graphic, `transform.svg`, a rectangle and some text are both first rotated through 90° about the center of the rectangle, then moved 450 user units right and 100 user units down to position it in the center of the canvas:

```
<svg width="12cm" height="4cm" viewBox="0 0 1200 400"
     xmlns="http://www.w3.org/2000/svg">
  <g transform="translate(450, 100) rotate(90, 150, 100)">
    <rect width="300" height="200" fill="#C00"
          stroke="black" stroke-width="20" />
    <text x="150" y="150" text-anchor="middle"
          font-size="120" fill="yellow">SVG</text>
  </g>
</svg>
```

The resulting graphic is the following:

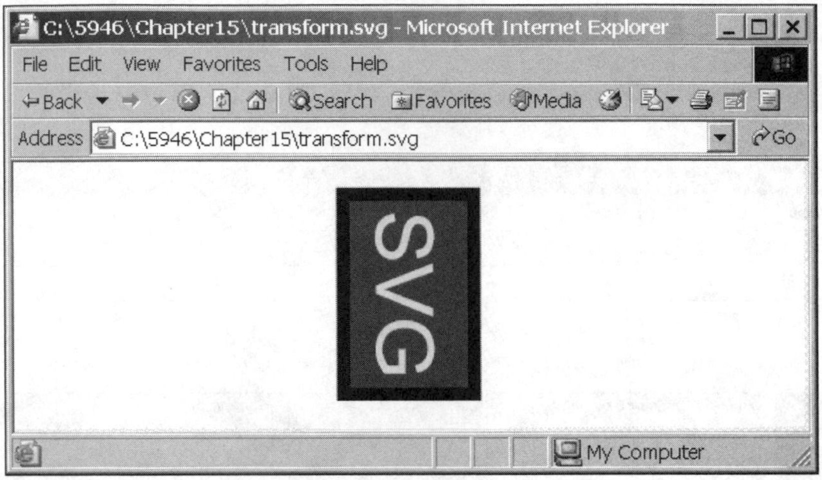

Linking from SVG

You can link from graphics within an SVG image using the <a> element. The <a> element works much like the <g> element; it groups together a bunch of graphic elements so that you can apply common presentational attributes to them, and so that you can move, scale, rotate, and skew them.

The <a> element also adds a behavior to the graphics that it contains, namely that if you click on them then the browser opens up the page that's linked to with the `xlink:href` attribute – the `href` attribute in the XLink namespace of `http://www.w3.org/1999/xlink`. The <a> element in SVG therefore works like the <a> element in HTML, except that it contains graphics rather than text (usually).

For example, you could change the <g> element from the last example into an <a> element and add an `xlink:href` attribute, not forgetting to add the namespace declaration for XLink, as in `linking.svg`:

```
<svg width="12cm" height="4cm" viewBox="0 0 1200 400"
     xmlns="http://www.w3.org/2000/svg"
     xmlns:xlink="http://www.w3.org/1999/xlink">
  <a xlink:href="http://www.w3.org/TR/svg"
     transform="translate(450, 100) rotate(90, 150, 100)">
    <rect width="300" height="200" fill="#C00"
          stroke="black" stroke-width="20" />
    <text x="150" y="150" text-anchor="middle"
          font-size="120" fill="yellow">SVG</text>
  </a>
</svg>
```

Now, when you click on the rectangle, the browser should take you to http://www.w3.org/TR/svg, the location of the SVG Recommendation.

Generating SVG with XSLT

Now that you have a rough idea of what you can achieve with SVG and how to achieve it, it's time to start trying to generate some SVG using XSLT. Our task will be to generate a graphical TV Guide, showing the programs that are showing between 7 pm and 10 pm on a particular day, looking something like the following:

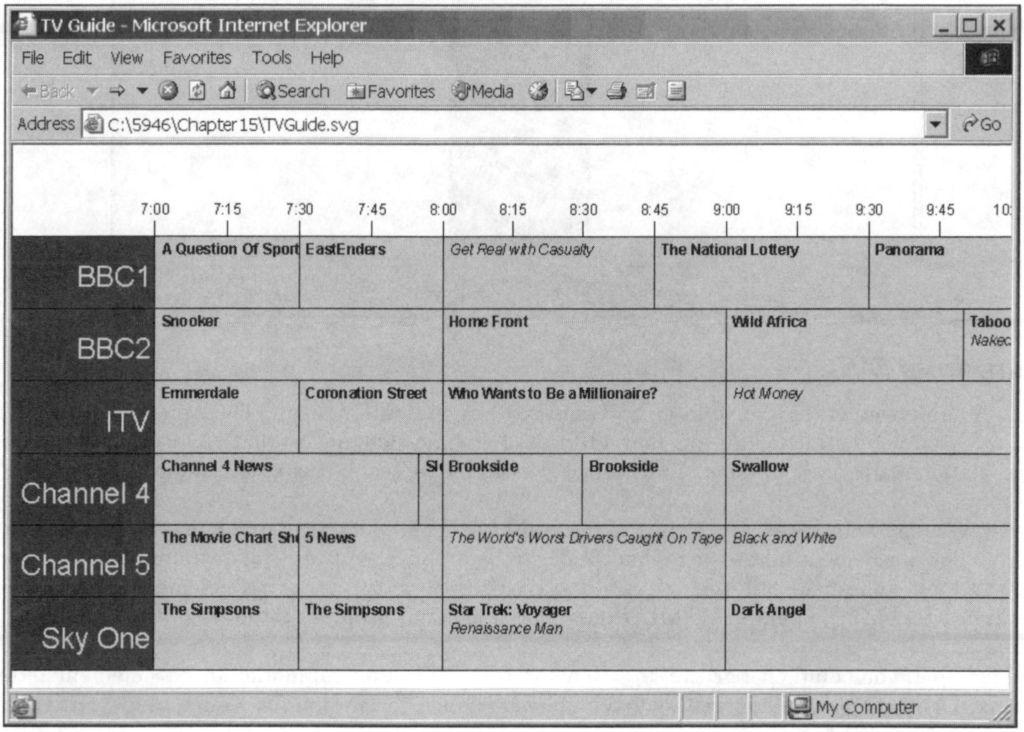

SVG Design

Our first task to create this image is to work out what SVG to use. The following SVG (`TVGuide.svg`) generates this image:

```
<svg xmlns="http://www.w3.org/2000/svg"
     xmlns:xlink="http://www.w3.org/1999/xlink"
     viewBox="0 0 1400 700">
  <title>TV Guide</title>
  <g text-anchor="middle" font-size="20" fill="black">
    <desc>Timeline markers</desc>
    <text x="200" y="70">7:00</text>
    <text x="300" y="70">7:15</text>
    ...
  </g>
  <g stroke="black" stroke-width="2">
```

```
    <desc>Vertical grid lines</desc>
    <line x1="200" y1="80" x2="200" y2="700"/>
    <line x1="300" y1="80" x2="300" y2="700"/>
    ...
  </g>
  <g transform="translate(0, 100)">
    <desc>BBC1</desc>
    <g>
      <desc>Channel Label</desc>
      <rect x="0" y="0" height="100" width="200" fill="#C00"/>
      <text x="195" y="70" text-anchor="end" font-size="40"
            fill="yellow">BBC1</text>
    </g>
    <g>
      <desc>Programs</desc>
      ...
      <g transform="translate(400)">
        <rect x="0" y="0" fill="#CCC" height="100" stroke="black"
              stroke-width="2" width="200"/>
        <text y="0" font-size="20" fill="black">
          <tspan font-weight="bold" x="0.5em" dy="25">EastEnders</tspan>
        </text>
      </g>
      ...
    </g>
  </g>
  ...
  <g stroke="black" stroke-width="2">
    <desc>Horizontal grid lines</desc>
    <line x1="0" y1="100" x2="1400" y2="100"/>
    <line x1="0" y1="200" x2="1400" y2="200"/>
    ...
  </g>
</svg>
```

The SVG is split into a number of <g> elements that demonstrate the structure of the graphic and allow groups of graphics to be positioned within the image and to share the same presentational attributes. There are four groups at the top level:

- A group holding the timeline markers displaying fifteen minute intervals; these timeline markers cover the top-most 100 user units of the graphic.
- A group holding vertical gridlines that start just below the timeline markers and continue to the bottom of the graphic, every 100 user units across the image, starting 200 user units from the left.
- Groups holding the information about a particular channel, each displayed in a single row within the graphic. Each channel takes up 100 user units vertically, with the label taking up 200 user units at the left. The more channels there are, the greater the height of the graphic.
- A group holding the horizontal gridlines that separate the information from each channel, every 100 user units down the image.

The groups are arranged in this order so that the vertical gridlines are painted over by programs (if there is a program at a particular time) whereas the horizontal gridlines are painted over the graphics for each channel.

The group for each channel contains two groups: a group giving the label for the channel, and a group holding the programs showing on that channel. The details for each program are displayed in their own group as well.

Constructing the Stylesheet

You're familiar by now with the content of the `TVGuide.xml` and `series.xml` documents that will form the source document for our transformation, and we've just looked at the `TVGuide.svg` document that we want to generate. Our task now is to create the stylesheet, `TVGuide.svg.xsl`, which will carry out the transformation from one to the other.

In the rest of this section, we'll build up the stylesheet bit by bit, first constructing the outline of the stylesheet and then adding the templates that we need to generate the result we want.

Basic Stylesheet

Our first step is to construct the document element, which controls namespaces, to work out how we're going to handle whitespace in our source document, and to decide what kind of output we're generating with this stylesheet.

Namespace Declarations and Management

Let's start at the beginning and consider what our `<xsl:stylesheet>` document element should look like. We certainly need to include the XSLT namespace declaration and a `version` attribute with the value `1.0`.

We also need namespace declarations for the namespaces that we'll use in the stylesheet. We don't have to worry about any namespaces on the source document because we're not using any. However, the SVG that we're generating does use a couple of namespaces:

- `http://www.w3.org/2000/svg` for the SVG elements
- `http://www.w3.org/1999/xlink` for the XLink attributes that are used to refer to elsewhere

Because most of the stylesheet will be concerned with generating SVG elements, we'll make the SVG namespace the default namespace. We'll use the standard prefix `xlink` for XLink attributes. The `<xsl:stylesheet>` document element for the stylesheet therefore looks as follows:

```
<xsl:stylesheet version="1.0"
                xmlns:xsl="http://www.w3.org/1999/XSL/Transform"
                xmlns="http://www.w3.org/2000/svg"
                xmlns:xlink="http://www.w3.org/1999/xlink">
...
</xsl:stylesheet>
```

Whitespace Stripping

Next up is managing the whitespace in our source document. The source document for this transformation is mainly data-oriented, so most of the whitespace that we have in TVGuide.xml is just there to make it easier to read. We should therefore strip the whitespace-only text nodes from the source node tree using the <xsl:strip-space> element, as follows:

```
<xsl:strip-space elements="*" />
```

There are a few document-oriented elements in TVGuide.xml in which whitespace matters, namely the <Description> element and the various styling elements that it contains. However, this SVG document isn't going to be including the content of the <Description> elements, so we don't have to worry about the fact that whitespace within them will be stripped from the tree.

Output Control

Our final job in setting up the stylesheet is to describe the result of the transformation using the <xsl:output> element. This stylesheet generates SVG, which is XML, so we need to use the xml output method. The media type for SVG is image/svg+xml, so we'll use that in the media-type attribute. We'll indent the output so that we can view it easily later on and set the encoding to ISO-8859-1 so that we can open it in normal text editors without having to worry about special characters. The <xsl:output> element is as follows:

```
<xsl:output method="xml" media-type="image/svg+xml"
            indent="yes" encoding="ISO-8859-1" />
```

Creating the SVG Element

The first element that we need to generate with our stylesheet is the <svg> element that holds the specification of the graphic. We can generate this element with a literal result element, without using a prefix, because the default namespace for the stylesheet is the SVG namespace. We'll create this element in the template for the document element, the <TVGuide> element, as follows:

```
<xsl:template match="TVGuide">
  <svg ...>
    ...
  </svg>
</xsl:template>
```

The namespace declarations that are specified on the <svg> element in TVGuide.svg will be automatically generated when the result tree is serialized, because the <svg> element in the stylesheet is in the SVG namespace and has a namespace node for the other namespace we need to use, XLink. As you'll remember from Chapter 8, the XSLT processor will add the namespace declarations automatically where necessary, so we don't have to add them explicitly. However, we do have to add the viewBox attribute.

Calculating the Height of the Coordinate System

In TVGuide.svg, the viewBox attribute has the value "0 0 1400 600". The coordinate system should always begin at (0, 0), and we'll always want it to be 1400 user units in width (200 for the labels, and 100 for every quarter hour between 19:00 and 22:00). However, the height of the graphic should change depending on how many channels we have; it should be 100 user units for each channel, plus the 100 user units needed to display the timeline markers.

Therefore the fourth value in the viewBox attribute (which gives the height of the graphic in user units) should be dependent on the number of channels that are specified within the source document. You can count the number of channels in TVGuide.xml using:

```
count(/TVGuide/Channel)
```

We'll assign the total height to a global variable so that we can refer to it from elsewhere, as follows:

```
<xsl:variable name="height"
              select="(count(/TVGuide/Channel) * 100) + 100" />
```

We can use an attribute value template to insert this value into the viewBox attribute, as follows:

```
<xsl:template match="TVGuide">
  <svg viewBox="0 0 1400 {$height}">
    ...
  </svg>
</xsl:template>
```

Now let's look at the content of the <svg> element. As we saw earlier, the content is broken up into four groups: one for the timeline markers, one for the vertical gridlines, one for each of the channels, and one for the horizontal gridlines. We'll get the <g> elements for each channel by applying templates to them and create the other groups with named templates. The content of the <svg> element in the stylesheet is therefore as follows:

```
<xsl:template match="TVGuide">
  <svg viewBox="0 0 1400 {$height}">
    <title>TV Guide</title>
    <xsl:call-template name="timelineMarkers" />
    <xsl:call-template name="verticalGridlines" />
    <xsl:apply-templates select="Channel"/>
    <xsl:call-template name="horizontalGridlines" />
  </svg>
</xsl:template>
```

Creating Timeline Markers

The timeline markers are a series of <text> elements displaying times specifying every quarter hour between 19:00 and 22:00. All these <text> elements have some things in common – the way they're anchored, the size of the font, and the color of the text, for example – so they're collected into a group. This also helps identify the timeline markers, separate from the other graphic elements.

In the stylesheet, the timeline markers need to be constructed with a template called timelineMarkers, which is called from the template that matches the <TVGuide> element. The template generates the <g> element, as follows:

```
<xsl:template name="timelineMarkers">
  <g text-anchor="middle" font-size="20" fill="black">
    <desc>Timeline markers</desc>
```

```
    ...
  </g>
</xsl:template>
```

The timeline markers are always going to be the same for this stylesheet, so we could just fill in the `timelineMarkers` template with the `<text>` elements directly, as follows:

```
<xsl:template name="timelineMarkers">
  <g text-anchor="middle" font-size="20" fill="black">
    <desc>Timeline markers</desc>
    <text x="200" y="70">7:00</text>
    <text x="300" y="70">7:15</text>
    <text x="400" y="70">7:30</text>
    <text x="500" y="70">7:45</text>
    <text x="600" y="70">8:00</text>
    <text x="700" y="70">8:15</text>
    <text x="800" y="70">8:30</text>
    <text x="900" y="70">8:45</text>
    <text x="1000" y="70">9:00</text>
    <text x="1100" y="70">9:15</text>
    <text x="1200" y="70">9:30</text>
    <text x="1300" y="70">9:45</text>
    <text x="1400" y="70">10:00</text>
  </g>
</xsl:template>
```

However, this is fairly long and error-prone, and it won't scale up well if we decide to make the stylesheet more flexible and show more of the evening's programs. Therefore, we'll use a recursive template to generate the timeline, which needs to keep track of three things:

- How far the text should be indented (the `x` attribute on the `<text>` elements), starting from 200 and incrementing by 100 each time the template recurses
- The hour that should be displayed, starting at 7 and incrementing by one if the minute for the previous `<text>` element is 45
- The minute that should be displayed, starting at 0 and incrementing by 15 (but going back to 0 if the result is 60)

These become the three parameters to the template: `$indent`, `$hour`, and `$minute`, as follows:

```
<xsl:template name="generateTimeLine">
  <xsl:param name="indent" select="200"/>
  <xsl:param name="hour" select="7"/>
  <xsl:param name="minute" select="0"/>
  ...
</xsl:template>
```

To create a `<text>` element for a particular indent, hour, and minute, we need to set the `x` attribute to the value of `$indent` and have the content show the hour, a colon, and then the minute (formatted so that it shows two decimal places):

```
<xsl:template name="generateTimeLine">
  <xsl:param name="indent" select="200"/>
  <xsl:param name="hour" select="7"/>
  <xsl:param name="minute" select="0"/>
  <text x="{$indent}" y="70">
    <xsl:value-of select="$hour"/>
    <xsl:text>:</xsl:text>
    <xsl:value-of select="format-number($minute, '00')"/>
  </text>
  ...
</xsl:template>
```

Finally, we need the recursive part of the template. The template only needs to call itself if we haven't reached the end of the timeline – if the hour is less than 10. If it does recurse, it needs to update the indent, hour, and minute for the next recursion. The indent should be the same as the current one, plus 100. The hour needs to increase by one, but only if the minute is on 45. The new minute is the old minute plus 15, mod 60:

```
<xsl:template name="generateTimeLine">
  <xsl:param name="indent" select="200"/>
  <xsl:param name="hour" select="7"/>
  <xsl:param name="minute" select="0"/>
  <text x="{$indent}" y="70">
    <xsl:value-of select="$hour"/>
    <xsl:text>:</xsl:text>
    <xsl:value-of select="format-number($minute, '00')"/>
  </text>
  <xsl:if test="$hour &lt; 10">
    <xsl:call-template name="generateTimeLine">
      <xsl:with-param name="indent" select="$indent + 100"/>
      <xsl:with-param name="hour">
        <xsl:choose>
          <xsl:when test="$minute = 45">
            <xsl:value-of select="$hour + 1"/>
          </xsl:when>
          <xsl:otherwise><xsl:value-of select="$hour"/></xsl:otherwise>
        </xsl:choose>
      </xsl:with-param>
      <xsl:with-param name="minute" select="($minute + 15) mod 60"/>
    </xsl:call-template>
  </xsl:if>
</xsl:template>
```

You could update the hour more simply using the expression `$hour + ($minute = 45)`. Because it is involved in an addition, the expression `$minute = 45` is converted to a number, 1 for true and 0 for false, so the new hour is the old hour plus 1 if `$minute` is equal to 45, and plus 0 if `$minute` is not equal to 45.

This `generateTimeLine` template needs to be called from the `timelineMarkers` template; you don't need to pass any parameters because the default values are the ones that you want to use anyway:

```
<xsl:template name="timelineMarkers">
  <g text-anchor="middle" font-size="20" fill="black">
    <desc>Timeline markers</desc>
    <xsl:call-template name="generateTimeLine" />
  </g>
</xsl:template>
```

Creating Vertical Gridlines

The next group is the group of vertical gridlines. The vertical gridlines are generated by the template named verticalGridlines, which looks like the following:

```
<xsl:template name="verticalGridlines">
  <g stroke="black" stroke-width="2">
    <desc>Vertical grid lines</desc>
    ...
  </g>
</xsl:template>
```

The method of generating the vertical gridlines is much the same as that for creating the timeline markers. We could generate them simply by adding the <line> elements explicitly to the group, but this would not be very flexible in the long run. Therefore, we'll generate them automatically using a recursive template called generateVerticalGridlines:

```
<xsl:template name="verticalGridlines">
  <g stroke="black" stroke-width="2">
    <desc>Vertical grid lines</desc>
    <xsl:call-template name="generateVerticalGridlines"/>
  </g>
</xsl:template>
```

When generating the timeline markers, we had to keep track of three things (the indent, the hour, and the minute). Here, we only need to worry about the indentation:

```
<xsl:template name="generateVerticalGridlines">
  <xsl:param name="indent" select="200"/>
  ...
</xsl:template>
```

Each line is created with a <line> element, starts 70 user units from the top of the graphic, and goes down to the bottom of the graphic. As you'll remember from when we created the coordinate system for this image, the height of the image might change depending on how many channels there are. We need to get the value of the maximum y-coordinate from the $height global variable that we used in the viewBox attribute when creating the <svg> element. The x-coordinate of the start and end of the line is the same – the x-coordinate specified by the $indent parameter:

```
<xsl:template name="generateVerticalGridlines">
  <xsl:param name="indent" select="200"/>
  <line x1="{$indent}" y1="80" x2="{$indent}" y2="{$height}"/>
  ...
</xsl:template>
```

Finally, let's look at the recursion. We need to have the gridlines appear right across the image – the last gridline is the one that appears at 1400 user units from the left. We can check whether this is the last one, or if we should carry on recursing, by looking at the `$indent` parameter; if we do carry on recursing, the `$indent` parameter needs to be incremented by 100:

```
<xsl:template name="generateVerticalGridlines">
  <xsl:param name="indent" select="200"/>
  <line x1="{$indent}" y1="80" x2="{$indent}" y2="{$height}"/>
  <xsl:if test="$indent &lt; 1400">
    <xsl:call-template name="generateVerticalGridlines">
      <xsl:with-param name="indent" select="$indent + 100"/>
    </xsl:call-template>
  </xsl:if>
</xsl:template>
```

Creating Horizontal Gridlines

Before we go on and look at how to generate the content for the grid, we'll just add the final group in the `<svg>` element – the group for the horizontal gridlines. The horizontal gridlines separate the channels from each other: there's a line right the way across the image above the row for each channel, plus a line at the bottom of the image.

These horizontal gridlines are generated by the `horizontalGridlines` template, which is called from the template that matches the `<TVGuide>` element. The `horizontalGridlines` template needs to create the `<g>` element, like the other named templates have done:

```
<xsl:template name="horizontalGridlines">
  <g stroke="black" stroke-width="2">
    <desc>Horizontal grid lines</desc>
    ...
  </g>
</xsl:template>
```

The horizontal gridlines need to be constructed slightly differently from the vertical gridlines and the timeline markers because the number of horizontal gridlines is dependent on the number of channels that are held in the source TV Guide. In fact, this makes creating them easier rather than harder – you can iterate over the `<Channel>` elements and create a horizontal gridline for each of them. You can use the `position()` of each `<Channel>` element to tell you how far down to place the gridline – the first at 100 user units, the second at 200 user units, and so on, as follows:

```
<xsl:template name="horizontalGridlines">
  <g stroke="black" stroke-width="2">
    <desc>Horizontal grid lines</desc>
    <xsl:for-each select="/TVGuide/Channel">
      <line x1="0"    y1="{position() * 100}"
            x2="1400" y2="{position() * 100}" />
    </xsl:for-each>
  </g>
</xsl:template>
```

What have we forgotten? We've left out the last gridline, which needs to appear right at the bottom of the graphic. We can add this last gridline by checking whether the `<Channel>` that we're on is the last `<Channel>` in the document. If it is, then we can add a final gridline, 100 user units below the one that we've just added:

```
<xsl:template name="horizontalGridlines">
  <g stroke="black" stroke-width="2">
    <desc>Horizontal grid lines</desc>
    <xsl:for-each select="/TVGuide/Channel">
      <line x1="0"    y1="{position() * 100}"
            x2="1400" y2="{position() * 100}" />
      <xsl:if test="position() = last()">
        <line x1="0"    y1="{(position() * 100) + 100}"
              x2="1400" y2="{(position() * 100) + 100}" />
      </xsl:if>
    </xsl:for-each>
  </g>
</xsl:template>
```

Creating Groups for Channels

At last we're on to the most important information that's displayed in the graphic – what's actually showing on each of the channels. Back in the template for the `<TVGuide>` element, we applied templates to the `<Channel>` elements to generate the groups for each channel. So we need a template that matches `<Channel>` elements to generate these groups:

```
<xsl:template match="Channel">
  <g ...>
    <desc><xsl:value-of select="Name"/></desc>
    ...
  </g>
</xsl:template>
```

If you look back at the source of `TVGuide.svg`, you'll see that each of the `<g>` elements for the channels uses a `transform` attribute to move its contents down the graphic. The amount that the group is moved down the graphic depends on the position of the channel – the first channel is moved down 100 user units, the second 200 user units, and so on. We can therefore use the `position()` attribute to work out how much the group should be translated by, as shown below:

```
<xsl:template match="Channel">
  <g transform="translate(0, {position() * 100})">
    <desc><xsl:value-of select="Name"/></desc>
    ...
  </g>
</xsl:template>
```

The content of the channel group is made up of two more groups: the label for the channel and the programs that are shown on the channel. These groups are purely there to add structure to the SVG document – the `<g>` elements don't provide default values for presentational attributes, nor do they move their contents anywhere:

```
<xsl:template match="Channel">
  <g transform="translate(0, {position() * 100})">
    <desc><xsl:value-of select="Name"/></desc>
    <g>
      <desc>Channel Label</desc>
      ...
    </g>
    <g>
      <desc>Programs</desc>
      ...
    </g>
  </g>
</xsl:template>
```

The channel label consists of a rectangle in red that is 200 user units wide and 100 user units in height, with some right-aligned yellow text on top giving the name of the channel. You can right-align the text by using the `text-anchor` attribute, set to `end`, so that the x, y anchor coordinate for the text specifies the coordinate of the end of the text, as follows:

```
<xsl:template match="Channel">
  <g transform="translate(0, {position() * 100})">
    <desc><xsl:value-of select="Name"/></desc>
    <g>
      <desc>Channel Label</desc>
      <rect x="0" y="0" height="100" width="200" fill="#C00"/>
      <text x="195" y="70" text-anchor="end" font-size="40" fill="yellow">
        <xsl:value-of select="Name"/>
      </text>
    </g>
    <g>
      <desc>Programs</desc>
      ...
    </g>
  </g>
</xsl:template>
```

Last but not least, we need to apply templates to generate the rectangles that display the details of each program. We'll do this simply by applying templates to all the `<Program>` elements within the `<Channel>` and let the template for the `<Program>` elements figure out whether they should be displayed or not:

```
<xsl:template match="Channel">
  <g transform="translate(0, {position() * 100})">
    <desc><xsl:value-of select="Name"/></desc>
    <g>
      <desc>Channel Label</desc>
      <rect x="0" y="0" height="100" width="200" fill="#C00"/>
      <text x="195" y="70" text-anchor="end" font-size="40" fill="yellow">
        <xsl:value-of select="Name"/>
      </text>
    </g>
```

```
    <g>
      <desc>Programs</desc>
      <xsl:apply-templates select="Program"/>
    </g>
  </g>
</xsl:template>
```

Creating Groups for Programs

Our last task is to generate the rectangles that display the details of each program. We'll do this in a template that matches `<Program>` elements:

```
<xsl:template match="Program">
  ...
</xsl:template>
```

The first task is to figure out whether the program should be displayed at all. We're only displaying programs that start after 19:00 and before 22:00 (and assuming that all the programs listed are on the same day). The start time of a program is stored in the `<Start>` child element of the `<Program>` element. This has the ISO 8601 date and time format *YYYY-MM-DD*T*hh*:*mm*:*ss*. The hour is specified in the 12th and 13th characters of this string, so we can use the `substring()` function to pull out these characters and work out in which hour the program starts. If it's between 19 and 22, then we go on with the rest of thc processing:

```
<xsl:template match="Program">
  <xsl:variable name="hour" select="substring(Start, 12, 2)"/>
  <xsl:if test="$hour &gt;= 19 and $hour &lt; 22">
    ...
  </xsl:if>
</xsl:template>
```

The `<Start>` element also gives us the location of the group for the program – it needs to be indented according to the start time, with a program starting at 19:00 indented 200 user units, one at 19:15 indented 300 user units, and so on. The actual formula is 200 user units (for the channel labels) plus 100 user units for every quarter hour after 19:00. To work this out, we first need to figure out the minute at which the program starts, which we can do in the same way as we got hold of the hour, using the `substring()` function:

```
<xsl:variable name="minute" select="substring(Start, 15, 2)"/>
```

Once we've got hold of the minute, we need to work out how many quarter hours there are between 19:00 and the start time of the program. This is the difference between the hour and 19, multiplied by 4, plus the number of minutes divided by 15:

```
(($hour - 19) * 4) + ($minute div 15)
```

The indent is this number of quarter hours, multiplied by 100, plus 200. In some cases, this will give us a fraction (for example, a program that starts at 19:05 should start 233.333333333 user units in from the side). We don't really need a high level of accuracy, though – two decimal places will be more than enough – so we'll format the number that we get to fix it to a maximum of two decimal places with the `format-number()` function:

```
<xsl:variable name="indent"
  select="format-number(
        (($hour - 19) * 4 + $minute div 15) * 100 + 200, '0.##')"/>
```

Now we've got the start x-coordinate for the rectangle for the program, we need to work out how wide the rectangle needs to be. The width of the rectangle depends on its duration – it should cover 100 user units for every quarter hour that it lasts. To work this out, we need to look at the `<Duration>` child of the `<Program>` element, which holds an ISO 8601 duration in the form `PT`*n*`H`*n*`M`.

> *We're only using a restricted syntax for the durations in our TV Guide because TV programs last for hours and minutes, not days or seconds.*

Either the hour or minute component of the duration could be missing, so we need to check the syntax that's being used for the duration to work out whether there's an hour and/or minute present. The duration's hour component is the part of the duration after the `PT` and before the `H`, if there's an `H` in the string, or `0` if there isn't:

```
<xsl:variable name="durHour">
  <xsl:choose>
    <xsl:when test="contains(Duration, 'H')">
      <xsl:value-of
        select="substring-before(substring-after(Duration, 'PT'), 'H')"/>
    </xsl:when>
    <xsl:otherwise>0</xsl:otherwise>
  </xsl:choose>
</xsl:variable>
```

The duration's minute component is the part of the duration before the `M` (if the duration contains an `M`) and after the `H` if the duration contains an `H`, or after the `PT` if it doesn't. If the duration doesn't contain an `M`, then the minute component is `0`:

```
<xsl:variable name="durMinute">
  <xsl:choose>
    <xsl:when test="contains(Duration, 'M')">
      <xsl:choose>
        <xsl:when test="contains(Duration, 'H')">
          <xsl:value-of select="substring-before(
                                  substring-after(Duration, 'H'), 'M')"/>
        </xsl:when>
        <xsl:otherwise>
          <xsl:value-of select="substring-before(
                                  substring-after(Duration, 'PT'), 'M')"/>
        </xsl:otherwise>
      </xsl:choose>
```

```
    </xsl:when>
    <xsl:otherwise>0</xsl:otherwise>
  </xsl:choose>
</xsl:variable>
```

The total duration, in minutes, is `$durMinute` plus `$durHour` multiplied by 60:

```
<xsl:variable name="duration" select="$durMinute + $durHour * 60" />
```

We've gathered together all the information that we need to position the group containing the program information now, and to draw the rectangle that forms the background to the text describing the program. The group needs to be moved right by the amount held in the `$indent` variable, and the background rectangle's width should be the `$duration` divided by 15, multiplied by 100, and formatted to two decimal places in the same way as the indent. The template looks as follows:

```
<xsl:template match="Program">
  <xsl:variable name="hour" select="substring(Start, 12, 2)"/>
  <xsl:if test="$hour &gt;= 19 and $hour &lt; 22">
    <xsl:variable name="minute" select="substring(Start, 15, 2)"/>
    <xsl:variable name="indent"
      select="format-number(
             (($hour - 19) * 4 + $minute div 15) * 100 + 200, '0.##')"/>
    <xsl:variable name="durHour">
      ...
    </xsl:variable>
    <xsl:variable name="durMinute">
      ...
    </xsl:variable>
    <xsl:variable name="duration"
                  select="$durMinute + (60 * $durHour)"/>
    <g transform="translate({$indent})">
      <rect x="0" y="0" fill="#CCC" height="100"
            stroke="black" stroke-width="2"
            width="{format-number(($duration div 15) * 100, '0.##')}" />
      ...
    </g>
  </xsl:if>
</xsl:template>
```

Now let's look at the text content of the program. We want to display the series name of the program, if it has one, followed on a new line by the series title of the program, if it has one. If we place both these pieces of text within the same `<text>` element, then they can be selected at the same time. It will also help us to position the text. So we'll create a `<text>` element in this template and use templates for the `<Series>` and `<Title>` templates to generate the `<tspan>` elements that contain the text itself.

> *Using `<tspan>` elements also helps us design the stylesheet because we can take advantage of the fact that you can position a `<tspan>` element relative to the previous `<tspan>` element, using the `dx` and `dy` attributes.*

We'll generate the <tspan> elements using separate templates for the <Series> and <Title> elements, but we only want to apply these templates, and generate the <tspan> elements, if there's something to generate information about. All the <Program> elements in TVGuide.xml have <Series> and <Title> child elements, but not all the <Series> and <Title> elements have any content – if a program doesn't belong to a series then its <Series> element is empty, for example. Rather than using a test within the templates, we'll only apply templates to the <Series> and <Title> elements if they contain some text, using a predicate as shown in the following:

```
<xsl:template match="Program">
  <xsl:variable name="hour" select="substring(Start, 12, 2)"/>
  <xsl:if test="$hour &gt;= 19 and $hour &lt; 22">
    <xsl:variable name="minute" select="substring(Start, 15, 2)"/>
    <xsl:variable name="indent"
      select="format-number(
             (($hour - 19) * 4 + $minute div 15) * 100 + 200, '0.##')"/>
    <xsl:variable name="durHour">
      ...
    </xsl:variable>
    <xsl:variable name="durMinute">
      ...
    </xsl:variable>
    <xsl:variable name="duration"
              select="$durMinute + (60 * $durHour)"/>
    <g transform="translate({$indent})">
      <rect x="0" y="0" fill="#CCC" height="100"
            stroke="black" stroke-width="2"
            width="{format-number(($duration div 15) * 100, '0.##')}" />
      <text y="0" font-size="20" fill="black">
        <xsl:apply-templates select="Series[string()]"/>
        <xsl:apply-templates select="Title[string()]"/>
      </text>
    </g>
  </xsl:if>
</xsl:template>
```

Displaying the Series Title

We're applying templates to the <Series> element within a <Program> to display the name of the series that the program belongs to. However, the <Series> element contains the series ID, not the full title of the series. To get hold of the full title of the series, we need to look in series.xml, which lists each series and gives its full title.

Because we'll be querying information from series.xml several times during the course of the transformation, we'll store the root node for the document in a global variable called $seriesDocument, as follows:

```
<xsl:variable name="seriesDocument" select="document('series.xml')" />
```

The second preparatory step to take is to create a key that gives us quick access to the information about a series, given the ID for that series. To create this key, we need an `<xsl:key>` element whose `match` attribute holds a pattern that matches the `<Series>` elements (in `series.xml`) and whose `use` attribute leads from the `<Series>` element to its `id` attribute:

```
<xsl:key name="series" match="Series" use="@id" />
```

Now let's see the template that matches `<Series>` element children of `<Program>` elements and generates a `<tspan>` holding the series title. To make it clear that the `<Series>` element that we're matching is a child of the `<Program>` element, we'll use a more specific match pattern than usual:

```
<xsl:template match="Program/Series">
  ...
</xsl:template>
```

The `<tspan>` element will make its content bold, using the `font-weight` attribute. To get hold of the text, we need to query `series.xml` (whose root node is held in `$seriesDocument`) using the `series` key. Remember that keys only search in the document that holds the current node. To use the key on a different document, we need to change the context, using an `<xsl:for-each>` to select the root node of `series.xml`. But that would mean that we lost track of the value of the `<Series>` element from `TVGuide.xml`, so we have to hold that in a variable called `$series`. Once we have the `<Series>` element from `series.xml`, we can find its `<Title>` element child and display its content as the value of the `<tspan>` element, as follows:

```
<xsl:template match="Program/Series">
  <tspan font-weight="bold" x="0.5em" dy="25">
    <xsl:variable name="series" select="."/>
    <xsl:for-each select="$seriesDocument">
      <xsl:value-of select="key('series', $series)/Title"/>
    </xsl:for-each>
  </tspan>
</xsl:template>
```

Displaying the Program Title

Displaying the program's title is easier than displaying the series title because the program's title is right there in the `<Program>` element's child `<Title>` element. The template is simply the following:

```
<xsl:template match="Title">
  <tspan x="0.5em" dy="25" font-style="italic">
    <xsl:value-of select="."/>
  </tspan>
</xsl:template>
```

Completed Stylesheet

The complete XSLT stylesheet is as follows:

```
<xsl:stylesheet version="1.0"
                xmlns:xsl="http://www.w3.org/1999/XSL/Transform"
xmlns="http://www.w3.org/2000/svg"
                xmlns:xlink="http://www.w3.org/1999/xlink">

<xsl:strip-space elements="*" />

<xsl:output method="xml" media-type="image/svg+xml"
            indent="yes" encoding="ISO-8859-1" />

<xsl:variable name="height"
              select="(count(/TVGuide/Channel) * 100) + 100" />

<xsl:template match="TVGuide">
  <svg viewBox="0 0 1400 {$height}">
    <title>TV Guide</title>
    <xsl:call-template name="timelineMarkers" />
    <xsl:call-template name="verticalGridlines" />
    <xsl:apply-templates select="Channel"/>
    <xsl:call-template name="horizontalGridlines" />
  </svg>
</xsl:template>

<xsl:template name="timelineMarkers">
  <g text-anchor="middle" font-size="20" fill="black">
    <desc>Timeline markers</desc>
    <xsl:call-template name="generateTimeLine" />
  </g>
</xsl:template>

<xsl:template name="generateTimeLine">
  <xsl:param name="indent" select="200"/>
  <xsl:param name="hour" select="7"/>
  <xsl:param name="minute" select="0"/>
  <text x="{$indent}" y="70">
    <xsl:value-of select="$hour"/>
    <xsl:text>:</xsl:text>
    <xsl:value-of select="format-number($minute, '00')"/>
  </text>
  <xsl:if test="$hour &lt; 10">
    <xsl:call-template name="generateTimeLine">
      <xsl:with-param name="indent" select="$indent + 100"/>
      <xsl:with-param name="hour">
        <xsl:choose>
          <xsl:when test="$minute = 45">
            <xsl:value-of select="$hour + 1"/>
          </xsl:when>
          <xsl:otherwise><xsl:value-of select="$hour"/></xsl:otherwise>
        </xsl:choose>
      </xsl:with-param>
      <xsl:with-param name="minute" select="($minute + 15) mod 60"/>
    </xsl:call-template>
  </xsl:if>
</xsl:template>
```

```
<xsl:template name="verticalGridlines">
  <g stroke="black" stroke-width="2">
    <desc>Vertical grid lines</desc>
    <xsl:call-template name="generateVerticalGridlines"/>
  </g>
</xsl:template>

<xsl:template name="generateVerticalGridlines">
  <xsl:param name="indent" select="200"/>
  <line x1="{$indent}" y1="80" x2="{$indent}" y2="{$height}"/>
  <xsl:if test="$indent &lt; 1400">
    <xsl:call-template name="generateVerticalGridlines">
      <xsl:with-param name="indent" select="$indent + 100"/>
    </xsl:call-template>
  </xsl:if>
</xsl:template>

<xsl:template name="horizontalGridlines">
  <g stroke="black" stroke-width="2">
    <desc>Horizontal grid lines</desc>
    <xsl:for-each select="/TVGuide/Channel">
      <line x1="0"    y1="{position() * 100}"
            x2="1400" y2="{position() * 100}" />
      <xsl:if test="position() = last()">
        <line x1="0"    y1="{(position() * 100) + 100}"
              x2="1400" y2="{(position() * 100) + 100}" />
      </xsl:if>
    </xsl:for-each>
  </g>
</xsl:template>

<xsl:template match="Channel">
  <g transform="translate(0, {position() * 100})">
    <desc><xsl:value-of select="Name"/></desc>
    <g>
      <desc>Channel Label</desc>
      <rect x="0" y="0" height="100" width="200" fill="#C00"/>
      <text x="195" y="70" text-anchor="end" font-size="40" fill="yellow">
        <xsl:value-of select="Name"/>
      </text>
    </g>
    <g>
      <desc>Programs</desc>
      <xsl:apply-templates select="Program"/>
    </g>
  </g>
</xsl:template>

<xsl:template match="Program">
  <xsl:variable name="hour" select="substring(Start, 12, 2)"/>
  <xsl:if test="$hour &gt;= 19 and $hour &lt; 22">
    <xsl:variable name="minute" select="substring(Start, 15, 2)"/>
```

```
    <xsl:variable name="indent"
  select="format-number((($hour - 19) * 4 + $minute div 15) * 100 + 200,
                        '0.##')"/>
    <xsl:variable name="durHour">
      <xsl:choose>
        <xsl:when test="contains(Duration, 'H')">
          <xsl:value-of select="substring-before(
                                  substring-after(Duration, 'PT'),
                                  'H')"/>
        </xsl:when>
        <xsl:otherwise>0</xsl:otherwise>
      </xsl:choose>
    </xsl:variable>
    <xsl:variable name="durMinute">
      <xsl:choose>
        <xsl:when test="contains(Duration, 'M')">
          <xsl:choose>
            <xsl:when test="contains(Duration, 'H')">
              <xsl:value-of select="substring-before(
                                      substring-after(Duration, 'H'),
                                      'M')" />
            </xsl:when>
            <xsl:otherwise>
              <xsl:value-of select="substring-before(
                                      substring-after(Duration, 'PT'),
                                      'M')"/>
            </xsl:otherwise>
          </xsl:choose>
        </xsl:when>
        <xsl:otherwise>0</xsl:otherwise>
      </xsl:choose>
    </xsl:variable>
    <xsl:variable name="duration"
                  select="$durMinute + (60 * $durHour)"/>
    <g transform="translate({$indent})">
      <rect x="0" y="0" fill="#CCC" height="100"
            stroke="black" stroke-width="2"
            width="{format-number(($duration div 15) * 100, '0.##')}" />
      <text y="0" font-size="20" fill="black">
        <xsl:apply-templates select="Series[string()]"/>
        <xsl:apply-templates select="Title[string()]"/>
      </text>
    </g>
  </xsl:if>
</xsl:template>

<xsl:variable name="seriesDocument" select="document('series.xml')" />

<xsl:key name="series" match="Series" use="@id" />

<xsl:template match="Program/Series">
  <tspan font-weight="bold" x="0.5em" dy="25">
    <xsl:variable name="series" select="."/>
    <xsl:for-each select="$seriesDocument">
```

```
      <xsl:value-of select="key('series', $series)/Title"/>
    </xsl:for-each>
  </tspan>
</xsl:template>

<xsl:template match="Title">
  <tspan x="0.5em" dy="25" font-style="italic">
    <xsl:value-of select="."/>
  </tspan>
</xsl:template>

</xsl:stylesheet>
```

Transforming `TVGuide.xml` with `TVGuide.svg.xsl` gives you the SVG graphic that we saw at the beginning of this section.

Embedding SVG in HTML Pages

The SVG graphics that we've looked at thus far in this chapter have been standalone files, created with a batch or server side process that we've opened individually. We haven't discussed either embedding the SVG within an HTML page or displaying SVG that is generated on the client side.

Different browsers support different methods of embedding SVG graphics within HTML pages. Some browsers, such as Mozilla or Xsmiles, allow you to embed SVG directly within an XHTML page. This enables you to generate SVG in the same process as generating other information from the same XML source.

Most browsers, however, require you to embed an SVG graphic within an HTML page using the `<object>` and/or `<embed>` elements. For example, `TVGuide.html` embeds `TVGuide.svg` as follows:

```
<object data="TVGuide.svg" type="image/svg+xml"
        width="700" height="350">
  <embed src="TVGuide.svg" type="image/svg+xml"
         width="700" height="350"
         pluginspage="http://www.adobe.com/svg/viewer/install/" />
</object>
```

The `<object>` element is the W3C-sanctioned method of embedding non-HTML formats within HTML pages. The `data` attribute specifies the source of the SVG graphic, the `type` attribute gives the content type of the graphic, and the `width` and `height` attributes determine the width and height of the graphic within the page, here set to `700` pixels by `350` pixels (such that each user unit is half a pixel wide).

The `<embed>` element is provided for legacy browsers that don't support HTML 4.01. The attributes have the same kind of effect – `src` is used rather than `data` to indicate the source of the graphic, with the `pluginspage` attribute directing people who don't have Adobe's SVG Viewer installed to Adobe's site. The semantics of the `<object>` element and HTML mean that the `<embed>` element will be ignored unless the browser doesn't support the `<object>` element or can't provide a viewer for the SVG graphic.

When you view `TVGuide.html`, if you have Adobe's SVG Viewer installed, you should see the following page:

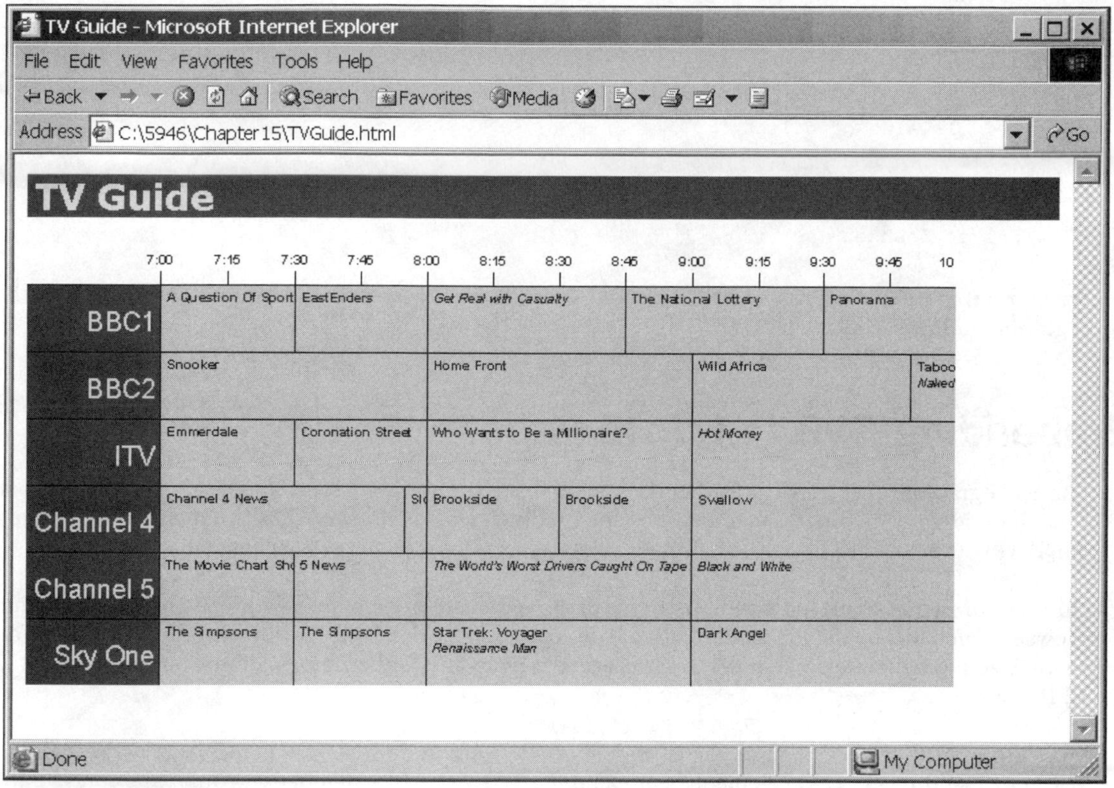

This can be a bit of a constraint because it makes it harder to create SVG and the rest of the page in one process. If you are processing the document in batch mode, from the command line, you can use extension elements to create multiple output documents, as we saw in Chapter 13. If you are processing the document server side, you can make sure that the request for the SVG graphic causes the server to generate the SVG dynamically from the XML source.

Embedding SVG within HTML pages when the transformation is carried out on the client side is a lot harder, and has to be done through scripts that perform DOM manipulation. For details and tools that support client side transformation involving SVG, see Chris Bayes's `domtodom.js` utility at http://www.bayes.co.uk/xml/index.xml?/xml/utils/domtodom.xml.

Summary

This chapter has introduced you to the basics of SVG and shown you how you can create nice-looking, interactive graphics using XSLT to transform your XML data to SVG. You've learned about how to draw graphics and text on the screen using SVG, how to control their presentation, how to move, rotate, stretch, and skew those graphics, and how to link to other documents.

In creating the stylesheet transforming XML to SVG, you've seen many of the techniques that were discussed theoretically in the first part of this book being used in practice:

- Declaring namespaces for use in the result tree
- Stripping whitespace from data-oriented XML
- Serializing the result tree as XML
- Counting the number of nodes in a document
- Performing calculations using XPath
- Creating and using global variables
- Using attribute value templates to insert calculated values into attribute values
- Using named templates to break up your stylesheet into manageable portions of code
- Creating recursive templates to generate repeated information
- Using the `position()` function as a counter
- Parsing strings with fixed formats and delimited formats
- Formatting numbers to certain numbers of decimal places
- Selecting subsets of nodes to apply templates to
- Using keys, in particular with external documents

Review Questions

1. Add stars to the programs to indicate how highly rated they are (the number of stars is held in the `rating` attribute on the `<Program>` element). A good polygon to use for a star is:

```
<polygon points="12,0 15,9 24,9 17,14 20,25 12,18 4,25 7,14 0,9 9,9" />
```

   You can wrap all the stars in a `<g>` element to use the same presentational attributes with each, and use the `transform` attribute on the `<polygon>` elements to move them to the right so that you don't have to come up with a new set of x-coordinates each time.

2. Highlight the `<Program>` elements with `flag` attributes by coloring them differently from the other programs. Use blue for programs with an 'interesting' flag and green for programs with a 'favorite' flag.

3. Some `<Series>` elements in `series.xml` have an `xlink:href` attribute that points to a home page for the series. When there is such an attribute, use an `<a>` element in the SVG so that when you click on the rectangle for a program, you get taken to the home page of the series.

4. Some of the titles of the programs are not displayed very well because the program only lasts for a short amount of time and SVG doesn't do any word wrapping. Assuming that each character takes up 11 user units, use a recursive template to split up the text and word breaks so that it can flow over several lines. You may need to adjust the font size or the height of the rows so that several lines of text can fit in the rectangle for a program. If the text can't be split up (because the words are too long), then rotate the text so that it fits in sideways.

5. Currently, if a program starts before 19:00 but ends after 19:00, it isn't shown, and if it lasts past 22:00 then its rectangle goes over the end of the graphic. Amend the template for `<Program>` elements so that programs that start before 19:00 are included in the graphic and so that the rectangles for programs that finish later are foreshortened.

6. Assuming that the `<Program>` elements held in `TVGuide.xml` do *not* share the same date, alter the stylesheet so that it displays the programs shown on a particular evening by storing the date in a `$date` stylesheet parameter.

7. Make the start and end time for the displayed SVG depend on `$startHour` and `$endHour` parameters passed in to the stylesheet.

8. Serve `TVGuide.xml` using `TVGuide.svg.xsl` from Cocoon 2, allowing the `$date`, `$startHour`, and `$endHour` parameters to be set through request parameters or parts of the URL.

9. Add a `$series` parameter to the stylesheet so that it highlights programs in a particular series within the SVG graphic.

10. Create a user preferences file to hold information about the fonts and colors that the user wants to be used in the graphic. Use the information from this file when creating the presentational attributes that are used in the SVG document.

Beginning
XSLT

16

Validating XML with Schematron

Early on in this book, you learned that XML is a meta-markup language, a specification of the syntax that a wide variety of markup languages all follow. You also learned the difference between well-formed XML documents, which follow the XML syntax, and valid XML documents, which adhere to the rules laid down by a particular markup language. In Chapter 2, we looked briefly at how to validate XML documents using DTDs and schemas to make sure that they contain the correct elements with the correct attributes and the right kind of values. In this chapter, we'll look at how to use XSLT and XPath to validate XML.

When you write a stylesheet, you need to have an understanding of the markup language that's used as the source of the transformation and the markup language that's used in the result of the transformation. You need to understand the source markup language so that you know where to find the information that you need to insert into the result. And you need to understand the result markup language so that you know what elements and attributes you need to create and how they fit together. A stylesheet is designed for a transformation between a specific pair of markup languages.

However, there's nothing explicit in an XSLT stylesheet that states what the source and result markup languages are. There's nothing that stops someone from trying to use an XSLT stylesheet on a markup language that it wasn't designed for, and nothing that stops a stylesheet from running on a document that isn't valid. The result of running a stylesheet on a document that doesn't follow the rules that the stylesheet expects is usually gobbledygook (garbage in, garbage out), but no error messages will be produced.

If you don't want your stylesheet to produce garbage, it's worth checking that the source document isn't garbage, and that it's valid XML. You can use DTDs and XML Schema to make these checks, but in this chapter, we'll look at Schematron, which is a schema language that uses XSLT and XPath to validate XML documents. We'll start by looking at how Schematron works at a general level. Then we'll explore how to test various aspects of an XML document using XPath expressions within Schematron. Finally, we'll see how to create meta-stylesheets, which operate on Schematron schemas to create validating stylesheets. Exploring how to use XSLT and XPath for validation should help bring home the power, and limitations, of XPath and XSLT.

In this chapter, you'll learn:

- How to create Schematron schemas
- How to generate Schematron validators
- How to construct XPaths that check elements, attributes, and values
- How to put together meta-stylesheets

Introducing Schematron

As you've seen in earlier chapters of this book, XSLT and XPath are powerful languages for extracting information about an XML document. Mostly, a transformation is concerned with extracting that information so that it can be included in the generated result document. However, there's nothing to stop you from using XSLT and XPath to check an XML document to see if it follows the rules that you expect it to. In fact, XSLT and XPath can be really powerful tools for checking XML documents because they are so flexible.

The power of XSLT and XPath as validation tools has led to the development of Schematron by Rick Jeliffe and others (see http://www.ascc.net/xml/schematron/ for more details). Schematron takes the idea of using XPaths to validate documents, and provides a language in which these XPaths can be explicitly associated with error messages.

Schematron schemas allow you to construct XSLT stylesheets that perform validation of an XML document. The result of the validating XSLT stylesheet can be anything that you like. They can:

- simply generate error messages
- create sets of HTML pages that provide an overall report on the validity of the XML document
- create other XML formats, such as RDF, or annotate the XML document with comments

Schematron simply provides a standard way of expressing the rules that govern a markup language; different applications can do different things as a result of processing an XML document with that schema.

A validating stylesheet is generated from a Schematron schema, usually using XSLT. The Schematron schema is used as the source of a transformation that creates a validating XSLT stylesheet. A stylesheet that uses a Schematron schema to produce a validating stylesheet is known as a **meta-stylesheet**. The validating XSLT stylesheet is run over the XML document in order to validate the document. The process is shown in the following diagram:

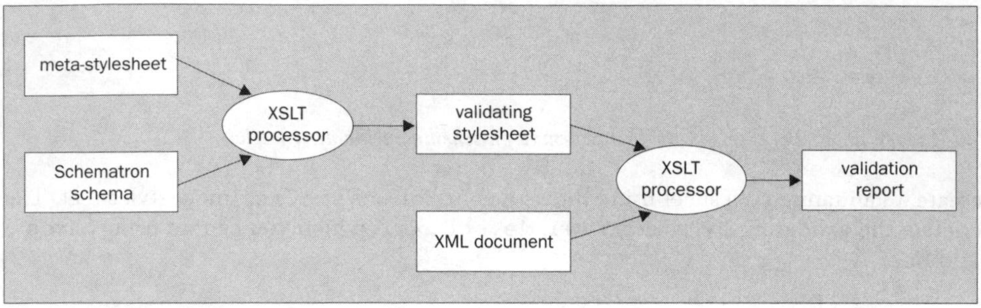

In this section, we'll first look at how to validate documents using Schematron. We'll then see how Schematron schemas are put together and get a quick introduction to some of the elements that are available within Schematron.

Validating with Schematron

The basic way of using Schematron to validate a document is in a two-step process using an XSLT processor: first, you create a validating stylesheet using a meta-stylesheet, and then you use the validating stylesheet to create a validation report. Using Saxon, for example, the command lines would be:

>saxon -o *validator*.xsl *schema*.sch *meta-stylesheet*.xsl

>saxon -o *report.txt document*.xml *validator*.xsl

There are a variety of meta-stylesheets that you can choose from at the Schematron web site at http://www.ascc.net/xml/resource/schematron/. Most of these are built on top of the basic stylesheet `skeleton1_5.xsl`.

You can also validate documents using Schematron with the Topologi Schema Validator, which uses the `schematron-report.xsl` meta-stylesheet to report the results of the validation and can also be used to validate against XML Schema schemas using MSXML4. The Topologi Schema Validators can be downloaded from http://www.topologi.com/.

Try It Out – Validating XML Documents with Schematron

To test out validating with Schematron, we'll use a simple Schematron schema, `TVGuide.sch`, which simply tests that the document element of the XML document is a `<TVGuide>` element:

```
<sch:schema xmlns:sch="http://www.ascc.net/xml/schematron">

<sch:title>TV Guide Schematron Schema</sch:title>

<sch:pattern name="TV Guide Structure">
  <sch:rule context="/">
    <sch:assert test="TVGuide">
      The document element must be a &lt;TVGuide&gt; element.
    </sch:assert>
  </sch:rule>
```

```
</sch:pattern>

</sch:schema>
```

You'll learn about the elements in this Schematron schema in the next section.

We'll create a validating stylesheet using the `schematron-basic.xsl` meta-stylesheet. The first step is to generate the validating stylesheet, `TVGuide.sch.xsl`, which you can do using Saxon with the command line:

>saxon -o TVGuide.sch.xsl TVGuide.sch schematron-basic.xsl

Once you've created `TVGuide.sch.xsl`, take a look at it. It should look something like the following XSLT stylesheet (I've changed the namespace prefix and the indentation so it's more readable):

```
<?xml version="1.0" encoding="utf-8" standalone="yes"?>
<xsl:stylesheet xmlns:xsl="http://www.w3.org/1999/XSL/Transform"
                xmlns:sch="http://www.ascc.net/xml/schematron"
                version="1.0">

<xsl:output method="text"/>

<xsl:template match="*|@*" mode="schematron-get-full-path">
  <xsl:apply-templates select="parent::*" mode="schematron-get-full-path"/>
  <xsl:text>/</xsl:text>
  <xsl:if test="count(. | ../@*) = count(../@*)">@</xsl:if>
  <xsl:value-of select="name()"/>
  <xsl:text>[</xsl:text>
  <xsl:value-of
    select="1+count(preceding-sibling::*[name()=name(current())])"/>
  <xsl:text>]</xsl:text>
</xsl:template>

<xsl:template match="/">
   <xsl:apply-templates select="/" mode="M0"/>
</xsl:template>

<xsl:template match="/" priority="4000" mode="M0">
  <xsl:choose>
    <xsl:when test="TVGuide"/>
    <xsl:otherwise>In pattern TVGuide:
      This schema tests TV Guide documents; the document element must be a
      &lt;TVGuide&gt; element.
    </xsl:otherwise>
  </xsl:choose>
  <xsl:apply-templates mode="M0"/>
</xsl:template>

<xsl:template match="text()" priority="-1" mode="M0"/>
<xsl:template match="text()" priority="-1"/>

</xsl:stylesheet>
```

The highlighted code shows where the rule from the Schematron schema has been translated into an action in the validating stylesheet. The template matches the root node (the context of the Schematron rule) and contains an `<xsl:choose>` that tests whether the root node has a `<TVGuide>` element child. If it does, then the stylesheet does nothing; if it doesn't, the stylesheet prints out the message that was included in the schema.

Try running `TVGuide.sch.xsl` over `TVGuide.xml`; you should get no error messages as a result. Now try running `TVGuide.sch.xsl` over `invalidTVGuide.xml`, which has a `<tvGuide>` document element. You should see the following result:

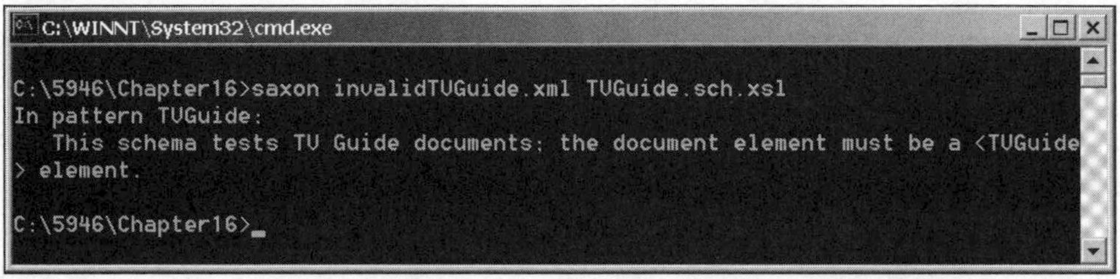

You can get a more sophisticated report if you use the Topologi Schema Validator. Navigate to the directories holding `TVGuide.xml` and `TVGuide.sch`, and highlight them in the Document and Schema selection lists:

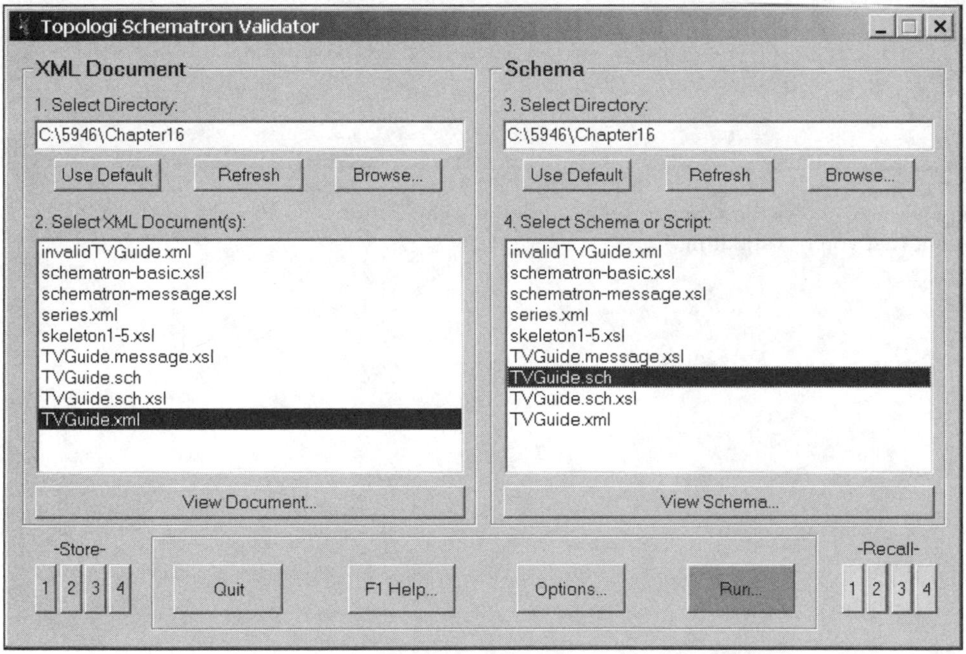

Hit the Run... button, and the following window should appear:

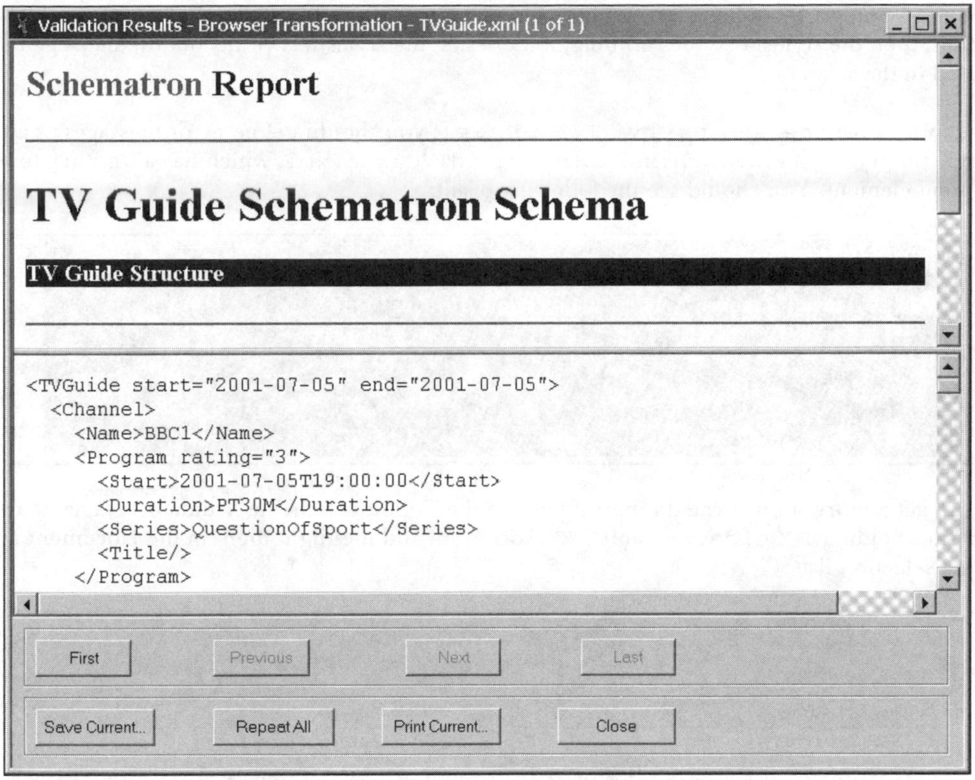

The top window shows the report on the validation. The bottom window shows the XML source of the document that you're validating.

Try validating invalidTVGuide.xml with TVGuide.sch instead. You should see the following report:

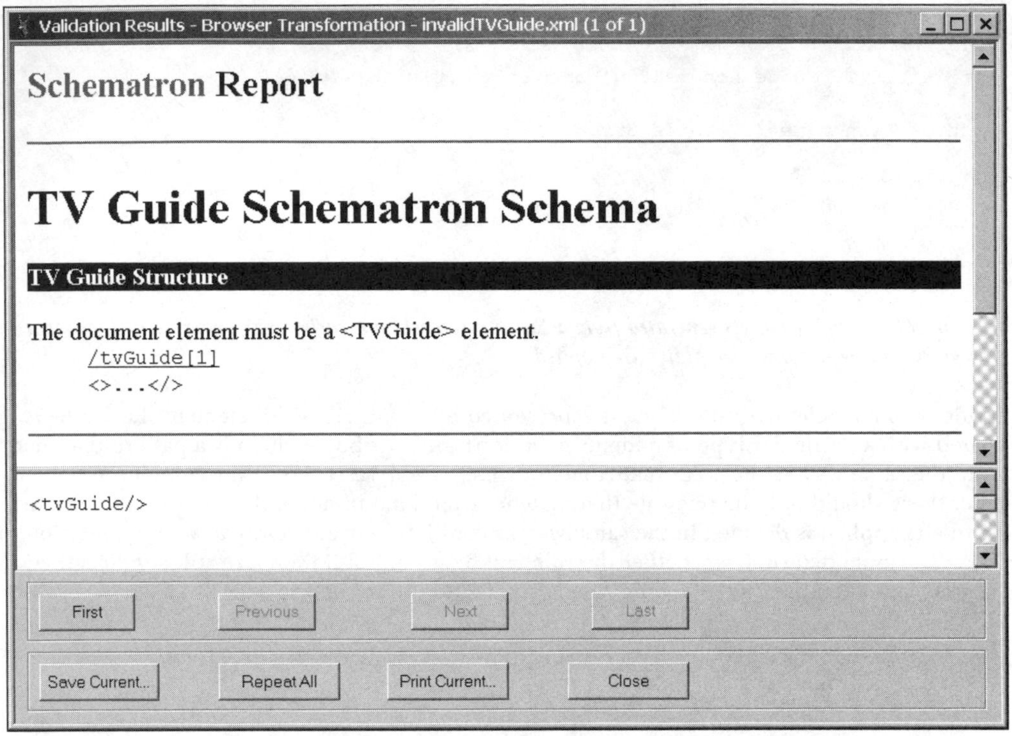

Clicking on the path /tvGuide[1] takes you to the <tvGuide> element that's generated the error; this facility can be useful when viewing a validation report for long documents.

Constructing Schematron Schemas

You've seen in the last section how to validate documents with Schematron schemas. Now we'll turn our attention to constructing those Schematron schemas.

The document element of a Schematron schema is a <sch:schema> element in the namespace http://www.ascc.net/xml/schematron (I'll use the prefix sch to refer to the Schematron namespace throughout the rest of this chapter). The <sch:schema> element contains a <sch:title> element, giving the title of the schema, followed by a number of <sch:pattern> elements, each of which contains a set of rules.

The <sch:pattern> elements each have a name attribute to indicate the kind of checking that the rules contain. For example, you might have one <sch:pattern> element to check the general element structure of the document, and another to check the <Description> elements and their content.

The general structure of a Schematron schema is thus as follows:

```
<sch:schema xmlns:sch="http://www.ascc.net/xml/schematron">

<sch:title>TV Guide Schematron Schema</sch:title>

<sch:pattern name="TV Guide Structure">
  ...
</sch:pattern>
...

</sch:schema>
```

In the validating stylesheets generated from a Schematron schema, each `<sch:pattern>` element becomes a mode in which templates are applied.

Each rule within a Schematron schema is represented by a `<sch:rule>` element. Each rule is associated with a particular type of node using a `context` attribute, which is a pattern that matches nodes in the same way as the `match` attribute of `<xsl:template>`. Within a single `<sch:pattern>` element, there should only be one rule that matches each kind of node; if there's more than one, then which rule is applied is decided in the same way as conflicts between templates – the precision of the `context` attribute determines whether the rule will be used, but if there are still conflicts then the last one is used. For example, the following rule is applied to the root node:

```
<sch:pattern name="TV Guide Structure">
  <sch:rule context="/">
    ...
  </sch:rule>
  ...
</sch:pattern>
```

In the validating stylesheets generated from a Schematron schema, each `<sch:rule>` element becomes an `<xsl:template>` element whose `match` attribute is the same as the value of the `<sch:rule>` element's `context` attribute.

Each rule contains a number of `<sch:assert>` and `<sch:report>` elements, each of which represents a constraint on the context node. Both types of element have a `test` attribute, which holds an XPath test, and have as their content a message. For `<sch:assert>` elements, the message is emitted if the test evaluates as `false`; in other words, they represent positive assertions about how the XML document should be structured. For `<sch:report>` elements, the message is emitted if the test evaluates as `true`; in other words, they represent situations that should be reported to the person validating the document. Which you use is up to you – some constraints are more naturally expressed as positive assertions about the document, while others can be thought of more easily as negative tests. For example, to test whether the document element was a `<TVGuide>` element, you could use:

```
<sch:rule context="/">
  <sch:assert test="TVGuide">...</sch:assert>
  ...
</sch:rule>
```

Or you could use:

```
<sch:rule context="/">
  <sch:report test="not(TVGuide)">...</sch:report>
  ...
</sch:rule>
```

If you find yourself putting a call to the `not()` *function around a test for an assertion or a report, you should probably be using the other one!*

Within the message held by the `<sch:assert>` and `<sch:report>` elements, you can access information about the structure of the document using `<sch:name>` and `<sch:value-of>` elements.

The empty `<sch:name>` element can be used to insert the name of a node. By default, it inserts the name of the node that's currently being tested (the context of the rule), which is particularly useful if the same rule is used for different kinds of elements. Alternatively, you can specify a `path` attribute that should hold an expression that evaluates to a node; the `<sch:name>` element then inserts the name of that element.

The empty `<sch:value-of>` element is just like `<xsl:value-of>` – the `select` attribute is an XPath expression specifying the value that you want to insert within the message.

As an example, here is a rule that tests various aspects of the `<TVGuide>` element:

```
<sch:rule context="TVGuide">
  <sch:report test="parent::*">
    The <sch:name /> element must be the document element in the TV guide
    (currently nested <sch:value-of select="count(ancestor::*)" /> levels).
  </sch:report>
  <sch:assert test="@start and @end">
    The <sch:name /> element must have start and end attributes.
  </sch:assert>
  <sch:assert test="Channel">
    The <sch:name /> element must contain &lt;Channel&gt; elements.
  </sch:assert>
  <sch:report test="*[not(self::Channel)]">
    The <sch:name /> element must not contain any other elements aside from
    &lt;Channel&gt; elements (it shouldn't contain
    <sch:name path="*[not(self::Channel)]" /> elements).
  </sch:report>
</sch:rule>
```

There are other elements available within Schematron for defining phases of validation and providing diagnostic information, but they are outside the scope of this book. To learn more about Schematron, visit the Schematron web site at http://www.ascc.net/xml/schematron/.

Testing XML with XPath

The previous section introduced you to Schematron, a schema language that uses XPath to express constraints on markup languages. This section goes through some of the kinds of constraints that you might want to include within a Schematron schema and how to express them using XPath.

A secondary purpose to this section is to practice using XPath to perform a variety of tasks. The paths in this section aren't just useful for validating; they're also handy if you need to test elements or attributes for other reasons. For example, you may need to generate different output depending on the structure or content of the XML document.

Checking the Document Element

We've already seen the first check that we can make using a Schematron schema: seeing whether the name of the document element, the top-most element in the source document, is the kind of element we expect it to be. In our example, we expect the document element of `TVGuide.xml` to be a `<TVGuide>` element.

There are a few ways that you can check the document element. The most obvious method is to use the `name()` function to give you the name of the document element as a string, and to match that name to the name that we expect. For example, to check whether the name of the document element is `'TVGuide'` as expected, you could use:

```
<sch:rule context="/">
  <sch:assert test="name(*) = 'TVGuide'">
    The document element must be a &lt;TVGuide&gt; element.
  </sch:assert>
</sch:rule>
```

However, you should be a little careful of using the `name()` function in this context, because the `name()` function gives you the name used in the source document, including the prefix that was declared for the element's namespace. The above test, for example, would return `true` even if the `<TVGuide>` element was in a particular namespace (as long as that namespace was the default namespace), whereas we expect the `<TVGuide>` element to be in no namespace.

A better test, therefore, is a path that tries to select the `<TVGuide>` document element. If it finds a `<TVGuide>` document element, then the node set returned by the path has a node in it and, when interpreted as a boolean, is `true`. If the XSLT processor doesn't find a `<TVGuide>` document element then the node set returned by the path is empty and, when interpreted as a boolean, is `false`. To test whether the document element is a `<TVGuide>` element, therefore, you can use the following:

```
<sch:rule context="/">
  <sch:assert test="TVGuide">
    The document element must be a &lt;TVGuide&gt; element.
  </sch:assert>
</sch:rule>
```

The reverse of this test is a check that confirms whether the element that we want to be the document element has a parent:

```
<sch:rule context="TVGuide">
  <sch:report test="parent::*">
    The <sch:name /> element must be the document element.
  </sch:report>
</sch:rule>
```

This kind of reverse test is sometimes helpful in Schematron; unlike other schema languages it can be hard to articulate constraints about the children of a node. On the other hand, it's easy to test whether a node appears in a legal context by matching that node and looking at its ancestors.

Checking Element Content

There are lots of different kinds of constraints that you can place on element content. In this section, we'll look at the types of element content that you might have in a document and how to test for them using XPaths.

Checking Empty Elements

You might think that empty elements are pretty simple. However, there are different interpretations of the word 'empty' that you might use, and the kind of 'empty' that you mean determines the test that you need to carry out.

No Contents

The basic type of empty element is an element that contains nothing whatsoever. These elements have no child nodes. Assuming that the current rule's context is the element that you want to test, you can check whether an element has a child node using the test:

```
<sch:report test="node()">
  <sch:name /> should not have any content.
</sch:report>
```

If the element contains any children at all, then the message will be shown. For example, the following elements would count as empty elements:

```
<Picture />
<Picture></Picture>
```

whereas the following elements would not count as empty elements:

```
<Picture>Null</Picture>
<Picture><Null /></Picture>
<Picture><Value>Null</Value></Picture>
<Picture><!-- No Picture --></Picture>
<Picture>
</Picture>
```

Whitespace-only text nodes are not stripped from XML documents prior to validation using Schematron. If they were then the line break in the last of the above examples would be excluded, and it would count as an empty element.

No Child Element or Text Content

A second form of empty element is an element that does not contain any child elements or any text, but may contain comments or processing instructions. You can test whether an element contains child elements or text with the following assertion:

```
<sch:report test="* or text()">
  <sch:name /> should not contain anything aside from comments
  or processing instructions.
</sch:report>
```

If the element contains any elements or text nodes, then this evaluates as `true`; otherwise it evaluates as `false`. For example, the following elements would count as empty elements:

```
<Picture />
<Picture></Picture>
<Picture><!-- No Picture --></Picture>
```

whereas the following elements would not count as empty elements:

```
<Picture>Null</Picture>
<Picture><Null /></Picture>
<Picture><Value>Null</Value></Picture>
<Picture>
</Picture>
```

No String Value

A third type of empty element is an element that doesn't have a string value – that contains no text content, and that contains no child elements that themselves have text content. You can test whether an element has a string value with the following expression:

```
<sch:report test="string()">
  <sch:name /> should not have a value.
</sch:report>
```

If the string value of the element contains any characters, then this evaluates as `true`; otherwise it evaluates as `false`. Taking the same elements as before, this time the following count as empty elements:

```
<Picture />
<Picture></Picture>
<Picture><!-- No Picture --></Picture>
<Picture><Null /></Picture>
```

whereas the following elements would not count as empty elements:

```
<Picture>Null</Picture>
<Picture><Value>Null</Value></Picture>
<Picture>
</Picture>
```

Checking Elements with Text Content

There are two aspects to checking elements with text content – checking whether the element only contains text, and checking whether that text is in the expected format. We'll come on to validating string values later in this chapter, and here concentrate on the first type of check, on the type of the element's contents.

Under the strictest interpretation of the meaning of elements with text content, the only nodes allowed within the element should be text nodes. You can check whether an element contains any other kinds of nodes with the following test:

```
<sch:report test="* or comment() or processing-instruction()">
  <sch:name /> should contain only text nodes.
</sch:report>
```

Like empty elements, you may want to allow an element that "contains only text" to contain comments and processing instructions as well, such that in fact the only things that aren't allowed in one of these elements are element nodes. The test that checks whether the element contains any elements is simply:

```
<sch:report test="*">
  <sch:name /> should not contain elements.
</sch:report>
```

Checking Elements with Element Content

The expected content of elements with element content is easy to express in DTDs, and fairly straight forward in XML Schema. In both schema languages, you can use model groups to express the expected content of the element: a sequence of a particular set of elements, a choice between this pair, this element repeated a certain number of times, and so on.

While Schematron gives you a lot of flexibility about the information that you test for in element structures, it's not designed to make testing for model groups particularly straightforward. In fact, it is far easier to test content where elements can occur in any order (which isn't something you can do in DTDs, and can only be done in certain circumstances in XML Schema) than it is to test whether elements occur in a particular order.

In the rest of this section, we'll look at how to test various aspects of content models. Naturally, these tests can be joined together with `and` and `or` and `not()` to check combinations of tests.

Testing Element-Only Content

Elements that only contain other elements should not have any significant content aside from those elements. In particular, they should not contain text nodes unless those text nodes consist purely of whitespace characters.

As mentioned before, Schematron does not automatically strip whitespace-only text nodes from documents prior to validation. Therefore, an element may contain text nodes perfectly innocently, those text nodes being used to indent the XML and make it easier to read. In this case, the only text nodes that make the element invalid are those that contain characters other than whitespace. You can test the text nodes that the element contains using the `normalize-space()` function – if the `normalize-space()` function returns a string with any characters in it, then the text node contains non-whitespace characters.

The test for text content when whitespace-only text nodes have not been stripped from the source tree is therefore:

```
<sch:report test="text()[normalize-space()]">
  <sch:name /> should not contain text (unless it's whitespace).
</sch:report>
```

Testing Element Presence and Repetition

You can test whether an element has a child element by trying to select that child element with a path. If you manage to select a child element of that name, then the child element exists; if you don't manage to select a child element, then it doesn't. For example, to check that the current `<Channel>` element has a `<Name>` element child, you can use:

```
<sch:rule context="Channel">
  <sch:assert test="Name">
    <sch:name /> should have a &lt;Name&gt; element as a child.
  </sch:assert>
</sch:rule>
```

The message is shown if the `<Channel>` element does not have a `<Name>` element child.

To test how many child elements of a particular type there are, you can use the `count()` function to count them. For example, to test that there are less than 300 `<Program>` elements within the current `<Channel>` element, you could use:

```
<sch:rule context="Channel">
  <sch:assert test="Name">
    <sch:name /> should have a &lt;Name&gt; element as a child.
  </sch:assert>
  <sch:assert test="count(Program) &lt; 300">
    <sch:name /> should contain less than 300 &lt;Program&gt; elements.
  </sch:assert>
</sch:rule>
```

You can also perform the equivalent of this test by reporting channels that have a 300th `<Program>` element:

```
<sch:rule context="Channel">
  <sch:assert test="Name">
    <sch:name /> should have a &lt;Name&gt; element as a child.
  </sch:assert>
  <sch:report test="Program[300]">
```

```
      <sch:name /> should contain less than 300 &lt;Program&gt; elements.
    </sch:report>
  </sch:rule>
```

This latter method can be more efficient in processors that don't optimize expressions involving the `count()` *function.*

Testing for Other Elements

As well as checking whether an element *does* contain the elements that it *should* contain, you often need to check whether an element *doesn't* contain any elements that it *shouldn't* contain. For example, the `<Channel>` element should only have two kinds of children: a `<Name>` element and any number of `<Program>` elements. No other elements should be present within the `<Channel>` element.

You can test whether an element contains elements other than the ones you expect by trying to select elements other than the ones you expect. Select all the element children:

```
*
```

And then filter that set of elements so that you don't include those that you expect the element to contain. In this example, the `<Channel>` element should have `<Name>` and `<Program>` children. You can test the identity of the elements you've selected using the `self::` axis.

Testing using the `self::` *axis is more robust than using the* `name()` *function because it deals properly with namespaces.*

To select elements that are neither `<Name>` nor `<Program>` elements, for example, you could use:

```
*[not(self::Name or self::Program)]
```

Within a Schematron rule, this would be:

```
<sch:rule context="Channel">
  <sch:assert test="Name">
    <sch:name /> should have a &lt;Name&gt; element as a child.
  </sch:assert>
  <sch:assert test="count(Program) &lt; 300">
    <sch:name /> should contain less than 300 &lt;Program&gt; elements.
  </sch:assert>
  <sch:report test="*[not(self::Name or self::Program)]">
    <sch:name /> should not contain elements other than &lt;Name&gt; and
    &lt;Program&gt; elements.
  </sch:report>
</sch:rule>
```

One type of "other element" that you may want to permit is "other elements" that do not belong to the same namespace as the elements you expect. Allowing elements from other namespaces within your XML documents makes the markup language more extensible. You might make a particular element a holder for elements from other namespaces, or allow elements from other namespaces anywhere within the document; either way, this allows your markup language to be tailored by other people to their particular requirements.

In our example, most of the elements in the TV Guide are in no namespace. To allow elements from other namespaces, we need to tighten the test so that it doesn't return `true` if the element that it's selected is in any namespace. You can test the namespace of an element using the `namespace-uri()` function; if it returns a string, then the element is in a namespace, if it doesn't then it is not. To locate elements from any namespace (but not from no namespace, aside from <Name> and <Channel> elements), you could use the following report:

```
<sch:report test="*[namespace-uri() or not(self::Name or self::Program)]">
  <sch:name /> should not contain elements other than &lt;Name&gt; and
  &lt;Program&gt; elements, unless they're in another namespace.
</sch:report>
```

If we were using a namespace for the TV Guide, and that namespace were associated with the `tv` prefix, we could use an alternative test. We can select all the elements in the TV Guide namespace, ignoring those that are not, with the path:

```
tv::*
```

This would return a node set containing any elements from the TV Guide namespace. In the <tv:Channel> element, we want to allow <tv:Name> and <tv:Program> elements, so the only elements in the TV Guide namespace that we're interested in and want to test for are those that are not <tv:Name> or <tv:Program> elements. The test is therefore:

```
<sch:report test="tv:*[not(self::tv:Name or self::tv:Program)]">
  <sch:name /> should not contain elements in the TV Guide namespace other
  than &lt;Name&gt; and &lt;Program&gt; elements.
</sch:report>
```

Testing Element Sequences

DTDs and XML Schemas are particularly good at making sure that elements occur in the order that they should do. Testing the same thing with Schematron is more troublesome. You can test whether the first element child of the current element is not what you expect it to be with a path that selects the first element child only if it is of the expected type. For example, to test whether the first element child of the current <Program> element is a <Start> element, you could use:

```
<sch:rule context="Program">
  <sch:assert test="*[1][self::Start]">
    The first child of the <sch:name /> element should be a &lt;Start&gt;
    element.
  </sch:assert>
</sch:rule>
```

The next child of the <Program> element should be a <Duration> element. You can test whether the second child of the <Program> element is a <Duration> element in several ways. Firstly, you can use the same kind of construction as that used to test the first child of the <Program> element:

```
<sch:rule context="Program">
  <sch:assert test="*[1][self::Start]">
```

```
      The first child of the <sch:name /> element should be a &lt;Start&gt;
      element.
    </sch:assert>
    <sch:assert test="*[2][self::Duration]">
      The second child of the <sch:name /> element should be a
      &lt;Duration&gt; element.
    </sch:assert>
  </sch:rule>
```

Using this test, you would generate an error if the <Program> element was as follows:

```
<Program>
  <Series>EastEnders</Series>
  <Start>2001-12-12T19:30:00</Start>
  <Duration>PT30M</Duration>
  ...
</Program>
```

Alternatively, since you know that the first child element is a <Start> element from the initial test that you performed, you could just test whether the immediately following sibling of the <Start> element is a <Duration> element:

```
<sch:rule context="Program">
  <sch:assert test="*[1][self::Start]">
    The first child of the <sch:name /> element should be a &lt;Start&gt;
    element.
  </sch:assert>
  <sch:assert test="Start/following-sibling::*[1][self::Duration]">
    The element after the &lt;Start&gt; element should be a
    &lt;Duration&gt; element.
  </sch:assert>
</sch:rule>
```

Technically, this checks that if the <Start> element has a following sibling, then it's a <Duration> element, which means that the following <Program> element would return `false` from this test:

```
<Program>
  <Start>2001-12-12T19:30:00</Start>
</Program>
```

Another alternative is looking at the <Duration> element and checking that its preceding sibling is a <Start> element:

```
<sch:rule context="Program">
  <sch:assert test="*[1][self::Start]">
    The first child of the <sch:name /> element should be a &lt;Start&gt;
    element.
  </sch:assert>
  <sch:assert test="Duration/preceding-sibling::*[1][self::Start]">
```

```
      The element before the &lt;Duration&gt; element should be a
      &lt;Start&gt; element.
    </sch:assert>
  </sch:rule>
```

Again, this path will only return a node (and hence evaluate as `true`) if the `<Duration>` element has a preceding sibling and it is a `<Start>` element.

Testing the preceding and following siblings is useful if the sequence of elements that you're testing contains optional elements. For example, the `<Program>` element has an optional `<CastList>` element child, which if it occurs should come after the `<Description>` element. The optional `<CastList>` may be followed by an optional `<Writers>` element. You can test that if the `<CastList>` element is there, it follows a `<Description>` element with:

```
  <sch:rule context="Program">
    ...
    <sch:assert test="CastList/preceding-sibling::*[1][self::Description]">
      The element before the &lt;CastList&gt; element should be a
      &lt;Description&gt; element.
    <sch:assert>
  </sch:rule>
```

And you can test whether the `<Writers>` element, if it's there, follows either the `<Description>` or the `<CastList>` element with:

```
  <sch:rule context="Program">
    ...
    <sch:assert test="CastList/preceding-sibling::*[1][self::Description]">
      The element before the &lt;CastList&gt; element should be a
      &lt;Description&gt; element.
    <sch:assert>
    <sch:assert test="Writers/preceding-sibling::*[1]
                          [self::Description or self::CastList]">
      The element before the &lt;Writers&gt; element should be either a
      &lt;Description&gt; element or a &lt;CastList&gt; element.
    </sch:assert>
  </sch:rule>
```

Testing Element Choices

Often a model will allow either one of two elements. For example, in `TVGuide.xml`, the `<Program>` element can either contain a `<Writers>` element or a `<Writer>` element, depending on whether there are several writers or only one for a particular program.

To check that the `<Program>` element does not contain both a `<Writers>` and a `<Writer>` element, you can use the following:

```
  <sch:rule context="Program">
    <sch:report test="Writers and Writer">
      <sch:name /> should not contain both a &lt;Writers&gt; and a
```

```
      &lt;Writer&gt; element.
    </sch:report>
  </sch:rule>
```

You may also wish to make sure that at least one of these elements is present. You can use a separate test for this:

```
  <sch:rule context="Program">
    <sch:report test="Writers and Writer">
      <sch:name /> should not contain both a &lt;Writers&gt; and a
      &lt;Writer&gt; element.
    </sch:report>
    <sch:assert test="Writers or Writer">
      <sch:name /> should contain either a &lt;Writers&gt; or a &lt;Writer&gt;
      element.
    </sch:assert>
  </sch:rule>
```

This will return `true` if there is either a <Writers> element or a <Writer> element within the current <Program>. Of course, you can join the two tests together to check that one or the other is present, but not both, as follows:

```
  <sch:rule context="Program">
    <sch:assert test="Writers or Writer and not(Writers and Writer)">
      <sch:name /> should contain either a &lt;Writers&gt; or a &lt;Writer&gt;
      element, but not both.
    </sch:assert>
  </sch:rule>
```

Testing Contiguity of Child Elements

A final kind of check that you might wish to make on the content of an element is that elements of the same type within its content are grouped together. For example, even if you wanted to allow the <Channel> element's <Name> element to appear before or after the channel's programs, you may not want to allow it to occur in the middle of the <Program> elements.

You can check that all the elements with a particular name occur contiguously by looking at each element's preceding siblings. If the elements are contiguous, then there should only be a maximum of one instance of that element that doesn't have a preceding sibling or whose preceding sibling is something different – for example, there should only be one <Program> element whose preceding sibling is not a <Program> element. If you manage to find two, then the element is invalid.

Given a <Program> element, you can get hold of its immediately preceding sibling element with the path:

```
  preceding-sibling::*[1]
```

You can check whether the immediately preceding sibling is a <Program> element as follows:

```
  preceding-sibling::*[1][self::Program]
```

Thus, you can find <Program> elements that don't have a preceding sibling or whose preceding sibling is a <Program> element with the following:

```
Program[not(preceding-sibling::*[1]) or
        preceding-sibling::*[1][self::Program]]
```

You can try to select a second of these <Program> elements by adding a positional predicate; if this path manages to select a <Program> element then the <Program> elements are not contiguous:

```
<sch:rule context="Channel">
  <sch:report
    test="Program[not(preceding-sibling::*[1]) or
                  preceding-sibling::*[1][not(self::Program)]][2]">
    All the &lt;Program&gt; element children of <sch:name /> should be next
    to each other.
  </sch:report>
</sch:rule>
```

Another method of going about the same test is to count how many <Program> elements there are whose immediately preceding sibling is a <Program> element and compare this to the number of <Program> elements overall. The number of <Program> elements overall should be one more than the number of <Program> elements with a <Program> element preceding sibling. You can therefore use the following test, which returns `true` if the <Program> elements are contiguous:

```
<sch:rule context="Channel">
  <sch:assert
    test="count(Program[preceding-sibling::*[1][self::Program]]) + 1 =
          count(Program)">
    All the &lt;Program&gt; element children of <sch:name /> should be next
    to each other.
  </sch:assert>
</sch:rule>
```

A final method that you could use in this case is to see whether the <Name> element child of the <Channel> element has <Program> elements both before and after it:

```
<sch:rule context="Channel">
  <sch:report test="Name/preceding-sibling::Program and
                    Name/following-sibling::Program">
    The &lt;Name&gt; element should not appear in the middle of the
    &lt;Program&gt; elements.
  </sch:report>
</sch:rule>
```

Checking Attributes

Aside from checking the values of attributes, which we'll come on to in the next section, the other important aspect of attributes that you might want to check is whether the attribute is present or not. In particular, some attributes are mandatory whereas others are optional.

Checking the presence of attributes using XPath is very similar to checking whether an element has particular child elements – if you can select the attribute, then it's there; if you can't, then it's missing. For example, the start and end attributes on the <TVGuide> element are required, and a message should be generated if they are missing. You can check whether the start attribute is missing using the rule:

```
<sch:rule context="TVGuide">
  <sch:assert test="@start">
    <sch:name /> should have a &lt;start&gt; attribute.
  </sch:assert>
</sch:rule>
```

Also like child elements, you probably want to check that the element does not have attributes that it shouldn't have. Performing this test is a bit more difficult with attributes than it is with elements, unfortunately, because you can't use the self:: axis to test the identity of attributes. In most cases, you can use the name() function to locate attributes aside from those you expect because, mostly, attributes have no namespace. For example, to select all attributes aside from the start and end attributes, you could use:

```
@*[not(name() = 'start' or name() = 'end')]
```

In the following, the message is displayed if the element has any attributes other than the start and end attributes:

```
<sch:rule context="TVGuide">
  <sch:report test="@*[not(name() = 'start' or name() = 'end')]">
    <sch:name /> should not have attributes other than start and end
    attributes.
  </sch:report>
</sch:rule>
```

To also allow the <TVGuide> element to have an xlink:href attribute (where xlink is associated with the namespace http://www.w3.org/1999/xlink), you need to check the namespace and local name of the attributes that you select as well:

```
<sch:rule context="TVGuide">
  <sch:report
    test="@*[not(name() = 'start' or name() = 'end') and
             not(local-name() = 'href' and
                 namespace-uri() = 'http://www.w3.org/1999/xlink')]">
    <sch:name /> should not have attributes other than start, end and
    xlink:href attributes.
  </sch:report>
</sch:rule>
```

Similarly, if you want to allow the <TVGuide> element to have any attribute in the XLink namespace, you could use:

```
<sch:rule context="TVGuide">
  <sch:report
```

```
    test="@*[not(name() = 'start' or name() = 'end') and
              not(namespace-uri() = 'http://www.w3.org/1999/xlink')]">
    <sch:name /> should not have attributes other than start, end and
    attributes in the XLink namespace.
  </sch:report>
</sch:rule>
```

To allow any attribute as long as it is not in no namespace (in other words, create a message if you find any attributes in no namespace, aside from `start` and `end` attributes), you can use:

```
<sch:rule context="TVGuide">
  <sch:report test="@*[not(name() = 'start' or name() = 'end') and
                      not(namespace-uri())]">
    <sch:name /> should not have attributes other than start, end and
    attributes in the XLink namespace.
  </sch:report>
</sch:rule>
```

Validating String Values

The string values of attributes and text-only elements can be treated in the same way. Unlike XML Schema, or even DTDs, XPath (and hence Schematron) really only natively recognizes two types of data: numbers and strings. However, the functions and operators supported by XPath mean that you can test a greater range of values within a Schematron schema.

There are string formats that XPath does have problems with, for example, splitting up a string of arbitrary length at spaces and testing each value within the space-delimited list. Checking these kinds of values requires a separate language, such as XSLT.

Ignoring Whitespace

The first decision to make when testing the value of an element or an attribute is whether whitespace around the value of the element or attribute should count as part of the value of the element or attribute. For example, given that the `<Duration>` element must contain a date/time in ISO 8601 format, should the following be allowed?

```
<Duration>
  2001-12-12T19:30:00
</Duration>
```

Usually, whitespace around a value can be safely ignored: it's only there to make the source document easier to read. Therefore, you need to test the normalized string value of the element or attribute rather than the actual string value. You can get the normalized string value of an element or attribute with the `normalize-space()` function.

Testing Enumerated Values

One of the simplest types of data that an element or attribute can hold is an enumerated value, where the value of the element or attribute must be one of a particular set of values. An example of an enumerated value is a boolean value: `true/false`, `1/0`, or `yes/no`.

You can test whether an element or attribute has one of these values simply by testing whether the normalized value of the element or attribute (assuming that you want to ignore leading and trailing whitespace) is equal to the allowed values. If it isn't, then you need to create an error. Given that the element or attribute is the context of the surrounding rule, you can use the following to test whether the value is one of `true`, `false`, `0`, or `1`, for example:

```
<sch:assert test="normalize-space() = 'true' or normalize-space() = 'false'
                  or normalize-space() = '0' or normalize-space() = '1'">
  <sch:name /> should have the value 'true', 'false', '1' or '0' (after
  whitespace normalization).
</sch:assert>
```

You have to be a little bit careful when using XPath to test enumerated values to make sure that you are allowing values that might not be precisely the strings that you are checking against. For example, you might want to test the value of an element or attribute case-insensitively. In that case, you need to use the `translate()` function to make sure that the value that you're testing uses the same case as the strings against which you're testing. To allow `True`, `TRUE`, `tRUe`, `False`, `FALSE`, `FAlsE`, and so on, you need the following:

```
<sch:assert test="translate(normalize-space(), 'FALSE', 'false') = 'false'
                 or translate(normalize-space(), 'TRUE', 'true') = 'true '
                 or normalize-space() = '0' or normalize-space() = '1'">
  <sch:name /> should have the value 'true', 'false', '1' or '0' (after
  whitespace normalization, and case insensitively).
</sch:assert>
```

The same kind of thing applies to numeric values. If you want to allow elements or attributes to hold numeric values and don't care about leading or trailing zeros, then you should convert the value to a number before testing it – the conversion to a number automatically strips leading and trailing whitespace:

```
<sch:assert test="translate(normalize-space(), 'FALSE', 'false') = 'false'
                 or translate(normalize-space(), 'TRUE', 'true') = 'true'
                 or number() = 0 or number() = 1">
  After whitespace normalization, <sch:name /> should have the value 'true'
  or 'false' (case insensitively), or the numeric value 1 or 0.
</sch:assert>
```

Testing String Data

Schema languages such as XML Schema highlight two important aspects of string data: the length of the string and the format of that string. These properties of string data can be tested using Schematron as well.

Testing the Length of a String

You can use the `string-length()` function to test the length of a string. For example, to make sure that the context element or attribute's value is between 2 and 32, you could use:

```
<sch:assert test="string-length() >= 2 and 32 >= string-length()">
  <sch:name />'s value should be between 2 and 32 characters long
  (inclusive).
</sch:assert>
```

To make sure that the length of the value of the context element or attribute is exactly 16 characters, you could use:

```
<sch:assert test="string-length() = 16">
  <sch:name />'s value should be 16 characters long.
</sch:assert>
```

The `string-length()` function with no arguments returns the length of the string value of the current node, including whitespace. If you want to ignore leading and trailing whitespace when assessing the length of the string, you should use `string-length(normalize-space())`.

There is one special case of testing the length of a string where you don't have to use the `string-length()` function, and that's to test that the string contains at least one character (with no upper limit). To test this, you can simply see whether the string value is equal to the empty string:

```
<sch:assert test="string() != ''">
  <sch:name />'s string value should not be empty.
</sch:assert>
```

Or you can use the fact that when a string is interpreted as a boolean, it is `true` if the string contains characters, and `false` otherwise:

```
<sch:assert test="string()">
  <sch:name />'s should have a string value.
</sch:assert>
```

Testing the Format of a String

The usual method of testing the format of a string, with most languages, is to use a regular expression. Unfortunately, XPath 1.0 does not support any regular expressions, so to test the format of a string you need to make imaginative use of the `substring()`, `substring-before()`, and `substring-after()` functions to break up the string.

The major restrictions on the types of tests that you can carry out are firstly that there are no automatic methods of changing the case of characters (aside from with the `translate()` function) and second that it's impossible to test whether characters are within certain character ranges. It's likely that XPath 2.0 will provide regular expression support as well as methods for changing the case of strings and comparing characters.

For fixed format strings, such as dates, you can use the `substring()` function to break apart the date into its component parts, which you can then test individually if you need to. You can test that a date is in ISO 8601 format, for example, by first making sure that the first four characters are a valid integer:

```
substring(., 1, 4) = floor(substring(., 1, 4))
```

Then, testing whether the sixth and seventh characters make up an integer between 1 and 12, we can use:

```
substring(., 1, 4) = floor(substring(., 1, 4)) and
substring(., 6, 2) = floor(substring(., 6, 2)) and
substring(., 6, 2) >= 1 and 12 >= substring(., 6, 2)
```

The third step is testing whether the ninth and tenth characters are an integer between 1 and 31:

```
substring(., 1, 4) = floor(substring(., 1, 4)) and
substring(., 6, 2) = floor(substring(., 6, 2)) and
substring(., 6, 2) >= 1 and 12 >= substring(., 6, 2) and
substring(., 9, 2) = floor(substring(., 9, 2)) and
substring(., 9, 2) >= 1 and 31 >= substring(., 9, 2)
```

Note that this test does not take account of shorter months or leap years.

Finally, you need to make sure that the fifth and eighth characters are hyphens:

```
substring(., 1, 4) = floor(substring(., 1, 4)) and
substring(., 6, 2) = floor(substring(., 6, 2)) and
substring(., 6, 2) >= 1 and 12 >= substring(., 6, 2) and
substring(., 9, 2) = floor(substring(., 9, 2)) and
substring(., 9, 2) >= 1 and 31 >= substring(., 9, 2) and
substring(., 5, 1) = '-' and substring(., 8, 1) = '-'
```

The rule to test whether the `start` and `end` attributes of the `<TVGuide>` element are dates would therefore look like the following:

```
<sch:rule context="@start | @end">
  <sch:assert
    test="substring(., 1, 4) = floor(substring(., 1, 4)) and
          substring(., 6, 2) = floor(substring(., 6, 2)) and
          substring(., 6, 2) >= 1 and 12 >= substring(., 6, 2) and
          substring(., 9, 2) = floor(substring(., 9, 2)) and
          substring(., 9, 2) >= 1 and 31 >= substring(., 9, 2) and
          substring(., 5, 1) = '-' and substring(., 8, 1) = '-'">
    <sch:name /> should be a date in the format YYYY-MM-DD.
  </sch:assert>
</sch:rule>
```

Flexible-format strings follow the same kind of pattern, except that the `substring-before()` and `substring-after()` functions are more important. As you can see, these tests can get very involved, particularly when the format of one component of the string is dependent on the format of another component.

The fact that XPath does not support a wide range of data types means that most data types need to be treated as strings when it comes to manipulating and validating them. The dates, durations, qualified names, URIs, and so on that you use in your XML document may each have their own constraints over and above those placed on their format. For example, durations in the TV Guide must be between 5 minutes and 24 hours; you cannot test this using the normal less-than operator, but instead must perform the comparison manually.

> *XPath 2.0 will support the same range of data types as XML Schema, as well as extending the set of comparisons and functions to deal with those data types.*

Testing Numerical Data

There are two aspects to testing numerical data: testing that it is in a numerical format and testing that it falls within particular limits. It is easy to test whether a number falls within a particular range using the less-than and greater-than operators, but it is sometimes harder to get at the number itself.

Numeric strings can only be converted to numbers in XPath 1.0 if they contain just digits and an optional decimal point. Strings in other formats – including those containing commas (which you might use for grouping separators), currency signs, `E` or `e` (which you might use in scientific notation), and so on – are all interpreted as `NaN` (Not a Number).

In most cases, numbers in XML documents follow the numeric format recognized by XPath, and you can test that the context element or attribute is a number using:

```
<sch:assert test="number() = number()">
  <sch:name /> should be a number.
</sch:assert>
```

This test works because `NaN` is unique amongst numeric values in that it does not equal itself – if the result of converting the value of the current node to a number is `NaN`, then the test returns false; otherwise, the numerical value is equal to the numerical value, and the test returns true.

If you wish to allow other characters within the numerical format, you can break apart the string value of the current element or attribute using the string manipulation functions, and calculate the number based on that. For example, if you wish to use numeric values in scientific notation, with an exponent, then you need to break apart the string at the `E` or `e`, and multiply the mantissa (the number before the `E` or `e`) by ten to the power of the exponent (the number after the `E` or `e`, removing the leading plus sign which XPath does not allow).

Validating Co-occurrence Constraints

As you've seen, Schematron is not particularly good at validating individual values from a range of data types, nor is it very hot on testing model groups. However, when you start looking at what are known as **co-occurrence constraints**, Schematron really comes into its own.

Co-occurrence constraints are constraints within a markup language where the value of or presence of one element or attribute affects the value of or presence of another element or attribute. Co-occurrence constraints often occur when a particular element is overloaded, with attributes determining its precise behavior. Strangely enough, XML Schema (which doesn't itself support validation of co-occurrence constraints) is a good source of examples of co-occurrence constraints:

- An <xs:attribute> element can either have a type attribute or have an <xs:simpleType> element child, but not both (attribute presence constrains element presence)
- An <xs:element> element can either have a default attribute or have a fixed attribute, but not both (attribute presence constrains attribute presence)
- If the use attribute has the value prohibited or required, then there must not be a default or fixed attribute (attribute value constrains attribute presence)
- The value of the minOccurs attribute must be less than the value of the maxOccurs attribute (attribute value constrains attribute value)

In other languages, the value of an attribute may constrain the presence of or value of a child element. These effects can cover many levels within the source tree (with grandparents constraining their grandchildren, for example). They can also affect various aspects of attribute values – their format or type, their actual value, the range in which the value falls, and so on.

As a language, XPath is flexible enough to deal with these constraints fairly easily, partly because it does not make any great distinction between attributes and elements and partly because it can extract values from all over the source tree. A rule that states that <attribute> elements should not have a type attribute as well as a simpleType child could be expressed as:

```
<sch:rule context="xs:attribute">
  <sch:report test="@type and xs:simpleType">
    <sch:name /> should not have a type attribute and a simpleType element
    child.
  </sch:report>
</sch:rule>
```

To test that there is no default or fixed attribute when the use attribute is prohibited or required, you could use:

```
<sch:rule context="xs:attribute">
  <sch:report test="@type and xs:simpleType">
    <sch:name /> should not have a type attribute and a simpleType element
    child.
  </sch:report>
  <sch:report test="(@use = 'prohibited' or @use = 'required') and
                    (@default or @fixed)">
    If its use attribute has the value 'prohibited' or 'required',
    <sch:name /> should not have a default or fixed attribute.
  </sch:report>
</sch:rule>
```

And to test that an <xs:element>'s minOccurs attribute is less than or equal to its maxOccurs attribute, you could use:

```
<sch:rule context="xs:element">
  <sch:assert test="@minOccurs &lt;= @maxOccurs">
    <sch:name />'s minOccurs attribute must have a value that's less than
or equal to its maxOccurs attribute.
```

```
    </sch:assert>
  </sch:rule>
```

Validating IDs and References

The final level of validation that Schematron offers through XSLT and XPath is the validation of IDs and references. When testing IDs, or what XML Schema calls identity constraints, the important factor is whether all the elements of a given type have distinct identities (based on some combination of element and attribute values). When testing references, you need to make sure that each reference actually refers to some element within a particular document.

Generating Identifiers

The simplest identifier of an element, used with DTDs, is an ID attribute. However, more complex identifiers can be made up of many components, including attributes, child elements, attributes on parent elements, and so on.

The first stage in testing identifiers is to construct the identifier that you want to test. With single-component identifiers, this is easy (since it is just the value of the component), but it is more complex if the identifier is made up of several components – in this case, you can construct the composite identifier with the `concat()` function.

When constructing an identifier from several components using the `concat()` function, you should separate each component from the previous one with a character or series of characters that cannot occur within the first component. For example, to construct an identifier for each `<Program>` element, you could use the `<Start>` child of the `<Program>` element combined with its parent `<Channel>`'s `<Name>` child element. You know that the `<Start>` element cannot contain the string `' on '`, for example, so you could use this as the separator when constructing the identifier for the `<Program>`:

```
concat(Start, ' on ', parent::Channel/Name)
```

For example, in the following snippet of XML, the `<Program>` will have an identifier of `'2001-12-24T21:00:00 on BBC1'`:

```
<Channel>
  <Name>BBC1</Name>
  <Program>
    <Start>2001-12-24T21:00:00</Start>
    ...
  </Program>
</Channel>
```

Testing Uniqueness

If an element has an identifier, you can construct a key that enables you to access that element through the identifier later on. Schematron allows you to assert keys in roughly the same way as you do in XSLT (which you saw in Chapter 10). In Schematron, keys are defined using a `<sch:key>` element within a rule. The rule's context indicates the things that are matched by the key (equivalent to the `match` attribute in `<xsl:key>`). The `name` attribute on `<sch:key>` names the key and the `path` attribute gives the identifier.

For example, you could construct a key that enabled you to quickly access the program that started at a particular time on a particular channel as follows:

```
<sch:rule context="Program">
  <sch:key name="programs"
           path="concat(Start, ' on ', parent::Channel/Name)" />
</sch:rule>
```

Once a key is set up for an identifier, you can retrieve all the elements with a particular identifier with that particular key using the `key()` function. For example, to return all the `<Program>` elements that start at 9 pm on Christmas Eve on BBC1, you could use:

```
key('programs', '2001-12-24T21:00:00 on BBC1')
```

Since this is a unique identifier, there should only be one such program. You can test how many there are by counting them explicitly, as follows:

```
count(key('programs', '2001-12-24T21:00:00 on BBC1')) = 1
```

For each `<Program>` element, then, you can test whether there is a duplicate program as follows:

```
<sch:rule context="Program">
  <sch:key name="programs"
           path="concat(Start, ' on ', parent::Channel/Name)" />
  <sch:assert
    test="count(key('programs',
                concat(Start, ' on ', parent::Channel/Name))) = 1">
    There should not be two Programs starting at the same time on the same
    channel.
  </sch:assert>
</sch:rule>
```

Checking References

You can also use the key when testing whether a reference is actually referring to an element in that same document. For example, if the details of the series that programs might belong to are held within the same document as the rest of the TV Guide, you can set up a key that indexes the `<Series>` elements by their `id` attribute:

```
<sch:rule context="Series">
  <sch:key name="series" path="@id" />
</sch:rule>
```

Then you can use this key to test whether the <Series> element children of the <Program> elements, if they have values, refer to one of these series, using:

```
<sch:rule context="Program">
  <sch:report test="string(Series) and not(key('series', Series))">
    <sch:name />'s &lt;Series&gt; element child's value should be the same
    as the id attribute on a &lt;Series&gt; element elsewhere in the
    document.
  </sch:report>
</sch:rule>
```

If the key returns some nodes, then there is a <Series> element with that ID; otherwise, there is not and the document is invalid.

Creating Validators for Schematron

As mentioned earlier, Schematron uses XSLT to carry out validation. The application that actually carries out the validation is an XSLT processor using a validating XSLT stylesheet on the XML document.

Part of the power of Schematron is that the same Schematron schema could be used to generate a number of different types of validating XSLT stylesheets. For example, you could use the same Schematron schema to create stylesheets that generate HTML reports on the validity of XML documents, command-line utilities that create error messages using <xsl:message>, or stylesheets that add comments to an XML document indicating problem areas within it. The validation rules stay the same; only the way the results are presented differs.

To get this range of behavior from the same Schematron schema, you need different meta-stylesheets that create the appropriate validator stylesheets. For example, you might have one meta-stylesheet that creates validators that emit HTML reports and another generator stylesheet that creates validators that emit messages.

XSLT stylesheets that generate XSLT stylesheets are at the more complicated end of the stylesheet spectrum, because it's very easy to get confused between the code that is being used to generate the stylesheet and the code that you're generating for the result stylesheet. Fortunately, several meta-stylesheets have already been developed for Schematron, so it's easiest to reuse or adapt those.

The basis of most meta-stylesheets is the skeleton1-5.xsl stylesheet. This stylesheet constructs the top level of the validating stylesheet and calls various named templates that you can override in order to customize the result of the validating stylesheet. If you are creating your own meta-stylesheet, you should import skeleton1-5.xsl so that you can override the named templates that it contains:

```
<xsl:stylesheet version="1.0"
                xmlns:xsl="http://www.w3.org/1999/XSL/Transform">
<xsl:import href="skeleton1-5.xsl" />
...
</xsl:stylesheet>
```

The most important of the templates to override is the process-message template, which deals with the messages held in the <sch:report> and <sch:assert> elements. The current node at the time the template is called is the <sch:report> or <sch:assert> element, so the value of the current node gives you the message, and you can also access the value of the test attribute on the element if you need to. The easiest thing to do to get the message is to apply templates in text mode. A minimal process-message template, for example, would look like:

```
<xsl:template name="process-message">
  <xsl:apply-templates mode="text" />
</xsl:template>
```

You can also generate elements within this template. For example, you could put the message inside a <p> element with a class attribute equal to assert or report depending on the name of the current element, with:

```
<xsl:template name="process-message">
  <p class="{local-name()}">
    <xsl:apply-templates mode="text" />
  </p>
</xsl:template>
```

If you want to generate XSLT elements to go in the validating stylesheet, then you should use the <xsl:element> element to create them. For example, to emit the message with an <xsl:message> element, you could use:

```
<xsl:template name="process-message">
  <xsl:element name="xsl:message">
    <xsl:apply-templates mode="text" />
  </xsl:element>
</xsl:template>
```

If you're creating lots of XSLT instructions within your template, there is an easier way than using <xsl:message>. You can set up an alias namespace for the XSLT namespace, and create elements in that namespace with literal result elements. Then, you can tell the processor that any elements in your alias namespace should actually be in the XSLT namespace, using the <xsl:namespace-alias> element.

The <xsl:namespace-alias> element goes at the top level of the stylesheet and has two attributes: stylesheet-prefix and result-prefix. The stylesheet-prefix attribute holds the prefix that you use for the alias namespace (the default namespace is specified with the value #default). The result-prefix attribute specifies the prefix of the namespace that you want that alias namespace to be mapped to in the result, usually xsl.

Try It Out – Creating a Meta-stylesheet

In this try it out, we'll create a simple meta-stylesheet that emits messages using <xsl:message> whenever there is something wrong in the source XML document. The <xsl:stylesheet> element needs to declare two namespaces: the XSLT namespace as usual, and an alias namespace, which we'll associate with the prefix axsl. This alias namespace can be anything you like, but remember to state that it's an alias of the XSLT namespace with the <xsl:namespace-alias> element:

```
<xsl:stylesheet version="1.0"
                xmlns:xsl="http://www.w3.org/1999/XSL/Transform"
                xmlns:axsl="http://www.w3.org/1999/XSL/TransformAlias">
...
<xsl:namespace-alias stylesheet-prefix="axsl" result-prefix="xsl" />
...
</xsl:stylesheet>
```

The stylesheet needs to import `skeleton1-5.xsl`, which provides the basic processing of Schematron schemas into validating stylesheets:

```
<xsl:stylesheet version="1.0"
                xmlns:xsl="http://www.w3.org/1999/XSL/Transform"
                xmlns:axsl="http://www.w3.org/1999/XSL/TransformAlias">

<xsl:import href="skeleton1-5.xsl" />

<xsl:namespace-alias stylesheet-prefix="axsl" result-prefix="xsl" />
...
</xsl:stylesheet>
```

It then needs to define a template called `process-message`, which determines what's done with the messages held in `<sch:assert>` and `<sch:report>` elements. We want this template to create an `<xsl:message>` element in the validating stylesheet. To create the `<xsl:message>` element in the validating stylesheet, we can use a literal result element in the alias namespace, as follows:

```
<xsl:template name="process-message">
  <axsl:message>
    <xsl:apply-templates mode="text" />
  </axsl:message>
</xsl:template>
```

This stylesheet is `schematron-message.xsl`. Try running `schematron-message.xsl` over the simple TV Guide schema that we saw at the beginning of this chapter, `TVGuide.sch`, to create `TVGuide.message.xsl`.

If you look at `TVGuide.message.xsl`, you should see the following template, which contains an `<xsl:message>` element generated by our stylesheet:

```
<xsl:template match="/" priority="4000" mode="M1">
  <xsl:choose>
    <xsl:when test="TVGuide"/>
    <xsl:otherwise>
      <xsl:message>
        The document element must be a &lt;TVGuide&gt; element.
      </xsl:message>
    </xsl:otherwise>
  </xsl:choose>
  <xsl:apply-templates mode="M1"/>
</xsl:template>
```

Don't worry if your stylesheet contains elements with the prefix `axsl` *rather than* `xsl` *– if you look at the namespace declarations on the* `<xsl:stylesheet>` *element, you'll see that the prefix* `axsl` *is bound to the XSLT namespace.*

Now try running `TVGuide.message.xsl` over `invalidTVGuide.xml`. You should see the following message:

```
C:\WINNT\System32\cmd.exe

C:\5946\Chapter16>saxon -o TVGuide.message.xsl TVGuide.sch schematron-message.xs
l

C:\5946\Chapter16>saxon -o log.xml invalidTVGuide.xml TVGuide.message.xsl
The document element must be a &lt;TVGuide&gt; element.

C:\5946\Chapter16>_
```

Summary

This chapter has given a quick introduction to Schematron, which is a schema language that uses XPath and XSLT to validate documents. Schematron is a very powerful schema language, particularly in areas where other schema languages (such as XML Schema) are not able to cope, such as co-occurrence constraints.

You've seen how Schematron works in general, using a meta-stylesheet to create a validating stylesheet from a schema, and then using the validating stylesheet on an XML document to create a report about the validity of the XML document.

You have learned how to create a Schematron schema for a markup language. In particular, you've explored some of the tests you can carry out with XPath to check the structure of an XML document. You've seen how to:

- Check the identity of the document element
- Test that elements are empty
- Check that elements have text (and only text) content
- Test that elements have particular elements as content
- Validate the order in which elements appear
- Test that elements occur consecutively
- Check the presence of attributes
- Validate the content of elements and attributes
- Check co-occurrence constraints
- Test the uniqueness of identifiers
- Check that references point to an existing element

Finally, in this section you've learned how to put together a simple meta-stylesheet so that you can customize the kinds of reports that the validating stylesheet generates. The `skeleton1-5.xsl` stylesheet forms the basis of most meta-stylesheets, and defines a number of named templates that you can override. For more documentation about the `skeleton1-5.xsl` stylesheet and what you can create from it see http://www.ascc.net/xml/schematron/1.5/.

Review Questions

1. Create a full Schematron schema for the TV Guide XML markup language.
2. Use `schematron-report-portable.xsl` to generate a validator stylesheet that creates an HTML document from the Schematron schema.
3. Write your own meta-stylesheet that creates a log of the results of the validation, including a deep copy of the node that caused the problem.

Beginning
XSLT

17

Interpreting RSS with XSLT

The TV Guide that we've been looking at throughout this book is a very useful resource; not only does it list all those programs, but it also includes ratings on each of them to help you choose what to watch. Throughout, the origin of this information has remained hidden; in this chapter, we'll look at how the information might be collected from other sites using the syndication format RSS (RDF Site Summary).

RSS is an XML-based markup language that holds metadata about a web site, and in particular it is used to notify sites of time-sensitive information such as site changes, news headlines, mails on discussion forums, and notifications and announcements of various kinds. RSS has its roots in the channels used in the "My Netscape Network" (MNN) portal site, which allowed content providers to provide summaries of their web sites that users could follow if they chose.

RSS 1.0, the version of RSS that we will be looking at in this chapter, is based on RDF (Resource Description Framework). RDF is a standard from the W3C that provides a framework for expressing metadata – information about information. RSS 1.0 is highly modularized – providers can put together their site information with the components that they need – and uses standards such as Dublin Core to provide **meta-information** about the content of the site.

In this chapter, you'll learn:

- The basics of RDF and RSS 1.0
- How to transform RSS descriptions into other XML
- How to pull information from two different RSS feeds together

RDF Basics

Before we launch into RSS, we'll take a quick look at the basics of RDF, the Resource Description Format. RDF is an XML-based markup language that was initially developed by the W3C as a means of expressing meta-information about documents, for example who wrote a particular document or when it was last modified.

RDF actually addresses a more general problem than how to express meta-information. RDF defines how to assert facts using XML. Some of these facts might concern documents (and therefore be meta-information for those documents). But other facts might be more general, such as "The capital of England is London" or "the Universe contains 1,000,000,000,000,000,000,000 stars".

RDF processors are able to make use of these facts to draw conclusions – to infer other facts. An RDF processor might take the fact "Amazon.com sells books published by Wrox" and the fact "Beginning XSLT is a book published by Wrox" and draw the conclusion that "Amazon.com sells Beginning XSLT". Also a search engine that understood RDF could search the metadata of a number of documents to create a list of the documents authored by a particular person or on a particular day.

The ability to express facts makes RDF one of the possible technologies at the heart of the Semantic Web. For more details, see the RDF home page at http://www.w3.org/RDF/.

RDF has been in development since 1997, before XML was even finalized. There are two parts to RDF: the RDF Model and Syntax Recommendation (http://www.w3.org/TR/REC-rdf-syntax/), which became a Recommendation in 1999, and the RDF Schema Specification (http://www.w3.org/TR/rdf-schema/), which has been a Candidate Recommendation since March 2000.

The Model and Syntax Recommendation defines how RDF is used to express meta-information, and gives the basic syntax and semantics for RDF, which is what we need to look at in order to understand RSS. RDF Schemas describe the vocabularies that are used by basic RDF to express metadata, in much the same way as XML Schemas describe the markup languages that are used by XML to express data.

RDF Schemas aren't important in RSS, so we're not going to address them in this chapter.

In this section, we'll look first at the model that underlies RDF and then go on to look at how that model is expressed in XML.

Statements, Resources, and Properties

The heart of RDF is the ability to assert facts, which are known as **statements** in RDF. For example, RDF allows you to say "The page at http://www.jenitennison.com/ is written by Jeni Tennison" and "Jeni Tennison's email address is jeni@jenitennison.com". An RDF document is essentially a collection of statements like these.

*Statements are made about things, which in RDF terms are known as **resources**. A resource is a thing that can be identified with a URI. The URI doesn't necessarily have to point to a physical resource – its main purpose is to act as an identifier for the resource so that assertions can be made about it. In the examples above, the resources involved are the web page http://www.jenitennison.com/ and the person "Jeni Tennison". Of course I am not a web-based resource, but you could make up a URI to identify me (for example, urn:person:Jeni-Tennison). All that matters is that the URI is used consistently, because that enables RDF processors to link together two statements about a particular resource, and infer a third statement.*

Each resource has a number of **properties** with values; a statement states that a resource has a particular value for a property. The values of properties can be literals (like strings or numbers) or other resources (again identified by their own URI). For example, in the statement "The page at http://www.jenitennison.com/ is written by Jeni Tennison", the resource http://www.jenitennison.com/ has the property "is written by", whose value is Jeni Tennison. As we'll see later, when we looks at bags, sequences, and alternatives, properties can sometimes have multiple values, for example a document could have multiple authors.

Different RDF applications are interested in different kinds of resources and properties. If you use RDF for metadata about pages on a web site, the resources will mostly be web pages and the properties will be document metadata such as the author, date of last modification, keywords, and so on. If you use RDF to represent virtual business cards, then the resources will be people and the properties will be things like name, role, address, and telephone number. Each RDF application thus has its own **vocabulary**.

Representing Statements in XML

Statements in RDF are made using XML elements and attributes. RDF provides elements and attributes that allow you to point to resources in order to make statements about them. A particular RDF vocabulary will also define the elements or attributes that specify the properties about those resources, but RDF itself does not provide any domain-specific information, which means that it doesn't say anything about what properties can apply to a particular resource.

The elements and attributes that are part of RDF are all members of the namespace:

```
http://www.w3.org/1999/02/22-rdf-syntax-ns#
```

In this chapter, we'll use the prefix `rdf` to indicate this namespace.

Describing Resources

The document element of an RDF document is the `<rdf:RDF>` element. Within the `<rdf:RDF>` element are a number of descriptions, each of which represent one or more statements about a resource.

The description elements can be either `<rdf:Description>` elements (for generic statements) or elements from another namespace, which allows you to give more information about the type of resource that the statement is about. We'll call the specialized elements that do the same job as `<rdf:Description>` **description elements**.

Both `<rdf:Description>` and description elements must have an `about` attribute that indicates the resource that the statement is talking about. The `about` attribute holds the URI that identifies the resource.

Officially, attributes from RDF can be in no namespace (unprefixed) or in the RDF namespace; I follow the model of XSLT and use no namespace for attributes on elements from the RDF namespace and the RDF namespace for attributes on elements from other namespaces. For example, I use no namespace for the `about` *attribute when it is used on* `<rdf:Description>`*, but the RDF namespace (*`rdf:about`*) when the* `about` *attribute is used on elements in other namespaces.*

For example, to make statements about the web page http://www.jenitennison.com/ and about the person Jeni Tennison, you could use the following RDF:

```
<rdf:RDF xmlns:rdf="http://www.w3.org/1999/02/22-rdf-syntax-ns#">

<rdf:Description about="http://www.jenitennison.com/">
  ...
</rdf:Description>

<rdf:Description about="urn:person:Jeni-Tennison">
  ...
</rdf:Description>

</rdf:RDF>
```

Alternatively, you could use elements in a different namespace as description elements, as follows:

```
<rdf:RDF xmlns:rdf="http://www.w3.org/1999/02/22-rdf-syntax-ns#"
         xmlns="http://www.example.com/websites">

<website rdf:about="http://www.jenitennison.com/">
  ...
</website>

<person rdf:about="urn:person:Jeni-Tennison">
  ...
</person>

</rdf:RDF>
```

Making Statements

The description elements contain a number of other elements that define the values of properties. These **property elements** usually come from another namespace because the properties that are relevant to a particular resource depend on the RDF application that you're using.

For literal values, the value of the property is given as the content of the property element. For example, to state that my email address is jeni@jenitennison.com, you could use:

```
<rdf:Description about="urn:person:Jeni-Tennison">
  <emailAddress>jeni@jenitennison.com</emailAddress>
</rdf:Description>
```

or:

```
<person rdf:about="urn:person:Jeni-Tennison">
  <emailAddress>jeni@jenitennison.com</emailAddress>
</person>
```

Properties can be given structured literal values by nesting XML inside them. However, if you do this you should add an attribute `rdf:parseType` with a value of `Literal` to the property element to indicate that the XML represents a literal value, not more RDF.

When a property's value is another resource, there are two options. The first option is to use the `rdf:resource` attribute to give the URI for this other resource. For example, to say that the web page http://www.jenitennison.com/ is written by Jeni Tennison (identified with the URN urn:jeni@jenitennison.com), you could use:

```
<rdf:Description about="http://www.jenitennison.com/">
  <author rdf:resource="urn:person:Jeni-Tennison" />
</rdf:Description>
```

or:

```
<website rdf:about="http://www.jenitennison.com/">
  <author rdf:resource="urn:person:Jeni-Tennison" />
</website>
```

Alternatively, you can nest the description of the resource within the property element, at the same time adding an `rdf:parseType` attribute with a value of `Resource` to the property element. This is particularly useful when there is additional information about the referenced resource because, the more nested the structure is, the easier it is to read and navigate than the flatter structure. For example, you could use:

```
<rdf:Description about="http://www.jenitennison.com/">
  <author rdf:parseType="Resource">
    <rdf:Description about="urn:person:Jeni-Tennison">
      <emailAddress>jeni@jenitennison.com</emailAddress>
    </rdf:Description>
  </author>
</rdf:Description>
```

or:

```
<website rdf:about="http://www.jenitennison.com/">
  <author rdf:parseType="Resource">
    <person rdf:about="urn:person:Jeni-Tennison">
      <emailAddress>jeni@jenitennison.com</emailAddress>
    </person>
  </author>
</website>
```

This latter example looks just like a normal XML document, but the RDF attributes allow any RDF processor to pull out useful information from it.

Bags, Sequences, and Alternatives

Sometimes properties have multiple values. A web page may have many authors, have gone through multiple changes, or be available in several different formats. These situations are supported by the RDF elements `<rdf:Bag>`, `<rdf:Seq>`, and `<rdf:Alt>`, which are collectively known as **container elements**:

- `<rdf:Bag>` is used when properties have several values in no particular order, such as the authors of a web page
- `<rdf:Seq>` is used when properties have several values and their order is important, such as a list of changes to the page
- `<rdf:Alt>` is used when there are multiple alternative values for the property, such as several formats for the same web page

Each of these container elements holds `<rdf:li>` elements, which behave just like property elements – they can hold a literal value, point to a resource, or even contain another resource. For example, I have an alternative email address of mail@jenitennison.com. To represent this, you could use:

```
<person rdf:about="urn:person:Jeni-Tennison">
  <emailAddress>
    <rdf:Alt>
      <rdf:li>jeni@jenitennison.com</rdf:li>
      <rdf:li>mail@jenitennison.com</rdf:li>
    </rdf:Alt>
  </emailAddress>
</person>
```

Introducing RSS

RDF Site Summary (RSS) documents provide summaries of (some of) the information available on a web site. Each web site could provide several RSS documents to describe different aspects of the web site – news about changes to the web site, announcements on particular product lines, or information provided as a service to all. RSS documents can be retrieved by other applications, either behind the scenes (which is particularly useful for portal sites) or directly to the user via headline readers.

> *For a list of readers for RSS documents see* http://blogspace.com/rss/readers.

Each RSS document describes a particular **channel** available from a web site. The body of the RSS document contains summaries of one or more **items** that are available on that web site or elsewhere. For example, if you're using RSS on a site that serves news stories, the channel would be the news service and the items would be news headlines, with links to the full story on your site. For our TV Guide, we can imagine RSS documents from the site for each TV channel, with the items providing links to details of the programs that are showing on that channel. Another RSS source might provide reviews of the programs. The TV Guide site itself might operate a channel for each subscriber, notifying them through a standard RSS reader when one of their favorite shows is about to start.

As with any standard that has been around for a while, there are several versions of RSS that are currently commonplace:

- RSS 0.9 – the original format developed by Netscape for My Netscape Network (http://my.netscape.com/)
- RSS 0.91 – a format that dropped RDF and incorporated elements from scriptingNews, a format from Userland (http://www.userland.com/)
- RSS 0.92 – further development on top of RSS 0.91, developed by Userland
- RSS 0.93 – a work currently in progress, developed by Userland based on RSS 0.92
- RSS 1.0 – separate development on top of RSS 0.91, which reintroduces RDF, developed by members of the RSS-DEV mailing list

As you can see, the development of RSS forked after version 0.91, with Userland developing versions 0.92 and 0.93 while members of RSS-DEV developed RSS 1.0. We're going to look at version 1.0 in this chapter because it uses RDF and Dublin Core, two standards that are useful in other areas aside from syndicated content, and because it provides a more meaty transformation due to its use of namespaces.

In this section, we'll have a look at the RSS format. We've already met RDF, on which RSS is based, so we'll look first at how the RSS markup language incorporates RDF, and then look at the Dublin Core and Syndication modules that plug in to RSS.

RSS Markup Language

As you've seen, any RDF document has to be supplemented with elements from other namespaces in order to create a specialized vocabulary that can be understood by a particular RDF application. These namespaces need to define property elements and can also define description elements to take the place of `<rdf:Description>`.

RSS is one such markup language. RSS documents are RDF documents that use elements from the RSS namespace as description and property elements. The RSS namespace is:

```
http://purl.org/rss/1.0/
```

We'll use the prefix `rss` for this namespace throughout the rest of this chapter.

In this section, we'll have a look at the description and property elements that RSS uses to describe channels and items.

Describing Channels

The first type of description element that RSS defines is the `<rss:channel>` element. The `<rss:channel>` element describes the web site whose content is being summarized by the RSS page.

Being an RDF description element, the `<rss:channel>` element has an `rdf:about` attribute that contains a URI that identifies the web site. Usually the URI is either the URL for the home page of the web site or the URL of the RSS document itself.

The `<rss:channel>` element contains a number of property elements, the most important of which are:

- <rss:title> – a literal property giving the name of the web site.
- <rss:link> – a literal property giving the URL for the web site.
- <rss:description> – a literal property that gives a brief description of the web site (in plain text).
- <rss:items> – a sequence property that points to the items listed for the channel. The <rss:items> element contains an <rdf:Seq> element whose <rdf:li> elements each have a resource attribute giving an identifier for each item described by the RSS page, which is usually the URL of the "full story" back on the web site.

Describing Items

The second type of description element that we'll look at is the <rss:item> element. Each RSS page should contain one or more such <rss:item> elements, each of which describes one of the items that are being summarized within the RSS page.

The <rss:item> element has an rdf:about attribute which references the URL summarized by the item. This URL is the same as the URL used in the resource attribute of one of the <rdf:li> elements within the <rss:items> element in the channel description outlined above. The <rss:item> element contains three property elements:

- <rss:title> – a literal property giving a title for the item
- <rss:link> – a literal property giving the URL for the item (this will usually be the same as the URL in the <rss:item> element's rdf:about attribute)
- <rss:description> – an optional literal property giving a more detailed description of the item (as opposed to the <rss:title>, which gives only the 'headline')

Example RSS Page

As examples of RSS, we'll look at two RSS documents that could provide useful material for our TV Guide.

The first is a site that provides reviews of the TV programs showing over the next 24 hours. The RSS page reviews.rss gives a summary of each review, with URLs referencing back to the main site so that you can get more details. One thing to note here is that the URLs provided by the site use the VIDEO Plus+ code for each program to identify them uniquely:

```
<rdf:RDF xmlns:rdf="http://www.w3.org/1999/02/22-rdf-syntax-ns#"
         xmlns:rss="http://purl.org/rss/1.0/">

<rss:channel rdf:about="http://www.example.com/reviews/reviews.rss">

  <rss:title>TV Reviews</rss:title>
  <rss:link>http://www.example.com/reviews/</rss:link>
  <rss:description>
    Reviews of TV programs showing in the next 24 hours.
  </rss:description>

  <rss:items>
```

```
      <rdf:Seq>
        <rdf:li resource="http://www.example.com/reviews/2571.html" />
        <rdf:li resource="http://www.example.com/reviews/85674.html" />
        ...
      </rdf:Seq>
    </rss:items>

  </rss:channel>

  <rss:item rdf:about="http://www.example.com/reviews/2571.html">
    <rss:title>EastEnders: They're Mad About the Boy</rss:title>
    <rss:link>http://www.example.com/reviews/2571.html</rss:link>
    <rss:description>
      Jamie Mitchell has never been so popular.
    </rss:description>
  </rss:item>

  <rss:item rdf:about="http://www.example.com/reviews/85674.html">
    <rss:title>Panorama: Current Issues</rss:title>
    <rss:link>http://www.example.com/reviews/85674.html</rss:link>
    <rss:description>
      Today's Panorama tackles the issue of pet cloning.
    </rss:description>
  </rss:item>
  ...
  </rdf:RDF>
```

VIDEO Plus+ numbers are the UK equivalent of VCR Plus+ numbers in the US.

The second example page is `listing.rss` and provides a program listing. Note that new programs are added at the top of the list, so that the most recent item is a program that's just been added to the listing. Also note that the program identifiers use the timing of the program, while the links from the `<rss:item>` elements point to pages that may contain details about lots of programs:

```
  <rdf:RDF xmlns:rdf="http://www.w3.org/1999/02/22-rdf-syntax-ns#"
           xmlns:rss="http://purl.org/rss/1.0/">

  <rss:channel rdf:about="http://www.example.com/bbc1/listing.rss">
    <rss:title>BBC1</rss:title>
    <rss:link>http://www.example.com/bbc1/</rss:link>
    <rss:description>
      Listings of BBC 1 programs over the next 24 hours
    </rss:description>

    <rss:items>
      <rdf:Seq>
        <rdf:li resource="http://www.example.com/bbc1#2001-07-05T21:30:00" />
        <rdf:li resource="http://www.example.com/bbc1#2001-07-05T20:45:00" />
        ...
      </rdf:Seq>
    </rss:items>
```

```
</rss:channel>

<rss:item rdf:about="http://www.example.com/bbc1#2001-07-05T21:30:00">
  <rss:title>Panorama</rss:title>
  <rss:link>http://www.bbc.co.uk/panorama</rss:link>
  <rss:description>
    Today discusses whether cloning pets is morally wrong.
  </rss:description>
</rss:item>

<rss:item rdf:about="http://www.example.com/bbc1#2001-07-05T20:45:00">
  <rss:title>The National Lottery</rss:title>
  <rss:link>http://www.bbc.co.uk/lottery/</rss:link>
  <rss:description>
    Stunning celebrity guests and a grand giveaway.
  </rss:description>
</rss:item>
...
</rdf:RDF>
```

RSS Modules

As we saw in the previous section, the required content in an RSS page is rather brief and doesn't give a lot of detail about either the channel or the items that it describes. However, this is part of the design of RSS – different types of channels require different kinds of supplementary information for their items, so RSS defines a number of modules that can be used to add extra information to the basic RSS pages. These extra modules define additional property elements that can be used within `<rss:channel>` or `<rss:item>` elements.

The two modules that we'll look at briefly here are the Dublin Core module, which provides standard metadata properties (particularly relevant for web documents), and the Syndication module, which provides properties to do with how often an RSS feed is updated. We'll also see how it's possible for RSS applications to use their own properties if they wish.

Dublin Core Module

Dublin Core is a standard set of metadata that is commonly associated with documents. Dublin Core Metadata isn't limited to XML representations, but Dublin Core elements and attributes are often used in XML-based markup languages to represent metadata. These elements and attributes are specified by the Dublin Core Metadata Initiative (http://dublincore.org/). The Dublin Core elements are all in the namespace:

```
http://purl.org/dc/elements/1.1/
```

We'll use the prefix `dc` for this namespace throughout the rest of this chapter.

The following elements can provide common metadata about a document:

- `<dc:title>` – the title of the document
- `<dc:creator>` – the creator of the document

- `<dc:subject>` – a code or set of keywords that indicates the subject of the document
- `<dc:description>` – a description of the document
- `<dc:publisher>` – the entity responsible for making the document available
- `<dc:contributor>` – a contributor to the document
- `<dc:date>` – a date associated with the document (such as the date the document was issued)
- `<dc:type>` – the type of the document, for example `Dataset`, `Image`, or `Text` (see http://dublincore.org/documents/dcmi-type-vocabulary/ for a list)
- `<dc:format>` – the media type of the document
- `<dc:identifier>` – an identifier for the document
- `<dc:source>` – a URL specifying the resource from which the document is derived
- `<dc:language>` – a language identifier specifying the language in which the document is written
- `<dc:relation>` – a URI of a resource related to the document in some way
- `<dc:coverage>` – the scope of the document, in terms of physical location, time period, or organizational entity
- `<dc:rights>` – a copyright statement about the document

When RDF is used to represent metadata about documents, it generally uses these Dublin Core elements to hold that metadata. Similarly, RSS uses these same elements within `<rss:channel>` and `<rss:item>` to provide metadata about the channel or items.

These elements are particularly useful in the RSS document that contains reviews of TV programs – you can use it to add information about the author of the review, the date it was published, and any copyright issues governing the review. For example:

```
<rss:item rdf:about="http://www.example.com/reviews/2571.html">
  <rss:title>EastEnders: They're Mad About the Boy</rss:title>
  <rss:link>http://www.example.com/reviews/2571.html</rss:link>
  <rss:description>
    Jamie Mitchell has never been so popular.
  </rss:description>
  <dc:creator>Georgina Holland (george@reviews.example.com)</dc:creator>
  <dc:date>2001-07-05</dc:date>
  <dc:rights>Copyright &#169; 2001 Example Reviews Plc.</dc:rights>
</rss:item>
```

The TV listing RSS feed could also use Dublin Core elements to add information about the item, for example supplementing the item with a unique identifier for the program; here we'll use the VIDEO Plus+ code for the program again:

```
<rss:item rdf:about="http://www.example.com/bbc1#2001-07-05T19:30:00">
  <rss:title>EastEnders</rss:title>
  <rss:link>http://www.bbc.co.uk/eastenders/</rss:link>
  <rss:description>
```

```
      Mark's health scare forces him to reconsider his future with Lisa, while
      Jamie is torn between Sonia and Zoe.
    </rss:description>
    <dc:identifier>2571</dc:identifier>
  </rss:item>
```

Syndication Module

The Syndication module for RSS defines a set of properties that can be specified for channels to describe how frequently they are updated. This is particularly useful for RSS documents that act as news feeds and are regularly updated – an application receiving the RSS document can work out when it next needs to check that more information has been made available. The namespace for the elements in the Syndication module is:

```
http://purl.org/rss/modules/syndication/
```

We'll use the prefix `sy` to indicate elements in this module in the rest of this chapter.

The Syndication module defines three elements:

- `<sy:updatePeriod>` – describes the period over which the channel is updated (`hourly`, `daily`, `weekly`, `monthly`, or `yearly`)
- `<sy:updateFrequency>` – states how many times the channel is updated during the update period (if missing, a value of `1` is assumed)
- `<sy:updateBase>` – specifies the date and time at which the channel started, from which the date and time of updates can be calculated

The `<sy:updateBase>` element contains dates and times without seconds, slightly different from the more standard ISO 8601 date format.

The Syndication module elements are important in both the channels that we're using as examples. The TV review channel is updated once a day, so simply needs an `<sy:updatePeriod>` element to be added:

```
<rss:channel rdf:about="http://www.example.com/reviews/reviews.rss">

  <rss:title>TV Reviews</rss:title>
  <rss:link>http://www.example.com/reviews/</rss:link>
  <rss:description>
    Reviews of TV programs showing in the next 24 hours.
  </rss:description>

  <sy:updatePeriod>daily</sy:updatePeriod>

  <rss:items>
    <rdf:Seq>
      <rdf:li resource="http://www.example.com/reviews/2571.html" />
      <rdf:li resource="http://www.example.com/reviews/85674.html" />
```

```
    ...
  </rdf:Seq>
</rss:items>

</rss:channel>
```

The TV listing channel is updated more frequently, with more programs being added to the listing every half hour (48 times per day). It therefore needs both an `<sy:updatePeriod>` element and an `<sy:updateFrequency>` element, as follows:

```
<rss:channel rdf:about="http://www.example.com/bbc1/listing.rss">
  <rss:title>BBC1</rss:title>
  <rss:link>http://www.example.com/bbc1/</rss:link>
  <rss:description>
    Listings of BBC 1 programs over the next 24 hours
  </rss:description>

  <sy:updatePeriod>daily</sy:updatePeriod>
  <sy:updateFrequency>48</sy:updateFrequency>

  <rss:items>
    <rdf:Seq>
      <rdf:li resource="http://www.example.com/bbc1#2001-07-05T21:30:00" />
      <rdf:li resource="http://www.example.com/bbc1#2001-07-05T20:45:00" />
      ...
    </rdf:Seq>
  </rss:items>

</rss:channel>
```

Other Modules

The Dublin Core and Syndication modules are just examples of the modules that you can plug in to RSS. The provider of an RSS document is able to add their own properties, in their own namespace, to the channel of items to provide appropriate supplementary information.

For example, as well as using the Dublin Core and Syndication module, the TV review channel could define its own properties in the namespace:

```
http://www.example.com/reviews
```

It could use a `<rev:rating>` element in this namespace to summarize the overall rating of the program, providing this information within the RSS feed:

```
<rss:item rdf:about="http://www.example.com/reviews/2571.html">
  <rss:title>EastEnders: They're Mad About the Boy</rss:title>
  <rss:link>http://www.example.com/reviews/2571.html</rss:link>
  <rss:description>
    Jamie Mitchell has never been so popular.
  </rss:description>
```

```
    <dc:creator>Georgina Holland (george@reviews.example.com)</dc:creator>
    <dc:date>2001-07-05</dc:date>
    <dc:rights>Copyright &#169; 2001 Example Reviews Plc.</dc:rights>
    <rev:rating>5</rev:rating>
  </rss:item>
```

Naturally, the more people use and understand elements from these other modules, the more useful the information is. If an application didn't know that the <rev:rating> element held a rating, then it wouldn't be able to use that information.

Transforming RSS

The two types of RSS document that we've looked at provide us with a lot of useful information for our TV Guide. The more important of the two types of document is the one giving the program listing, because we can use that to generate the XML that we've been using as the source of our TV Guide. The review document is interesting too, because we can use that to provide the rating for each program. Rather than creating the TV Guide document by hand, we can create it automatically by collecting the feeds together. The overall process might look as shown in the following diagram:

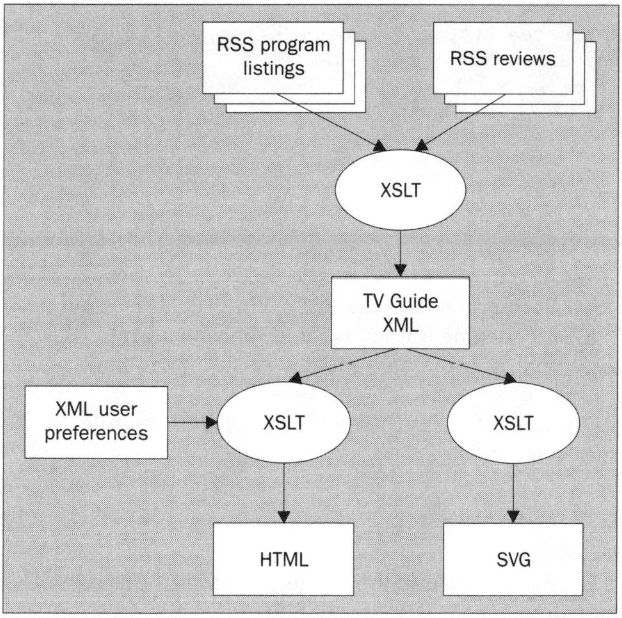

In the remaining part of this chapter, we'll look at how to generate the TV Guide XML that we've been using throughout this book from a collection of RSS documents.

Sample Documents

We need to design a stylesheet that combines the two RSS files, `listing.rss` and `reviews.rss`, into a single XML document, `TVGuide.xml`. It's a good idea to look at the documents that we have and what we aim to get from them before we start. `listing.rss` is as follows:

```
<rdf:RDF xmlns:rdf="http://www.w3.org/1999/02/22-rdf-syntax-ns#"
         xmlns:rss="http://purl.org/rss/1.0/"
         xmlns:dc="http://purl.org/dc/elements/1.1/"
         xmlns:sy="http://purl.org/rss/modules/syndication/">

<rss:channel rdf:about="http://www.example.com/bbc1/listing.rss">
  <rss:title>BBC1</rss:title>
  <rss:link>http://www.example.com/bbc1/</rss:link>
  <rss:description>
    Listings of BBC 1 programs over the next 24 hours
  </rss:description>

  <sy:updatePeriod>daily</sy:updatePeriod>
  <sy:updateFrequency>48</sy:updateFrequency>

  <rss:items>
    <rdf:Seq>
      <rdf:li resource="http://www.example.com/bbc1#2001-07-05T21:30:00" />
      <rdf:li resource="http://www.example.com/bbc1#2001-07-05T20:45:00" />
      ...
    </rdf:Seq>
  </rss:items>

</rss:channel>

<rss:item rdf:about="http://www.example.com/bbc1#2001-07-05T21:30:00">
  <rss:title>Panorama</rss:title>
  <rss:link>http://www.bbc.co.uk/panorama</rss:link>
  <rss:description>
    Today discusses whether cloning pets is morally wrong.
  </rss:description>
  <dc:identifier>85674</dc:identifier>
</rss:item>

<rss:item rdf:about="http://www.example.com/bbc1#2001-07-05T20:45:00">
  <rss:title>The National Lottery</rss:title>
  <rss:link>http://www.bbc.co.uk/lottery/</rss:link>
  <rss:description>
    Stunning celebrity guests and a grand giveaway.
  </rss:description>
  <dc:identifier>7129</dc:identifier>
</rss:item>
...
</rdf:RDF>
```

The reviews.rss document looks like the following:

```
<rdf:RDF xmlns:rdf="http://www.w3.org/1999/02/22-rdf-syntax-ns#"
         xmlns:rss="http://purl.org/rss/1.0/"
         xmlns:dc="http://purl.org/dc/elements/1.1/"
         xmlns:sy="http://purl.org/rss/modules/syndication/"
         xmlns:rev="http://www.example.com/reviews">

<rss:channel rdf:about="http://www.example.com/reviews/reviews.rss">

  <rss:title>TV Reviews</rss:title>
  <rss:link>http://www.example.com/reviews/</rss:link>
  <rss:description>
    Reviews of TV programs showing in the next 24 hours.
  </rss:description>

  <sy:updatePeriod>daily</sy:updatePeriod>

  <rss:items>
    <rdf:Seq>
      <rdf:li resource="http://www.example.com/reviews/2571.html" />
      <rdf:li resource="http://www.example.com/reviews/85674.html" />
      ...
    </rdf:Seq>
  </rss:items>

</rss:channel>

<rss:item rdf:about="http://www.example.com/reviews/2571.html">
  <rss:title>EastEnders: They're Mad About the Boy</rss:title>
  <rss:link>http://www.example.com/reviews/2571.html</rss:link>
  <rss:description>
    Jamie Mitchell has never been so popular.
  </rss:description>
  <dc:creator>Georgina Holland (george@reviews.example.com)</dc:creator>
  <dc:date>2001-07-05</dc:date>
  <dc:rights>Copyright &#169; 2001 Example Reviews Plc.</dc:rights>
  <rev:rating>5</rev:rating>
</rss:item>

<rss:item rdf:about="http://www.example.com/reviews/85674.html">
  <rss:title>Panorama: Current Issues</rss:title>
  <rss:link>http://www.example.com/reviews/85674.html</rss:link>
  <rss:description>
    Today's Panorama tackles the issue of pet cloning.
  </rss:description>
  <dc:creator>Christian Taylor (chris@reviews.example.com)</dc:creator>
  <dc:date>2001-07-05</dc:date>
  <dc:rights>Copyright &#169; 2001 Example Reviews Plc.</dc:rights>
  <rev:rating>6</rev:rating>
</rss:item>
...
</rdf:RDF>
```

And the `BBC1.xml` document that we need to generate from this is simply:

```
<Channel>

<Name>BBC1</Name>

<Program videoPlus="620">
  <Start>2001-07-05T19:00:00</Start>
  <Duration>PT30M</Duration>
  <Series>A Question of Sport</Series>
  <Title/>
  <Description>
    Sports quiz hosted by Sue Barker.
  </Description>
</Program>

<Program videoPlus="2571" rating="5">
  <Start>2001-07-05T19:30:00</Start>
  <Duration>PT30M</Duration>
  <Series>EastEnders</Series>
  <Title/>
  <Description>
    Mark's health scare forces him to reconsider his future with Lisa,
    while Jamie is torn between Sonia and Zoe.
  </Description>
</Program>
...
</Channel>
```

The stylesheet that we'll construct for this task is `RSS2Channel.xsl`. This stylesheet will exercise all the XSLT and XPath that you've learned over the course of this book, so hold tight!

Basic Stylesheet

Before we launch into the body of the stylesheet, we need to set up the basics – look at the namespaces that we need to be able to handle, consider what whitespace management we want to use, and decide what control we want over the output.

Managing Namespaces

RSS documents use a lot of namespaces, especially if the extra modules are used as well. The namespaces that are used in the source documents are:

- The RDF namespace – `http://www.w3.org/1999/02/22-rdf-syntax-ns#`
- The RSS namespace – `http://purl.org/rss/1.0/`
- The Dublin Core namespace – `http://purl.org/dc/elements/1.1/`
- The Syndication namespace – `http://purl.org/rss/modules/syndication/`
- The TV Review namespace – `http://www.example.com/reviews`

All except the Syndication namespace are used for elements or attributes that we're interested in, so our stylesheet needs to declare these namespaces, as well as the XSLT namespace, within the <xsl:stylesheet> element as follows:

```
<xsl:stylesheet version="1.0"
                xmlns:xsl="http://www.w3.org/1999/XSL/Transform"
                xmlns:rdf="http://www.w3.org/1999/02/22-rdf-syntax-ns#"
                xmlns:rss="http://purl.org/rss/1.0/"
                xmlns:dc="http://purl.org/dc/elements/1.1/"
                xmlns:rev="http://www.example.com/reviews">
...
</xsl:stylesheet>
```

On the other hand, the result of the transformation doesn't involve any namespaces. If we leave the <xsl:stylesheet> element as above, then any elements that we construct within the stylesheet will be given namespace nodes for each of these namespaces, with the end result that the output of the transformation will include namespace declarations for the RDF, RSS, Dublin Core, and TV Review namespaces, despite the fact that they are never used within the document itself.

To prevent this from happening, we can use the exclude-result-prefixes attribute on <xsl:stylesheet>, listing the prefixes of the namespaces that we don't want to be included in the result. The <xsl:stylesheet> element therefore looks as follows:

```
<xsl:stylesheet version="1.0"
                xmlns:xsl="http://www.w3.org/1999/XSL/Transform"
                xmlns:rdf="http://www.w3.org/1999/02/22-rdf-syntax-ns#"
                xmlns:rss="http://purl.org/rss/1.0/"
                xmlns:dc="http://purl.org/dc/elements/1.1/"
                xmlns:rev="http://www.example.com/reviews"
                exclude-result-prefixes="rdf rss dc rev">
...
</xsl:stylesheet>
```

Managing Whitespace

Our next preparatory task is to decide what to do about whitespace-only text nodes in the source RSS documents. If we can strip out the whitespace-only text nodes that we're not interested in, we'll end up with a much smaller tree and run less risk of numbering going awry (if we ever add it) because we have whitespace that we don't want in the result document.

Fortunately, in general RDF documents tend to avoid mixed content, so you can usually strip whitespace-only text nodes throughout the document. This is true in the case of the RSS documents that we're dealing with, so we can use <xsl:strip-space> to strip all whitespace-only text nodes from the two source documents, as follows:

```
<xsl:strip-space elements="*" />
```

Managing Output

The final setup task for the stylesheet is to construct an `<xsl:output>` element that describes the format that we want to generate. In this case, we're generating a basic XML format, with no special media type, no DTD, and no elements that should contain CDATA sections. Therefore the `<xsl:output>` element is pretty simple – the only thing that I think we should include is an instruction to the processor to indent the output, as that will make it easier for us to read and debug:

```
<xsl:output indent="yes" />
```

Creating the Program Listing

The first task that we'll attempt with our stylesheet is to generate the `<Channel>` and `<Program>` elements from `listing.rss`. To help us do this, let's look at the mappings between the information available within the RSS document and the format in `TVGuide.xml`:

- The document element `<rdf:RDF>` maps to the document element, `<Channel>`
- The content of the `<rss:channel>` element's child `<rss:title>` element maps to the `<Name>` child of the `<Channel>` element
- Each `<rss:item>` maps to an equivalent `<Program>` element
- The `<dc:identifier>` element maps to the `videoPlus` attribute on the `<Program>` element
- The end of the `rdf:about` attribute provides the value for the `<Start>` element
- The `<rss:title>` element within the `<rss:item>` element maps to the `<Series>` element in the `<Program>` element
- The `<rss:description>` element maps to the `<Description>` element

We can construct a template for each of these mappings, matching the relevant element or attribute in the source RSS document and using it to generate the required element or attribute in the result.

First the document element: the `<rdf:RDF>` element maps to the `<Channel>` element. Inside the `<Channel>` element comes the result of applying templates to the `<rdf:RDF>` elements' children, first the `<rss:channel>` element, and then the `<rss:item>` elements, in reverse order. We can make sure that the `<rss:item>` elements are processed in reverse order by adding an `<xsl:sort>` element to the `<xsl:apply-templates>`, sorting in descending order on the position of the `<rss:item>` (remembering that this is a numerical sort, not an alphabetical one). Sorting in reverse order is simpler than trying to work out the time of each program and using that. The resulting template is:

```
<xsl:template match="rdf:RDF">
  <Channel>
    <xsl:apply-templates select="rss:channel" />
    <xsl:apply-templates select="rss:item">
      <xsl:sort select="position()" order="descending" data-type="number" />
    </xsl:apply-templates>
  </Channel>
</xsl:template>
```

The <rss:channel> element doesn't have an equivalent as such – the only relevant thing about the <rss:channel>, for this transformation, is its title. We can therefore use a template that matches the <rss:channel> element to focus the processing on to its <rss:title> element child, nothing more:

```
<xsl:template match="rss:channel">
  <xsl:apply-templates select="rss:title" />
</xsl:template>
```

The template for the <rss:title> element needs to map this element on to a <Name> element with the same value. The mapping itself is straightforward, but we have to watch out here – <rss:title> elements occur in two places in the source RSS document (the <rss:channel> element and the <rss:item> elements). We're going to need to process the <rss:title> elements within the <rss:item> elements in a different way (to produce a <Series> element), so we'll make sure that this template only matches those <rss:title> elements that appear within <rss:channel> elements, as follows:

```
<xsl:template match="rss:channel/rss:title">
  <Name><xsl:value-of select="." /></Name>
</xsl:template>
```

That's all we have to worry about for the channel information, so we'll now move on to the <rss:item> elements, each of which maps on to a <Program> element:

```
<xsl:template match="rss:item">
  <Program>
    ...
  </Program>
</xsl:template>
```

The first interesting property of this <Program> element is that it has a videoPlus attribute whose value comes from the <dc:identifier> child element of the <rss:item>. We could generate this attribute by applying templates to the <dc:identifier> element, but it's simpler in this case to just use an attribute value template, as follows:

```
<xsl:template match="rss:item">
  <Program videoPlus="{dc:identifier}">
    ...
  </Program>
</xsl:template>
```

To create the element content of the <Program> element, we need to make sure that the relevant attribute and child elements of the <rss:item> element are processed in the correct order – first the rdf:about attribute to generate the <Duration> element, then the <rss:title> element, and then the <rss:description> element:

```
<xsl:template match="rss:item">
  <Program videoPlus="{dc:identifier}">
    <xsl:apply-templates select="@rdf:about" />
    <xsl:apply-templates select="rss:title" />
```

```
    <xsl:apply-templates select="rss:description" />
  </Program>
</xsl:template>
```

The other thing we need to do in this template is to add the empty <Title> element (here I'm assuming that the RSS feed gives series names rather than program titles):

```
<xsl:template match="rss:item">
  <Program videoPlus="{dc:identifier}">
    <xsl:apply-templates select="@rdf:about" />
    <xsl:apply-templates select="rss:title" />
    <Title />
    <xsl:apply-templates select="rss:description" />
  </Program>
</xsl:template>
```

The templates for the <rss:title> and <rss:description> elements are straightforward, although again we need to take a little bit of care over the match pattern for the <rss:title> element because there are <rss:title> elements in other contexts that need to be treated in a different way. The two templates are:

```
<xsl:template match="rss:item/rss:title">
  <Series><xsl:value-of select="." /></Series>
</xsl:template>

<xsl:template match="rss:description">
  <Description><xsl:value-of select="." /></Description>
</xsl:template>
```

The final template is the template for the `rdf:about` attribute. We're using this attribute as the source of the start time of the program, since the start time is used in the fragment identifier. For example, the `rdf:about` attribute for the <rss:item> representing the EastEnders program has the value:

```
http://www.example.com/bbc1#2002-01-07T20:00:00
```

The start time of the program is given after the # in this URI. Since the URI can only contain a single #, we can simply use the `substring-after()` function to retrieve the value. The template for the `rdf:about` attribute is therefore:

```
<xsl:template match="@rdf:about">
  <Start><xsl:value-of select="substring-after(., '#')" /></Start>
</xsl:template>
```

Adding Duration Information

The one bit of information available in the TV listing RSS document that we've missed out so far is the <Duration> element. In this section, we'll look at how to create this element.

The RSS TV listing doesn't explicitly provide us with a duration for each program. However, if we know when a program starts and know when it ends, then we should be able to work out the duration of the program, and we can work out when the program ends by looking at when the next program begins. Calculating the duration is going to take a bit of work, so we'll create a separate template, matching the `<rss:item>` element in `duration` mode, to do it, just to make the stylesheet more modular:

```
<xsl:template match="rss:item" mode="duration">
  ...
</xsl:template>
```

We can "call" this template from the main template for the `<rss:item>` elements by applying templates to the `<rss:item>` element we're on, but in `duration` mode, as follows:

```
<xsl:template match="rss:item">
  <Program videoPlus="{dc:identifier}">
    <xsl:apply-templates select="@rdf:about" />
    <xsl:apply-templates select="." mode="duration" />
    <xsl:apply-templates select="rss:title" />
    <Title />
    <xsl:apply-templates select="rss:description" />
  </Program>
</xsl:template>
```

We've seen how to get the start time for the current program using the `substring-after()` function on the `rdf:about` attribute. To get the start time for the next program, we need to look at the `rdf:about` attribute of the immediately preceding `<rss:item>` element (remember that the RSS listing gives the programs in reverse order). We can get this `<rss:item>` using the `preceding-sibling::`axis, as follows:

```
preceding-sibling::rss:item[1]
```

Of course we might not be able to find an item at all – the latest program in the listing (which is the first `<rss:item>` in the RSS document) doesn't have a preceding sibling. In these cases, we won't generate a `<Duration>` element, so the first job in the `duration`-mode template is to test whether the `<rss:item>` actually has a preceding sibling at all. Since we'll be using the preceding sibling if it exists, we may as well hold it in a variable:

```
<xsl:template match="rss:item" mode="duration">
  <xsl:variable name="nextProgram"
                select="preceding-sibling::rss:item[1]" />
  <xsl:if test="$nextProgram">
    <Duration>
      ...
    </Duration>
  </xsl:if>
</xsl:template>
```

Since programs always last a whole number of minutes (at least in the schedules!), we only need to worry about the hour and minute of the start times of the two programs. Since the date time format that's being used here is fixed format, we can work these out using the `substring()` function, as follows:

```
<xsl:variable name="start" select="substring-after(@rdf:about, '#')" />
<xsl:variable name="end"
              select="substring-after($nextProgram/@rdf:about, '#')" />
<xsl:variable name="startHour" select="substring($start, 12, 2)" />
<xsl:variable name="startMin" select="substring($start, 15, 2)" />
<xsl:variable name="endHour" select="substring($end, 12, 2)" />
<xsl:variable name="endMin" select="substring($end, 15, 2)" />
```

The duration format that we're using represents the duration in terms of hours and minutes. To work out the number of hours the program lasts for, we can subtract the start hour from the end hour; if the end hour is less than the start hour (because the program extends over midnight), then adding 24 hours to the end hour will deal with the difference. Also, if the end minute is less than the start minute, then we need to subtract 1:

```
<xsl:variable name="durHours">
  <xsl:variable name="minAdjust" select="$startMin > $endMin" />
  <xsl:choose>
    <xsl:when test="$startHour > $endHour">
      <xsl:value-of select="($endHour + 24) - $startHour - $minAdjust" />
    </xsl:when>
    <xsl:otherwise>
      <xsl:value-of select="$endHour - $startHour - $minAdjust" />
    </xsl:otherwise>
  </xsl:choose>
</xsl:variable>
```

A similar method can be used to calculate how many additional minutes the program lasts for. This time, if the start minute is more than the end minute then adding 60 will deal with the difference:

```
<xsl:variable name="durMins">
  <xsl:choose>
    <xsl:when test="$startMin > $endMin">
      <xsl:value-of select="($endMin + 60) - $startMin" />
    </xsl:when>
    <xsl:otherwise>
      <xsl:value-of select="$endMin - $startMin" />
    </xsl:otherwise>
  </xsl:choose>
</xsl:variable>
```

Once the duration hours and minutes have been calculated, creating the duration format is straightforward:

```
<xsl:text>PT</xsl:text>
<xsl:if test="number($durHours)">
  <xsl:value-of select="$durHours" />
  <xsl:text>H</xsl:text>
</xsl:if>
<xsl:if test="number($durMins)">
  <xsl:value-of select="$durMins" />
```

```
    <xsl:text>M</xsl:text>
  </xsl:if>
```

The completed template is as follows:

```
<xsl:template match="rss:item" mode="duration">
  <xsl:variable name="nextProgram"
                select="preceding-sibling::rss:item[1]" />
  <xsl:if test="$nextProgram">
    <Duration>
      <xsl:variable name="start"
        select="substring-after(@rdf:about, '#')" />
      <xsl:variable name="end"
        select="substring-after($nextProgram/@rdf:about, '#')" />
      <xsl:variable name="startHour" select="substring($start, 12, 2)" />
      <xsl:variable name="startMin" select="substring($start, 15, 2)" />
      <xsl:variable name="endHour" select="substring($end, 12, 2)" />
      <xsl:variable name="endMin" select="substring($end, 15, 2)" />
      <xsl:variable name="durHours">
      <xsl:variable name="minAdjust" select="$startMin > $endMin" />
        <xsl:choose>
          <xsl:when test="$startHour > $endHour">
            <xsl:value-of select="($endHour + 24) - $startHour -
                                  $minAdjust" />
          </xsl:when>
          <xsl:otherwise>
            <xsl:value-of select="$endHour - $startHour - $minAdjust" />
          </xsl:otherwise>
        </xsl:choose>
      </xsl:variable>
      <xsl:variable name="durMins">
        <xsl:choose>
          <xsl:when test="$startMin > $endMin">
            <xsl:value-of select="($endMin + 60) - $startMin" />
          </xsl:when>
          <xsl:otherwise>
            <xsl:value-of select="$endMin - $startMin" />
          </xsl:otherwise>
        </xsl:choose>
      </xsl:variable>
      <xsl:text>PT</xsl:text>
      <xsl:if test="number($durHours)">
        <xsl:value-of select="$durHours" />
        <xsl:text>H</xsl:text>
      </xsl:if>
      <xsl:if test="number($durMins)">
        <xsl:value-of select="$durMins" />
        <xsl:text>M</xsl:text>
      </xsl:if>
    </Duration>
  </xsl:if>
</xsl:template>
```

Adding Rating Information

The remaining piece of information that we need to insert in the TVGuide.xml document is from the TV review feed – the rating of those programs that have been reviewed. This information is stored in the <rev:rating> child element of the <rss:item> representing a particular program review within the review RSS document.

The TV review RSS document, reviews.rss, is a separate document, which doesn't act as the main source for the transformation. Therefore it has to be accessed from the stylesheet using the document() function. Because we'll be referring to it multiple times during the course of the transformation, we'll create a global variable to hold the root node of the review document, as follows:

```
<xsl:variable name="reviews" select="document('reviews.rss')" />
```

In real life, this reviews.rss document might come from a completely different web site. You could use document('http://www.example.com/reviews/reviews.rss') to retrieve it from http://www.example.com/reviews/reviews.rss, for example.

Within the review RSS document, each program review is represented by an <rss:item> element. The <rss:item> indicates what program it's talking about via the name of the file referenced by the <rss:link> element (and the rdf:about attribute). The file name of the HTML file containing the review of a program is named via the VIDEO Plus+ number for the program.

Luckily, we know the VIDEO Plus+ code for the program, because it's held in the <dc:identifier> child element of the <rss:item> representing the program in the listing document. We can therefore use the code as a link between the two sources of information – retrieve the VIDEO Plus+ number from the TV listing, and use that to identify the relevant review in the review RSS document.

As you saw in Chapter 10, the most efficient way to retrieve the element with a particular value for an attribute or child element is via a key. You can use <xsl:key> to set up a key to index an element on practically anything, and then use the key() function to retrieve the element based on its key value.

In this case, we need to index <rss:item> elements from the review RSS document by the VIDEO Plus+ number. The VIDEO Plus+ number can be retrieved from the <rss:link> child element of the <rss:item> element by taking the substring after the directory name 'http://www.example.com/reviews/' and before the file extension '.html', as follows:

```
substring-before(
  substring-after(rss:link, 'http://www.example.com/reviews/'), '.html')
```

We'll call this key reviews. The <xsl:key> element needs to match <rss:item> elements and use the path above to calculate a key value (the VIDEO Plus+ code) for each item:

```
<xsl:key name="reviews" match="rss:item"
   use="substring-before(
        substring-after(rss:link, 'http://www.example.com/reviews/'),
        '.html')" />
```

Now, given a VIDEO Plus+ code in the $videoPlus variable, and assuming that the current node is in the review RSS document, we can retrieve the <rss:item> that reviews that program using:

```
key('reviews', $videoPlus)
```

From there, we can get the rating of the program by accessing the <rev:rating> child element as follows:

```
key('reviews', $videoPlus)/rev:rating
```

To retrieve the relevant <rss:item> from the TV review RSS document, we need to make sure that the current node is in the TV review RSS document. We can do this by using <xsl:for-each> as a context-changer – selecting a single node so that it is used as the context node. To apply templates to the <rev:rating> child element of the relevant <rss:item>, for example, we need the following:

```
<xsl:for-each select="$reviews">
  <xsl:apply-templates select="key('reviews', $videoPlus)/rev:rating" />
</xsl:for-each>
```

This code appears in the template for the <rss:item> elements (which are matched in the TV listing document), while creating <Program> elements, as follows:

```
<xsl:template match="rss:item">
  <xsl:variable name="videoPlus" select="dc:identifier" />
  <Program videoPlus="{$videoPlus}">
    <xsl:for-each select="$reviews">
      <xsl:apply-templates select="key('reviews', $videoPlus)/rev:rating" />
    </xsl:for-each>
    <xsl:apply-templates select="@rdf:about" />
    <xsl:apply-templates select="." mode="duration" />
    <xsl:apply-templates select="rss:title" />
    <Title />
    <xsl:apply-templates select="rss:description" />
  </Program>
</xsl:template>
```

The template matching the <rev:rating> elements needs to generate a rating attribute for the <Program> element, using <xsl:attribute>, as follows:

```
<xsl:template match="rev:rating">
  <xsl:attribute name="rating">
    <xsl:value-of select="." />
  </xsl:attribute>
</xsl:template>
```

Final Result

The `RSS2Channel.xsl` stylesheet can now be used to take the `listing.rss` and `reviews.rss` documents and generate `BBC1.xml`. The `listing.rss` document needs to be the main source document for the transformation; `reviews.rss` gets pulled into the transformation using the `document()` function from within the stylesheet.

The command line for running the transformation, with Saxon for example, is:

```
>saxon -o BBC1.xml listing.rss RSS2Channel.xsl
```

If you run this transformation, you should generate `BBC1.xml`, which looks as follows when you view it in Internet Explorer:

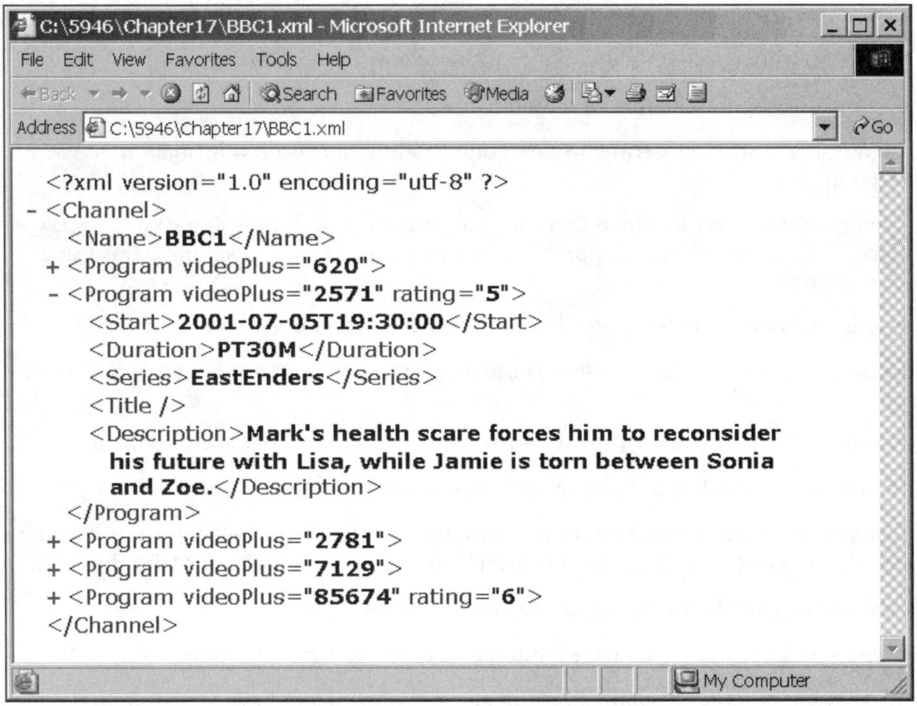

The information from `listing.rss` has been interpreted into the markup language that we've been using to represent channels throughout this book. Ratings have been added to those programs that have been reviewed, from `reviews.rss`. Thus RSS documents, made available on channel and reviewers' web sites, can be combined to create the TV Guide XML document that we can use on our online TV Guide site to create HTML pages, SVG, and other formats.

Summary

This chapter has introduced you to the basics of RDF, for representing information about resources, Dublin Core, for representing metadata about documents, and RSS, for representing syndicated information or general site summaries. We've concentrated on the XML syntax of RSS, but hopefully this chapter has also given you an idea about how XSLT applications can use RSS as both the source and result of transformations.

In the process of generating a stylesheet to use information from RSS documents, we've looked at the following techniques, which you learned in the first part of this book:

- Using namespaces in XML documents to distinguish between elements and attributes from different markup languages
- Declaring namespaces for use in XSLT stylesheets, and preventing them from appearing in the result
- Stripping whitespace-only text nodes from data-oriented XML structures
- Controlling the indentation of output using `<xsl:output>`
- Identifying mappings between source information and result information, to use as the basis of templates
- Changing the order in which items appear in the result, both using `<xsl:apply-templates>` to select the appropriate information and by reversing items using `<xsl:sort>`
- Using attribute value templates to insert information into generated attributes
- Extracting information from strings using `substring()`, `substring-before()`, and `substring-after()`
- Using modes to break up your stylesheet into more manageable components
- Identifying preceding siblings using the `preceding-sibling::`axis
- Conditionally adding elements and attributes using explicit flow control instructions (such as `<xsl:if>`) or by applying templates, which can only be used on nodes that exist
- Performing calculations using arithmetic operators
- Using `<xsl:text>` to manage whitespace added to the result tree
- Working with multiple source documents, including using keys across multiple documents

Review Questions

1. Construct an XML document that points to a list of RSS documents containing TV listings.

2. Amend the stylesheet developed during this chapter so that it creates multiple `<Channel>` elements wrapped within a `<TVGuide>` element, based on the XML document from Exercise 1. The stylesheet should retrieve the RSS documents using the `document()` function.

3. Construct a separate XML document that lists RSS documents supplying TV program ratings.

4. Amend the stylesheet developed in Exercise 2 so that it accesses the TV rating RSS documents from Exercise 3 and calculates average ratings to include in the `rating` attribute of the `<Program>` element.

5. Construct an RSS document containing reminders when someone's favorite programs are showing.

6. Create a stylesheet that generates the reminders RSS document from `TVGuide.xml`, assuming the `<Program>` elements in `TVGuide.xml` have `flag` attributes with a value of `favorite` for the user's favorite programs.

Beginning
XSLT

A

XPath Quick Reference

Node Types

Nodes can be of the following types:

Node Type	Name	String Value
`root`	-	Concatenation of all text nodes in the document
`element`	Element name	Concatenation of all text nodes descended from the element
`attribute`	Attribute name	Attribute value
`text`	-	Text
`comment`	-	Text held within the comment
`processing`	Processing instruction target	Text in the processing instruction after the space after the target name
`namespace`	Namespace prefix	Namespace URI

Object Types

Values in XSLT can be one of the following five types:

Object Type	Description
`boolean`	`true` or `false`
`number`	A floating-point number: a double-precision 64-bit format IEEE 754 value

Table continued on following page

Object Type	Description
string	A sequence of XML characters
node set	An unordered collection of nodes
result tree fragment	The root node of a generated node tree

The various object types can be converted to each other by the following rules.

Object	Boolean	Number	String
boolean	–	1 if the boolean is true, 0 if the boolean is false	'true' if the boolean is true, 'false' if the boolean is false
number	false if the number is 0 or NaN, otherwise true	-	A string version of the number with no leading or trailing zeros; 'NaN' if the number is NaN, 'Infinity' if the number is infinity, and '-Infinity' if the number is negative infinity
string	false if the string is an empty string, otherwise true	The number held by the string, as long as it is a valid XPath number (which doesn't include exponents or grouping separators); otherwise NaN	-
node set	true if the node set holds nodes; false if the node set is empty	The result of converting the string value of the first node in the node set to a number	The string value of the first node in the node set
result tree fragment	true	The result of converting the string value of the result tree fragment to a number	The string value of the result tree fragment

Booleans, numbers, and strings cannot be converted to node sets or result tree fragments.

Paths

Paths are made up of a number of steps, separated by /s. Each step is made up of an optional axis (defaults to child), a node test, and any number of predicates (held in square brackets).

Axes

Axes dictate the relationship between the context node and the selected nodes. The direction of an axis determines how the `position()` of a node is calculated – forward axes look at document order, reverse axes look at reverse document order.

Axis	Direction	Description
`self`	Forward	Selects the context node itself
`child`	Forward	Selects the children of the context node
`parent`	Reverse	Selects the parent of the context node
`attribute`	Forward	Selects the attributes of the context node
`descendant`	Forward	Selects the descendants of the context node at any level
`descendant-or-self`	Forward	Selects the descendants of the context node, and the context node itself
`ancestor`	Reverse	Selects the ancestors of the context node
`ancestor-or-self`	Reverse	Selects the ancestors of the context node, and the context node itself
`following-sibling`	Forward	Selects the siblings of the context node that follow the context node in document order
`preceding-sibling`	Reverse	Selects the siblings of the context node that precede the context node in document order
`following`	Forward	Selects the nodes (aside from attribute and namespace nodes) that follow the context node in document order and that are not descendants of the context node
`preceding`	Reverse	Selects the nodes (aside from attribute and namespace nodes) that precede the context node in document order and that are not ancestors of the context node
`namespace`	Forward	Selects the namespace nodes on the context node

Node Tests

Node tests match different kinds of nodes as follows:

Node Test	Description
`node()`	Matches nodes of all types
`*`	Matches elements with any name (or attributes if you're using the attribute axis)
`name`	Matches elements with the given name (or attribute if you're using the attribute axis)
`text()`	Matches text nodes
`comment()`	Matches comment nodes
`processing-instruction()`	Matches processing instruction nodes
`processing-instruction('target')`	Matches processing instruction nodes with the given target

Abbreviated Syntax

You can use several abbreviations in XPath expressions, as described in the following table.

Abbreviation	Full Equivalent	Description
`.`	`self::node()`	The context node
`..`	`parent::node()`	The parent of the context node
`//`	`/descendant-or-self::node()/`	Supplies quick access to descendants of the context node
`@`	`attribute::`	Shortens expressions that access attributes

Operators

The operators in XPath can be split into four groups:

- Logical operators
- Comparisons
- Numerical operators
- Node set operators

The precedence of the operators (from lowest to highest) is as follows:

1. `or`
2. `and`
3. `=, !=`
4. `<=, <, >=, >`
5. `+, -`
6. `*, div, mod`
7. unary -
8. `|`

Logical Operators

Operator	Description
`or`	`true` if either operand is `true` when converted to booleans; the right operand is not evaluated if the left operand is `true`
`and`	`true` if both operands are `true` when converted to booleans; the right operand is not evaluated if the left operand is `false`

Comparisons

Operator	Description
`=`	Equal to
`!=`	Not equal to
`<`	Less than
`<=`	Less than or equal to
`>`	Greater than
`>=`	Greater than or equal to

Comparisons between node sets and values are true if the comparison is true for the string value of any node in the node set.

The numeric comparisons (<, <=, >, and >=) can only be used to do numeric comparisons – you can't use them to test whether one string is alphabetically less than another string.

Numerical Operators

Operator	Description
+	Addition
-	Subtraction
*	Multiplication
`div`	Floating-point division
`mod`	Remainder from integer division
unary -	Negation

Node Set Operator

Operator	Description
|	Creates a union of two node sets

Functions

XPath and XSLT together define the following functions:

boolean()

Syntax: *`boolean`* `boolean(`*`object`*`)`
See also: `string()`, `number()`

Converts the argument to a boolean value (either `true` or `false`). Usually this is done automatically, for example in `test` attributes.

ceiling()

Syntax: *`number`* `ceiling(`*`number`*`)`
See also: `floor()`, `round()`

Rounds the argument up to the nearest integer. For negative numbers, this means rounding nearer to 0, so `ceiling(-1.5)` is `-1`.

concat()

Syntax: *string* concat(*string*, *string+*)

Concatenates the strings passed as arguments into a single string.

contains()

Syntax: *boolean* contains(*string*, *string*)
See also: starts-with()

Returns true if the string passed as the first argument contains the string passed as the second argument or if the second argument is an empty string, and false otherwise.

count()

Syntax: *number* count(*node*-set)
See also: last(), position(), <xsl:number>

Counts the number of nodes in the node set passed as the argument.

current()

Syntax: *node-set* current()
See also: the path .

Returns the current node – the node that's currently being processed within the <xsl:for-each> or <xsl:template> as opposed to the *context node*, which is the node currently being looked at within an XPath.

document()

Syntax: *node-set* document(*object*, *node-set*?)

If the first argument is a string, returns the node found at the URL specified by that string (usually the root node of a document). The URL is resolved relative to the location of the file containing the first node in the node set passed as the second argument (which is usually used to resolve the URL relative to the source document). If the second argument is missing, the URL is resolved relative to the stylesheet itself. If the first argument is a node set, then the result is a node set containing all the nodes that are retrieved by calling the document() function with the string values of the nodes in the node set.

element-available()

Syntax: *boolean* element-available(*string*)
See also: function-available(), <xsl:fallback>

Returns `true` if the processor supports the extension element or new XSLT instruction named by the string passed as the argument. The string should be a qualified name, with a prefix.

false()

Syntax: *boolean* `false()`
See also: `true()`, `boolean()`

Returns `false`.

floor()

Syntax: *number* `floor(`*number*`)`
See also: `ceiling()`, `round()`

Rounds the number down to the nearest integer. If the number is negative, then it gets rounded away from zero, so `floor(-1.5)` returns `-2`.

format-number()

Syntax: *string* `format-number(`*number*, *string*, *string*?`)`
See also: `number()`, `<xsl:decimal-format>`, `<xsl:number>`

Returns the number passed as the first argument formatted according to the format pattern passed as the second argument. The format pattern usually contains # to mean an optional digit, `0` to indicate a required digit, `.` to indicate the decimal point, and `,` to indicate a grouping separator. For example, `format-number(1234.5, '#,##0.00')` returns `1,234.50`. If the third argument is specified, it gives the name of a decimal format, declared with the `<xsl:decimal-format>` element, which can define other characters to be used instead of #, `0`, `,`, and `.`.

function-available()

Syntax: *boolean* `function-available(`*string*`)`
See also: `element-available()`

Returns `true` if the processor supports the function named by the argument string. The string usually includes a prefix to test for the availability of extension functions.

generate-id()

Syntax: *string* `generate-id(`*node-set?*`)`

Returns an ID for the first node in the node set passed as the argument which is both unique and a valid XML ID. If no argument is given, it returns a unique ID for the context node. The unique IDs are not stable – they are different from processor to processor, and even for the same processor operating over the same stylesheet with the same source XML document.

id()

Syntax: *node-set* id(*object*)
See also: key()

Returns the nodes with the XML IDs specified by the argument. If the argument is a string, then it's split up at the whitespace, and the function returns all the nodes in the current document that have any of the IDs. If the argument is a node set, the same is done but with the string values of each of the nodes in the node set. You have to have declared an attribute as an ID function within a DTD for the id() attribute to work, and the context node must be in the same document as the nodes that you want to retrieve.

key()

Syntax: *node-set* key(*string*, *object*)
See also: id(), <xsl:key>

Returns the nodes that are indexed by the value specified by the second argument in the key named by the first argument. If the second argument is a node set, then all the nodes with any of the values are returned. You have to have declared the key with an <xsl:key> declaration, and the context node must be in the same document as the nodes that you want to retrieve.

lang()

Syntax: *boolean* lang(*string*)

Returns true if the language of the context node (as specified with the xml:lang attribute) matches the language specified by the argument. This test is aware of sub languages and is case-insensitive, so for example lang('en') would return true even if the context node's language was specified as EN-US.

last()

Syntax: *number* last()
See also: position(), count()

Returns the index of the last node in the list that's currently being looked at (or the number of nodes that are currently being looked at, depending on how you like to view it).

local-name()

Syntax: *string* local-name(*node-set*?)
See also: name(), namespace-uri()

Returns the local name of the first node in the node set – the part of the name after any prefix that there might be. If no argument is passed, then returns the local name of the context node.

name()

Syntax: *string* `name` *(node-set?)*
See also: `local-name()`, `namespace-uri()`

Returns the full name of the first node in the node set, including the prefix for its namespace as declared in the source document. If no argument is passed, then returns the full name of the context node.

namespace-uri()

Syntax: *string* `namespace-uri` *(node-set?)*
See also: `name()`, `local-name()`

Returns the namespace URI for the first node in the node set, or an empty string if the node is in no namespace. If no argument is passed, then returns the namespace URI of the context node.

normalize-space()

Syntax: *string* `normalize-space(`*string?*`)`
See also: `string()`, `<xsl:strip-space>`

Returns the argument string with leading and trailing whitespace stripped, and any sequences of whitespace converted to single spaces. If no argument string is specified, then it returns the normalized string value of the context node.

not()

Syntax: *boolean* `not(`*boolean*`)`
See also: `true()`, `false()`, `boolean()`

Returns `false` if the argument is `true`, and `true` if the argument is `false`.

number()

Syntax: *number* `number(`*object?*`)`
See also: `string()`, `boolean()`, `format-number()`, `<xsl:number>`

Converts the argument to a number; if no argument is given, returns the numerical value of the context node. You don't usually need to use this function because values are converted to numbers automatically if they need to be numbers.

position()

Syntax: *number* `position()`
See also: `last()`, `count()`, `<xsl:number>`

Returns the position of the context node amongst the list of nodes that are currently being looked at. Unlike the numbers generated through `<xsl:number>`, the `position()` function depends on the order in which nodes are processed regardless of their original order in the source document.

round()

Syntax: *`number`* `round(`*`number`*`)`
See also: `floor()`, `ceiling()`

Rounds the argument number to the nearest integer. If the number is exactly between two integers, then it rounds up (the same as `ceiling()`).

starts-with()

Syntax: *`boolean`* `starts-with(`*`string`*`, `*`string`*`)`
See also: `contains()`

Returns `true` if the first argument string starts with the second argument string, or if the second argument string is empty, and returns `false` otherwise.

string()

Syntax: `string string(object?)`
See also: `boolean()`, `number()`

Converts the argument to a string; if no argument is given, returns the string value of the context node. You don't normally need to use this function because values are converted to strings automatically if they need to be strings.

string-length()

Syntax: *`number`* `string-length(`*`string`*`?)`
See also: `substring()`

Returns the length of the string passed as the argument. If no argument is passed, then returns the length of the string value of the context node.

substring()

Syntax: *`string`* `substring(`*`string`*`, `*`number`*`, `*`number`*`?)`
See also: `substring-before()`, `substring-after()`

Returns a substring of the first argument string starting from the number passed as the second argument and a number of characters long equal to the third argument number. If the third argument isn't specified, then it returns the rest of the string, to the last character. The first character in the string is numbered `1`.

substring-after()

Syntax: *string* `substring-after(`*string*, *string*`)`
See also: `substring-before()`, `substring()`

Returns the substring of the first argument string that occurs after the second argument string. If the second string is not contained in the first string, or if the second string is empty, then it returns an empty string.

substring-before()

Syntax: *string* `substring-before(`*string*, *string*`)`
See also: `substring-after()`, `substring()`

Returns the substring of the first argument string that occurs before the second argument string. If the second string is not contained in the first string, or if the second string is empty, then it returns an empty string.

sum()

Syntax: *number* `sum(`*node-set*`)`

Returns the sum of the values of the nodes in the node set. If any of the nodes' values isn't numeric, then this function returns `NaN`. If the node set is empty, it returns `0`.

system-property()

Syntax: *object* `system-property(`*string*`)`
See also: `element-available()`, `function-available()`

Supplies information about the processor that's being used to run the stylesheet. The argument string specifies the kind of information that's returned. There are three standard arguments:

- `xsl:version` – the version of XSLT supported by the processor (usually `1.0` in current XSLT processors)
- `xsl:vendor` – the name of the vendor of the XSLT processor
- `xsl:vendor-url` – a URL for the vendor of the XSLT processor

Processors can support their own system properties. For example, MSXML supports the system property `msxsl:version` which returns the version of MSXML that's being used.

translate()

Syntax: *string* `translate(`*string*, *string*, *string*`)`

Returns the first argument string with all occurrences of the characters in the second argument string replaced by their corresponding characters in the third string. If a character in the second string doesn't have a corresponding character in the third string, then the character is deleted from the first string.

true()

Syntax: *boolean* `true()`
See also: `false()`, `boolean()`

Returns `true`.

unparsed-entity-uri()

Syntax: *string* `unparsed-entity-uri(`*string*`)`

Returns the URI of the unparsed entity whose name is passed as the argument. Unparsed entities are declared within DTDs as a way of pointing to non-XML files, but they aren't very common nowadays.

Beginning
XSLT

B

XSLT Quick Reference

XSLT Elements

This section describes each of the XSLT 1.0 elements in alphabetical order. The syntax for each element is shown, followed by a description. Within the syntax descriptions, attributes that are attribute value templates are indicated by curly braces ({}) within the attribute value. Required attributes and default values are shown in bold.

xsl:apply-imports

Syntax:

```
<xsl:apply-imports />
```

See also: `<xsl:import>`, `<xsl:apply-templates>`

The `<xsl:apply-imports>` instruction tells the XSLT processor to take the current node and try to find a template in an imported stylesheet that (a) is in the same mode as the current template and (b) matches the current node. If the processor locates a template, it uses that template to process the current node; otherwise it uses the default templates.

The `<xsl:apply-imports>` instruction must be within an `<xsl:template>` element, and is not allowed as a descendant of an `<xsl:for-each>` – the current node at the point at which the `<xsl:apply-imports>` instruction is used must be the same as the current node of the template it's in.

xsl:apply-templates

Syntax:

```
<xsl:apply-templates select="node-set-expression"
                     mode="qualified-name">
  (xsl:sort | xsl:with-param)*
</xsl:apply-templates>
```

See also: <xsl:sort>, <xsl:with-param>, <xsl:template>, <xsl:call-template>, <xsl:for-each>, <xsl:apply-imports>

The <xsl:apply-templates> instruction tells the processor to gather together a set of nodes and to process each of the nodes by finding a template that matches it and using that template. The nodes that the processor applies templates to are selected by the path held in the `select` attribute. If the `select` attribute is missing, then the processor applies templates to the child nodes of the current node.

The nodes are processed in the order determined by the <xsl:sort> elements that are contained by the <xsl:apply-templates> instruction. See the description of <xsl:sort> for details. If there are no <xsl:sort> elements within the <xsl:apply-templates> instruction, the processor goes through the nodes in document order (the order in which they appeared in their document).

The only templates that can match the nodes to which the processor applies templates are those whose `mode` attribute has the same value as the value of the `mode` attribute on the <xsl:apply-templates>. If the <xsl:apply-templates> instruction doesn't have a `mode` attribute, then the only templates that are applied are those without a `mode` attribute.

The templates that are used are passed the parameters specified by the <xsl:with-param> elements within the <xsl:apply-templates> instruction. See the description of <xsl:with-param> for details.

xsl:attribute

Syntax:

```
<xsl:attribute name="{qualified-name}"
               namespace="{namespace-URI}">
  template
</xsl:attribute>
```

See also: <xsl:attribute-set>, <xsl:element>

The <xsl:attribute> instruction creates an attribute. When adding attributes to an element, any <xsl:attribute> instructions must come before any instructions that add content to the element. The <xsl:attribute> instruction can also be included within an <xsl:attribute-set> element; see the description of <xsl:attribute-set> for details.

The name of the attribute that's created is determined by its name and namespace attributes. The name attribute gives the qualified name for the attribute and the namespace attribute gives the namespace for the attribute. If the name held in the name attribute doesn't include a prefix and the namespace attribute has a value, then the generated attribute will be given a prefix generated by the XSLT processor.

If the namespace attribute is missing, then the qualified name specified by the name attribute is used to identify the namespace for the attribute – the namespace associated with the qualified name's prefix. If the qualified name doesn't have a prefix, then the attribute is in no namespace.

Both the name and namespace attributes are attribute value templates, so their values can be calculated on the fly.

The value of the created attribute is the result of processing the content of the <xsl:attribute> instruction. The instructions within the <xsl:attribute> must not generate any nodes aside from text nodes.

xsl:attribute-set

Syntax:

```
<xsl:attribute-set name="qualified-name"
                   use-attribute-sets="list-of-qualified-names">
  xsl:attribute*
</xsl:attribute-set>
```

See also: <xsl:attribute>, <xsl:element>, <xsl:copy>, xsl:use-attribute-sets

The <xsl:attribute-set> declaration defines a set of attributes that can then all be added to an element at once through the use-attribute-sets attribute on <xsl:element> or <xsl:copy>, or the xsl:use-attribute-sets attribute on literal result elements. It is located at the top level of the stylesheet, as a child of <xsl:stylesheet>.

The name attribute holds the qualified name of the attribute set, by which it can be referred to later on. The <xsl:attribute-set> element contains a number of <xsl:attribute> elements. The use-attribute-sets attribute contains a space-delimited list of the qualified names of other attribute sets. The attributes from the used attribute sets are added to this one.

xsl:call-template

Syntax:

```
<xsl:call-template name="qualified-name">
  xsl:with-param*
</xsl:call-template>
```

See also: <xsl:template>, <xsl:apply-templates>

The <xsl:call-template> instruction calls a template by name. The name of the called template is held in the name attribute. The <xsl:with-param> elements held within the <xsl:call-template> are used to define parameters that are passed to the template. See the description of <xsl:with-param> for more details.

xsl:choose

Syntax:

```
<xsl:choose>
  (xsl:when+, xsl:otherwise?)
</xsl:choose>
```

See also: <xsl:when>, <xsl:otherwise>, <xsl:if>

The <xsl:choose> instruction is a conditional construct that causes different instructions to be processed in different circumstances. The XSLT processor processes the instructions held in the first <xsl:when> element whose test attribute evaluates as true. If none of the <xsl:when> elements' test attributes evaluate as true, the content of the <xsl:otherwise> element, if there is one, is processed.

xsl:comment

Syntax:

```
<xsl:comment>
  template
</xsl:comment>
```

See also: <xsl:processing-instruction>

The <xsl:comment> instruction generates a comment node. The instructions within the <xsl:comment> element determine the value of the comment. These instructions must not generate any nodes apart from text nodes, and the text nodes that they generate must not contain two hyphens next to each other ('--'), as this sequence isn't allowed in comments.

xsl:copy

Syntax:

```
<xsl:copy use-attribute-sets="list-of-qualified-names">
  template
</xsl:copy>
```

See also: <xsl:copy-of>, <xsl:attribute-set>

The <xsl:copy> instruction creates a shallow copy of the current node. For most nodes, this is equivalent to a deep copy, but for element and root nodes it's slightly different.

If the current node is an element or root node, the children of the copy are the results of processing the contents of the <xsl:copy> instruction. If the current node is an element, then any namespace nodes from the original element are copied over. The attributes from the attribute sets named in use-attribute-sets are added to the copied element (along with any attributes that might be added through <xsl:attribute> instructions within the <xsl:copy>).

xsl:copy-of

Syntax:

```
<xsl:copy-of select="expression" />
```

See also: <xsl:copy>, <xsl:value-of>

The <xsl:copy-of> instruction creates a deep copy of whatever is selected by the expression held in its select attribute. If the expression evaluates to a string, number, or boolean, then it creates a text node whose value is that value. If the expression evaluates to a node set or a result tree fragment, then it creates a deep copy of the nodes in the node set or the result tree fragment. This deep copy includes child nodes, attributes, and namespace nodes.

xsl:decimal-format

Syntax:

```
<xsl:decimal-format name="qualified-name"
                    digit="character"
                    zero-digit="character"
                    decimal-separator="character"
                    grouping-separator="character"
                    minus-sign="character"
                    pattern-separator="character"
                    percent="character"
                    per-mille="character"
                    infinity="string"
                    NaN="string" />
```

See also: format-number()

<xsl:decimal-format> elements define methods of interpreting the format pattern strings that are used as the second argument of the format-number() function. They live at the top level of the stylesheet, as children of <xsl:stylesheet>. There can be many decimal formats, but they must all have different names, specified by the name attribute. If the name attribute is missing, the decimal format is used as the default decimal format.

When you use the format-number() function, the XSLT processor identifies a decimal format to use to interpret the pattern that you specify as the second argument. If the format-number() function is passed three arguments, the third argument is taken as the name of a decimal format, and that decimal format is used. If the format-number() function is passed two arguments, then the default decimal format is used; if you haven't specified a default decimal format, then the XSLT processor uses one with all attributes set to their default values.

When the XSLT processor formats the number, it looks first to see if it is infinity or not a number. If it is infinity, then the XSLT processor returns the string held in the `infinity` attribute. If it is not a number, then the XSLT processor returns the string held in the `NaN` attribute.

If the number is a number, and not infinity, the XSLT processor has to format it according to the pattern string passed as the second argument of `format-number()` and the decimal format that is identified. The processor splits the pattern into a positive pattern and a negative pattern at the character held by the `pattern-separator` attribute, which defaults to the semicolon character (`;`). The minus sign is indicated by the character held by the `minus-sign` attribute, which defaults to the hyphen character (`-`), within the negative pattern. If there's no negative pattern, then it defaults to the same as the positive pattern, prefixed by the character held in the `minus-sign` attribute of the decimal format.

If the pattern contains the character held by the `percent` attribute (which defaults to the percent character, `%`), then the number being formatted is multiplied by 100 prior to formatting, and that character is included as specified by the pattern. If the pattern contains the character held by the `per-mille` attribute (which defaults to the per-mille character, ‰ or `‰`), then the number being formatted is multiplied by1000 prior to formatting, and that character is included as specified by the pattern.

The remaining pattern string is interpreted to indicate how many digits should occur before and after the decimal point and if the digits should be grouped, and if so what by. Within the pattern, essential digits are indicated by the character held in the `zero-digit` attribute (which defaults to the zero character, `0`), and optional digits are indicated by the character held in the `digit` attribute (which defaults to the hash character, `#`). The decimal point is the character held in the `decimal-point` attribute of the decimal format (which defaults to the period character, `.`). Groups of digits are separated by the character held in the `grouping-separator` attribute (which defaults to the comma character, `,`).

xsl:element

Syntax:

```
<xsl:element name="{qualified-name}"
             namespace="{namespace-uri}"
             use-attribute-sets="list-of-qualified-names">
  template
</xsl:element>
```

See also: `<xsl:attribute-set>`

The `<xsl:element>` instruction creates an element. The name of the element that's created is determined by its `name` and `namespace` attributes. The `name` attribute gives the qualified name for the element and the `namespace` attribute gives the namespace for the element. If the `namespace` attribute is missing, then the qualified name specified by the `name` attribute is used to identify the namespace for the element – the namespace associated with the qualified name's prefix, or the default namespace if it doesn't have a prefix. Both the `name` and `namespace` attributes are attribute value templates, so their values can be calculated on the fly – in fact, this is the only reason you should use `<xsl:element>` rather than a literal result element.

If the `use-attribute-sets` attribute is present, then the attributes held in the attribute sets named within this attribute are added to the created element. Other attributes and the content of the element are generated as the result of processing the content of the `<xsl:element>` instruction.

xsl:fallback

Syntax:

```
<xsl:fallback>
  template
</xsl:fallback>
```

The <xsl:fallback> element provides alternative processing in the event that an implementation does not support a particular element. When an XSLT processor comes across an instruction that it doesn't understand (such as an XSLT 2.0 instruction or an extension element), it looks for an <xsl:fallback> element amongst its children. If it finds one, it processes the content of that <xsl:fallback> element; if it doesn't, it stops processing and the transformation fails.

xsl:for-each

Syntax:

```
<xsl:for-each select="node-set-expression">
  (xsl:sort, template)
</xsl:for-each>
```

See also: <xsl:sort>, <xsl:apply-templates>

The <xsl:for-each> instruction tells the XSLT processor to gather together a set of nodes and process them one by one. The nodes are selected by the expression held in the `select` attribute. If there are any <xsl:sort> elements, these change the order in which the nodes are processed; if there aren't any, then they are processed in document order. Each of the nodes is then processed according to the instructions held in the <xsl:for-each> after any <xsl:sort> elements.

xsl:if

Syntax:

```
<xsl:if test="boolean-expression">
  template
</xsl:if>
```

See also: <xsl:choose>, <xsl:when>

The <xsl:if> instruction performs some conditional processing. The content of the <xsl:if> is only processed if the expression held in its `test` attribute evaluates to boolean `true`.

xsl:import

Syntax:

```
<xsl:import href="URI" />
```

See also: <xsl:include>, <xsl:apply-imports>

The <xsl:import> element imports a stylesheet into this one. This gives you access to all the declarations and templates within that stylesheet, and allows you to override them with your own if you need to. The href attribute gives the location of the imported stylesheet. Any <xsl:import> elements must be the very first elements within the stylesheet, the first children of the <xsl:stylesheet> document element.

xsl:include

Syntax:

```
<xsl:include href="URI" />
```

See also: <xsl:import>

The <xsl:include> element includes a stylesheet in this one. This gives you access to all the declarations within that stylesheet, exactly as if they had been specified in your stylesheet. The href attribute gives the location of the included stylesheet. The <xsl:include> element is a top-level element, and must appear as a direct child of the <xsl:stylesheet> document element.

xsl:key

Syntax:

```
<xsl:key name="qualified-name"
         match="pattern"
         use="expression" />
```

See also: key()

The <xsl:key> element declares a key, which indexes all the nodes in a document by a particular value. Each key is identified by its name attribute. The nodes that are indexed by a key are those that match the pattern held in its match attribute.

The value by which each node is indexed is specified through the use attribute. The expression held in the use attribute is evaluated for each matched node. If it results in a string, number, or boolean, then that value is used to index the node. If the expression evaluates as a node set, then there are multiple entries for the matched node, one for each of the selected nodes, using the string value of each of those nodes. This enables you to access a node through multiple values using the key() function.

The <xsl:key> elements are top-level elements, direct children of the <xsl:stylesheet> document element. There can be multiple keys with the same name within a stylesheet; they are combined for the purpose of retrieving nodes using the key() function.

xsl:message

Syntax:

```
<xsl:message terminate="yes | no">
  template
</xsl:message>
```

The <xsl:message> instruction sends a message to the XSLT processor, which will usually forward the message on to the person running the transformation. If the terminate attribute is present with the value yes, then the transformation ends with the error message, otherwise it continues. The content of the <xsl:message> instruction provides the message itself.

xsl:namespace-alias

Syntax:

```
<xsl:namespace-alias stylesheet-prefix="namespace-prefix | #default"
                     result-prefix="namespace-prefix | #default" />
```

The <xsl:namespace-alias> element tells the XSLT processor that a namespace as used in the stylesheet should be substituted by another namespace in the result tree. This is usually used when creating stylesheets that create stylesheets: a namespace alias enables you to create the XSLT elements for the result as literal result elements, without the XSLT processor confusing them with instructions that it should follow.

The stylesheet-prefix attribute holds the prefix associated with the alias namespace within the stylesheet. The result-prefix attribute holds the prefix associated with the namespace that should be used instead, in the result (which is usually xsl when generating XSLT). The keyword #default can be used to indicate the default (unprefixed) namespace in either attribute.

xsl:number

Syntax:

```
<xsl:number level="single | multiple | any"
            count="pattern"
            from="pattern"
            value="numeric-expression"
            format="{format-pattern}"
            lang="{language-code}"
            letter-value="{alphabetic | traditional}"
            grouping-separator="{character}"
            grouping-size="{integer}" />
```

See also: format-number(), position()

The <xsl:number> instruction inserts a number into the result tree. The <xsl:number> instruction actually has two roles: generating a number and formatting that number.

By default, <xsl:number> generates a number based on the position of the current node amongst its similarly named siblings within the source XML document. You can control what number is generated more precisely using the `level`, `count`, and `from` attributes. The `level` attribute determines what kinds of numbers are generated. The value `single` numbers nodes amongst their siblings. The value `any` numbers nodes throughout the source tree. The value `multiple` creates multilevel numbering based on the hierarchical structure of the source tree. Only nodes that match the pattern held in the `count` attribute will be counted when creating a number. The `from` attribute holds a pattern matching the node from which numbering should start afresh.

If you already know the number that you want, you can use the `value` attribute to specify the number directly, rather than using the number-generating aspect of <xsl:number>.

The number is formatted according to the format pattern held in the `format` attribute. This works in a different way from the format pattern used by the `format-number()` function, because it's used to number integers rather than decimal numbers.

The format pattern can hold any punctuation characters and placeholders that indicate where the number should be included and in what format. There are five standard placeholders: `1` for decimal numbers, `a` for lowercase alphabetical numbers, `A` for uppercase alphabetical numbers, `i` for lowercase Roman numbers, and `I` for uppercase Roman numbers. Processors can support other numbering schemas as well. The `lang` and `letter-value` attributes help the processor decide which alphabet and numbering scheme to use.

If the number is large, then the digits may be grouped into groups of the size specified by the `grouping-size` attribute and separated by the character specified by the `grouping-separator` attribute.

xsl:otherwise

Syntax:

```
<xsl:otherwise>
  template
</xsl:otherwise>
```

See also: <xsl:choose>, <xsl:when>

The <xsl:otherwise> element appears only within an <xsl:choose> element, containing the instructions that are processed if none of the expressions held in the `test` attributes of the <xsl:when> elements evaluate as `true`.

xsl:output

Syntax:

```
<xsl:output method="xml | text | html | qualified-name"
            media-type="content-type"
            version="version-number"
            encoding="encoding"
            indent="yes | no"
            doctype-public="string"
            doctype-system="URI"
            omit-xml-declaration="yes | no"
            standalone="yes | no"
            cdata-section-elements="list-of-name-tests" />
```

The `<xsl:output>` element describes how the result of the transformation should be serialized into a file. The `method` attribute has the most effect on the serialization, determining whether the stylesheet creates XML, text, HTML, or some other format defined by a processor implementer. The `media-type` and `version` attributes give tighter definition about the format being generated.

The `encoding` attribute determines the character encoding used during serialization, and defaults to `UTF-8` or `UTF-16`. The `indent` attribute determines whether whitespace-only text nodes are added to the result tree in order to make it easier to read; this is `yes` by default for HTML and `no` by default for XML.

The `doctype-public` and `doctype-system` attributes hold the public and system identifiers for the result, which are included in a DOCTYPE declaration at the top of the generated file.

When generating XML, a processor will add an XML declaration at the start of the output, unless the `omit-xml-declaration` attribute is present with the value `yes`. Even if this attribute is present, the XML declaration will still be added if the encoding is something other than UTF-8 or UTF-16, or if the `standalone` attribute is present (in which case the XML declaration contains a `standalone` pseudo-attribute with the specified value).

The `cdata-section-elements` attribute lists the names of elements in the result whose text content should be wrapped within CDATA sections.

The `<xsl:output>` element should appear at the top level of the stylesheet, as a child of the `<xsl:stylesheet>` document element. There can be multiple `<xsl:output>` elements in a stylesheet, in which case they are combined on an attribute-by-attribute basis; it is an error for more than one `<xsl:output>` element to specify the same attribute with different values.

xsl:param

Syntax:

```
<xsl:param name="qualified-name"
           select="expression">
  template
</xsl:param>
```

See also: <xsl:with-param>, <xsl:variable>, <xsl:template>

The <xsl:param> element declares a parameter for a template (if it's within a template) or for the stylesheet as a whole (if it's at the top level of the stylesheet). The name attribute holds the name of the parameter. The select attribute or the content of the <xsl:param> element holds the default value for the parameter, which will be used if no value is explicitly passed in to the stylesheet or template for that parameter. It is an error to specify both a select attribute and some content; use the select attribute if you can, otherwise you'll create a result tree fragment.

xsl:preserve-space

Syntax:

```
<xsl:preserve-space elements="list-of-name-tests" />
```

See also: <xsl:strip-space>

The <xsl:preserve-space> element specifies the elements whose child whitespace-only text nodes should be preserved within the source node tree. The elements attribute holds a whitespace-separated list of name tests (which can include specific names, or * to mean any element, for example). Whitespace-only text nodes are preserved by default, so this element is only required if <xsl:strip-space> has been used to strip whitespace-only text nodes from the node tree.

xsl:processing-instruction

Syntax:

```
<xsl:processing-instruction name="unqualified-name">
  template
</xsl:processing-instruction>
```

See also: <xsl:comment>

The <xsl:processing-instruction> instruction creates a processing instruction whose target is the name held in the name attribute and whose value is the result of processing the template that it contains. The content of the <xsl:processing-instruction> element must not result in the generation of any nodes aside from text nodes, and the text nodes that it generates must not contain the string '?>'.

xsl:sort

Syntax:

```
<xsl:sort select="string-expression"
          data-type="{text | number | qualified-name}"
          order="{ascending | descending}"
          lang="{language-code}"
          case-order="{upper-first | lower-first}" />
```

See also: <xsl:apply-templates>, <xsl:for-each>

The <xsl:sort> element specifies a method of sorting a set of nodes. For each of the nodes selected in the surrounding <xsl:apply-templates> or <xsl:for-each> instruction, the <xsl:sort> element creates a sort key by evaluating the expression held in the select attribute with the node as the current node and converting it to a string. The nodes are then sorted according to this sort key and the other attributes on the <xsl:sort> element.

The data-type attribute determines whether the nodes are sorted by their sort key in alphabetical order (text), in numeric order (number), or in some other order supported by the implementation. The order attribute determines whether the nodes are sorted in ascending order or descending order. The lang and case-order attributes are used if it's an alphabetical sort; the default language is determined from the system environment, while the case ordering (whether uppercase letters are sorted before lowercase letters or vice versa) is based on the language being used.

If there are multiple <xsl:sort> elements, then they define sub-sort keys on which nodes are sorted only if they have the same value for their sort key according to the previous sort.

xsl:strip-space

Syntax:

```
<xsl:strip-space elements="list-of-name-tests" />
```

See also: <xsl:preserve-space>, normalize-space()

The <xsl:strip-space> element specifies the elements whose child whitespace-only text nodes are removed from the node tree when it is created. The elements attribute holds a whitespace-separated list of name tests (which can include specific names, or * to mean any element, for example). The <xsl:preserve-space> element can override this specification.

xsl:stylesheet

Syntax:

```
<xsl:stylesheet version="1.0"
                id="identifier"
                extension-element-prefixes="list-of-namespace-prefixes"
                exclude-result-prefixes="list-of-namespace-prefixes">
  (xsl:import*, top-level-elements)
</xsl:stylesheet>
```

See also: <xsl:transform>

The <xsl:stylesheet> element is the document element for a stylesheet, and holds all the top-level elements such as global variable and parameter declarations, templates, decimal format and attribute set definitions, key declarations, output declarations, and so on. Any <xsl:import> elements that the stylesheet contains must come before anything else within the <xsl:stylesheet> element.

The <xsl:stylesheet> element must have a version attribute indicating the version of XSLT being used, which for now should always be 1.0. If you're embedding a stylesheet within an XML document, the id attribute can be used as an identifier so that you can point to the stylesheet.

The extension-element-prefixes attribute lists the prefixes of namespaces that are used for extension elements. The exclude-result-prefixes attribute lists the prefixes of namespaces that shouldn't be included in the result document, which are usually those namespaces that are used in the source XML document.

xsl:template

Syntax:

```
<xsl:template match="pattern"
              mode="qualified-name"
              priority="number"
              name="qualified-name">
  (xsl:param*, template)
</xsl:template>
```

See also: <xsl:apply-templates>, <xsl:call-template>

The <xsl:template> element declares a template. Templates can be used in two ways within a stylesheet – they can be applied to nodes or they can be called by name. Each template must specify either a match attribute, so that it can be applied to nodes, or a name attribute, so that it can be called by name.

When templates are applied to a node set using <xsl:apply-templates>, they might be applied in a particular mode; the mode attribute on <xsl:template> indicates the mode in which templates need to be applied for this template to be used. If templates are applied in the relevant mode, then the match attribute is used to determine whether the template can be used with the particular node. The match attribute holds a pattern against which nodes are matched. If a node matches the pattern, then the template can be used to process that node. If there's more than one template that matches a node in the specified mode, then the priority attribute is used to determine which one should be used – the highest priority wins. If no priority is specified explicitly, the priority of a template is determined from its match pattern.

Whether templates are applied or called, they can be passed parameters through the <xsl:with-param> element. To receive a parameter, however, the template must contain an <xsl:param> element that declares a parameter of that name. These parameters are given before the body of the template, which is used to process the node and create a result.

xsl:text

Syntax:

```
<xsl:text disable-output-escaping="yes | no">
  text
</xsl:text>
```

The <xsl:text> element is used to add some text to the result tree. Unlike elsewhere within an XSLT stylesheet, whitespace-only text nodes within <xsl:text> elements are included, so <xsl:text> is the only way to add whitespace-only text nodes to the result tree (aside from those automatically added if you tell the processor to indent the output using the indent attribute on <xsl:output>). The <xsl:text> element is also useful for limiting the amount of space that's included around text when it's added to the result.

If the disable-output-escaping attribute is specified with the value yes then the content of the <xsl:text> element is output without special characters such as < and & being escaped with < or &.

xsl:transform

Syntax:

```
<xsl:transform version="1.0"
               id="identifier"
               extension-element-prefixes="list-of-namespace-prefixes"
               exclude-result-prefixes="list-of-namespace-prefixes">
  (xsl:import*, top-level-elements)
</xsl:transform>
```

See also: <xsl:transform>

The <xsl:transform> element is an alias for <xsl:stylesheet>; see the definition of <xsl:stylesheet> for details.

xsl:value-of

Syntax:

```
<xsl:value-of select="string-expression"
              disable-output-escaping="yes | no" />
```

See also: <xsl:copy-of>

The <xsl:value-of> instruction adds the string value of the selected expression to the result tree. The select attribute holds the expression that's evaluated. If the result is a node set, then <xsl:value-of> adds the string value of the first node in that node set; none of the structure of the node is preserved (you need <xsl:copy-of> for that).

If the disable-output-escaping attribute is specified with the value yes then the value is output without special characters such as < and & being escaped with < or &.

xsl:variable

Syntax:

```
<xsl:variable name="qualified-name"
              select="expression">
  template
</xsl:variable>
```

See also: <xsl:param>

The <xsl:variable> element declares a variable. If the <xsl:variable> element appears at the top level of the stylesheet, as a child of the <xsl:stylesheet> document element, then it is a global variable with a scope covering the entire stylesheet. Otherwise, it is a local variable with a scope of its following siblings and their descendants.

The name attribute specifies the name of the variable. After declaration, the variable can be referred to within XPath expressions using this name, prefixed with the $ character.

The value of the variable is determined either by the select attribute or by the contents of the <xsl:variable> element. It is an error to have both a select attribute and some content. If you can, use the select attribute to set the variable; otherwise the variable holds a result tree fragment.

xsl:when

Syntax:

```
<xsl:when test="boolean-expression">
  template
</xsl:when>
```

See also: <xsl:choose>, <xsl:otherwise>, <xsl:if>

The <xsl:when> element appears within an <xsl:choose> instruction and specifies a set of processing that could occur and the condition when it occurs. The XSLT processor processes the content of the first <xsl:when> within the <xsl:choose> whose test attribute contains an expression that evaluates as true.

xsl:with-param

Syntax:

```
<xsl:with-param name="qualified-name"
                select="expression">
  template
</xsl:with-param>
```

See also: <xsl:param>, <xsl:apply-templates>, <xsl:call-template>

The <xsl:with-param> element specifies the value that should be passed to a template parameter. It can be used when applying templates with <xsl:apply-templates> or calling templates with <xsl:call-template>. The name attribute holds the name of the parameter for which the value is being passed.

The value of the parameter is determined either by the select attribute or by the contents of the <xsl:with-param> element. It is an error to have both a select attribute and some content. If you can, use the select attribute to set the parameter; otherwise the parameter will be passed a result tree fragment as its value.

XSLT Attributes

There are four attributes from the XSLT namespace that can be added to any literal result element.

xsl:extension-element-prefixes

Syntax:

```
<element xsl:extension-element-prefixes="list-of-namespace-prefixes">
  template
</element>
```

See also: <xsl:stylesheet>

The xsl:extension-element-prefixes attribute lists the prefixes of namespaces that are being used for extension elements. This works exactly like the extension-element-prefixes attribute on <xsl:stylesheet>, but only within the scope of the literal result element.

xsl:exclude-result-prefixes

Syntax:

```
<element xsl:exclude-result-prefixes="list-of-namespace-prefixes">
  template
</element>
```

See also: <xsl:stylesheet>

The xsl:exclude-result-prefixes attribute lists the prefixes of namespaces that should not be included within the result tree. This works exactly like the exclude-result-prefixes attribute on <xsl:stylesheet>, but only within the scope of the literal result element.

xsl:use-attribute-sets

Syntax:

```
<element xsl:use-attribute-sets="list-of-qualified-names">
  template
</element>
```

See also: <xsl:attribute-set>, <xsl:element>, <xsl:copy>

The xsl:use-attribute-sets attribute lists the names of attribute sets that contain attributes that should be added to the literal result element, in exactly the same way as the use-attribute-sets attribute works with <xsl:element> and <xsl:copy>.

xsl:version

Syntax:

```
<element xsl:version="1.0">
  template
</element>
```

See also: <xsl:stylesheet>

The xsl:version attribute specifies the version of XSLT that is being used within its content (which is currently always 1.0). This attribute is required on the document element of simplified stylesheets, which have a literal result element as their document element.

Beginning
XSLT

C

Tools

XSLT Processors

Saxon

http://saxon.sourceforge.net/

- Java (and "instant" version)
- 6.5.1 supports XSLT 1.0/1.1
- 7.0 has limited support for XSLT 2.0
- lots of extension elements and functions
- supports user-defined extension functions in XSLT and Java
- supports TrAX (JAXP 1.1 conformant)

Xalan-J

http://xml.apache.org/xalan-j/

- Java
- current version 2.3.1
- several extension elements and functions
- supports user-defined extension functions through Bean Scripting Framework
- supports TrAX (JAXP 1.1 conformant)

MSXML

http://msdn.microsoft.com/xml

- C++
- MSXML3 supports XSLT 1.0 (and WD-xsl)
- MSXML4 supports XSLT 1.0 and XML Schema (adds some extensions)
- supports user-defined extension functions in JScript, JavaScript, VBScript
- some extension elements and functions

Other XSLT Processors

- 4XSLT (Python) – http://4suite.org/
- DGXT (Java) – http://www.datapower.com/products.shtml#dgxt
- EZ/X – http://www.activated.com/products/products.html
- FastXML (C++) – http://www.geocities.com/fastxml/
- jd.xslt (Java) – http://www.aztecrider.com/xslt/
- libxslt (C++) – http://xmlsoft.org/XSLT
- Napa – http://homepage.ntlworld.com/kjjones/
- MDC-XSL (C++) – http://mdc-xsl.sourceforge.net/
- OracleXSLT (Java, C, C++) – http://technet.oracle.com/tech/xml/
- Sablotron (C++) – http://www.gingerall.com/charlie/ga/xml/p_sab.xml
- TransforMiiX (C++) – http://www.mozilla.org/projects/xslt/
- Unicorn XSLT Processor (C++) – http://www.unicorn-enterprises.com/products_uxt.html
- Xalan-C (C++) – http://xml.apache.org/xalan-c/
- xesalt (C++) – http://www.inlogix.de/products.html
- XMLPartner (C++) – http://www.turbopower.com/products/xmlpartner/
- XML::XSLT (Perl) – http://xmlxslt.sourceforge.net/
- XSLJIT (Java)* – http://www.xsljit.com/
- XSLTC (Java)* – http://xml.apache.org/xalan-j/xsltc_usage.html
- xt (Java) – http://www.jclark.com/xml/xt.html

* XSLJIT and XSLTC are both compilers rather than interpreters like the rest of the XSLT processors. They compile the XSLT stylesheet into Java byte code, and you then run those Java programs over your XML documents to do the transformation.

XSLT Editors

Extensions to Other Editors

Visual XSLT

http://www.activestate.com/Products/Visual_XSLT/

- plug-in for Visual Studio .NET
- syntax highlighting
- auto-completion
- preview of the result of running the stylesheet (with either the System.Xsl .NET component or Xalan)
- browsers for navigating through the stylesheet
- breakpoints in the source document or the stylesheet
- testing XPath expressions

XSLAtHome

http://www.vbxml.com/xslathome/

- plug-in for Macromedia's HomeSite web development tool
- syntax highlighting
- auto-completion
- reformatting
- running XSLT processors
- testing XPath expressions

XSlide

http://www.menteith.com/xslide/

- major mode for emacs
- syntax highlighting
- auto-completion
- processing XML files with xt and Saxon

XSLT-Process

http://xslt-process.sourceforge.net/index.php

- minor mode for emacs
- process XML files with Saxon, Xalan, and other Java-based XSLT processors
- view the results within emacs, within a web browser, or as PDF via FOP
- set breakpoints in the source or the stylesheet
- watch local and global variables

Mapping Tools

CapeStudio

http://capeclear.com/products/capestudio/

- supports mapping from value to value with tables
- includes XPath editor for more complicated mappings

Whitehill <xsl>Composer

http://www.whitehill.com/Products/xslcomposer/

- visual editor for XML to HTML transformations

XMapper

http://www.nalasoftware.com/DOCS/Xmapper/overview.cfm

- web-based mapping tool

XSLWiz

http://www.induslogic.com/products/products2.html

- graphical "funclets" to merge or split information
- supports grouping in mappings

XSLerator

http://www.alphaworks.ibm.com/tech/xslerator

- written in Java

Basic Editors

XFinity Designer

http://www.b-bop.com/products_xfinity_designer.htm

- automatic generation of XPaths
- integrated HTML viewer for result

XL-Styler

http://www.seeburger.de/xml/

- syntax highlighting
- auto-completion
- integrated HTML viewer for result

XTrans

http://www.simx.com/pub/XTrans/

- syntax highlighting
- built-in XPath evaluator
- integrated HTML viewer for result

Integrated Development Environments

Cooktop

http://xmleverywhere.com/cooktop/

- supports transformations with a whole range of XSLT processors
- syntax highlighting
- some debugging support
- chat with other Cooktop users over the Internet

Komodo

http://aspn.activestate.com/ASPN/Downloads/Komodo/

- supports JavaScript, Perl, Python, and other languages as well as XSLT
- syntax highlighting
- auto-completion

- set breakpoints in the source and stylesheet
- view or change global or local variables and parameters

MarrowSoft Xselerator

http://www.vbxml.com/xselerator/default.asp

- syntax highlighting
- auto-completion
- set breakpoints in the source or stylesheet
- step through XSLT instructions
- view the values of variables and parameters

Stylus Studio

http://www.stylusstudio.com/

- syntax highlighting
- auto-completion
- construct simple stylesheets based on mappings
- set breakpoints
- step through, into, and over instructions
- view the values of parameters and variables

XMLOrigin

http://www.xmlorigin.com/

- syntax highlighting
- auto-completion
- set breakpoints
- supports processing with Xalan, MSXML 3, MSXML 4, and Napa
- step through, into, and over instructions
- view the values of parameters and variables
- watch the results of XPath expressions

XML Spy

http://www.xmlspy.com/

- syntax highlighting
- auto-completion
- XSLT Designer (bought separately) gives a drag-and-drop interface for construction of HTML pages from an XML document

XSLT Support Tools

XPath Constructors

XPath 1.0: Interactive Expression Builder

http://staff.develop.com/aarons/bits/xpath-builder/

- web or offline as a browser-based tool
- dynamically highlights the selected nodes in a source view of an XML document

XPath Tester

http://www.fivesight.com/downloads/xpathtester.asp

- Java-based tool (uses Xalan-J)
- displays selected nodes within an XML document displayed as a tree structure

XPath Visualizer

http://www.vbxml.com/xpathvisualizer/

- browser-based tool
- evaluate any XPath expression (not only location paths)
- highlights the relevant nodes in a source document
- set up keys and variables

XSLT Debuggers

XSLDebugger

http://www.vbxml.com/xsldebugger/

- integrated with XPath Visualizer
- step through stylesheet, source, and result in parallel
- view the values of parameters and variables

XSL Trace

http://www.alphaworks.ibm.com/tech/xsltrace

- Java-based XSL debugger (uses Xalan-J)
- step through stylesheets while viewing the source and result
- set breakpoints on the source or stylesheet

Zvon XSL Tracer

http://www.zvon.org/xxl/XSLTracer/Output/introduction.html

- Perl-based tool (uses Saxon)
- step through a transformation with the stylesheet alongside either the source or the result

XSLT Profilers

CatchXSL

http://www.xslprofiler.org/

- provides detailed profile of stylesheet performance
- uses Saxon or Xalan

XSL Lint

http://www.nwalsh.com/xsl/xslint/

- checks stylesheets for basic omissions

XSLT Test Tool

http://www.netcrucible.com/xslt/xslt-tool.htm

- runs stylesheets with multiple XSLT processors

XSLTMark

http://www.datapower.com/XSLTMark/

- provides benchmarking for XSLT processors

XSLTUnit

http://xsltunit.org/

- provides unit-testing environment for XSLT

Documentation Generation

XSLDoc

http://www.xsldoc.org/

- generates Javadoc-style documentation for stylesheets

XSLTDoc

http://grillade.griotte.com/xml/xsltdoc/xsltdoc.html

- generates an HTML page summarizing the stylesheet

XSLTDoc

http://www.jenitennison.com/xslt/utilities

- displays explanation of stylesheet, including automatically-generated descriptions of XPaths

XSLT-Enabled Browsers

Antenna House XSL Formatter

http://www.antennahouse.com/

- uses MSXML3
- expects transformation result to be XSL-FO

Internet Explorer

http://www.microsoft.com/ie

- uses MSXML3.0 (IE 6.0, or IE 5.0+ if MSXML3 installed in replace mode)
- expects transformation result to be HTML

Mozilla

http://www.mozilla.org

- uses TransforMiix
- expects transformation result to be HTML

Netscape

http://browsers.netscape.com/

- uses TransforMiix
- expects transformation result to be HTML

XSmiles

http://www.xsmiles.org/

- uses JAXP-compatible processor (default Xalan)
- expects transformation result to be XHTML, XSL-FO, SMIL, SVG, or XForms

Server Side Support

AxKit

http://www.axkit.org/

- Apache module
- uses Sablotron or libxslt

Cocoon

http://xml.apache.org/cocoon

- Java servlet
- uses JAXP-compatible processor (default Xalan)

UWOBO

http://www.cs.unibo.it/helm/uwobo/

- Java servlet
- uses Xalan

XSQL

http://otn.oracle.com/tech/xml/xdk_java

- Java servlet over SQL database
- uses Oracle's XSLT processor

Beginning
XSLT

Index

A Guide to the Index

The index is arranged hierarchically, in alphabetical order, with symbols preceding the letter A. Most second-level entries and many third-level entries also occur as first-level entries. This is to ensure that users will find the information they require however they choose to search for it.

Symbols

A

B

C

D

E

F

G

M

N

O

P

Q

R

S

T

U

V

W

X

Y

Notes

Notes

Notes

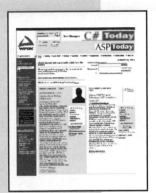

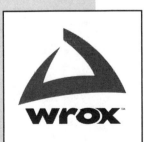

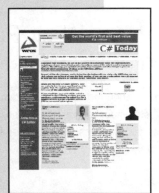

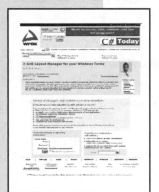

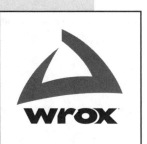

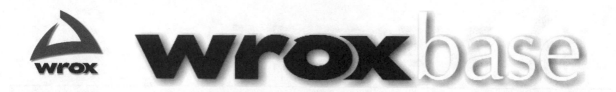

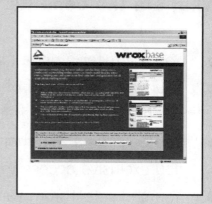

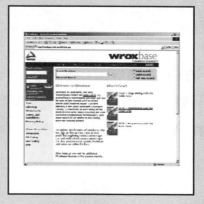

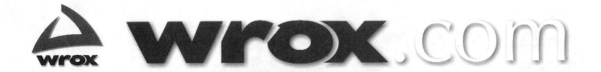

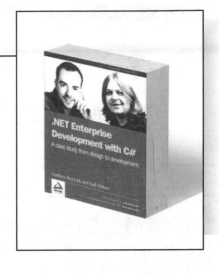

Beginning
XSLT

About the Author

Jeni Tennison

Jeni is an independent consultant and author on XML, XSLT, and related technologies. She has a background in knowledge engineering: her PhD was on developing ontologies collaboratively over the Web. Her interest in representing information led to XML, and the requirement to support different views of information to XSLT. She seems to spend most of her time answering people's email about XSLT and XML Schemas. She lives in Nottingham, England, with one man, two cats, three games consoles, four computers, and lots of Lego.

Trademark Acknowledgements

Wrox has endeavored to provide trademark information about all the companies and products mentioned in this book by the appropriate use of capitals. However, Wrox cannot guarantee the accuracy of this information.

Credits

Author
Jeni Tennison

Technical Architect
Timothy Briggs

Lead Technical Editor
Nick Manning

Technical Editor
Girish Sharangpani

Technical Reviewers
David Carlisle
Michael Corning
Jon Duckett
James Fuller
David Pawson
Linda van den Brink

Project Administrators
Helen Cuthill
Vicky Idiens

Indexer
Andrew Criddle

Proof Reader
Lisa Stephenson

Production Co-ordinator
Sarah Hall

Illustrations
Sarah Hall

Cover
Chris Morris

Beginning XSLT

First Published May 2002

wrox

Published by Wrox Press Ltd,
Arden House, 1102 Warwick Road, Acocks Green,
Birmingham, B27 6BH, UK
Printed in the United States
ISBN 1861005946

Beginning XSLT

Jeni Tennison

Wrox Press Ltd. ®